lonely planet

Slovenia

Steve Fallon

Slovenia

2nd edition

Published by
Lonely Planet Publications
Head Office: PO Box 617, Hawthorn, Vic 3122, Australia
Branches: 150 Linden Street, Oakland, CA 94607, USA
10a Spring Place, London NW5 3BH, UK
71 bis rue du Cardinal Lemoine, 75005 Paris, France

Printed by
Colorcraft Ltd, Hong Kong

Photographs by

Steve Fallon   Dušan Podgornik
Aleš Fevzer   Promotion Centre Ljubljana
Tomo Jeseničnik   Damien Simonis
Bogdan Kladnik   Slovenian Tourist Board (CPTS)
Renata Picej   Joco Žnidaršič

Front cover: Predjama Castle (Notranjska), Stuart Dee (The Image Bank)

First Published
October 1995

This Edition
September 1998

Although the authors and publisher have tried to make the information as accurate as possible, they accept no responsibility for any loss, injury or inconvenience sustained by any person using this book.

National Library of Australia Cataloguing in Publication Data

Fallon, Steve.
Slovenia.

2nd ed.
Includes index.
ISBN 0 86442 538 4.

1. Slovenia – Guidebooks. 2. Slovenia – Description and travel. I. Title.

914.9704

text & maps © Lonely Planet 1998
photos © photographers as indicated 1998
Bled and Koper climate charts compiled from information supplied by Patrick J Tyson, © Patrick J Tyson, 1998

All rights reserved. No part of this publication may be reproduced, stored in a retrieval system or transmitted in any form by any means, electronic, mechanical, photocopying, recording or otherwise, except brief extracts for the purpose of review, without the written permission of the publisher and copyright owner.

Steve Fallon

Born in Boston, Massachusetts, Steve Fallon can't remember a time when he was not obsessed with travel, other cultures and languages. As a teenager he worked an assortment of jobs to finance trips to Europe and South America, and he graduated from Georgetown University with a Bachelor of Science in modern languages. The following year he taught English at the University of Silesia near Katowice, Poland.

After he had worked for several years for a Gannett newspaper and obtained a master's degree in journalism, his fascination with the 'new' Asia took him to Hong Kong, where he lived for 13 years and worked on a variety of publications and was editor of *Business Traveller* magazine. In 1987, he put journalism on hold when he opened Wanderlust Books, Asia's only travel bookshop.

Steve lived in Budapest for 2½ years from where he wrote Lonely Planet's *Hungary* and *Slovenia* before moving to London in 1994. He has written or contributed to a number of other Lonely Planet titles.

From the Author

In the 'year of the majority', this one too (this two one) is for Michael Rothschild, forever patient, understanding and loyal. A star.

A number of people assisted in the research and writing of this 2nd edition of *Slovenia*, and I'd like to say a heartfelt *'Najlepša hvala'* to the following: Irena Bezjak of Ptujske Vedute, Ptuj; Andrej Blatnik of Cankarjeva Založba, Ljubljana; Tjaša Borštnik of the Ljubljana Promotion Centre; Jana Hojnik & the staff at the Park hotel, Ljubljana; Aleš & Tanja Hvala of the Hvala hotel, Kobarid; Matej & Mitja Karun of ABC, Brnik Airport; Rok V Klančnik of the Slovenian Tourist Board, Ljubljana; Matjaž Kos of the Geodesic Institute of Slovenia (GZS), Ljubljana; Ivana Leskovec of the Cerkno Museum; Amadeja Ličen of the Vila Viktorija, Bled; Renata Mlakar of Planšar, Stara Fužina; Tatjana Radovič of the Ljubljana Promotion Centre; the Ravbar family in Novo Mesto; Ivana Rizmal of

Adria Airways, London; Aleksander Riznič of Video Art, Črnomelj; Miha Rott of the Government Public Relations & Media Office, Ljubljana; Danilo Miklavž Sbrizaj of the Alpine Association of Slovenia (PZS), Ljubljana; Janko Štebej of Kompas Holidays, Ljubljana; Darko Viler of the Idrija Municipal Museum; and Olga Žvanut of Slovenian Railways (SŽ), Ljubljana.

Finally a very special acknowledgment for Črtomir Šoba for showing me a side of Slovenia even I'd never seen before. *Hvala lepa, zlati knez Štajerske.*

From the Publisher

The coordinating editor of this book was Craig MacKenzie. He was assisted by Wendy Owen, Anne Mulvaney, Janet Austin and Susannah Farfor. Lyndell Taylor and Ann Jeffree prepared the maps, and Ann took the book the rest of the way through production. Thanks to Dan Levin for weaving his font magic. Marcel Gaston, Mary Neighbour and Jane Hart conducted the artwork check. The cover was designed by David Kemp. Quentin Frayne edited the Language Guide.

Thanks

Many thanks to the travellers who wrote to us with information and suggestions:

Jaroslav Adamec, Taja Albolena, Ivo Andrea, Bergamo Andreis, Steven Austermiller, Maureen Ball, Vladislav Bevc, Paul Blazko, Paul Borstnik, Ann Bryant, Patrick Burke, Jean Cooke, Maria Demsar, Anne DeMuth, Christy Duijvelaar, A Edwards, Wes Eichenwald, Derek Emson, Igor Fabjan, Simon Hewison, Mark Hodge, Francis & Catherine King, Kobarid Museum, P Larkin, Maire Lynam, Mary McElhinney, Graham Owers, A Pettegree, Stephanie Polutnik, Candy Poon, Murray Rahn, Joanne Rebec, Graham Rhind, Matt Salmon, Johan Segers, Carol Stuckey, D Swabey, Edward Sykes, D Thomas, Magda Thurhner, Mirko Toporis, Joan Utting, Leon Vermys, Ron Wilson, Christine Wilson.

Warning & Request

Things change – prices go up, schedules change, good places go bad and bad places go bankrupt – nothing stays the same. So, if you find things better or worse, recently opened or long since closed, please tell us and help make the next edition even more accurate and useful. Julie Young coordinates a small team who read and acknowledge every letter, postcard and email, and ensure that information finds its way to the appropriate authors, editors and publishers. Everyone who writes to us will find their name in the next edition of the appropriate guide and will also receive a free subscription to our quarterly newsletter, *Planet Talk*. The very best contributions will be rewarded with a free Lonely Planet guide.

Excerpts from your correspondence may appear in new editions of this guide; in our newsletter, *Planet Talk*; or in updates on our Web site – so please let us know if you don't want your letter published or your name acknowledged.

Contents

BOXED ASIDES

Map Legend

Map Legend

BOUNDARIES

.... International Boundary
.... Provincial Boundary
.... Disputed Boundary

ROUTES

..... Freeway, with Route Number
.... Major Road
.... Minor Road
.... Minor Road - Unsealed
.... City Road
.... City Street
.... City Lane
.... Train Route, with Station
.... Metro Route, with Station
.... Cable Car or Chairlift
.... Ferry Route
.... Walking Track

AREA FEATURES

.... Building
.... Cemetery
.... Beach
.... Market
.... Park, Gardens
.... Pedestrian Mall
.... Reef
.... Urban Area

HYDROGRAPHIC FEATURES

.... Canal
.... Coastline
.... Creek, River
.... Lake, Intermittent Lake
.... Rapids, Waterfalls
.... Salt Lake
.... Swamp

SYMBOLS

✪ CAPITAL	National Capital	✈ .... Airport
◉ CAPITAL	Provincial Capital	.... Ancient or City Wall
● CITY	City	❸ .... Bank
● Town	Town	⋔ .... Beach
● Village	Village	⌒ .... Cave
		⛪ 🕆 .... Church
■	Place to Stay	.... Cliff or Escarpment
𝍫	Camping Ground	◩ .... Dive Site
⚏	Caravan Park	◐ .... Embassy
⌂	Hut or Chalet	⚑ .... Golf Course
		✚ .... Hospital
▼	Place to Eat	☀ .... Lookout
◉	Pub or Bar	⚱ .... Monument
		◙ .... Mosque
		▲ .... Mountain or Hill
		⛫ .... Museum
		⚓ .... National Park

←	One Way Street
℗	Parking
)(	Pass
⛽	Petrol Station
★	Police Station
✉	Post Office
∴	Ruins
❖	Shopping Centre
◎	Spring
⚑	Surf Beach
▭	Swimming Pool
☎	Telephone
⛩	Temple
▣	Tomb
❶	Tourist Information
◒	Transport
⛺	Zoo

Note: not all symbols displayed above appear in this book

Map Index

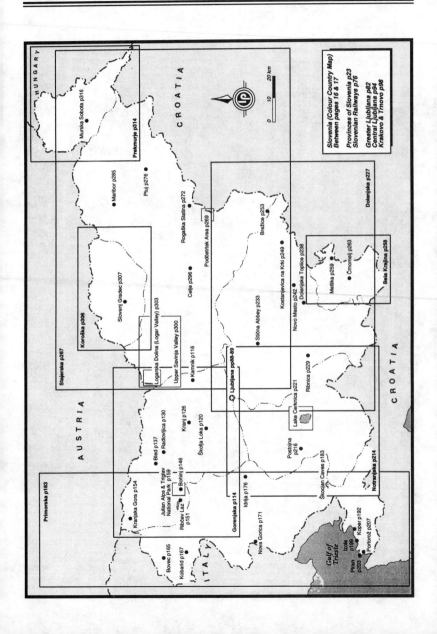

Introduction

It's a tiny place – there's no disputing that fact – with a surface area of just over 20,000 sq km and less than two million people. But 'good things come in small packages', and never was that old chestnut more appropriate than in describing Slovenia (Slovenija), an independent republic bordering Italy, Austria, Hungary and Croatia.

Slovenia has been dubbed a lot of different things by its promoters – 'Europe in Miniature', 'The Sunny Side of the Alps', 'The Green Piece of Europe' – and they're all true. Slovenia has everything, from beaches, snowcapped mountains, hills awash in grape vines and wide plains blanketed in sunflowers to Gothic churches, baroque palaces and Art Nouveau civic buildings. Its incredible mixture of climates brings warm Mediterranean breezes up to the foothills of the Alps, where it can snow in summer. And with more than half of its total area covered in forest, Slovenia really is one of the 'greenest' countries in the world.

But there are several important things to know about Slovenia, points that are often misunderstood or overlooked.

First, this is Slovenia not Slovakia. The latter declared itself independent from its erstwhile sibling, the Czech Republic, in January 1993 and has stagnated ever since under the strong-arm government of a former boxer.

Second, Slovenia is not part of the Balkans – geographically (the Kolpa River is the border), historically or psychologically – and no more resembles the nations of that traditionally volatile region than do Austria, Hungary or Italy. Throughout their history, the Slovenian people have had very close cultural and economic ties with Europe and have been influenced much more from the west than the east or south. This may seem odd when you take a close look at a map of the country. If you imagine the city of Murska Sobota to be an 'eye', the Julian Alps and the north-west to be a clump of 'tail

feathers' and Bela Krajina and southern Primorska to be 'feet', you'll see what looks like a chicken scurrying eastward. In fact, Slovenia is heading in the opposite direction – and fast – in these last years of the 20th century.

Third, Slovenia has always been a very safe place to live and to visit. Except for 10 days in late June/early July 1991 when rump Yugoslavia attempted to prevent its smallest child from leaving its decayed and collapsing House of Usher, there was no further fighting, war or terrorism here and there is none now. While Croatia and Bosnia-Hercegovina became embroiled in the bitterest conflict in Europe since WWII, Slovenia got on with what it has always done best: working hard, earning money and making progress.

In a very short time, Slovenia has gone from being a *narod* (nation of people) with no political foundation to a fully fledged *nacija* (nation-state), and that's just what the vast majority – 88% in fact – of its people wanted when they voted for independence in December 1990. Not everything has gone according to plan since then, and the 'evening of dreams' that President Milan Kučan spoke about on that first Independence Day in June 1991 brought a 'new day' with all the usual shams and drudgeries.

No, Slovenia ain't paradise; like everywhere, it has got its own share of problems and difficulties. But when I die – and they've confirmed that I'm headed north and not south – I'll take along a copy of Petrol's *Large Atlas for Motorists & Travellers*. You never know – it might prove useful.

'God's blessing on all nations,
Who long and work for that bright day
When o'er earth's habitations
No war, no strife shall hold its sway;
Who long to see
That all men free
No more shall foes, but neighbours be.'
A Toast to Freedom, **France Prešeren (1800-49)**

Facts about the Country

HISTORY
Early Inhabitants

The area of present-day Slovenia and its immediate borders has been settled since the Palaeolithic Age. Tools made of bone and dating back to between 100,000 and 60,000 BC have been discovered in a cave at Mt Olševa, north of Solčava in the Upper Savinja Valley. In 1995 one of the most important archaeological finds from the Stone Age was made in a cave at Divje Babe near Cerknica in Primorska: a primitive bone flute dating back some 35,000 years. It is now considered to be the world's oldest known musical instrument (see boxed text entitled Stone Age Music, in the Cerkno section of the Primorska chapter).

During the Bronze Age (around 2000 to 900 BC), marsh dwellers farmed and raised cattle in the area south of present-day Ljubljana called the Ljubljansko Barje and at Lake Cerknica. They lived in round huts set on stilts and traded with other peoples along the so-called Amber Route linking the Balkans with Italy and northern Europe. Finds dating from this period are extensive and include daggers, hatchets, pots and hoes.

Around 700 BC the Ljubljana Marsh people were overwhelmed by Illyrian tribes from the south who brought with them iron tools and weapons. They settled largely in today's province of Dolenjska, built hill-top forts and reached their economic and cultural peak between 650 and 550 BC during what is now called the Hallstatt period. Priceless objects like iron helmets, gold jewellery and embossed pails *(situlae)* have been found in tombs near Stična and at Vače near Litija.

In about 400 BC, Celtic tribes from France, Germany and the Czech lands began pushing southward towards the Balkans. They mixed with the local population and established the first 'state' on Slovenian soil, the Noric kingdom.

The Romans

In 181 BC, the Romans established the colony of Aquileia (Oglej in Slovene) on the Gulf of Trieste in order to protect the empire from tribal incursions (see boxed text entitled Patriarchate of Aquileia). Among its visitors would be Julius Caesar himself, for whom the Julian Alps are named. In the 2nd decade AD, the Romans annexed the Celtic

---

Patriarchate of Aquileia

You'd never guess from its present size and population (less than 3500 people) but the Italian town of Aquileia (Oglej in Slovene), north of Grado on the Gulf of Trieste, played a pivotal role in Slovenian history and for many centuries its bishops (or 'patriarchs') ruled much of Carniola (Kranjska).

Founded as a Roman colony in the late 2nd century BC, Aquileia fell to a succession of tribes during the Great Migrations and had lost its political and economic importance by the end of the 6th century. But it had been made the metropolitan see for Venice, Istria and Carniola and when the church declared some of Aquileia's teachings heretical, Aquileia broke from Rome. The schism lasted only a century and when it was resolved Aquileia was recognised as a separate patriarchate.

Aquileia's ecclesiastical importance grew during the mission of Paolino II to the Avars and Slovenes in the late 8th century and it acquired feudal estates and extensive political privileges (including the right to coin money) from the Frankish and later the German kings. It remained a feudal principality until 1420 when the Venetian Republic conquered Friuli and Venetians were appointed patriarchs for the first time. Aquileia retained some of its holdings in Slovenia and elsewhere for the next 300 years. But the final blow came in 1751 when Pope Benedict XIV created the archbishoprics of Udine and Gorizia. The once powerful Patriarchate of Aquileia had outlasted its usefulness and was dissolved. ■

Noric kingdom and moved into the rest of Slovenia and Istria.

The Romans divided the area into the provinces of Noricum (today's southern Austria, Koroška and western Štajerska), Upper and Lower Pannonia (eastern Štajerska, Dolenjska and much of Gorenjska) and Histria (Primorska and Croatian Istria) and built roads connecting their new military settlements. From these bases developed the important towns of Emona (Ljubljana), Celeia (Celje), Poetovio (Ptuj) and Virunum (near Klagenfurt in Austria), which had a forum, sophisticated fortifications, housing, baths, gymnasiums, temples and later Christian chapels. Many reminders of the Roman presence can still be seen in Ljubljana, Ptuj, Celje and Šempeter.

The Great Migrations

In the middle of the 5th century AD, the Huns, led by Attila, invaded Italy via Slovenia, attacking Poetovio, Celeia and Emona along the way. Aquileia fell to the Huns in 452, but Attila's empire was short-lived and was soon eclipsed by the Germanic Ostrogoths. In their wake came the Langobards, another Germanic tribe that had also occupied much Slovenian territory. In 568 the Langobards struck out for Italy, taking Aquileia and eventually conquering the Venetian mainland.

The Early Slavs

The ancestors of today's Slovenes arrived from the Carpathian Basin in the 6th century and settled in the Sava, Drava and Mura river valleys and the eastern Alps. Under pressure from the Avars, a powerful Mongol people with whom they had formed a tribal alliance, the early Slavs then migrated farther west to the Friulian plain and the Adriatic Sea, north to the sources of the Drava and Mura rivers and east as far as Lake Balaton in Hungary. In the end they occupied a total land area of about 70,000 sq km and numbered about 200,000 people.

At that time these people were called Sclavi or Sclaveni, as were most Slavs. Later these 'proto-Slovenes' would be identified by their region: Carniola, Styria, Carinthia. It wasn't until the late 18th century during a period of national consciousness that the name Sloveni or Slovenci (Slovenians) came into common use.

In their original homelands – bordered by the Baltic Sea to the north, the Carpathians to the south, the Oder River to the east and the Dnieper to the west – these Sclavi were a peaceful people, living in forests or along rivers and lakes, breeding cattle and farming by slash-and-burn methods. They were a superstitious people who saw *vile* (both good and bad fairies or sprites) everywhere and paid homage to a pantheon of gods and goddesses: Svarog, the creator of light; Perun, the god of storms, lightning and thunder; Vales, the protector of cattle. As a social group they made no class distinctions, which is why some historians believe they never succeeded in establishing a kingdom. But a leader – a *župan* (now 'mayor') or *vojvoda* (duke) – was selected in times of great danger.

The docile nature of these people changed, however, during the migratory periods, and they became more war-like and aggressive.

The Duchy of Carantania

When the Avars failed in their bid to take Byzantium in 626, the Alpine Slavs united under their leader Veluk and joined forces

The coat of arms of the Duchy of Carantania, the first Slavic state

with the Frankish chief Samo to fight them. The Slavic tribal union became the Duchy of Carantania (Karantanija) with its seat at Krn Castle (now Karnburg in Austria). Carantania was the first Slavic state, and its borders extended from the valley of the Sava River as far as Leipzig, including Moravia, Bohemia and Lower Austria.

By the early 8th century, a new class of ennobled commoners *(kosezi)* had emerged, and it was they who publicly elected and crowned the new *knez* (grand duke) on the 'duke's rock' *(knežji kamen)* in the courtyard of Krn Castle. Such a democratic process was unique in the feudal Europe of the early Middle Ages, and it is believed to have influenced Thomas Jefferson in the formation of his contractual theory and the writing of the American Declaration of Independence in 1775-76.

Expansion of the Franks

In 748 the Frankish empire of the Carolingians incorporated Carantania as a vassal state called Carinthia and attempted to convert the population to Christianity. Because of this foreign domination, the new religion was resisted at first. But Irish monks under the auspices of the Diocese of Salzburg in the late 8th century made use of the vernacular and were more successful.

By the early 9th century, religious authority on Slovenian territory was shared between Salzburg and the Patriarchate of Aquileia (the Drava River remained the border until the 18th century) so that no local ecclesiastical centre could develop on its own. At the same time, the weakening Frankish authorities replaced the Slovenian nobles with German counts to help retain what little power they had left. They were absorbed into the new system while the local peasantry was reduced to serfdom. The German nobility was thus at the top of the feudal hierarchy for the first time in Slovenian lands. This would later become one of the key obstacles to Slovenian national and cultural development.

Prince Kocelj & the Carinthian Kingdom

With the total collapse of the Frankish state in the second half of the 9th century, a Carinthian prince named Kocelj established an independent Slovenian 'kingdom' (869-74) in Lower Pannonia, the area stretching south-east from Styria (Štajerska) to the Mura, Drava and Danube rivers. It was to Lower Pannonia that the Macedonian brothers Cyril and Methodius, the 'apostles of the southern Slavs', had first brought the translations of the Scriptures to the Slovenes (863). And it was here that calls for a Slavic archdiocese were first heard.

Magyar Invasion & German Ascendancy

The Carinthian kingdom was not to last long. In about 900, the fearsome Magyars, expert horsemen and archers, invaded and subjugated the Slovenian regions of Lower Pannonia and along the Sava, cutting them off from Carinthia. They intended to go farther but were defeated by German and Slovenian forces under King Otto I at Augsburg in 955.

The Germans decided to re-establish Carinthia, dividing the area into a half-dozen border counties or marches. By the early 11th century, these would develop into the Slovenian provinces that would remain basically unchanged until 1918: Carniola (Kranjska), Carinthia (Koroška), Styria (Štajerska), Gorica (Goriška) and the White March (Bela Krajina).

A drive for complete Germanisation of the Slovenian lands began in the 10th century. Land was divided between the nobility and various church dioceses (Brixen, Salzburg and Freising), and German gentry were settled on it. But except for the foreign nobles and administrators, the territory remained essentially Slovene. That these people were able to preserve their identity through German and later Austrian rule was due largely to intensive educational work conducted by the clergy.

Most of Slovenia's important castles were built between the 10th and 13th centuries, and many Christian monasteries (eg Stična and Kostanjevica) were established. Towns also developed as administrative, trade and social centres. Eventually landowners, traders, merchants, artisans and manual workers would find their way to them.

Early Habsburg Rule

The Austro-German monarchy (known as the Habsburg Empire from 1804) held control over Slovenian territory from the early 14th century until the end of WWI. It dominated the local population in every sense, stifled national aspirations and stunted political and cultural development.

In the early Middle Ages, the Habsburgs were just one of many German aristocratic families struggling for hegemony on Slovenian soil. Others, such as the Andechs, Spanheims and Žoneks (later the Counts of Celje), were equally powerful at various times. But as dynasties intermarried or died out, the Habsburgs consolidated their power.

Between the late 13th and early 16th centuries, almost all the lands inhabited by the Slovenes passed into Habsburg hands with the exception of Istria and the Littoral, which were controlled by Venice until 1797, and Prekmurje, which belonged to the Hungarian crown. Most of Kranjska, Koroška and western Štajerska were united under the Habsburgs by the middle of the 14th century, and the area around Celje, Gorica and parts of Prekmurje followed in the 15th and 16th centuries. Until the 17th century rule was not directly imposed but administered by diets (parliaments) of 'resident princes', prelates, feudal lords and representatives from the towns, who dealt with matters such as taxation.

By this time Slovenian territory totalled about 24,000 sq km, about 15% larger than its present size. Not only did more towns and boroughs receive charters and rights, but the country began to develop economically with the opening of ironworks (eg at Kropa) and mines (Idrija). And as economic progress reduced the differences among the repressed peasants, they united against their feudal lords.

Peasant Uprisings & the Reformation

More than 100 peasant uprisings and revolts occurred between 1358 (at Stična) and 1848 (at Ig), but they reached their peak between 1478 and 1573. Together with the Protestant Reformation at the end of the 16th century, they are considered a watershed of the Slovenian national awakening.

Attacks by the Ottoman Turks on south-eastern Europe began in 1408 and continued for more than two and a half centuries, almost reaching Vienna on several occasions. By the start of the 16th century, thousands of Slovenes had been killed or taken prisoner. The assaults helped to radicalise the peasants and landless labourers who were required to raise their own defences *and* continue to pay tribute and work for their feudal lords. At the same time, the population was growing and small farms were being divided up even further.

In most of the uprisings, peasant 'unions' demanded a reduction in feudal payments, the democratic election of parish priests and, in at least one case, the formation of a peasant state under direct control of the emperor. The three most violent uprisings took place in 1478 in Koroška; in 1515, encompassing almost the entire Slovenian territory; and in 1573, when Ambrož 'Matija' Gubec led some 12,000 Slovenian and Croatian peasants in revolt. Castles were occupied and pulled down and lords executed. But none of the revolts succeeded.

The Protestant Reformation in Slovenia was closely associated with the nobility from 1540 onward and was generally ignored by the rural population except for those who lived or worked on lands owned by the church (though of Ljubljana's 5000 residents in 1570, two-thirds were Protestant). The effects of this great reform movement cannot be underestimated. Though only 1% of the current population is Protestant, the Reformation gave Slovenia its first books in the vernacular – some 50 in all. Not only did this raise the educational level of Slovenes, but it also lifted the status of the language itself, the first real affirmation of Slovenian culture.

Counter-Reformation & Progress

The wealthy middle class had lost interest in the Reformation by the time it peaked in the 1580s because of the widening economic gap between that class and the nobility. They turned to the Catholic resident princes who quashed Protestantism among the peasants through religious commissions and trials and

BOGDAN KLADNIK

STEVE FALLON

STEVE FALLON

STEVE FALLON

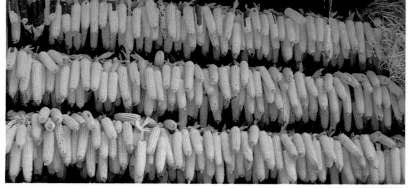

STEVE FALLON

A
B	C	D
E

A: Bringing in the sheaves, Dolenjska

B: Double-linked hayrack (toplar)

C: Linden tree

D: Toplar with corn and hay drying on it's side racks

E: Corn hanging out to dry on a toplar

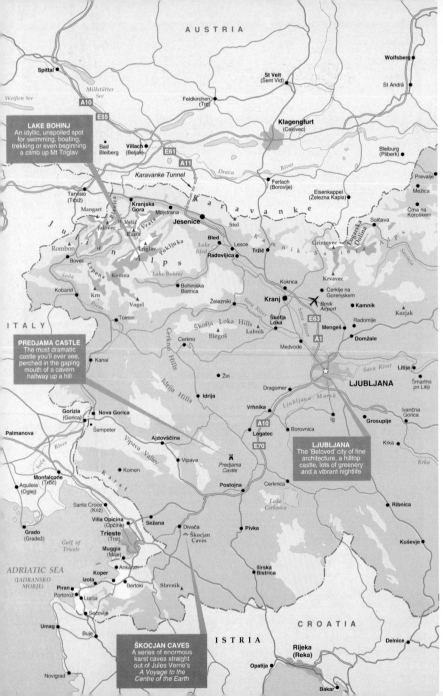

LAKE BOHINJ
An idyllic, unspoiled spot for swimming, boating, trekking or even beginning a climb up Mt Triglav

PREDJAMA CASTLE
The most dramatic castle you'll ever see, perched in the gaping mouth of a cavern halfway up a hill

LJUBLJANA
The 'Beloved' city of fine architecture, a hilltop castle, lots of greenery and a vibrant nightlife

ŠKOCJAN CAVES
A series of enormous karst caves straight out of Jules Verne's *A Voyage to the Centre of the Earth*

AUSTRIA

Spittal
Weißen See
Millstätter See
A10
E55
Bad Bleiberg
Villach (Beljak)
E61
A11
Karavanke Tunnel
Tarvisio (Trbiž)
Mangart
Vršič
Jalovec
Razor
Kranjska Gora
Mojstrana
Rombon
Bovec
Triglav
Pokljuka
Kobarid
Krn
Komna
Lake Bohinj
Vogel
Bohinjska Bistrica
Tolmin
Železniki
Cerkno
Idrija Hills
Idrija
Žiri
Kanal
Gorizia (Gorica)
Nova Gorica
Šempeter
Palmanova
Vipava Valley
Ajdovščina
Vipava
Komen
Monfalcone (Tržič)
Aquileia (Oglej)
Santa Croce (Križ)
Villa Opicina (Opčine)
Sežana
Grado (Gradež)
Gulf of Trieste
Trieste (Trst)
Muggia (Milje)
Divača
Škocjan Caves
ADRIATIC SEA (JADRANSKO MORJE)
Koper
Izola
Ankaran
Bertoki
Piran
Portorož
Lucija
Sečovlje
Slavnik
Umag
Buje
ISTRIA
Novigrad

St Veit (Šent Vid)
Wolfsberg
St Andrä
Feldkirchen (Trg)
Klagenfurt (Celovec)
Bleiburg (Pliberk)
Prevalje
Mežica
Ferlach (Borovlje)
Eisenkappel (Železna Kapla)
Črna na Koroškem
Soičava
Jesenice
Stol
Bled
Lesce
Radovljica
Tržič
Grintovec
Logarska Dolina
Krvavec
Kokrica
Savinja
Kranj
Brnik Airport
Cerklje na Gorenjskem
Kamnik
Kozjak
Radomlje
Škofja Loka Hills
Škofja Loka
Lubnik
Blegoš
Mengeš
E63
A1
Domžale
Medvode
Cerkno Hills
Dragomer
LJUBLJANA
Litija
Šmartno pri Litiji
Vrhnika
Ljubljana Marsh
A10
Logatec
E70
Borovnica
Ig
Grosuplje
Ivančna Gorica
Krka
Predjama Castle
Postojna
Cerknica
Lake Cerknica
Ribnica
Pivka
Ilirska Bistrica
Koševje
CROATIA
Rijeka (Reka)
Opatija
Delnice
Bakar

ITALY
Soča River
Idrija Hills
Karst

banished noble families or individuals who persisted in the new belief.

After almost a century of Habsburg decline brought on by the losses of the Counter-Reformation and the Thirty Years' War (1618-48) to gain control of Germany, economic improvements began in the early 18th century and Empress Maria Theresa (1740-80) introduced a series of reforms. These included the establishment of a new state administration with a type of provincial government, the abolition of customs duties between provinces of the empire, the building of new roads, and the introduction of obligatory elementary school in German and state-controlled secondary schools. Her son, Joseph II (1780-90), went several steps further. He abolished serfdom in 1782, paving the way for the formation of a Slovenian bourgeoisie, and allowed complete religious freedom to Calvinists, Lutherans and Jews. He also dissolved the all-powerful (and often corrupt) Catholic religious orders.

Though Joseph II rescinded many of these reforms (including the emancipation of the peasantry) on his death bed, they had a major effect on the economy. Agricultural output improved, manufacturing intensified and shipping from Austria's main port at Trieste increased substantially. The reforms also produced a flowering of the arts and letters in Slovenia, with the playwright and historian Anton Tomaž Linhart and the poet and journalist Valentin Vodnik producing their finest and most influential works at this time. The first newspaper in Slovene – *Lublanske Novize* – was launched by Vodnik in 1797.

Napoleon & the Illyrian Provinces

The French Revolution of 1789 convinced the Austrian rulers that the reform movement should be nipped in the bud, and a period of reaction began that continued until the Revolution of 1848. In the meantime there was a brief interlude – almost a footnote in history – that would have a profound effect on Slovenia and the future of the Slovenian nation.

Following his defeat of the Austrians at Wagram in 1809, Napoleon decided to cut the Habsburg Empire off from the Adriatic. To do this he created six 'Illyrian Provinces' from Slovenian and Croatian regions, including Koroška, Kranjska, Gorica, Istria and Trieste, and made Ljubljana the capital.

Though the Illyrian Provinces lasted only from 1809 to 1813, France instituted a number of reforms, including equality before the law and the use of Slovene in primary and lower secondary schools and in public offices, and gained the support of certain Slovenian intellectuals, including Vodnik. Most importantly, the Illyrian Provinces and the progressive influence of the French Revolution brought the issue of national awakening to the Slovenian political arena for the first time.

Romantic Nationalism & the 1848 Revolution

Austrian rule, restored in 1814, was now guided by the iron fist of Prince Clemens von Metternich. He immediately reinstituted the Austrian feudal system and attempted to suppress every national movement from the time of the Congress of Vienna (1815) to the Revolution of 1848. But the process of change in the wake of industrial revolution had started in Europe and among the Slovenes too. It could no longer be stopped.

The period of Romantic Nationalism (1814-48) in Slovenia was one of intensive literary and cultural activity and set the stage for the promulgation of the first Slovenian political program. Though many influential writers published at this time (Matija Čop, Bishop Anton Martin Slomšek, Andrej Smole), no one so dominated the period as the poet France Prešeren (see boxed text entitled France Prešeren: A Poet for the Nation). His bitter-sweet verse, progressive ideas, demands for political freedom and longings for the unity of all Slovenes caught the imagination of the nation then, and to an extent have never let it go.

Despite this, the revolution that swept Europe in early 1848 found Slovenia politically weak and relatively unprepared. But it did bring two positive results. First, it did away with absolutism and freed the peasantry from its remaining feudal obligations (though at a price – literally). Second, it provided intellectuals with the opportunity to launch their first national political program, one that came under the banner Zedinjena Slovenija (United Slovenia).

The United Slovenia program, first drawn up by the Slovenija Society in Vienna, basically called for the unification of all historic Slovenian regions within an autonomous unit of the Austrian monarchy. It also called for the use of Slovene in all schools and offices and the establishment of a local university. But the demands were rejected as they would have required the reorganisation of the empire along ethnic lines.

It must be remembered that the Slovenes of the time were not contemplating total independence. Indeed, most looked upon the Habsburg Empire as a protective mantle for small nations against larger ones they considered predators like Italy, Germany and Serbia.

Constitutional Period

The only tangible results for the Slovenes in the resulting 1848 Austrian Constitution were that laws would henceforth be published in Slovene and that the Slovenian flag should be three horizontal stripes of white, blue and red. But the United Slovenia program would remain the basis of all Slovenian political demands up to 1918 and political-cultural clubs and circles began to appear all over the territory.

The rest of the 19th century and the decade before WWI were marked by economic development for the ruling classes – the railway from Vienna to Ljubljana opened in 1849, industrial companies were formed at Kranj and Trbovlje, and a mill began operating at Ajdovščina. However, material conditions declined for the peasantry whose traditional sources of income were being eroded. Between 1850 and 1910, more than 300,000 Slovenes – 56% of the population – emigrated to other countries.

Some advances were made on the political side. Out of the *čitalnice* (reading clubs) and the *tabori* (camps in which Slovenes of many different beliefs rallied) grew political movements. Parties first appeared toward the end of the 19th century, with the Clerical Party of newspaper editor Janez Bleiweis representing the conservative side, the Liberal Party on the left, and the Social Democratic Party advocating a new idea: union with the other southern Slavs. The 'Yugoslav' idea was propounded from the 1860s onward by the distinguished Croatian Bishop Josip Strossmayer, whose name still adorns streets in many Slovenian towns and cities. The writer and socialist Ivan Cankar even called for an independent Yugoslav state in the form of a federal republic.

WWI & the Kingdom of Serbs, Croats & Slovenes

Slovenian political parties generally remained faithful to Austria-Hungary (as the empire was known from 1867). With the heavy loss of life and destruction of property during WWI, however, support was growing for an autonomous democratic state within the Habsburg monarchy, principles put forward in the May 1917 Declaration of the Yugoslav Club. With the defeat of Austria-Hungary and the dissolution of the Habsburg dynasty in 1918, Slovenes, Croats and Serbs banded together and declared themselves to be an independent state with the capital at Zagreb. Due to a perceived threat from Italy, however, the state joined up with Serbia and Montenegro in December 1918 under the name of the Kingdom of Serbs, Croats and Slovenes. The Serbian statesman Stojan Protić became prime minister while the Slovene leader of the Clerical Party, Anton Korošec, was named vice-premier.

The peace treaties signed at Paris and Rapallo had given large amounts of Slovenian and Croatian territory to Italy (Primorska and Istria), to Austria (Koroška) and Hungary (part of Prekmurje) and almost half a million Slovenes now lived in those countries (some, like the Slovenes in Koroška, had voted to do so, however). The loss of more than a quarter of its population and a third of its land would remain the single most important issue facing Slovenia between the wars.

The kingdom, which lasted in one form or another until 1940, was dominated by the notion of 'Yugoslav unity', Serbian control, imperialistic pressure from Italy and political intrigue. Slovenia was reduced to little more than a province in this centralist kingdom – a position supported by both the liberal bourgeoisie and the socialist parties for entirely different reasons. The Slovenes did enjoy cultural and linguistic autonomy, however, and economic progress was rapid.

Following the assassination of the leaders of the most powerful Serbian and Croatian parties, King Alexander seized absolute power, abolished the constitution and proclaimed the Kingdom of Yugoslavia in 1929. But Alexander himself was murdered by a Croatian-backed Macedonian in Marseilles in 1934 during an official visit to France and his cousin, Prince Paul, was named regent until Alexander's son, Peter, came of age.

The political climate changed in Slovenia when the Clerical Party joined the new centralist government of Milan Stojadinović in 1935, proving how hollow that party's calls for Slovenian autonomy had been. As a result, splinter groups from both the Clerical and the Liberal parties began to seek closer contacts with the workers' movements. In 1937 the Communist Party of Slovenia (KPS) was formed under the tutelage of Josip Broz Tito (1892-1980) and the Communist Party of Yugoslavia (KPJ).

WWII & the Partisan Struggle

Yugoslavia avoided getting involved in the war until March 1941 when Prince Paul, under pressure from Berlin and Rome, signed a treaty with the Axis powers. He was overthrown in a coup backed by the British, who installed King Paul II. Paul at first attempted neutrality, but German armies invaded Yugoslavia in April, and the Yugoslav army capitulated in less than two weeks.

Slovenia was split up among Germany (Štajerska, Gorenjska and Koroška), Italy (Ljubljana, Primorska, Notranjska, Dolenjska and Bela Krajina) and Hungary (Prekmurje). Repression and deportations

were the order of the day in Štajerska and Koroška.

To counter this the Slovenian communists and other left-wing groups formed a Liberation Front (Osvobodilne Fronte; OF), and Slovenes took up arms for the first time since the peasant uprisings to resist the occupiers. The OF, dedicated to the principles of a united Slovenia in a Yugoslav republic, joined the all-Yugoslav Partisan army of the KPJ and its secretary-general, Tito. Under the Dolomites Proclamation (1943), the KPS was given the leading role in the front. The Partisans received assistance from the Allies and, given the terrain and long tradition of guerrilla warfare in the Balkans, were the most organised and successful of any resistance movement during WWII.

After Italy capitulated in 1943, the anti-OF Slovenian Domobranci (Home Guards) were active in Primorska and, in a bid to prevent the communists from gaining political control in liberated areas, began supporting the Germans.

Despite this assistance and the support of the fascist Ustaša nationalists in Croatia and later the Četniks in Serbia, the Germans were forced to evacuate Belgrade in 1944. Slovenia was not totally liberated until May 1945.

As many as 12,000 Domobranci and anti-communist civilians were sent back to Slovenia from refugee camps in Austria by the British in June. Most of them were executed by the communists over the next two months, their bodies thrown into caverns at Kočevski Rog in Dolenjska.

Postwar Division

Of immediate concern to Slovenia after the war was the status of liberated areas along the Adriatic, especially Trieste, which the Partisans had occupied for 40 days at the end of the war. A peace treaty signed in Paris in 1947 put Trieste and its surrounds under Anglo-American administration (the so-called Zone A) and the Koper and Buje (Istria) areas under Yugoslav control in Zone B. In 1954, Zone A (with both its Italian and ethnic Slovenian populations) became the

Italian province of Trieste. Koper and a 47km stretch of coast later went to Slovenia and Istria to Croatia. The Belvedere Treaty (1955) guaranteed Austria its 1938 borders, including most of Koroška.

Tito & Socialist Yugoslavia

Tito had been elected head of the Anti-Fascist Assembly for the National Liberation of Yugoslavia (AVNOJ) in November 1943, which provided for a federal republic. Immediately after the war he moved quickly to consolidate his power under the communist banner.

It soon became clear that, despite the efforts of Slovenian communist leader Edvard Kardelj to have them enshrined in the new constitution, Slovenia's rights to self-determination and autonomy within the framework of a federal Yugoslavia would be very limited beyond educational and cultural matters. Serbian domination from Belgrade would continue and in some respects be even more centralist than under the Kingdom of Yugoslavia.

Josip Broz Tito, whose domination of post-WWII Yugoslavia ended with his death in 1980

Tito distanced himself from Stalin and domination by the Soviet Union as early as 1948, risking invasion, but efforts to create a communist state, with all the usual arrests, show trials, purges and concentration camps (such as the one on the island of Goli in the Adriatic), continued into the mid-1950s. Industry was nationalised, private ownership of agricultural land limited to 20 hectares, and a planned central economy put in place.

But isolation from the markets of the Soviet bloc soon forced Tito to look to the west. Yugoslavia introduced features of a market economy (including workers' self-management) though what was by then called the League of Communists would retain its decisive political role. Greater economic reforms in the mid-1960s (especially under Stane Kavčič in Slovenia) as well as relaxed police control and border controls for both foreign tourists and Yugoslavs brought greater prosperity and freedom of movement, but the Communist Party saw such democratisation as a threat to its power. A purge against the reformists in government was carried out in 1971-72, and many politicians and directors were pensioned off for their 'liberalism' and 'entrepreneurial thinking'. A new constitution in 1974 gave the Yugoslav republics more independence (and autonomy to the ethnic Albanian province of Kosovo in Serbia), but what were to become known as the 'leaden years' in Yugoslavia lasted throughout the 1970s until Tito's death in 1980. Economically, though, Slovenia was the most advanced republic in Yugoslavia by the end of the decade.

Crisis, Renewal & Change

The economic decline in Yugoslavia in the early 1980s led to inter-ethnic conflict, especially between Serbs and ethnic Albanians in autonomous Kosovo, which persists to this day. Serbia proposed scrapping elements of the 1974 constitution in favour of more uniformity of the state in economic and cultural areas. This, of course, was anathema to Slovenes who saw themselves threatened.

In 1987, the liberal magazine *Nova Revija*

in Ljubljana published an article outlining a new Slovenian national program: political pluralism, democracy, a market economy and independence for Slovenia, possibly within a Yugoslav confederation. The new liberal leader of the Slovenian communists, Milan Kučan, did not oppose the demands and opposition parties began emerging. The *de facto* head of the central government in Belgrade, the Serbian communist leader Slobodan Milošević, resolved to put pressure on Slovenia.

In June 1988, three Slovenian journalists working for the *Mladina* (Youth) weekly and a junior army officer who had given away 'military secrets' were put on trial by a military court and sentenced to prison. (One of the journalists, Janez Janša, would serve as defence minister for the first 15 months after independence.) Mass demonstrations were held throughout the country in support of the four.

In the autumn, Serbia unilaterally scrapped the autonomy of Kosovo (where 80% of the population is ethnically Albanian). Slovenes were shocked by the move, fearing the same could happen to them. A rally organised jointly by the Slovenian government and the opposition in Ljubljana in February 1989 condemned the move.

In the spring of that year the new opposition parties published the May Declaration demanding a sovereign state for Slovenes based on democracy and respect for human rights. It wasn't all about political altruism, of course. In September, the Slovenian parliament amended the constitution to legalise management of its own resources – much more money was still going out of Slovenia than coming in – and peace-time command of the armed forces. Serbia announced plans to hold a 'meeting of truth' in Ljubljana on its intentions. When Slovenia banned it, Serbia and all the other republics except Croatia announced an economic boycott of Slovenia, cutting off 25% of its exports. In January 1990 Slovenian delegates walked out on an extraordinary congress of the League of Communists, thereby sounding the death knell of the party.

Independence

In April 1990, Slovenia became the first Yugoslav republic to hold free elections and shed 45 years of communist rule. DEMOS, a coalition of seven opposition parties, won 55% of the vote and Kučan, head of what was now called the Party of Democratic Renewal, was elected 'president of the presidency'. The leader of the Christian Democrats, Lojze Peterle, became prime minister.

In the summer, after Serbia had rejected Slovenian and Croatian proposals for a confederation and threatened to declare a state of emergency, the Slovenian parliament adopted a 'declaration on the sovereignty of the state of Slovenia'. Henceforth Slovenia's own constitution would direct its political, economic and judicial systems; federal laws would apply only if they were not in contradiction to it. A referendum on the question of independence was scheduled for just before Christmas.

On 23 December 1990, 88% of the electorate voted for an independent republic – effective within six months. The presidency of the Yugoslav Federation in Belgrade labelled the move secessionist and an anticonstitutional act. Serbia then proceeded to raid the Yugoslav monetary system and misappropriated almost the entire monetary issue planned for Yugoslavia in 1991 – US$2 billion. Seeing the handwriting on the wall all too clearly, the Slovenian government began stockpiling weapons and on 25 June 1991 Slovenia pulled out of the Yugoslav Federation for good. 'This evening dreams are allowed,' President Kučan told the jubilant crowd in Ljubljana's Kongresni trg the following evening. 'Tomorrow is a new day.'

Indeed it was. On 27 June the Yugoslav army began marching on Slovenia but met great resistance from the Territorial Defence Forces, the police and the general population. Within several days, units of the federal army began disintegrating; Belgrade threatened aerial bombardment and total war, as would soon follow in the Croatian cities of Vukovar and Dubrovnik.

The military action had not come totally

unprovoked. To dramatise their bid for independence and to generate support from a less than sympathetic west, which wanted to see Yugoslavia continue to exist in some form or another, Slovenian leaders had baited Belgrade by attempting to take control of the border crossings first. Belgrade apparently never expected Slovenia to resist to the degree that it did, believing that a show of force would be sufficient for it to back down.

As no territorial claims or minority issues were involved, the Yugoslav government agreed on 7 July to a truce brokered by leaders of the European Community (EC). Under the so-called Brioni Declaration, Slovenia would put further moves to assert its independence on hold for three months provided it was granted recognition by the EC after that time. The war had lasted just 10 days and taken the lives of 66 people.

To everyone's surprise, Belgrade announced that it would withdraw the federal army from Slovenian soil within three months, which took place on 25 October. In late December, Slovenia got a new constitution and the EC formally recognised the country on 15 January 1992. Slovenia was admitted to the United Nations on 22 May 1992 as the 176th member-state.

GEOGRAPHY & GEOLOGY

Slovenia is a central European country with a surface area of only 20,256 sq km – about 0.2% of Europe's total land mass. Compare it with Wales, Israel or half of Switzerland and you'll get the picture. It borders Austria for 324km to the north and Croatia for 546km to the south and south-east. Much shorter frontiers are shared with Italy (235km) to the west and Hungary (102km) to the north-east.

Geographers divide Slovenia into as many as 13 different areas, but there are basically six topographies: the Alps, including the Julian Alps, the Kamnik-Savinja Alps, the Karavanke chain and the Pohorje Massif to the north and north-east; the pre-Alpine hills of Idrija, Cerkno, Škofja Loka and Posavje spreading across the entire southern side of

the Alps; the Dinaric karst below the hills and encompassing the 'true' or 'original' Karst plateau (from which all other karst regions around the world take their name) between Ljubljana and the Italian border; the Slovenian littoral, 47km of coastline along the Adriatic Sea; the 'lowlands', comprising about one-fifth of the territory in various parts of the country; and the essentially flat Pannonian plain to the east and north-east.

Much of the interior of Slovenia is drained by the rivers Sava, which rises near Bohinj and Kranjska Gora, and Drava from Austria; they both empty into the Danube. Other important rivers are the Soča to the west, which flows into the Adriatic, the Mura in the north-east, the Krka to the south-east and the Kolpa, which forms part of the southeastern border with Croatia. There are several 'intermittent' rivers (eg the Unica, Pivka and Reka), which disappear into karst caves, only to resurface again later under different names. Slovenia's largest lakes are Cerknica, which is dry for part of the year, and Bohinj.

Main Regions

The topographical divisions do not accurately reflect Slovenia's cultural and historical differences nor do the 147 *občine* (administrative communes or municipalities) help the traveller much. Instead, Slovenia is best viewed as a country with a capital city (Ljubljana) and eight traditional *regije* (regions or provinces): Gorenjska, Primorska, Notranjska, Dolenjska, Bela Krajina, Štajerska, Prekmurje and Koroška.

Greater Ljubljana, by far the nation's largest city, is pinched between two groups of hills to the west, east and south-east and a non-arable marshland (Ljubljansko Barje) to the south. It is not in the exact centre of the country but close to it.

Gorenjska, to the north and north-west of the capital, is the country's most mountainous province and contains Slovenia's highest peaks, including Mt Triglav (2864m). The provincial centre is Kranj. Primorska, a very diverse region of hills, valleys, karst and a short coastline on the north-western side of

Provinces
of Slovenia

0   25   50 km

the Istrian peninsula, forms the country's western border. It has two 'capitals', Nova Gorica and Koper, and the Italian minority is based here. Notranjska, to the south and south-west of Ljubljana, is an underdeveloped area of forests and karst – Slovenia's 'last frontier'. Its main towns are Cerknica and Postojna.

Dolenjska lies south of the Sava River and counts several distinct areas, including the Krka Valley, the hilly Kočevje and the Posavje regions. Novo Mesto is the main city here. Bela Krajina, a land of rolling hills, birch groves and folk culture below Dolenjska, has its centres at Metlika and Črnomelj.

Štajerska, Slovenia's largest *regija*, stretches to the east and north-east and is a land of mountains, rivers, valleys, vineyards and ancient towns. Maribor and Celje are the centres and Slovenia's second and third largest cities respectively. Prekmurje, 'beyond the Mura River' in Slovenia's extreme north-east, is basically a flat plain though there are hills to the north. The Hungarian minority lives within its borders, and the centre is Murska Sobota. Sitting on top of Štajerska, little Koroška, with its

centre at Slovenj Gradec, is all that is left of the once great historical province of Carinthia.

CLIMATE
In general, Slovenia is temperate with four distinct seasons, but the topography creates three individual climates. The north-west has an Alpine climate with strong influences from the Atlantic and abundant precipitation. Temperatures in the Alpine valleys are moderate in summer but cold in winter. The coast and a large part of Primorska as far as the Soča Valley has a Mediterranean climate with warm, sunny weather much of the year and mild winters (though the *burja*, a cold and dry north-easterly wind from the Adriatic, can be fierce at times). Most of eastern Slovenia has a Continental climate with hot (in recent years *very* hot) summers and cold winters.

Slovenia gets most of its rain in the spring (March and April) and autumn (October and November); precipitation amounts vary but average about 800mm in the eastern part of the country, 1400mm in the centre, 1000mm on the coast and 3500mm in the Alps. January is the coldest month with an average annual temperature of -2°C and July is the

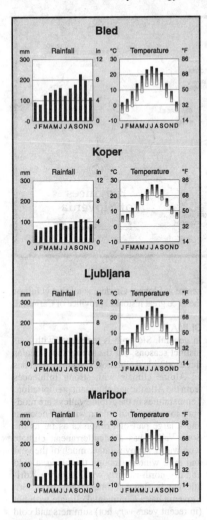

Bled

mm Rainfall in °C Temperature °F
J F M A M J J A S O N D

Koper

mm Rainfall in °C Temperature °F
J F M A M J J A S O N D

Ljubljana

mm Rainfall in °C Temperature °F
J F M A M J J A S O N D

Maribor

mm Rainfall in °C Temperature °F
J F M A M J J A S O N D

ECOLOGY & ENVIRONMENT

Habitation

Slovenia is predominantly hilly or mountainous; about 90% of the surface is more than 300m above sea level. Forest, some of it virgin, covers more than half of the country, making Slovenia the greenest country in Europe outside Finland. Agricultural land (fields, orchards, vineyards, pastures etc) accounts for just under 43% of the total.

The population density is just over 98 people per sq km, with the urban-rural ratio split almost exactly in half. The five largest settlements in Slovenia are Ljubljana (270,000), Maribor (101,700), Celje (39,700), Kranj (36,700) and Koper (24,400).

Cities and towns like Ljubljana, Celje, Ptuj and Koper were built on the foundations of Roman or even pre-Roman settlements while others are essentially new (eg Nova Gorica). Many cities in Slovenia are ringed by housing estates. Traditional farmhouses are quite different in the Alps, the Karst region, Pannonia and central Slovenia though modern 'European-style' housing appears everywhere nowadays. The hayrack *(kozolec)*, the most distinctly Slovenian of all folk architecture, can be seen everywhere in the country except in Prekmurje and some parts of Primorska.

Pollution

Though Slovenia is a very 'green' country in both senses of the word, pollution is a problem, particularly in the Sava, Mura and lower Savinja rivers. Rain has washed all sorts of filth dumped in the Karst region underground, and waste carried by the 'disappearing' Unica and Ljubljanica rivers threatens the Ljubljana Marsh.

Air pollution is also a big worry. Nitrogen oxide emitted by cars on the highway connecting Gorenjska with the coast is hurting the pine forests of Notranjska, and it's also damaging buildings, outdoor sculptures and other artwork in many historical cities. Sulphur dioxide levels are high in cities and towns like Šoštanj, Trbovlje and Ljubljana where coal is burned in thermo-electric power

warmest (21°C). The mean average temperature in Ljubljana is 9.5°C. The number of hours of sunshine ranges between 1700 and 2300, with Ljubljana on the low end of the scale, Portorož on the top. The climate charts on these pages show you what to expect and when to expect it in various parts of the country.

stations and heating plants. The nation's sole nuclear power plant (at Krško in Dolenjska) currently provides 37% of electric power but half is owned by Croatia and Slovenia plans to stop using it altogether in 2023.

Steps have been taken to clean up the mess with the construction of water-purifying plants, the monitoring of companies discharging waste and the introduction of gas heating. Indeed, over the 10-year period from 1985 to 1995, sulphur dioxide emissions were cut almost in half and nitrogen oxide levels reduced by about 20%. Pollution levels rarely exceed those permitted in the rest of central and western Europe, and warnings are issued periodically.

FLORA & FAUNA
Flora
Slovenia is home to some 2900 plant species and about 70 of them – many in the Alps – are unique to the country or were first classified here. Triglav National Park is especially rich in endemic flowering plants, including the Triglav 'rose' (actually a pink cinquefoil), the blue Clusi's gentian, yellow hawk's-beard, Julian poppy, Carniola lily and the purple Zois bell flower.

Fauna
Common European animals live in Slovenia in abundance such as deer, boar, chamois,

The brown bear is one of a number of European animals living in one of the world's most forested countries.

brown bears, wolves and lynx as well as some rare species like the moor tortoise, cave hedgehog, scarab beetle and various types of dormice. Two species unique to Slovenia are *Proteus anguinus*, the unique 'human fish' that lives in karst cave pools, and the marbled Soča trout *(Salmo marmorata)*. Slovenia provides a habitat for 344 bird species.

National Parks
At present, there is only one national park – the 83,807-hectare Triglav National Park encompassing almost all of the Julian Alps – although proposals have been made to set aside four more: in the Kamnik Alps, the Pohorje Massif, the Karst and the Kočevje-Kolpa region. There are another two-dozen zones designated as regional parks. These can range in size from the Sečovlje salt pans (835 hectares) south of Portorož and the Robanov Kot (1423 hectares), a pristine valley in Štajerska, to the Logar Valley (2475 hectares).

GOVERNMENT & POLITICS
Slovenia's constitution provides for a parliamentary system of government. The National Assembly (Državni Zbor), which has exclusive jurisdiction over the passing of laws, consists of 90 deputies elected for four years by proportional representation. The 40 members of the Council of State (Državni Svet), which performs an advisory role, are elected for five-year terms by regions and interest groups. The head of state, the president, is also the supreme commander of the armed forces and is elected directly for a maximum of two five-year terms. Executive power is vested in the prime minister and his or her 15-member cabinet. The judicial system consists of a supreme court, four high courts which serve as appeals courts, 11 circuit courts, and 44 district courts which are the courts of first instance. Judges exercise full judicial authority and their appointment by the National Assembly is for life. There is no death penalty in Slovenia.

Slovenia counts seven political parties represented in parliament: the Liberal Democrats of Slovenia (LDS), the Slovenian

People's Party (SLS), the Social Democratic Party of Slovenia (SDS), the Slovenian Christian Democrats (SKD), the United List of Social Democrats (ZLSD), the Democratic Party of Pensioners of Slovenia (DeSUS), and the Slovenian National Party (SNS). Their political leanings run the spectrum from the far right (SNS) and right (SLS) to the centre (LDS) and the centre-left (ZLSD).

In the first elections held in independent Slovenia (December 1992), a coalition of four parties (Liberal Democrats, Christian Democrats, United List and Social Democrats) won more than 60% of the vote with 63 deputies taking seats. The leader of the Liberal Democrats, Janez Drnovšek, was named prime minister. Milan Kučan was elected president of the republic with 64% of the vote.

President Milan Kučan was elected for a second term in November 1997.

In the November 1996 parliamentary elections, a centrist alliance of the Liberal Democrats, the People's Party and DeSUS garnered more than 55% of the vote, seating 49 MPs. Drnovšek was retained as prime minister. The Christian Democrats, wracked by infighting and split into factions, sat 10 MPs while support for the ZLSD tumbled to just 9%. In November 1997 56-year-old President Kučan was returned for his second term after winning nearly 56% of the popular vote. Janez Podobnik of the SLS came in second with just 18%.

The Hungarian and Italian ethnic communities are guaranteed certain rights under the constitution including education in their own language and the right to use it in public administration and the courts. They are also guaranteed representation in the National Assembly of one deputy each. The law on foreigners applies to those individuals of other nationalities in Slovenia who did not obtain citizenship by December 1991.

Slovenia is a member of the Alps-Adriatic Association, a regional group bringing together Hungary, Croatia, Bavaria and adjacent regions of Austria and Italy for multilateral cooperation in many fields. It is also a member of CEFTA (Central European Free Trade Association), including Hungary, the Czech Republic, Slovakia, Poland and Romania.

Slovenia's relations with Austria are good, in spite of neo-Nazi attacks on a Slovene-language school and publishing house in Klagenfurt in 1993 and 1994; the rights of ethnic Slovenes there are enshrined in the Austrian constitution. Relations between Slovenia and Hungary are warm though coloured by the 8500 ethnic Magyars living in Prekmurje and the estimated 5000 Slovenes in south-west Hungary. An agreement signed by both countries in 1992 ensures each group's rights.

Difficulties with Slovenia's neighbour to the west stem from the land claims of Italian citizens who either left Slovenia (then Yugoslavia) willingly after WWII (the 'optants') or those who were expelled. Italy even went so far as to grant citizenship to everyone born in Italian-occupied land up to 1943, which included such 'un-Italian' places as Idrija and Postojna.

Slovenia has a long list of disputes with Croatia, including ones over Slovenian property rights in Croatia and the precise position of state borders, especially those in Piran Bay off Sečovlje, which Slovenia claims entirely.

Slovenia was admitted into the Council of Europe in May 1993. Negotiations over membership of the European Union (EU) were blocked by Italy until March 1995 when Rome dropped its veto. All political parties have signed a declaration in favour of joining NATO. In June 1996 Slovenia became an associate member of the Western European Union (WEU) council and a year later an associate member of the EU. Though desire to join the EU is by no means universal in Slovenia, a poll taken in September 1997 suggested that over 60% of citizens would vote in favour of it in a referendum. Slovenia has now been invited to begin negotiations for EU membership.

ECONOMY

After a few tough years following independence, Slovenia has emerged as one of the strongest economies of the former socialist countries of eastern and central Europe. Inflation has dropped, employment is on the rise and its per-capita gross domestic product (GDP) – currently 60% of the EU average – is expected to surpass those of Greece and Portugal by 2002.

But for many Slovenes, the economic picture remains unclear. Real wages continue to grow – but faster than inflation, which puts Slovenia's international competitiveness at a disadvantage. Inflation zoomed up to 200% after independence and has steadily decreased since; it stood at about 9.5% in 1997. Unemployment continues to hover around 14.5%.

Slovenia has never been a poor country. Prior to independence it was by far the wealthiest republic of Yugoslavia. Although they represented only 8% of the total population, the industrious Slovenes produced up

to 20% of the GDP and exported more than a quarter of its goods. A favourite saying in those days was: 'The laws are written in Belgrade, read in Zagreb and carried out in Slovenia.'

The negative effects of the loss of its markets in the former Yugoslavia (once 30% of Slovenia's exports) and the pain caused by reforms needed to modernise the economy have long since faded away. The country has been able to bounce back principally because its highly educated population quickly re-oriented itself towards western Europe. Some 70% of Slovenia's foreign trade is now with the EU, especially Germany, Italy, France and Austria.

With hindsight, Slovenia was fortunate not to have had many large industrial conglomerates that in today's economic climate would prove unviable to maintain. Although Slovenia still has its share of communist-style dinosaur industrial plants, the country's furniture, textile and paper sectors produce high-quality goods that can be sold throughout Europe. Skis, for example, are one of the country's niche products.

Anyone searching for smokestacks and mines can find steelworks at Jesenice, textile mills at Kranj and coal mines east of Ljubljana at Trbovlje and Hrastnik. But more typically, the landscape is now dotted with upgraded factories thanks to foreign investment. French Renault cars are assembled at the Revoz plant in Novo Mesto and the Gorenje kitchen appliance manufacturer in Velenje does subcontract manufacturing for Germany's AEG and Quelle and MFI in the UK.

But foreign investment has not been as high as originally expected; Slovenia got a slow start in reforming laws that would entice large companies into the country. An amendment to Slovenia's constitution allowing the sale of land to foreigners was only passed in July 1997 as part of the association amendment with the EU.

Also, foreign investors are forbidden to take part directly in privatisations. They may buy shares only from the Slovenian Development Fund, a government agency that receives 20% of all shares in enterprises that are being sold by the state. However, foreign enterprises have no restrictions on participating with joint ventures and can own 100% of a company.

Mass privatisation in Slovenia of unprofitable industries built up by the former regime came about much later than in some other eastern European countries. A complicated 'transformation of ownership' scheme was put in place in 1994 but got off to a slow start; by 1996 less than a third of the more than 1400 eligible companies had actually been privatised. By the end of 1997, however, that figure had increased to more than 80%.

One of the fastest-growing sectors in the Slovenian economy is tourism, though the numbers of tourists have yet to reach pre-1991 levels. In 1997, Slovenia earned US$1.18 billion from tourism, twice the receipts of 1994 but an actual drop of 4% in earnings over the previous year, blamed on the strong US dollar, lower duty-free and petrol sales along the Italian border and falling casino revenues. The majority of visitors come from Italy, Germany and Austria – in that order.

Agriculture plays a remarkably minor role in the economy, considering how rural Slovenia appears at first. It comprises only 6% of GDP, as opposed to industry at 39% (manufacturing accounts for 30% of that figure) and services at 55%.

A little more than one in 10 Slovenes now lives off farming alone – in 1960 nearly half the population were engaged full-time in agriculture. But as Slovenes love the countryside, it is estimated that a quarter of the population farms at some point, growing grapes or raising bees for honey. The most important farm products are wheat, corn, potatoes, pears, apples and grapes. Štajerska hops for beer are a small but important export crop.

POPULATION & PEOPLE

Slovenia's last census (1991), conducted every 10 years, counted just under 1,966,000 people; the estimated population now is 1,991,000, 99% of whom are citizens. The vast majority (87%) of the population are Slovenes, descendants of the South Slavs who settled in what is now Slovenia and parts of Italy, Austria and Hungary from the 6th century AD.

There are just over 8500 ethnic Hungarians and some 2300 Gypsies largely in Prekmurje as well as 3060 Italians in Primorska. 'Others', accounting for 11.5% of the population, include Croats, Serbs, ethnic Albanians and those who identify themselves simply as 'Muslims'.

The Italians and Hungarians are considered indigenous minorities with rights protected under the constitution, and they have special deputies looking after their interests in parliament. Though some members of the other groups have lived and worked in Slovenia for many years, most are recent arrivals – refugees and economic immigrants from the fighting in the former Yugoslav republics. Their status as noncitizens in Slovenia remains hazy, and many Slovenes have very racist feelings about them. Several thousand migrants cross over the border from Croatia each day to work in Slovenia.

Ethnic Slovenes living outside the national borders number as many as 400,000, with the vast majority (almost 75%) in the USA and Canada. (Cleveland, Ohio, is the largest 'Slovenian' city outside Slovenia.) In addition, some 50,000 Slovenes or more live in the Italian regions of Gorizia, Udine and Trieste, another 15,000 in Austrian Carinthia (Kärnten) and 5000 in south-west Hungary.

Life expectancy has increased dramatically in Slovenia in recent years and is almost at western European levels – 70 years for men and almost 78 years for women. The birth rate in Slovenia is low – under 10 per 1000 population against 12.5 in the UK and 15.5 in the USA.

The age structure is therefore relatively old, with the average age for men about 35 years and for women just over 38. About 30% of the parents of the 19,000 children born in 1995 were unmarried.

EDUCATION

Slovenia is a highly educated society with a literacy rate of over 99.6% for those over 10 years of age. Indeed, being able to read and write is ingrained in the culture. 'What is your surname?' in Slovene is '*Kako si pišete?*' or 'How do you write yourself?'

Primary school *(osnovna šola)* is compulsory and free for eight years until the age of 15. Secondary school *(srednja šola)* usually lasts for four years. Some schools are orientated toward a particular profession (eg nursing); others – like the *gimnazije* (high schools) – prepare pupils for university. Those attending a three-year vocational course go to a *poklicna šola* (technical college). Ethnic Italians and Hungarians can choose to be taught in their mother tongues at 18 elementary schools and 46 secondary-school departments largely in Prekmurje and Primorska.

Slovenia has only two universities – the University of Ljubljana and a smaller one at Maribor – with a total enrolment of just under 50,000 students. Competition for places is stiff, and secondary-school pupils must take exams to be accepted into most faculties. The largest number of students are enrolled at the Faculty of Economics in Ljubljana and at the Technical Faculty of the University of Maribor.

The university course of study usually lasts four years with another year for students to take their degree *(visoka stopnja)*, which usually requires writing a thesis. But there are other programs, including a two-year '1st stage' degree *(višja stopnja)*, which is equivalent to a college or associate degree abroad and prepares students for administrative work and the like. Study at graduate levels is more individualised and involves independent research. A medical degree takes about seven years to complete.

The academic year for primary and secondary schools lasts from 1 September to 25 June with 10 days holiday around Christmas and the New Year, a week off in early February and another one at Easter. The university year is from 1 October to 30 May, with exams in June and early July.

Slovenia has a strong tradition in the sciences and has produced many great scientists – from the 17th century polymath Janez Vajkard Valvasor and Gabriel Gruber, who regulated the Ljubljanica River in the late 18th century, to the patron Žiga Zois and Friderik Pregl, who won the Nobel Prize in 1923 for organic chemistry. The Slovenian Academy of Arts and Sciences has a research centre with 14 institutes studying all aspects of science as well as history and culture.

ARTS
Architecture, Sculpture & Painting

Examples of Romanesque architecture can be found in many parts of Slovenia, including the churches at Stična Abbey, at Muta and Dravograd in Koroška and Podsreda Castle, but fine art from the period is rare, surviving only in illuminated manuscripts.

Gothic painting and sculpture is another matter, with excellent works – some commissioned by burghers and wealthy landowners – at Ptujska Gora (the carved altar in the Church of the Virgin Mary), at Bohinj (frescoes in the Church of St John the Baptist) and Hrastovlje (Dance of Death wall painting at the Church of the Holy Trinity). Important painters of this time were Johannes de Laibaco (John of Ljubljana), who decorated the Church of the Assumption in Muljava; Jernej of Loka, who worked mostly around Škofja Loka; and Johannes Aquila of Radgona, who did the frescoes in the magnificent church at Martjanci in Prekmurje. Much Gothic architecture in Slovenia is of the late period; the earthquake of 1511 took care of many buildings erected before then (though Koper's Venetian Gothic Loggia and Praetorian Palace date back a century earlier). Renaissance architecture is mostly limited to civil buildings (eg the town houses in Škofja Loka and Kranj and Brdo Castle).

Italian-influenced baroque abounds in Slovenia, and you'll find many great architectural examples, particularly in Ljubljana (Ursuline Church of the Holy Trinity and the cathedral). For sculpture, look at Jožef Straub's plague pillar in Maribor, the golden altar in the Church of the Annunciation at

Crngrob or the work of Francesco Robba in Ljubljana (Fountain of the Carniolan Rivers in Mestni trg). Fortunat Bergant, who painted the Stations of the Cross in the church at Stična Abbey, was a master of baroque painting.

Classicism prevailed in Slovenian architecture in the first half of the 18th century (the Kazina building in Kongresni trg in Ljubljana, the Tempel pavilion in Rogaška Slatina) but also in the works of the painter Franc Kavčič and the Romantic portraits and landscapes of Josip Tominc and Matevž Langus. Realism arrived in the second half of the century in the work of artists like Ivana Kobilca, Jurij Šubic and Anton Ažbe, but the most important painters of that time were the impressionists Rihard Jakopič, Matija Jama, Ivan Grohar and Matej Sternen, who exhibited together in Ljubljana in 1900.

The turn of the century was also the time when the Secessionist (or Art Nouveau) architects Maks Fabiani and Ivan Vurnik began changing the face of Ljubljana (Miklošičev Park, Prešeren monument, Cooperative Bank on Miklošičeva cesta)

Jože Tisnikar, from Slovenj Gradec, is one of Slovenia's most interesting and original artists.

after the devastating 1895 earthquake. But no architect has had a greater impact on their city or nation than Jože Plečnik, a man who defies easy definition (see boxed text entitled Jože Plečnik, Architect Extraordinaire in the Ljubljana chapter).

In the 20th century, the expressionist school of Božidar Jakac and the brothers France and Tone Kralj gave way to the so-called Club of Independents (the painters Zoran Mušič, Maks Sedej and France Mihelič) and later the sculptors Alojzij Gangl, Franc Berneker, Jakob Savinšek and Lojze Dolinar. The last two would later create 'masterpieces' of socialist realism under Tito without losing their credibility or (sometimes) their artistic sensibilities. Favourite artists of recent years include Janez Bernik, Rudi Španzel (who designed the tolar notes in circulation) and Jože Tisnikar, a painter with a very unique style from Slovenj Gradec.

Postmodernist painting and sculpture has been more or less dominated since the 1980s by the multimedia group Neue Slowenische Kunst (NSK) and the five-member artists' cooperative IRWIN.

The apogee of folk painting in Slovenia over the past few centuries has been the traditional beehive panel *(panjska končnica)* illustrated with folk motifs. For more information, see the boxed text entitled The Boards and the Bees in the Radovljica section of the Gorenjska chapter.

Music
The conversion of the Slavs to Christianity from the 8th century brought the development of choral singing – the oldest Slovenian spiritual song dates from 1440 – in churches and monasteries. By the end of the Middle Ages, secular music had developed to the same degree as music elsewhere in Europe. The most important composer in the late 16th century was Jakob Gallus, who wrote madrigals and choral songs as well as 16 Masses. An outstanding composer of Renaissance music was Izak Poš.

Baroque music had gone out of fashion by the time the Filharmonija was founded in

Ljubljana in 1701, and classicist forms had become all the rage. *Belin*, the first Slovenian opera, was written by Jakob Francisek Zupan in 1780, and Janez Novak composed classicist music for a comedy written by Slovenia's first playwright, Anton Tomaž Linhart. The 19th century Romantics like Benjamin Ipavec, Fran Gerbič and Anton Foerster incorporated traditional Slovenian elements into their music as a way of expressing their nationalism. Perhaps Slovenia's most well known composer was Hugo Wolf, who was born in Slovenj Gradec in 1860 and died in 1903.

Slovenian music between the wars is best represented by the expressionist Marij Kogoj and the modernist Slavko Osterc. Contemporary composers whose reputations go well beyond the borders of Slovenia include Primož Ramovš, Marjan Kozina, Lojze Lebič and the ultramodernist Vinko Globokar, who lives in Paris. Opera buffs won't want to miss the chance to hear Marjana Lipovšek, the country's foremost mezzo-soprano.

Popular music runs the gamut from Slovenian *chanson* (best exemplified by Vita Mavrič) and folk to jazz and techno, but it was punk music in the late 1970s and early 1980s that put Slovenia on the world stage. The most celebrated groups were Pankrti, Borghesia and Laibach, and they were imitated throughout eastern Europe. (Laibach's leader, Tomaž Hostnik, died tragically in 1983 when he hanged himself from a kozolec, the traditional Slovenian hayrack.)

Folk music *(ljudska glasba)* in Slovenia has developed independently from other forms of music over the centuries, and the collection and classification of children's songs, wedding marches and fables set to music began only in the nationalistic Romantic period of the 19th century. Today the Institute of Music and National Manuscripts (Glasbeno Narodopisni Institut) is charged with this task. Traditional folk instruments include the *frajtonarica* (button accordion), cymbalom (a curious stringed instrument played with sticks), zither, *zvegla*

(wooden cross flute), *okarina* (a clay flute), *šurle* (Istrian double flute), *trstenke* (reed pipes), Jew's harp, *lončeni bajs* (earthenware bass), and *brač* (eight-string guitar). Folk groups and individuals to watch out for include the Avseniki, Lojzeta Slaka, the Alpski Kvintet led by Oto Pestner and the Gypsy band Šukar.

Dance

Much of Slovenian dance finds its origins in folk culture, and folk dance *(ljudski ples)* has a long tradition in Slovenia, including polkas, circle dances and Hungarian-style czardas. The first ballet group was established in 1918 as part of the Ljubljana Opera and a ballet school set up within the National Theatre. The Ljubljana Ballet still performs at the Opera and there's another company in Maribor.

Avant-garde dance is best exemplified by Betontanc, an NSK dance company that mixes live music and theatrical elements (called 'physical theatre' here) with sharp political comment. In the rock ballet *Thieves of Wet Handkerchiefs*, members of the troupe murder one another and then are resurrected.

Literature

Christian monks from Ireland probably introduced the Latin alphabet to the early Slavs living in Slovenia in the 8th century, and St Cyril and St Methodius gave them their first translations of the Scriptures a century later.

The oldest example of written Slovene (or any Slavic language for that matter) is contained in the three *Freising Texts (Brižinski Spomeniki)* dating from around 970. They contain a sermon on sin and penance and instructions for general confession. Oral poetry, such as the seminal tale of *Lepa Vida (Fair Vida)*, flourished throughout the Middle Ages, but it was the Reformation that saw the first book in Slovene, a catechism published by Primož Trubar in 1550. A complete translation of the Bible by Jurij Dalmatin followed in 1584, and Adam Bohorič published a grammar of Slovene in Latin (with the evocative title *Spare Winter*

Hours) in the same year. Most everything else published until the late 18th century was in Latin or German, including Janez Vajkard Valvasor's laudatory account of Slovenia, *The Glory of the Duchy of Carniola* (1689).

The Enlightenment and the reforms of the Habsburg rulers Maria Theresa and Joseph II raised the educational and general cultural level of the Slovenian nation. In large part due to the support and philanthropy of Baron Žiga Zois (1747-1819), Slovenia gained its first dramatist (Anton Tomaž Linhart), poet (Valentin Vodnik) and modern grammarian (Jernej Kopitar) at this time. But it was during the Romantic period when Slovenian literature truly came of age. This period produced the nation's greatest poet France Prešeren (see boxed text entitled France Prešeren: A Poet for the Nation). The *Car-*

niolan Bee (Kranjska Čebelica), an anthology to which Prešeren contributed, was an important literary and nationalist forum in the 1830s and 1840s.

In the latter half of the 19th century, Fran Levstik (1831-87) brought the writing and interpretation of oral folk tales to new heights with his *Martin Krpan* (see boxed text entitled Big Men for Big Times in the Notranjska chapter), but it was Josip Jurčič (1844-81) who published the first full-length novel in Slovene, *The 10th Brother (Deseti Brat*; 1866). The lyrical poets Simon Jenko (1835-69) and Simon Gregorčič (1844-1906) wrote original and powerful verse.

The period from the turn of the 20th century up to WWII is dominated by two men who single-handedly introduced modernism into Slovenian literature: the poet

---

France Prešeren: A Poet for the Nation

Slovenia's most beloved poet was born in Vrba near Bled in 1800 and educated in Ribnica, Ljubljana and Vienna, where he received a law degree in 1828. Most of his working life was spent as an articled clerk in the office of a Ljubljana lawyer. By the time he opened his own practice in Kranj in 1846 he was already a sick and dispirited man. He died in 1849.

Although Prešeren published only one volume of poetry during his lifetime *(Poezije,* 1848), he left behind a legacy of work printed in the literary magazines *Kranjska Čbelica (Carniolan Bee)* and the German-language *Illyrisches Blatt (Illyrian Sheet).* His verse set new standards for Slovenian literature at a time when German was the literary language, and his lyric poems, such as the masterpiece *Sonetni Venec (A Garland of Sonnets,* 1834), are among the most sensitive, original and eloquent works in Slovene. In later poems he expressed a national consciousness that he tried to instil in his compatriots. *Krst pri Savici (Baptism at the Savica Waterfall,* 1836) is such a work.

Prešeren's life was one of sorrow and disappointment, which he met with stoicism and resignation. The sudden death of his close friend and mentor, the literary historian Matija Čop, in 1835 and an unrequited love affair with an heiress called Julija Primic brought him close to suicide. (Julija later married a German, and Slovenes like to point out, with a certain amount of *Schadenfreude,* that she was unhappy with her husband.) But this was when he produced his best poems.

In reality, Prešeren was a drunkard, a philanderer, a social outcast and perhaps even vain. He refused to have his portrait done and any likeness you see of him – including the rather dashing one on the 1000 SIT note – were done from memory after his death.

But Prešeren was the first to demonstrate the full literary potential of the Slovenian language and his body of verse – lyric poems, epics, satire, narrative verse – has inspired Slovenes at home and abroad for generations. And continues to do so. ∎

Oton Župančič (1878-1949) and the novelist and playwright Ivan Cankar (1876-1918). The latter has been called 'the outstanding master of Slovenian prose' and his works, notably *The Ward of Our Lady of Mercy (Hiša Marije Pomočnice)* and *The Bailiff Yerney and His Rights (Hlapec Jernej in Njegova Pravica)* influenced a generation of young writers.

Slovenian literature immediately before and after WWII was influenced by socialist realism and the Partisan struggle as exemplified in the novels of Voranc Prežihov (1893-1950) and the poems by Matej Bor (1913-), but since then Slovenia has tended to follow western European literary trends: late expressionism, symbolism (the poetry of Edvard Kocbek, 1904-81) and existentialism (the novels of Vitomil Zupan, 1914-87, and the drama of Gregor Strniša, 1930-87). Contemporary writers and poets using avante-garde techniques include Drago Jančar (1948-), Tomaž Šalamun (1941-), Kajetan Kovič (1931-), Andrej Hieng (1925-) and Rudi Šeligo (1935-).

Film

Slovenia was never on the cutting edge of film-making as were some of the other republics (eg Croatia) in the former Yugoslavia, but it still managed to produce about a dozen full-length features annually, some of which – like Jože Gale's *Kekec* (1951) and France Štiglic's *Dolina Miru (Valley of Peace*, 1955) – won international awards. Today that number has dropped to about three per year. Indeed, the panoply of feature films produced in Slovene from the first *(V Kraljestvu Zlatoroga* or *In the Realm of the Goldenhorn)* in 1931 until 1998 numbers only around 140.

Only two films were produced in Slovenia between the wars and after WWII and into the 1950s Slovenian film tended to focus on subjects like the Partisan struggle – eg Štiglic's *Na Svoji Zemlji (On Our Land*, 1948) and *Akcija (Action*, 1960) by Jane Kavčič – and life among the Slovenian bourgeoisie under the Austro-Hungarian Empire *(Jara Gospoda* or *Parvenus*, 1953) by Bojan

Stupica. The 1960s brought a new wave of modernism to Slovenian film best exemplified in the work of Boštjan Hladnik *(Ples v Dežju* or *Dance in the Rain*, 1961) and Matjaž Klopčič *(Na Papirnatih Avionih* or *On Wings of Paper*, 1967). Since the 1970s, the most popular films in Slovenia like everywhere have been those dealing with crime and suspense and comedies (eg Franci Slak's *Hudodelci* or *The Felons*, 1987; Jure Pervanje's *Do Konca in Naprej* or *To the Limit and Beyond*, 1990; and Vinči Vogue Anžlovar's *Babica Gre na Jug* or *Grandma Goes South*, 1991). More recent successes have been *Ekspres, Ekspres (Express, Express)* by Igor Šterk, *Herzog* by Mitja Milavec and Andrej Košak's *Outsider*, all released in 1997.

Declining audience figures in the 1990s have led to the closure of more than 35% of cinemas around the country though some 115 remain open. The best place to see Slovenian films is the Kinoteka (☎ 061-311 391) at Miklošičeva cesta 38 in Ljubljana. A Festival of Slovenian Film is held in Portorož in March.

RELIGION

Although Protestantism gained a very strong foothold in Slovenia in the 16th century, the majority of Slovenes today – just under 72% – identify themselves as Roman Catholic. An archbishop (currently Alojzij Šuštar) sits in Ljubljana and there are bishoprics at Maribor and Koper.

Other religious communities in Slovenia include Eastern Orthodox Christians (2.4%), Muslims (1%) and Protestants (1%). Most Protestants belong to the Evangelical (Lutheran) church based in Murska Sobota in Prekmurje.

Jews have played a very minor role in Slovenia since they were first banished from the territory in the 15th century. Although the remains of a synagogue still stand in Maribor and there was one in Ljubljana until WWII, no temple functions in Slovenia today. The rabbi from Zagreb occasionally holds services for the tiny community in Ljubljana when there is a minyan.

As in most of central and western Europe today, religion doesn't appear to be much of an issue in Slovenia, particularly among the young, and churches are seldom more than half-full outside the most important holy days like Easter, Christmas and the Assumption of Mary (15 August). One Slovenian friend's only memory of ever having been into a church as a child was when his granny brought him to see the *božične jaslice* (crèche) one Christmas.

LANGUAGE

The French novelist Charles Nodier (1780-1844), who lived and worked in Ljubljana for a couple of years in the early 19th century, once wrote that Slovenia was like 'an Academy of Arts and Sciences' because of the people's flair for speaking foreign languages. Monsieur Nodier would be happy to know that Slovenci still have that talent almost two centuries down the track.

Virtually everyone in Slovenia speaks at least one other language. In the 1991 census, 88% said they knew Croatian and Serbian, 45% German, 37% were conversant in English and 17% spoke Italian. But those figures require further explanation.

Italian is really only useful in Primorska and small parts of Notranjska. German, once the language of education and the elite, is spoken mostly by older people, especially in Koroška, Štajerska and northern Gorenjska. There may be fewer speakers of English than German overall, but it is definitely the preferred language of the young, with 84% of all students claiming some knowledge of it. Most speak English very well indeed, even if they pepper their speech with 'Slovenglish' slang like 'full cool', meaning 'trendy' or 'fashionable'.

The fact that you will rarely have difficulty in making yourself understood and that you will probably never 'need' Slovene shouldn't stop you from learning a few words and phrases of this rich and wonderful language.

More than anything else, Slovene has kept the Slovenian nation *(narod)* alive and united as a culture over centuries of domination and brutality. And despite all attempts to destroy it from outside, Slovene is very much alive, dynamic and organic. Any effort on your part to speak it will be rewarded one hundred-fold (see the Language Guide at the back of the book).

Facts for the Visitor

PLANNING

When to Go

Snow can linger in the mountains as late as June, but spring (April and May) is a great time to be in the lowlands and valleys of Slovenia when everything is fresh and in blossom. (April can be a bit wet though.) In July and August, hotel rates are increased and there will be lots of tourists, especially on the coast. September is an excellent month to visit as the days are long and the weather warm, the summer crowds will have vanished and it's the best time for hiking and climbing. October and November can be rainy, but winter (December to March) is for skiers. Remember, though, that Slovenian school kids have their Christmas holidays in December/January and a week off in early February. The slopes could be heaving at those times.

Maps

The Geodesic Institute of Slovenia (Geodetski Zavod Slovenije; GZS), the country's principal map-making company, produces national (1:300,000), regional (1:50,000) and topographical maps to the entire country (64 1:50,000-scale sheets) as well as city plans. Its Ljubljana map (1:20,000; 850 SIT) is excellent. The Alpine Association of Slovenia (Planinska Zveza Slovenije; PZS) produces some 30 different hiking maps with scales as large as 1:25,000.

If you can afford it, the 385-page *Atlas of Slovenia* (Založba Mladinska Knjiga & GZS) is the most complete in the land, with 109 1:50,000-scale maps of the country and a dozen town plans. A lot more user-friendly, though, is the *Veliki Atlas za Voznike in Izletnike (Large Atlas for Motorists & Travellers;* Petrol; 2520 SIT) with two dozen 1:250,000 motoring maps, town plans and practical tips.

What to Bring

You don't have to remember any particular items of clothing – a warm sweater (even in summer) for the mountains at night, perhaps, and an umbrella in the spring or autumn – unless you plan to do some serious hiking or other sport. In general, Slovenian society dresses casually (though a bit smarter in Ljubljana than in the provinces) when it goes out on the town.

A swimsuit for the beach, pool or mixed-sex thermal spas (not always required) and a towel and thongs (flip-flops) for mouldy showers in hostels and camping grounds are mandatory. Soap, toothpaste and toilet paper are readily obtainable almost anywhere as are tampons and condoms, both locally made and imported.

A sleeping sheet with pillow cover (case) is a good idea if you plan to stay in hostels or college dormitories. A padlock is useful to secure your hostel locker. A Swiss Army knife is helpful for all sorts of things. Make sure it includes such essentials as a bottle opener and strong corkscrew!

One peculiarity here is that, while Slovenes drink lots of herbal teas, black tea is hard to find. Bring along a cup, coil water heater and tea bags and make your own cuppa.

Other optional items include a compass (to help orient yourself in the mountains and while driving), a flashlight (torch), an adapter plug for electrical appliances, sunglasses, a few clothes pegs (pins) and premoistened towelettes or a large cotton handkerchief that you can soak in fountains and use to cool off while touring towns and cities in the hot summer months. And don't forget sunblock – even in the cooler months. Those rays in the mountains can be fierce.

SUGGESTED ITINERARIES

Depending on the length of your stay, you might want to see and do the following in Slovenia:

Two days
    Visit Ljubljana

One week
  Visit Ljubljana, Bled and Bohinj or Škocjan
  Caves and Piran
Two weeks
  Visit Ljubljana, Bled, Bohinj, Soča Valley,
  Škocjan Caves, Piran and Ptuj

HIGHLIGHTS
Historic Towns
The most attractive cities and towns – and the ones where you'll get a real feel for the past – are Ljubljana, Ptuj, Škofja Loka, Radovljica, Piran and Kranj.

Museums
The following museums stand out not just for what they contain but for how they display it: the Dolenjska Museum in Novo Mesto, the Posavje Museum in Brežice, the Blacksmith Museum in Kropa, the Municipal Museum in Idrija, the Saltworks Museum in Sečovlje, the Beekeeping Museum in Radovljica, the Kobarid Museum and, in Ljubljana, the Museum of Modern History and the Slovenian Ethnographic Museum.

Castles
Slovenia was once known as the 'country of castles' and counted over 1000, but wars and development have taken care of most of them. Of the remaining ones, the most dramatic (open to the public and in varying states of repair) are Bled Castle, Predjama Castle near Postojna, Ljubljana Castle, Snežnik Castle in Notranjska, Bogenšperk Castle in Dolenjska, Podsreda Castle in the Kozjansko region of Štajerska, Celje Castle and Ptuj Castle. For more information contact the Association of Castles in Slovenia (Skupnost Gradov na Slovenskem; ☎ 062-773 145; fax 062-771 618), Na gradu 1, 2250 Ptuj.

Churches
The following are a half-dozen of Slovenia's most beautiful houses of worship: the Church of St John the Baptist at Bohinj, the Church of the Holy Trinity at Hrastovlje (Primorska), the Church of the Virgin Mary at Ptujska Gora near Ptuj, the Chapter Church of St Nicholas in Novo Mesto, the Church of the Assumption at Nova Štifta near Ribnica and the Church of the Annunciation at Crngrob near Škofja Loka.

Natural Wonders
You won't soon forget the Vršič Pass and the Julian Alps in Triglav National Park, the Škocjan Caves, the Vintgar Gorge near Bled, the Upper Savinja Valley in Štajerska, the Soča River and the (True or Original) Karst region.

TOURIST INFORMATION
Local Tourist Offices
The Slovenian Tourist Board (Center za Promocijo Turizma Slovenije; CPTS; ☎ 061-189 1840; fax 061-189 1841; lucka .letic@cpts.tradepoint.si), in the World Trade Centre at Dunajska cesta 160 in Ljubljana, is the umbrella organisation for tourist offices in Slovenia and produces brochures and pamphlets. It can handle requests for information in writing or you can check out its page on the Internet (see Online Services later in this chapter).

The best office for face-to-face information in Slovenia – bar none – is the Ljubljana Tourist Information Centre (TIC; ☎ 061-133 0111; fax 061-133 0244) in Ljubljana. The staff know *everything* about the capital and a lot about Slovenia. There are also TICs in Bled, Bohinj, Kranjska Gora, Maribor, Portorož and Ptuj and smaller, independent or community-run offices in other cities and towns. If the place you're visiting doesn't have one, seek assistance at a branch of one of the big travel agencies (eg Kompas, Emona Globtour or Slovenijaturist) or from hotel or museum staff.

Travel Agencies
The head offices (all in Ljubljana, where the telephone code is 061) of Slovenia's most important travel agencies appear below. For the addresses and telephone numbers of branch offices in Ljubljana and the provinces, see the Information sections under each town or city.

Emona Globtour
(☎ 140 1044; fax 441 325), Šmartinska cesta 130
Kompas Holidays
(☎ 125 2065; fax 219 111), Slovenska cesta 36
Kompas Turizem
(☎ 132 7127; fax 319 888), Pražakova ulica 4
Slovenijaturist
(☎ 131 5055; fax 328 884), Slovenska cesta 58

Tourist Offices & Agencies Abroad

The Slovenian Tourist Board maintains tourist offices in the following eight countries:

Austria
(☎ 0222-715 40 10), Hilton Center, Landstrasser Hauptstrasse 2, 1030 Vienna
Germany
(☎ 089-2916 1202), Maximilliansplatz 12a, 80333 Munich
Hungary
(☎ 1-156 8223), Gellérthegy utca 28, 1013 Budapest
Italy
(☎ 02-29 51 11 87), Via Lazzaro Palazzi 2a/III, 20124 Milan
Netherlands & Belgium
(☎ 0118-635 790), Goudent 10-13, 4330 GC Middelburg
Switzerland
(☎ 01-212 63 94), Löwenstrasse 54, 8001 Zürich
UK
(☎ 0171-372 3767), 2 Canfield Place, London NW6 3BT
USA
(☎ 212-358 9686), 345 East 12th St, New York, NY 10003

In addition, Kompas has representative offices in many cities worldwide, including:

Australia
(☎ 07-3831 4400), 323 Boundary St, Spring Hill, 4000 Queensland
Canada
(☎ 514-938 4041), 4060 Ste-Catherine St West, Suite 535, Montreal, Que H3Z 2Z3
Croatia
(☎ 052-451 100), Obala Maršala Tita 16, 51440 Poreč
Czech Republic
(☎ 02-2423 5070), Ul Rytirska 26/II, 11000 Prague I
France
(☎ 01 53 92 27 80), 14 Rue de la Source, 75016 Paris

Germany
(☎ 030-8060 2780), Glienickerstrasse 40, 14109 Berlin
(☎ 069-233 024/6), Mainluststrasse 6/VI, 60329 Frankfurt
Italy
(☎ 041-528 6545), San Marco 1497, 30124 Venice
Netherlands
(☎ 010-414 0903), Nieuwehaven 106, 3011 VT Rotterdam
South Africa
(☎ 011-884 8555), Norwich Towers, 3/F, 13 Fredman Drive, Sandton, Johannesburg
Spain
(☎ 93-246 6777), Calle Valencia 414, Escderecha, I/2a, 08013 Barcelona
Switzerland
(☎ 041-410 8515), St Leodegarstrasse 2, 6006 Lucerne
USA
(☎ 954-771 9200), 2826 East Commercial Blvd, Fort Lauderdale, FL 33308

Tourist Publications

The CPTS and other offices produce many brochures, pamphlets and booklets in English, some of them overly colourful and 'sing-song', others quite useful and well written. The titles below are general ones; more specialised publications and local ones appear under other headings in this chapter or in the Information sections for each town.

Calendar of Events of Slovenia
An annual list of everything happening in Slovenia – from concerts and folk festivals to trade fairs and conferences.
Facts about Slovenia: Useful Dates
Names, addresses and contact numbers for ministries, business institutions, universities, embassies etc.
Fishing in Slovenia/Ribolov v Sloveniji
Details, seasons and prices for angling in a dozen different rivers and lakes.
Hotel Rates in Slovenia
Virtually every type of accommodation (not just hotels) appears in this annual publication.
Camp Sites in Slovenia
Descriptions and photographs of the more than 40 registered camping grounds in the country.
A Merry Wintertime on the Sunny Side of the Alps
This slim brochure describes the facilities and nearby accommodation at some 47 ski resorts and grounds in Slovenia – from Kranjska Gora to tiny Janina Hill in Rogaška Slatina.

Slovenian Health Resorts
> This pamphlet covers all aspects of spa tourism in Slovenia, with a listing of 16 resorts, their facilities and prices.

Slovenia in Figures
> Every statistic you may – or may not – need to know about Slovenia – from unemployment rates to how much the average family spends on bread.

Welcome to Slovenia
> A colourful introduction to the country and its attractions.

Castles in Slovenia
> Castles, palaces and mansions across the country.

VISAS & DOCUMENTS
Passport
Most everyone entering Slovenia must have a valid passport, though citizens of the EU and Switzerland need only produce their national identity card on arrival for stays of up to 30 days. It's a good idea to carry your passport or other identification at all times.

Visas
Citizens of Australia, Canada, Israel, Japan, New Zealand and the USA do not require visas for stays of up to 90 days. Those who do require visas (including South African passport holders at the time of writing) can get them at any of the Slovenian embassies or consulates listed below for up to 90 days. They cost DM50 (or equivalent), and you may have to show a return or onward ticket. Photographs are not required.

Visas are also available at international border crossings (see Car & Motorcycle in the Getting There & Away chapter) and at Brnik airport near Ljubljana. There they cost 3500 SIT and, again, photos are not necessary. Visas can also be acquired on trains, but you may have to get off and queue, in which case you could miss your onward connection. If you do plan to enter Slovenia by rail, it is strongly advised that you organise your visa in advance at a Slovenian embassy or consulate.

Your hotel, hostel, camp site or private room arranged through an agency will register your name and address with the municipal government *(občina)* office as required by law; that's why they have to take your passport away – at least for the first night. If you are staying elsewhere (eg with relatives or friends), your host is supposed to take care of this for you within three days.

If you want to stay in Slovenia longer than three months, the easiest thing to do is simply cross the border into Italy or Austria and return. Otherwise you will have to apply for a temporary residence permit at the Foreigners Office (Urad za Tujce; ☎ 061-131 0166) in the Kresija building at Adamič-Lundrovo nabrežje 2 in Ljubljana.

Contact any Slovenian embassy, consulate or tourist office abroad for any recent changes in the above regulations. The staff at any branch of Adria Airways, the Slovenian national carrier, should also be able to help. For addresses, see Air in the Getting There & Away chapter.

Photocopies
The hassles brought on by losing your passport can be considerably reduced if you have a record of its number and issue date, or even better, photocopies of the relevant data pages. A photocopy of your birth certificate can also be useful.

Also add the serial numbers of your travellers cheques (cross them off as you cash them) and photocopies of your credit cards, airline ticket and other travel documents. Keep all this emergency material separate from your passport, cheques and cash, and leave extra copies with someone you can rely on back home. Add some emergency money (US$50 in cash, say) to this separate stash as well. If you do lose your passport, notify the police immediately to get a statement, and contact your nearest consulate.

Travel Insurance
A travel insurance policy to cover theft, loss and medical problems is a must, so consider this before you leave home. Remember, however, that some policies specifically exclude 'dangerous activities' such as skiing, mountaineering or even trekking.

Your policy should also cover cancellation or delays in your travel arrangements. (You could fall seriously ill two days before departure, for example.) Cover depends on your insurance and type of airline ticket, so ask both your insurer and your ticket-issuing agency to explain where you stand. Ticket loss is also covered by travel insurance.

Paying for your airline ticket with a credit card often provides limited travel accident insurance, and you may be able to reclaim the payment if the operator doesn't deliver. In the UK, for instance, institutions issuing credit cards are required by law to reimburse consumers if a company goes into liquidation and the amount in contention is more than UK£100. Ask your credit card company what it's prepared to cover.

Driving Licence & Permits
If you don't hold a European driving licence and plan to drive in Slovenia, obtain an International Driving Permit from your local automobile association before you leave – you'll need a passport photo and a valid licence. They are usually inexpensive and valid for one year only.

Camping Card International
Your local automobile association also issues the Camping Card International (CCI), which is basically a camping ground ID. These cards are also available from your local camping federation, and sometimes on the spot at camping grounds. They incorporate third-party insurance for damage you may cause, and some camping grounds in Slovenia offer discounts of 5 to 10% if you sign in with one.

Hostel Card
No hostels in Slovenia require that you be a hostelling association member, but they sometimes charge a little less if you have a card. Mladi Turist (☎ 061-125 9260), at Salendrova ulica 4 in Ljubljana, is the office of the Slovenian Youth Hostel Association and sells hostel cards (800 SIT for those under 18 years of age, 1200 SIT for those between 18 and 26, 1800 SIT for those over 26).

Student & Youth Cards
The most useful of these is the International Student Identity Card (ISIC), a plastic ID-style card with your photograph, which provides discounts on some forms of transport and cheap or free admission to museums, sights and even films. If you're aged under 26 but not a student, you can apply for a GO25 card issued by the Federation of International Youth Travel Organisations (FIYTO), which gives much the same discounts and benefits as an ISIC. The Erazem backpacker travel agency (☎ 061-133 1076) at Trubarjeva cesta 7 in Ljubljana sells both ISIC cards (800 SIT) and GO25 cards (700 SIT).

EMBASSIES
Slovenian Embassies Abroad
In addition to the embassies and general consulates listed here, Slovenia has honorary consuls in Sydney, Australia (☎ 02-9314 5116), and in Cleveland, Ohio (☎ 216-589 9220) and Venice, California (☎ 310-392 5820) in the USA.

Australia
> (☎ 06-243 4830), Advance Bank Centre, Level 6, 60 Marcus Clark St, Canberra, ACT 2601

Austria
> (☎ 0222-586 1307), Nibelungengasse 13, 1010 Vienna

Belgium
> (☎ 02-646 90 99), Ave Louise 179, 1050 Brussels

Canada
> (☎ 613-565 5781), 150 Metcalfe St, Suite 2101, Cttawa, Ont K2P 1P1

Croatia
> (☎ 01-612 1503), Savska cesta 41/IX, 10000 Zagreb

Czech Republic
> (☎ 02-2431 5106), Pod Hradbami 15, 16000 Prague 6

France
> (☎ 01 47 55 65 90), 21 Rue Bouquet de Longchamp, 75016 Paris
> (☎ 03 88 36 60 25), 40 Allée de la Robertsau, 67000 Strasbourg

Germany
> (☎ 0228-858 031), Siegfriedstrasse 28, 53179 Bonn 2
> (☎ 089-543 9819), Lindwurm Strasse 10, 80045 Munich

Hungary
> (☎ 1-325 9202), Cseppkő utca 68, 1025 Budapest

Italy
> (☎ 06-808 1272), Via Ludovico Pisano 10, 00197 Rome

Russia
  (☎ 095-209 0203), Ul Chehova 14, 103006 Moscow
Spain
  (☎ 91-441 6893), Calle Hermanos Becquer 7-2, 28006 Madrid
Switzerland
  (☎ 031-312 4418), Schwanengasse 9/II, 3011 Bern
UK
  (☎ 0171-495 7775), Suite One, Cavendish Court, 11-15 Wigmore St, London W1H 9LA
USA
  (☎ 202-667 5363), 1525 New Hampshire Ave NW, Washington, DC 20036

Foreign Embassies & Consulates in Slovenia

Selected countries with representation in Ljubljana – either full embassies or consulate holdovers from pre-independence days – appear below. If telephoning from outside the capital but still within Slovenia, remember to dial 061 first.

Australia
  (☎ 125 4252), Trg Republike 3/XII
Austria
  (☎ 179 0700), Dunajska cesta 51
Bosnia-Hercegovina
  (☎ 132 4042), Likozarjeva ulica 6
Canada
  (☎ 130 3570), Miklošičeva cesta 19
Croatia
  (☎ 125 7287), Gruberjevo nabrežje 6
Czech Republic
  (☎ 339 257), Riharjeva ulica 1
France
  (☎ 126 4525), Barjanska cesta 1
Germany
  (☎ 216 166), Prešernova cesta 27
Hungary
  (☎ 152 1882), Ulica Konrada Babnika 5
Italy
  (☎ 126 2194), Snežniška ulica 8
Macedonia
  (☎ 168 4454), Dunajska cesta 104
Netherlands
  (☎ 328 978), Dunajska cesta 22
Romania
  (☎ 268 702), Nanoška ulica 8
Russia
  (☎ 125 6875), Rožna Dolina, Cesta II, No 7
UK
  (☎ 125 7191), Trg Republike 3/IV
USA
  (☎ 301 485), Pražakova ulica 4

CUSTOMS

Travellers can bring in the usual personal effects, a couple of cameras and electronic goods for their own use, 200 cigarettes, a generous 4L of spirits but only 1L of wine (remember, viniculture is big business here). The import or export of more than 300,000 SIT in Slovenian tolars or securities without permission from the Bank of Slovenia is forbidden.

Customs inspections at most border crossings and Brnik airport are cursory or nonexistent and visitors need only make an oral declaration. However, officers are rather strict about enforcing laws regarding pets, and you may have to turn around – as I almost had to once – if Fido's (or Pussy's) papers aren't in order. Basically, a rabies vaccination certificate (in English, German or Italian if you can't manage Slovene) must be at least 30 days old but no older than six months. A veterinarian's certificate of health must be no more than 10 days old.

MONEY
Currency

The Slovenian tolar, abbreviated SIT after the international currency-coding system, is a relatively new currency with a distinguished pedigree (see boxed text entitled The Almighty Tolar). In theory the tolar is divided into 100 stotinov, but nowadays you'll come across only the 50 stotin version of these worthless aluminium coins. More substantial brassy coins of one tolar, two tolarja and five tolarji have been in circulation since 1992.

Slovenia's truly colourful paper money designed by the superb postmodernist artist Rudi Španzel comes in nine denominations: 10, 20, 50, 100, 200, 500, 1000, 5000 and 10,000 SIT. They bear the likenesses of Slovenian writers, historians, artists, scientists, architects and musicians; gratefully, there's not a general among them.

The 10 SIT note bears the portrait of Primož Trubar (1508-86), the Protestant reformer and translator, while the 20 SIT one portrays the historian and geographer Janez Vajkard

Valvasor (1641-93). The 50 SIT note features the mathematician Jurij Vega (1754-1802).

The 100 SIT bill takes us into the 20th century with the stern-faced impressionist painter Rihard Jakopič (1869-1943). Jakob Gallus (1550-91), a composer who worked mostly in Prague, is on the 200 SIT note while the architect Jože Plečnik (1872-1957) is portrayed on the 500 SIT one. The Romantic poet and patriot France Prešeren (1800-49) is on the 1000 SIT and, in a bow to political correctness, a woman – the realist painter Ivana Kobilca (1861-1926) – takes pride of place on the 5000 SIT note. The 10,000 SIT note features Ivan Cankar (1876-1918), the writer who has been called the 'outstanding master of Slovenian prose'.

Currency Exchange

As the tolar remains tied to the Deutschmark, it will continue to reflect fluctuations in the German currency's value for the foreseeable future.

Australia	A$1	=	110 SIT
Austria	ASch 1	=	13.50 SIT
Canada	C$1	=	117 SIT
Croatia	Kuna 1	=	26 SIT
Czech Republic	Kčs 1	=	5 SIT
European Union	Euro 1	=	184 SIT
France	FF1	=	28 SIT
Germany	DM1	=	94 SIT
Hungary	Ft100	=	80 SIT
Italy	L 100	=	10.60 SIT
Japan	¥100	=	127 SIT
New Zealand	NZ$1	=	93 SIT
South Africa	Rand 1	=	33 SIT
Switzerland	Sfr 1	=	112 SIT
UK	UK£1	=	280 SIT
USA	US$1	=	168 SIT

Costs

Though prices have increased, with imported items costing as much as they do in western Europe, Slovenia remains much cheaper than nearby Italy and Austria. But don't expect it to be a bargain basement like Hungary; everything costs about 50% more here.

If you stay at private rooms or guesthouses, eat at medium-priced restaurants and travel 2nd class on the train or by bus, you should get by on under US$40 a day. Those putting up at hostels or college dormitories, eating *burek* (meat or cheese-filled pastries) for lunch and at self-service restaurants at night will cut costs considerably. Travelling in a little more style and comfort – occasional restaurant splurges with bottles of wine, an active nightlife, small hotels/guesthouses with 'character' – will cost about US$65 a day.

Prices in shops, at restaurants and train and bus fares are always in tolars, but hotels,

---

The Almighty Tolar

The Slovenian tolar, the currency that sounds suspiciously like 'dollar', actually shares the same etymology as its more worldly cousin.

Both 'tolar' and 'dollar' are modified forms of the German word *thaler*, the name of a silver coin first struck in 1518 under Emperor Charles V of Germany, who was also King of Spain and the Spanish colonies in the New World. The silver was mined at a place called St Joachimsthal (Joachim's Dale) in Bohemia and the coin circulated in Germany from the 16th century onward under various names: thaler, daler, dalar and tallero. The thaler was replaced by the mark as the German monetary unit only after unification in 1873.

Spanish pesos – the celebrated 'pieces of eight' of sea ditties – circulated in the Spanish and English colonies in 17th century America and were known as 'dollars' to English speakers. In 1792, the fledgling American government bowed to this familiarity and adopted it as its official currency. Canada adopted the name in 1858, Australia in 1966 and New Zealand a year after that.

In October 1991, as the last soldier of the Yugoslav army left Slovenia, the central bank issued its own tolar coupons to replace the Yugoslav dinars in circulation. A year later Slovenia had its own currency. ∎

guesthouses and even camping grounds often use Deutschmarks as the tolar is linked to it. For that reason, the prices of many types of accommodation and a few other items listed in this guide are quoted in Deutschmarks. You are never required to pay in the German currency though.

Cash & Travellers Cheques

It is very simple to change cash and travellers cheques at banks, post offices, tourist offices, travel agencies and *menjalnice*, the private exchange offices that have sprung up everywhere in recent years. Look for any of the words *Menjalnica* or *Devizna Blagajna* to guide you.

There's no black market in Slovenia, but exchange rates can vary substantially, so it pays to keep your eyes open. Banks take a commission *(provizija)* of 1% or none at all, but tourist offices, travel agencies, exchange bureaus and hotels have ones of 3 to 5%.

Banks often pay a higher rate for travellers cheques than for cash but some private exchange offices (not travel agencies) do the opposite. Post offices are not the best places to change money as some may only want to accept cash and when they do take travellers cheques, it will be at a relatively poor rate.

You can easily change excess tolars back into US dollars or Deutschmarks (the exchange office at Ljubljana's train station is a good place); keep your exchange receipts just in case. Slovenia, which had relatively liberal currency-exchange laws even while part of Yugoslavia, is also a good place to trade one foreign currency for another – US dollars for Deutschmarks, say – without having to have it converted into tolars first. You can also receive cash dollars or Deutschmarks for your travellers cheques at most banks for a flat 3% commission.

Credit Cards & ATMs

Visa, MasterCard/Eurocard and American Express credit cards are widely accepted at upmarket restaurants, shops, hotels, car-rental firms and some travel agencies; Diner's Club less so.

SKB Banka maintains more than 50 Cirrus-linked ATMs throughout the country; their locations are noted in the Information sections of the individual towns and cities. At the time of writing, no other ATMs in Slovenia were open to foreign-account holders. Clients of Visa, however, can get cash advances in tolars from any A Banka branch, MasterCard and Eurocard holders from a Nova Ljubljanska Banka or an SKB Banka, and American Express clients from the representative in Ljubljana.

Though an English-language option is available on the ATM screen, the following are the Slovenian words on the buttons to push and their English equivalents:

ATM Words
  Prekinitev – Cancel
  Popravek – Correction
  Sprememba – Change/Modification
  Potrditev – Enter/Confirm

If you have problems with your Visa card, call the Visa Card Centre (☎ 061-302 055) in Ljubljana or go to the A Banka (☎ 061-131 1031) at Slovenska cesta 50. They can't replace a lost or stolen card, but they can put a stop-payment order on it. MasterCard/ Eurocard holders should go to the Nova Ljubljanska Banka (061-125 0155) at Trg Republike 2.

American Express customers who want to report lost or stolen travellers cheques or a card or need an advance should contact Atlas Express (☎ 061-133 2024 or ☎ 061-131 9020) at Trubarjeva cesta 50 in Ljubljana. They can replace cards (though you must know the account number) and make refunds for lost or stolen American Express travellers cheques. Green Card holders can get up to US$200 in cash tolars and US$300 in US dollar travellers cheques (US$1000 if you can write a personal cheque). Anyone with a Gold Card can get the tolar cash equivalent of US$500 and US$1500 in dollar cheques. The advance must be approved by the head office in Zagreb, but that usually only takes a few minutes. Payment is actually made by the Nova Ljubljanska Banka on Trg Republike.

Guaranteed Cheques

Nova Ljubljanska Banka branches will cash Eurocheques for up to 25,000 SIT (or the equivalent).

Tipping & Bargaining

Tipping is not really necessary at Slovenian restaurants (some take a 10% service charge anyway), bars or hotels, but no one is going to complain if you hand them a gratuity. Taxi drivers are almost never tipped, but you can round up if you have been happy with the ride or for the sake of convenience.

As in eastern Europe, bargaining was not the done thing under communism; everyone paid the same amount by weight and volume. Nowadays people selling folk crafts on the street and especially vendors at flea markets will be very open to haggling. At hotels enjoying less than full occupancy during the off season, you may be able to wangle a *popust* (discount) of up to 25%.

Taxes & Refunds

A 'circulation tax' called *prometni davek* (PD) and not unlike Value-Added Tax (VAT) covers the purchase of most goods and services in Slovenia, from imported electronic equipment and top-class hotels (20%) and wine (10%) to books and car rentals (5%). It is *usually* included in the quoted price of goods but not some services, so beware.

Visitors can claim refunds on total purchases of 12,500 SIT or more (not including tobacco products or spirits) through Kompas MTS, which has offices at Brnik airport and some 26 border crossings; they are marked with an asterisk (*) in the Car & Motorcycle section of the Getting There & Away chapter. There's also an MTS cash-refund office (☎ 061-132 5285) in Ljubljana north-east of the train station at Neubergerjeva ulica 19. In order to make the claim, you must have a European Tax-Free Shopping (ETS) cheque correctly filled out by the salesperson at the time of purchase and have it stamped by a Slovenian customs officer at the border. You can then collect your refund – minus commission – from the nearby Kompas MTS payment office in cash, and have it sent by bank cheque or deposited into your credit-card account.

Most towns and cities levy a 'tourist tax' on visitors staying the night (100 to 300 SIT per person per night).

POST & COMMUNICATIONS

The Slovenian postal system (Pošta Slovenije), recognised by its bright yellow sign, offers a wide variety of services – from selling stamps and telephone cards and the now rare telephone tokens to sending faxes and changing money. The queues are never very long, but you can avoid a trip to the post office if you just want to mail a few postcards by buying stamps *(znamke)* at certain newsstands and dropping your mail into any of the yellow letterboxes on the street.

Postal Rates

Look for the signs *Sprejem Pisemskih Pošiljk* if you're posting a letter and *Sprejem Paketov* or *Paketi* if you've got a parcel. Domestic mail costs 14 SIT for up to 20g and 26 SIT for up to 100g. Postcards are 13 SIT. For international mail, the base rate is 90 SIT for 20g or less, 186 SIT for up to 100g and 70 to 90 SIT for a postcard, depending on the size. Then you have to add on the air-mail charge for every 10g: 16 SIT for Europe, 21 SIT for North America, 22 SIT for most of Asia and 28 SIT for Australasia. An aerogram is 120 SIT.

Sending & Receiving Mail

Something mailed within Slovenia takes only a day or two. Post to neighbouring countries and ones close by like Germany should take about three days. For the UK, count on about five days and the USA between a week and 10 days. Mail to Asia and Australia takes between 10 days and two weeks.

Poste restante is sent to the main post office in a city or town (in the capital, it goes to the one at Slovenska cesta 32, 1101 Ljubljana) where it is held for 30 days. American Express card members can have their mail addressed c/o Atlas Express, Trubarjeva cesta 50, 1000 Ljubljana.

Telephone

The easiest – and most private – place to make long-distance calls as well as send faxes and telegrams is from a post office or telephone centre; the one at Trg OF near the train and bus stations in Ljubljana is open 24 hours a day. Simply go into one of the booths (sometimes you have to take a number first), make your call and then pay the cashier. Some booths have electronic meters telling you exactly how much you're spending in tolars as you chat away.

Public telephones on the street never accept coins; they require a telephone card *(telefonska kartica)* or a phone token *(žeton)*; the latter are being used less and less these days. Both are available at all post offices and some newsstands. Phone boxes that accept cards are marked with a 'K' or say 'Telekartica'; those taking tokens have a 'Ž'.

Phone cards issued by Telekom Slovenije cost 550/750/1300/2900 SIT for 20/50/100/300 impulses. A local two-minute call absorbs one impulse, and a three-minute call from Slovenia to neighbouring countries will cost about 756 SIT, 924 SIT to western Europe (including the UK), 1596 SIT to the USA or Australia and 2226 SIT to most of Asia. Rates are 50% cheaper between 7 pm and 7 am.

Tokens come in three types. Token A (63 SIT) has five impulses and is used for brief local calls. Token B, with 25 impulses for 221 SIT, can be used for longer local or domestic calls. Token C costs 442 SIT and has 50 impulses. You can only use the tokens once; they are not returned for later use.

Slovenian call boxes do not display their telephone numbers so it's impossible for the other party to phone you back. There are no 'country direct' services yet available, and most telephone credit cards like Sprint and AT&T still can't be used from Slovenia.

Mobile telephones are becoming increasingly common in Slovenia with about 40,000 subscribers by the end of 1997 and 70% of the country's surface covered. Mobitel, the only GSM system operator in the country, has an office (☎ 064-363 000) at Brnik airport renting phones but, at the time of writing, foreigners were still not allowed to hire the cell phones directly. A Slovenian contact may rent one for you, however. The office is open weekdays from 7 am to 10 pm and at the weekend from 8 am to 3 pm.

To call Slovenia from abroad, dial the international access code, 386 (the country code for Slovenia), the area code (minus the initial zero) and the number. There are 12 area codes in Slovenia and these are listed in the Information section of each city and town. Most have three digits (eg 061 in Ljubljana, 062 in Maribor) but a few areas of Koroška and Dolenjska have four digits (0602 is the code for Slovenj Gradec, 0608 for Brežice). The codes for mobile telephones are 0609 and 041. Slovenian telephone numbers themselves can have between four and seven digits.

When making a domestic call from one area to another, you must use the code. To call abroad, dial 00 followed by the country and area codes and then the number.

Telephone numbers you may find useful include:

☎ 981 – general information
☎ 988 – directory assistance for Slovenia
☎ 989 – international directory assistance
☎ 900 – domestic operator
☎ 901 – international operator/collect calls
☎ 95 – time (in Slovene)

BOOKS

There's no shortage of books on Slovenia but the big problem is price: printed material of any kind is terribly expensive here. The useful *Atlas of Slovenia*, for example, will set you back a cool 19,320 SIT. An attractive, but by no means lavish, picture book on the history of urban development called *Settlement Culture in the Slovene Lands (Naselbinska Kultura na Slovenskem)* costs a whopping 10,500 SIT. *Discover Slovenia*, a 136-page paperback, is priced at 2900 SIT and even maps or simple town plans cost 850 to 1200 SIT each. Remember that Slovenes, who earn a lot less than many of us, have to pay those prices too. Slovenia is the third smallest literature market in Europe and a fiction 'best seller' in this country means 500 copies. They still manage to publish 15 books per 10,000 people a year, though, against the EU average of 10 books.

Most of the following books can be purchased at any branch of Mladinska Knjiga or Cankarjeva Založba. See the Information section of individual towns for addresses.

Lonely Planet

Lonely Planet's *Slovenia* remains the only complete guidebook to the country in the English language and is available in most Ljubljana bookshops for 3235 SIT. *Eastern Europe*, *Central Europe* and *Mediterranean Europe*, also published by Lonely Planet, all contain a brief chapter on Slovenia.

The Lonely Planet *Mediterranean Europe phrasebook* contains sections of useful words and phrases in Slovene.

Guidebooks

The only other guide devoted exclusively to the country is the Italian-language *Slovenia* (ClupGuide, Milan) by Aldo Pavan, but it's outdated and not very practical.

Good local guides to the whole country are thin on the ground, but the richly illustrated *Slovenia Tourist Guide* (Založba Mladinska Knjiga) is a decent if expensive (11,130 SIT) choice. For something more specialised, the *Slovenia Art Guide* (Marketing 013 ZTP; 8190 SIT) by Nace Šumi is an excellent introduction to the architecture of Slovenia.

For Ljubljana, choose *Walks in Old Ljubljana* (Marketing 013 ZTP; 6300 SIT) by Ivan Stopar, *Plečnik's Ljubljana* (Cankarjeva Založba; 1300 SIT) or *Outdoor Sculpture in Ljubljana* (DZS; 1490 SIT) by Špelca Čopič et al.

History & Politics

Janko Prunk's revised *Brief History of Slovenia* (Založba Grad; 1995 SIT) is a good start, but if you want something more in-depth, pick up a copy of *Independent Slovenia: Origins, Movements, Prospects* (Macmillan; 5254 SIT) edited by Jill Benderly & Evan Craft. A dozen chapters written by Slovenian experts examine the country's history, political system and economy both past and present.

General

Art & Culture *Discover Slovenia* (Cankarjeva Založba; 2900 SIT) is not exclusively devoted to things artistic or cultural but contains very enlightening, easy-to-read sections on them and is updated annually. It also introduces the nation's history, geography and key cities and towns. *Traditional Arts & Crafts in Slovenia* (Domus; 10,500 SIT) by Edi Berk is a lavishly illustrated guide to local folk craft and lore.

Picture Books There are plenty of these. The 80-page *Greetings from Slovenia* (Založba Mladinska Knjiga; 4400 SIT), available in English, German and Slovene, introduces the country's natural and cultural heritage with shots of daily life. The 244-page *Slovenia from the Air* (Založba Mladinska Knjiga; 10,800 SIT) in English, German and Slovene by Matjaž Kmecl et al has the standard 'Gosh!' photographs of Slovenia's mountains, lakes, coast and towns from on high; *Treasures of Slovenia* (Cankarjeva Založba), also by Kmecl, is a more serious look at the country's natural beauty spots.

Other flashy coffee-table books are *Slovenia: A Portrait* (Založba Zaklad; 8820 SIT) and *Slovenia* (Flint River Press, London; 9975 SIT).

An excellent all-rounder, with superb photos and text that delves into Slovenian culture, history and folklore, is *Mountains of Slovenia* (Cankarjeva Založba; 11,676 SIT) by Kmecl et al.

Ljubljana: City of Culture (City of Ljubljana; 6510 SIT) was published to coincide with Ljubljana's European Month of Culture celebrations in 1997 and is a decent pictorial overview of the capital. *Ljubljana* (Avante Garde; 8990 SIT) by Bogdan Kladnik & Daniel Rojšek is a basic introduction to the capital.

Language The best compact dictionary is the English-Slovene/Slovene-English *Moderni Slovar/Modern Dictionary* (Cankarjeva Založba; 7875 SIT) by Daša Komac.

If you want to learn Slovene on your own, choose *Colloquial Slovene* (Routledge, London; 8328 SIT; UK£29.99), a course pack containing a 324-page book and two 60-minute cassettes. Another self-paced course is *Teach Yourself Slovene* (Hodder & Stoughton; 3526 SIT; UK£14.95), which includes a 196-page book and one cassette.

CD ROM

Two CD ROMs available on Slovenia include the multimedia *Welcome to Slovenia* from the CPTS and *Slovenia* from Vitrum Publishing. Both are in English. The CPTS also produces a diskette called *Gremo v Dobro Gostilno*, which lists hundreds of inns and country restaurants across Slovenia. But it's really just a listing of names, addresses, telephone numbers, opening hours etc; there are no reviews or recommendations.

ONLINE SERVICES

Slovenia has gone Internet crazy and everyone from TV and radio stations to sports clubs has a Web site. About 7% of all Slovenes use the Internet regularly and some 30% own a PC.

The best single source of information on the Internet is the SloWWWenia site: www.ijs.si:90/slo/. It has an interactive map where you can click on to more than two dozen cities, towns, ski resorts etc as well as information on culture, history, food and wine, getting to and from Slovenia and what's on. Other useful Web sites wholly or partly in English include:

www.kabi.si/si21/aa/
    Adria Airways. Schedules and routes
www.tourist-board.si
    Corporate and promotional site of the Slovenian Tourist Board
www.sigov.si
    Slovenian government. General, business and economic news. Index of institutions
www.sigov.si/zrs/index.html
    Statistical Office of Slovenia. Facts and figures

www.gzs.si
    Chamber of Economy of Slovenia (Gospodarska Zbornica Slovenije; GZS)
www.ijs.si/slo/resources/alphabet/
    Organisations in Slovenia
www.sigov.si./uzp/city
    Government Office for Women's Affairs
www.pzs.si
    Alpine Association of Slovenia (Planinska Zveza Slovenije; PZS)
www.arnes.si/ljzavodrib6/
    Fisheries Institute (Zavod za Ribištvo)
www.arctur.si/slovenia/first.html
    Slovenian Emigrants' Centre (Slovenska Izseljenska Matica; SIM)
www.ljudmila/org/most/
    MOST-SIC volunteer work organisation
www.rtvslo.si/
    RTV Slovenija
www.skb.si/
    SKB Banka
www.kompas-holy.si
    Kompas travel agency

See also the Online Services section in the Ljubljana chapter for more sites.

NEWSPAPERS & MAGAZINES

Slovenia counts four daily newspapers, the most widely read being *Delo (Work)* and *Večer (Evening)*. Some 30 weeklies, fortnightlies and monthlies cover topics as diverse as agriculture, finance and women's fashion. *Mladina (Youth)* is a liberal weekly covering political and social issues.

There are no English-language newspapers though a good 20-page political and business newsletter called *Slovenia Weekly* is available by subscription or on the Internet. Contact Vitrum Publishing (☎ 061-126 1412; fax 061-140 2027; vitrum-lj@eunet.si) at Hradeckega ulica 38 in Ljubljana. An annual subscription costs DM126. The Slovenian Emigrants' Centre (see Useful Organisations later in this chapter) publishes a glossy quarterly magazine in English called *Slovenija* and has a site on the Internet (see Online Services). Single copies cost US$7, an annual subscription US$25/DM40.

MM Slovenija is an English-language monthly magazine (1800 SIT) published by Delo and focuses on management, marketing and promotion. Many of the articles on tourism are well written and useful.

Western newspapers in English available on the day of publication at kiosks, hotels and department stores in Ljubljana include the *International Herald Tribune*, the *Guardian International*, the *Financial Times* and *USA Today*. The European edition of the *Wall Street Journal* and the *Independent* are usually available the following day.

RADIO & TV

Radiotelevizija Slovenija (or RTV Slovenija for short) incorporates both radio and television. Radio Slovenija has three national channels (Radio Slovenija 1, 2 & 3), a regional one in Maribor (MM1) and special ones for the Hungarian minority in Murska Sobota (Radio Murski Val) and the Italian one in Koper (Radio Koper-Capodistria).

In July and August both Radio Slovenija 1 and 2 broadcast a report on the weather, including conditions on the sea and in the mountains, in English, German and Italian at 7.15 am. News, weather, traffic and tourist information in the same languages follows on Radio 1 at 9.35 am daily, except Sunday. Also at this time Radio 2 broadcasts weekend traffic conditions after each news bulletin from Friday afternoon through Sunday evening.

There's a nightly news bulletin at 10.30 pm throughout the year on Radio 1.

You can listen to Radio 1 on MHz/FM frequencies 88.5, 90.0, 90.9, 91.8, 92.0, 92.9, 94.1 and 96.4 as well as AM 326.8. Radio 2 can be found on MHz/FM 87.8, 92.4, 93.5, 94.1, 95.3, 96.9, 97.6, 98.9 and 99.9.

Televizija Slovenija broadcasts on two channels, Slovenija 1 and Slovenija 2. A subsidiary called TV Koper-Capodistria broadcasts in Italian on the coast. There are three private commercial channels, including Kanal A, TV3 and the immensely popular Pop TV, and about 20 local cable stations in cities and towns across the country. In general, public television is not very good in Slovenia – you may have noticed all those satellite dishes on the roof tops pulling in Sky, CNN and the Cartoon Network – with 'talking heads' droning on for hours about the state of privatisation and the like.

VIDEO SYSTEMS

If you want to record or buy video tapes to play back home, you won't get the picture if the image registration systems are different. Like most of Europe and Australia, Slovenia uses the PAL (Phase Alternative Line) system, which is incompatible with the North American and Japanese NTSC standard or the SECAM system used in France.

PHOTOGRAPHY & VIDEO

Film and basic camera equipment (batteries, lens cleaner etc) are available throughout Slovenia, though the largest selection is in Ljubljana. Film prices vary but 24 exposures of 100 ASA Kodacolor II, Agfa or Fujifilm will cost about 650 SIT and 36 exposures 750 SIT. Ektachrome 100 (36 exposures) is 1110 SIT.

Photo developers can be found in towns and cities nationwide, and you can have your film processed in a matter of hours. Developing print film costs about 2500 SIT for 36 prints (10 x 15cm). For 36 framed transparencies, expect to pay around 1200 SIT.

Large outfits with fast processing in Ljubljana are Kodak Express at Slovenska cesta 55, which is open weekdays from 8 am to 7 pm and on Saturday till 1 pm, and Mikrokop Kodak Express at Gregorčičeva ulica 9 (open weekdays only from 8 am to 4 pm). Some smaller agencies offer professional service at competitive rates. One good example in the capital is Foto Grad at Miklošičeva cesta 36. It is open from 8 am to 6 pm on weekdays and till noon on Saturday.

TIME

Slovenia lies in the central European time zone. Winter time is GMT/UTC plus one hour while in summer it's GMT/UTC plus two hours. Clocks are advanced by one hour at 2 am on the last Sunday in March and turned back on the last Sunday in October. Without taking daylight savings time into account, the table below shows time differences using Ljubljana as a reference point.

Times in Other Cities When it is Noon in Ljubljana	
Auckland	11 pm
Athens	1 pm
Belgrade	noon
Berlin	noon
Bucharest	1 pm
Budapest	noon
Hong Kong	7 pm
London	11 am
Moscow	2 pm
New York	6 am
Paris	noon
Prague	noon
Rome	noon
San Francisco	3 am
Sydney	9 pm
Tokyo	8 pm
Toronto	6 am
Warsaw	noon
Vienna	noon
Zagreb	noon

Like a lot of other European languages, Slovene tells the time by making reference to the next hour – not the last one. Thus 1.15 is 'one quarter of two', 1.30 is 'half of two' and 1.45 is 'three quarters of two'.

ELECTRICITY
The electric current in Slovenia is 220V, 50Hz AC. Plugs are the standard European type with two round pins. Do not attempt to plug an American appliance into a Slovenian outlet without a transformer.

WEIGHTS & MEASURES
Slovenia uses the metric system exclusively. In supermarkets and outdoor markets, fresh food is sold by weight or by piece (kos). When ordering by weight, you specify by kilo or decagramme (dekagram) – 50 decagrammes is equal to half a kilo or roughly one pound. Fresh fish is almost always sold in restaurants by decagramme, usually abbreviated as dag. For those who need help with the metric system, there's a conversion table at the back of this book.

Beer in a pivnica (pub) is served in either a 0.5L glass (veliko pivo) or one measuring 0.3L (malo pivo). Wine comes in 1L bottles or is ordered by the deci (decilitre, 0.1L). A 'normal' glass of wine is about 0.2L (dva deci), but no one is going to blink an eye if you order three or more.

LAUNDRY
With 94% of all Slovenian households owning washing machines ... well, good luck trying to find a self-service laundrette! The best place to look for do-it-yourself washers and dryers is at hostels, college dormitories and camp sites (about a dozen have them), and there are a couple of places in Ljubljana that will do your laundry reasonably quickly (see Laundry in the Information section of that chapter). Hotels will take care of it too. A smaller one in the provinces will wash, dry and fold a load for around 2000 to 2500 SIT. Prices in Ljubljana will be much, much higher (eg 9500 SIT at the Slon hotel for the same load!).

HEALTH
No special inoculations are needed before visiting Slovenia, and tap water is 100% safe everywhere (though over-chlorinated on the coast). There are no troublesome snakes or creepy-crawlies to worry about, but mosquitoes can be a real pain around lakes and ponds. Make sure you're armed with insect repellent.

The standard of medical care in Slovenia is high and a constituent part of the nation's welfare system. And it is generous – women get a full year off after having a child and now the child's father can opt to take the leave instead, if that's what the couple decides.

Citizens of certain EU countries (Austria, Benelux, Germany, Italy and the UK) as well as some eastern European countries get free emergency medical aid. Everyone else is entitled to it at the very least, but they must bear the cost of the services. Your country's agreement with Slovenia may require carrying a special form so check with your Ministry of Health or equivalent before leaving home.

Subsequent treatment must be paid for in cash and medical care and medicine can be expensive in Slovenia for foreigners. The best idea if you're not covered by travel insurance (see the preceding Visas & Documents section) is to buy temporary health insurance through the Health Insurance Institute of Slovenia (Zavod za Zdravstveno Zavarovanje Slovenije; ZZZS; ☎ 061-172 1200) at Miklošičeva cesta 24 in Ljubljana or the Emona Globtour travel agency.

Every city in Slovenia has a health centre where clinics operate from 7 am to 7 pm. Pharmacies are usually open from 7 am to 8 pm and at least one in a town or city is open round the clock. A sign on the door of any pharmacy (lekarna) will help you locate the closest 24-hour service.

Remember that travel health depends on your predeparture preparations, your day-to-day health care while travelling and how you handle any medical problem or emergency that does develop.

TOILETS

Finding a public lavatory is not always easy in Slovenia and when you do you'll probably have to pay anything from 30 to 50 SIT for the convenience. All train stations have toilets as do most shopping centres and department stores. The standard of hygiene is usually acceptable.

WOMEN TRAVELLERS

Women do not suffer any particular form of harassment in Slovenia, though rape and domestic violence get little media coverage here. Most men – even drunks – are effusively polite with women. Women may not be made to feel especially welcome when eating or drinking alone, but it's really no different here than in many other countries in Europe. If you can handle yourself in a less than comfortable situation, you'll be fine.

The Društvo Mesto Žensk (City of Women Association), part of the Government Office for Women's Affairs (☎ 061-125 112; fax 061-125 6057) at Tomšičeva ulica 4 in Ljubljana, sponsors an international festival of contemporary arts (usually in October) called City of Women. In the event of an emergency ring ☎ 080 124 or any of the following six numbers: ☎ 9780 to ☎ 9785.

GAY & LESBIAN TRAVELLERS

The gay association Roza Klub (☎ 061-130 4740; fax 061-328 185), at Kersnikova ulica 4 in Ljubljana, publishes a quarterly called Revolver and organises a disco every Sunday night at the Klub K4 in Ljubljana for gays and lesbians. Magnus (☎ /fax same), the gay branch of the Student Cultural Centre (Študentski Kulturni Center; ŠKUC), puts out the monthly broadsheet Kekec. A new independent gay newsletter now being distributed at bars and clubs around Ljubljana is Sestre (Sisters).

Lesbians should contact the ŠKUC-affiliated organisation LL (☎ /fax same) at Metelkova ulica 6 in Ljubljana. It publishes a political, cultural and social review call Lesbo.

The GALfon (☎ 061-132 4089) is a hotline and source of general information for gays and lesbians. It operates daily from 7 to 10 pm. The Queer Resources Directory (www .ljudmila.org/siqrd/) for gays and lesbians on the Internet leaves no stone unturned.

DISABLED TRAVELLERS

Facilities found throughout Slovenia include public telephones with amplifiers for the deaf, special traffic lights at pedestrian crossings that make a beeping noise for the blind, sloped pavements and ramps in government buildings for wheelchairs, and reserved spaces in many car parks.

Zveza Paraplegikov Republike Slovenije (☎ 061-132 7138; fax 061-132 7286) at Štihova ulica 14 in Ljubljana, a group that looks after the interests and special needs of paraplegics, produces a special guide for its members but it is in Slovene only. Some cities produce useful brochures outlining which local sights and attractions are accessible for wheelchairs. The Guide through Slovenj Gradec is an outstanding example of this.

SENIOR TRAVELLERS

Senior citizens may be entitled to discounts in Slovenia on things like transport (eg those over 60 years of age holding an international RES card get from 30% to 50% off on Slovenian Railways), museum admission fees etc, provided they show proof of their age. The minimum qualifying age is generally 60.

TRAVEL WITH CHILDREN

They might not have a lot of kids – the average family numbers just three people – but Slovenes love them and this is a very children-friendly country. The family goes everywhere together, and you'll see youngsters dining with their parents in even the poshest restaurants.

Successful travel with young children requires planning and effort. Don't try to overdo things; even for adults, packing too much into the time available can cause problems. And make sure the activities include the kids as well – balance that morning at Ljubljana's National Museum with an afternoon at the zoo on Rožnik Hill or a performance at the Puppet Theatre. Include children in the trip planning; if they've helped to work out where you will be going, they will be much more interested when they get there. Lonely Planet's *Travel with Children* is a good source of information.

Several farmhouses in Slovenia organise programs for children that may include horse riding, caving, skiing, learning traditional crafts or just messing around with farm animals. A great place to visit with the kids (or even deposit them) is the Kaja & Grom Ranch (☎ /fax 061-743 234) in the village of Petkovec (house No 59) near Rovte, 32km south-east of Ljubljana. This *ranč* offers week-long riding and sports programs for children on their own from nine years and up. Two other farmhouses with holidays for children aged five to 14 are Podmalčan (☎ /fax 064-688 001) in the village of Jarčje Brdo near Selca, 12km west of Škofja Loka, and Urška (☎ 063-762 180) in the village of Križevec near Stranice, 18km north-east of Celje.

Most car-rental firms in Slovenia have children's safety seats for hire for between DM5 and DM10, but it is essential that you book them in advance. The same goes for highchairs and cots (cribs); they're standard in some restaurants and hotels but numbers are limited. The choice of baby food, infant formulas, soy and other types of milk, disposable nappies (diapers) and the like can be as great in Slovenian supermarkets these days as it is back home, but the opening hours may be quite different. Don't get caught out at the weekend.

STUDENT TRAVELLERS

The Student Organisation of the University of Ljubljana (Študentska Organizacija Univerze Ljubljani; ŠOU; ☎ 061-133 7219) at Kersnikova ulica 4 in the capital is a good place to mix with like-minded people. There's a small club/cybercafé there for socialising and surfing the net, and the organisation produces a useful brochure called *Slovenia for Foreign Students* in which, among lots of other things, the dates and locations of weekly student parties are listed. The Student Cultural Centre (ŠKUC; ☎ 061-130 4740; fax 061-329 185) at the same address organises cultural activities such as theatre productions.

Two agencies in Ljubljana – Erazem and Mladi Turist – deal specifically with students and young travellers. See the Visas & Documents section earlier in this chapter for more information.

USEFUL ORGANISATIONS

In addition to the organisations listed elsewhere in this chapter, the following may be helpful for visitors to Slovenia with special interests.

Archives of the Republic of Slovenia (Arhiv Republike Slovenije; ☎ 061-125 1222; fax 061-216 551), Gruber Palace, Zvezdarska ulica 1, 1000 Ljubljana. If you are searching for your Slovenian roots, check first with the municipal government *(mestna občina)* or country office *(občina)*; they have birth and death certificates going back a century. Vital records beyond the 100-year limit are kept at the archives.

Slovenian Emigrants' Centre (Slovenska Izseljenska Matica; SIM; ☎ 061-126 3284; fax 061-210 732), Cankarjeva ulica 1, 1000 Ljubljana. This office deals with ethnic Slovenes living abroad and publishes the quarterly magazine *Slovenija* in English (see Newspapers & Magazines earlier).

DANGERS & ANNOYANCES

Slovenia is hardly a violent or dangerous society. Firearms are strictly controlled, drunks are sloppy but docile and you'll see little of the vandalism that plagues cities like New York or London.

Though graffiti is on the increase in big cities, about as bad as the 'handwriting on the wall' gets here is anti-papist stuff sprayed on the outside walls of the Church of the Annunciation in Ljubljana to coincide with Pope John Paul II's visit to Slovenia in May 1996.

At the special traffic lights for the blind, which bear the sign *'Samo za Slepe'* (Only for the Blind), wags frequently erase the second 'S', making it *'Samo za Lepe'* (Only for Beautiful Women). The organised crime tormenting Russia and eastern European countries has arrived in Slovenia, notably in Ljubljana and Maribor, but nowhere to the same degree.

Police say that 90% of all crimes reported in Slovenia involve thefts so take the usual precautions. Be careful of your purse or wallet in bus and train stations and where you may consider leaving it unattended (on the beach, in a hut while hiking). Lock your car at all times, park in well lit areas and do not leave valuables visible.

In cities like Ljubljana, Maribor (sometimes called 'Mafiabor' because of organised crime based there) or Celje, you might be approached occasionally by beggars who ask for and then demand money. But it's usually nothing serious. One problem can be drunks on the road – literally or behind the wheel – especially around St Martin's Day (Martinovanje, 11 November) when grape juice (or *must)* legally becomes new wine and everybody has got to have a sip or three.

In the event of an emergency, the following are the most important numbers which can be dialled nationwide:

Police (Policija)	☎ 113
Fire (Gasilci)	☎ 112
First Aid (Prva Pomoč)	
Ambulance (Reševalci)	
Automobile Assistance (AMZS)	☎ 987

LEGAL MATTERS

The permitted blood-alcohol level for motorists is 0.5g/kg.

BUSINESS HOURS

The opening time *(delovni čas)* of shops, groceries and department stores is usually from about 7 or 8 am to 7 pm on weekdays and till 1 pm on Saturday. In winter they may close an hour earlier.

Bank hours vary but generally they're from 8 am to 5 or 6 pm weekdays (often with a lunchtime break of one or two hours) and till noon on Saturday. The main post office in any city or town (almost always the ones listed in the Information sections of the individual towns and cities) is open from 7 am to 8 pm weekdays, till 1 pm on Saturday and occasionally from 9 to 11 am on Sunday. Branch offices close earlier on weekdays and at noon on Saturday. They are always closed on Sunday.

Museums are usually open from 10 am to 6 pm Tuesday to Sunday from April to October; winter opening hours are shorter or at weekends only.

PUBLIC HOLIDAYS & SPECIAL EVENTS

Slovenia celebrates 14 holidays *(prazniki)* a year. If any of the following fall on a Sunday, then the Monday becomes the holiday.

1 & 2 January
   New Year's holidays
8 February
   Prešeren/Slovenian Culture Day
March/April
   Easter & Easter Monday
27 April
   Insurrection Day
1 & 2 May
   Labour Day holidays
25 June
   National Day
15 August
   Assumption Day
31 October
   Reformation Day
1 November
   All Saints' Day
25 December
   Christmas Day
26 December
   Independence Day

Though not a public holiday, St Martin's Day (11 November) is important since on this day, *must* (pressed grape juice) officially becomes wine and can be sold as such. That evening families traditionally dine on goose and some restaurants offer a *Martinovanje* dinner of goose and young wine accompanied by folk music.

On Palm Sunday (the Sunday before Easter), people carry a complex arrangement of greenery and ribbons called a *butara* to church to be blessed. These *butare* end up as home decorations or are placed on the graves of relatives. On the eve of St Gregory's Day (11 March), children in certain Gorenjska towns and villages (eg Tržič, Železniki) set afloat hundreds of tiny boats bearing candles.

Many towns celebrate Midsummer's Night (Kresna Noč; 23 June) by burning a large bonfire, and St John's Eve (30 April) is the night for setting up the maypoles and more bonfires. A *žegnanje* is a fair or some sort of celebration held on the feast day of a church's patron saint. Naturally a lot of them take place throughout Slovenia on 15 August, the Assumption of the Virgin Mary, especially at Ptujska Gora in Štajerska and at Sveta Gora, north of Nova Gorica.

Major cultural and sporting events in Slovenia appear in the Special Events section of the individual towns and cities. The following abbreviated list gives you a taste of what to expect.

January
  Women's World Cup Slalom and Giant Slalom Competition (Golden Fox), Pohorje – one of the major international ski events for women held on the slopes south-west of Maribor.
February
  Kurentovanje, Ptuj – a 'rite of spring' celebrated for 10 days up to Shrove Tuesday and the most popular Mardi Gras celebrations in Slovenia (other important pre-Lenten festivals take place in Cerknica and Cerkno).
March
  Ski Jumping World Cup Championships, Planica – three days of high flying on skis near Kranjska Gora.
April
  International Kayak and Canoe Competition, Osilnica – five days of wild-water racing on the Kolpa River in Notranjska.

  Day of Tulips, Volčji Potok – Slovenia's largest flower and gardening show.
May
  International Cycling Marathon, Novo Mesto – international bicycle race starting in Dolenjska.
June
  Festival Lent, Maribor – a two-week extravaganza of folklore and culture held in late June/early July with stages set up throughout the old part of town.
July
  International Summer Festival, Ljubljana – the nation's premier cultural event (music, theatre and dance) from mid-July through August.
  Piran Musical Evenings & Primorska Summer Festival – concerts, theatre and dance events held in various locations in Piran, Koper, Izola and Portorož from early July to mid-August.
  International Motocross Grand Prix of Slovenia, Orehova Vas (Štajerska).
August
  Brežice Festival of Early Music, Brežice – a series of concerts of ancient music.
September
  Kravji Bal (Cows' Ball), Bohinj – a zany weekend in September of folk dance, music, eating and drinking to mark the return of the cows from their high pastures to the valleys.
October
  Dormouse Night (Polharska Noč), Cerknica – celebration and feast during the very short dormouse-hunting season.
December
  Christmas concerts, Ljubljana and Postojna Cave.

ACTIVITIES

Slovenes have a strong attachment to nature, and most lead active, outdoor lives from an early age. From skiing and cycling to caving and birdwatching, Slovenia has it all and it's always affordable.

Skiing

Skiing is by far the most popular recreational pursuit in Slovenia – counting some 300,000 enthusiasts – and some people believe the sport was actually invented in the 17th century on the Bloke Plateau in Notranjska province. Everybody seems to take to the slopes or trails in season (mainly December to March) and you can too at ski resorts and grounds across the country (see boxed text entitled Slovenian Ski Resorts). They are most crowded over the Christmas holidays and in early February.

Slovenian Ski Resorts

Slovenia has four dozen ski resorts and grounds. Most of the biggest and best equipped ones are in the Julian Alps – Kranjska Gora, Vogel above Bohinj and Krvavec east of Kranj – but other large ones are in the Pohorje Massif, including those at Maribor Pohorje and Rogla. Kanin, near Bovec, offers the highest-altitude skiing in Slovenia and the season there sometimes extends into May. These and other resorts have multiple chair lifts, tows and cable cars, ski schools, equipment rental and large resort hotels.

The following is a selected list of the country's ski resorts and grounds and their facilities arranged by province. For further information – contact numbers, ski pass prices, tuition, transport to and from the ski fields, accommodation etc – see the appropriate chapter.

Dolenjska

Rog-Črmošnjice – this ski centre 16km south of Dolenjske Toplice usually operates five T-bar tows on the slopes of Mt Gače at altitudes of between 730 and 930m, but it may still be under renovation.

Travna Gora – about 10km north-west of Ribnica near Sodražica, this is one of the smallest ski centres in the country. One T-bar tow serves a 200m-long piste at altitudes of between 860 and 910m.

Gorenjska

Bled – the closest 'real' ski resort to the lake is Zatrnik on the slopes of the Pokljuka Plateau 8km west of Bled with skiing up to 1264m, a chair lift and four T-bars. On the lake itself the mini-ski centre of Straža has a chair lift that goes to the top of a 646m hill and the start of a 1200m-long piste.

Kanin – this ski centre in the mountains north-west of Bovec has skiing up to almost 2300m – the only real high-altitude Alpine skiing available in the country. The ski fields, 14km of pistes and some 12km of cross-country runs served by three chair lifts and two T-bars, are reached by cable car. The season here can continue until May.

Kobla – this resort about 1km east of Bohinjska Bistrica has 23km of slopes (skiing up to 1480m) and 10km of cross-country runs with three chair lifts and three T-bars.

Kranjska Gora – the twin ski centres at Kranjska Gora and Podkoren, 3km apart, are the largest and best equipped in the country. Skiing in Kranjska Gora is on the eastern side of Vitranc and some runs join up with those at Podkoren on Vitranc's northern face (up to about 1600m). Kranjska Gora has two chair lifts and 10 tows; Podkoren has another two chair lifts and five tows. In all, the two centres have 30km of pistes and 40km of cross-country runs.

Krvavec – this ski centre 17km north-east of Kranj is at 1450m and is served by a cable car. It counts a dozen chair lifts and T-bar tows, 25km of slopes and 6km of cross-country runs with skiing up to 1971m.

Planica – the ski-jumping centre at Planica, across the motorway from Rateče and 6km west of Kranjska Gora, has six jumps with lengths of 25, 120 and 180m. The short lift near the Dom Planica hut reaches an altitude of only 900m, but there are some 20km of cross-country runs in the Tamar Valley.

Stari Vrh – some 12km west of Škofja Loka, Stari Vrh is situated at an altitude of 1200m and covers 18km of ski slopes and 3km of trails. There are four T-bar tows and a chair lift.

Velika Planina – this centre is reached by cable car from the lower station, about 11km north of Kamnik. A chair lift ferries skiers up to Gradišče from the upper cable-car station to 6km of slopes, which are served by T-bars. Skiing is between 1666 and 1888m.

Vogel – some 1540m above the Lake Bohinj's south-western corner and accessible by cable car, Vogel counts 36km of ski slopes and cross-country runs served by three chair lifts and five T-bar tows with skiing up to 1840m.

Koroška

Kope – some 1380m above the Mislinja Valley on the western edge of the Pohorje Massif and 16km south-east of Slovenj Gradec, this centre counts 9km of slopes and seven T-bars on Mala Kopa and Velika Kopa peaks (skiing up to 1542m). There are also 15km of cross-country runs.

Primorska

Cerkno – this ski centre 10km north-east of Cerkno is on Črni Vrh (1290m) and covers just over 7km of runs served by four tows and three chair lifts.

Štajerska

Golte – from Žekovec, 4km north-west of Mozirje, a cable car runs to this ski centre that has 10km of pistes at up to 1500m and 12.5km of ski trails.

Maribor Pohorje – with 60km of slopes, 25km of cross-country runs and 16 ski lifts, this ski centre south-west of Maribor is Slovenia's largest (skiing up to 1347m). You can reach it by road (20km) or by cable car in 15 minutes from Zgornje Radvanje, 6km south-west of Maribor.

Rogaška Slatina – this spa town has a tiny ski slope on Janina Hill (404m) with 3km of trails and two tows.

Rogla – the 15km of slopes and 30km of cross-country trails at this ski centre in the Pohorje are served by two chair lifts and 11 tows with skiing up to 1517m. ■

Slovenia has joined Austria and Italy in a three-country bid to host the 2006 Winter Olympics in a 'game without borders'. In Slovenia, the events would be held at Planica and in Ljubljana, around Klagenfurt in the Austrian province of Kärnten (Koroška) and at Cortina in north-east Italy.

Hiking & Climbing

Almost as many Slovenes hike as they do ski and one of the nicest things about this activity is that it gives you a chance to meet local people in an informal environment. Though many Slovenes are expert climbers, you don't have to be a mountaineer to 'conquer' Mt Triglav (2864m), the nation's highest peak.

Slovenia has an excellent system of trails – some 7000km of them – and they are most commonly marked by a red circle with a white centre. At crossings, there are signs indicating distances and walking times given in hours or fractions thereof.

The Julian Alps, the Kamnik-Savinja Alps and the Pohorje Massif are the most popular places for hiking, but there are some wonderful trails in the lower hills and valleys as well.

The E6 European Hiking Trail running from the Baltic to the Adriatic seas enters Slovenia at Radlje in Koroška and continues for some 280km to a point south of Mt Snežnik in Notranjska.

The E7 European Hiking Trail, which connects the Atlantic with the Black Sea, crosses into Slovenia at Robič in Primorska, runs along the Soča Valley and then continues through the southern part of the country eastward to Bistrica ob Sotli in Štajerska before exiting into Croatia. The E6 and the E7 trails are marked by a red circle with a yellow centre.

The Slovenian Alpine Trail, which opened in 1953, runs from Maribor to Ankaran on the coast via the Pohorje Massif, the Kamnik-Savinja Alps, the Julian Alps and the Cerkno and Idrija hills. You can also follow the Slovenian Geological Trail (Slovenska Geološka Pot) system in various parts of the country.

The Alpine Association of Slovenia (Planinska Zveza Slovenije; PZS; ☎ 061-

134 3022; fax 061-132 2140) in Ljubljana, the umbrella organisation of 185 clubs with 90,000 paid members, is the font of all information and can organise guides. It also publishes hiking maps and has a very useful list of 165 mountain huts, refuges and bivouacs throughout Slovenia.

It can tell you which huts are open and when and whether you can book in advance via mobile telephone. It also provides information about weather conditions and specific trails in Triglav National Park and elsewhere.

More detailed information about the PZS and the park appears in the Ljubljana and Gorenjska chapters or check out their Web site (see Online Services earlier in this chapter). A bivouac (bivak) is the most basic hut, providing shelter only, while a refuge (zavetišče) has refreshments, sometimes accommodation but usually no running water. A hut (koča) or house (dom) can be a simple cottage or a fairly grand establishment just like some of the ones close to Mt Triglav.

A bed for the night runs from 1320 to 2750 SIT in a Category I hut depending on the number of beds in the room and from 1000 to 1760 SIT in a Category II. (A hut is Category I if it is more than 1km or one hour's walk away from motorised transport – everything closer is Category II.) Members of recognised international hiking or climbing associations get a 30% discount. Holders of a Hostelling International card may also get a small discount.

Food prices are regulated at PZS huts as well. A simple meal of jota, ričet, špageti or golaž (see Menu Items in the Food section) should cost between 500 and 800 SIT in a Category I hut, from 400 to 600 SIT in a Category II one. Tea is 80 to 120 SIT, 1L of mineral water 400 to 600 SIT and 0.5L of beer 300 to 550 SIT.

The main centre for rock climbing is Lake Bohinj (see the Gorenjska chapter).

Swimming

In warmer months, swimming is extremely popular on the coastal areas as well as in Bled and Bohinj lakes and the Krka and Kolpa rivers. Many towns have a swimming pool open to the public and some, like the one at Portorož, use heated sea water.

Pools sometimes require you to wear a bathing cap; disposable plastic ones are usually available from the pool attendant.

Boating & Windsurfing

Sailing is big on the Adriatic, and you can rent sailing boats at several locations along the coast, including the Portorož Marina. You can windsurf here too as well as on lakes Bled and Bohinj.

Kayaking, Canoeing & Rafting

These sports are practised anywhere there's running water but especially on the Krka River in Dolenjska (at Žužemberk, Krka, Novo Mesto), the Kolpa in Bela Krajina (Vinica), the Sava River in Gorenjska (Šobec camp site near Bled, Bohinj), and the Savinja River in Štajerska (Logarska Dolina near Radmirje).

The best white-water rafting in the country is on the Soča River, one of only a half-dozen rivers in the European Alps whose upper waters are still unspoiled. The centre is at Bovec, which is covered in the Primorska chapter.

Diving

You can dive in all Slovenian rivers, lakes and of course the sea with the sole exception of the fish hatchery at Lake Bohinj. The sport is popular at Lake Bled and Fiesa, Ankaran and Portorož on the coast and you can even take lessons and qualify. Just remember that you're diving for the sport here; there ain't a whole lot in those waters. For more information contact the Slovenian Divers Union (☎ 061-133 9308) at Celovška cesta 25 in Ljubljana. For information about cave diving, see Caving below.

Fishing

Slovenia's rivers, streams and lakes are teeming with trout, grayling, pike and other fish. The best rivers for angling are the Soča, the Krka, the Kolpa, the Sava Bohinjka near Bohinj and the Unica in Notranjska. Lake fishing is good at Bled, Bohinj and Cerknica. But fishing is not a cheap sport in Slovenia; a daily permit at the popular river spots will cost you from 8500 to 13,700 SIT.

For information, licences and seasons, contact the Fisheries Institute (Zavod za Ribištvo; ☎ 061-126 2019; fax 061-125 5185) at Župančičeva ulica 9 in Ljubljana.

Hunting

Hunting is big business in Slovenia, and many Europeans (especially Italians) will pay big, um, bucks to bag a deer, a brace of grouse, a boar or even a bear. Among the best areas are the virgin forests of Kočevski Rog and the Gorjanci Hills in Gorenjska. The Slovenian Hunting Association (Lovska Zveza Slovenije; ☎ 061-214 950; fax 061-214 947), at the same address as the Fisheries Institute in Ljubljana, can organise a guide or include you in a hunting party. In addition to a daily fee, you will be charged for each animal or bird killed.

Horse Riding

Slovenia is a nation of horse riders, and the world's most famous horse, the Lipizzaner of the Spanish Riding School in Vienna, was first bred at Lipica in Primorska. More than a dozen centres registered with the Equestrian Association of Slovenia offer riding and lessons, but there are just as many smaller stables renting privately. One of the biggest – and most professional – outfits is the Kaval Equestrian Centre (☎ 067-54 506) at Prestranek Castle, about 6.5km south of Postojna. You can contact it directly or get information from ABC Farm and Countryside Holidays (☎/fax 061-576 127) in Ljubljana.

Cycling

Slovenia is a wonderful country for bicycling and mountain biking; the *Tourist Map of Slovenia*, available for free everywhere, lists cycling itineraries. Many towns and cities, including Ljubljana, Maribor, Ptuj, Novo Mesto, Kranj and Škofja Loka, have bicycle lanes and some even have special traffic lights.

Mountain bikes are for rent at Bled and Bohinj, and the uncrowded roads around these resorts are a joy to cycle on. Other excellent areas for cycling are the Upper Savinja Valley in Štajerska, the Soča Valley, the Krka Valley and, in Koroška, the Drava Valley. Remember that bikes are banned from the trails in Triglav National Park and all motorways.

It is not always easy to rent bicycles and mountain bikes in Slovenia. Places to rent them are listed in the Getting Around sections of each town, and the tourist office in Ljubljana can arrange bike rentals throughout the year. Otherwise, your best bet is always camp sites.

Prava Pot-Goodway (☎ 061-131 7114; fax 061-131 7186) at Slovenska cesta 55b in Ljubljana organises cycling tours of Slovenia between June and September, including an eight-day 250km one of Dolenjska following the Krka River for US$446 and a more difficult 290km eight-day one of Gorenjska for US$415. Prices include meals and accommodation; if you don't have your own wheels you'll have to pay US$60 extra.

Caving

Of Slovenia's 6700 registered caves, about two dozen are open to tourists. The vast majority of the richest ones – Škocjan, Postojna, Križna, Planina, Pivka, Predjama – are in the karst areas of Primorska and Notranjska, but there are many ice caves as well including one open to the public above the Upper Savinja Valley in Štajerska. Not all of the limestone caves are lit by electricity or open regularly though. You can learn to 'pothole' – descending with a guide through tunnels into the bowels of the earth – in the Kanin Mountains near Bovec.

Cave diving is a popular sport in Slovenia but is permitted only under the supervision of a professional guide. Cave diving has been done at Postojna, Škocjan and in the tunnel at Wild Lake (Divje Jezero) near Idrija. Sadly, three divers have drowned at Wild Lake over the past several years.

Thermal Spas

Slovenia counts some 16 thermal spa resorts, most of them in Štajerska, Dolenjska and Prekmurje and covered in this guide. They are excellent places not just for 'taking the cure' but for relaxing and meeting people.

Only two – Dolenjske Toplice and Radenci – are really spa towns as such, with that distinctive fin-de-siècle feel about them. Others, like Atomske Toplice and Čatež Terme, are loud, brash places dedicated to all the hedonistic pursuits you care to imagine. The Banovci spa near Veržej, about 13km south of Murska Sobota in Prekmurje, is reserved for naturists.

Many resorts use the trendier Italian terme for 'spa' instead of the proper Slovene word toplice or zdravilišče (health resort).

Paragliding, Ballooning & Flying

Paragliding is becoming increasingly popular in Slovenia, especially around Lake Bohinj and at Bovec in Gorenjska; at the latter you can jump in tandem paragliding from the upper cable-car station to the Kanin ski slopes and descend some 2000m down into the Bovec Valley.

One of the most active ballooning outfits is the Little Dragon Club (☎ 061-127 2534) at Ižanska cesta 350 in Ljubljana. See Activities in that chapter for details.

Every self-respecting town or city in Slovenia seems to have an airstrip or aerodrome these days complete with an enthusiastic aeroklub whose members will take you 'flight-seeing'. The Ljubljana-based Aeronautical Association of Slovenia (Letalska Zveza Slovenije; ☎/fax 061-222 504) at Tržaška cesta 2 has a complete list or see Activities in the following sections for details: Novo Mesto (Dolenjska); Lake Bled (Gorenjska); Slovenj Gradec (Koroška); Portorož (Primorska).

Golf

There's a 27-hole golf course at Bled, an 18-hole one at Mokrice Castle in Dolenjska and a nine-hole course in Lipica (Primorska).

Birdwatching

Although many Slovenes don't know it, Slovenia has some of the best birdwatching in central Europe with well over 300 species spotted here. The Ljubljana Marsh (Ljubljansko Barje), Lake Cerknica and Sečovlje saltworks are especially good for sighting aquatic and other birds like the black heron and kestrel, and the arrival of the white storks in Prekmurje in April is a wonderful sight. There's no guidebook devoted specifically to the birds of Slovenia, but the *Hamlyn Guide to the Birds of Britain and Europe* (UK£8.99) is very useful as is *Where to Watch Birds in Eastern Europe* (Hamlyn) by Gerard Gorman (UK£16.99).

LANGUAGE COURSES

The most famous school for learning Slovene is the Centre for Slovene as a Second Language (☎ 061-176 9382 or ☎ 061-176 9238; fax 061-125 7055) at the University of Ljubljana's Faculty of Arts, Aškerčeva cesta 2. There are two-week winter courses in February for US330, four-week summer ones in July for US$625 as well as an intensive course running from October to May for US$1850. Prices do not include room and board.

Other private schools offering Slovene as a discipline in Ljubljana are the Miklošič Educational Centre (☎ 061-322 791 or ☎ 061-133 4016) at Miklošičeva cesta 26 and Cene Štupar Center (☎ 061-132 7223) at Vojkova cesta 71. Courses of about 100 hours start at about US$450. The TIC in Ljubljana has a list of private tutors used to teaching foreigners.

WORK

Travellers on tourist visas in Slovenia are not supposed to accept employment, but many end up teaching English (going rate from DM25 per hour) or even doing a little work for foreign firms without work permits. An organisation called MOST (☎ 061-125 8067; fax 061-217 208) at Breg 12 in Ljubljana, which is part of the Service International Civil (SIC), organises summer work camps in Slovenia on projects ranging from ecology research in Novo Mesto to working with Gypsies near Murska Sobota.

ACCOMMODATION

Accommodation in Slovenia runs the gamut from riverside camp sites, cosy *gostišča* (inns) and farmhouses to elegant castle hotels in Dolenjska and Štajerska. Slovenia counts some 78,000 beds in total – more than a third of them in hotels – so you'll seldom have trouble finding accommodation to fit your budget except at the height of the season (July and August) on the coast, at Bled or Bohinj or in Ljubljana.

Accommodation is never really cheap in Slovenia, and there are a lot of 'hidden' costs. First of all, virtually every municipality levies a tourist tax that can add 100 to 300 SIT to your bill (per person per night) and some places charge fees for registration and insurance (100 SIT or under) and 30% or higher extra for stays of less than three nights. Hotels and camping grounds almost always insist on holding your passport or identity document during your stay. This can be a real pain when trying to change money and even disastrous when the staff are not as efficient as they should be. I almost left town twice without mine.

Camping

In summer, camping is the cheapest way to go, and there are conveniently located camping grounds *(kampi)* – about three-dozen official ones and lots more independent ones – in all areas of the country. You don't always need a tent; some camp sites have tents on site and inexpensive bungalows available as well. The three best camping grounds for those who want to experience the mountains or the sea are Zlatorog on Lake Bohinj, Špik at Gozd Martuljek near Kranjska Gora and Jezero Fiesa near Piran, though they can be jammed in summer. Prices vary according to the site and the season, but expect to pay anywhere between 600 and 1600 SIT per person a night. About one-third of the official camping grounds here offer discounts of 5 to 10% if you sign in with a Camping Card International (CCI).

It is forbidden to camp 'rough' in Slovenia though many Slovenes do – without ever lighting a fire.

Hostels & Student Dormitories

Only a half-dozen hostels in Slovenia are registered with the Holiday Association of Slovenia (Počitniška Zveza Slovenije; PZS), the national hostel organisation. They are in Bled, Koper, Ljubljana (two), Maribor and Rogla. Contact Mladi Turist (☎ 061-125 9260) at Salendrova ulica 4 in Ljubljana. You are never required to have a Hostelling International (HI) card to stay at hostels here, but it sometimes earns you a small discount or cancellation of the tourist tax.

A large portion of Slovenian pupils and students live away from home during the school year and sleep in a college dormitory (dijaški dom). Some of the ones in Ljubljana, Maribor, Idrija etc accept foreign travellers in summer for between 1200 SIT for a bed in a dormitory to 2500 SIT for a single room.

Private Rooms & Apartments

The system of letting private rooms to travellers is not as developed or as widespread as it is in, say, Hungary, but you'll find them available through tourist offices and travel agencies at Bled, Bohinj, Bovec, Celje, Izola, Koper, Kranjska Gora, Ljubljana, Piran, Portorož, Postojna, Radenci and Rogaška Slatina. Make sure you understand exactly where you'll be staying; in cities some private rooms are quite far from the centre.

You don't have to go through agencies or tourist offices; any house with a sign reading 'Sobe' means that rooms are available. Of course, you have no recourse if things don't work out, but if you've seen the room and understand the price, what could go wrong?

In Slovenia, private rooms are ranked according to category. Category I rooms have their own shower or bath, Category II ones have running water in the room and a shower or bath in the corridor, Category III rooms have no basin or tap in the room. Prices vary according to the town and season but in Bohinj at present, for example, Cat-

egory I rooms are DM16 to DM20 per person, Category II ones are DM13 to DM16 and Category III rooms DM11 to DM13.

The price quoted is usually for a minimum three nights. If you're staying a shorter time (and you are usually welcome to), you'll have to pay 30% and sometimes as much as 50% more. The price of a private room never includes breakfast (DM6 to DM9 if available) or tourist tax. An extra bed is 20% on top.

Some of the offices in the towns and cities mentioned earlier also have holiday apartments available that can accommodate up to six. One for two people could go for as low as DM45 or as high as DM75 per night.

Pensions & Guesthouses

Pensions and guesthouses come by several names in Slovenia. A penzion is, of course, a pension but more commonly it's called a gostišče, an inn or restaurant with accommodation (prenočišče) upstairs or somewhere out back. They are more expensive than hostels but cheaper than hotels and often your only choice in small towns and villages. Generally speaking, a gostilna serves food and drink only but some have rooms available as well. The distinction between a gostilna and a gostišče isn't very clear – even to most Slovenes nowadays.

Farmhouses

Some 230 working farms in Slovenia offer accommodation to paying guests and, for a truly relaxing break, they can't be beaten. You either stay in private rooms in the farmhouse itself or in alpine-style guesthouses somewhere nearby. Many of the farms offer activities such as horse riding, kayaking, trekking or cycling and allow you to help out with the farm work – if you're interested.

The farms themselves can range from places where Old MacDonald would feel at home to not much more than a modern pension with a vegetable patch and orchard. The latter is especially true at tourist destinations like Bled and near the coast. You'll find much more isolated farmsteads with livestock and vineyards in Štajerska and Dolenjska.

ABC Farm and Countryside Holidays (☎/fax 061-576 12,') at Ulica Jožeta Jama 16 in Ljubljana or at Brnik airport (☎ 064-261 684; fax 064-261 669) oversees much of the farmhouse accommodation in Slovenia. Its agent in the UK is Slovenia Pursuits (☎ 01763-852 646; fax 01763-852 387), 14 Hay Street, Steeple Morden, Royston, Herts SG8 0PE, England.

Roughly expect to pay about DM30 per person in a 2nd category room with shared bath and breakfast in the low season (from September to mid-December and from mid-January to June) to DM45 per person for a 1st category room with private bath and meals in the high season (July and August). Apartments for groups of up to eight people are also available. There's no minimum stay but you must pay 30% more if it's less than three nights. Prices at very popular destinations like Bled and Logarska Dolina are higher.

Hotels

Slovenia's 180 hotels are more expensive than the other accommodation options and the rates vary according to season, with July and August being the peak season and September/October and May/June the shoulder ones. In Ljubljana prices are constant all year. Many resort hotels, particularly on the coast, are closed in winter. As hotels seldom levy a surcharge for stays of one or two nights, they're worth considering if you're only passing through.

As with many other countries in the region, hotel standards in Slovenia vary enormously, and it's often difficult to tell what's what until you've stepped (or slept) inside. Hopefully the Slovenian Tourist Board's new star-rating system will sort that out.

Among the finest and most expensive places to stay in Slovenia are the castle hotels at Otočec and Mokrice. The Protocol Service of the Republic of Slovenia owns several magnificent properties with accommodation, including Brdo and Strmol castles near Kranj in Gorenjska and the Vila Podrožnik at Rožna Dolina in Ljubljana. For informa-tion, contact the Protocol Service (☎ 064-221 133; fax 064-221 551) at Brdo Castle in Predoslje.

FOOD

The most important thing to remember about Slovenian food is that it is heavily influenced by its neighbours' cuisines. From Austria, it's sausage *(klobasa)*, strudel *(zavitek)* filled with fruit, nuts and/or *skuta* (curd cheese), and Wiener schnitzel *(Dunajski zrezek)*. The ravioli-like *žlikrofi*, *njoki* (potato dumplings) and *rižota* (risotto) obviously have Italian origins, and Hungary has contributed *golaž* (goulash), *paprikaš* (piquant chicken or beef 'stew') and *palačinke*, thin pancakes filled with jam or nuts and topped with chocolate. Distinctively Slovenian dishes are prepared with *žganci*, groats that can be made from buckwheat, barley or corn. Slovenian bread *(kruh)* is generally excellent, especially the braided loaves made around the holidays. A real treat is 'mottled bread' *(pisan kruh)* in which three types of dough (buckwheat, wheat and corn) are rolled up and baked.

Most Slovenian meals start with soup, usually chicken or beef broth with little egg noodles *(kokošja* or *goveja juha z rezanci)* and move on to a main course. This is for the most part meat *(meso)* with the favourites being pork *(svinjina)*, veal *(teletina)*, beef *(govedina)* and, in season, game like deer *(srna)*. One excellent prepared meat is *pršut*, air-dried, thinly sliced ham that is nothing like the slimy Italian *prosciutto* from where it gets its name.

For some reason chicken *(piščanec)* is not as common on a Slovenian menu as turkey *(puran)* and goose *(gos)*. Slovenes are big eaters of fish *(riba)* and other seafood, though away from the coast it's usually trout *(postrv)*.

Slovenia is hardly paradise for vegetarians though this is changing and you're sure to find a fair few meat-less dishes on any menu. Dumplings made with cheese *(štruklji)* and often with chives or tarragon added are widely available as are dishes like *gobova rižota* (mushroom risotto) and deep-fried cheese *(ocvrti sir)*. Another boon for veggies is that Slovenes love fresh salad *(solata)* – a most un-Slavic partiality – and you can get one any place, even in a countryside gostilna. A milk bar *(mlečna restavracija)* sells yoghurt and other dairy products as well as *krofi*, jam-filled raised doughnuts that are very tasty.

Slovenian cuisine boasts two excellent and very different desserts. *Potica*, almost a national institution, is a kind of nut roll (though often made with savoury fillings too) eaten after a meal or with coffee or tea during the day. *Gibanica* from Prekmurje is a rich concoction of pastry filled with poppy seeds, walnuts, apples and/or sultanas and cheese and topped with cream. It's definitely not for dieters.

You should have no problem getting a snack between meals in Slovenia; many people eat something hot at about 10 am. The most popular is a Balkan import called *burek*, flaky pastry stuffed with meat, cheese or even apple not unlike Greek *tiropita* and sold at outside stalls throughout the land. It is very cheap and filling but can be quite greasy. Other snack foods include:

Čevapčiči – spicy meatballs of beef or pork
Pica – another way to spell 'pizza'
Pljeskavica – spicy, Serbian-style meat patties
Pomfri – chips (French fries)
Ražnjiči – shish kebab
Vroča hrenovka – hot dog

Potica, a Slovenian speciality, is traditionally baked in a round ceramic mould.

Restaurants

Restaurants go by many names in Slovenia, but the distinction is not always very precise. At the top of the heap, a *restavracija* is a restaurant where you sit down and are served. A *gostilna* or *gostišče* – there's supposed to be a difference – has waiters too but it's more like an inn, with rustic décor and usually (but not always) national dishes. A *samopostrežna restavracija* is a self-service establishment where you order from a counter and sometimes eat standing up. An *okrepčevalnica* and a *bife* serve simple, fast food like grilled meats and sausages; a *krčma* may have snacks, but the emphasis here is on drinking. A *slaščičarna* sells sweets and ice cream while a *kavarna* provides coffee and pastries.

Many restaurants and inns have an inexpensive set menu at lunch *(dnevno kosilo)* advertised on a blackboard outside. Three courses can cost less than 600 SIT.

It's important to remember that not many Slovenes eat in restaurants in cities or towns unless they have to because of work or they're entertaining. At the weekend, most will head 5 or 10km out of town for a gostilna or gostišče they know will serve them good, home-cooked food and local wine at affordable prices. For the traveller without a car, it can be difficult reaching these little 'finds' but I've included as many as practical.

Menu Items

Almost every sit-down restaurant in Slovenia has a multilingual menu with dishes translated into English, Italian, German and sometimes even French. But the language used is sometimes inaccurate or less then appetising; 'Beef Mouth in Salad' and 'Farinaceous Dishes' would have most would-be diners scratching their heads or running for the door. And then there are all those lists with 'daily recommendations' *('Danes priporočamo ...')* that are frequently in Slovene only.

The following is a menu *(jedilni list)* sampler with dishes listed in the way most Slovenian restaurants would group them. It's not complete by any means, but it will give you a good idea of what to expect. For more food and ordering words, see the Language Guide at the back of the book.

It's customary to wish others at your table *'Dober tek!'* ('Bon appetit!') before starting your meal.

Cold Starters – *Hladne Začetne Jedi* or *Hladne Predjede*

Domača salama – home-style salami
Francoska solata – diced potatoes and vegetables with mayonnaise
Gnjat/šunka s hrenom – smoked/boiled ham with horseradish
Kraški pršut z olivami – air-dried Karst ham (prosciutto) with salty black olives
Narezek – assorted smoked meats/cold cuts
Riba v marinadi – marinated fish

Soups – *Juhe*

Dnevna juha – soup of the day
Gobova kremna juha – creamed mushroom soup
Goveja juha z rezanci – beef broth with little egg noodles
Grahova juha – pea soup
Paradižnikova juha – tomato soup
Prežganka – toasted rye-flour soup thickened with cream
Zelenjavna juha – vegetable soup

Warm Starters – *Tople Začetne Jedi* or *Tople Predjedi*

Drobnjakovi štruklji – dumplings of cottage cheese and chives
Ocvrti sir s tatarsko omako – deep-fried cheese with tartar sauce
Omlet s sirom/šunko – omelette with cheese/ham
Rižota z gobami – risotto with mushrooms
Špageti po bolonjska – spaghetti bolognese
Žlikrofi – ravioli of cheese, bacon and chives

Ready-Made Dishes – *Pripravljene Jedi* or *Gotova Jedilna*

Bograč golaž – beef goulash served in a pot
Jota – beans, sauerkraut and potatoes or barley cooked with salt pork in a pot
Kuhana govedina s hrenom – boiled beef with horseradish
Kurja obara z ajdovimi žganci – chicken stew or 'gumbo' with buckwheat groats
Pečen piščanec – roast chicken
Prekajena svinjska rebrca s kislim zeljem – smoked pork ribs with sauerkraut
Ričet – barley stew with smoked pork ribs
Svinjska pečenka – roast pork

Dishes Made to Order – *Jedi po Naročilu*

Čebulna bržola – braised beef with onions
Ciganska jetra – liver Gypsy-style
Dunajski zrezek – Wiener schnitzel (breaded cutlet of veal or pork)
Kmečka pojedina – 'farmer's feast' of smoked meats and sauerkraut
Kranjska klobasa z gočico – Carniolan sausage with mustard
Ljubljanski zrezek – breaded cutlet with cheese
Mešano meso na žaru – mixed grill
Ocvrti piščanec – fried chicken
Pariški zrezek – cutlet fried in egg batter
Puranov zrezek s šampinjoni – turkey steak with white mushrooms

Fish – *Ribe*

Brancin z maslom – sea bass in butter
Kuhana/pečena postrv – boiled/grilled trout
Lignji ali kalamari na žaru – grilled squid
Morski list v belem vinu – sole in white wine
Ocvrti oslič – fried cod
Orada na žaru – grilled sea bream
Pečene sardele – grilled sardines
Ribja plošča – seafood plate
Škampi – scampi (prawns)
Školjke – shellfish (clams, mussels etc)

Side Dishes – *Priloge* or *Prikuhe*

Ajdovi/koruzni žganci – buckwheat/corn groats
Bučke – squash or pumpkin
Cvetača or *karfijola* – cauliflower
Grah – sweet peas
Korenje – carrots
Kruhovi cmoki – bread dumplings
Mlinci – small pancakes
Ocvrti krompir or *pomfri* – chips (French fries)
Pire krompir – mashed potatoes
Pražen krompir – fried potatoes
Riž – rice
Špinača – spinach
Stročji fižol – string beans
Testenine – pasta
Zelenjavne prikuhe – side vegetables

Salads – *Solate*

Fižolova solata – bean salad
Kisle kumarice – pickled cucumbers
Kumarična solata – cucumber salad
Paradižnikova solata – tomato salad
Rdeča pesa – pickled beetroot (beets)
Sezonska/mešana solata – seasonal/mixed salad
Srbska solata – 'Serbian salad' of tomatoes and green peppers
Zelena solata – lettuce salad
Zelnjata solata – cabbage salad

Fruit – *Sadje*

Ananas – pineapple
Breskev – peach
Češnje – cherries
Češplja – plum
Grozdje – grapes
Hruška – pear
Jabolko – apple
Jagode – strawberries
Kompot – stewed fruit (many types)
Lešniki – hazelnuts
Maline – raspberries
Marelica – apricot
Orehi – walnuts
Pomaranča – orange
Višnje – sour cherries (morellos)

Desserts/Cheese – *Sladice/Siri*

Jabolčni zavitek – apple strudel
Krofi – raised doughnuts
Orehova potica – Slovenian nut roll
Palačinke z marmelado/orehi/čokolado – thin pancakes with marmelade/nuts/chocolate
Prekmurska gibanica – layers of flaky pastry with fruit, nut, cheese and poppy-seed filling and topped with cream
Sadna kupa – fruit salad with whipped cream
Sirova polšča – cheese plate
Sladoled – ice cream
Torta – cake

DRINKS
Wine

Slovenia has been making wine since the time of the Romans, and many of its wines today are of a very high quality indeed. Unfortunately, most foreigners know Slovenian wine – if at all – from the 'el cheapo' bottles of white Ljutomer Riesling or Laški Riesling served at college parties. For the most part, these are dull, unmemorable wines (the Ljutomer can be slightly sweet), but a trip to Slovenia will convince you that most of the best wines stay at home. For more detailed information, contact the Slovenian Academy of Wine (☎ 062-779 198; fax 062-779 009; sva-veitas@sva-veritas.si) at Grajska ulica 2, 2250 Ptuj.

Slovenia counts 14 distinct wine-growing areas with some 22,000 hectares under cultivation, but there are just three major regions. Podravje ('on the Drava') extends from north-east Štajerska into Prekmurje and produces whites almost exclusively. Eschew the insipid Ljutomer and Laški Rieslings in favour of Renski Rizling (a true German Riesling), Beli Pinot (Pinot Blanc), Traminec (Traminer) or Šipon (Furmint), all whites.

Posavje is the region running from eastern Štajerska across the Sava River into Dolenjska and Bela Krajina. This region produces both whites and reds, but its most famous wine is Cviček, a dry light red, almost rosé wine that is distinctly Slovenian.

The Primorska wine region concentrates on reds, the most famous being Teran made from Slovenian Refošk grapes in the Karst region. It is a ruby-red, peppery wine with high acidity that goes perfectly with pršut ham and game. Other wines from this region are Malvazija, a yellowish white from the coast that is light and dry and good with fish, and red Merlot, especially the one from the Vipava Valley.

On a Slovenian wine label, the first word usually identifies where the wine comes from and the second the grape varietal: Vipavski Merlot, Mariborski Traminec etc. But it's not always like that. Some bear names according to their place of origin such as Jeruzalemčan, Bizeljčan, Haložan.

There is no *appellation contrôlée* as such in Slovenia; *kontrolirano poreklo* is a trademark protection that usually – but not in every instance – suggests a certain standard. When choosing wine, look for the words *vrhunsko vino* (premium wine) and a gold label, *kakovostno vino* (quality wine) and a silver one, and *namizno vino* (table wine) with a bronze-coloured label. They can be red, white or rosé and dry, semi-dry, semi-sweet or sweet. Vintage is not as important with most Slovenian wines as it is with French and Californian ones.

The best sparkling wine is Zlata Radgonska Penina from Gornja Radgona.

Slovenes usually drink wine with meals or socially at home; it's rare to see people sit down to a bottle at a café or pub. As elsewhere in central Europe, a bottle or glass of mineral water is ordered along with the wine when eating. It's a different story in summer when spritzers (wine coolers) of red or white wine mixed with mineral water are consumed in vast quantities.

All of the wine-producing areas have a 'wine road' *(vinska cesta)* or two – 20 in all – that you can follow in a car or on a bicycle. These are outlined on the useful and updated *Slovenian Wine Map* (Imago) available from most bookshops in Ljubljana. Along the way, you can stop at the occasional cellar *(klet)* offering wine tastings or at a *vinoteka* in wine towns or cities (Maribor, Metlika, Ptuj, Rogaška Slatina, Dobrovo near Nova Gorica and Brežice).

Some important wine words are:

Arhivsko vino – vintage wine
Belo vino – white wine
Brizganec or *špricar* – spritzer (wine cooler)
Buteljka – bottle
Črno vino – red (literally 'black') wine
Kakovostno vino – quality wine
Kozarec – glass
Kuhano vino – mulled wine
Namizno vino – table wine
Peneče vino – sparkling wine
Polsladko – semi-sweet
Polsuho – semi-dry/medium
Rose – rosé wine
Sladko or *Desertno* – sweet wine
Suho – dry
Vino – wine
Vinoteka – wine shop with tastings
Vinska karta – wine list
Vinska klet – wine cellar
Vinski hram – wine bar/room
Vrhunsko vino – premium wine

Beer

Beer is very popular in Slovenia, especially outside the home and among younger people. Štajerska hops *(hmelj)* grown in the Savinja Valley are used locally and widely sought after by brewers from around the world. They have been described as having the flavour of lemon grass.

Slovenia has three breweries: Union in Ljubljana, Laško in the town of that name south of Celje, and the small Gambrinus in Maribor. Union is lighter-tasting and sweeter than Zlatorog, the excellent and ubiquitous beer (it has about 50% of the market) brewed by Laško. Union also produces an alcohol-free beer called Uni, a decent stout called

Črni Baron and a shandy called Radler. Laško's alcohol-free brew is called Gren and its shandy is called Roler. It also makes a 'light' beer called Lahko.

In a pub *(pivnica)* draught beer is drunk in 0.5L mugs or 0.3L ones. Both locally brewed and imported beers are also available at pubs, shops and supermarkets in 0.5L bottles or cans measuring 0.3L. *'Na zdravje!'* is how you say 'Cheers!' in Slovene.

Important beer words:

Malo pivo – beer measuring 0.3L
Pivo – beer
Pivnica – pub/beer hall
Svetlo pivo – lager
Temno pivo – dark beer/stout
Točeno pivo – draught beer
Veliko pivo – beer measuring 0.5L
Vrček – mug

Other Drinks

An alcoholic drink as Slovenian as wine is *žganje*, a strong brandy or *eau de vie* distilled from a variety of fruits but most commonly apples, plums and cherries. Another type is *medeno žganje* (or *medica*) flavoured with honey, but the finest is Pleterska Hruška, a pear brandy (or *viljemovka*) made by the Carthusian monks at Pleterje Monastery near Kostanjevica na Krki in Dolenjska. They let a pear grow into a bottle that has been placed upside-down on a branch, then 'pick' bottle and pear together and pour brandy inside. Drink too much of this stuff and you'll see visions of the place the monks warn us all about.

Many Slovenes enjoy a *špička* – slang for a little glass of schnapps – during the day as a pick-me-up. You'll probably get the invitation *'Pridite na kupico'* ('Come and have a drop') more than once.

Most international brands of soft drinks are available in Slovenia, but mineral water from Radenci (Radenska) or Rogaška Slatina seems to be the most popular libation for teetotallers in pubs and bars. Juice *(sok)* is usually boxed fruit 'drink' with lots of sugar or a drink made with syrup.

Italian espresso is the type of coffee most commonly served but thick, sweet Turkish coffee is also popular, especially at home. If you don't want it too sweet, say *'Ne sladko, prosim'*. Coffee is good everywhere except at hotel breakfasts when you'll almost invariably be served a cup of lukewarm, milky, ersatz coffee.

Local people drink lots of herbal teas and seem to prefer anything made with a berry, a blossom or a leaf over what they call 'Russian' (black) tea. It's also difficult to find in the shops so bring your own supply of tea bags.

Useful words include:

Brezalkoholne pijače – soft drinks
Brinjevec – juniper-flavoured brandy
Čaj – tea
Češnjevec – cherry brandy (kirsch)
Jabolčni sok – apple juice
Jabolčnik – apple cider
Kapučino – cappuccino
Kava – coffee
Kava s smetano – coffee with whipped cream
Limonada – lemonade
Mineralna voda – mineral water
Planinski čaj – mountain-flower tea
Pomarančni sok – orange juice
Sadjevec – apple brandy (apple jack)
Slivovka – plum brandy
Sok – juice
Tonik z ledom – tonic water with ice
Viljemovka – pear brandy
Vinjak – wine brandy
Zeliščni čaj – herbal tea

There are more words and phrases in Slovene in the Language Guide and the Glossary at the back of the book.

ENTERTAINMENT

Cinema

Foreign films are never dubbed into Slovene but are shown in their original language with subtitles. The choice, even in Ljubljana, is not very great – one film usually travels from one cinema to the next – but you're sure to find something of interest.

Discos & Clubs

Discos are the most popular form of entertainment for young people and are always good fun. The biggest and most rollicking are in Ljubljana and on the coast, but you'll even find them in small provincial towns.

Classical Music, Opera, Ballet & Theatre

Slovenia has a lot of excellent, high-brow entertainment on offer – particularly classical music and theatre. Ljubljana alone counts seven theatres, an opera house where ballets are also performed, and two symphony orchestras. Maribor has a resident opera company as well as a symphony orchestra, a ballet company and two theatres. There are also theatres in Celje, Kranj and Koper. Many other towns have chamber orchestras and string quartets that perform in churches, castles, museums and civic centres.

Folk & Traditional Music

Folk-music performances are usually local affairs and are very popular in Dolenjska, Bela Krajina and even Bled (especially in July and August during the Okarina World Music Festival). Črnomelj is the centre of Slovenian folk music and as many as 50 bands playing stringed instruments like the *tamburica*, the *berdo* (contrabass), the guitar-like *brač* and the *bisernica* (lute) are active in the area. Flyers and posters in these areas are always announcing folk nights at halls and cultural centres.

SPECTATOR SPORT

In a land where skiing *(smučanje)* is king, Slovenia counts some world-class champions, including Roman Perko in cross-country racing and Mitja Dragšič in alpine slalom. But the national hero in this sport is the young Primož Peterka, World Cup holder in ski-jumping once again in 1998. Peterka reached the 200m mark in Planica in 1994.

Oddly, Slovenia is one of the few countries in Europe where football *(nogomet)* is not a national passion; some wags have suggested that in a nation of only two million it's almost impossible to get 11 people on the ground and go for the same goal. Perhaps that explains why basketball *(košarka)*, with only five a side, is so popular here. The Union Olimpija team reigns supreme and one of its members, the slam dunker Marko

Milič, was hunted by the American NBA in 1996. Other popular spectator sports are ice hockey *(hokej)*, with Olimpija Ljubljana at the top, and volleyball *(rokomet)*, with the team from Celje excelling.

The first Olympic medal won by a Slovene was a silver won by Rudolf Cvetko at Stockholm in 1912 as part of the Austrian sabre team. But the most celebrated Slovenian Olympic athlete is the gymnast Leon Štukelj (born 1899), who took gold medals at Paris in 1924, bronze at Amsterdam in 1928 and silver at Berlin in 1936. Štukelj is the oldest Olympic champion in the world and still trains.

Since independence, Slovenia has won two bronze medals in rowing (Iztok Čop and Denis Žvegelj at Barcelona in 1992) and two silvers at Atlanta in 1996 (Andraž Vehovar in white-water kayaking and Brigita Bukovec in 100m hurdles). At the 1994 Winter Olympics at Lillehammer in Norway skiers Katja Koren, Alenka Dovžan and Mitja Košir all won bronze medals.

THINGS TO BUY

For folk craft and other souvenirs in Slovenia, it's best to go to the source where you'll find the real thing and not mass-produced kitsch: Idrija or Železniki for lace, Ribnica for wooden household utensils, Bohinj for carved wooden pipes with silver lids, Prekmurje for Hungarian-style black pottery, Kropa for objects made of wrought iron and Rogaška Slatina for crystal. Some people think they're tacky, but I like the traditional beehive panels *(panjske končnice)* painted with folk motifs, especially the ones showing a devil sharpening a gossip's tongue on a grindstone. I know a few people who should hang that one up at home as an icon and light votive candles in front of it.

The silver-filigree jewellery you'll see for sale in shops around the country, but especially on the coast, is not really Slovenian but a good buy nonetheless. Almost all of the shops are owned and run by ethnic Albanians who brought the craft here from Kosovo in southern Serbia.

Ski equipment and skiwear are of very high quality. Elan skis and snowboards are made in Begunje na Gorenjskem near Bled and Alpina boots at Žiri, north-east of Idrija.

Natural remedies, herbal teas and apian products like beeswax, honey, pollen, propolis and royal jelly can be found in speciality shops around the country.

A bottle or two of Slovenian wine makes a great gift. Buy it from a vinoteka or a dealer with a large selection like Simon Bradeško or Vino Boutique in Ljubljana (see that chapter). A couple of monasteries in Dolenjska – the Cistercian one at Stična near Ivančna Gorica and the Carthusian one at Pleterje – sell their own brand of firewater made from fruits and berries. It's fragrant but very potent stuff.

Getting There & Away

AIR
Airports & Airlines
While there are international airports at Maribor in Štajerska and Portorož on the coast in Primorska, only Brnik airport (☎ 064-222 700), 23km north-west of Ljubljana, receives regularly scheduled flights. The airport is open daily from 6 am to 10 pm and has a hotel booking board with telephone in the arrivals hall and an information desk in the departures area. The Kompas travel agency has a representative office, and there are car-rental firms, including ABC, Alpetour, Avis, Budget, Europcar, Eurodollar and Hertz. There's also a post office, duty-free shop, the Edvard Rusjan à la carte restaurant and the Ikar self-service one. You can change money in the departures area at the Nova Ljubljanska Banka branch (open weekdays 8 am to 3 pm) or at the Kompas newsagents (open daily from 7 am to 8 pm). In arrivals there's a Cirrus-linked SKB Banka ATM dispensing tolars and a machine that can exchange 15 different currencies into tolars.

The Slovenian national carrier, Adria Airways (JP; ☎ 061-133 4336 in Ljubljana, ☎ 064-223 555 at Brnik airport), flies nonstop to Ljubljana from 17 cities, including Amsterdam, Barcelona, Copenhagen, Frankfurt, London (LHR), Manchester (seasonal), Moscow, Munich, Ohrid in Macedonia, Paris (CDG), Sarajevo, Skopje, Split, Tel Aviv, Tirana, Vienna and Zürich. It also has charters during summer months to several other destinations, including Athens, Istanbul and Malta.

Adria has about a dozen offices abroad, including the following:

Austria
    (☎ 0222-522 3740), Mariahilferstrasse 32-34, 1070 Vienna
Croatia
    (☎ 01-481 0011), Praška ul 9, 10000 Zagreb
France
    (☎ 01 47 42 95 00), 38 Ave de l'Opéra, 75002 Paris

Germany
    (☎ 069-290 27 4), Grosse Eschenheimer Strasse 43, 60313 Frankfurt
    (☎ 089-228 39 74), Maximilliansplatz 12a, 80333 Munich
Spain
    (☎ 3-28 04 890), Paseo Manuel Girona 71, 08034 Barcelona
Switzerland
    (☎ 01-212 63 93), Löwenstrasse 54, CH-8001 Zürich
UK
    (☎ 0171-734 4630), 49 Conduit Street, London W1R 9FB

Other airlines that serve Ljubljana include Aeroflot (SU) from Moscow, Austrian Airlines (OS) from Vienna, Avioimpex (M4) from Skopje and Swissair (SR) from Zürich.

Buying Tickets
In early 1998 Adria's cheapest excursion fare (with one-week advance purchase, fixed dates and a Saturday overnight) from London to Ljubljana was UK£210 plus taxes of around UK£30 (against a regular full-fare economy return ticket of UK£688); the fare increases by about UK£25 in summer. APEX fares on the same route with Lufthansa via Frankfurt and Swissair via Zürich were UK£245 and UK£255 respectively. Adria's Frankfurt-Ljubljana-Frankfurt excursion fare was DM530 (full economy fare DM1216). Travellers to the Balkans might like to know that Adria offers very attractive return fares from London to Croatia, Macedonia and Bosnia-Hercegovina via Ljubljana; to Split and Sarajevo it's UK£240 and to Skopje UK£280.

Travellers with Special Needs
If you have special needs of any sort – you're vegetarian or require a special diet, you're travelling in a wheelchair, taking the baby, terrified of flying, whatever – let the airline people know as soon as possible so that they can make the necessary arrangements. Remind them when you reconfirm your

booking (at least 72 hours before departure) and again when you check in at the airport. It may also be worth ringing around the airlines before you make your booking to find out how they can handle your particular needs.

Airports and airlines can be surprisingly helpful, but they do need advance warning. Most international airports will provide escorts from check-in desk to plane where needed, and there should be ramps, lifts, accessible toilets and reachable phones. Aircraft toilets, on the other hand, are likely to present a problem; travellers should discuss this with the airline at an early stage and, if necessary, with their doctor.

Guide dogs for the blind will often have to travel in a specially pressurised baggage compartment with other animals, away from their owner, though smaller guide dogs may be admitted to the cabin. All guide dogs will be subject to the same quarantine laws (six months in isolation etc) as any other animal when entering or returning to countries currently free of rabies such as Britain or Australia.

Deaf travellers can ask for airport and in-flight announcements to be written down for them.

Children aged under two travel for 10% of the full fare (or free on some airlines) as long as they don't occupy a seat. They don't get a baggage allowance in this case. 'Skycots', baby food and nappies (diapers) should be provided by the airline if requested in advance. Push chairs can often be taken as hand luggage. Children aged between two and 12 can usually occupy a seat for half to two-thirds of the full fare. They do get a standard baggage allowance.

LAND
Bus

International buses do not just arrive and depart from Ljubljana; you can catch them from cities and towns around Slovenia. For an indication of international bus fares from the capital, see Getting There & Away in the Ljubljana chapter.

Italy Nova Gorica is the easiest exit/entry point between Slovenia and Italy as you can catch up to five buses a day to/from the Italian city of Gorizia or simply walk across the border at Rožna Dolina (Casa Rossa in Italian). Between eight and 11 buses a day make the run from Ankaran, the first resort on the Slovenian coast, to the Italian border crossing at Lazaret, but you'll have to change again to reach Trieste to the north-east.

To reach Trieste from the coast it's easier to leave from Koper. Up to 17 buses a day go to/from Trieste, 20km to the north-east. Buses run from 6 am to 7.30 pm on weekdays only – though there is one bus on Saturday at 7.30 pm. The bus station in Trieste is immediately south-west of the train station in Piazza Libertà.

There's a bus from Ljubljana to Trieste Monday to Saturday at 6.25 am. Tarvisio in north-east Italy is linked with Kranjska Gora by two buses, which run Monday to Saturday at 9.35 and 11.45 am.

Croatia & Yugoslavia The coastal towns of Koper, Piran and Portorož are the best places for making your way by bus to Croatian Istria. There are frequent services to Novigrad, Poreč, Pula and Rovinj. There's also at least one bus a day Monday to Saturday to Rijeka.

For cities in north-western Croatia like Varaždin and the capital, Zagreb, the gateways apart from Ljubljana are in eastern Štajerska and Dolenjska. For Varaždin count on one morning bus on Saturday and Sunday from Celje, two a day from Maribor and up to six from Ptuj. Zagreb-bound buses go from Ptuj (three a day), Maribor (two) and Novo Mesto (three).

From Ljubljana there's a daily bus to Novigrad, Rovinj and Umag at 1.45 pm and to Split and Rijeka at 7.40 pm. Four buses a day leave for Zagreb and there's a departure on Saturday and Sunday at 6.35 am to Varaždin.

In Ljubljana a company called Yatras (☎ 061-316 975) runs buses to Croatian and Yugoslav cities and towns from the old Yugoslav Airlines office at Slomškova ulica

Air Travel Glossary

Apex Tickets Apex ('advance purchase excursion') fares are usually between 30 and 40% cheaper than full economy ones, but there are restrictions. You must purchase the ticket at least 21 days (sometimes more) in advance, be away for a minimum period (normally 14 days) and return within a maximum period (90 or 180 days). Stopovers are not allowed, and if you have to change your travel dates or routing, there will be extra charges. These tickets are not fully refundable; if you cancel your trip, the refund is often considerably less than what you paid for the ticket. Take out travel insurance to cover yourself in case you have to call off your trip unexpectedly (eg due to illness).

Baggage Allowance This will be written on your ticket; you are usually allowed one item weighing 20 kg to go in the hold, plus one item of hand luggage. Many airlines flying transatlantic routes allow for two pieces of luggage with relatively generous limits on their dimensions and weight.

Bucket Shops At certain times of the year and/or on certain routes, many airlines fly with empty seats. This isn't profitable (or good PR) and it's often more cost-effective for them to fly full, even if that means having to sell a certain number of drastically discounted tickets. They do this by off-loading them onto bucket shops (or consolidators), travel agents who specialise in such discounted fares. The agents, in turn, sell them to the public at reduced prices. These tickets are often the cheapest you'll find, but you usually can't purchase them directly from the airlines, restrictions abound and long-haul journeys can be extremely time-consuming, with several stops along the way. Availability varies widely, so you'll not only have to be flexible in your travel plans, you'll also have to be quick off the mark as soon as an advertisement appears in the press.

Bucket-shop agents advertise in newspapers and magazines, and there's a lot of competition – especially in places like Amsterdam, London and Hong Kong which are crawling with them. It's always a good idea to telephone first to ascertain availability before rushing to some out-of-the-way shop. Naturally, they'll advertise the cheapest available tickets, but by the time you get there, these may be sold out (or were nonexistent in the first place), and you may be looking at something slightly more expensive.

Bumping Just because you have a confirmed seat doesn't mean you're going to get on the plane (see Overbooking).

Cancellation Penalties If you have to cancel or change an Apex or other discounted ticket, there may be heavy penalties involved; travel insurance can sometimes be taken out against these penalties. Some airlines now impose penalties on regular tickets as well, particularly against 'no show' passengers.

Check In Airlines ask you to check in a certain time ahead of the flight departure (usually two hours on international flights but longer on particularly security-conscious ones like El Al, the Israeli carrier). If you fail to check in on time and the flight is overbooked, the airline can cancel your reservation and give your seat to somebody else.

Confirmation Having a ticket written out with the flight and date on it doesn't mean you have a seat until the agent has confirmed with the airline that your status is 'OK' and has written or stamped that on your ticket. Prior to this confirmation, your status is 'on request'.

Courier Fares Businesses often send their urgent documents or freight through courier companies. These companies hire people to accompany the package through customs and, in return, offer cheap tickets that used to be phenomenal bargains but nowadays are just like decent discounted fares. In effect, what the courier companies do is ship their goods as your luggage on regular commercial flights; you are usually only allowed carry-on. This is a legitimate operation – all freight is completely legal. There are two drawbacks, however: the short turnaround time of the ticket (usually not longer than a month) and the limitation on your baggage allowance.

Discounted Tickets There are two types of discounted fares: officially discounted (such as Apex) ones and unofficially discounted tickets (see Bucket Shops). The latter can save you more than money – you may be able to pay Apex prices without the associated advance-purchase and other requirements. The lowest prices often impose drawbacks, such as flying with unpopular airlines, inconvenient schedules, or unpleasant routings and connections.

Economy Class Economy-class tickets are usually not the cheapest way to go, but they do give you maximum flexibility and they are valid for 12 months. If you don't use them, most are fully refundable, as are unused sectors of a multiple ticket.

Full Fares Airlines traditionally offer first class (coded F), business class (coded J) and economy class (coded Y) tickets. These days there are so many promotional and discounted fares available that the only passengers paying full fare are on expense accounts or at the gate and in a hurry.

Lost Tickets If you lose your ticket, an airline will usually treat it like a travellers cheque and, after inquiries, issue you with a replacement. Legally, however, an airline is entitled to treat it like cash, so a loss could be permanent. Consider them as valuables.

MCO An MCO (Miscellaneous Charges Order) is a voucher for a given amount, usually issued by an airline as a refund or against a lost ticket. It can be used to pay for a flight with any IATA (International Air Transport Association) airline. MCOs, which are more flexible than a regular ticket, may satisfy the irritating onward ticket requirement, but some countries are now reluctant to accept them.

No Shows No shows are passengers who fail to turn up for their flight for whatever reason. Full-fare no shows are sometimes entitled to travel on a later flight. The rest are penalised (see Cancellation Penalties), but it all depends on the circumstances and availability of space.

Open-Jaw Tickets These are return tickets that allow you to fly to one place but return from another, and travel between the two 'jaws' by any means of transport at your own expense. If available, this can save you backtracking to your arrival point.

Overbooking Airlines hate to fly with empty seats, and since every flight has some passengers who fail to show up, they often book more passengers than there are seats available. Usually the excess passengers balance those who fail to show up, but occasionally somebody gets bumped – usually the last passenger(s) to check in.

Promotional Fares These are officially discounted fares, such as Apex ones, which are available from travel agents or direct from the airline.

Reconfirmation If you break your journey, you must contact the airline at least 72 hours prior to departure of the ongoing flight to 'reconfirm' that you intend to fly. If you don't do this, the airline is entitled to delete your name from the passenger list.

Restrictions Discounted tickets often have various constraints placed on them, such as advance purchase, limitations on the minimum and maximum period you must be away, restrictions on breaking the journey or changing the booking or routing etc.

Round-the-World Tickets These tickets have become very popular in the last decade and basically there are two types: airline RTW tickets and agent (or 'tailor-made') RTW tickets. An airline RTW ticket is issued by two or more airlines that have joined together and allows you to fly around the world in one continuous direction on their combined routes. Other restrictions are that you (usually) must book the first sector in advance and cancellation penalties then apply. There may be restrictions on how many stopovers you are permitted. The RTW tickets are usually valid for from 90 days up to a year.

The other type of RTW ticket is a combination of cheap fares strung together by an experienced travel agent. These may be much cheaper than airline RTW tickets, but the choice of routes will be limited.

Standby This is a discounted ticket where you only fly if there is a seat free at the last moment. Standby fares are usually only available directly at the airport, but may sometimes also be handled by an airline's city office. To give yourself the best possible chance of getting on the flight you want, get there early and have your name placed on the waiting list immediately. It's first come, first served.

Student Discounts Some airlines offer student-card holders 15% to 25% off on certain fares. The same often applies to anyone under the age of 26. These discounts are generally only available on normal economy-class fares; you wouldn't get one, for instance, on an Apex or an RTW ticket, since these are already discounted. Take a calculator and do the sums; discounted tickets – both the official and bucket-shop ones – are often better value than student fares.

Tickets Out An entry requirement for many countries is that you have an onward (ie out of the country) ticket. If you're not sure of your travel plans, the easiest solution is to buy the cheapest onward ticket to a neighbouring country or a ticket from a reliable airline that can be refunded later if you do not use it.

Transferred Tickets Airline tickets cannot be transferred from one person to another. Travellers sometimes try to sell the return half of their ticket, but officials can ask you to prove that you are the person named on the ticket. This may not be checked on domestic flights, but on international flights tickets are usually compared with passports. Remember that if you are flying on a transferred ticket and something goes wrong with the flight (hijack, crash), there will be no record of your presence on board.

Travel Periods Some officially discounted fares – Apex fares in particular – vary with the seasons. There is often a low (off-peak) season and a high (peak) season. Sometimes there's an intermediate (or shoulder) season as well. At peak times, when everyone wants to fly, both officially and unofficially discounted fares will be higher and discounted tickets may not be available. Usually the fare depends on your outward flight – if you depart in the high season and return in the low season, you still pay the high-season fare.

1 on the corner of Kolodvorska ulica. Destinations, frequencies and one-way fares are: Belgrade via Novi Sad daily at 2.30 and 6 pm, 5000 SIT; Belgrade direct via Croatia, Tuesday and Thursday at 10.15 pm, 6500 SIT; Vrnjačka Banja via Kragujevac and Kraljevo daily at 6 pm, 6000 SIT; Dijakovica daily at 2.30 pm, 8000 SIT.

Austria & Germany Many towns in Gorenjska, Koroška and Štajerska have bus services to Austria and Germany. They can also be reached from Ljubljana. Be ready for a quick change of buses on the Austrian or German borders.

One daily bus in summer goes to Villach (Beljak in Slovene) in Austria from Kranjska Gora, and there are daily buses to Klagenfurt (Celovec in Slovene) from Dravograd and Graz from Maribor.

From Maribor, count on one bus a day to Graz and, from Ptuj, a twice weekly service. Daily buses also reach Frankfurt and Stuttgart from Maribor.

From Ljubljana, there's a bus to Berlin with a stop in Frankfurt on Wednesday at 7.30 pm, to Munich from Tuesday to Thursday at 5.05 or 5.30 am, to Stuttgart on Wednesday at 7.30 pm and to Klagenfurt on Wednesday at 6.15 am.

Hungary From Ljubljana you can catch a bus to Budapest on Tuesday, Thursday and Friday at 10 pm. There's also a service on Thursday at 5.30 am to Lenti. Otherwise take one of up to five daily buses to Lendava; the Hungarian border is 5km north. The first Hungarian train station, Rédics, is only 2km beyond the border. From Rédics, there are up to 10 trains a day (49km; 1¼ hours) to Zalaegerszeg, from where there are three direct trains (3¾ hours) and five buses to Budapest.

Lenti is also served by two buses a week from Maribor and Celje (on Thursday and Saturday).

Some bus and train timetables in Slovenia use the names in Slovene of cities and towns in neighbouring countries (Celovec for Klagenfurt, for example, or Trst for Trieste).

See the Alternative Place Names appendix at the back of this book.

Train

Slovenian Railways (Slovenske Železnice; SŽ) links up with the European railway network to Austria (Villach, Salzburg, Graz, Vienna), Germany (Leipzig, Munich), Switzerland (Geneva), Italy (Trieste, Venice, Milan), Hungary (Budapest) and Croatia (Zagreb, Karlovac, Rijeka, Pula). SŽ trains are hardly luxurious, but they are clean and punctual.

The international trains listed below are expresses, and some require a seat reservation costing 460 SIT. The InterCity (IC) supplement is 150 SIT; the one EuroCity (EC) train which serves Slovenia (the air-conditioned *Mimara* linking Berlin and Zagreb via Munich, Salzburg and Ljubljana) charges a supplement of 250 SIT.

On some trains, including the *Venezia Express*, *Simplon Express*, *Lisinski* and *Opatija*, sleepers are available in 1st (8335 SIT) and 2nd class (5560 SIT); couchettes in 2nd class cost 2540 SIT. Surprisingly not all express trains have dining or even buffet cars; bring along some snacks and drinks as vendors can be few and far between.

To reduce confusion, specify your train by the name listed under the country sections below or on the posted schedule when requesting information or buying a ticket. You can do both at the train stations, of course, but it is often easier to deal with the less-harried staff at Slovenijaturist offices. They sell train tickets of all types and have branches at the train stations in Celje, Ljubljana, Koper and Maribor. Other Slovenijaturist offices can be found in either city or town centres.

Tickets on SŽ trains are valid for two months.

Tickets & Discounts All fares to Croatia are reduced by 20%. Wasteels 26 (BIJ) tickets, available to people under 26 for 2nd class travel on selected routes, offer discounts of between 30 and 40%. Students up to 26 years old and holding an ISIC card get 30% off the fare on certain other trains. Both types of tickets must be purchased at Slovenijaturist offices – not the regular ticket windows in the train stations – or at the Wasteels office at the Ljubljana train station. Fare reductions are also available to children between six and 15 years of age (50%) and those over 60 years holding an international RES (Rail Europe S) card (30 to 50%).

Sample international one-way fares for 2nd class travel from Ljubljana include Amsterdam 31,395 SIT, Berlin 25,945 SIT, Budapest 6110 SIT, Graz 3480 SIT, Munich 9400 SIT, Paris (via Geneva) 22,655 SIT, Rijeka 1270 SIT, Rome (via Venice) 7335 SIT, Salzburg 5435 SIT, Trieste 1786 SIT, Vienna 7500 SIT, Villach 2030 SIT and Zagreb 1365 SIT.

SŽ and Slovenijaturist sell Inter-Rail passes to those under 26. Theoretically, you must have resided in the country of purchase for six months. Inter-Rail divides Europe into seven zones (A to G). Passes for one, two, three or all seven are available. A 15-day pass valid in Zone G only (which includes Slovenia, Italy, Greece and the ferry companies serving the last two) costs 38,915 SIT. Other passes are valid for a month. A two-zone pass is 46,345 SIT, three zones 51,890 SIT and a pass for all seven zones (called Global) is 58,280 SIT. Inter-Rail cards should be treated as cash for you can make no claims in the event of loss or theft. Eurail passes and Flexipasses are not valid or sold in Slovenia.

Adult and youth Euro Domino passes, allowing three, five or 10 days of midnight-to-midnight travel over a one-month period, are also available from SŽ. A five-day adult pass costs 5545 SIT and it's 3855 SIT for those under 26. Passengers holding Euro Domino passes get a 25% discount on domestic fares in Slovenia.

SŽ also sells its own SlovenijaRail pass for domestic travel only. See Train in the Getting Around chapter for details.

Italy Four trains a day link Trieste with Ljubljana (165km, three hours) via Pivka year round, including the *Venezia Express*

from Venice to Zagreb and Budapest, the *Simplon Express* from Geneva to Zagreb, the IC *Drava* from Venice to Budapest and the IC *Kras* to Zagreb.

Croatia To Zagreb (160km, 2½ hours), there are eight trains a day from Ljubljana via Zidani Most – the EC *Mimara* from Berlin, the *Venezia Express*, the *Arena* from Pula, the *Simplon Express*, the *Lisinski* from Munich, the IC *Kras*, the *Bled* from Villach and the *Sava*.

To Rijeka (155km, 2½ hours), there are two trains a day from Ljubljana via Pivka; depending on the day and the season, these might be the IC *Emona*, *Opatija*, *Ljubljana* and/or *Snežnik*. Trains operating between the Slovenian capital and Pula (4½ hours) in Istria go via Divača. These include the *Arena* and a spur of the IC *Kras*.

Austria & Germany The main train routes into Slovenia from Austria are Vienna to Maribor and Salzburg to Jesenice. There are two trains a day between Munich (453km, seven hours) and Ljubljana via Salzburg. The EC *Mimara* travels by day while the IC *Lisinski* goes overnight in each direction. Four more trains make the run between Ljubljana and Salzburg, one with a change at Villach.

To get to Vienna (460km, six hours) from Ljubljana, you have a choice between the morning IC *Croatia* from Zagreb (but you must change at Maribor) or the afternoon IC *Emona* from Rijeka. When travelling by train to Austria, it's somewhat cheaper to take a local train to Maribor or Jesenice and buy your ticket on to Vienna or Salzburg from there. Domestic fares in Slovenia are much lower than the international ones.

Hungary The *Venezia Express* and the IC *Drava* link Ljubljana directly to Budapest (500km, 7½ hours) via north-western Croatia.

Car & Motorcycle
Slovenia maintains some 150 border crossings with Italy, Austria, Hungary and Croatia

though not all are open to citizens of third countries.

The following is a list of border crossings with each of Slovenia's four neighbours that are open to all international traffic at present. They run clockwise from the south-western border with Italy. The name of the Slovenian border post appears first, followed by its location in brackets. Those crossings marked with an asterisk (*) have a Kompas MTS office, which is authorised to make sales-tax refunds to foreigners (see Taxes & Refunds in the Money section of the Facts for the Visitor chapter).

Italy
    Lazaret* (between Trieste and Ankaran)
    Škofije* (between Trieste and Koper)
    Kozina* (between Trieste and Rijeka)
    Lipica* (near Trieste)
    Sežana* (between Trieste and Ljubljana)
    Vrtojba* (near Nova Gorica)
    Rožna Dolina (between Gorizia and Nova Gorica)
    Robič (32km north-east of Udine)
    Učeja (16km south-west of Bovec)
    Predel* (13km south of Tarvisio)
    Rateče* (12km east of Tarvisio)

Austria
    Korensko Sedlo* (20km south-west of Villach)
    Karavanke* (at the 7km tunnel between Jesenice and Villach)
    Ljubelj* (between Klagenfurt and Kranj)
    Jezersko (35km north-east of Kranj)
    Holmec* (49km east of Klagenfurt)
    Vič* (between Klagenfurt and Maribor)
    Radlje (43km west of Maribor)
    Jurij* (13km north-west of Maribor)
    Šentilj* (17km north of Maribor)
    Trate (16km east of Šentilj)
    Gornja Radgona* (41km north-east of Maribor)
    Gederovci (10km west of Murska Sobota)
    Kuzma (28km north of Murska Sobota)

Hungary
    Hodoš (60km west of Zalaegerszeg)
    Dolga Vas* (between Lendava and Rédics)

Croatia
    Petišovci (5km south of Lendava)
    Razkrižje (10km east of Ljutomer)
    Središče ob Dravi* (20km west of Čakovec)
    Ormož (25km east of Ptuj)
    Zavrč* (19km south-east of Ptuj)

    Gruškovje* (18km south of Ptuj)
    Dobovec (7km south-east of Rogatec)
    Rogatec (7km east of Rogaška Slatina)
    Bistrica ob Sotli (9km north-east of Podsreda)
    Dobova (8km south-east of Brežice)
    Obrežje* (3km south-east of Mokrice)
    Križevska Vas (1km south of Metlika)
    Vinica (18km south of Črnomelj)
    Petrina (between Kočevje and Rijeka)
    Čabar (25km south of Sodražica)
    Babno Polje (30km south-west of Cerknica)
    Jelšane* (between Ilirska Bistrica and Rijeka)
    Starod* (between Trieste and Opatija)
    Sočerga* (between Trieste and Rijeka)
    Dragojna* (between Koper and Buje)
    Sečovlje* (7km south-east of Portorož)

Bicycle

Cycling is a cheap, convenient, healthy, environmentally sound and above all fun way of travelling. One note of caution if you are bringing your bicycle to Slovenia – before you leave home, go over it with a fine-tooth comb and fill your repair kit with every imaginable spare. As with cars and motorcycles, you won't necessarily be able to buy that crucial gizmo for your machine when it breaks down somewhere in the back of beyond in Notranjska.

Bicycles can travel by air, which can be surprisingly inexpensive. Adria, for instance, charges only UK£15 to transport a bicycle from London to Ljubljana and it has even carried tandems. You *can* take your vehicle to pieces and put it in a bike bag or box, but it's much easier simply to wheel your bike to the check-in desk where Adria will treat it as a piece of baggage. You must remove the pedals and turn the handlebars sideways so that it takes up less space in the aircraft's hold; Adria will put them into a box for you. Check all this with whatever airline you fly well in advance. For information about transporting your bicycle by train in Slovenia, see the Getting Around chapter.

SEA

An alternative way of getting to Slovenia from Italy is by boat. Between late March and October on Friday, Saturday and Sunday the *Prince of Venice*, a 40m Australian-made catamaran seating 330 passengers, sails between Portorož and Venice (2½ hours; DM90 return). For information in Portorož contact Kompas (☎ 066-747 032) at Obala 41; in Venice the Kompas office (☎ 041-528 6545) is at San Marco 1497. Another boat making return trips to Venice from Portorož from Tuesday to Saturday between late May and September is the *Santa Eleonora* catamaran (☎ 066-73 583 in Portorož; ☎ 041-520 8966 in Venice). The trip takes only 1½ hours and costs DM95 to DM110 return. Another catamaran called *Marconi* links Trieste with Piran (35 minutes; 4000 SIT return) on Thursday between late March and October. For more information, see Cruises in the Piran section and Boating & Cruises under Portorož in the Primorska chapter.

DEPARTURE TAX

A departure tax of DM25/US$14 is collected from all passengers leaving Slovenia by air. This is almost always included in the ticket price.

WARNING

The information in this chapter is particularly vulnerable to change – prices for international travel are volatile, routes are introduced or cancelled, schedules change, special deals come and go, and rules and visa requirements are amended.

Airlines seem to take a perverse pleasure in making price structures and regulations as complicated as possible; you should check directly with the airline or travel agent to make sure you understand how a fare (and ticket you may buy) works.

In addition, the travel industry is highly competitive, and there are many specials and bonuses.

The upshot of this is that you should get opinions, quotes and advice from as many airlines and travel agents as possible before you part with your hard-earned cash.

Therefore the details given in this chapter should only be regarded as pointers; they are not a substitute for your careful, up-to-date research.

Getting Around

AIR

Little Slovenia has no scheduled domestic flights, but a division of Adria called Aviotaxi (☎ 064-223 555 at Brnik airport) will fly chartered Pipers (four seats) and Cessnas (eight seats) to airports and aerodromes around the country. Sample return fares for three passengers are DM95 to Bled, DM185 to Slovenj Gradec and DM360 to Portorož or Maribor.

Smelt Air (☎ 061-378 704) located at Dunajska cesta 160 in Ljubljana is another small-aircraft charter company.

BUS

Except for long journeys, taking the bus is preferable to the train in Slovenia and departures are frequent. In some cases you don't have a choice; by bus is the only practical way to get to Bled, the Julian Alps, much of Dolenjska, Koroška and Notranjska and to Croatian Istria. But for a large part of the rest of the country you do have a choice.

You can buy your ticket at the bus station (avtobusna postaja) or simply pay the driver as you enter the bus everywhere in Slovenia. In Ljubljana you should book your seat (120 SIT) a day in advance, particularly if you're travelling on Friday or to popular destinations in the mountains or along the coast before a public holiday. Be aware that bus services are severely restricted on Sunday and holidays (and sometimes on Saturday too). Plan your trip accordingly or you'll find yourself marooned until Monday morning.

Different national companies serve the country. It's Integral and ESAP in Ljubljana, Kambus in Kamnik, Alpetour in Škofja Loka and Kranj, Avrigo in Nova Gorica and I & I in Koper. But this means little to travellers, and prices are uniform when services overlap or compete. For some sample domestic and international bus fares from the capital, see Getting There & Away in the Ljubljana chapter.

Some, but not all, bus stations have a left-luggage office (garderoba) and charge 150 to 180 SIT per piece per day. Be careful as some of them have almost bankers hours. A better (and safer) bet is to leave your luggage at the train station, which is usually nearby and has longer hours. If your bag has to go in the luggage compartment below the bus, it will be about 170 SIT extra, though most drivers don't mind you carrying it on the bus if it will fit between your seat and the one in front of it.

The timetables in the station or posted on a wall or column outside list all bus routes, and times are usually up to date. If you cannot find your bus listed or don't understand the schedule, seek assistance from the information or ticket window (usually combined). Odhodi means 'Departures' while Prihodi is 'Arrivals'. Blagajna Vozovnice is the place for tickets.

Slovenian bus timetables use coloured plastic numbers or abbreviation footnotes to denote which days of the week and during what seasons the buses run. The following lists cover most of the combinations you'll encounter. (Please note that a different colour scheme may be in operation at some stations.)

Bus Timetable Colours

white	(bela barva)	daily
green	(zelena barva)	Monday-Saturday
blue	(modra barva)	Monday-Friday
orange	(oranža barva)	Monday-Friday and working Saturdays
yellow	(rumena barva)	days when school is in session
red	(rdeča barva)	Sunday and public holidays

Bus Timetable Abbreviations

Č	Thursday	PP	Monday-Friday
D	workdays	So	Saturday
D+	Monday-Friday	SN	Saturday and Sunday
N	Sunday	ŠP.	days when school is
NP	Sunday and		in session
	holidays	Sr	Wednesday
Pe	Friday	To	Tuesday
Po	Monday	V	daily

74

TRAIN

SŽ runs trains on just over 1200km of track, about 40% of which are electrified. Large stretches of the main line need to be upgraded and though SŽ rolling stock is not the most modern, the service is reliable, fairly punctual and inexpensive, if a little slow. Very roughly, figure on covering about 60 to 65km per hour.

Although many secondary lines link provincial cities and towns, all main ones converge on Ljubljana and to get from A to B it's usually easier to return to the capital. Going from Maribor to Novo Mesto, for example, takes two or more changes if you refuse to backtrack. At the same time, large sections of the country (the Alps, Notranjska, western Dolenjska, central Primorska) are not served by rail, making the bus your only choice. Aside from Ljubljana, other important rail crossings are at Pivka, Divača, Zidani Most and Pragersko.

The domestic service runs regional trains (regionalni vlaki) and city trains (primestni vlaki), but the fastest are InterCity and Green Trains (Zeleni Vlaki). IC trains levy a surcharge of 150 SIT. Fares on the Green Trains, which are calculated by the route not per kilometre like IC trains, include the supplement, but you must book your seat on these for 300 SIT. If seat reservations are obligatory, the 'R' on the timetable will be boxed. An 'R' without a box means seat reservations are available.

Tickets are usually purchased in advance at the železniška postaja (train station) or a Slovenijaturist office. If you haven't been able to buy a ticket in advance, seek out the conductor who will sell you one and charge you a supplement of 180 SIT. The extra charge is not made if the ticket window at the station was closed (yes, the conductor will know) or your connecting train was late. An invalid ticket or trying to avoid paying will earn you a fine of 2000 SIT.

A return ticket (povratna vozovnica) is 20% less than double the price of a one-way ticket (enosmerna vozovnica). A 1st class ticket costs 50% more than a 2nd class one.

SŽ is still under government subvention though it is free to set its own prices. It has tried to keep them down in competition with the more extensive bus network, so travelling by train is generally cheaper than going by bus. It's difficult to give an exact per-kilometre charge as the price decreases as the journey lengthens. But, in rough terms, a 100km journey costs 685 SIT in 2nd class and 1035 SIT in 1st class.

Here are some one-way 2nd/1st class domestic fares from Ljubljana: Bled 451/677 SIT (51km), Jesenice 545/827 SIT (64km), Koper 940/1410 SIT (163km), Maribor 940/1410 SIT (156km), Murska Sobota 1260/1880 SIT (216km) and Novo Mesto 611/912 SIT (75km).

SŽ sells SlovenijaRail passes that are valid for 10, 20 or 30 days of travel over a two-month period. They are available to individuals or to groups of two or more at a discount. Thus a 10-day pass is 7962 SIT for one person and 13,160 SIT for a couple. Remember, though, that trains are generally convenient only for long-distance travel in Slovenia; once you reach a regional centre, you'll be making most day trips by bus. The only other discount scheme in effect for foreigners (students get 30% off only if they are enrolled in a Slovenian school) is a 30% discount for groups of six or more adults and 'mini-groups' of two adults and a child. Children up to the age of six travel for free if they don't occupy a seat. Otherwise they pay half the fare.

Depending on the station, departures and arrivals are announced by loudspeaker or on an electronic board and are always on a printed timetable. The yellow one with the heading Odhod or Odhodi Vlakov means 'Departures' and the white one with the words Prihod or Prihodi Vlakov is 'Arrivals'. Other important train words that appear often are čas (time), peron (platform), sedež (seat), smer (direction) and tir (rail). Timetable symbols include:

✗   Monday-Saturday (except public holidays)

Ⓧ   Monday-Friday (except public holidays)

✪   Monday-Saturday and public holidays

Ⓥ   Saturday and Sunday

Slovenian Railways (SŽ)

V Saturday, Sunday and public holidays

P Sunday and public holidays

7 no Sunday service

† holiday service

If you expect to be taking a lot of trains in Slovenia, buy a copy of the official timetable book, *Vozni Red Slovenske Železnice*, which is available at the Slovenijaturist branch at the Ljubljana train station for 700 SIT. It is published every year at the end of May and has explanatory notes in Slovene, German and French. Remember, too, when planning your trips that almost two-thirds of all rail passengers in Slovenia are commuters who only travel at peak times in the morning and late afternoon.

Left-luggage offices at some 32 stations around the country are supposed to be open 24 hours a day, but double-check the hours

before you leave your bag behind. The charge is about 150 SIT per piece. Ljubljana's garderoba is definitely open round the clock.

You can freight an automobile on the Maribor-Koper route for between 3000 and 4000 SIT one way (4800 to 6400 SIT return), depending on the size of the vehicle. The charge for a bicycle, which can be transported on most trains with the exception of the Green Trains, is a flat 300 SIT.

Scenic Routes

Slovenia's most scenic rail route runs from Jesenice to Nova Gorica via Bled (Bled Jezero station), Bohinjska Bistrica and Most na Soči. This 89km route through the Julian Alps and Soča River Valley opened for service in 1906. If you are travelling south, sit on the right-hand side of the train to see the cobalt-blue Soča at its most sparkling. A half-dozen local trains a day cover this route in each direction. The trip takes about two hours.

The 160km train ride from Ljubljana to Zagreb is also worth taking as the line follows the Sava River along most of its route through a picturesque gorge. Sit on the right side eastbound, the left side westbound.

Steam Trains

SŽ has a stock of five steam locomotives and antique wagons – a train spotter's dream come true – and puts them to good use every year with its Oldtimer Train excursions in summer. Routes and timetables change frequently but popular excursions include Jesenice to Bohinj via Bled (5760/3600 SIT for adults/children) and from Jesenice, Bled or Bohinjska Bistrica through the Soča Valley to Most na Soči (6350/3950 SIT). Fares include lunch, side trips and transfers. Contact the Slovenijaturist office (☎ 061-131 5055 or ☎ 061-131 5206) in Ljubljana for the latest information.

CAR & MOTORCYCLE

Roads in Slovenia are generally good – if a bit narrow at times. Driving in the Alps can be hair-raising, but never dangerous, with a gradient of up to 18% at the Korensko Sedlo pass into Austria. Many mountain roads are closed in winter and early spring. Motorways and highways are very well signposted, but secondary and tertiary roads are not; be sure to have your *Large Atlas for Motorists & Travellers* (see Maps under Planning in the Facts for the Visitor chapter) at the ready.

But there aren't all that many roads in the first place. Slovenia counts a total of 14,836km, of which only 280km are motorways. These go partially round Ljubljana as an outer ring road and extend south-west almost to Divača on the way to the coast and soon to Sežana en route to Italy; north-west to Naklo past Kranj and from Lesce via Jesenice to the Karavanke Tunnel; and south-east to Grosuplje heading for Zagreb. There's also a stretch from Hoče, south of Maribor, to Vransko past Celje. They are numbered up to 10 and preceded by an 'A' (for *avtocesta*).

International roads are preceded by an 'E'. The most important of these are the E70 to Zagreb via Novo Mesto, the E61 to Villach via Jesenice and the Karavanke Tunnel and the E57 to Graz via Maribor.

National highways contain a single digit and link cities. Secondary and tertiary roads have two sets of numbers separated by a hyphen; the first number indicates the highway that the road runs into. Thus road No 10-5 from Nova Gorica and Ajdovščina joins the A10 motorway at Razdrto.

A toll is payable on the motorways from Ljubljana to Kranj (26km), Ljubljana to Razdrto via Postojna (56km) and Maribor to Celje (54km), but it's not terribly expensive. From the capital to the turn-off onto highway No 10 for Koper and the coast, for example, it costs 470 SIT for cars and motorcycles and 300 SIT from Maribor to Celje. If you take the highway between Ljubljana and Brnik airport, you must pay a 150 SIT toll at Torovo. Using the 7km Karavanke Tunnel (1991) between Jesenice and Austria, however, is a different matter. That will set you back by 1100 SIT.

Private-car ownership in Slovenia (365 vehicles per 1000 inhabitants) is as high as it is in Germany and the UK so expect a lot of traffic, especially on Friday afternoons when entire cities and towns move to the countryside and in the summer. The roads between Ljubljana and Celje, Celje and Maribor and Ljubljana and Koper can get very busy, and traffic jams are frequent. Lorries weighing more than 5.5 tonnes are banned from the highways between 6 am and 1 pm on Saturday and from 6 am to 10 pm on Sunday and public holidays so you might think of travelling those stretches then. Also, work is being carried out on major roads throughout the country so factor in the possibility of delays and diversions *(obvozi)*.

Petrol stations are usually open Monday to Saturday from about 7 am to 8 pm, though larger towns have a 24-hour one as you enter (and often leave) the limits. Fuels of 91 (increasingly hard to find) and unleaded 95 and 98 octane are available and are relatively cheap by European standards: 94.80, 99.10 and 111.40 SIT per litre respectively at the time of writing. Most stations also have diesel fuel costing 95.30 SIT per litre. Payment by foreign credit card is still uncommon at Slovenian petrol stations; expect to pay cash.

International vehicle insurance is compulsory in Slovenia. If your car is registered in the EU it is assumed you have it, and Slovenia has concluded special agreements with Croatia, Hungary, Macedonia and Slovakia. Other motorists must buy a Green Card valid for Slovenia at the border (DM52 for 15 days, DM75 for a month).

The national automobile club is the Avto-Moto Zveza Slovenije (AMZS). For emergency roadside assistance, motorists should call it on ☎ 987. For information on road and traffic conditions, contact the AMZS in Ljubljana (☎ 061-341 341; fax 061-342 378; info.center@amzs.si; www. amzs.si). All accidents should be reported to the police (☎ 113) immediately.

Road Rules

You must drive on the right. Speed limits for cars and motorcycles are the same throughout the country: 60km/h in towns and villages; 80km/h on secondary and tertiary roads; 100 km/h on highways; 120km/h on motorways. These limits are being more and more strictly enforced and should you exceed them you'll hit a speed trap for sure. I know I did.

The use of seat belts is compulsory and motorcyclists must wear helmets. Neither they nor motorists are required to show their headlights throughout the day outside built-up areas as is the case in some other European countries but many now do. The permitted blood-alcohol level for drivers is 0.5g/kg.

You now must pay to park in the centre of most large towns in Slovenia – from Izola and Novo Mesto to Slovenj Gradec and Ptuj – and illegally parked vehicles are routinely towed away nowadays, especially in Ljubljana and the historic towns on the coast. In general you'll have to seek out car parks (indicated on most maps by a 'P') where fees are charged (from 100 SIT per hour) or buy a special parking coupon from newsstands, kiosks or vending machines and place it on the dashboard.

Car Rental

Car rentals from international firms like Eurodollar, Budget, Avis and Kompas Hertz (all have offices in Ljubljana and in some provincial cities) vary widely in price, but expect to pay from about US$55/315 a day/week with unlimited mileage for a Renault 5, Nissan Micra or Ford Fiesta with Eurodollar. Optional collision insurance to reduce the excess/deductible is about US$8 a day extra, theft protection another US$8 and personal accident insurance US$5. There's also a 'circulation tax' similar to value-added tax levied on car rentals. Independent agencies like ABC, Alpetour and Avtoimpex (which rents Czech Škodas only) have more competitive rates. See Car & Motorcycle in the Getting Around section of the Ljubljana chapter for a full list of agencies.

Hertz will rent to drivers aged from 21 to 25 only if they pay an additional 'young driver's fee' of US$8 a day. Budget rents to those 21 years and over in possession of a licence of at least two years, Avis only to those 23 and over. Ask about one-way rentals with free drop-offs at other offices in Slovenia.

BICYCLE

Cycling is permitted on all roads except motorways. Many towns and cities, including Ljubljana, Maribor, Ptuj, Novo Mesto, Kranj and Škofja Loka, have bicycle lanes and some even have special traffic lights. The *Tourist Map of Slovenia*, available everywhere, lists itineraries and some tourist offices have special cycling maps for their town or region.

HITCHING

Hitchhiking is legal everywhere except on motorways and some major highways and is generally easy; even young women do it in Slovenia. Hitching can be difficult on Friday afternoon, before school holidays and almost impossible on Sunday. If you're heading north, don't count on many rides from Austrian motorists; they seem to have an aversion to this method of travel.

Hitching from bus stops is fairly common in Slovenia. Otherwise use motorway access roads or other areas where the traffic is not disturbed. See Hitching in the Getting There & Away section of the Ljubljana chapter for the best routes out of the capital.

Hitching is never a totally safe way of getting around and, although we may occasionally mention it as an option, we don't recommend it.

ORGANISED TOURS

The big travel agencies like Kompas, Emona Globtour and Slovenijaturist, as well as some smaller ones, organise excursions and tours for individuals and groups, usually out of Ljubljana. If you're pressed for time or want to squeeze in as much as possible over a short period, you can 'do' the entire country with Kompas in a week in summer for US$850 (single supplement US$160), including all meals, accommodation and transportation, or take in Austria, Hungary and the Czech Republic as well as Slovenia in two weeks for US$1910 (single supplement US$430). Kompas also has several very good specialised tours, from horse riding in Rogla and rafting in the Soča River to thermal spa and castle tours.

ADDRESSES & PLACE NAMES

Streets are well signposted in Slovenian towns and cities though the numbering system can be a bit confusing, with odd and even numbers sometimes running on the same sides of streets and squares.

Ljubljana and other cities have changed some of their street names since independence, and most anything recalling the *ancien régime* has been dropped. This can cause some confusion as many people still use the old names and, in some cases, streets have had to be renumbered. For example, Ljubljana's main drag, Slovenska cesta, and its northern extension, Dunajska cesta, were both Titova cesta until 1991. The houses and buildings on the latter have since had to be given new numbers.

In small towns and villages, houses are usually numbered off a single street, which

bears the same name as the community. Thus Ribčev Laz 13 is house No 13 in the village of Ribčev Laz on Lake Bohinj. As Slovenian villages are frequently made up of one road with houses clustered on or just off it, this is seldom confusing.

Places with double-barrelled names like Novo Mesto (New Town) and Črna Gora (Black Hill) put the second word in lower case (Novo mesto, Črna gora) almost as if the names were Newtown and Blackhill. It is proper orthography in Slovene, but we have opted to go with the English-language way of doing it to avoid confusion.

Slovene uses the possessive case frequently in street names. Thus a road named after the poet Ivan Cankar is Cankarjeva ulica while a square honouring France Prešeren is Prešernov trg. Also, when nouns are turned into adjectives they often become unrecognisable to a foreigner. The town is 'Bled', for example, but 'Lake Bled' is Blejsko Jezero. A street leading to a castle *(grad)* is usually called Grajska ulica. The words 'pri', 'pod' and 'na' in place names mean 'at the', 'below the' and 'on the' respectively.

There are a lot of different words for 'street' in Slovene, and the following list will at least help you distinguish between the boulevards, roads and alleys used in addresses. A more extensive list of words for use in reading maps appears in the Glossary at the back of this book.

avtocesta – motorway
breg – river bank
cesta (abbreviated *c*) – road
drevored – avenue
dvorišče – courtyard
nabrežje – embankment
naselje – colony, hamlet, estate
obvoznica – ring road, bypass
pot – trail
prehod – passage, crossing
sprehajališče – walkway, alley
steza – path
trg – square
ulica (abbreviated *ul*) – street

Ljubljana

• *pop 270,000* • *area code* ☎*061* • *postcode 1000*

Though it doesn't even count 300,000 inhabitants, Ljubljana is by far and away Slovenia's largest and most populous city. It is also the nation's political, economic and cultural capital. As such, virtually everything of national importance begins, ends or is taking place in Ljubljana.

But it can be difficult to get a grip on the place. In many ways the city whose name almost means 'beloved' *(ljubljena)* in Slovene does not feel like an industrious municipality of national importance but a pleasant, self-contented town with responsibilities only to itself and its citizens. You might think that way too, especially in spring and summer when café tables fill the narrow streets of the Old Town and street musicians (both free agents and hired help) entertain passers-by on Čopova ulica and Prešernov trg. Then Ljubljana becomes a little Prague without the crowds or a more manageable Paris.

With some 25,000 students attending Ljubljana University's 14 faculties and three art academies, the city feels young and offers all the facilities you'll need during your stay. And among the fine baroque churches, palaces and quaint bridges, you'll see a lot of greenery. A large park called Tivoli and the hills beyond it form the city's western border and willow-lined walkways follow the Ljubljanica River and its canals. A much longer trail, a legacy of WWII, completely encircles the city as a kind of pedestrian 'ring road' and is a boon for those who want to escape the early morning fog endemic to the city in autumn and winter.

HISTORY

Ljubljana first appeared in print in 1144 as the town of Laibach but a whole lot more had taken place here before that. The area to the south, an infertile bog, was settled during the Bronze Age by marsh dwellers who lived in round huts on stilts sunk into the soggy soil.

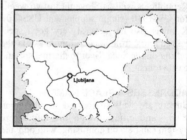
Remnants of these dwellings can be seen in the National Museum. These early people were followed by the Illyrians and, in about 400 BC, the Celts, who settled along the Ljubljanica.

The first important settlement in the area, however, came with the arrival of the Romans who built a military camp here in the century preceding the birth of Christ. Within 100 years, what had become known as Emona was a thriving town and a strategic crossroads on the routes linking Roman Pannonia in the south with colonies at Noricum and Aquileia. Legacies of the Roman presence – walls, dwellings, early churches – can still be seen throughout Ljubljana.

Emona was sacked and eventually destroyed by the Huns, Ostrogoths and Langobards from the 5th century, but the 'Ljubljana Gate' remained an important crossing point between east and west. Tribes of early Slavs settled here in the 6th century.

Ljubljana changed hands frequently in the Middle Ages. In the 12th century the fortified town between Castle Hill and the Ljubljanica River was in the possession of the Dukes of Carinthia. Within 100 years, it was transferred to the rulers of the new Duchy of Carniola, who made it their capital. The last and most momentous change came in 1335 when the Habsburgs became the town's new rulers. Except for a brief interlude in the early 19th century, they would remain the city's (and the nation's) masters until the end of WWI in 1918.

The Habsburgs turned Ljubljana into an important trading centre and made it an episcopal seat; it would later become the centre of the Protestant Reformation in Slovenia. The town and its new hill-top castle (1415) were able to repel the Turks in the 15th century, but a devastating earthquake in 1511 reduced much of medieval Ljubljana to rubble. This led to a period of frantic construction in the 17th and 18th centuries which provided Ljubljana with many of its pale-coloured baroque churches and mansions – and the nickname 'Bela Ljubljana' (White Ljubljana). The town walls were pulled down to allow Ljubljana to expand, and the southern marsh was partly drained. But the most important engineering feat was the construction of a canal to the south and east of Castle Hill that regulated the flow of the Ljubljanica and prevented flooding.

When Napoleon established his Illyrian Provinces in 1809 in a bid to cut Habsburg Austria's access to the Adriatic, he made Ljubljana the capital, as it remained until 1813. In 1821 members of the Holy Alliance (Austria, Prussia, Russia and Naples) met at the Congress of Laibach to discuss measures to suppress the democratic revolutionary and national movements in Europe.

The railway linking Trieste and Vienna reached Ljubljana in 1849 and stimulated development of the town. By then Ljubljana had become the centre of Slovenian nationalism under Austrian rule. Writers and nationalists like France Prešeren and Ivan Cankar produced the bulk of their work here. Slovenes began to join the town government and emerged as a majority in 1882. But in 1895 another earthquake struck Ljubljana, forcing the city to rebuild once again. To Ljubljana's great benefit, the Secessionist and Art Nouveau styles were all the rage in central Europe at the time, and many wonderful buildings were erected – structures the Communists would later condemn as 'bourgeois' and 'decadent' and raze to the ground.

Slovenia and its capital joined the Kingdom of the Serbs, Croats and Slovenes after WWI. During WWII the city was occupied by the Italians and then the Germans, who encircled the city with barbed-wire fencing creating, in effect, an urban concentration camp. Ljubljana became the capital of the Socialist Republic of Slovenia within Yugoslavia in 1945 and remained the capital after Slovenia's independence in 1991.

ORIENTATION

Ljubljana lies in the Ljubljana Basin (Ljubljanska Kotlina), which runs to the north and north-west along the Sava River to Kranj. The basin forms two distinct parts: the non-arable Ljubljana Marsh (Ljubljansko Barje) to the south and the fertile Ljubljana Plain (Ljubljansko Polje) to the north and east. The city is wedged between the Polhov Gradec Hills to the west and Golovec Hills (including Castle Hill) to the east and southeast. The Ljubljanica River and the Gruber Canal have effectively turned a large part of central Ljubljana into an island.

All this geography is important in order to understand how the city has developed and continues to grow. If you look at a map or stand atop Ljubljana's landmark Skyscraper, you'll see that the city has had to expand fan-like to the north and east; hills and unstable

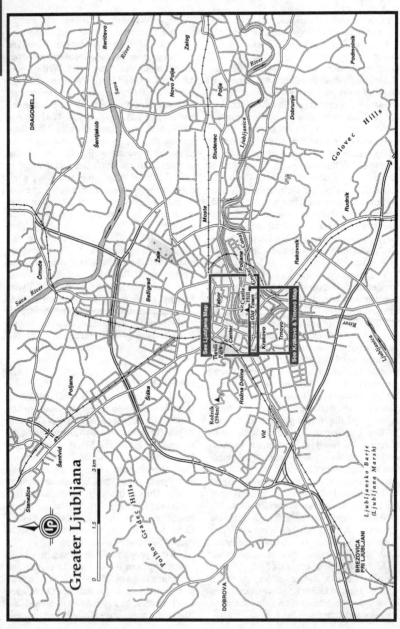

Greater Ljubljana

ground have prevented growth in the other directions.

Ljubljana is traditionally divided into five districts but only a few are of any importance to travellers.

Center is the commercial area on the left bank of the Ljubljanica to the west and north of Castle Hill and the Old Town. Tabor and Poljane are the easternmost parts of Center, and Bežigrad, where the bulk of the university buildings are, lies to the north. Two old suburbs to the south of Center – Krakovo and Trnovo – retain a lot of their old character.

Certain streets and squares (Čopova ulica, Trubarjeva cesta, Prešernov trg) and much of the Old Town are reserved for pedestrians and cyclists. The Ljubljanica is crossed by a dozen vehicular bridges and footbridges and three of them – Shoemaker Bridge (Čevljarski Most), Triple Bridge (Tromostovje) and Dragon Bridge (Zmajski Most) – are historically important.

The train and bus stations are opposite one another on Trg Osvobodilne Fronte (known as Trg OF) at the northern end of Center. Slovenska cesta, the capital's main thoroughfare, is 350m to the south-west. To get to central Prešernov trg, head south on Miklošičeva cesta (600m).

Maps

The tourist office as well as many hotels hand out a free map of Ljubljana that should take care of most people's needs. If you intend staying longer in the capital or exploring it in depth, pick up a copy of the 1:20,000-scale *Ljubljana City Map* published by the Geodesic Institute of Slovenia (GZS; 850 SIT). The 1:15,000 *Ljubljana Euro City* map from RV Verlag is also widely available.

INFORMATION
Tourist Offices

The best office anywhere for information not just on Ljubljana but all of Slovenia is the Tourist Information Centre (TIC; ☎ 133 0111; fax 133 0244) in the historical Kresija building south-east of Triple Bridge at Mačkova ulica 1. The Ljubljana Promotion Centre, which runs the TIC, employs students during summer months who are very enthusiastic about their country and your interest in it. Though they can book accommodation only in Ljubljana, they can help with information on all of Slovenia. The TIC is open weekdays from 8 am to 7 pm and on Saturday from 9 am to 5 pm. The TIC branch

---

The Ljubljana Triangle

If you're feeling pretty good about yourself and the world in general while in Ljubljana, you might want to pay homage to the Union Brewery on Celovška cesta, but credit could go to the city's fabulous ley lines.

According to those who dibble-dabble in geomancy, which deals with an environment's invisible dimensions as well as its psychic and spiritual levels, Ljubljana is in the exact centre of Slovenia – not the geographical one (that's near Litija to the east) but at the axis of three energy currents (or ley lines) that cross Slovenia and meet to form the 'Ljubljana Triangle'.

Marko Pogačnik, a Ljubljana-based geomancer, says that the west-east ley line heading for Zagreb runs through Tivoli, down the Jakopičevo sprehajališče designed by Plečnik and over the Triple Bridge through the Cathedral. The north-south one from Prague hits the east-west ley line in the park before carrying on to Trnovo Bridge and the Church of St John the Baptist. The current coming from Graz in the north-east meets the east-west line at the Cathedral and travels south-west to the Trnovo church, where it mates with the north-south line.

So where can you feel all this energy at its buzziest best? The Trnovo Bridge, says Pogačnik, concentrates the forces of birth while Triple Bridge is the centre of creativity and maturing. The centre for the forces of transformation and destruction (read death) is in the little park called Navje, just north of the train station and east of Slovenian Youth Theatre. This too was designed by Plečnik but is clearly outside the Ljubljana Triangle – at least according to my map. I'm happy to report that the Union Brewery, where my ley line is heading, is a mere 700m to the west. ■

office (☎ 133 9475) at the train station between the main ticket hall and platform No 1 is open daily (including Sunday) June to September from 8 am to 9 pm. During the rest of the year the daily hours are 10 am to 6 pm. The TIC is worth visiting just to pick up its free maps and brochures especially the *Ljubljana: Capital of the Republic of Slovenia* map and the *Ljubljana Where?* tourist guide, which is a goldmine of information.

Backpackers and students should head for the Erazem travel office (☎ 133 1076) at Trubarjeva cesta 7. The staff provide information, make bookings, sell Lonely Planet guidebooks and have a message board. They also sell ISIC cards (800 SIT) and, for those under 26 but not studying, FIYTO cards (700 SIT). Erazem is open weekdays from 10 am to 5 pm. Mladi Turist (☎ 125 9260), at Salendrova ulica 4 near the Municipal Museum, is the office of the Slovenian Youth Hostel Association and sells hostel cards (800 SIT for those under 18 years of age, 1200 SIT for those between 18 and 26, 1800 SIT for those over 26). The office is open from 9 am to 3 pm on Monday and Friday and to 5 pm Tuesday to Thursday.

The Cultural Information Centre (☎ 214 025) next to Trg Francoske Revolucije 7 can answer questions about what's on in Ljubljana and has a free booklet listing all the city's museums, galleries and exhibitions. It's open from 10 am to 6 pm and on Saturday to 1 pm (and again from 4 to 7 pm in summer).

The main office of the Alpine Association of Slovenia (PZS; ☎ 134 3022) is at Dvoržakova ulica 9, a small house set back from the street. It has information about hiking throughout the country and some excellent maps and guides for sale. The office is open weekdays from 8 am to 2 pm (till 6 pm on Monday).

Motorists in need of assistance or advice can contact the Avto-Moto Zveza Slovenije (AMZS; ☎ 341 341) at Dunajska cesta 128, about 3km north of Center. It's open weekdays from 7 am to 7.30 pm and on Saturday till noon, but you can telephone for information daily between 5.30 am and 9 pm.

Money

There's a currency exchange bureau run by Slovenijaturist in the train station next to the TIC office. It is open daily from 6 am to 10 pm. The *bureau de change* at the bus station is open daily from 5.30 am to 9 pm.

You'll find SKB Banka Cirrus-linked automatic teller machines (ATMs) scattered throughout the city, including ones at Trg Ajdovščina 4, in the very centre of the big shopping mall; outside the Emona Globtour agency in the Emona Maximarket passageway connecting Trg Republike with Plečnikov trg; and in the Gledališka pasaža connecting Čopova ulica with Nazorjeva ulica. Next to the SKB Banka ATM on Trg Ajdovščina is a currency-exchange machine that changes the banknotes of 18 countries into tolar.

Some of the best rates of exchange in Ljubljana are available at Nova Ljubljanska Banka at Trg Republike 2. It is open weekdays from 8 am to 5 pm and on Saturday from 9 am till noon. Three other central Nova Ljubljanska Banka branches are at Šubičeva ulica 2 (open weekdays 8 am to 5 pm, till 6 pm on Wednesday); in the beautiful Art Nouveau City Savings Bank building (Mestna Hranilnica Ljubljanska) at Čopova ulica 3 (open 9 am to noon and 2 to 5 pm weekdays, till noon Saturday) and at Mestni trg 16 in the Old Town (open 9 am to noon and 2 to 5 pm weekdays, till 6 pm on Wednesday).

Ljubljana is full of private exchange bureaus *(menjalnice)* taking no commission and offering good exchange rates. One called Hida has a branch in the Central Market at Pogarčarjev trg 1 open weekdays from 7 am to 7 pm and on Saturday to 2 pm, and another one at Čopova ulica 42 open weekdays from 8 am to 8 pm and on Saturday to 1 pm.

Credit Cards A Banka, with a branch at Slovenska cesta 50 (open weekdays from 8 am to 5 pm and till noon on Saturday) and another one to the south at Slovenska cesta 9 (open weekdays from 9 am to 4 pm, to 3 pm on Friday), is a local rep for Visa and can issue a tolar cash advance on your card. It takes a 1% commission for cashing travellers cheques, though. If you have problems with your Visa card when A Banka is closed, call the Visa Centre (☎ 302 055).

Eurocard and MasterCard holders should go to Nova Ljubljanska Banka (☎ 125 0155) at Trg Republike 2.

Atlas Express (☎ 133 2024 or ☎ 131 9020) at Trubarjeva cesta 50 is the Slovenian representative for American Express and can replace cards, make cash advances and hold clients' mail. It is open weekdays from 9 am to 5 pm and Saturday till noon.

Post & Communications

The post office where poste restante is sent and held for 30 days only is at Slovenska cesta 32 on the corner of Čopova ulica; have the folks at home use the post code 1101. It also sells boxes for sending things home from 170 to 280 SIT. The Slovenska cesta post office is open weekdays from 7 am to 8 pm and on Saturday to 1 pm.

You can make long-distance telephone calls from booths here as well as send faxes and telexes, but the main telephone centre is in the post office at Pražakova ulica 3, to the north near the bus and train stations. It is open from 7 am to 8 pm weekdays and to 3 pm on Saturday. Next door at No 5 is Telekom Slovenije.

To mail a parcel you must go to the special customs post office at Trg OF 5, due west of the train station and opposite the bus station. Make sure you bring your package open for inspection; the maximum weight is about 15kg, depending on the destination. This post office is open 24 hours a day.

Online Services

Here are some Ljubljana-based organisations and associations with Web sites:

www.ljubljana.si/
    City of Ljubljana
www.cd-cc.si
    Cankarjev Dom
www.festival-lj.si/
    Ljubljana Summer Festival/Križanke

www.uni-lj.si
    Ljubljana University (check out the Welcome chapter with practical information for foreign students)
www.nuk.uni-lj.si
    National and University Library
www.ljudmila/org/
    Ljubljana Digital Media Lab (links with the multi-media group Neue Slowenische Kunst, the MOST-SIC volunteer work organisation etc)
www.ljudmila.org/srce/
    Student Resource Centre
www.ljudmila.org/siqrd/
    Queer Resources Directory for gays and lesbians
www.ng-slo.si
    National Gallery
www.mglc-lj.si
    International Centre of Graphic Arts
www.arnes.si/
    Academic and Research Network of Slovenia

For more listings see Online Services in the Facts for the Visitor chapter.

Ljubljana counts two cybercafés with public-access Internet sites:

Klub K4 Café
    Kersnikova ulica 4 (☎ 131 7010). Open daily 10 am to 9 pm.
Club Podhod
    In the underpass passage (podhod) between Kongresni trg and Plečnikov trg (☎ 121 4100). Open weekdays from 7.30 am to 2.30 or 3 am, on Saturday from 8 am to 3 am and on Sunday from 7 pm to 2 am. Computers can be used until 8 pm.

Travel Agencies

All of the big agencies have offices in Center. Kompas Holidays (☎ 125 2065) is at Slovenska cesta 36 and at Miklošičeva cesta 11 (☎ 132 1053) while Emona Globtour (☎ 213 843) is in the Emona Maximarket passageway connecting Trg Republike with Plečnikov trg. Slovenijaturist (☎ 131 5055 or ☎ 131 5206) at Slovenska cesta 58 and at the train station is your best source of information for details of rail travel. These offices are generally open from 8.30 or 9 am to 6 or 7 pm weekdays and till noon or 1 pm on Saturday.

Bookshops

Mladinska Knjiga at Slovenska cesta 29 is the biggest bookshop in Ljubljana and has picture books, guides and maps to every corner of the country as well as books in English on other subjects. It is open weekdays from 8 am to 7.30 pm and on Saturday to 1 pm. MK (as it's known) has several smaller branches in the city, including one opposite the train station at Miklošičeva cesta 40 and another at Nazorjeva ulica 1.

A smaller chain with knowledgeable and helpful staff is Cankarjeva Založba with an outlet at Slovenska cesta 37. They keep the same hours as MK. Cankarjeva Založba's Oxford Center at Kopitarjeva ulica 2 stocks English-language titles only, including some novels, but is really aimed at Slovenes studying our language. DZS, with branches at Šubičeva ulica 1a and Mestni trg 26, has academic titles and reference books.

The best selection of maps in Ljubljana can be found at a shop called Kod & Kam – meaning roughly 'Whence & Whither' – at Trg Francoske Revolucije 7 opposite the Križanke. It stocks most city, regional and hiking maps produced in the country as well as imported maps and guides, including the Lonely Planet series. It is open weekdays from 9 am to 7 pm and on Saturday from 8 am to 1 pm. The Geographical Museum is also based here. There's a second-hand/antiquarian bookshop called Trubarjev Antikvariat at Mestni trg 25.

For foreign newspapers, go to the Ljubljanček gift shop in the lobby of the Grand Hotel Union. The shop is open weekdays from 8 am to 2 pm and 5 to 9 pm, on Saturday from 8 am to 1 pm, and on Sunday from 6 to 9 pm.

Cultural Centres

The British Council (☎ 125 9292) is located on the 3rd floor of the Skyscraper at Štefanova ulica 1. It is open Monday, Wednesday and Friday from 10 am to 3 pm, Tuesday and Thursday from 2 to 7 pm and from 9 am to 1 pm on the first Saturday of every month.

The American Center (☎ 210 190), Cankarjeva cesta 11, is open Monday, Tuesday, Thursday and Friday from noon to 4 pm and Wednesday from 9 am to 4 pm.

The Institut Français Charles Nodier (☎ 224 883) is at Slovenska cesta 19 and opens on weekdays only from 8 am to 7 pm. Outside is a bust of the French Gothic novelist Nodier (1780-1844), who lived and worked in Ljubljana in 1812-13.

The Deutscher Lesesaal (☎ 176 3725) at Trg Republike 3 is open on Monday from 9 am to 1 pm and 2 to 6 pm, in the afternoon only on Tuesday, and in the morning only from Wednesday to Friday.

Laundry

Getting your clothes washed is a problem in Ljubljana, as it is everywhere in Slovenia. A couple of the student dormitories have washing machines and dryers that you can use – the Dijaški Dom Poljane (see Hostels & Student Dormitories under Places to Stay) and the Dijaški Dom Kam (Building C) at Kardeljeva ploščad 14, north of the centre in Bežigrad and near the Dijaški Dom Bežigrad – as does the Ježica camp site. Mehurček is a self-service place at Viška cesta 54 open weekdays from 8 am to 8 pm and Saturday to 1 pm, but it's about 3.5km south-west of Center (bus No 6 to Vič). Alba at Wolfova ulica 12 near Prešernov trg is an old-style laundry and dry cleaner open weekdays from 7 am to 6 pm.

Medical Services

You can see a doctor at the medical centre (*klinični center*; ☎ 133 6236 or ☎ 131 3123) at Zaloška cesta 7, which is in Tabor east of the Park hotel. The emergency unit (*urgenca*; ☎ 323 060) is open 24 hours a day. The dental clinic (☎ 325 288) is almost opposite at Zaloška cesta 2.

For a pharmacy (*lekarna*) head for the Centralna Lekarna (Central Pharmacy; ☎ 133 5044), Prešernov trg 5, open weekdays from 8 am to 7 pm and on Saturday morning to 1 pm, or Lekarna Miklošič (☎ 314 558) at Miklošičeva cesta 24, open daily from 8 am to 8 pm.

THINGS TO SEE

The easiest way to see the best that Ljubljana has to offer and still enjoy a leisurely stroll is to follow the walking tour outlined on the map *Ljubljana: Capital of the Republic of Slovenia*, available free from the TIC as well as at many hotels and some restaurants around the city.

I've broken the tour up into eight sections which can be done individually or together with preceding or subsequent ones. If you run straight though them and make no stops, all eight shouldn't take much more than half a day. But count on a full day if you expect to see everything and even longer if you intend visiting all the museums too. Many sights have plaques outside identifying and providing historical information in four languages, including English.

Around Prešernov Trg

Begin the tour at **Prešernov trg**, a beautiful square that forms the link between Center and the Old Town and always a hub of activity. Taking pride of place in the square is the **Prešeren monument** designed by Maks Fabiani and Ivan Zajc and erected in 1905 in honour of Slovenia's greatest hero. In summer, the steps at the base of the plinth (with motifs from Prešeren's poems) become a sitting-out area for Ljubljana's young bloods and foreigners alike.

To the east of the monument at No 5 is the Italianate **Central Pharmacy**, which was a famous café frequented by intellectuals in the 19th century, and to the north, on the corner of Trubarjeva cesta and Miklošičeva cesta, the delightful Secessionist **Urbanc** building (1903), now the Centromerkur department store. Diagonally across the square at No 1 is another Secessionist gem. The **Ura** building, now marred by a Citizen watch sign above it, was once a shop for painters and thus is very gaily decorated. Peer two doors down Wolfova ulica and at No 4 you'll see a terracotta figure peeking out from a 'window'. It's Julija Primic looking at the monument to her life-long admirer France Prešeren.

The 17th century **Franciscan Church of the Annunciation** stands on the northern side of the square. The interior is not so interesting with its six side altars and enormous choir but to the left (west) of the main altar, designed by the Italian sculptor Francesco Robba, is a glass-fronted coffin with the spooky remains of a saint. Like many churches in Ljubljana, the Franciscan church is open from morning till dusk but closes from about noon to 3 pm.

Attached to the church on the western side is the **Franciscan monastery**, with a very important library. Nearby in the south-west corner of the square is a bronze **relief map** of the city.

Walk north along Miklošičeva cesta from the Urbanc building and don't miss the several fine buildings along the way. The cream-coloured **People's Loan Bank** (1908) at No 4 is topped with the figures of two women holding a beehive and a purse – symbols of industry and wealth. The **Cooperative Bank** at No 8 was designed by Ivan Vurnik, and the red, yellow and blue geometric patterns were painted by his wife Helena in 1922. Just opposite is the newly renovated **Grand Hotel Union**, the *grande dame* of Ljubljana hotels. A short distance to the north-west is **Miklošičev Park**, laid out by Maks Fabiani in 1902. All the buildings facing it are Art Nouveau masterpieces, with the exception of the unspeakable Gorenjska Banka to the south on Dalmatinova ulica.

Market Area

From Prešernov trg, cross into the Old Town via the **Triple Bridge** (Tromostovje), once the Špital Bridge dating from 1842. The prolific architect Jože Plečnik added the two sides almost a century later to create something quite unique for Slovenia and the world. He also designed the covered walkway along the river, the recently renovated **Plečnik Colonnade**, which forms part of the city's **Central Market**.

Walk through Pogarčarjev trg with its wonderful open-air market and old men and women selling everything from forest berries and wild mushrooms to home-made cheeses like soft white *sirček* and honey.

The strange **cone** in Pogarčarjev trg was erected in honour of Plečnik in 1993. It represents the Parliament building he designed

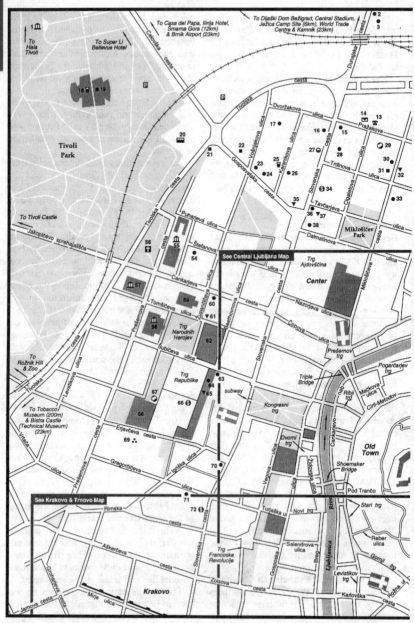

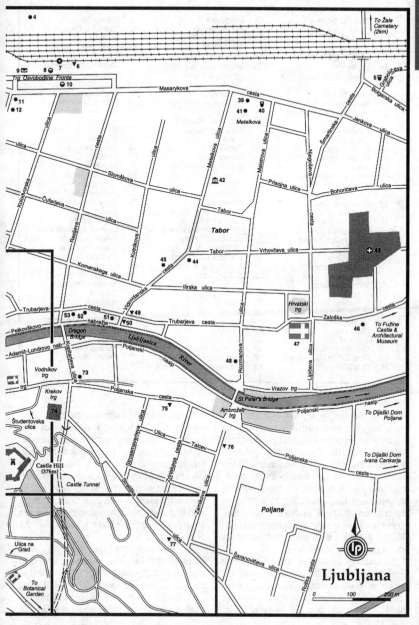

PLACES TO STAY
21 Tivoli Hotel
22 Lev Hotel
31 Austrotel &
   Ljubljana Casino
44 Park Hotel
45 Dijaški Dom Tabor

PLACES TO EAT
6 McDonald's
32 M Monroe Restaurant
   & Kinoteka
35 Evropa Café
37 Tavčarjev Hram
49 Špageterija
50 Čerin Pizzeria
61 Operna Klet
65 Emona Maximarket &
   Maxim Self-Service
   Restaurant
75 Shanghai Chinese
   Restaurant
76 Zlati Pav Chinese
   Restaurant
77 Meson Dun Felipe

OTHER
1 Modern History
   Museum
2 Vinoteka Simon
   Bradeško
3 Ljubljana Fairgrounds
4 Youth Theatre
5 Propoganda Klub &
   Onto Bar
7 Train Station
8 City Airport Buses
9 Post Office (Customs)
10 Bus Station

11 Mladinska Knjiga
   Bookshop
12 Kompas Cinema
13 Telekom Slovenije
14 Main Post Office
15 Slovenijaturist Travel
   Agency & Burek
   Stand
16 Kodak Express
17 Alpine Association of
   Slovenia (PZS)
18 Zlati Klub Sauna &
   Klub Manhattan
   Disco
19 Tivoli Recreation
   Centre
20 Ilirija Swimming Pool
23 Lovec Riding Shop
24 Adria Airways &
   Lufthansa
25 Miriam's Pub
26 Klub K4, ŠOU Centre
   & Klub Metropol
27 City Bus Ticket Kiosks
28 Visa Card Centre
29 US Embassy
30 Kompas Travel Agency
   & Hertz Car Rentals
33 ZZZS (Health
   Insurance Institute
   of Slovenia)
34 A Banka
36 Bicycle Club
38 Slovenijašport
39 Gala Dvorana Club
40 Club Tiffany
41 Channel Zero Club
42 Ethnographic Museum
43 University Clinic Centre

46 Dental Clinic
47 Orthodox Church of
   St Peter
48 Rog Bicycle Shop
51 Atlas Express
   (American Express)
52 Hard Rock Music Shop
53 Laura Crafts Shop
54 Eurodollar Car Rentals
55 National Gallery
56 Serbian Orthodox
   Church
57 Museum of Modern Art
58 National Museum
59 Opera House
60 American Center
62 Parliament
63 DZS Bookshop
64 Emona Globtour Travel
   Agency & SKB ATM
66 Nova Ljubljanska
   Banka
67 UK Embassy,
   Deutscher Lesesaal
   & Adria Airways
68 Cankarjev Dom
   (Cultural Centre)
69 Ferant Garden &
   Roman Ruins
70 National Drama
   Theatre
71 Mikrokop Kodak
   Express
72 A Banka & Jakopič
   Gallery
73 Oxford Book Centre
74 Puppet Theatre & St
   James Theatre

but never built for the top of Castle Hill. The building on the south-west side of Pogarčarjev trg is the Renaissance **Bishop's Palace** (Škofijski Dvorec) with a lovely arcaded courtyard. The **Seminary** (Semenišče; 1749) to the east, with its pock-marked Atlases outside, contains valuable baroque furnishings and a library with price-less incunabula and 16th century manu-scripts. It can be visited by appointment only. There's a market with meat, fish and dairy products on the ground floor.

Dominating the square is the **Cathedral** (Stolnica) dedicated to Saint Nicholas, the patron of boatmen and fishermen (closed noon to 3 pm). A church has stood here since the 12th century, but the existing twin-towered building is from the early 18th century. Inside it's a baroque palace of pink marble, white stucco and gilt with frescoes by Matevž Langus. Have a look at the mag-nificent carved choir stalls, organ and the sweet faces of the angels on the main altar, another creation of Francesco Robba. The Pietà in the glass case on the outside southern wall is a copy. Nearby is a stunning bronze door (1996) depicting six bishops and the dead Christ in relief.

If you want a closer look at what Ljubljančani like to eat, continue eastward to Vodnikov trg where there's yet another outdoor market. From here you could cross Ciril-Metodov trg and begin walking up Študentovska ulica to the castle, a relatively steep, 15-minute climb. Instead, we'll continue walking west along Ciril-Metodov trg to one of the prettiest squares in the city.

Old Town

Mestni trg has two major landmarks. The **Magistrat** (town hall), seat of the city government, was erected in the late 15th century but rebuilt in 1718. The Gothic courtyard inside, arcaded on two levels, is where theatrical performances once took place and contains some lovely sgraffiti. If you look above the south portal leading to a second courtyard you'll see a relief map of Ljubljana as it appeared in the second half of the 17th century.

The town hall is topped with a golden dragon, a symbol of Ljubljana but quite a recent one. A wily mayor at the turn of the century apparently convinced the authorities in Vienna that Ljubljana needed a new crossing over the Ljubljanica River and the **Dragon Bridge** (Zmajski Most) was built to the northeast. City folk say the dragons wag their tails whenever a virgin crosses the bridge.

In the middle of Mestni trg stands the **Robba Fountain** (1751) modelled after one in Rome. But the Titons with their gushing urns here represent something totally Slovenian, the three rivers of Carniola (the Sava, Krka and Ljubljanica). To protect it

It's said that the statues on Dragon Bridge wag their tails whenever a virgin passes by.

from decay, it may soon be moved to the courtyard between the old and new wings of the National Gallery and a copy put in its place.

From Mestni trg you can make a small detour west into **Ribji trg** with perhaps the oldest house (1528) in Ljubljana still standing at No 2 and a golden fountain with a girl in classical dress pouring water.

Mestni trg leads into **Stari trg**, the true heart of the Old Town. More of a street than a square with 19th century wooden shop fronts, quiet courtyards and cobblestone passageways, Stari trg is a positive delight to explore. From behind the houses on the eastern side, paths once led to Castle Hill, a source of water. The buildings fronting the river had large passageways built to allow drainage in case of flooding.

Tranča at No 4 was a prison until the 18th century, and those condemned to death were executed at a spot nearby in some fairly unpleasant ways (strangulation, drowning, being burned at the stake). Later it became the city's monopoly bakery – the only place where bread could be sold. Unscrupulous bakers who cheated customers got a dunking in the cold waters of the Ljubljanica.

A small street called **Pod Trančo** just beyond leads to **Shoemaker Bridge** (Čevljarski Most). Like all the bridges here in the Middle Ages, this was a place of trade and a gateway to the town. Craftsmen worked and lived on the bridges (in this case 16 cobblers) to catch the traffic and avoid paying town taxes – a kind of medieval duty-free setup.

Between Stari trg 11 and 15 – the house that *should* bear the number 13 – there's a lovely rococo building called **Schweiger House** with a large Atlas supporting the upper balcony. The figure has his finger raised to his lips as if asking passers-by to be quiet. But the owner, whose name meant the 'Silent One' in German, might have had something other than self-promotion in mind. In this part of the world, bordellos were traditionally located at house No 13 of a street and he probably got quite a few unsolicited calls.

In the middle of **Levstikov trg**, the southern extension of Stari trg, the **Hercules Fountain** is a favourite meeting place in summer. Perhaps that's why a copy has replaced the original 17th century statue, which is now in the town hall.

The big church farther south on Stari trg is the **Church of St James**. Far more interesting than the main altar (1732) by Francesco Robba is the one in the church's **Chapel of St Francis Xavier** with statues of a 'White Queen' and a 'Black King'. The **Column of Mary** outside to the south of the church was designed by Janez Vajkard Valvasor (well, at least the statue on top was) and erected in 1682 in memory of the victory over the Turks at Monošter (now Szentgotthárd in Hungary) 18 years earlier.

Across Karlovška cesta is **Gruber Palace** (Gruberjeva Palača). Gabriel Gruber, who built the canal (Gruberjev Prekop) regulating the Ljubljanica, lived here until 1784. The palace is in Zopf style, a transitional art style between late baroque and neoclassicism, and now contains the national archives. If you look eastward on Karlovška cesta to No 1, you'll see a 'bridge of sighs' that was once the Balkan Gate, the easternmost point of the Old Town. From here the town walls ran halfway up Castle Hill. If you were to continue south-east along Karlovška cesta for 800m and cross the Ljubljanica, you'd reach the **Botanical Garden** (Botanični Vrt) at Ižanska cesta 15 with some 4500 species of plants and trees. It is open April to October from 7 am to 7 pm and to 5 pm the rest of the year. Entry is free. You can also reach here on bus No 3 (stop: Strelišče).

Gornji trg is the eastern extension of Stari trg. The five **medieval houses** at Gornji trg 7 to 15 have narrow side passages where rubbish was once deposited so it could be washed down into the river.

The most important building on this elongated square is the **Church of St Florian** built in 1672 and dedicated to the patron saint of fires after a serious blaze destroyed much of the Old Town. Beyond the church is an area of small houses once inhabited by Ljubljana's struggling artists. Venture into a courtyard or peer through an open door or window, and you'll see that they left their mark.

A footpath called Ulica na Grad leads from the Church of St Florian up to Castle Hill.

Ljubljana Castle

There have been fortifications of some kind or another on Castle Hill at least since Celtic times, but the existing Ljubljana Castle (Ljubljanski Grad) mostly dates from after the 1511 earthquake. It is now frequently used as a venue for concerts and other cultural activities.

The climb up the double wrought-iron staircase (150 steps) of the 19th century **Castle Tower** and a walk along the **ramparts** is worth the effort for the views down into the Old Town and across the river to Center. The ceiling in the **Chapel of St George** (1489) is covered in frescoes and the coats of arms of the Dukes of Carniola; the **Pentagonal Tower** of the southern wing hosts changing exhibits. In the corridor beneath the courtyard is an exhibition on the castle and urban development of Ljubljana.

On some days weddings are held in the wing facing the south-east, so the castle and Pentagonal Tower (admission 200/100 SIT) have complicated opening hours: from 11 am to 6 pm on Tuesday, Thursday and Sunday and from 1 to 6 pm on Wednesday and Friday. The Castle Tower, however, is open every day from 10 am to dusk.

A path from below the **Western Gate** will bring you to Reber ulica and Stari trg. Return to Pod Trančo and cross Shoemaker Bridge; the very narrow street a few steps to the north-west called Židovska ulica was once the site of a synagogue and the centre of Jewish life in the Middle Ages.

Center

A lot of this district on the left bank of the Ljubljanica is worth exploring. If you go south from Shoemaker Bridge to **Breg**, the city's port when the Ljubljanica was still navigable this far (a steamboat once called from Vrhnika), and then west up **Novi trg**, you'll pass the **Academy of Arts and Sci-**

ences (Akademija Znanosti in Umetnosti) on your left at No 3, which was once the seat of the Provincial Diet under the Habsburgs. The **National & University Library** (Narodna in Univerzitetna Knjižnica; 1941), Plečnik's masterpiece, is across Gosposka ulica. To appreciate more of this great man's philosophy, enter through the main door on Turjaška ulica and you'll find yourself almost in darkness with all the black marble. But as you ascend the steps, you'll enter a colonnade full of light – the light of knowledge, according to Plečnik's plans. The reading room with huge glass walls has some interesting lamps also designed by Plečnik.

The **Municipal Museum** (Mestni Muzej) is a few steps to the south-east at Gosposka ulica 15. It has a well preserved collection of Roman artefacts (some of them recovered from the archaeological dig in the museum courtyard) plus a scale model of Emona to help it all make sense. Upstairs rooms contain period furniture and household objects and one is devoted to the work of the poet Oton Župančič (1878-1949). The museum is open Tuesday to Saturday from 9 am to 7 pm with guided tours on the hour. Admission is 400/300 SIT.

Diagonally opposite the museum in **Trg Francoske Revolucije** is the **Križanke**, a monastery complex that once belonged to the Teutonic Order of Knights and now serves as the headquarters of the Ljubljana Summer Festival. Its outside theatre alone seats 2000 people. The **Ilirija Column** in the square is dedicated to Napoleon and his Illyrian Provinces (1809-13), when Slovene was taught in schools for the first time. Monsieur

---

Jože Plečnik, Architect Extraordinaire

Few architects anywhere in the world have had as great an impact on their birthplace as Jože Plečnik – a name you'll hear again and again during your travels in Slovenia. And with good reason. His work is eclectic, inspired, unique – and found everywhere.

Born in Ljubljana in 1872, Plečnik was educated at the College of Arts in Graz and studied under the architect Otto Wagner in Vienna. From 1911 to 1921 he lived in Prague where he taught and later helped renovate Prague Castle.

Plečnik's work in Ljubljana began in 1921 and continued until his death in 1957. Almost single-handedly, he transformed the city, adding elements of classical Greek and Roman architecture with Byzantine, Islamic, ancient Egyptian and folkloric motifs to its baroque and Secessionist faces. The list of his creations and renovations are endless – from the National and University Library, the colonnaded Central Market and the cemetery at Žale in Ljubljana to the delightful churches in Bogojina in Prekmurje and Ribnica in Dolenjska.

Plečnik was also a city planner and designer. Not only did he redesign the banks of the Ljubljanica River (including the Triple Bridge), entire streets (Zoisova ulica) and Tivoli Park,

Plečnik's St Michael on the Marsh, near Ljubljana

but he also set his sights elsewhere on monumental stairways (Kranj), public buildings (Kamnik) and outdoor shrines (Bled). An intensely religious man, Plečnik designed many furnishings and liturgical objects (especially chalices and candlesticks) for churches throughout the land (eg Škofja Loka's Church of St James).

Plečnik's eclecticism and individuality alienated him from the mainstream of modern architecture during his lifetime. But in the 1980s he was 'rediscovered' and hailed as a prophet of postmodernism. Oddly, he remained more or less in favour under the Communists because of his classicist phase.

One of Plečnik's designs that was never realised was an extravagant Parliament, complete with an enormous cone-shaped structure, to be built on Castle Hill after WWII. But such an extravagant building would have alarmed the federalist Josip Broz Tito and the Slovenes backed off. ■

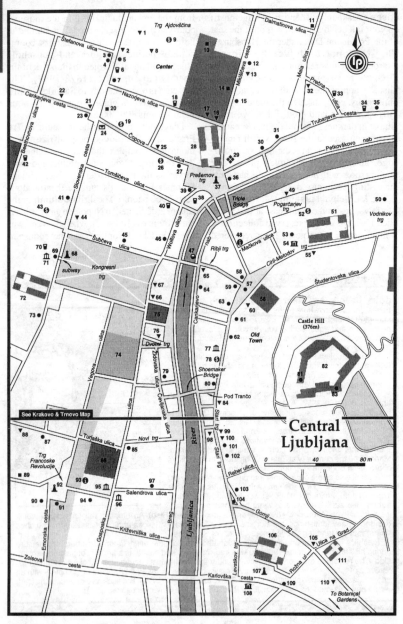

Central Ljubljana

See Krakovo & Trnovo Map

Trg Ajdovščina

Center

Štefanova ulica

Cankarjeva cesta

Beethovnova ulica

Slovenska cesta

Nazorjeva ulica

Čopova ulica

Tomšičeva ulica

Wolfova ulica

Prešernov trg

Triple Bridge

Pogačarjev trg

Vodnikov trg

Mackova ulica

Ribji trg

Cankarjevo nab

Ciril-Metodov trg

Študentovska ulica

Castle Hill (376m)

Old Town

Shoemaker Bridge

Pod Trančo

Vegova ulica

Zidovska ulica

Cerkljanska ulica

Gosposka ulica

Turjaška ulica

Novi trg

Trg Francoske Revolucije

Salendrova ulica

Breg

Emonska cesta

Križevniška ulica

Zoisova cesta

Karlovška cesta

Ljubljanica

River

Stari trg

Levstikov trg

Reber ulica

Gornji trg

Rožna ul.

Ulica na Grad

To Botanical Gardens

Dalmatinova ulica

Miklošičeva cesta

Maia ulica

Prečna

Trubarjeva cesta

Petkovškovo nab

Šubčeva ulica

Kongresni trg

subway

Dvorni trg

Mestni trg

0   40   80 m

Bonaparte actually visited his 'capital' during this period and stayed at the Bishop's Palace. South-west of the square on Emonska cesta, where a new university

library is being built, more archaeological excavations are in progress.

Vegova ulica runs north from Trg Francoske Revolucije past a row of busts of

PLACES TO STAY
10 Holiday Inn
11 Turist Hotel & Klub
    Central Disco
14 Grand Hotel Union
20 Slon Best Western
    Hotel
89 Mrak Guesthouse

PLACES TO EAT
1 Super 5 Fast-Food
   Restaurant
2 Šestica
8 Skriti Kot Self-Service
   Restaurant
13 Triglav Self-Service
    Restaurant
16 Grand Hotel
    Union Café
17 Smrekarjev Hram &
    Union Cinema
21 Dairy Queen
22 Daj-Dam Fast-Food
    Restaurant
25 McDonald's & City
    Theatre
32 Napoli Pizzeria
44 Rio Ham Ham
    Fast-Food
    Restaurant
49 Ribca Seafood Bar
55 Kolovrat
60 Rotovž
65 Zlata Ribica
66 Burja Delicatessen
67 Delikatesa
76 Ljubljanski Dvor
84 Čajna Hiša Teahouse
88 Foculus Pizzeria
98 Pizzeria Romeo
99 Julija Café
100 Nostalgia Café
105 Sichuan Chinese
    Restaurant
110 Špajza Restaurant

OTHER
3 Skyscraper/British
   Council
4 Cankajena Založba
   Bookshop &
   Little Gallery
5 Vino Boutique
6 Holidays Pub

7 Kompas Holidays
   Travel Agency &
   Flex Jazz Club
9 SKB Banka & ATM
12 Peko Shoe Shop
15 Art Nouveau Bank
    Buildings
18 Eldorado Disco
19 Hida Exchange
    Bureau
23 Komuna Cinema
24 Post Office
    (Poste Restante)
26 Art Nouveau City
    Savings Bank, Nova
    Ljubljanska Banka
    & Bik Butik
    Delicatessan
27 Peko Shoe Shop
28 Franciscan Church
29 Urbanc Building &
    Centromerkur
    Department Store
30 Erazem Travel
    Agency
31 Carniola Antiqua
33 Patrick's Irish Pub
34 TrueBar
35 Apiteka Honey Shop
36 Central Pharmacy
37 Prešeren Monument
38 Horse's Tail Café-Pub
39 Ura Building
40 Cutty Sark Pub
41 Mladinska Knjiga
    Bookshop
42 Gajo Jazz Club
43 Nova Ljubljanska
    Banka
45 Sidro Herbal Shop
46 Big Bang Music Shop
    & Alba Laundry
47 Emona Boat Tours
48 Tourist Office (TIC)
50 Fruit & Vegetable
    Market
51 Cathedral of Saint
    Nicholas
52 Seminary & Hida
    Exchange Bureau
53 Market
54 Bishop's Palace
56 Town Hall
57 Robba Fountain
58 Antika Ferjan

59 Trubarjev Antikvariat
    Bookshop
61 Mestna Galerija &
    Caffé Galerija
62 Atlas Travel Agency
    (American Express)
63 Dom Crafts Shop
64 Kože Grčar Hide Shop
68 Citizen of Emona
    Statue
69 Club Podhod
    (Internet Café)
70 Rock Café
71 School Museum
72 Ursuline Church
73 Institut Français
    Charles Nodier
74 Ljubljana University
75 Filharmonija
77 Theatre Museum
78 Nova Ljubljanska
    Banka
79 Galerija Lala
80 Tranča
81 Castle Tower
82 Castle
83 Pentagonal Tower
85 Academy of Arts
    & Sciences
86 National &
    University Library
87 Glej Theatre &
    Equrna Gallery
90 New University
    Library Site
91 Križanke Ticket Office
92 Ilirija Column
93 Cultural Information
    Centre
94 Križanke & Plečnikov
    Hram Café
95 Kod & Kam Bookshop
    & Geographical
    Museum
96 Municipal Museum
97 Mladi Turist
101 Schweiger House
102 Parazol Crafts Shop
103 ŠKUC Gallery
104 Hercules Fountain
106 Church of St James
107 Column of Mary
108 Gruber Palace
109 Former Balkan Gate
111 Church of St Florian

Slovenian writers, scientists and musicians to the central building of **Ljubljana University**, established in 1919. The proclamation of independence was announced from the balcony facing **Kongresni trg** in 1991.

Named in honour of the Congress of the Holy Alliance convened by Austria, Prussia, Russia and Naples in 1821 and hosted by Ljubljana, Kongresni trg contains several important buildings. **Philharmonic Hall** (Filharmonija) on the south-east corner is home to the Slovenian Philharmonic Orchestra founded in 1701 and one of the oldest in the world. Haydn, Beethoven and Brahms were honorary members and Gustav Mahler was resident conductor for a season (1881-82). The **Ursuline Church of the Holy Trinity** (1726) to the west is the most beautiful baroque building in Ljubljana and contains a multicoloured altar by Robba made of African marble. It is open daily from 7.30 to 9.30 am and 10.30 am to 4.30 pm.

As you descend into the subway that will take you under Slovenska cesta, keep an eye open for a small gilded statue on top of a column. It's a copy (the original is in the National Museum) of the **Citizen of Emona**, dating from the 4th century. It was unearthed nearby in 1836 and probably formed part of a Roman necropolis.

Trg Republike is the main square in Center and contains the ugly **Parliament** (1959) to the north-east festooned with revolutionary reliefs and, to the south-west, **Cankar Hall** (Cankarjev Dom), Center's main cultural and congress centre. To the south beyond Erjavčeva cesta in **Ferant Garden** are the remains of an early Christian church porch and baptistery with mosaics from the 4th century.

Museum Area

Ljubljana's three most important museums are situated to the north-west of Trg Republike.

The **National Museum** (Narodni Muzej) at Muzejska ulica 1 at the western end of park-like Trg Narodnih Herojev has sections devoted to history and natural history as well as fine coin and mineral collections (the latter amassed by the philanthropic Baron Žiga Zois in the early 19th century). The Roman glass and the jewellery found in 6th century Slavic graves is pretty standard fare; the highlight here is the **Vače situla**, a Celtic pail from the 5th or 6th century BC unearthed in a town east of Ljubljana. The relief around the situla shows men hunting stags, driving chariots, playing reed pipes and wrestling.

Other items on display – 16th century crossbows, a tiny 17th century strong box with a complicated locking system, an Art Nouveau mirror from the turn of the century – are interesting but say little about Slovenian history and few are labelled in English. Still, the museum building (1885) itself is impressive. Check out the ceiling fresco in the foyer featuring an allegorical Carniola surrounded by important Slovenes from the past and the statues of the Muses and Fates relaxing on the stairway banisters. The National Museum is open Tuesday to Sunday from 10 am to 6 pm (to 8 pm on Wednesday). Admission is 200/100 SIT.

The graceful **Opera House** on Župančičeva ulica to the north-east was opened in 1892 as the Provincial Theatre, and plays in both German and Slovene were performed here. After WWI it was renamed the Opera House and is now home to the Slovenian National Opera and Ballet companies. No doubt you'll hear someone singing scales as you walk by.

The **National Gallery** (Narodna Galerija; 1896) at Cankarjeva cesta 20 offers portraits and landscapes from the 17th to 19th centuries, copies of medieval frescoes and wonderful Gothic statuary in its old south wing. Although the subjects of the earlier paintings are the usual foppish nobles and lemon-lipped clergy, some of the later works are remarkable and provide a good introduction to Slovenian art. Take a close look at the works of the impressionists Jurij Šubic and Rihard Jakopič (eg *Birches in Snow*), the pointillist Ivan Grohar *(Škofja Loka in the Snow)* and Slovenia's most celebrated woman painter Ivana Kobilca *(Summer)*. The bronzes by Franc Berneker are truly

A: France Marolt folk group,
Shoemaker Bridge, Ljubljana

B: Detail of Schweiger House,
on Stari trg, Ljubljana

C: Apple seller, central market,
Ljubljana

D: Old Town and Ljubljana Castle

A	
B	C

A: Shoemaker Bridge (Cevljarski Most), Ljubljana
B: Prešernov trg from pedestrian Čopova ulica, Ljubljana
C: Brass band, Mestni trg, Ljubljana

exceptional and, as long as you're here, have a look at the Art Deco toilets, all black marble and green glass. The gallery's new wing to the north at Puharjeva ulica 9 (separate entrance) has a permanent collection of European paintings from the Middle Ages to the 20th century and is used for temporary exhibits. Eventually a glassed-in walkway will link the two buildings and the original Robba Fountain may be moved here from Mestni trg. The National Gallery is open Tuesday to Saturday from 10 am to 6 pm and Sunday to 1 pm. Admission is 300/200 SIT for adults/seniors and children or 500/400 SIT during special exhibits.

The **Museum of Modern Art** (Moderna Galerija) south-west of the National Gallery at Cankarjeva cesta 15 is housed in an ugly modern building that is like stepping into a cold shower after walking around the other museums. The gallery shows part of its permanent collection of 20th century Slovenian art, which helps put some of the socialist-inspired work of sculptors like Jakob Savinšek into artistic perspective. A large part of the building is given over to temporary exhibitions that a lot of people would consider 'fun' rather than 'serious' art. The Museum of Modern Art hosts the International Biennial of Graphic Arts in odd-numbered years. The museum keeps the same hours as the National Gallery.

The interior of the Serbian Orthodox **Church of Sts Cyril & Methodius** north of the Museum of Modern Art is covered from floor to ceiling with colourful modern frescoes and has a richly carved iconostasis separating the nave from the sanctuary. It is open Tuesday to Saturday from 3 to 6 pm.

Tivoli Park

You can reach the city's leafy playground via a subway from Cankarjeva cesta. Straight ahead, at the end of a monumental promenade designed by Plečnik (Jakopičevo sprehajališče), is the 17th century **Tivoli Castle** (Tivolski Grad) which contains the **International Centre of Graphic Arts** (Mednarodni Grafični Likovni Center) open

Tuesday to Saturday from 10 am to 7 pm and Sunday till 1 pm.

Along with making use of the sport facilities at the Tivoli Recreation Centre (see Activities later in this chapter), you can climb to the top of **Rožnik Hill** (394m) for wonderful views of the city. The 45-hectare **Ljubljana Zoo** (Živalski Vrt), on the hill's southern slope along Večna pot and containing some 800 animals representing 120 species, is open every day, except Monday, from 9 am to 7 pm in summer, till 4 pm in winter. Admission is 600/350 SIT.

The **Museum of Modern History** (Muzej Novejše Zgodovine) at Celovška cesta 23 just beyond the Tivoli Recreation Centre has gone from being a temple to the Partisans to a first-class museum tracing the history of Slovenia in the 20th century via multimedia. It's highly recommended for a better understanding of how Slovenes view themselves and their nation yesterday and today. The museum is open daily, except Monday, from 10 am to 6 pm and admission costs 400/300 SIT.

Krakovo & Trnovo

These two attractive districts south of Center are Ljubljana's oldest suburbs and have a number of interesting buildings and historic sites. The Krakovo neighbourhood around Krakovska ulica with its two-storey cottages was once called the 'Montmartre of Ljubljana' because of all the artists living here.

If you walk along Barjanska cesta, the short southern extension of Slovenska cesta, you'll reach the **Roman Wall** (Rimski Zid) from Emona times running along Mirje. The **pyramid** is a Plečnik addition and the young people holding onto the bricks in the wall with their fingertips aren't being subjected to some cruel and unusual punishment – this is where many novice mountaineers practice their sport. Within the **Jakopič Garden** to the south-east at Mirje 4 where the impressionist painter once worked in his summerhouse, there are more **Roman ruins** including household artefacts and the remains of a sophisticated heating system. It's open from 10 am to 1 pm and 4 to 6 pm.

Barjanska cesta ends at a picturesque canal called **Gradaščica**, which is a pleasant place for a stroll on a warm day. Spanning the canal to the east from Emonska ulica is the little **Trnovo Bridge**, designed by Plečnik in 1932. Birch trees actually grow on the bridge and the railings are topped with five curious pyramids. The **Church of St John the Baptist**, where France Prešeren met the love of his life, Julija Primic, is on the southern side.

Farther south at Karunova ulica 4 is the house where Jože Plečnik lived and worked for almost 40 years. Today it houses the Ljubljana Architectural Museum's **Plečnik Collection**, an excellent introduction to this almost ascetically religious man, his inspiration and his work. It is open Tuesday and Thursday from 10 am to 2 pm only. Admission costs 500/200 SIT.

Other Museums & Galleries

Ljubljana contains many other interesting museums besides the ones mentioned above, most notably the new **Slovenian Ethnographic Museum** (Slovenski Etnografski Muzej) at Metelkova ulica 2. At present it offers only a hint of what's to come: a selection of objects amassed by the 19th century Slovenian missionary Frederick Baraga, who preached among the Chippewa Indians of Michigan; an inventive look at birth and early childhood in Slovenia across the centuries; and a well chosen display of Slovenian folk objects. But when more of the National Museum's collection is moved here, the Ethnographic Museum (open Tuesday to Sunday from 10 am to 6 pm) is sure to be a winner.

The following is a list of other museums in the Ljubljana area that may interest you. Some – but not all – can be visited while following the walking tours and are noted on

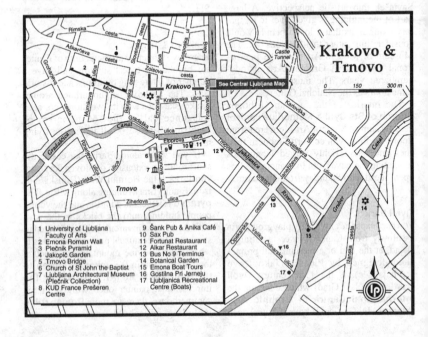

Krakovo & Trnovo

1 University of Ljubljana
   Faculty of Arts
2 Emona Roman Wall
3 Plečnik Pyramid
4 Jakopič Garden
5 Trnovo Bridge
6 Church of St John the Baptist
7 Ljubljana Architectural Museum
   (Plečnik Collection)
8 KUD France Prešeren
   Centre

9 Šank Pub & Anika Café
10 Sax Pub
11 Fortunat Restaurant
12 Alkar Restaurant
13 Bus No 9 Terminus
14 Botanical Garden
15 Emona Boat Tours
16 Gostilna Pri Jerneju
17 Ljubljanica Recreational
   Centre (Boats)

the Ljubljana, Central Ljubljana and Krakovo & Trnovo maps. They can have very convoluted and abbreviated opening times so check with the TIC before setting out.

Architectural Museum (Arhitekturni Muzej)
    Fužine Castle, in the eastern suburb of Studenec
    (bus No 20 to Fužine)
City Gallery (Mestna Galerija)
    Mestni trg 5
Equrna Gallery (Galerija Equrna)
    Gregorčičeva ulica 3
Jakopič Gallery (Jakopičeva Galerija)
    Slovenska cesta 9
Little Gallery (Mala Galerija)
    Slovenska cesta 35
Slovenian Film Museum (Slovenski Filmski Muzej)
    Kinoteka, Miklošičeva cesta 28
Slovenian School Museum (Slovenski Šolski Muzej)
    Plečnikov trg 1
Slovenian Theatre Museum (Slovenski Gledališki Muzej)
    Mestni trg 17
Technical Museum of Slovenia (Tehniški Muzej Slovenije)
    Bistra Castle, 23km south-west of Ljubljana (bus to Bistra pri Vrhniki)
Tobacco Museum (Tobačni Muzej)
    Tobačna ulica 5 (bus No 6 to Tobačna)

ACTIVITIES

The Tivoli Recreation Centre (☎ 131 5155), at Celovška cesta 25 in Tivoli Park, has bowling alleys, tennis courts, an indoor swimming pool, a fitness centre, a roller-skating rink and a popular sauna called Zlati Klub with saunas, a steam room, cold and warm splash pools and a small outside pool surrounded by high walls so you can sunbathe au naturel. The Zlati Klub is open daily from 10 am to 10 pm (to 8 pm from July to September) and to midnight on Friday. Women-only days are all day Tuesday and Friday to 2 pm; otherwise it's mixed days (men and women together in the buff). Entrance costs 1100 SIT (950 SIT until 1 pm) for adults and 500 SIT for children. It costs 300 SIT extra if you don't have your own towel.

The Ilirija outdoor pool opposite the Tivoli hotel at Celovška cesta 3 is open in summer from 10 am to 7 pm.

You can rent rowing boats on the river from the Ljubljanica Recreational Centre (☎ 214 906) at Velika Čolnarska ulica 20 in Trnovo mid-May to September from 10 am to 7 pm.

The Zmajček Ballooning Club (☎ 127 2534), south of the Botanical Garden at Ižanska cesta 350, has half-hour/one-hour flights over the city for DM125/250.

If you fancy a long but easy walk, you could follow the marked Trail of Remembrance (Pot Spominov), which runs for some 34km along where German barbed wire once completely enclosed Ljubljana during WWII. Today it is especially popular with joggers. The easiest places to reach it from are the AMZS (Automobile Association of Slovenia) headquarters at Dunajska cesta 128 north of the Bežigrad student dormitory or from Trg Komandanta Staneta just north-west of the LPP central office (see Getting Around later in this chapter) at Celovška cesta 160. You can also join it from the south-western edge of Tivoli Park near the zoo or the northern side of Žale Cemetery.

Ljubljana Casino (☎ 302 988), next to the Austrotel at Miklošičeva cesta 9, has American roulette, black jack, poker and slot machines. It's open daily from noon to 2 am (3 am on Friday and Saturday).

ORGANISED TOURS

From June to September, a two-hour guided tour in English (700/500 SIT adults/seniors, students and children) sponsored by the TIC departs daily at 5 pm from the town hall in Mestni trg. During the rest of the year there are tours at 11 am on Sunday only.

In summer a boat called the Emona II (☎ 448 112 or mobile ☎ 041-627 857) offers excursions on the Ljubljanica River Tuesday to Sunday at 5 and 7 pm from the footbridge just west of Ribji trg to Livada, east of Trnovo, and back for 500 SIT per person (children under 12 free).

SPECIAL EVENTS

The No 1 event on Ljubljana's social calendar is the International Summer Festival of music, theatre and dance held in venues throughout the city but principally at the open-air theatre of the Križanke on Trg Francoske Revolucije. The festival, now in its fourth decade, begins in early July and runs through August.

A festival of alternative and world music called Druga Godba (Other Music) takes place in the Križanke in June as does the Photo Antique Fair, where old photographs, cameras and other equipment are traded. There's a Jazz Festival at the Križanke in late June.

Vino Ljubljana is an international wine fair in early June for the trade and general public alike. It takes place at the Ljubljana Fairgrounds (Gospodarsko Razstavišče) north of the train station at Dunajska cesta 10 and the opening is marked with delivery of wine from the Vipava Valley to Ljubljana via the ancient *vinska magistrala* (wine trading route). Some restaurants, *gostilne* and bars serve special dishes and selected wines during the fair. They are identified by grape-shaped wreaths made of wood shavings.

Ljubljana is at its most vibrant in July and August during the so-called Summer in the Old Town season when there are three or four cultural events a week in the city's historic squares and courtyards. All are free. The KUD Summer Festival takes place in Trnovo in August.

The International Biennial of Graphic Arts, at the Museum of Modern Arts, the International Centre of Graphic Arts in Tivoli and other venues, takes place throughout the summer during odd-numbered years. The 23rd is in 1999.

Numerous church concerts and street fairs are held throughout Ljubljana in December during the build-up to Christmas and the New Year.

PLACES TO STAY
Camping

The only camping ground convenient to Ljubljana is the *Ježica* site (☎ 168 3913 or ☎ 371 382) on the Sava River at Dunajska cesta 270, about 6km north of the train and bus stations. You can reach it on bus No 6 or 8. Ježica, which is open all year, has an outdoor swimming pool, a fitness studio, bowling alley, tennis courts and a laundry room and costs 860 to 1100 SIT per person. Bicycles are available for rent, and there are daily permits (1300 SIT) for fishing in the Sava. There are also three-dozen cramped little bungalows with two rooms costing from 7000 SIT.

The *Smlednik* camp site (☎ 627 002) in Dragočajna, 17km north-west of Ljubljana, is located between two small lakes; the big draw here seems to be the nudist beach. Smlednik, open from May to mid-October, charges 720 to 1100 SIT per person.

Hostels & Student Dormitories

Four student dormitories *(dijaški dom)* open their doors to foreign travellers in summer and are clean, cheap and friendly places in which to stay. A couple are near Center but, as you would expect, most are quite a way out.

The closest one, which is affiliated with Hostelling International (HI), is *Dijaški Dom Tabor* (☎ 321 067), Vidovdanska ulica 7, which can accommodate up to 60 people. It charges 2370 SIT for a single room with breakfast and 2000 SIT per person for a bed in a double, triple or quad. If you don't have an HI card, breakfast costs 360 SIT. As usual, toilets and showers are on the corridor, but all rooms have running water. Though there's a 'curfew' between 10 pm and 6 am, the security guard will let you in when you ring the bell. The Tabor is open late June to August. It is a short walk from the bus and train stations.

The *Dijaški Dom Poljane* (☎ 327 471 or ☎ 327 494) about 1.5km east of the Old Town at Potočnikova ulica 3 has 80 two-bedded rooms and is open from mid-June to late July. The charge here is 2000 SIT for a single and 3000 SIT for a double with shower. You can eat in the student cafeteria and there's a laundry room. To reach it, take bus No 5 from Tavčarjeva ulica or No 13 from Kongresni trg and get off at the Gornje Poljane stop.

A bit closer to town but still in Poljane is the *Dijaški Dom Ivana Cankarja* (☎ 133

5177) at Poljanska cesta 26-28 (Building B). It has 160 three-bedded rooms and charges 1200/1530 SIT per person with/without an HI card. Rooms don't have running water, but there are showers, toilets and TVs on each floor. The Ivana Cankarja is open mid-June to August, but you may be able to find a bed here on weekends at other times of the year. You can also reach here on bus Nos 5 and 13.

The *Dijaški Dom Bežigrad* (☎ 342 867) is at Kardeljeva ploščad 28 in the Bežigrad district 2km north of the train and bus stations. It has doubles/triples with shower and toilet for 3600/4500 SIT and rooms with one to three beds with shared facilities for 1200 SIT per person. None of the rates include breakfast. An HI card gets you about 10% off, and the hostel is open throughout the night. The Bežigrad has 70 rooms available from late June to late August but only about 20 for the rest of the year. There's a laundry in the Dijaški Dom Kam (Building C) at Kardeljeva ploščad 14 which is open from 8 am till noon and 2 to 6 pm weekdays and 8 am to 3 pm on Saturday. To get here from Slovenska cesta, take bus No 6, 8 or 21 and get off at the Mercator/Triglavska stop.

Private Rooms & Apartments

The TIC has about 40 private rooms on its list, but just a handful are in Center. Most of the others would require a bus trip up to Bežigrad. Prices range from 2500 SIT for singles and 4000 SIT for doubles. It also has eight apartments and two studios – four of which are central – for one to four people starting at 7500 SIT. Reception is at the Meredita agency (☎ 131 1102; fax 131 1096) at Kotnikova ulica 5.

Pensions & Guesthouses

The closest thing to a guesthouse in Ljubljana proper is the *Mrak* pension (☎ 223 412; fax 301 197), west of Trg Francoske Revolucije at Rimska cesta 4, with 30 rooms. It's decent enough and the *Gostilna Pri Mraku* downstairs has reasonably priced and generous Slovenian set menus, but the rooms are small and quite expensive – 6390 SIT for

a single with shower and breakfast and 8930 SIT for a double.

The 11-room *Lieber* (☎ 161 2123; fax 372 862), 7km north of Ljubljana in Srednje Gameljne (house No 32e), charges from 6000 SIT for singles and from 8000 SIT for doubles. The Lieber has a fine restaurant (see Places to Eat).

Hotels – budget

One of the best deals in Ljubljana is the 15-room *Super Li Bellevue* hotel (☎ 133 4049) on the northern edge of Tivoli Park at Pod Gozdom 12. There are no rooms with private baths, but bright and airy singles with basins are 3050 SIT, doubles 6000 SIT. The nightclub gets pretty noisy at the weekend.

The 124-room *Park* hotel (☎ 133 1306; fax 133 0546) at Tabor 9 is where most people usually end up in Ljubljana as it's the city's only large budget hotel close to Center and the Old Town. It's pretty basic, but the price is right: DM53/72 for singles/doubles with buffet breakfast and shared shower and DM72/90 with private shower. Students with cards get a 20% discount. The staff are very helpful and friendly.

If you're desperate, the *Tivoli* (☎ 133 6131; fax 302 671), a former hostel for workers at Tivolska cesta 30, has 31 tiny double rooms with showers that cost 5500/7720 SIT for singles/doubles. The Tivoli faces the park but is on the corner of two very busy and noisy streets.

Hotels – mid-range

The 128-room *Ilirija* hotel (☎ 159 3337; fax 159 3048) at Trg Prekomorskih Brigad 4, off Celovška cesta, is neither here nor there – in location or aesthetics. It's a far walk from Center and the stations and although this two-storey hotel was renovated not so long ago there is already a sad feeling of neglect. It does back on to Debeli Hill and the Šiška district's leafy recreation area however. Singles range from 6370 to 8650 SIT, doubles from 8830 to 11,830 SIT.

The 190-room *Turist* hotel (☎ 132 2343; fax 319 291) at Dalmatinova ulica 15, a mere 200m from Prešernov trg, is very central, but this six-storey place has a lot of drawbacks and desperately needs to be renovated. Rooms are very small, the hotel drab and noisy and the service substandard. If you do stay here, request a room looking southward to the Old Town and Castle Hill. Rates are 7740 SIT for a single and 11,350 SIT for a double, including a generous breakfast buffet.

Hotels – top end

Most of the expensive hotels in Ljubljana have all the things you'd expect from such high prices: satellite and cable TV, direct-dial telephones, minibars in the rooms etc.

In the thick of things is the 171-room *Slon Best Western* hotel (☎ 170 1100; fax 217 164) at Slovenska cesta 34, but try to get a room facing east toward Castle Hill. The 'Elephant' has a history going back more than four centuries – it is said that this was the spot where a pachyderm presented to the Habsburg emperor by an African king tarried on its way to Vienna – though the present hotel dates from this century. There are several categories of single rooms starting at a minimum of about 12,150 SIT and hitting 16,850 SIT, with doubles from 17,250 to 22,050 SIT. The Slon has a floor reserved for nonsmokers, and popular Slovenian and Italian restaurants.

The *Lev* hotel (☎ 133 2155; fax 321 994) at Vošnjakova ulica 1, south-west of the landmark Pivovarna Union (Union Brewery), has been busy over the last several years metamorphosing from a huge old nondescript hotel into a glass-and-mirror tower. The 95 new rooms start at 24,300/31,500 SIT for a single/double, but the 61 old rooms are much cheaper – from 13,050/15,750 SIT for a single/double. The Lev is within easy walking distance of the stations and most everything in Center.

Hotels – luxury

The 62-room *Austrotel* (☎ 132 6133; fax 301 181) at Miklošičeva cesta 9 is among Ljubljana's most modern hotels with distinctly 'modern' prices – from 16,300 SIT for a single and from 25,480 SIT for a double. The Austrotel's pricey *Steakhouse* restaurant

and its salad bar are excellent and a welcome change from an overdose of *burek*. The only problem with this four-storey hotel is that the rooms facing Miklošičeva cesta can be noisy. Parking is available.

The hotel with the most character in Ljubljana is the renovated Art Nouveau *Grand Hotel Union* (☎ 125 4133; fax 217 910), Miklošičeva cesta 1, which was built in 1905. But beware, this 187-room hotel has rooms of different categories in an old wing and in a boring new one from the late 1960s. Singles with breakfast and shower range from 14,100 to 16,800 SIT, with doubles between 19,600 and 22,300 SIT. The hotel has a cellar and a lovely garden restaurant, and guests get to use the swimming pool and fitness centre (open from 3 to 10 pm) and car park of the *Holiday Inn* (☎ 125 5051; fax 125 0323) next door. This 133-room hotel looks and feels like Holiday Inns from Cleveland, Ohio, to Kuala Lumpur and charges from 19,400 SIT for a single and 26,900 SIT for a double.

The Protocol Service of the Republic of Slovenia owns several magnificent properties available for hire in Slovenia, including *Vila Podrožnik* on Večna pot in Rožna Dolina with apartments for – wait for it – 77,200 SIT. For information, contact the Protocol Service (☎ 064-221 133; fax 064-221 551) at Brdo Castle in Predoslje.

PLACES TO EAT
Restaurants

Slovenian An old standby – it's been around since 1776 – with national dishes is *Šestica* at Slovenska cesta 40. It's a very popular place with local people and serves up plates of goveji golaž (beef goulash) and fat Kranjska sausage with cabbage. Main courses are in the 600 to 1200 SIT range, salads from 250 SIT and there's a set menu for 1200 SIT. The back courtyard is pleasant but gets a bit stuffy in summer. Šestica is from open Monday to Saturday to 11 pm.

The *Kolovrat* at Ciril-Metodov trg 14 opposite the cathedral is a renovated *gostilna* with reasonably priced Slovenian meals. However, a better choice than this would be the *Tavčarjev Hram* at Tavčarjeva ulica 4. It is open daily, except Sunday, from 8 am to 10 pm.

A welcome arrival in the Old Town is *Špajza* (☎ 125 3094) at Gornji trg 28. The 'Pantry' couldn't be more nicely decorated with its rough-hewn tables and chairs, wooden floors, frescoed ceilings and nostalgic bits and pieces. But there are problems: the menu is handwritten, almost indecipherable and in Slovene only; the food is ordinary and very expensive (starters 900 to 1200 SIT, main courses 1200 to 2800 SIT – expect to pay about 4300 SIT per person for two courses and a drink); and the restaurant is understaffed. Špajza is open daily, except Sunday, from noon to 1.30 am.

Arguably the most stylish restaurant in Ljubljana is the *Smrekarjev Hram* (☎ 216 810), an Art Nouveau jewel run by the Grand Hotel Union at Nazorjeva ulica 2. But without the rich aunt or uncle in tow, enter at your own peril as this place is very expensive. It's open weekdays only from noon to 11 pm.

A couple of gostilne that are a bit out of the way but get rave reviews from both local and foreign residents of Ljubljana alike are *Pri Jerneju* (☎ 221 951) at Velika Čolnarska ulica 17, about 400m south-east of Eipprova ulica and the Gradaščica canal (open daily noon to 11 pm), and *Pri Gorjancu* (☎ 123 1111) at Tržaška cesta 330, 5km south-west of Center. The latter is open Sunday to Friday from noon to 10 pm.

Continental The *Rotovž* (☎ 212 839) next to the town hall at Mestni trg 2 is a relatively expensive – around 350 SIT for soups and salads, 1500 SIT for main courses – restaurant that caters mostly to foreign tourists; you'll be lucky to get a seat, especially on the outside terrace in the warmer months. Some of the dishes like the roast kid (pečen kolíček; 1950 SIT) are unusual and quite tasty; service is multilingual but somewhat cavalier. It's open daily, except Sunday, from 11 am till midnight. Expect to pay about 8000 SIT for a two-course meal for two with a bottle of wine.

Ljubljanski Dvor (☎ 216 555) at Dvorni trg 1 south-east of Kongresni trg is both an upmarket restaurant serving decent international fare and a pizzeria (see Italian). It opens daily, except Sunday, from noon till midnight.

M Monroe opposite the Austrotel at Miklošičeva cesta 28 is an attractively decorated modern restaurant popular with office workers and staff from Kompas and the US Embassy nearby. It has three-course daily set lunches for less than 1000 SIT.

Pod Rožnikom (☎ 213 446) at Cesta na Rožnik 18 is famous for its south Slav-style grills like pljeskavica (spicy meat patties; 900 SIT) served with ajvar (roasted red peppers, tomatoes and eggplant cooked into a purée) as well as starters like prebranac (onions and beans cooked in an earthenware pot; 500 SIT) and šampinjoni na žaru (grilled mushrooms; 850 SIT); even a food reviewer with the *New York Times* couldn't get enough of this place. It's open daily from noon till 11 pm. The *Dva Fazana* (☎ 316 480) in a renovated gostilna at Dunajska cesta 61 specialises in game and fish dishes. The 'Two Pheasants' is open Monday to Saturday to 11 pm and on Sunday for lunch from noon to 5 pm.

The restaurant at the *Lieber* pension (☎ 161 2123), in Srednje Gameljne 7km north of Ljubljana, is a Maison de Qualité restaurant and comes highly recommended. Its specialities include dishes based on žganci, groats made from buckwheat. It is open Monday to Saturday from noon to 10 pm.

Italian If you hanker after real Italian cuisine, you should head for the upmarket *Atrij* restaurant (☎ 170 1100) in the Slon hotel or, in a pinch, the *Fortunat* at Eipprova ulica 2 in Trnovo (open daily, except Saturday, to 11 pm). Otherwise, 'Italian' usually means pizza or a bit of pasta in Ljubljana.

There's an ongoing argument who has the best pizza: *Napoli* off Trubarjeva cesta at Prečna ulica 7 (enter from Mala ulica; open to 11 pm Monday to Saturday, 10 pm on Sunday) or *Ljubljanski Dvor* at Dvorni trg 1 north of Breg. Actually my vote goes to the newer *Foculus*, next to the Equrna Gallery and Glej Theatre at Gregorčičeva ulica 3, which is open daily from noon till midnight. Small/large pizzas here cost 650/850 SIT and the salad bar from 390 SIT.

The *Špageterija*, at Trubarjeva cesta 52 and close to the Park hotel, has more pasta dishes (about 1000 SIT) than pizza and is an old favourite (though the decor suggests the owner might originally have had a Mexican or Spanish restaurant in mind). *Čerin*, just down the hill from the Špageterija on Znamenjska ulica, has so-so pizza but an excellent salad bar where you pay by the weight.

A central place serving unexceptional pizzas (700 to 900 SIT) and with a rather sad salad bar (400 SIT) is *Pizzeria Romeo* at Stari trg 6. It is open every day from 11 am to 1 am. As is fitting in a city whose name sounds almost like 'beloved' in Slovene, opposite the Romeo is a bar/café called *Julija*.

Spanish & Mexican *Casa del Papa* (☎ 134 3158), the new kid in town at Celovška cesta 54a, is a Spanish (and maybe a little Cuban – the 'Papa' refers to Ernest Hemingway) restaurant decorated in a hotchpotch of styles: Spanish here, French there and African somewhere over there. Somehow it all works and well heeled Ljubljančani can't seem to get enough of the place. On the 1st floor is the *American Bar* and in the cellar the *Cuba Club* (see Entertainment). The restaurant is open daily from noon to 1 am.

Meson Don Felipe (☎ 134 3862), southeast of Krekov trg at Streliška ulica 22, is Ljubljana's first – and only – tapas bar (300 to 800 SIT). It's open daily from noon till midnight.

There's Mexican food available at the *Eldorado*, behind Nazorjeva ulica 6, weekdays from 11 am to 5 pm.

Chinese If you're looking for a fix of Chinese food, the location of the *Sichuan* below St Florian's Church at Gornji trg 23 is wonderful, but the food is much more authentic at the *Zlati Pav* (☎ 171 0701), Zarnikova ulica 3 (enter from Poljanska

cesta 20). Main courses like hui guo rou (twice-cooked pork), mapo doufu (spicy bean curd) and beef with bamboo shoots and black mushrooms at the 'Golden Peacock' start at about 900 SIT, soups from 300 SIT. Another place close by with seriously over-the-top decorations and slightly lower prices is *Shanghai* at Poljanska cesta 14. Both Zlati Pav and Shanghai are open daily from 11 or 11.30 am to 11 pm.

Fish For a quick and very tasty lunch, try the fried squid (250 SIT) or whitebait (370 SIT) at *Ribca*, a basement seafood bar below the Plečnik Colonnade in Pogarčarjev trg. Other fish dishes go for 600 to 950 SIT. *Zlata Ribica*, a small pub-restaurant at Cankarjevo nabrežje 5, serves simple fish dishes at lunch. It is open from 8 am to 10 pm weekdays, to 3 pm on Saturday and from 7 am to 3 pm on Sunday. *Alkar*, at Trnovski pristan 4 in Trnovo, is a similar place and open daily, except Tuesday, until 10 pm.

The *Operna Klet* (☎ 214 715) near the Opera at Župančičeva ulica 4 (enter from Tomšičeva ulica) is a more upmarket place for fish, open daily from noon till 10 pm.

Cafés
The coffee house *(kavarna)* is nowhere near as much a part of the social fabric and daily routine in Ljubljana as it is in, say, Budapest or Vienna but one or two may be worth a visit. Always look for the Barcaffè brand-name on display – it's the best quality coffee available.

The renovated café at the *Grand Hotel Union*, open from 9 am to 10 pm and to 2 am on Friday and Saturday, was once *the* venue to rub shoulders with the movers and shakers of Ljubljana. It still attracts an interesting assortment of characters.

For coffee and cakes you might also try the truncated *Evropa* café at Gosposvetska cesta 2 on the corner of Slovenska cesta or the *Slon* café in the Slon hotel. Better still (at least for the views) is the *Nebotičnik Terasa* café on the top (12th) floor of the Art Deco Skyscraper building on the corner of Slovenska cesta and Štefanova ulica. This was Ljubljana's tallest building for decades after it was built in 1933 and, though it's in pretty sad shape, it still looks like it could be part of a set for a King Kong film. The views – of the Old Town, Ljubljana Castle, Tivoli Park, the Ljubljana Marsh to the south and the glass-and-steel 72m World Trade Centre to the north – are the best in town and the café is open daily from 10 am till 11 pm.

The *Plečnikov Hram*, more of a café than a restaurant (though it does a set lunch for 820 SIT) in the Križanke on Trg Francoske Revolucije, is a great meeting place, especially for a quiet *tête à tête*.

There's only one real teahouse in town, *Čajna Hiša* at Stari trg 1, serving any number of green and black teas just the way you like it. The 'China House' is open weekdays from 9 am to 11 pm and on Saturday to 3 pm.

The *Anika* café at Eipprova ulica 19 in Trnovo is said to have the best ice cream in the city.

Self-Service Restaurants & Cafeterias
One of the cheapest places for a meal in Ljubljana is at the *Maxim* self-service restaurant in the basement of the Emona Maximarket shopping arcade on Trg Republike. Main dishes are between 250 and 450 SIT, and there are set menus from 750 SIT. It's open from 9 am to 6 pm and on Saturday till 3 pm. But don't expect cordon bleu food at those prices; it's real school cafeteria stuff.

A similar place is *Daj-Dam* at Cankarjeva cesta 4. There are set menus (pay the cashier first), which you eat standing up, and a sitdown restaurant in the back with regular table service. Mains with meat cost from 450 SIT and Daj-Dam is open weekdays from 6 am to 9 pm, Saturday from 7 am to 4 pm and Sunday from 9 am to 4 pm. *Triglav*, a self-service restaurant in the courtyard at Miklošičeva cesta 12, is open Monday to Thursday from 11 am to 8 pm and Friday to Sunday from 11 am to 4 pm.

The best self-service restaurant in Ljubljana, according to cognoscenti, is *Skriti Kot*, very much a 'Hidden Corner' in the shopping arcade below Trg Ajdovščina. Hearty main courses go for 450 to 750 SIT, roast chicken and ričet

for around 350 SIT. It's open weekdays from 7 am to 4 pm and till 2 pm on Saturday.

Snacks & Fast Food
There are *burek stands* at several locations in Ljubljana for a quick and filling lunch or snack, and one of the best is the one next to Slovenijaturist on Pražakova ulica. Cheese, meat or apple bureks go for 250 SIT. If you want something more substantial, head for *Super 5*, which faces Slovenska cesta from the shopping mall on Trg Ajdovščina. It serves cheap and cheerful Balkan grills like čevapčiči (600 SIT), pljeskavica (540 SIT) and klobasa and is open 24 hours.

The best sandwiches in town are available at *Nostalgia* in the Old Town at Stari trg 9, where every bit of wall space is covered with old Slovenian film posters, photos etc. It's open daily from 9 or 10 am to 1 am.

If you *must* have western-style fast food, Ljubljana can oblige. *Dairy Queen* has an outlet at Cankarjeva cesta 2 on the corner of Slovenska cesta (open Monday to Thursday from 9 am to 11 pm, to midnight on Friday and Saturday and from 4 to 10 pm on Sunday). *McDonald's* is up the stairs at Čopova ulica 14. It is open Monday to Saturday from 9 am to 11 pm and on Sunday from 10 am. The best thing that can be said about this place is that it looks directly at the wonderful decorations of the Art Nouveau City Savings Bank building (1904) opposite at No 3.

The *McDonald's* outlet at the train station is open daily from 7 am to 2 am. A local version of fast food is available at *Rio Ham Ham*, Slovenska cesta 28 (open weekdays from 8 am to 10 pm, from 10 am on Saturday and Sunday).

Food Markets & Self-Catering
The large *outdoor market* in Vodnikov trg, selling mostly produce, is open Monday to Saturday from 6 am to 5 or 6 pm in summer and to 4 pm in winter. The *indoor market* on the ground floor of the Seminary on Pogarčarjev trg – good for meats, fish, dairy products etc – is open weekdays from 6 am to 4 pm and on Saturday to 2 pm.

The *supermarket* in the basement of the Emona Maximarket shopping arcade on Trg Republike has about the largest selection in town. It is open weekdays from 9 am to 8 pm and on Saturday from 8 am to 3 pm.

Fancy delicatessens where you can stock up on pršut, cheese and other picnic fare have sprung up around Ljubljana like mushrooms after rain. Some of the best are: *Bik Butik*, Čopova ulica 5 (open weekdays from 8 am to 7 pm, till 1 pm Saturday); *Delikatesa*, Kongresni trg 8 (7 am to 8 pm weekdays, till 1 pm Saturday); and *Burja*, Kongresni trg 11 (7.30 am to 7 pm weekdays, till 1 pm Saturday).

ENTERTAINMENT
Ljubljana enjoys a very rich cultural and social life for its size so ask the TIC for its monthly program of events in English *(Where to? in Ljubljana)* as well as any flyers it might have for various theatres and concert halls.

Cinema
For first-run films, head for any of the following cinemas: the *Komuna* at Cankarjeva cesta 1; the *Union* at Nazorjeva ulica 2; or the *Šiška* near the Ilirija hotel at Trg Prekomorskih Brigad 3. They generally have three screenings a day.

The *Kompas* cinema, Miklošičeva cesta 38, shows art and classic films as does the *Kinoteka* at No 28 of the same street, with screenings at 6, 8 and 10 pm. Cinema tickets generally cost 300 to 500 SIT, and discounts are usually available on Monday.

Discos & Clubs
The most popular conventional discos are *Eldorado*, behind Nazorjeva ulica 6 and open daily to at least 2 am (cover charge 500 SIT on Wednesday, Friday and Saturday) and *Klub Central* next to the Turist hotel at Dalmatinova ulica 15.

The student *Klub K4* at Kersnikova ulica 4 has a disco on some nights (Sunday is for gays and lesbians). Two other popular venues for Ljubljana's young bloods are the *Klub Manhattan* next to the Zlati Klub sauna in the Tivoli Recreation Centre in Tivoli Park (Celovška cesta 25) and the *Klub Metropol* next door to the K4 at Kersnikova ulica 6. *Cuba Club* below the *Casa del Papa* restaurant at Celovška cesta 54a has Latino and salsa music and opens daily from 3 pm to 2 am.

Gay & Lesbian Venues
Ljubljana may not be the gayest city in central Europe, but there are a few decent options. For general information and advice, ring Roza Klub (☎ 130 4740), the gay branch of the Student Cultural Centre (Študentski Kulturni Center; ŠKUC) at Kersnikova ulica 4 or the GALfon hotline (☎ 132 4089; daily between 7 to 10 pm).

A popular spot for both gays and lesbians alike on Sunday night is the *Roza Klub* at the *Klub K4*. The music takes no risks, but the crowd is lively and friendly. It's open from 10 pm to 4 am and costs 800 SIT (600 SIT for students).

In Metelkova, Ljubljana's version of Christiania in Copenhagen, between Metelkova ulica and Maistrova ulica, there's a café-pub for gays called *Club Tiffany*. It's in the small blue building to the left (east) as you enter the squat. Tiffany is open daily Sunday to Thursday from 9 pm till midnight or 1 am and on Friday and Saturday to 4 am. Wednesday night is video night and for gays only; Thursday night is reserved for lesbians.

The *Propaganda Klub* has a gay and lesbian night on Friday called 'Does Your Momma Know?' from 10 pm to 4 am. It is next to the landmark *Orto Bar* at Graboličeva ulica 1, which begins a short distance north-west of Metelkova. Entry costs 500 SIT.

The *Caffè Galerija* at the City Gallery, Mestni trg 5 (open 10 am till midnight), attracts a gay crowd as does the *Zlati Klub* sauna in Tivoli Park. If you prefer to meet friends *en plein air*, the walkways behind the Tivoli Recreation Centre and Modern History Museum in the park as far as the Hala Tivoli sport centre are notoriously cruisy after dark as are the car parks just in front of the recreation centre and to the east across the train tracks along Tivolska cesta. The path along the Sava River near the Gostilna Žagar (Gameljska ulica 1) in Črnuče (bus No 6) is a popular meeting place in warmer weather.

Multicultural Centres

The *Klub K4* in the basement of the Študentska Organizacija Univerze Ljubljani (ŠOU; Student Organisation of the University of Ljubljana; ☎ 133 7219) building at Kersnikova ulica 4 is a very popular venue featuring both canned and live music nightly – from hiphop, rap and techno to acid jazz and folk. Ask for its monthly program and make your choices. It's open from 10 to 2 or 4 am and admission is 500 SIT (400 SIT for students) except on Friday and Sunday night when it costs 800/600 SIT respectively.

The *KUD France Prešeren* (☎ 332 288), a 'non-institutional culture and arts society' at Karunova ulica 14 in Trnovo, stages concerts of all kinds and is the headquarters of the Ana Monro Theatre, the only street theatre in Slovenia. KUD also has a great high-tech pub-café open daily from 3 to 10 pm where you can meet people.

The *ŠKUC Galerija* (☎ 216 540 or ☎ 121 3142), run by the student cultural association at Stari trg 21, has information, music performances and art exhibitions, especially by the Neue Slowenische Kunst (NSK) multimedia group and the IRWIN artists' cooperative.

For a truly alternative scene, head for the two music clubs at Metelkova – *Channel Zero* and *Gala Dvorana* – with all sorts of music as well as performance arts and theatre.

Theatre

Ljubljana has a half-dozen theatres – not including the new *Café Teater* (☎ 216 390), at the Grand Hotel Union – so there should be something for everyone. Slovenian theatre is usually quite visual with a lot of mixed media so you don't always have to speak the lingo to enjoy the production.

The home of the national company is the *National Drama Theatre* (Slovensko Narodno Gledališče; SNG; ☎ 126 4549 or ☎ 221 462) at Erjavčeva cesta 1; the box office there is open daily from 10 am to 1 pm and from 6 pm till the performance. The *Slovenian Youth Theatre* (Slovensko Mladinsko Gledališče; ☎ 310 610) in the Festival Hall (Festivalna Dvorana) at

Vilharjeva ulica 11 has staged some highly acclaimed productions (eg *Scheherazade*, *Alice in Wonderland* and *Family Album*) at home and abroad in recent years. The *City Theatre of Ljubljana* (Mesto Gledališče Ljubljansko; ☎ 125 8222) is at Čopova ulica 14.

The *Glej Theatre* (☎ 216 679), Gregorčičeva ulica 3, is Ljubljana's foremost experimental theatre with three resident or affiliated companies, including the Betontanc dance and Grapefruit acting troupes. They're often on tour and the theatre is closed in July and August; in other months, your best chance to see a performance is on Thursday or Friday night. The box office is open weekdays from 10 am to 2 pm and 5 to 7 pm and on Saturday from 10 am to 1 pm.

The *Ljubljana Puppet Theatre* (Lutkovno Gledališče Ljubljana; ☎ 314 966) performs at the St James Theatre at Krekov trg 2 south of Vodnikov trg.

Classical Music, Opera & Dance

Ljubljana is home to two orchestras: the Slovenian Philharmonic and the Symphony Orchestra of RTV Slovenija. Concerts are held in various locations all over town, but the main venue – with up to 700 cultural events a year – is *Cankarjev Dom* on Trg Republike. It has two large auditoriums (the Gallus Hall has perfect acoustics) and a number of smaller ones. The ticket office (☎ 222 815) in the basement of the nearby Emona Maximarket shopping arcade is open weekdays from 10 am to 2 pm and 4.30 to 8 pm, Saturday from 10 am to 1 pm and an hour before performances. Also check for concerts at the beautiful *Filharmonija* at Kongresni trg 10. Tickets run anywhere between 300 and 2000 SIT, but most are in the 600 to 900 SIT range.

The ticket office (☎ 125 4840) of the *Opera House*, where ballets are also performed, at Župančičeva ulica 1 is open Monday to Saturday from 11 am to 1 pm and an hour before each performance.

For tickets to the Ljubljana Summer Festival and anything else staged at the *Križanke*, go to the booking office (☎ 126 4340 or ☎ 226 544) opposite the Ilirija

Column at Trg Francoske Revolucije 1-2. It is open weekdays from 9 am to 2 pm and from 6 pm till the performance and on Saturday from 10 am to 1 pm.

Rock & Jazz

Ljubljana has a number of excellent music clubs and the ones listed below are highly recommended. The *Rock Café* on Plečnikov trg 1 opposite the Slovenian School Museum is open till midnight daily, except Sunday, with a DJ Thursday to Saturday from 8 pm.

The *Gajo Jazz Club* at Beethovnova ulica 8 just up from the Parliament building is Ljubljana's premier venue for live jazz and attracts both local and international talent. It's open daily from 10 am to 2 am weekdays and from 7 pm to midnight on Saturday and Sunday. The capital's other jazz club, the *Flex Club* below Nazorjeva ulica 12, doesn't hold a candle to Gajo but it's open later – to 4 am daily, except Sunday.

Pubs & Bars

One of the best places for a drink in Ljubljana if you just want to sit outside and watch the passing parade is the roped-off café-pub on the southern side of Prešernov trg that local people call the *Konjski Rep* (Horse's Tail). You'll probably bump into half the people you've met along the way in Slovenia here. It's open from June to October till at least midnight. A pleasant and congenial place for a *pivo* or glass of *vino* nearby is the *Cutty Sark* in the courtyard behind Wolfova ulica 6 on Knafljev Prehod.

Trubarjeva cesta, pedestrianised from just north-east of the Dragon Bridge to Prešernov trg, is a lively street with plenty of pubs, bars, cafés and late-night pizzerias. One of my favourite places – especially for its name – is the *TrueBar* at No 53 open nightly to 2 am. *Patrick's Irish Pub* nearby at Prečna ulica 6 is also a pleasant place for a drink.

Holidays Pub next to the Kompas travel agency at Slovenska cesta 36 is a very popular meeting place in the evening and can get very crowded. A favourite place for students is *Miriam's Pub* opposite the ŠOU at Kersnikova ulica 5. A popular place for a

drink among the well heeled set is the *American Bar* above the Casa del Papa restaurant at Celovška cesta 54a. It's open Monday to Saturday to 2 am.

Down in the Trnovo district, the *Sax* pub at Eipprova ulica 7, decorated with wonderful murals and graffiti, takes the spillover from the nearby KUD France Prešeren centre. The *Šank* in the same building as the Anika café at Eipprova ulica 19 isn't half as much fun but is sometimes easier to get into than the Sax.

SPECTATOR SPORT

For a schedule of sporting events in the capital, check the monthly *Where to? in Ljubljana* available from the TIC.

Football matches take place at the Central Stadium (Centralni Stadion) at Dunajska cesta, designed by Jože Plečnik in 1925. It's an easy bus ride (bus No 6, 8 or 21 to the Stadion stop) or a 20-minute walk north up Dunajska cesta from Center. For basketball, ice hockey and volleyball, the venue is the Hala Tivoli sport centre in Tivoli Park.

THINGS TO BUY

For general souvenirs and folk crafts, check out what's on offer at the Galerija Zibka in the Slon hotel, the Dom at Mestni trg 24, Parazol at Stari trg 15 and Laura at Trubarjeva cesta 40. They all have Slovenian things like Prekmurje black pottery, Idrija lace, beehive panels with folk motifs, decorated heart-shaped honey cakes, painted Easter eggs, Rogaška glassware and so on. The best place in town for distinctly Ljubljana souvenirs is the Ljubljanček gift shop in the lobby of the Grand Hotel Union.

Don't expect any bargains, but Carniola Antiqua at Trubarjeva cesta 9 and Antika Ferjan at Mestni trg 21 in the Old Town have superb antiques. Galerija Lala at Židovska ulica 5 is one of the finest galleries in the capital, with both old and new art.

Big Bang is a music shop with CDs and cassettes of all kinds of music, including Slovenian folk, at Wolfova ulica 12. It's open from 9 am to 7 pm and to 1.30 pm on

Saturday. Another good place for music is the Hard Rock shop at Trubarjeva cesta 40.

If you've forgotten your fishing rod, ski poles, hiking boots or knapsack, head for Slovenijašport at Slovenska cesta 44. It's open weekdays from 8.30 am to 7 pm and on Saturday to 1 pm. For those into ridin', fishin' and shootin', Lovec at Gosposvetska 12 has all the kit and equipment you'll need. It's open weekdays from 8 am to 7 pm and on Saturday to 1 pm.

A shop called Kože Grčar at Cankarjevo nabrežje 13 sells sheepskins and cow hides (to be used as floor coverings). It's open from 9.30 am till noon and 5 to 7 pm on weekdays only.

The city of Tržič north-west of Ljubljana has always been synonymous with quality shoes and the Peko branches at Čopova ulica 1 and Miklošičeva cesta 12 (both open weekdays 8 am to 7.30 pm, Saturday to 1 pm) stock a wide range.

Sidro at Kongresni trg 3 sells natural remedies, herbal teas and other concoctions, some produced by the monks at Stična Abbey in Dolenjska. The shop is open from 8 am to 6 pm and on Saturday to 1 pm. An interesting shop called Apiteka in a courtyard to the east of Trubarjeva cesta 53 sells all manner of bee-related items: wax candles, honey, pollen, propolis etc. It's usually open from 9 am to 2 pm weekdays and till noon on Saturday.

Vinoteka Simon Bradeško at Dunajska cesta 18 has a selection of some 400 Slovenian wines. It's open weekdays from 10 am to 7 pm and on Saturday from 9 am to 1 pm. Vino Boutique at Slovenska cesta 38 may not have as many choices, but it's more conveniently located and most wines are under 1000 SIT. It is open weekdays from 10 am to 7.30 pm and on Saturday to 1.30 pm.

Flea Market

There's an antiques flea market on Cankarjevo nabrežje every Sunday from 8 am to 1 pm.

GETTING THERE & AWAY
Air

The main ticket office for Adria Airways is at Gosposvetska cesta 6 (☎ 313 312) near the

Lev hotel, open weekdays from 8 am to 7 pm and Saturday to 1 pm. A more convenient branch (☎ 126 2262) but open weekdays only (8 am to 4 pm) is on the ground floor of Trg Republike 3.

Other airlines with offices in Ljubljana include:

Aeroflot
    (☎ 313 350), Dunajska cesta 21
Austrian Airlines
    (☎ 168 4099), Dunajska cesta 107
Lufthansa
    (☎ 326 669), Gosposvetska cesta 6
Swissair
    (☎ 317 647), Hotel Lev, Vošnjakova ulica 1

Bus

Buses to destinations both within Slovenia and abroad leave from the same bus station – no more then a shed, really – opposite the train station at Trg OF 4. For information, ring ☎ 133 6136 or ☎ 133 4344 (and good luck getting through). There's an information window, inside the station across from the ticket ones, open from 5.30 am to 9 pm. The staff are multilingual and quite helpful.

For the most part, you do not have to buy your ticket in advance; just pay as you board the bus. But for long-distance trips on Friday, just before the school break and public holidays, you are running the risk of not getting a seat. Book one the day before and reserve a seat for 120 SIT.

The bus station has a left-luggage office open from 5.30 am to 8.30 pm. If you think you'll arrive after closing time, leave your bags at the one in the train station; it's open 24 hours a day. The exchange office at the bus station is open daily from 5.30 am to 9 pm.

You can reach virtually anywhere in the country by bus – as close as Kamnik (at least every half-hour) or as far away as Vinica in Bela Krajina (three a day). If you're planning a trip to Bled or Bohinj, take the bus and not the train. The train from Ljubljana to the former will leave you at the Lesce-Bled station, 4km south-east of the lake. The closest railway station to Lake Bohinj is at Bohinjska Bistrica, 6km to the east. It's on the line linking Nova Gorica with Jesenice.

The timetable in the bus station lists all bus routes and times but here are some sample frequencies and one-way fares (return fares are double): Bled (hourly, 740 SIT), Bohinj (hourly, 1110 SIT), Jesenice (hourly, 830 SIT), Koper (nine to 13 a day, 1430 SIT), Maribor (every half-hour, 1550 SIT), Murska Sobota (eight a day, 2260 SIT), Novo Mesto (up to 10 a day, 880 SIT), Piran (six to 10 a day, 1600 SIT) and Postojna (half-hourly, 670 SIT).

Buses from Ljubljana serve a number of international destinations as well, including: Belgrade (one daily, 5460 SIT), Berlin (Wednesday at 7.30 pm, 15,546 SIT), Budapest (Tuesday, Thursday and Friday at 10 pm, 6770 SIT), Frankfurt (Wednesday at 7.30 pm, 12,663 SIT), Klagenfurt (Wednesday at 6.15 am, 1230 SIT), Lenti (Thursday at 5.30 am, 2860 SIT), Munich (Tuesday to Thursday at 5.05 or 5.30 am), Novigrad (daily at 1.45 pm, 2380 SIT), Prague (Tuesday, Thursday and Saturday at 9 pm, 6580 SIT), Rijeka (daily at 7.40 pm, 1020 SIT), Rovinj (daily at 1.45 pm, 3100 SIT), Split (daily at 7.40 pm, 3830 SIT), Stuttgart (Wednesday and Thursday at 7.30 pm), Trieste (Monday to Saturday at 6.25 am, 1370 SIT), Varaždin (Saturday and Sunday at 6.35 am, 2620 SIT) and Zagreb (four a day, 1900 SIT).

For more details on domestic and international bus services see the Getting There & Away and Getting Around chapters.

Train
All trains – both Slovenian and foreign – arrive at and depart from the train station (☎ 131 5167 for information) at Trg OF 6. The lemon-yellow building has finally got its long-awaited face-lift and now has quite a few amenities, including a bar, café, *okrepčevalnica* (snack bar), McDonald's outlet (open 7 am to 2 am daily) and grocery store. There's a currency-exchange bureau next to the TIC branch office, open daily from 6 am to 10 pm. The left-luggage is on platform No 1 (open 24 hours a day; 150 SIT per piece), and there are now lockers too.

Nearby is the Wasteels office for BIJ tickets (open weekdays from 9 am to 5 pm).

You can seek information from window No 11 and buy domestic tickets from window Nos 3 to 8 and international ones from window Nos 9 and 10. For Croatia, go to window No 1 or 2.

The following are some one-way 2nd class domestic fares from Ljubljana: Bled 451 SIT, Jesenice 545 SIT, Koper 940 SIT, Maribor 949 SIT, Murska Sobota 1260 SIT and Novo Mesto 611 SIT. Return fares are usually 20% cheaper than double the price, and there's a small surcharge on domestic IC train tickets.

Sample one-way 2nd class fares on international trains include Berlin 25,945 SIT, Budapest 6110 SIT, Munich 9400 SIT, Trieste 1786 SIT and Villach 2030 SIT. Seat reservations (460 SIT) are mandatory on some trains and available on others. An extra 150 SIT is levied on foreign IC train tickets and 250 SIT on the one EC train.

For more information on trains leaving Ljubljana, turn to the Getting There & Away and Getting Around chapters.

Hitching
If you are leaving Ljubljana by way of thumb, take one of the following city buses to the terminus and begin hitching there. Do not actually go on to the motorway; use one of the access areas where the traffic is not disturbed.

Postojna, Koper, Croatian Istria & Italy (Trieste)
　　Bus No 6 south-west (stop: Dolgi Most)
Bled, Jesenice & Austria (Salzburg)
　　Bus No 1 north-west (stop: Vižmarje)
Novo Mesto & Croatia (Zagreb)
　　Bus No 3 south-east (stop: Rudnik)
Maribor & Austria (Vienna)
　　Bus No 6 north-east (stop: Črnuče)

GETTING AROUND
To/From the Airport
Bus No 28 (350 SIT) makes the run between Ljubljana and Brnik airport, 23km to the north-west, 15 times a day Monday to Friday and eight times daily at the weekend. The first bus departs for the airport at 5.20 am

(6.10 am on Saturday and Sunday), the last at 7.10 pm. From Brnik to the city the first bus is at 6 am (7 am on Saturday and Sunday) and the last at 8 pm. Catch the airport bus at Ljubljana's bus station from stop No 28 just east of the post office.

There are also three to seven buses a day from Brnik to Kamnik, between five and 16 to Kranj and six to 10 buses to Zagreb and Rijeka.

A taxi from Brnik airport to Ljubljana will cost between 4000 and 4500 SIT. To Bled, expect to pay about 5000 SIT and double that to Kranjska Gora. The SuperShuttle service (mobile ☎ 041-640 839) picks up and drops off passengers at the Slon, Holiday Inn, Grand Union, Austrotel and Lev hotels between 6 am and 10 pm, but you must book in advance. The fare is 2500 SIT per passenger.

Public Transport
From 1898 until 1958 public transport around Ljubljana was provided by trams; there's a wonderful picture book available in most of Ljubljana's bookshops recalling those nostalgic times. Until 1971 electric trolley buses did the job when they were replaced by the polluting diesel buses that carry commuters around the city today.

The system, run by LPP (Ljubljanski Potniški Promet), is excellent and very user-friendly. Every bus stop has a name, which appears on the plan in the bus shelter or is posted somewhere near the stop. There are a total of 22 lines with five of them (Nos 1, 2, 3, 6 and 11) considered main ones. These start at 3.15 am and run till midnight. The rest operate between 5 am and 10.30 pm. The main lines run about every five to 15 minutes throughout the day. Service is less frequent on other lines and on Saturday, Sunday and holidays.

The system is fool-proof. You can pay on board, which costs 100 SIT (the driver does not give change but accepts notes) or use a tiny yellow plastic token (žeton) costing only 70 SIT and available at many newsstands, kiosks, tobacco shops and post offices.

Bus passes (as well as tokens, of course) can be purchased from LPP's central office (☎ 159 4114) at Celovška cesta 160 or from the two kiosks marked 'LPP' on the pavement at Slovenska cesta 55 opposite what is, in fact, the system's central stop (Bavarski Dvor). Passes are available for a day (dnevna vozovnica, 240 SIT), a week (tedenska vozovnica, 1200 SIT) or even a month (mesečna vozovnica, 3150/1600 SIT for adults/students). The LPP office on Celovška cesta is open from 6.45 am to 7 pm Monday to Friday and to 1 pm on Saturday. You can reach it on bus Nos 1, 8 and 15 (stop: Avtomontaža). The kiosks on Slovenska cesta are open Monday to Saturday from 5.30 am to 8 pm and on Sunday from 9 am.

From the bus or train stations, bus No 2 will take you down Slovenska cesta to Mestni trg (bus stop: Magistrat) in the Old Town. To reach Trnovo, catch bus No 9 to the terminus.

Car & Motorcycle
Parking is not easy in central Ljubljana and, if you're not prepared to pay in some form or another, you're bound to get a ticket with a fine of up to 3000 SIT. In order to park on any street with blue lines painted by the kerb you should buy coupons from Delo or Tobak kiosks or petrol stations for 150 SIT (valid for one or two hours, depending on the location) and place them on the dashboard inside.

There are car parks throughout the city and their locations are indicated on most maps. To park in the underground garage beneath Miklošičev Park, for example, you'll pay 400 SIT for the first two hours (minimum) and 200 SIT for every additional hour. The open car park on Trg Republike costs 200 SIT per hour.

Car Rental Both big international car-rental firms and local companies have offices in Ljubljana, including:

ABC (☎ 064-261 684; fax 064-261 669), Brnik airport

Alpetour (☎ /fax 064-221 600), Brnik airport

Avis (☎ 168 7204; fax 374 151), World Trade Centre, Dunajska cesta 156, or through any Adria office

Avtoimpex (☎ 555 025; fax 322 615), Celovška cesta 150

Eurodollar (☎ 126 3118; fax 213 947), Štefanova ulica 13

Kompas Hertz (☎ 311 241; fax 572 088), Miklošičeva cesta 11

For sample rates and information on conditions, see the Car & Motorcycle section in the Getting Around chapter.

Taxi
Taxis, which can be hailed on the street or hired from ranks such as those near the train station, in front of the Slon hotel on Slovenska cesta or on Mestni trg, cost 150 to 200 SIT at flag fall and 130 to 160 SIT for each additional kilometre, depending on which zone you are travelling in. The per-hour waiting charge is between 1600 and 2000 SIT. You can call a taxi on 10 numbers: ☎ 9700 to ☎ 9709. Private taxis include Laguna (☎ 161 1204) and Katana (☎ 639 358).

Bicycle
Ljubljana is a city of cyclists and there are bike lanes and special traffic lights everywhere. Unfortunately, only a very few places rent them (1500 SIT per day). The TIC will give you a list of the following names, but you must make your own arrangements:

Društvo Koloklub (Bicycle Club; ☎ 133 9188), Tavčarjeva ulica 2, open weekdays 8 am to 4 pm

Kos Damjan (☎ 553 606), just north-west of the Ilirija hotel at Tugomerjeva ulica 35, open weekdays 9 am to 5 pm, Saturday and Sunday 9 am to 1 pm

Rog (☎ 315 868), Rozmanova ulica, open weekdays 8 am to 7 pm, Saturday till noon

Rog, which is just north of Ambrožev trg, is also a good place to buy new and reconditioned used bikes.

For information about organised bike tours, see Cycling in the Activities section of the Facts for the Visitor chapter.

AROUND LJUBLJANA
Let's face it, an awful lot in little Slovenia is 'around Ljubljana' and most of the towns and cities in Gorenjska, Primorska and Notranjska could actually be day trips from the capital. You can be in Bled in an hour, for example, and on the coast in less than two. Škofja Loka, Kamnik and Velika Planina are less than 30km away, and Cerknica is only 50km to the south-west.

Žale
Another Plečnik masterpiece, the monumental **Žale Cemetery** (Pokopališče Žale), 3km to the north-east of Center, has a series of chapels dedicated to the patron saints of Ljubljana's churches, and the entrance is an enormous two-storey arcade. It is a very peaceful, green place and 'home' to a number of Slovenian actors, writers, painters and a certain distinguished architect – Gospod Plečnik himself. You can reach Žale on bus No 2 or 7 (stop: Žale).

Šmarna Gora
This 669m hill above the Sava River, 12km north-west of Ljubljana, is a popular walking destination from Ljubljana and a mecca for hang-gliders and paragliders. Take bus No 15 from Slovenska cesta or Gosposvetska cesta to the Medno stop and begin walking. Another way to go is via the Smlednik bus from the main station and then follow the marked path from the 12th century **Smlednik Castle**. There's swimming and boating in **Zbilje Lake** nearby.

Gorenjska

Mountains and lakes are the big attraction in Gorenjska (Upper Carniola), the province that in many ways feels more 'Slovenian' than any other. The start of the Kamnik-Savinja Alps are a short drive from Ljubljana, and Triglav National Park contains most of Slovenia's share of the Julian Alps, with many peaks rising to well over 2000m. There's a lot of skiing here, and Gorenjska offers some of the best hiking in Europe. A mountain trek is an excellent way to meet other Slovenes in a relaxed environment so take advantage of this opportunity if you're in Gorenjska during the hiking season.

The lakes at Bled and Bohinj are also popular centres for any number of outdoor activities, but Gorenjska also has many of Slovenia's most attractive, historical towns. Škofja Loka, Kamnik, Kranj and Radovljica – to name just a few – are treasure troves of Gothic, Renaissance and baroque art and architecture and wonderful bases from which to explore this diverse and visually spectacular province.

Because of the difficulty of eking out a living in mountainous areas, the people of Gorenjska have a reputation in Slovenia for being on the, well, let's just say 'thrifty' side. You won't see evidence of this yourself, but you'll probably hear a fair few jokes like the ones made about the Scots.

KAMNIK
• *pop 9800* • *area code ☎061* • *postcode 1240*
This historical town 'in the bosom of the mountains' just 23km north-east of Ljubljana, is frequently given a miss by travellers en route to Bled or Bohinj. But Kamnik's tidy and attractive medieval core, with its houses and portals of hewn stone, balconies and arcades, is well worth a visit. It was declared a cultural and historical monument in 1986.

History
Established early in the 13th century under the Counts of Andechs and later claiming its

HIGHLIGHTS

• Take in the view from Mt Triglav, Slovenia's tallest peak
• Enjoy the trip by cable car to Velika Planina near Kamnik
• Gaze upon the painted burgher houses of Mestni trg in Škofja Loka
• Visit the fascinating Beekeeping Museum at Radovljica
• Discover the ironmongering village of Kropa
• Marvel at the Church of St John the Baptist at Bohinj, the most beautiful and evocative house of worship in Slovenia
• Explore Vintgar Gorge near Bled
• Experience the hair-raising drive up to and descent from Vršič Pass in the Julian Alps

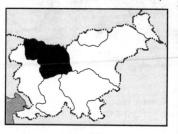

own mint and school, Kamnik (Stein in German) competed with Ljubljana and Kranj for economic and cultural dominance in Kranjska (Carniola) throughout the Middle Ages. The town was known for its large numbers of artisans and craftspeople, and it was on this rising middle class that Emperor Charles IV bestowed the massive forests around Kamniška Bistrica in the 14th century.

For centuries Kamnik controlled the pass in the Tuhinj Valley to the east that was indispensable for moving goods from the coastal areas to Štajerska and Koroška. But when the route was redirected via Trojane to the southeast in the 1600s, Kamnik fell into a deep sleep and only awakened in the late 19th century when the town was linked by rail to Ljubljana.

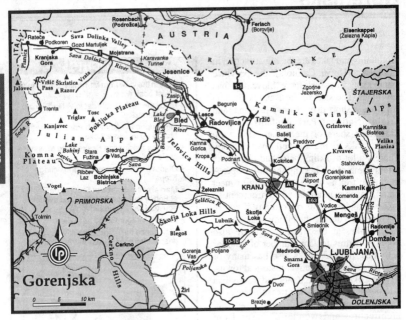

Gorenjska

Kamnik became a mecca for holidaying *Ljubljančani* at the turn of the century due to easy access to the Kamnik Alps and their popular thermal baths. The baths were destroyed during WWI and, though it remained a gateway in subsequent decades for hikers and skiers headed for the Velika Planina to the north, Kamnik began to industrialise and expand.

Orientation

Kamnik lies on the right bank of the Kamniška Bistrica River and south of the Kamnik Alps, which form part of the Kamnik-Savinja chain. The Old Town consists of two parts: medieval Glavni trg and the newer 'suburb' of Šutna, really just the southern continuation of the square.

Kamnik's bus station is near the river east of Glavni trg at the end of Prešernova ulica. The town has three train stations. The main one is on Kranjska cesta, south-west of

Šutna. Kamnik-Mesto, which is convenient for the Old Town and its sights, is on Kolodvorska ulica west of the Little Castle. Kamnik-Graben, the terminus of the Ljubljana-Kamnik line, is north-west of Glavni trg on Tunjiška cesta.

Information

Tourist Offices The tourist office (☎ 831 470; fax 831 176) at Glavni trg 23 can arrange bookings, find keys to locked sights and organise guides for excursions into the mountains. It also publishes a very useful English-language booklet called *What & Where – Guide to Kamnik and Environs*. The office is open daily June to September from 8 am to 6 pm. During the rest of the year weekday hours are 8 am to 4 pm and 9 am to 1 pm on Saturday. The Kamnik Alpine Society (☎ 831 345) at Šutna 42 will advise you on hiking guides for walking in the Kamnik Alps and weather conditions there.

The office is open weekdays from 8 am till noon (on Wednesday also from 1 to 5 pm).

Money SKB Banka, which has an ATM, is at Glavni trg 13. It is open from 8.30 am till noon and 2 to 5 pm on weekdays only. Just north, at No 14, you'll find a private exchange bureau called Publikum open to 6 pm weekdays and from 8.30 am till noon on Saturday.

Post & Communications The post office, open from 7 am to 7 pm weekdays and till noon on Saturday, is at Glavni trg 27.

Medical Services Kamnik's medical centre (☎ 831 611) is at Novi trg 26 on the opposite side of the Kamniška Bistrica River, over the bridge from Šolska ulica.

Things to See & Do

The **Franciscan monastery** (1492), a short distance to the south-west of the tourist office at Frančiškanski trg 2, has a rich library of theological, philosophical and sci- entific manuscripts and incunabula dating from the 15th to 18th centuries (including an original copy of the Bible translated by Jurij Dalmatin in 1584), and some valuable paint- ings by early Slovenian artists. Ask one of the priests in residence at the monastery (☎ 831 155) if you can have a look. Next door is the **Church of St James** with a chapel designed by Jože Plečnik, who also did the attractive beige-and-orange house with the glassed-in loggia (now the R Bar) on the eastern side of Glavni trg.

The **Little Castle** (Mali Grad), on a low hill above the southern end of Glavni trg, is Kamnik's most important historical sight. It has foundations going back to the 11th century, and this is where the town mint once stood. Behind the castle stand the ruins of a unique two-storey **Romanesque chapel** with 15th century frescoes in its lower nave and wall paintings by Janez Potočnik (1749-1834) in the presbytery. Ask the tourist office for the key if you care to have a look.

The Little Castle is home to Veronika, a legendary countess who was turned partly into a snake when she refused to help the Christian faithful build a church. Not only was the old gal mean but she was spiteful too. In her rage at having been asked to contrib- ute, she struck the entrance to the castle with her fist. If you look to the right of the portal as you go in, you'll see the imprint of her hand. Veronika continues to rule the treasure of the Little Castle and, in a way, the com- munity of Kamnik too. She appears both on the town seal and on the licence plate of every car registered here.

From the Little Castle, a walk along the quiet and attractive main street of **Šutna** is a trip back in time; check out the fine neoclas- sical house with columns at No 24, the stone relief of the Pascal lamb above the door at No 36 and the fresco indicating a butcher's shop sign at No 48.

In the centre of Šutna stands the **Parish Church of the Annunciation**, erected in the mid-18th century but with a detached belfry that shows an earlier church's Gothic origins. A short distance beyond at Šutna 33 is the **Sadnikar Collection**, a private museum – the first in Slovenia (1893) – of Gothic artwork, period furniture and paintings from the 18th century amassed by Josip Nikolaj Sadnikar (1863-1952), a local veterinarian and painter. It is opened by arrangement with the tourist office.

Zaprice Castle, with towers, ancient stone walls and an interesting chapel at Muzejski pot 3, was built in the 16th century but later converted into a baroque manor house. Today it's the home of the **Kamnik Museum**, with some dullish exhibits devoted to Kamnik's glory days and 18th century furniture. More interesting are the **granaries** from the 18th and 19th centuries outside that have been moved from the Tuhinj Valley. The museum is open May to September from Tuesday to Saturday at 9 am to noon and on Tuesday, Thursday, Friday and Saturday from 4 to 6 pm. During the rest of the year it opens in the morning from Tuesday to Sunday and in the afternoon only on Tuesday and Thursday.

The **Miha Maleš Gallery** on Glavni trg 1 contains works by the eponymous painter and graphic artist who was born in Kamnik in 1903. It keeps the same hours as the Kamnik Museum.

The **Old Castle** (Stari Grad), a 13th century ruin on Bergantov Hill east of the centre, can be reached from the end of Maistrova ulica on foot in about 20 minutes. There are excellent views of the Alps and the town from the top of this 585m hill.

On a hill east of Stahovica, a village about 4.5km north of Kamnik, is the **Church of Sts Primus & Felician** with some of the best medieval frescoes in Slovenia. It's about a

40-minute walk up from the village of **Črna** but make this 'pilgrimage' only on Saturday and Sunday when the church door is open. The frescoes on the north wall depict the Flight into Egypt, the Adoration of the Magi and Maria Misericordia – the Virgin Mary sheltering supplicants under her cloak in a scene similar to the one at the church in Ptujska Gora (see Around Ptuj in the Štajerska chapter). The painting on the south wall shows scenes from the life of Mary and is dated 1504.

Some 4km south of Kamnik is **Volčji**

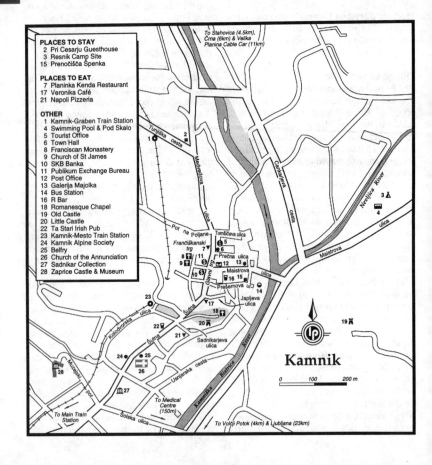

PLACES TO STAY
2 Pri Cesarju Guesthouse
3 Resnik Camp Site
15 Prenočišča Špenka

PLACES TO EAT
7 Planinka Kenda Restaurant
17 Veronika Café
21 Napoli Pizzeria

OTHER
1 Kamnik-Graben Train Station
4 Swimming Pool & Pod Skalo
5 Tourist Office
6 Town Hall
8 Franciscan Monastery
9 Church of St James
10 SKB Banka
11 Publikum Exchange Bureau
12 Post Office
13 Galerija Majolka
14 Bus Station
16 R Bar
18 Romanesque Chapel
19 Old Castle
20 Little Castle
22 Ta Stari Irish Pub
23 Kamnik-Mesto Train Station
24 Kamnik Alpine Society
25 Belfry
26 Church of the Annunciation
27 Sadnikar Collection
28 Zaprice Castle & Museum

Kamnik

0   100   200 m

Potok, Slovenia's largest and most beautiful arboretum. With the heart-shaped park of a former castle as its core, the 88-hectare arboretum counts more than 4500 varieties of trees, shrubs and flowers from all over the world. Volčji Potok's greenery, ponds and nearby Kamniška Bistrica make it a lovely place to visit on a warm summer's day. It's open daily March to October from 8 am to 6 pm, and the entry fee is 500/350 SIT for adults/children. Though five buses a day arrive here directly from Kamnik on weekdays, there's only one on Saturday and Sunday. If you're stuck, take the Radomlje bus, which stops close by.

The outdoor **swimming pool** near the camp site on Maistrova ulica is open mid-June to mid-September from 10 am to 6 pm (9 pm at weekends). Licences for fishing in the Kamniška Bistrica are available at the Gostilna Pri Planinskem Orlu (see Places to Stay) and cost DM28 a day.

Special Events

The big festival in Kamnik is National Costume Days (Dnevi Narodnih Noš), a festival held on the second Friday, Saturday and Sunday in September. A half-dozen stages are set up around town, and there's music, dancing, parades and general merrymaking. The event attracts people from all over Slovenia. Kamnik Evenings is a four-day festival of concerts held in mid-October.

There are big flower and horticultural shows at Volčji Potok in late April/early May and in early September.

Places to Stay

The tiny *Resnik* camp site (☎ 817 314) is north-east of the Old Town on the Nevljica River at Maistrova ulica 32. It is open from May to September and charges 300/200/200 SIT per person/car/tent site. There's a tennis court and the public swimming pool is adjacent, as is a popular gostilna called *Pod Skalo*, open till 10 pm (midnight on weekends).

With Ljubljana so close, Kamnik doesn't seem to have much need for a hotel – or budget accommodation. *Prenočišča Špenka*

(☎ 817 330), Prešernova ulica 14c, offers basic but very central accommodation in 11 rooms and breakfast for DM40 per person. *Pri Cesarju* (☎ 832 917), a 12-room guesthouse a bit farther afield at Tunjiška cesta 1, charges DM55/100 for singles/doubles.

Other accommodation can be found at a couple of gostilne in Stahovica on the road to Velika Planina and the village of Kamniška Bistrica. *Pri Planinskem Orlu* (☎ 825 410) at Stahovica 20 and *Pri Gamsu* (☎ 825 588) at Stahovica 31 have four or five rooms each and charge about DM30 per person for accommodation only.

Places to Eat

The *Napoli*, a pizzeria at Sadnikarjeva 5 south-west of the Little Castle, is open from 9 am to 10 pm from Monday to Saturday and from 1 pm on Sunday. The most convenient restaurant in Kamnik is *Planinka Kenda* opposite the tourist office at Glavni trg 19. It is open from Monday to Saturday from 8 am to 10 pm and on Sunday from 9 am to 5 pm. Lunch menus at 500 to 750 SIT are good value.

The *Kavarna Veronika*, on the corner of Glavni trg and Japljeva ulica, is a good place to cool your heels over a cup of something warm and a slice of cake. It's the most popular café in town and doubles as an art gallery. The Veronika is open daily till midnight or 1 am.

Entertainment

Lira, Slovenia's first choir (founded in 1882) and still going strong, occasionally gives local concerts. Ask the staff at the tourist office for information.

There are a couple of good pubs in town, including the *R Bar* in the house that Plečnik built on Glavni trg and *Ta Stari*, yet another Slovenian 'Irish pub' at Šutna 8. Ta Stari is open till midnight (10 pm on Sunday).

Things to Buy

Check out the interesting old clockmaker's at Maistrova ulica 1 near the post office. At No 11 of the same street, the Galerija Majolka sells souvenirs, paintings, porcelain and antiques. It is open from 9 am to 7 pm weekdays and till noon on Saturday.

Getting There & Away

Bus service is frequent – at least one departure every half-hour to and from Domžale, Komenda, Ljubljana, Mengeš, Radomlje and Stahovica. You can also reach Gornji Grad on between two and six buses a day, Kamniška Bistrica (three), Kranj (seven on weekdays, two on Saturday), Ljubno (two to five), Logarska Dolina (Logar Valley; one on Sunday at 6.45 am), Mozirje (one), Šentjakob (six) and Volčji Potok (five on weekdays, one daily at weekends).

Kamnik is on a direct rail line from Ljubljana (24km, one hour) via Domžale. Count on up to 17 trains a day in each direction. The line terminates at the Kamnik-Graben station.

VELIKA PLANINA
• *area code* ☎ 061

The so-called Great Highlands area, which reaches a height of 1666m, is a wonderful place to explore and is accessible to 1418m by cable car *(žičnica)* from the lower station 11km north of Kamnik. The six-minute ride is not for the skittish! You can also walk to Velika Planina from Stahovica, taking in the Church of Sts Primus & Felician above Črna along the way, in about three hours.

Velika Planina is where traditional dairy farmers graze their cattle between June and September. If you follow the road from the upper station up the hill for about 2km, you'll reach a highland plain filled with more than 50 shepherds huts and a small church dedicated to Our Lady of the Snows. The low-lying rounded buildings with conical roofs are unique to Velika Planina, and the design may be a legacy of ancient shepherds dating back as far as the Bronze Age. Today's silver-grey huts are replicas; the originals from around the turn of the century were burned to the ground by the Germans in WWII.

A circular walk of the plain and **Mala Planina** (1569m) to the south will take only a few hours. In summer, the friendly shepherds in their pointed green felt hats will sell you curd, sour milk and white cheese.

Velika Planina is a popular ski area with 6km of slopes. Depending on the snowfall, a chair lift ferries skiers up to Gradišče from the upper cable-car station daily between December and April (Friday to Sunday every hour, between 8 am and 5 pm at other times) and some of the six T-bars may be running. For information, contact the tourist office in Kamnik or the Kamnik Ski Club (☎ 817 228) at Medvedova ulica 10.

Places to Stay & Eat

There's quite a choice of accommodation in Velika Planina. Just a few steps from the upper station, the *Gostišče Šimnovec* (☎ 831 425) has 24 rooms with shared showers for DM17 per person. Among the mountain lodges offering accommodation, daily between June and September and at the weekend during the rest of the year, are *Domžalski Dom* (☎ 713 137 or mobile ☎ 0609-647 524) in Velika Planina and *Črnuški Dom* (☎ 724 316 or mobile ☎ 0609-639 317) in Mala Planina, each with nine multi-bed rooms.

At the lower cable-car station you'll find something to eat at the simple *Bife Pri Žičnici* (along with picnic tables and barbecue pits) open from 7.15 am to 8 pm (10 pm at weekends). In Velika Planina, the *Šimnovec* has a full restaurant open daily from 8 am to 10 pm, and there's an *okrepčevalnica* (snack bar) at Zeleni Rob about a kilometre up the hill open daily in season.

Getting There & Around

The cable-car station can be reached from Kamnik on three buses a day. From mid-June to September, the cable car runs every half-hour Monday to Thursday from 8 am to 6 pm and Friday, Saturday and Sunday till 8 pm. In winter (mid-December to March) the daily schedule is from 8 am to 6 pm. During the rest of the year it goes Monday to Thursday at 8 and 8.30 am, noon and 12.30, 4.30 and 5 pm and Friday to Sunday every hour from 8 am to 7 pm.

KAMNIŠKA BISTRICA

This pretty little settlement in a valley near the source of the Kamniška Bistrica River is 3km north of the Velika Planina lower cable-car station, and the *Dom v Kamniški Bistrici* (☎ 825 544) offers hostel-like accommodation in multi-bed rooms for DM22 per person (DM16 for members of the PZS or other climbing association). Check-in is from 7 am to 9 pm in summer, 8 am to 8 pm in winter.

Kamniška Bistrica is the springboard for some of the more ambitious and rewarding Kamnik Alps treks such as the ones to **Grintovec** (2558m; 11 hours return), **Brana** (2251m; eight hours) and **Planjava** (2394m; 10 hours).

The most popular hikes, though, are the easier, 3½-hour ones north-west to the mountain pass or saddle at **Kokra Saddle** (Kokrško Sedlo; 1791m) and north to **Kamnik Saddle** (Kamniško Sedlo; 1903m). On the other side of the latter lies Rinka Waterfall and Logarska Dolina (see the Upper Savinja Valley section of the Štajerska chapter). Each saddle has a mountain hut (☎ 831 345 for both): *Cojzova Koča* on Kokrško Sedlo and *Kamniška Koča* on Kamniško Sedlo. Both are open from 20 June to 10 October.

The main trails in the Kamnik Alps are well marked and pass numerous springs, waterfalls and caves. Guides are available from the tourist office in Kamnik, but the less energetic may be content to picnic around the lake near the hostel, cooling their drinks (or feet) in the blue Alpine water.

Kamniška Bistrica can be reached from Kamnik on three buses a day.

ŠKOFJA LOKA

• *pop 12,400* • *area code* ☎*064* • *postcode 4220*
Škofja Loka – 'Bishop's Meadow' – vies with Ptuj and Piran for being among the oldest settlements in Slovenia. Today the Old Town is protected as a historical and cultural monument (1987) and is among the most beautiful in Slovenia. When the castle and other old buildings are illuminated at night at the weekend, Škofja Loka takes on the appearance of a fairy-tale village.

History

In 973 German Emperor Otto II presented the Bavarian Bishops of Freising with the valleys along the Poljanščica and Selščica rivers. The point where the two tributaries merge to form the Sora River began to develop as a town.

The Freising bishops held control over Škofja Loka (Bischafflack in German) for more than eight centuries – and two actually met their maker in the town. Bishop Leopold drowned in the late 14th century when his horse slipped off the new bridge (no guard rails in those days) and Conrad was murdered three decades later by a greedy footman who wanted the bishop's 5000 gold ducats.

In the Middle Ages Škofja Loka developed as a trade centre along the Munich-Klagenfurt-Trieste route, doing particularly well in iron, linen and furs. A circular wall with five gates protected by guard towers was built around the town in 1318 to ensure that this success continued.

But it was all for naught. An army of the Counts of Celje breached the wall and burned the town to the ground in 1457; two decades later the Turks attacked. Then natural disasters struck: an earthquake in 1511 badly damaged the town, and several great fires at the end of the 17th century reduced most of Škofja Loka's finest buildings to ashes.

In 1803 the Habsburgs took possession of the town, and the advent of the railway later in the century put Škofja Loka on the road to industrialisation, especially in the field of textiles.

Orientation

The new part of Škofja Loka – without any redeeming qualities except that things of a practical nature are centred around Kapucinski trg – lies north of the Selščica River. The Old Town to the south consists of two squares – long streets really – called Mestni trg and Spodnji trg, which run southward from Cankarjev trg and the river. Mestni trg, which is the more beautiful and historically important, bans cars altogether while Spodnji trg (also known as Lontrg) remains a busy thoroughfare.

Škofja Loka's bus station is in Kapucinski trg at the footbridge leading to Cankarjev trg. The train station is 3km to the north-east, at the end of Kidričeva cesta, in the industrial suburb of Trata.

Information

Tourist Offices Škofja Loka's tourist office (☎/fax 620 268) is at Mestni trg 5 and opens on weekdays from 9 am to 7 pm and on Saturday till noon. The office sells maps and

souvenirs and has a series of handouts on a wide range of subjects – from the history of the town and local lace-making to hiking, fishing and what farms in the area offer accommodation. It also offers guided tours of the town and Loka Museum (600/450 SIT for adults/children).

The Škofja Loka Alpine Society (☎ 620 667) is at Mestni trg 38.

Money Gorenjska Banka, next to Kompas and the Transturist hotel at Kapucinski trg 7, is open Monday to Friday from 8 am to 6 pm

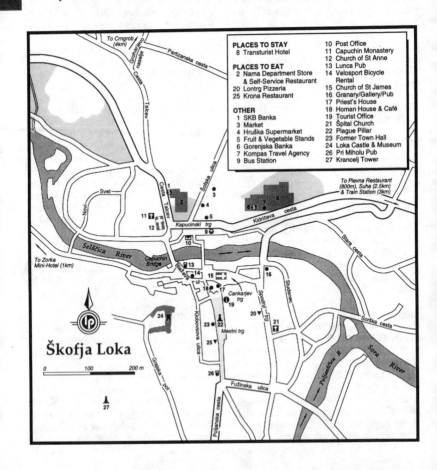

PLACES TO STAY
8 Transturist Hotel

PLACES TO EAT
2 Nama Department Store & Self-Service Restaurant
20 Lontrg Pizzeria
25 Krona Restaurant

OTHER
1 SKB Banka
3 Market
4 Hruška Supermarket
5 Fruit & Vegetable Stands
6 Gorenjska Banka
7 Kompas Travel Agency
9 Bus Station
10 Post Office
11 Capuchin Monastery
12 Church of St Anne
13 Lunca Pub
14 Velosport Bicycle Rental
15 Church of St James
16 Granary/Gallery/Pub
17 Priest's House
18 Homan House & Café
19 Tourist Office
21 Špital Church
22 Plague Pillar
23 Former Town Hall
24 Loka Castle & Museum
26 Pri Miholu Pub
27 Krancelj Tower

Škofja Loka

0   100   200 m

and on Saturday till noon. There's an SKB Banka branch with an ATM at Kapucinski trg 3 in the same building as the Nama department store. It is open on weekdays only from 8.30 am till noon and from 2 to 5 pm.

Post & Communications The post office, open on weekdays from 7 am to 7 pm and on Saturday till noon, is just west of the bus station between the footbridge and Capuchin Bridge at Kapucinski trg 9.

Travel Agency Kompas (☎ 624 027) has an office next to the Transturist hotel at Kapucinski trg 8. It is open weekdays from 9 am to 7 pm and on Saturday till noon.

Old Town
Parts of the **Parish Church of St James** in Cankarjev trg date back to the 13th century, but its most important elements – the nave, the presbytery with star vaulting (1524) and the tall bell tower (1532) – were added over the next three centuries. On either side of the choir are altars made of black marble that were designed in about 1700. These are very unusual for a time and place when baroque-style gilded wood and gypsum were all the rage. On the vaulted ceiling are bosses showing portraits of the Freising bishops, saints, workers with shears and a blacksmith, who probably contributed handsomely to the church. Two crescent moons in the presbytery are reminders of the Turkish presence in Škofja Loka. The dozen or so modern lamps and the baptismal font were designed by Jože Plečnik.

Opposite the church's main entrance on the south side is the **Priest's House**, part of a fortified aristocratic manor house built in the late 16th century. Below the rounded projection on the corner are strange consoles of animal heads.

The colourful 16th century burgher houses on **Mestni trg**, rebuilt after that terrible earthquake in 1511, have earned the town the nickname 'Painted Loka'. Almost every one is of historical and architectural importance, and plaques in English and Slovene explain their significance. Among the more

impressive is **Homan House** at No 2 with bits of frescoes of St Christopher and of a warrior. The **former town hall** at No 35 is remarkable for its three-storey Gothic courtyard and the 17th century frescoes on its façade. **Martin House** at No 26 leans on part of the old town wall. It has a wooden 1st floor, a late Gothic portal and a vaulted entrance hall. The **plague pillar** erected in the square in 1751 has recently been renovated.

Klobovsova ulica, a narrow street west of Homan House, leads to Loka Castle and the remains of **Krancelj Tower**.

Spodnji trg to the east of Mestni trg was where the poorer folk lived in the Middle Ages; after the devastating fire of 1698, most of them couldn't afford to rebuild the square so the houses remained two-storey and relatively modest. Of interest at the northern end at No 2 is the 16th century **granary** (kašča), where the town's grain stores, collected as taxes, were once kept. It now contains a pub and winery, a bank and the **France Mihelič Gallery**, with the works of the artist born in nearby Virmaše in 1907 (open Tuesday to Sunday from noon to 5 pm). The **Špital Church** at Spodnji trg 9 has an opulent baroque gold altar. The church was built in 1720 around the town's almshouse, and the poor lived in the cells of the courtyard building behind.

Loka Castle
The town castle, which looks down over Škofja Loka from a grassy hill west of Mestni trg at Grajska pot 13, was built in the 13th century but extensively renovated after the earthquake. Today it houses the **Loka Museum** (Loški Muzej), which has one of the best ethnographical collections in Slovenia.

The area around Škofja Loka was famous for its smiths and lace-makers, and there are lots of ornate guild chests on display. The copies of the 15th century frescoes from the churches at Crngrob and Suha (see Around Škofja Loka) in the corridors are much clearer than most of the originals *in situ*. Have a good look at these before you make the trip

– and don't miss the spectacular **Golden Altars** taken from a church destroyed during WWII in Dražgoše, north-west of Škofja Loka.

The Loka Museum is open daily, except Monday, from April to October from 9 am to 5 pm. During the rest of the year it's open on Saturday and Sunday only. Entry is 350/250 SIT for adults/children or 400/300 SIT if you want a guided tour.

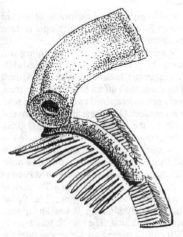

Combs made from cattle and rams' horns are on display in the Loka Museum.

Other Sights

The 18th century **Capuchin monastery** west of the bus station at Kapucinski trg 2 has a priceless **library** of medieval manuscripts, including the *Škofja Loka Passion*, a processional with dramatic elements, from around 1720. The library can be visited by prior arrangement. Contact the tourist office or the monastery directly (☎ 620 970).

The stone **Capuchin Bridge** leading from the monastery's **Church of St Anne** (1710) dates from the 14th century and is an excellent vantage point for the Old Town and castle as well as the river with its deep gorge, dams, abandoned mills and 18th century barracks. The area north-west of the bridge is called Novi Svet (New World) because it was settled after the Old Town. The statue on the bridge is of St John Nepomucen, a Bohemian prelate who was martyred in the 14th century by being thrown from Charles Bridge in Prague, the city where executioners usually favoured windows.

A dry goods **market** is held on Mestni trg and Cankarjev trg on the second Wednesday of every month.

Activities

The Škofja Loka Hills to the west, an area of steep slopes, deep valleys and ravines, is an excellent area for day-long walks or hikes of a longer duration and there are several huts with accommodation in the area. Before you set out, buy a copy of the 1:50,000 hiking map *Škofjeloško in Cerkljansko Hribovje* (Škofja Loka and Cerkno Hills) available from the tourist office for 1070 SIT, and ask the tourist office for a copy of its *Crngrob-Planica-Križna Gora* hiking pamphlet in English.

One of the easiest trips is to **Lubnik**, a 1025m peak north-west of the Old Town, which can be reached on foot in two hours via Vincarje or the castle ruins near Gabrovo. Start the walk from Klobovsova ulica in Mestni trg. A mountain hut near the summit called *Dom na Lubniku* (☎ 620 501 or ☎ 631 453) has 18 beds and is open daily from April to December and at the weekend from January to March.

A hike to 1562m **Blegoš** farther west would be much more demanding, but it only takes about three hours from Hotavlje, a village a couple of kilometres from Gorenja Vas and accessible by bus from Škofja Loka. There are two huts in the area. *Koča na Blegošu* (☎ 620 667 or mobile ☎ 0609-614 587) has 61 beds and is open daily from June to September and at weekends in May and October. *Zavetišče na Jelencih* (☎ 681 240), about 2km to the south-west, has 20 beds and is open at weekends only from November to April. If you don't want to hike all the way to Blegoš, there's the eight-bed *Dom na Slajki* (☎ 681 662), which is less than 3km from Hotavlje. It's only open at weekends in summer though.

The ski centre at **Stari Vrh** (1217m), 12km west of Škofja Loka, is situated at an altitude of 1200m and covers 65 hectares of ski slopes and 3km of trails. There are four T-bar tows and a chair lift. Accommodation here is at the *Koča na Starem Vrhu* (☎ 688 007), open daily in summer and winter and on Saturday and Sunday only in spring and autumn, with five rooms and 16 beds, or at *farmhouse No 3* (☎ 688 032) in the village of Zavpreval.

Special Events
A music festival called Pod Homanovo Lipo takes place under the big linden trees in front of Homan House on Mestni trg every Friday evening in July and August.

Places to Stay
Smlednik camp site (☎ 627 002) in Drago-čajna, 11km to the east, is the closest camping ground to Škofja Loka. It is situated between two small lakes and has a nudist beach. Smlednik, open from May to mid-October, charges 720 SIT per person per night.

Škofja Loka is not overly endowed with places to lay your weary head. The tourist office can organise *private rooms*, including one at Grajska pot 8 (☎ 620 509) for DM25 to DM35 per person, but it has a very short list. There are lots of *farmhouses* with accommodation but most are around Poljane, 13km to the south-west.

Zorka (☎ 620 986), a 'mini-hotel' in the suburb of Vincarje (house No 15) about a kilometre west of the bus station, has rooms with showers for about DM35 per person. The 48-room *Transturist* (☎ 624 026; fax 624 096) at Kapucinski trg 9 is grey, tall, depressing and relatively expensive. Singles with breakfast and shower are 5710 SIT, doubles 8620 SIT.

Places to Eat
There's a *self-service restaurant* on the 2nd floor of the *Nama* department store at Kapucinski trg 1 opposite the post office; enter from Cesta Talcev. *Plevna*, a 'gallery restaurant' at Kidričeva cesta 16 about 800m

to the east, is a very popular spot with Lokans. Dishes are simple but tasty and inexpensive. Plevna is open from Wednesday to Sunday from noon to 11 pm. It closes in August.

The *Homan* in historical Homan House at Mestni trg 2 is essentially a pub and a café but serves pizza and salads too. In warm weather, tables are set out on Mestni trg under the giant linden trees. Homan is open daily till 11 pm. There's more pizza available at the *Lontrg* at Spodnji trg 33. It's open from 9 am to 10 pm daily.

Krona, in an old town house at Mestni trg 32, is the best restaurant in Škofja Loka, with tasteful artwork on the walls, flowers on the table, friendly service and reasonably priced meals. It is open daily from 10 am to 10 pm (9 pm at the weekend).

There are *fruit and vegetable stands* on Kapucinski trg across from the bus station; the *market* is held on Tuesday, Thursday and Saturday mornings on Šolska ulica. The *Hruška* supermarket at Šolska ulica 2 is open weekdays from 8 am to noon and 3 to 7 pm and on Saturday morning.

Entertainment
Škofja Loka has a number of pleasant pubs including *Lunca* at Blaževa ulica 10 and *Pri Miholu*, built into part of the defence walls at Poljane Gate at Mestni trg 24. They are usually open daily till about 11 pm. There's a pleasant wine and beer cellar called *Kašča* in the old town granary at Spodnji trg 2 open till midnight (8 pm on Sunday).

Getting There & Away
Count on at least hourly buses to Kranj and Ljubljana but otherwise bus service from Škofja Loka is only adequate. Other destinations include: Bled via Radovljica (one bus a day), Cerkno (one to three), Nova Gorica (one at the weekend), Piran (one from late June to September), Sorica (four to seven), Soriška Planina (two at the weekend), Zali Log (five), Železniki and Žiri (six to 10).

Škofja Loka can be reached by up to 15 trains a day from Ljubljana (20km; 20 minutes) via Medvode. An equal number continue on to Kranj, Radovljica, Lesce-Bled and Jesenice (44km; 50 minutes). About 10 of these cross the border for Villach in Austria.

Getting Around

Local buses make the run between the train station in Trata and the bus station on Kapucinski trg. You can order a taxi on ☎ 622 195. Velosport at Blaževa ulica 2 rents mountain bikes and bicycles. It is open weekdays from 9 am till noon and 4 to 7 pm and on Saturday morning.

AROUND ŠKOFJA LOKA

Suha

The 15th century **Church of St John the Baptist** at Suha, about 2.5km east of the bus station in Škofja Loka, is unexceptional except for the presbytery which has an interior completely covered with amazing **frescoes** by Jernej of Loka. The paintings on the vaults show scenes from the life of Christ, the coronation of Mary and various Apostles. The panels below depict the five wise and five foolish virgins (the latter forgot to put oil in their lamps and were thus excluded from the wedding celebrations, according to Christ's parable reported in the Gospel of St Matthew). Inside the arch is a frightening scene from the Last Judgment.

If the church is locked, request the key from the house at No 45, the first building on the right as you enter Suha village and about 150m beyond the church.

Crngrob

The **Church of the Annunciation** at Crngrob, about 4km north of Škofja Loka, has one of the most priceless frescoes in Slovenia. Look for it on the outside wall under a 19th century portico near the church entrance. Called **Holy Sunday** (Sveta Nedelja) and produced in the workshop of Johannes de Laibaco (John of Ljubljana) in 1470, it explains in pictures what good Christians do on Sunday (pray, go to Mass, help the sick) and what they do *not* do (gamble, drink, play bowls or fight). The consequence of doing any of the latter, of

course, is damnation – vividly illustrated with souls being swallowed whole by a demon. On the south wall there's a large fresco of St Christopher from the same era.

The interior of the church, which was built and modified between the 14th and 17th centuries, contains more medieval frescoes on the north wall as well as the largest gilded altar in Slovenia, built by Jurij Skarnos in 1652. The spectacular organ was made around the same time. The stellar vaulting of the presbytery, painted in light red, blue and yellow, has a number of bosses portraying the Virgin Mary, the Bishops of Freising and a man on a horse who was probably a benefactor.

The people at the house (No 10) nearest the church hold the keys. You can eat at *Gostilna Crngrob* at house No 13, which is open every day, except Wednesday, till 11 pm, and there is accommodation and horses for rent at the four-room *Pri Marku* farmhouse (☎ 631 626) at house No 5.

Crngrob is easily accessible on foot or by bicycle from Škofja Loka via Groharjevo naselje, which runs north from Cesta Talcev and the Capuchin monastery. An alternative is to take the bus bound for Kranj, get off at the village of Dorfarje and walk west for about 1.5km.

KRANJ

• pop 36,700 • area code ☎064 • postcode 4000

Situated at the foot of the Kamnik-Savinja Alps with the snowcapped peak of Storžič (2132m) and others looming to the north, Kranj is Slovenia's fourth largest and most industrialised city with its fair share of unemployment and graffiti (one favourite is the ubiquitous 'Kranjsterdam'). But the casual traveller wouldn't have to know anything about all that. The attractive Old Town, sitting on an escarpment above the confluence of the Sava and Kokra rivers that barely measures 1km by 250m, contains everything of interest in Kranj.

History

A secondary Roman road linking Emona (Ljubljana) and Virunum (near today's

Klagenfurt in Austria) ran through Kranj until about the 5th century; 100 years later the Langobards established a base here. They were followed by the early Slavs, whose large burial grounds can be partly seen below the floor of the Gorenjska Museum.

In the 11th century, Kranj (Krainburg in German) was an important border stronghold of the German Frankish counts in their battles with the Hungarians, and the town gave its name to the entire region – Kranjska (Carniola in English). It was also an important market and ecclesiastical centre and, within 200 years, Kranj was granted town status by the new rulers, the Bavarian Counts of Andechs. More wealth came with the development of iron mining and foundries and when the progressive Protestant movement reached Gorenjska, it was centred in Kranj.

Kranj grew faster after the arrival of the railway in 1870 and is home to much of Slovenia's textile industry and Iskra, the electrical appliance company. As was the case in the Middle Ages, Kranj is known for its trade and industrial fairs.

Orientation

Kranj's Old Town is essentially three pedestrian streets running north to south. The main one begins as Prešernova ulica at Maistrov trg and changes its name to Cankarjeva ulica at Glavni trg, the main square and market place in medieval times. Cankarjeva ulica ends, like everything else, at Pungert, the 'Land's End' at the tip of the promontory.

'New Kranj' spreads in every direction but especially northward to Zlato Polje and to the south-east to Planina. Brnik airport is 15km south-east of Kranj.

Kranj's bus station is about 600m north of Maistrov trg on Stošičeva ulica. The train station lies below the Old Town to the west, on the right bank of the Sava. To reach the Old Town from the station, follow Kolodvorkska cesta south then east, cross the bridge over the Sava and walk up Vodopivčeva ulica to the Plečnik stairway. If you're headed for the Jelen or Creina hotels,

continue north along Ljubljanska cesta after crossing the bridge.

Information

Tourist Offices The tourist office (☎ 211 361; fax 221 880) at Koroška cesta 29 is open from 7.30 am to 7 pm on weekdays and 9 am to 1 pm on Saturday. The office stocks the English-language *Tourist Guide of Kranj & Its Environs* (500 SIT), which could be very useful if you plan to spend a fair bit of time in this part of Gorenjska. It has eight motoring day trips.

The Kranj Alpine Society (☎ 225 184) is at Koroška cesta 27.

Money Gorenjska Banka has a branch at Prešernova ulica 6, open from 9 to 11.30 am and 2 to 5 pm on weekdays and till noon on Saturday. The main branch is on Bleiweisova cesta near the tourist office. SKB Banka in the Creina hotel building at Koroška cesta 5 has an ATM and is open weekdays from 8.30 am till noon and 2 to 5 pm.

Post & Communications The main post office in Kranj is several hundred metres north-east of the bus station at Dražgoška ulica 8. A much more convenient branch is at Poštna ulica 4 east of Glavni trg. It is open weekdays from 7 am to 7 pm and on Saturday till noon.

Travel Agency Kompas (☎ 224 100) at the Creina hotel opens weekdays from 8 am to 7 pm and till noon on Saturday.

Bookshop Mladinska Knjiga at Maistrov trg 1 has maps as well as English-language guides and books. It is open from 8 am to 7 pm on weekdays and till noon on Saturday.

Walking Tour

You can see virtually everything of note in Kranj by following Prešernova ulica and Cankarjeva ulica to Pungert and returning to Maistrov trg via Tomšičeva ulica. Most of the important sights have plaques in English and are also marked with numbers. These

GORENJSKA

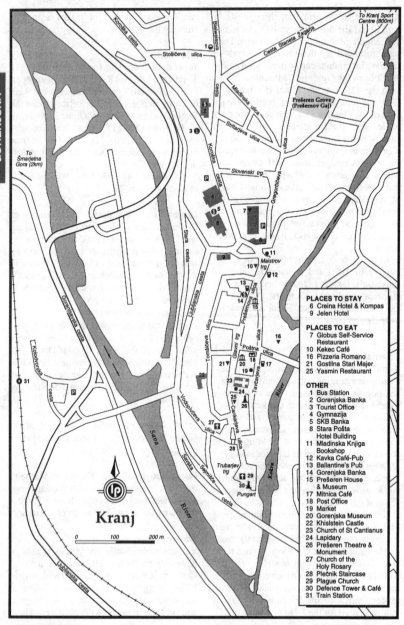

Kranj

0   100   200 m

PLACES TO STAY
6 Creina Hotel & Kompas
9 Jelen Hotel

PLACES TO EAT
7 Globus Self-Service
   Restaurant
10 Kekec Café
16 Pizzeria Romano
21 Gostilna Stari Majer
25 Yasmin Restaurant

OTHER
1 Bus Station
2 Gorenjska Banka
3 Tourist Office
4 Gymnazija
5 SKB Banka
8 Stara Pošta
   Hotel Building
11 Mladinska Knjiga
   Bookshop
12 Kavka Café-Pub
13 Ballantine's Pub
14 Gorenjska Banka
15 Prešeren House
   & Museum
17 Mitnica Café
18 Post Office
19 Market
20 Gorenjska Museum
22 Khislstein Castle
23 Church of St Cantianus
24 Lapidary
26 Prešeren Theatre &
   Monument
27 Church of the
   Holy Rosary
28 Plečnik Staircase
29 Plague Church
30 Defence Tower & Café
31 Train Station

correspond to the map included with the *Tourist Guide of Kranj & Its Environs.*

Maistrov trg was the site of the upper town gates in the 15th century and was the most vulnerable part of Kranj; the steep Kokra Canyon protected the town on the eastern side and thick walls did the trick on the west from Pungert as far as the square. The **Špital Tower**, one of seven along the wall, forms part of a shop at Maistrov trg 3. The unusual Art Deco building with the three statues facing the square to the north is the **former Stara Pošta hotel** built in the 1930s.

Prešeren House (Prešernova Hiša) at Prešernova ulica 7 was home to the poet France Prešeren (1800-49) for the last two years of his life, and he died in the front bedroom. The **Prešeren Memorial Museum** contained in five rooms here is devoted to his life and work but, sadly, the explanatory notes next to his letters, diaries and manuscripts are in Slovene only. From May to September, the museum is open Tuesday to Friday from 10 am till noon and from 5 to 7 pm. On Saturday and Sunday it opens in the morning only. During the rest of the year the hours are the same, except the museum opens in the afternoon from Tuesday to Friday from 4 to 6 pm. The 200/100 SIT admission charge for adults/children allows entry to the Gorenjska Museum as well. Prešeren is buried in the parish cemetery, now called **Prešeren Grove** (Prešernov Gaj), about 500m to the north.

Glavni trg is a beautiful square of Gothic and Renaissance buildings; the ones on the western side with their painted façades, vaulted hallways and arched courtyards are masterpieces. The 16th century one (actually *ones* as they were formerly two houses joined together) opposite at Glavni trg 4 was once the town hall. Today it contains the **Gorenjska Museum**.

Below the floor of the vaulted vestibule, **Slavic tombs** from the 9th and 10th centuries can be seen through glass panels. The museum's upper floors contain a lovely Renaissance **Great Hall** with carved wooden doors and ceiling (it is now used for civil wedding ceremonies), awful bronze sculp-

tures by Lojze Dolinar (1893-1970) – he did the revolutionary ones still standing in Slovenski trg, opposite the attractive **Gymnazija** (1898) and the Creina hotel – and history and folk art collections. Among the eye-catching bits and bobs lying around is a large porcelain stove topped with a Turk's turbaned head, an embroidered sheepskin coat called a *kožuh* and a child's toy of a devil sharpening a gossip's tongue on a grindstone (a common motif in Slovenian folk art and one that always makes me wonder whether or not Slovenes like a bit of gossip). The museum keeps the same hours as Prešeren House.

Glavni trg's pride and joy, though, is the **Church of St Cantianus** (Sveti Kancijan), which was built onto part of an older church starting in about 1400. It is the best example of a hall church – one with nave and aisles of equal height – in Slovenia and was the model for many others. There are some 15th century frescoes of angels with musical instruments on the stellar vaulting of the nave. The Mount of Olives relief in the arch above the main portal is worth a look, as is the modern altar designed by Ivan Vurnik (1884-1971).

Below the northern side of the church there are more old bones from early Slav graves and a medieval **ossuary**. On the south wall is a **lapidary** of medieval tombstones and nearby the **Fountain of St John Nepomucen**, with a stone statue of the 14th century Bohemian martyr complete with a doleful looking octopus.

The **Prešeren Theatre** is across the plaza at Glavni trg 6. The portico near the **Prešeren Monument** (showing a rather rugged-looking and heroic Dr France) was designed by Jože Plečnik in the early 1950s.

Walk down Cankarjeva ulica and you'll pass the **Church of the Holy Rosary**, built in the 16th century and a Protestant sanctuary during the Reformation. The church was 'attacked' by neo-Gothic restorers in 1892 and 'so renovated that it is of little importance artistically or historically', we are told on the outside. Beside the church are arcades, a fountain and a **staircase** designed in the late 1950s by Plečnik to give Kranj a monumental entrance up from the Sava River. This was where the lower town gates once stood.

Pungert is the end of the line for the Old Town. Here you'll find another old church, sometimes called the **Plague Church**, built during a time of pestilence in the 1470s. It contains some important artwork, including a painting dedicated to the three 'intercessors against the plague' – Sts Rok, Fabian and Sebastian – by the Austrian baroque artist Martin Johann Kremser-Schmidt (1718-1801). It is now used by Serbian Orthodox Christians. A three-storey **defence tower**, the only one in Kranj entirely preserved, was built in the 16th century. There is a café-gallery on the ground floor.

If you return to the Church of the Holy Rosary and head north on Tomšičeva ulica, you'll come to a restored section of the **town wall** and **Khislstein Castle** at No 44. Part of this stronghold was built during the Turkish invasions of the 15th century but mostly it's Renaissance. Today its glassed-in arcades and upper floors house the offices of several cultural institutes.

Activities

The Kranj Sport Centre (☎ 211 176) at Partizanska cesta 37, about 1.5km north-east of Maistrov trg, has tennis courts and both a covered and outdoor swimming pool.

A very easy destination for a walk is **Šmarjetna Gora**, a 643m hill 3km to the north-west of the Old Town, where a fort stood during the Hallstatt period. On top of the hill is the reconstructed **Church of St Margaret** and the Bellevue hotel. The views from here of Kranj, the Alps and the Sava River are astonishing; on a clear day you might be able to see Bled and Ljubljana, each some 30km away in opposite directions.

Special Events

It may sound like a bit of a schlep but if you happen to be in Kranj in mid-July, follow the flocks to **Jezersko** for the annual Shepherds' Ball (Ovčarski Bal). It's a day and evening of folk music, dancing and drinking *žganje* (brandy) – an ovine alternative to the bovine

event in Bohinj (see Special Events in that section). Jezersko, on the Austrian border 28km north-east of Kranj and easily accessible by car or bus, was a popular health resort before WWII. Today it is an unspoiled area in the shadow of Grintovec with a delightful Alpine lake, hiking trails, old farmhouses and mountain huts. A good hiking map for this area is the 1:50,000 *Karavanke* one from PZS.

Places to Stay

The tourist office can arrange *private rooms* for about DM25 per person, but most are in the boring and distant (5 to 7km) housing estates to the north or north-east.

For what it is, the *Jelen* hotel (☎ 211 466; fax 211 857), a run-down, three-storey pile at Ljubljanska cesta 1, is pretty pricey: singles/doubles/triples with shower cost 4550/6100/6750 SIT.

Just opposite at Koroška cesta 5, the brick-and-wood *Creina* hotel (☎ 224 550; fax 222 483) with 89 rooms is vastly superior in comfort and style at a price; this is the place for Austrian business people, tour groups headed for the Alps and airline crews who don't want to travel all the way to Ljubljana from Brnik. Singles with shower and breakfast are DM75 to DM95, doubles DM100 to DM140. Most rooms have TV and direct-dial telephones. There's a wine cellar *(vinoteka)* in the basement open Monday to Saturday from noon to 11 pm.

The *Bellevue* hotel (☎ 311 211; fax 312 122) atop Šmarjetna Gora (see Activities) has 31 beds and a very pleasant restaurant open 9 am till midnight (to 2 am Friday and Saturday).

Places to Eat

The cheapest place for a meal in Kranj is the *Globus* self-service restaurant in the north-west corner of the Globus department store on Koroška cesta. For 450 SIT you get half a chicken with potatoes or macaroni with some sort of meat and salad. It's open weekdays from 8 am to 7 pm and till 1 pm on Saturday.

Pizzeria Romano at Tavčarjeva ulica 31 north-east of the post office, serves a novel triumvirate: pizza, pasta and 'dishes made

STEVE FALLON

STEVE FALLON

STEVE FALLON

A: Wayside shrine, Trg Kropa, Kropa, Gorenjska

B: Medieval fresco in Bohinj's Church of St John the Baptist, Gorenjska

C: Looking across Lake Bled to the Island Church, Bled Castle and Mt Stol (2236m), Gorenjska

STEVE FALLON

Sheep grazing near the Vršič Pass in the Julian Alps, Gorenjska

from horsemeat'. It's open from 10 am to 10 pm (from 4 pm on Sunday).

Kekec, a café at Maistrov trg 13 and open Monday to Saturday till 7 pm, has decent sandwiches and salads while the stick-to-the-ribs Slovenian dishes at *Gostilna Stari Majer* at Glavni trg 16 will keep you going for longer than you'd think.

A favourite place to eat in Kranj is the *Yasmin* at Cankarjeva ulica 1, a combined café-restaurant, which serves well prepared Continental food with a Slovenian touch and some good vegetarian dishes; try the cheese štruklji (dumplings). The café is open daily from 9 am till midnight, the restaurant from noon.

The large *market* selling fruit and vegetables north-east of the Church of St Cantianus is open from 6 am to 6 pm from mid-March to mid-October and from 7 am to 3 pm during the rest of the year.

Entertainment

Prešeren Theatre (☎ 222 701) at Glavni trg 6 is very active, staging four plays with up to 200 performances a year. Concerts – both classical and popular – are held in the courtyard of Khislstein Castle in summer and sometimes at the Church of St Cantianus during the year.

Maistrov trg and Prešernova ulica are home to a number of pleasant pubs and cafés. One of the more unusual ones is *Kavka*, a lively café-bar-gallery up the stairs at Maistrov trg 8. It is open from 8 or 9 am till midnight Monday to Saturday and from 6 pm on Sunday. *Mitnica*, a lovely *kavarna* in the basement of a 16th century toll house at Tavčarjeva ulica 35, is just the place to relax in Kranj on a warm afternoon. There's live music on Thursday and Sunday from 6 pm. Another decent pub is *Ballantine's* at Prešernova ulica 2.

The *Trezor* disco at the Creina hotel caters to a mature and well heeled set Thursday to Saturday from 9 pm to 4 am.

Getting There & Away

Bus Buses leave Kranj for Bled, Bohinj, Brnik airport, Cerklje, Jesenice, Ljubljana, Medvode, Piran, Preddvor, Predoslje, Rad-

ovljica, Rateče-Planica via Kranjska Gora, Škofja Loka, Tržič and Vodice.

You can also reach Bašelj via Preddvor six times a day, Bohinjska Bistrica (one), Bovec via Kranjska Gora and the Vršič Pass (one bus a day in July and August), Brezje (one from May to September), Jezersko (five), Kamnik (two), Kropa (one or two), Maribor (one at weekends), Novo Mesto (one or two), Vinica (one at weekends) and Zali Log (on Sunday from May to September). There's a bus to Varaždin in Croatia on Saturday and Sunday.

Train Up to 15 trains a day pass through Kranj from Ljubljana (29km; 30 minutes) via Medvode and Škofja Loka. They carry on to Radovljica, Lesce-Bled and Jesenice (35km; 40 minutes), where about 10 cross the border for Villach in Austria.

Getting Around

Local buses make the run from the train station to the bus terminus on Stošičeva ulica if you don't feel like walking. You can ring a local taxi on ☎ 226 100.

Valy (☎ 245 007) at Cesta na Brdo 52, north-east of the Old Town, rents bikes for 1000 SIT a day.

AROUND KRANJ
• *area code* ☎ 064
Brdo Castle
Until recently, 16th century Brdo Castle at Predoslje, about 5km north-east of Kranj, was for official state guests only. Though it is still managed by the Protocol Service of the Republic of Slovenia, now anyone can visit or even stay, provided they have the dosh.

The castle was long the property of the aristocratic and philanthropic Zois (sometimes spelled Cois) family, the Slovenian equivalent to the Széchenyi clan in Hungary. It has two towers on the northern side, corridors crammed with artwork and a library containing a priceless copy of the Bible translated by Protestant reformer Jurij Dalmatin (1547-89). Brdo is surrounded by lovely parkland and a protected 500-hectare forest. You can fish in one of 11 lakes stocked with trout, carp and pike (1500 SIT per day),

GORENJSKA

play tennis or ride horses for 1000 SIT per hour (1500 SIT for a one-hour lesson). Visitors not staying at Brdo may have to pay a fee of 500 SIT to enter the park.

Accommodation for most people here is at the 68-room *Kokra* hotel (☎ 221 133; fax 221 551), where very run-of-the-mill singles are DM82 to DM116 and doubles DM128 to DM190, or its sister hotel, the 32-room *Gaber* (☎ /fax same) next door with singles for DM75 to DM95 and doubles DM114 to DM154. Of course if you're not 'most people' and are very flush indeed, a 1st class suite in *Brdo Castle* (☎ /fax same) can be had for DM1833 (or a mere DM1078 for a 3rd class one). State guests, who are still put up here, probably get a discount.

Strmol Castle

The 13th century Strmol Castle (☎/fax at Brdo Castle), near Cerklje 8km east of Brdo, is another manor house in the Protocol Service's stable. There are not a lot of recreational facilities here, but if you want to live like a count or countess for a day, DM1078 gets you a suite and DM430 a single room. The tourist tax is DM1.20.

Krvavec

The ski centre at Krvavec (☎ 421 180 or ☎ 222 579 in Kranj), 17km to the north-east of Kranj, is one of the most popular (and crowded) in Slovenia. A cable car transports you up to the centre at 1450m and a dozen chair lifts and T-bar tows serve the 25km of slopes and 6km of cross-country runs. Krvavec is also an excellent starting point for hikes in summer to **Kriška Planina** or **Jezerca**, about an hour's walk from the upper station of the cable car.

RADOVLJICA

• *pop 6200* • *area code ☎064* • *postcode 4240*
A charming town full of historical buildings, Radovljica enjoys an enviable position atop an outcrop 75m above a wide plain called the Dežela (Country). A short distance to the west, two branches of the Sava come together to form Slovenia's longest and mightiest river.

Radovljica (Ratmansdorf in German) was settled by the early Slavs and grew into an important market town by the early 14th century. With increased trade on the river and the iron forgeries at nearby Kropa and Kamna Gorica, Radovljica expanded and the town was built around a large rectangular square fortified with a wall and defence towers. Radovljica's affluence in the Middle Ages can be seen in the lovely buildings still lining Linhartov trg today.

Radovljica is an easy day trip from Bled, just 6km to the north-west.

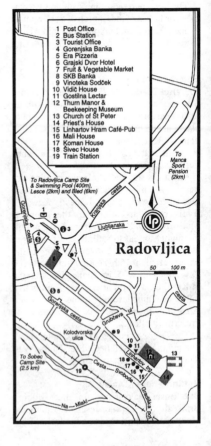

1 Post Office
2 Bus Station
3 Tourist Office
4 Gorenjska Banka
5 Era Pizzeria
6 Grajski Dvor Hotel
7 Fruit & Vegetable Market
8 SKB Banka
9 Vinoteka Sodček
10 Vidič House
11 Gostilna Lectar
12 Thurn Manor & Beekeeping Museum
13 Church of St Peter
14 Priest's House
15 Linhartov Hram Café-Pub
16 Mali House
17 Koman House
18 Šivec House
19 Train Station

Radovljica

0   50   100 m

Orientation

The centre of old Radovljica is Linhartov trg, a protected historical and cultural monument; everything of importance in Radovljica is on it. The new town extends primarily northward along Gorenjska cesta toward Lesce.

Radovljica's bus station is 500m northwest of Linhartov trg on Kranjska cesta. The train station is below the town on Cesta Svobode. To reach the square from the train station, walk up steep Kolodvorska ulica and turn right (east).

Information

The tourist office (☎ /fax 715 300) is at Kranjska cesta 13. From May to September it is open weekdays from 8 am till noon and 4 to 7 pm and on Saturday morning. During the rest of the year it is open weekdays from 8 am to 3 pm and on Saturday morning.

There's an SKB Banka branch with a Cirrus-linked ATM at Gorenjska 10, open weekdays only from 8.30 am till noon and 2 to 5 pm. About 150m north at No 16 of the same street is a Gorenjska Banka open Monday to Friday from 8 am to 6 pm and on Saturday morning till noon. The post office is beside the bus station at Kranjska cesta 1.

Beekeeping Museum

Though it may not sound like a crowd-pleaser, the Beekeeping Museum (Čebelarski Muzej) at Linhartov trg 1 is one of the most fascinating in Slovenia, and there isn't a whole lot you won't know about things apiarian after an hour inside.

The museum is housed in **Thurn Manor**, the largest and most important public building on the historical square and worth a look in itself. Thurn Manor began life as Ortenburg Castle in the early Middle Ages but was rebuilt with a large hall on the ground floor after the earthquake of 1511. Subsequent alterations and expansions gave it the appearance of a large baroque manor house. The cream-and-white structure has interesting reliefs and stucco work on its façade.

The museum's exhibits take a close look at the history of beekeeping in Slovenia (which was at its most intense in the 18th and 19th centuries), the country's unique contribution to the industry with the development of the Carniolan grey bee species *(Apis mellifera carnica)* and the research of men like Anton Janša (1734-73), who set up a research station in the Karavanke and is considered around the world to be the father of modern beekeeping. And the museum doesn't fail to pass on a few 'fun facts to know and tell'. Did *you* realise that bees cannot see the colour red but go gaga over yellow? The museum's collection of illustrated beehive panels *(panjske končnice)* from the 18th and 19th centuries, a folk art unique to Slovenia, is the largest in the country. Gratefully, everything here is labelled in English and German along with Slovene.

The Beekeeping Museum has extremely complicated hours but this much is certain: it is always closed in January and February. From May to August it is open daily, except Monday, from 10 am to 1 pm and again from 4 to 6 pm. In March, April, November and December it is open from 10 am till noon and 3 to 5 pm on Wednesday, Saturday and Sunday only. The hours in September and October are Tuesday to Sunday from 10 am till noon and 3 to 5 pm. The entry fee is 300/200 SIT for adults/children.

Bees have played an integral part in Slovenian agriculture since the 16th century.

The Boards & the Bees

The keeping of honeybees (species *Apis*) has been an integral part of Slovenian agriculture since the 16th century when buckwheat *(ajda)* was first planted on fallow ground to allow the more intensive use of farm land. Bees favour buckwheat and Slovenia, especially the Alpine regions of Carniola (Kranjska), was soon awash with honey for cooking and beeswax for candles. Valvasor discussed the subject at some length in his *The Glory of the Duchy of Carniola* published in 1689.

Originally bees were kept in hollow logs or woven baskets, but the entire hive was damaged when the honeycomb was removed. The invention of the *kranjič* hive, with removable boxes that resembled a chest of drawers, solved the problem by creating individual hives. It also led to the development of Slovenia's most important form of folk art.

Kranjič hives have front boards *(panjske končnice)* above the entrance, and painting and decorating these panels with religious motifs soon became all the rage. Ethnographers are still out to lunch over whether the illustrations were religious appeals to protect the hives from fire or disease, meant to guide the bees – they can distinguish colour – back home or to help beekeepers identify their hives.

The first panels (from the mid-18th century) were painted in a 'folk baroque' style and the subjects were taken from the Old and New Testaments (Adam and Eve, the Virgin Mary, St Florian and St George and, especially, patient Job, the patron of beekeepers) and history (the Turkish invasions, the Counter-Reformation with Martin Luther being driven to hell by a devil, Napoleon and the Illyrian Provinces). The most interesting panels show the foibles, rivalries and humour of the human condition. A devil may be sharpening a gossip's tongue on a grindstone or two women fighting over a man's trousers (ie his hand in marriage). A very common illustration shows the devil exchanging old wives for nubile young women – to the delight of the husbands. Another – in a 'world turned upside down' – has gun-toting deer and bears laying the hunter in his grave.

It is important to remember that these paintings were not 'art for art's sake'; the painters were primarily concerned with content and subject matter. But in their attempt to express the simple world around them, ordinary people and artisans between jobs produced some beautiful work.

The painting of beehive panels in Slovenia enjoyed its golden age between about 1820 and 1880; after that the art form went into decline. The introduction of a new and much larger hive by Anton Žnidaršič at the end of the 19th century obviated the need for small illustrations and the art form degenerated into kitsch.

Nowadays you'll see the best examples of painted panjske končnice in museums (eg in Radovljica and Maribor), but there are still a few traditional – and protected – ones around, such as those at Muljava in Dolenjska. An interesting twist is the beehive at Brdo Castle near Kranj, painted in the 1970s by some of Slovenia's most outstanding artists. Nowadays, the most common hives are the large box ones painted bright yellow (a colour bees like) and the 'hives on wheels', which can be moved into the sun or to a promising meadow.

Bees are still kept in Slovenia for their honey and wax but much more lucrative are by-products like pollen, propolis and royal jelly, used as elixirs and in homeopathic medicine. Propolis is a brownish, waxy substance collected from certain trees by bees and used to cement or caulk their hives. Royal jelly, so beloved by the European aristocracy of the 1920s and 1930s and by the Chinese, is the substance fed to the queen bee by the workers. ∎

Linhartov Trg

Radovljica's main square, named in honour of Slovenia's first dramatist and historian Anton Tomaž Linhart (1756-95) who was born here, is lined with painted houses mostly from the 16th century and is an absolute delight to explore. The sad part, however, is that you'll frequently find it jammed with cars. It has been called 'the most homogeneous old town core in Slovenia' and has interesting details at every step.

There are several lovely buildings opposite the Beekeeping Museum, including **Koman House** at No 23 with a baroque painting on its front of St Florian, the patron saint of fires (he douses, not sets, them) and **Mali House** at No 24 with a picture of St George slaying the dragon. But the most important one is 16th century **Šivec House** at No 22.

Šivec House is an interesting hybrid – Renaissance on the outside and Gothic on the inside. The fresco on the exterior shows the Good Samaritan performing his corporal work of mercy; inside there is a vaulted hall on the ground floor and a wood-panelled drawing room with a beamed ceiling on the first. The hall is now used as a gallery and the drawing room as a wedding hall. The gallery is open from 10 am to noon and from 4 or 5 pm to between 6 and 8 pm, depending on the season.

East of Thurn Manor, in an oddly shaped, shady courtyard, is the Gothic **Parish Church of St Peter**, a hall church modelled after the one in Kranj. The three portals are flamboyant Gothic and the sculptures inside were done by Angelo Pozzo in 1713. The building with the arcaded courtyard south of the church is the **Priest's House**. Parts of the old **town wall** can still be seen nearby.

To the north-west at Linhartov trg 3 is the 17th century **Vidič House** with a corner projection and colourfully painted in red, yellow and blue. Past the city park on Gorenjska cesta is the former **Savings Bank building** (1906) with a marvellous mosaic flowering tree, in Secessionist style, decorating the front.

Activities

There's a public swimming pool open in summer near the camp site at the northern end of Kopališka cesta and tennis courts nearby.

The Sport Riding Centre at Podvin Castle (☎ 738 881) in Mošnje, about 4km south-east of Radovljica, has horses available for riding individually or with an instructor. The centre also has a covered hippodrome.

Radovljica-based Tina Raft (☎ 715 005 or mobile ☎ 0609-646 255) offers a number of rafting trips on the Sava Dolinka and Sava Bohinjka rivers lasting between one hour and five hours and costing 2700 to 4500 SIT. You can also rent two-person canoes for 2700/4500 SIT per half day/day.

Places to Stay

Radovljica's tiny *camp site* (☎ 715 770) is next to the public swimming pool on Kopališka cesta. It is open from June to mid-September and costs between 600 SIT and 1000 SIT per person, with an extra 200 SIT charged for a tent.

The largest (and some say the best equipped) camping ground in Slovenia, *Šobec* (☎ 718 006), is in Lesce about 2.5km north-west of Radovljica. Situated on a small lake near a bend of the Sava Dolinka River, the camp site is huge – 20 sq hectares – and can accommodate up to 1500 people, which this popular place often does in summer. Šobec is open from May to September and costs from DM12.50 to DM14.50 for adults and DM10.50 to DM11 for children, depending on the month. There are also *bungalows* costing DM80 a night (DM65 from the third night).

You'll find lots more budget accommodation in nearby Bled but if you're determined to stay in Radovljica, the *Manca Šport* pension (☎ 714 120), which is a couple of kilometres north of Linhartov trg at Gradnikova cesta 2, charges between 4700 and 5200 SIT for singles with shower and breakfast and 6600 and 7520 SIT for doubles.

Radovljica's only hotel, a four-storey concrete block called the *Grajski Dvor* (☎ 715 585; fax 715 878), is at Kranjska cesta 2 opposite the bus station and the tourist office. Singles and doubles with shower and breakfast are DM60 and DM86. The hotel has 60 rooms and a swimming pool.

If money is no object, you might treat yourself to a night at the *Grad Podvin* hotel (☎ 738 881; fax 738 885) in Podvin Castle, a rather boxy affair about 4km south-east of Radovljica in the village of Mošje. Depending on the season, singles with shower and breakfast are 8000 to 9000 SIT while doubles are 11,000 to 12,500 SIT. Podvin Castle is surrounded by a lovely park and has tennis courts and a popular horse riding centre. Its restaurant gets high marks.

Places to Eat

Era is a popular pizzeria at the Grajski Dvor hotel. *Gostilna Lectar*, in yet another historical building at Linhartov trg 2, is open every day, except Tuesday, from 11 am till midnight. Across from Thurn Manor at No 26 is *Linhartov Hram*, a café-pub with snacks. There's a small *fruit and vegetable market* opposite the Grajski Dvor hotel.

Things to Buy

There's an excellent selection of Slovenian wines at *Vinoteka Sodček*, Linhartov trg 8. It's open weekdays from 9 am to 7 pm and on Saturday from 8 am to noon.

Getting There & Away

Buses leave Radovljica almost every half-hour for Bled and Ljubljana. They go hourly to Bohinj (via Bled), Kranj, Kranjska Gora and Kropa. Other destinations and their daily frequencies include: Begunje na Gorenjskem (up to nine), Bovec via Kranjska Gora and the Vršič Pass (one bus a day in summer), Brezje (one), Jesenice via Vrba (six), Novo Mesto (one to two), Podnart (four), Škofja Loka (one), Tržič (up to four), Vinica (one) and Zagreb in Croatia (one).

Radovljica is on the rail line linking Ljubljana (48km; 50 minutes) with Jesenice (16km; 20 minutes) via Škofja Loka, Kranj and Lesce-Bled. Up to 15 trains a day pass through the town in each direction. About 10 of the northbound ones carry on to Villach in Austria.

KROPA

• *pop 1025* • *area code ☎064* • *postcode 4245*

While in Radovljica, don't miss the chance to visit Kropa, a delightful little village tucked away in a narrow valley below the Jelovica Plateau some 10km to the south-east. Kropa has been a 'workhorse' for centuries, mining iron ore and hammering out the nails and decorative wrought iron that can still be seen in many parts of Slovenia. Today Kropa (Cropp in German) has turned its attention to screws – the Plamen factory is based here – but artisans continue their work, clanging away in the workshop on the village's single street, and the work of their forebears is evident in ornamental street lamps shaped like birds and dragons, weather vanes and shutters.

Blacksmith Museum

The fascinating collection at the Blacksmith Museum (Kovaški Muzej) at house No 10 traces the history of iron mining and forging in Kropa and nearby Kamna Gorica in English, German and Slovene from the 14th to the early 20th centuries. Nail manufacturing was the town's main industry for most of that period, and it is difficult to imagine that so many different types of nails existed, never mind that they were all made here. From giant ones that held tne pylons below Venice together to little studs for snow boots, Kropa produced some 130 varieties in huge quantities. In Kropa you did not become a master blacksmith until you could fit a horseshoe around an egg – without cracking the shell.

The museum has working models of forges, a couple of rooms showing how workers and their families lived in very cramped quarters (up to 45 people in one house) and a special exhibit devoted to the work of Joža Bertoncelj (1901-76), who turned out exquisite wrought-iron gratings, candlesticks, chandeliers and even masks. The museum shows a fascinating black-and-white documentary film about the town and its work produced in the very socialist 1950s. It's a real period piece.

The house itself was owned by a 17th century iron baron called Klinar and contains some valuable furniture and paintings. Among the most interesting pieces is a 19th century wind-up 'jukebox' from Bohemia. Ask the friendly caretaker to insert one of the large perforated rolls and watch the piano, drums, triangle and cymbals make music.

The Blacksmith Museum keeps the same hours as the Beekeeping Museum in Radovljica (see that section), including winter closure. The entrance charge is 300/200 SIT for adults/children.

Other Sights

The **UKO forgers' workshop** across from the museum at house No 7b is open for visits from 7 am to 2 pm on weekdays and from 9 am till noon on Saturday. The artisans sell their wares – none of them even approaching the work of Master Bertoncelj – at the shop next door (house No 7a), which keeps the same hours.

An 18th century furnace called **Purgatory Forge** (Vigenj Vice) lies a short distance north of the museum near the Kroparica, a fast-flowing stream that once turned the wheels that powered the furnaces for the forges. Close by is the birthplace of the Slovenian painter Janez Potočnik (1749-1834), whose work can be seen in the baroque **Church of St Leonard** on the hill to the east and in Kamnik. Kropa has many other lovely old houses, including several around Trg Kropa, the main square, which also has an interesting old wayside shrine.

A medieval smelter – the so-called **Slovenian Furnace** – dating from the 13th century is at Jamnik, about 3.5km south of Kropa along a tortuously twisting road. There are trails from Trg Kropa into the Jelovica Hills to the west, an area once rich in iron ore and timber for charcoal. In the early 19th century over 800 charcoal burners worked in this area alone.

Places to Eat

There's no accommodation in Kropa, which is just as well as you'd never get any sleep with all the banging and clanging going on. However, you can eat at *Gostilna Pri Kovač* just north of the museum at house No 30 or *Pri Jarmu*, a gostilna at the southern end of Kropa in house No 2.

BLED

• *pop 5664* • *area code ☎064* • *postcode 4260*

With its emerald-green lake, picture-postcard church on an islet, medieval castle clinging to a rocky cliff and some of the highest peaks of the Julian Alps and the Karavanke as backdrops, Bled is Slovenia's most popular resort and its biggest tourist money spinner. Not surprisingly, it can be overpriced, swarming with tourists and often less than welcoming. Many travellers make a beeline for the larger and far less developed Lake Bohinj, 26km to the south-west.

But as is the case with many popular destinations around the world, people come in droves – and will continue to do so – because the place *is* special. On a clear day you can make out Mt Stol (2236m) and Slovenia's highest peak, Mt Triglav (2864m), in the distance and then the bells start ringing from the belfry of the little island church. You should visit Bled too – at least for a look.

History

Bled was the site of a Hallstatt settlement in the early Iron Age but, as it was far from the main trade routes, the Romans gave it short shrift. More importantly, from the 7th century the early Slavs – no doubt attracted by the altitude (501m), the mild climate and the natural protection afforded by the mountains – came in waves, establishing themselves at Pristava below the castle, on the tiny island and at a dozen other sites around the lake. Bled has been linked with the myths and legends of these people for centuries, particularly the ancient Slavic goddess Živa, the priestess Bogomila and the man who loved her, Črtomir. France Prešeren gave this relationship new life in his epic poem *Krst pri Savici (Baptism by the Savica Waterfall)* in 1836.

Around the turn of the first millennium, the German Emperor Henry II presented Bled Castle and its lands to the Bishops of Brixen in South Tyrol, who retained secular control of the area until the early 19th century when the Habsburgs took it over. By that time a number of small villages, including Mlino, Želeče and Rečica, had grown up around the lake.

Bled's beauty and its warm waters were well known to medieval pilgrims who came to pray at the island church; the place made it into print in 1689 when Janez Vajkard Valvasor described the lake's thermal springs in *The Glory of the Duchy of Carniola*, his seminal work on Slovenian geography, history and culture. But Bled's wealth was not fully appreciated at that time, and in the late 18th century the keeper of the castle seriously considered draining Lake Bled and using the clay to make bricks.

Fortunately, along came a Swiss doctor named Arnold Rikli who saw the lake's full potential. In 1855 he opened baths where the casino now stands, taking advantage of the springs, the clean air and the mountain light. With the opening of the railway from Ljubljana to Tarvisio (Trbiž) in 1870, more and more guests came to Bled and the resort was a favourite of wealthy Europeans from the turn of the century right up to WWII. In fact, under the Kingdom of Serbs, Croats and Slovenes, Bled was the summer residence of the Karadžordževići, the Yugoslav royal family.

Orientation

'Bled' refers both to the lake and the settlements around it, particularly the built-up area to the north-east where most of the hotels are located. This development is dominated by a modern shopping complex called the Triglav centre but known locally as the 'Khaddhafi centre' because it was originally slated for Tripoli. Bled's main road, Ljubljanska cesta, runs eastward from here. Footpaths and a road called Cesta Svobode and then Kidričeva cesta circle the lake.

Bled's bus station is at the northern end of Cesta Svobode just up from the Jelovica hotel. There are two train stations. The station called Lesce-Bled is 4km to the south-east on the road to Radovljica and on the line linking Ljubljana with Jesenice and Austria. Bled Jezero, on Kolodvorska cesta

north-west of the lake and the Zaka Regatta Centre, connects Jesenice to the north with Nova Gorica, Sežana and Italy to the south-west.

Information

Tourist Offices Bled's tourist office (☎ 741 122; fax 741 555) is next to the Park hotel at Cesta Svobode 15. Essentially it is a souvenir shop with information, maps and guides. It also does currency exchange (3% commission) and sells fishing licences (trout, grayling) for the lake. Ask for the helpful (and free) English-language publication *Bled Tourist Information*. From April to October the office is open Monday to Saturday from 8 am to 7 pm (to 10 pm in July and August) and from 10 am to 6 pm on Sunday (to 10 pm in July and August). From November to March the hours are 8 am to 3 pm Monday to Saturday and noon to 4 pm on Sunday.

An important office to visit if you are headed for *the* mountain is the Triglav National Park information centre (☎ 741 188) in the Vila Rog at Kidričeva cesta 2 on the lake's northern shore. It is open from 8 am to 3 pm on weekdays only. The staff provide information about the park and climbing Triglav, and can arrange guides.

Money Gorenjska Banka in the Park hotel shopping complex and opposite the casino on Cesta Svobode is open from 9 to 11.30 am and 2 to 5 pm on weekdays and 8 to 11 am on Saturday. SKB Banka has a branch with an ATM in the Triglav shopping centre. It is open from 8.30 am till noon and from 2 to 5 pm weekdays only.

Post & Communications The main post office, open weekdays from 7 am to 7 pm and on Saturday till noon, is at Ljubljanska cesta 10.

Travel Agencies Kompas (☎ 741 515) has an office in the Triglav shopping centre at Ljubljanska cesta 4. It is open daily from 8 am to 7 pm (to 8 pm from June to September and on Sunday from 8 am till noon and 4 to

GORENJSKA

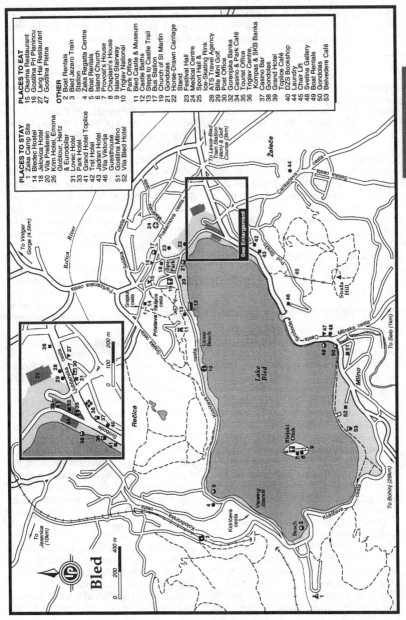

PLACES TO STAY
1   Zaka Camp Site
14 Bledec Hostel
18 Jelovica Hotel
20 Vila Prešeren
26 Krim Hotel, Emona
     Globtour, Hertz
     & Eurodollar
31 Lovec Hotel
33 Park Hotel
41 Grand Hotel Toplice
42 Trst Hotel
43 Jadran Hotel
46 Vila Viktorija
51 Guesthouse
     Mlino
52 Vila Bled Hotel

PLACES TO EAT
15 Okarina Restaurant
16 Gostilna Pri Planincu
21 Lang Hal Restaurant
47 Gostilna Pletna

OTHER
2   Boat Rentals
3   Bled Jezero Train
     Station
4   Zaka Regatta Centre
5   Boat Rentals
7   Provost's House
8   Chaplain's House
9   Island Stairway
10 Triglav National
     Park Office
11 Bled Castle & Museum
12 Castle Baths
13 Steps to Castle Trail
17 Bus Station
19 Church of St Martin
21 Gondolas
22 Horse-Drawn Carriage
     Stand
23 Festival Hall
24 Medical Centre
25 Sport Hall &
     Ice-Skating Rink
28 ATS Travel Agency
29 Bife Mini Golf
30 Post Office
34 Gorenjska Banka
35 Casino & Park Café
36 Tourist Office
     Triglav Centre,
     Kompas & SKB Banka
37 Casino Bar
38 Gondolas
39 Grand Hotel
40 Toplice Café
44 Laundry
45 Chair Lift
48 Prešernа Gallery
49 Boat Rentals
50 Gondolas
53 Belvedere Café

Bled

8 pm). Emona Globtour (☎ 741 821) is in the eastern wing of the Krim hotel at Ljubljanska cesta 7. It is open Monday to Saturday from 8 am to 7 pm and on Sunday from 8 am till noon and 5 to 7 pm.

Bookshop The DZS bookshop opposite the Grand Hotel Toplice on Cesta Svobode has maps of the region and some guidebooks in English. It is open weekdays from 7.30 am to 7 pm and till noon on Saturday.

Laundry If you're running low on clean laundry, Bled is the place to wash those dirty clothes. A machine load washed and dried should only cost about 500 SIT at the Bledec hostel, and there's a laundry south of the centre at Cankarjeva cesta 23c, open from 6 am to 2 pm.

Medical Services Bled's medical centre (☎ 741 400) is at Mladinska cesta 1.

Bled Castle

Perched on a steep cliff more than 100m above the lake, Bled Castle (Blejski Grad) is how most people imagine medieval forts to be – with towers, ramparts, moats and a terrace offering magnificent views on a clear day. The castle, which is built on two levels, dates back to the 11th century (though most of what stands here now is from the 16th century) and was the seat of the Bishops of Brixen, who apparently redecorated the place regularly, for 800 years.

The baroque southern wing houses a **museum collection** that traces the history of Lake Bled and its settlements from the Bronze Age to the mid-19th century. None of the furniture is original to the castle, but it helps give you an idea of how the leisured class lived in the Middle Ages.

There's a large collection of armour and weapons (swords, halberds and firearms from the 16th to 18th centuries), jewellery found at the early Slav burial pits at Pristava, and a few interesting carvings, including a 16th century one of the overworked St Florian, dowsing yet another conflagration. The small 16th century **chapel**, strewn with

coins and notes left by favour-seekers, contains a painting of Henry II and his wife Kunigunda above the altar.

The castle is open daily March to October from 8 am to 7 pm. During the rest of the year it opens at 9 am and closes at 4 pm. Admission costs 300/150 SIT for adults/children.

You can reach the castle via two trails: from behind the hostel (see Places to Stay) or from just north of the neo-Gothic **Parish Church of St Martin** on Riklijeva cesta. The church (1905) was designed by Friedrich von Schmidt, who also did the city hall and Votive Church in Vienna. The frescoes illustrating the Lord's Prayer were painted by Slavko Pengov in the 1930s. Outside there's a small shrine designed by Jože Plečnik and the remains of defence walls built to subdue the Turks in the 15th century.

Bled Island

Tiny, tear-shaped Blejski Otok, the only true island in Slovenia, has been the site of a Christian church since the 9th century. But excavations have shown that the early Slavs worshipped at a pagan temple here at least a century before that.

Getting to the island is half the fun. The easiest way is to climb aboard a hand-propelled gondola (*pletna* in Slovene) docked next to the casino, to the east of the Castle Baths pool complex or in Mlino. The return fare is 1000 SIT, and you get about a half-hour to explore the island; all in the trip takes about 1½ hours. Alternatively, you can rent a boat from the Castle Baths (see Activities), in Mlino or at the large beach to the southwest. You could even swim to the island, but if you choose that method you're going to have to drag some clothes along in a plastic bag. The powers-that-be will not let you into the island church in your swimming gear.

The boat lets you off on the island's south side at the monumental stairway built in 1655; as you walk up you'll pass the **Chaplain's House** and the **Provost's House** from the 17th and 18th centuries with the Brixen bishops' coat of arms on the façade.

The baroque **Church of the Assumption** contains some fresco fragments from the

14th century, a large gold altar and, under the floor of the nave, part of the apse of the **pre-Romanesque chapel**, the only one in Slovenia. Models in the porch illustrate the development of the site from an 8th century wattle-and-daub structure to the 17th century church standing here today. Outside is a 15th century **belfry** with a 'wishing bell' that visitors can ring if they want to ask a favour.

Naturally everyone and their grandmother does it – again and again and again. The church is open daily from 8 am to dusk.

Lake Walk

Lake Bled is not a large body of water – it measures only 2km by 1380m – and the second best way to see it is from the shore. A walk around the lake (6km) shouldn't take

Zlatorog & His Golden Horns

The oft-told tale of Zlatorog, the mythical chamois (*gams* in Slovene) with the golden horns who lived on Mt Triglav and guarded its treasure, almost always involves some super-human (or, in this case, superantelopine) feat that drastically changed the face of the mountain. But don't let Slovenes fool you into believing that their ancient ancestors passed on the tale. The Zlatorog story first appeared in the *Laibacher Zeitung (Ljubljana Gazette)* in 1868 during a period of Romanticism and national awakening. This one tells of how the chamois created the Triglav Lakes Valley, a wilderness of tumbled rock almost in the centre of Triglav National Park.

Zlatorog roamed the valley (at that time a beautiful garden) with the White Ladies, good fairies who kept the mountain pastures green and helped humans whenever they found them in need.

Meanwhile, down in the Soča Valley near Trenta, a greedy plot was being hatched. It seemed that an innkeeper's daughter had been given jewels by a rather wealthy Venetian merchant. The girl's mother demanded that her daughter's lover, a poor but skilled hunter, match the treasure with Zlatorog's gold which was hidden under Mt Bogatin and guarded by a multiheaded serpent. If not, he was at least to bring back a bunch of Triglav 'roses' (actually pink cinquefoils) to prove his fidelity – an impossible task in mid-winter.

The young hunter, seething with jealousy, climbed the mountain in search of the chamois, figuring that if he were to get even a piece of the golden horns, the treasure of Bogatin – and his beloved – would be his. At last the young man spotted Zlatorog, took aim and fired. It was a direct hit.

The blood gushing from Zlatorog's wound melted the snow and up sprang a magical Triglav rose. The chamois nibbled on a few petals and – presto! – Zlatorog was instantly back on his feet. As the chamois leapt away, roses sprang up from under his hooves, luring the hunter onto higher and higher ground. But as they climbed, the sun caught Zlatorog's shiny horns. The hunter was blinded, lost his footing and plunged into a gorge.

The once kind and trusting chamois was enraged that a mere mortal would treat him in such a manner. In his fury he gored his way through the Triglav Lakes Valley, leaving it much as it looks today. He left the area with the White Ladies, never to return.

And the fate of the others? The innkeeper's daughter waited in vain for her lover to return home. As spring approached, the snow began to melt, swelling the Soča River. One day it brought her a sad gift: the body of her young swain, his lifeless hand still clutching a Triglav rose. As for the inn keeper's rapacious wife, we know nothing. Perhaps she learned Italian and moved to Venice.

Observant travellers will see the face of Zlatorog no matter where they go in Slovenia. It's on the label of the country's best beer. ∎

much longer than two hours, and it is at its best in the early morning. Along the way, you'll pass linden, chestnut and willow trees hanging over the water, boat slips, wooden walkways, innumerable anglers, the start of several hikes and a couple of interesting sights. Start at the Grand Hotel Toplice and walk clockwise.

In Mlino, the **Svetina Gallery** at Cesta Svobode 39 and beside the sculptor's house at Mlinska cesta 10 exhibits the work of Tone Svetina. They're curious things really, made out of bits of old weapons, bombs, shrapnel and scrap metal and, like Svetina's popular *Boy's Own*-style historical novels, all express his anti-war sentiments.

Around the bend and past the camp site is the **Zaka Regatta Centre** from where a rowing competition is staged every June. The bronze statue of the *Boatman* by Boris Kalin is attractive but does little to obscure the dreadful staging to the south that was built for an international rowing championship in 1989. It is *very* unpopular in these parts. The **Triglav National Park** (TNP) office at Kidričeva cesta 2 has a small **nature exhibit** concerned with mountain ecology and what you might encounter in the park. It's unlikely you'll spot Zlatorog, the fearsome and immortal 'golden horn' chamois *(Rupicara reupicara)* who guards the golden treasure of Mt Triglav (see boxed text entitled Zlatorog & His Golden Horns). The **Castle Baths** are a bit farther on.

An alternative to circling the lake on foot is to rent a bicycle (see Getting Around) or to take a horse-drawn carriage *(fijakar)* from the stand near the Festival Hall (☎ 741 121) on Cesta Svobode. A twirl around the lake for four people costs 3000 SIT, and it's the same price for two people up to the castle. You can even get a carriage for four to Bohinj (20,000 SIT for a half-day return trip), Kropa (12,000 SIT), Radovljica (7000 SIT) and Vintgar (6000 SIT).

Activities
Swimming & Boating Bled's warm (23°C at source), crystal-clear water makes it suitable for swimming well into the autumn, and

there are decent beaches around the lake, including a big gravel one near the camp site and a grass lido with a big water slide to the east of the TNP office. Just beyond the latter is the large Castle Baths (Grajsko Kopališče) complex with an indoor pool and protected enclosures in the lake itself where you can splash around. Entry is 500/300 SIT for adults/children with cabins costing 400 SIT. The baths are open from mid-April to October from 7 am to 7 pm.

This is also a place to rent boats for rowing on the lake or getting to the island (motor boats are banned here). Boats accommodating three/five people cost 1000/1200 SIT per hour, 2500/3000 SIT for a half day and 4000/5000 for a full day. There's a 1000 SIT deposit on all rentals. Boats for two to four people are also for rent in front of the Gostilna Pletna in Mlino, or farther west near the entrance to the camp site, for 800 to 1000 SIT per hour.

Four hotels in Bled have indoor pools filled with thermal water as well as saunas: the Grand Hotel Toplice, the Park, the Jelovica and the Golf (Cankarjeva ulica 6). The pool in the basement of the Grand Hotel Toplice costs about 1000 SIT to use.

Horse Riding The Vila Viktorija pension has horses available for 2000 SIT per hour, a wonderful way to climb up Straža Hill, tour the lake or follow a section of the Sava River. The stables are open from 10 am till noon and from 2 to 7 pm daily.

Tennis There are four tennis courts at the Zaka Regatta Centre at the western end of the lake, open March to November.

Golf The Bled Golf & Country Club's 27-hole, 109-par course (☎ 718 230) is about 3km to the east of the lake near Lesce. The club is open daily from April to October from 8 am to 7 pm. The green fees for a round are DM65, a set of clubs costs DM19 and hand cart is DM6 to rent. There's also a driving range (DM4 for 36 balls) and a pro who gives lessons for DM35 to DM50 per hour. Miniature golf is available at the Bife Mini Golf opposite the Lovec hotel for 350 SIT.

Flying The Alpine Flying Centre (Alpski Letalski Center; ☎ 733 431) at Begunjska cesta 10 in Lesce has panoramic flights over Bled (7000 SIT for three people), Bohinj (11,000 SIT) and even Triglav (16,400 SIT), and in winter you can go 'para-skiing' (21,000 SIT) in which you are dropped by parachute over a precipitous snowbound slope – wearing skis!

Ice Skating The lake usually freezes in winter but if you're in Bled during a warm spell or in summer (open August to May) and feel like cutting up the ice, visit the ice skating rink (drsališče) in the Sport Hall (Športna Dvorana) at Ljubljanska cesta 5 in the park behind the Krim hotel.

Skiing The closest 'real' ski resort to Bled is **Zatrnik** (☎ 741 133), on the slopes of the Pokljuka Plateau 8km west of Bled with skiing up to 1250m, a chair lift and four T-bars. But beginners will be content with the mini-ski centre at **Straža** (same ☎) southwest of the Grand Hotel Toplice. A chair lift takes you to the top of the 646m hill in three minutes; you'll be down the short slope in no time.

Steam Train Slovenijaturist's Oldtimer Train has excursions in the warmer months (roughly from April to September) that either originate in Bled or pass through the resort. Others leave from Jesenice, 13km to the north-west, or Most na Soči. Routes and timetables change frequently, but popular excursions include Bled-Ljubljana via Kranj and Škofja Loka (5760/3600 SIT for adults/children) and Bled-Most na Soči via Bohinjska Bistrica (6350/3650 SIT). Fares include lunch and side trips.

Special Events
A number of special events take place during the summer in Bled, including the International Rowing Regatta in early June, the Okarina World Music Festival in July and

August, and Rikli's Days, a multimedia festival in late July when there are fireworks and the entire lake is illuminated by candlelight.

Summertime concerts (most often on Monday afternoon and Friday evening) take place at the castle, the island church and the parish church. While the island is a far more romantic venue for Bach or Handel, don't miss a concert at the Church of St Martin – it has one of the finest organs in Slovenia.

Places to Stay
Befitting a resort of such popularity, Bled has a wide range of accommodation – from Slovenia's first hostel to a five-star hotel in a villa that was once the summer retreat of Josip Broz Tito. The lake and surrounding areas count some 4000 beds, more than 5% of the total available in Slovenia.

Camping Zaka (☎ 741 117) is a six-hectare camp site accommodating 750 people in a quiet valley at the western end of the lake, about 2.5km from the bus station. The location is good, and there's a decent beach, tennis courts, a large restaurant facing the lake and a supermarket, but Zaka fills up very quickly in summer. The camp site is open from May to October and costs about DM12 per person.

Šobec (☎ 718 006), the largest camping ground in Slovenia, is in Lesce. See Places to Stay in the Radovljica section for details. It is strictly forbidden to camp elsewhere on the lake, and the law is enforced.

Hostel The Bledec hostel (☎ 745 250), at Grajska cesta 17 and open year round, except in November, has a total of 56 beds in 13 rooms and costs DM20 per person (or DM26 with breakfast). Check-in is from 7 am to 10 pm, and you'll be given a key to the front door if you expect to return late.

Private Rooms Kompas, Emona Globtour and the ATS travel agency (☎ 741 736) at Ljubljanska cesta 1a have thousands of private rooms and apartments on their books. In the low season, the price per person for a room without breakfast ranges from DM13 to DM22, depending on the category. In July and August, expect to pay between DM17 and DM26. Apartments for two range from DM42 to DM60. You'll have to pay 30% more if you stay in a private room or apartment for less than three days.

If you want to do your own investigating and strike a private deal, there are lots of houses with sobe (rooms available) signs around Bled, particularly to the north in Rečica. It's not exactly in the centre of things but it's a quiet area.

Farmhouses Believe it or not, you can actually stay at a farm very close to Bled. It may not exactly be a Štajerska-style spread, but it will be a working farm nonetheless. Selo, a village 1km south of Mlino, has several farmhouses with accommodation, including *Povšin* (☎ 77 334) at Selo 22 with eight rooms and *Stojan* (☎ 78 617) with four rooms at No 20. Prices range from about DM30 to DM45 per person, depending on the season and room category.

Pensions The attractive *Vila Viktorija* (☎ 742 485) below Straža Hill at Cesta Svobode 27a charges from DM35 to DM50 for singles and DM40 to DM70 for doubles, depending on the season. It has six rooms and two suites (DM30 to DM50 per person) with enormous balconies facing the lake – among the most romantic places to stay at Bled. The *Mlino* pension (☎ 741 404) in the next village at Cesta Svobode 45, better known for its restaurant than its accommodation, has 15 rooms available. They're more expensive than the Viktorija, with singles (including shower and breakfast) costing DM50 to DM60 and doubles DM70 to DM90. The attractive *Vila Prešeren* (☎ 741 608), with only 14 beds facing the lake at Kidričeva cesta 1, charges from DM65/100 for singles/doubles.

Hotels Not surprisingly, the cheapest hotels in Bled are a bit away from the water and on noisy streets. The *Lovec* (☎ 741 500; fax 741 021), Ljubljanska cesta 6, has 138 beds in both an interesting old building and an ugly

modern extension. Singles with shower and breakfast are DM48 to DM68 while doubles are DM66 to DM106. About 200m up the same street and on the left at No 7, the sprawling *Krim* (☎ 7970; fax 77 698), with 218 beds, has almost exactly the same rates: DM50 to DM70 for singles, DM70 to DM110 for doubles. Close to the bus station and fronting a pretty park that leads to the lake, the 188-bed *Jelovica* (☎ 7960; fax 741 550) has singles for DM65 to DM85 and doubles for DM100 to DM140.

Bled's largest hotel, the 400-bed *Park* (☎ 7930; fax 741 505) is opposite the casino and the lake and about as central as you are going to get. Singles are DM75 to DM110 while doubles are DM110 to DM180. Reception is on the 1st floor at Cesta Svobode 15.

If you really want to splurge or have the rich uncle or aunt in tow, there are two choices – both of them on the lake. The 110-room *Grand Hotel Toplice* (☎ 7910; fax 741 841), Cesta Svobode 12, is Bled's 'olde worlde' hotel, with attractive public areas (though some rather dark rooms) and superb views of the lake on its northern side. The cheapest singles are DM110 and DM120, depending on the season, while doubles are from DM150 and DM180. The hotel's two extensions opposite – the *Trst* at Cesta Svobode 19 and the more attractive *Jadran* on the hill at No 23 – are about one-third cheaper.

The five-star *Vila Bled* (☎ 7915; fax 741 320), where Tito and his foreign guests once put their feet up and their heads down, is even more expensive: DM215 to DM230 for a single and DM330 to DM360 for a double. Vila Bled is surrounded by a large park and has its own private beach and boat dock. It is at Cesta Svobode 26, west of Mlino village, and has 31 rooms and suites.

Places to Eat
Bled is blessed with a lot of restaurants – good, bad or otherwise. For pizza and vegetarian food, head for the large garden café and pub called the *Pod Kostanji* at the Jelovica hotel.

The *Lang Hai* is a – come on now, guess

– Chinese restaurant at Ulica Narodnih Herojev 3 almost opposite the Krim hotel. The hui guo rou (twice-cooked pork) and ma po doufu (spicy beancurd) aren't exactly what you'd get in Chengdu but this is Slovenia after all. Soups average about 250 SIT, rice and noodle dishes 750 SIT, and main courses run from 900 to 1250 SIT. Lang Hai is open daily till 11 pm.

There are a couple of *gostišča* in Mlino, the main village on the lake's southern shore: *Pletna* at Cesta Svobode 37, with a decent lunch menu for 880 SIT and open daily from 8 am to 11 pm, and *Mlino* at No 45. The latter has decent Slovenian dishes with an emphasis on fish and is open till 11 pm.

My favourite restaurant in Bled remains the homely *Pri Planincu* at Grajska cesta 8 just down the hill from the Bledec hostel. Excellent mushroom soup and roast chicken with chips and salad shouldn't cost much more than 1600 SIT and the grilled Balkan specialities like čevapčiči (spicy meatballs of beef or pork) and the tasty pljeskavica z kajmakom (Serbian-style meat patties with mascarpone-like cream cheese; 1050 SIT) are very well prepared. Pri Planincu is open daily from 9 am to 11 pm.

Bled's most upmarket restaurant is the *Okarina* at Riklijeva cesta 9. It has a lovely covered back terrace lit with torches, traditional musical instruments (an *okarina* is a small clay flute) and even stages special cultural events from time to time. But it's not cheap: soups and starters range from 600 to 1000 SIT, with mains (a dozen of them vegetarian) from 1300 to 2500 SIT. Expect to pay about 3000 SIT per person for two courses and a drink. The Okarina is open daily from 5 pm to midnight (from noon Friday to Sunday).

Entertainment

Several pubs have lovely terraces with great views open in the warmer months. Two of the better ones are the *Park* café above the casino on Cesta Svobode and the *Grand Hotel Toplice* café at Cesta Svobode 12a. But nothing beats the *Belvedere*, a café on top of a tall tower near the Vila Bled. It closes in winter though. The *Casino Bar* opposite the Grand Hotel Toplice café at Cesta Svobode 19a is more down to earth – in every respect.

Bled Casino (☎ 741 811), with roulette, black jack, baccarat and 80 slot machines, is open every day of the week – from 7 pm Monday to Thursday and from 5 pm at the weekend – till late.

Getting There & Away

Bus Buses are very frequent to Radovljica (via both Lesce and Begunje), and there is at least one an hour to Bohinj, Kranj, Ljubljana, Podhom and Zasip. Other destinations served from Bled include: Bovec via Kranjska Gora and the Vršič Pass (one bus a day in July and August, on Saturday and Sunday in June and September), Celje (one), Jesenice via Vrba (five), Kranjska Gora (three or four), Piran (one a day in summer), Pokljuka (one or two from late June to October) and Škofja Loka (one). One bus a day heads for the Croatian capital of Zagreb via Ljubljana.

Train Lesce-Bled station gets up to 15 trains a day from Ljubljana (51km; 55 minutes) via Škofja Loka, Kranj and Radovljica. They continue on to Jesenice (13km; 15 minutes), from where about 10 cross the border for Villach in Austria.

Up to eight daily trains from Jesenice via Podhom pass through Bled Jezero station on their way to Bohinjska Bistrica (18km; 20 minutes), Most na Soči and Nova Gorica (79km; 1¾ hours), from where you can make connections for Sežana, 40km to the south-east, and Italy. This mountain railway is one of the most picturesque in Slovenia. If you are headed south-west to Nova Gorica, sit on the right-hand side of the train to see the valley of the cobalt blue Soča River at its best.

Car Hertz (☎ 741 519) rents cars from its office at the Krim hotel at Ljubljanska cesta 7. It is open weekdays from 7 am till noon and from 5 to 7 pm. It closes at 1 pm on Saturday. Emona Globtour is affiliated with Eurodollar and rents cars from its office on the other side of the same building. Budget (☎ 742 183) has an office in the Triglav shopping centre.

Getting Around

Parking in Bled is restricted to seven city-maintained car parks around the resort and costs 500 SIT (or 1000 SIT right on the lake) per day. You can order a local taxi on ☎ 741 118.

Kompas, Emona Globtour and ATS rent bicycles and mountain bikes. Prices are 400 SIT an hour, 900 SIT for half a day and 1400 SIT for a full day. Kompas has the biggest selection.

AROUND BLED

The area around Bled offers endless possibilities for excursions: the **Pokljuka Plateau** beneath Triglav to the west with a gorge 2km long; the village of **Vrba** where France Prešeren was born (house No 2) and the site of the Romanesque-Gothic Church of St Mark with 14th century frescoes; **Begunje** with the ruins of Kamen Castle, the

---

Climbing Mt Triglav from Pokljuka

The shortest – but hardly the most enjoyable – way to reach the summit of Mt Triglav is from Bled. But you must drive first to Rudno Polje (1347m) on the Pokljuka Plateau, 18km south-west of the lake. From the 45-room Šport hotel (☎ 064-725 090; fax 064-211 235) a trail leads west below Mt Viševnik (2050m) to the Jezerce Valley, where it then turns south-west, zigzags over the Studor Saddle (1892m) and crosses the southern flank of Mt Tosc (2275m). Within three hours of setting out from Rudno Polje, you should be at the *Vodnikov Dom na Velem Polju* mountain hut (mobile ☎ 0609-615 621) at 1817m. It has 53 beds. The 62-bed *Dom Planika pod Triglavom* (mobile ☎ 0609-614 773), at 2401m, is two hours walk north-west from here. You can reach Triglav's summit in an hour from Dom Planika.

The super fit might attempt to do this trip in a day (Slovenian teenagers seem to manage), but most of us mortals stay at one of the huts overnight. ■

Church of St Peter, containing some of the most valuable medieval frescoes in Gorenjska done by Jernej of Loka, and the Hostages Museum (Muzej Talcev) in an old manor house (house No 55) dedicated to over 12,000 people held here by the Gestapo during WWII. All of these destinations can be reached by well marked trails that are outlined on the 1:25,000-scale map *Bled z Okolico (Bled and Environs*; 500 SIT) and the 1:50,000 *Gorenjska* map from GZS (1000 SIT), both available from the tourist office.

Vintgar Gorge

One of the easiest and most satisfying day trips is to Vintgar Gorge, a mere 4.5km north-west of Bled. A wooden footbridge built in 1893 hugs the rock wall for 1600m along the Radovna River, crisscrossing the raging river four times over rapids, waterfalls and pools before reaching **Šum Waterfall**. The entire walk is spectacular though it can get pretty wet and slippery. There are little snack bars at the beginning and the end of the walkway and picnic tables at several locations along the way. Admission to the gorge costs 300 SIT for adults and 200 SIT for children, and it is open from mid-April to October from 8 am to 8 pm.

It's an easy walk to the gorge from Bled. Head north-west on Prešernova ulica then north on Partizanska cesta to Cesta v Vintgar. This will take you to Podhom, where signs show the way to the gorge entrance. To return, you can either retrace your steps or, from Šum Waterfall, walk over Hom Hill (834m) eastward to the ancient pilgrimage **Church of St Catherine**, which retains some 15th century fortifications. From there it's due south through Zasip to Bled.

Those unable or unwilling to walk all the way can take the bus or the train (from Bled Jezero station) to Podhom. From there it's a 1.5km walk westward to the main entrance. From late June to mid-September an Alpetour bus makes the run from Bled's bus station daily at 9.30 am, stopping at the castle car park, and returns just before noon. One way is 200 SIT.

BOHINJ

• area code ☎ 064

Bohinj, a larger and much less developed glacial lake 26km to the south-west of Bled, is a wonderful antidote to the latter and one of my favourite spots in Slovenia. OK, so it doesn't have a romantic little island or a castle looming high on a rocky cliff. But it does have Triglav itself visible from the lake when the weather clears and a wonderful naturalness that doesn't exist at Bled. The Bohinj area's handful of museums and historical churches will keep culture vultures busy during their visit, and for action types there are activities galore – from kayaking and mountain biking to scaling Triglav via one of the southern approaches (see boxed text entitled Climbing Mt Triglav from Bohinj). The only drawback is the lake's propensity for attracting fog, especially in the morning.

History

Bohinj (Wochain in German) was densely settled during the Hallstatt period due to the large amounts of iron ore in the area, and a trade route linked the lake with the Soča Valley and the Adriatic Sea via a pass at Vrh Bače, south-east of Bohinjska Bistrica. During the Middle Ages, when the area fell under the jurisdiction of the Bishops of Brixen at Bled, Bohinj was known for its markets and fairs, which were held near the Church of St John the Baptist. Here peasants from the Friuli region around Trieste traded salt, wine and foodstuffs with their Slovenian counterparts for iron ore, livestock and butter. As the population grew, herders went higher into the Julian Alps in search of pasture land while charcoal burners cleared the upper forests for timber to fuel the forges.

The iron industry continued to flourish

Climbing Mt Triglav from Bohinj

There are several ways to reach Triglav from Bohinj though many climbers prefer to use these paths to descend after scaling the mountain from the north or the east side. One good route is to ascend from Savica Waterfall and return via Stara Fužina.

From the Savica Waterfall a path zigzags up the steep Komarča Crag. From the top of this cliff (1340m), there's an excellent view of Lake Bohinj. Farther north, three to four hours from the falls, is the Koča pri Triglavskih Jezerih (☎ 061-312 645 or mobile ☎ 0609-615 235; 1685m), a 104-bed hut at the southern end of the fantastic Triglav Lakes Valley where you'll spend the night. If you want a good overview of the valley and its seven permanent lakes (the others fill up in spring only), you can climb to Mt Tičarica (2091m) to the north-east in about one hour. An alternative – though longer – route from the waterfall to the Triglav Lakes Valley is via Dom na Komni (☎ 064-721 475 or mobile ☎ 0609-611 221; 1520m) and the Komna Plateau, a major battlefield in WWI.

On the second day you hike up the valley, which the immortal chamois Zlatorog is said to have created, past the largest glacial lakes then north-east to the desert-like Hribarice Plateau (up to 2448m). You descend to the Dolič Saddle (2164m) where the Tržaška Koča na Doliču (☎ 061-314 339 or mobile ☎ 0609-614 780; 2151m) has 60 beds. You would have walked about four hours by now from the Koča pri Triglavskih Jezerih and could well carry on to Dom Planika pod Triglavom (☎ 064-78 069 or mobile ☎ 0609-614 773; 2401m), about 1½ hours to the north-east. But this 80-bed hut is often packed; it's better to stay where you're sure there's a bed unless you've booked.

From Dom Planika it's just over an hour to the summit of Triglav (2864m), a well trodden path indeed. Don't be surprised if you find yourself being turned over and your bottom beaten with a birch switch. It's a long-established tradition for Triglav 'virgins'.

You could return the way you came, but it's far more interesting to go back to Bohinj southward via Stara Fužina. This way passes the 50-bed Vodnikov Dom na Velem Polju (☎ 064-723 070 or mobile ☎ 0609-615 621; 1817m) less than two hours from Dom Planika. There are two routes to choose from between Vodnikov Dom and Stara Fužina: down the Voje Valley or over Uskovnica, a highland pasture at about 1100m. The former takes about four hours; the route via Uskovnica is a little longer but affords better views. The trail to Rudno Polje and the road to Bled branches off from the Uskovnica route (see Climbing Mt Triglav from Pokljuka).

If you decide to do the trip in reverse – starting from Stara Fužina and returning via the Savica Waterfall – count on walking about seven hours to Dom Planika through the Voje Valley and eight hours via Uskovnica. ■

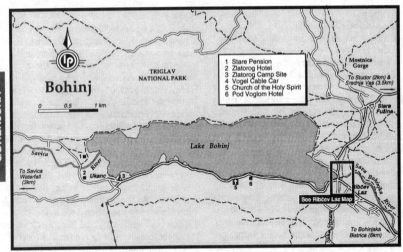

Bohinj

1 Stare Pension
2 Zlatorog Hotel
3 Zlatorog Camp Site
4 Vogel Cable Car
5 Church of the Holy Spirit
6 Pod Voglom Hotel

here until the late 19th century when it moved on to Jesenice. But all was not lost for Bohinj; a railway connecting the Sava Valley with Gorica and the coast opened in 1906, providing Bohinj with its first modern communications link.

Triglav was 'conquered' from Bohinj for the first time in the late 18th century. Bohinj has also figured prominently in Slovenian literary history. The poet Valentin Vodnik (1758-1819) lived and worked in nearby Gorjuše and even left his name in pencil on the back of the high altar at St John the Baptist's Church. And most of the events in France Prešeren's epic poem *Baptism at the Savica Waterfall*, including the demise of our hero Črtomir, take place around Bohinj. For those reasons Bohinj enjoys a much more special place than Bled in the hearts and minds of many Slovenes.

Orientation

Lake Bohinj, some 4.5km long and up to 45m deep, lies in a valley basin 523m above sea level on the southern edge of Triglav National Park. The Savica River flows into the lake to the west while the Sava Bohinjka flows out from the south-eastern corner.

There is no town called Bohinj; the name refers to the entire valley, its settlements and the lake. The largest town in the area is Bohinjska Bistrica (pop 3080; postcode 4264), 6km to the east of the lake. Small villages on or near the southern and eastern shores include: Ribčev Laz, Ukanc, Stara Fužina at the mouth of the Mostnica Gorge, Studor, a veritable 'village of hayracks', and Srednja Vas. There are no settlements on the northern side.

You'll find everything of a practical nature in Ribčev Laz – more specifically in the shopping complex south-east of the Jezero hotel.

In Ribčev Laz buses stop near the tourist office and in Bohinjska Bistrica on Triglavska cesta near the combination police station/post office and at the train station. Bohinjska Bistrica's train station is about 700m north-east of the town centre at Triglavska cesta 1.

Information

Tourist Office The helpful and very efficient tourist office (☎ 723 370; fax 723 330) at Ribčev Laz 48 is open daily July through mid-September from 7 am to 8 pm. During the rest of the year, it is open Monday to Saturday from 8 am to 7 pm and on Sunday from 8 am to 3 pm.

Money The tourist office can change money but the rate is not good and it takes a 3% commission. The post offices in Ribčev Laz and Bohinjska Bistrica give a better rate. Gorenjska Banka has a branch in Bohinjska Bistrica at Trg Svobode 2b, about 100m east of Slovenijaturist. It is open weekdays from 9 to 11.30 am and 2 to 5 pm and on Saturday from 8 to 11 am.

Post & Communications The post office at Ribčev Laz 47 is open Monday to Friday from 8 am to 6 pm with a couple of half-hour breaks and on Saturday till noon. Bohinjska Bistrica's post office, just east of Slovenijaturist at Triglavska cesta 35, is open weekdays nonstop from 8 am to 6 pm and on Saturday till noon.

Travel Agencies The Alpinum travel agency (☎ 723 441), which can organise any number of sport activities in Bohinj, is a couple of doors down from the tourist office at Ribčev Laz 50. It is open weekdays from 7 am to 7 pm and till 3 pm at the weekend. The Alpinsport kiosk (☎ 723 486) at Ribčev Laz 53 to the right, just before you cross the stone bridge to the Church of St John the Baptist, also has programs available but primarily rents equipment. It is open daily June to August from 9 am to 7 pm and from 10 am to 6 pm the rest of the year. Another such agency is Alpisclub at the Pod Voglom hotel (☎ 723 461) farther west.

Slovenijaturist (☎ 721 032) has a branch in Bohinjska Bistrica at Triglavska cesta 45. It is open Monday to Saturday from 8 am to 8 pm and on Sunday in summer from 9 am till noon. In winter, the Monday to Saturday hours are 8 am till noon and 2 to 6 pm. It also opens on Sunday morning.

Churches
The **Church of St John the Baptist**, on the northern side of the Sava Bohinjka across the stone bridge from the Jezero hotel, is what

every medieval church should be: small, on a lake and full of exquisite frescoes. To my mind, it is the most beautiful and evocative church in all of Slovenia, with the possible exception of the Church of the Holy Trinity at Hrastovlje in Primorska.

The nave is Romanesque while the Gothic presbytery dates from about 1440. A large portion of the latter's walls, ceilings and arches are covered with **15th and 16th century frescoes** too numerous to appreciate in one viewing. As you face the arch from the nave, look for the frescoes depicting the beheading of the church's patron saint on either side. On the opposite side of the arch to the left is Abel making his offering to God and, to the right, Cain with his inferior one. Upon the shoulder of history's first murderer sits a white devil – a very rare symbol. Behind you on the lower walls of the presbytery are rows of angels with vampire-like teeth; look for the three men above them singing. Some of them have goitres, once a common affliction in mountainous regions due to the lack of iodine in the diet. The carved wooden head of – guess who? – on one of the side altars dates from 1380.

Several paintings on the outside southern wall, one dating back to the early 14th century, depict St Christopher. In the Middle Ages people believed they would not die on the day they had gazed upon an icon of the patron saint of travellers. No fools our ancestors, they painted them on churches near roads and villages, but apparently they forgot to look at least once in their lives as they're all now dead. The 18th century **Church of the Holy Spirit**, a couple of kilometres to the west on the lake shore, has a painting of St Christopher on the outside as well.

The Church of St John the Baptist is open daily, mid-June to mid-September, from 9 am till noon and 3 to 6 pm. At other times a staff member from the tourist office will accompany you (150 SIT).

Museums
The **Alpine Dairy Museum** (Planšarski Muzej) at house No 181 in Stara Fužina, about 1.5km north of Ribčev Laz, has a small

collection related to Alpine dairy farming in the Bohinj Valley, once the most important such centre in Slovenia. Until the late 1950s large quantities of cheese were still being made on 28 highland pastures, but now a modern dairy in nearby Srednja Vas does it all.

The four rooms of the museum, a cheese dairy itself once upon a time, contain a mock-up of a 19th century herder's cottage, fascinating old photographs, cheese presses, wooden butter moulds, copper rennet vats, enormous snowshoes and sledges, and wonderful hand-carved crooks. It is open every day, except Monday, in July and August from 11 am to 7 pm. During the rest of the year (with the exception of November and December, when it is closed), the Tuesday to Sunday hours are 10 am till noon and from 4 to 6 pm. Admission is 300/150 SIT for adults/children.

While you're in Stara Fužina, take a walk over to the village of **Studor**, a couple of kilometres to the east. **Oplen House** (Oplenova Hiša) at No 16 is an old peasant's cottage with a chimney-less 'smoke kitchen' that has been turned into a museum (same hours and admission as the Alpine Dairy Museum). Studor's real claim to fame, however, is its many *toplarji*, double-linked hayracks with barns or storage areas at the top. Look for the ones at the entrance to the village, which date from the 18th and 19th centuries.

The **Tomaž Godec Museum** (Muzej Tomaža Godca) in Bohinjska Bistrica at Zoisova ulica 15 (about 100m south of Triglavska cesta) is a mixed bag of a place that does have its moments. Housed in a reconstructed tannery owned by Mr Godec (1905-42), a Partisan who played a role in the formation of the Yugoslav Communist Party, the exhibits trace the history of iron forging in the valley from earliest times, explain the long process of making leather – the small mill over the Bistrica River here still turns – and examine the life of Comrade Godec.

Above the mill there is a small but fascinating collection dealing graphically and often very poignantly with the horrors of the Isonzo Front in the Soča Valley during WWI. Along with weapons and bombs are many personal items from soldiers, including models of churches made from matchsticks by Russian prisoners of war and Italian helmets with holes punched into them for use as colanders when making pasta. It's really a peace museum and in many ways more moving and immediate than the much promoted museum in Kobarid. Josip Tito, who spent a few days in Bohinjska Bistrica in 1939, returned 40 years later to open the museum – something the curator is very proud of. The Tomaž Godec Museum is open May to October, Tuesday to Sunday, from 10 am till noon and 4 to 6 pm. From January to April it is open the same hours but on Wednesday, Saturday and Sunday only. Admission is 300/150 SIT for adults/children.

Savica Waterfall

Savica is one of the reasons people come to Bohinj – to gaze at this magnificent 60m waterfall cutting deep into a gorge and perhaps carry on to the Triglav Lakes Valley or even Triglav itself (see boxed text entitled Old Mr Three Heads).

The waterfall, the source of Slovenia's longest and mightiest river, is 4km from the Zlatorog hotel in Ukanc and can be reached by footpath from there. Cars and the bus in summer go via a gravel road. From the Savica restaurant, it's a 20-minute walk over rapids and streams to the falls. Entrance to the trail costs 300/150 SIT and it is open April to October from 9 am to 5 pm. It costs 350 SIT to park.

The falls are among the most impressive sights in the Julian Alps, especially after a heavy rain, but bring something waterproof or you may be soaked to the skin by the spray. Two huts to the west at just over 1500m – *Dom na Komni* (☎ 721 475 or mobile ☎ 0609-611 221) and *Koča pod Bogatinom* (☎ 723 070 or mobile ☎ 0609-621 943) – can be reached in about 2½ hours. Though both have accommodation and food, the former is open year round, the latter from late June to September only.

Old Mr Three Heads

The 2864m limestone mountain called Triglav has been a source of inspiration and devotion for Slovenes for more than a millennium. The early Slavs believed the mountain to be the home of a three-headed deity who ruled the sky, the earth and the underworld, but no one managed (or dared) to reach the summit until just two centuries ago. Today Triglav figures prominently on the national flag and seal.

As the statue of four men at Ribčev Laz constantly reminds visitors, Triglav's summit was first reached from Lake Bohinj by an Austrian climber and his three Slovenian associates in 1778 on the initiative of Žiga Zois (1747-1819), an iron magnate and patron of the arts. Under the Habsburgs in the 19th century, the 'pilgrimage' to Triglav became, in effect, a confirmation of one's Slovenian identity, and this tradition continues to this day.

You can do the hike to the summit too, even if you have no experience in this sort of thing. But first a few words of advice and caution. Do some physical exercise for a few days before setting out – bicycling, walking, swimming – and don't ignore the mental preparations; that's usually more than half the battle.

Triglav is inaccessible from late October to early June. June and July are the rainiest (and sometimes snowiest) summer months so August and particularly September and October are the best times to go. Weather can be very unpredictable at altitudes above 1500m, with temperatures varying by as much as 20°C and violent storms appearing out of nowhere.

Under *no* circumstances should you make the trek by yourself. If you are travelling alone, hire a guide (roughly 3000 to 4000 SIT a day) through the Triglav National Park office in Bled or a travel agency in Bohinj or join a group that is just setting out. Do the volunteer Mountain Rescue Service (Gorska Reševalna Služba; GRS) a favour; each year they have had to save dozens of people who went on their own, ignored the trail markings and weather warnings or tried to do something beyond their experience. Keep to the track marked with a red circle and a white centre and rest frequently. People die every year on Triglav.

What to bring depends on personal preference, but you want to travel absolutely as light as possible. Leave most of your kit down below but wear sturdy hiking boots and warm, waterproof clothing. You might also consider carrying a compass and a torch (flashlight). Food, except for snacks like nut bars, is unnecessary as the mountain huts are well supplied. You should bring some water but tea and other hot drinks are better for thirst.

There are 56 mountain huts in the Julian Alps, most of them open between June and September. But others may extend their season a month in either direction and some huts at lower altitudes are open all year. Huts are never more than five hours apart at the most. A mountain hut *(planinska koča* or *planinski dom)* almost always has accommodation (usually costing between from 1320 to 2750 SIT in a Category I hut depending on the number of beds in the room and from 1000 to 1760 SIT in a Category II one) and food, with hearty dishes like *enoloncnica* (hotpot), *golaž* (goulash) and *ješprenj* (barley gruel). You'll never be turned away if the weather looks bad, but some huts on Triglav can be unbearably crowded at weekends – especially in August and September. Try to do the trek mid-week and phone the hut ahead if it has a mobile telephone; some take bookings.

There are about 20 different ways to reach the top of Triglav with the main approaches from the south (Bohinj, Pokljuka) and the north (Vrata, Kot). All offer varying degrees of difficulty and have their pluses and minuses. Experienced hikers tend to go for the more forbidding northern approaches, descending via one of the gentle southern routes. Novices usually ascend and descend near Bohinj. The route from Trenta in the Soča Valley is steep but not impossible and less frequented due to its relatively remote start. Most treks require two overnights in the mountains.

Before you begin, arm yourself with a copy of *How to Climb Triglav*, a superb booklet with a dozen of the best routes and published by the Alpine Association of Slovenia (Planinska Zveza Slovenije; PZS). This 65-page publication, available everywhere for about 1000 SIT, also has an illustrated section on Triglav's remarkable flora that is useful.

Several maps to the area are available. Freytag and Berndt's 1:50,000-scale *Julische Alpen Wanderkarte* covers the whole of Triglav National Park. The Alpine Association publishes a two-sheet 1:50,000-scale map of the Julian Alps; for Triglav and the park you want the eastern part *(Julijske Alpe – Vzhodni Del).* They also do a more detailed 1:20,000-scale *Triglav* map. ■

Activities

Hiking For information about climbing Triglav from Bohinj see boxed text – though it's not all just Triglav at Bohinj. A circular walk around the lake (12km) from Ribčev Laz should take between three and four hours. Or you could just do parts of it by following the hunters' trail in the forest above the south shore of the lake to the Zlatorog hotel and taking the bus back or walking along the more tranquil northern shore under the cliffs of Pršivec (1761m). Much more difficult is the hike to **Mt Vogel** (1922m) from the cable car's upper station (see Skiing below). Be very careful of the fog in these parts and don't set out if it looks like rain; Vogel is especially prone to lightning strikes. The whole trip should take about four hours.

The Bohinj area map available at the tourist office for 500 SIT lists some 10 excellent walks and hikes. The Alpinum and Alpisclub agencies can arrange guides and excursions for DM30 to DM40. You can also take guided climbs ranging in grades from I to VI (DM150 to DM400). Serious stuff indeed ...

Swimming & Boating Some of the beaches on Lake Bohinj's northern shore are reserved for nude bathing in summer. Two hotels have their own indoor swimming pools (should the fog drive you inside), the Zlatorog and Jezero. Outsiders can use the former seven days a week between 3 pm and 8 pm and on Saturday and Sunday morning from 9 am till noon. Admission is 600 SIT; for 400 SIT more you get to use the sauna as well.

Alpinum and Alpinsport rent kayaks and canoes for DM5 or DM6 an hour or DM25 to DM30 a day; a kayak with all equipment for the day is DM30. As at Bled, no motor boats of any kind are allowed on the lake.

Alpisclub organises a number of sporting activities including rafting trips on the Sava Bohinjka River daily at 10 am and 2 pm and 'canyoning' through the rapids of the Mostnica Gorge, with participants safely stuffed into a neoprene body suit, life jacket and helmet for DM80.

Fishing Lake Bohinj and the jade-coloured Sava Bohinjka are rich in various types of trout and grayling and are among the most popular places for angling in Slovenia. But don't expect licences to come cheaply; you'll pay 4500 SIT a day for the lake and 8500 SIT for the river as far as Soteska. The season on the lake extends from March to September, depending on the fish, while on the river it's from May to October. The Alpinum travel agency and Stare pension in Ukanc sell the permits.

Tennis The tennis courts at the Kompas, Bellevue and Zlatorog hotels and Danica camp site cost between DM6 and DM10 per hour to hire. Two rackets and balls are about DM5.

Skiing The main skiing station for Bohinj is **Vogel** (☎ 723 466), some 1540m above the lake's south-western corner and accessible by cable car. With skiing up to 1840m, the season can be long, sometimes from late November to early May. Vogel counts 36km of ski slopes and cross-country runs served by three chair lifts and five T-bar tows. A ski pass costs 3500/19,800 SIT for a day/week, equipment costs about 2000 SIT a day and there is accommodation near the cable car's upper station at the 63-bed *Ski* hotel (☎ 721 471; fax 723 446), with singles at DM35 to DM45 and doubles DM50 to DM70.

The cable car's lower station is about 250m up the hill opposite the Zlatorog hotel in Ukanc, about 5km from Ribčev Laz. The cable car runs every half-hour year round, except in November, from 7.30 am to 6 pm (till 8 pm in July and August). Adults pay 1000 SIT for a return ticket while children pay 700 SIT.

The smaller and lower (skiing up to 1480m) ski centre of **Kobla** (☎ 721 058 or ☎ 715 860) is about 1km east of Bohinjska Bistrica. It has 23km of slopes and 10km of cross-country runs with three chair lifts and three T-bars.

Alpinsport rents downhill ski equipment for 1450/8700 SIT a day/week and cross-country gear for 1000/6000 SIT. Snowboards are 1100/6600 SIT a day/week.

An hour's individual lesson at its ski school costs 2500 SIT.

Paragliding Alpinsport has a four-hour introductory paragliding course available for DM50 and a much more intense five-day one for DM250. A tandem jump from Vogel costs DM80, from Studor (1002m) DM65.

Steam Train The Oldtimer Train run by Slovenijaturist has several excursions in summer that pass through Bohinjska Bistrica to or from Jesenice and Most na Soči. For details about itineraries, schedules and prices, contact Slovenijaturist (☎ 721 032) in Bohinjska Bistrica.

Special Events

The Cows' Ball (Kravji Bal) is a wacky event staged every year, on the third weekend in September, in a field north of the Zlatorog hotel. Although it traditionally marked the return of the cows to the valley after a spring and summer on highland pastures of up to 1700m, the ball has now degenerated into a day-long knees-up of folk dance and music, eating and drinking and haggling over baskets, painted beehive panels and bowls carved from tree roots. Of course, if you want to say you've seen cows dance, then by all means go.

On Midsummer's Night (Kresna Noč; 23 June), everyone goes out on the lake in boats with candles and there are fireworks.

Places to Stay

Camping The Bohinj area has two camping grounds. The large *Zlatorog* camp site (☎ 723 441) on the lake near the Zlatorog hotel is expensive, ranging from DM7 to DM16 depending on the season (mid-May to September). Campers get to use the tennis courts at the Zlatorog hotel.

The three-hectare *Danica* (☎ 721 055) some 200m west of the bus stop in Bohinjska Bistrica is open from May to September and costs DM8 to DM10 to camp or DM70 (DM50 after three days) to rent one of the *caravans* available on site. Danica has its own tennis courts.

Private Rooms The tourist office can arrange private rooms in Ribčev Laz, Stara Fužina and neighbouring villages for as little as DM11 per person per night in the low season and DM20 in July and August (though there's a 30% surcharge for stays of less than three days and guests on their own pay an additional 20%). Breakfast usually costs about DM6 more, though you are sometimes allowed to use the kitchen yourself. Two of the best places to stay are at the *Ardjelan* house (☎ 723 262) at Ribčev Laz 13 and *Planšar* (☎ 723 095), better known for its fabulous cheeses (see Places to Eat), at Stara Fužina 179. The latter offers accommodation in three rooms and one apartment for DM20 per person.

Apartments for two people arranged through the tourist office run from DM47 to DM63, depending on the season. The Alpinum travel agency has rooms and apartments, however they are more expensive.

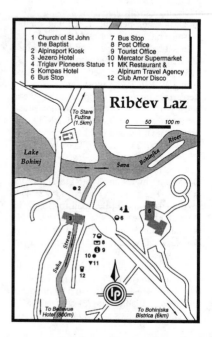

1 Church of St John	7 Bus Stop
the Baptist	8 Post Office
2 Alpinsport Kiosk	9 Tourist Office
3 Jezero Hotel	10 Mercator Supermarket
4 Triglav Pioneers Statue	11 MK Restaurant &
5 Kompas Hotel	Alpinum Travel Agency
6 Bus Stop	12 Club Amor Disco

Ribčev Laz

Slovenijaturist in Bohinjska Bistrica also has apartments.

Farmhouses Several farmhouses in the area offer accommodation, including the four-room *Agotnik* (☎ 723 014) at house No 145 in Stara Fužina and *Pri Andreju* (☎ 723 509) with three apartments for two, four or six people at house No 31 in picturesque Studor.

Pension The *Stare* pension (☎ 723 403) with nine rooms on the Sava Bohinjka River, at Ukanc 128 north of the Zlatorog hotel, has singles with shower and breakfast for DM40 to DM50, depending on the season, and doubles for DM64 to DM76. If you really want to get away from it all without having to climb mountains, this is the place.

Hotels Bohinj has no shortage of hotels but the cheapest, the 49-room *Pod Voglom* (☎ 723 461; fax 723 446) on the lake's southern shore at Ribčev Laz 60, is not very nice. It has singles with shared showers for DM33 to DM47 per person, depending on the season, and doubles for DM46 to DM74.

In Ribčev Laz proper, you have a choice of three hotels. The 50-room *Jezero* (☎ 723 375; fax 723 446), used by the Gestapo during WWII, is the most central – a few steps from the tourist office and the lake at house No 51. Single rooms with shower and breakfast start at DM69 and DM89 and doubles at DM98 and DM138. The 59-room *Bellevue* (☎ 723 331; fax 723 684), on a hill about 800m south of the Jezero at Ribčev Laz 65, charges a minimum of DM40 to DM56 for singles and DM60 to DM92 for doubles. The 55-room *Kompas* (☎ 723 471; fax 723 161), along the road to Bohinjska Bistrica north-east of the post office at No 45, has singles for DM56 to DM76 and doubles for DM72 to DM112, depending on the season.

Out of the way and pleasant for that is the 43-room *Zlatorog* (☎ 723 381; fax 723 384), a hotel in Ukanc at house No 64 with lots of activities available. Singles start at DM67 and DM85, doubles DM94 and DM130.

Places to Eat

The *MK*, a restaurant and pizzeria next to the Alpinum travel agency at house No 50 in Ribčev Laz, is one of the most popular places to eat and a good place to hang out.

If you've got wheels of any sort, head for *Gostišče Rupa* at house No 87 in Srednja Vas, about 5km from Ribčev Laz. It has excellent home-cooked food, including spectacular Bohinj trout and ajdova krapi, crescent-shaped dumplings made from buckwheat and cheese.

In Stara Fužina, the *Gostilna Mihovc* at house No 118 is a popular place and opens daily from 11 am till midnight. But if you want something light, head for *Planšar* opposite the Alpine Dairy Museum at house No 179. It specialises in home-made dairy products – hard Bohinj cheese, a soft, strong-tasting cheese called mohant, cottage cheese, curd pie, sour milk etc – and you and a friend can taste a number of them for about 700 SIT or make a meal of cheese and different types of grain dishes (600 SIT) like žganci made from buckwheat, ješprenj from barley or močnik from white corn. Other dishes available include štruklji (cheese dumplings; 700 SIT) and jota (bean 'stew' cooked with salt pork; 600 SIT). Planšar is open Tuesday to Sunday from 10 am to about 8 pm but only at weekends in winter. It's a taste sensation and highly recommended.

The *Zoisova Grad*, at Grajska ulica 14 in Bohinjska Bistrica about 200m east of the Tomaž Godec Museum, is a standard Slovenian restaurant in an old manor house with set menus from 990 SIT and pizzas. It's open daily from 11 am till midnight. Another place with pizza and cheaper set menus (from 400 SIT) in Bohinjska Bistrica is the *Bistrica* at Trg Svobode 1.

The *Mercator* supermarket at Ribčev Laz 49 is open weekdays from 7 am to 6.30 pm and to 5 pm on Saturday.

Entertainment

The only late-night venue in these parts is *Club Amor*, a disco next to the MK Restaurant and Alpinum travel agency.

Things to Buy

The traditional craft of Bohinj is a small, handcarved wooden pipe with a silver cover (*gorjuška čedra*) for smoking tobacco or whatever. The real thing isn't so easy to find these days, but the tourist office sells them and can tell you which masters are still carving.

Getting There & Away

Bus Bus services from Ribčev Laz to Ljubljana via Bled, Radovljica, Kranj, the Zlatorog hotel and Bohinjska Bistrica are very frequent. There are also about six buses a day to Bohinjska Bistrica via Stara Fužina, Studor and Srednja Vas.

From mid-June to September a bus leaves Bled bus station every day at around 10 am for Savica Waterfall, returning at about 12.45 pm. The one-way fare is 250 SIT.

Train Lake Bohinj is not on a train line, though Bohinjska Bistrica is on the scenic one linking Jesenice (28km; 35 minutes) and Bled Jezero to the north-east and Most na Soči and Nova Gorica (61km; 1¼ hours) to the south-west. Up to eight trains a day pass through Bohinjska Bistrica in each direction. From Nova Gorica you can carry on another 40km south-east to Sežana from where there are trains to Italy.

Car Alpinum in Ribčev Laz rents cars.

Getting Around

From mid-June to mid-September, a bus runs from Bohinjska Bistrica via Ribčev Laz to Savica Waterfall. From Monday to Saturday there's one departure in the morning and three in the afternoon. On Sunday, the schedule is increased by one early morning run.

Alpinsport and the Kompas hotel rent bicycles and mountain bikes for DM5/20 per hour/day.

KRANJSKA GORA

• *pop 2800* • *area code ☎064* • *postcode 4280*
The town of 'Carniolan Mountain', 40km north-west of Bled, is the largest and best equipped ski resort in the country, but somehow it just doesn't seem Slovenian. The fact that the Italian *and* Austrian borders are a half-dozen kilometres to the west and north-west might help explain that impression. But there's a clinical feel here too – one that speaks with a Teutonic accent rather than a Slavic one – and service staff are some of the most unfriendly I've encountered anywhere in the country.

Kranjska Gora is situated at 810m in the Sava Dolinka Valley separating the Karavanke range from the Julian Alps. The valley has been an important commercial route between Gorenjska and Koroška for centuries; the 853m pass at Rateče is the lowest Alpine link between the Sava and Drava valleys. The first railway in Gorenjska – from Ljubljana to Tarvisio (Trbiž) in Italy – made use of this pass when it opened in 1870.

Kranjska Gora was just a small valley village called Borovška Vas until the late 19th century, when skiing enthusiasts began to flock here. Planica, the cradle of ski jumping south of Rateče, helped put the town on the world map earlier this century.

Kranjska Gora is at its best under a blanket of snow, but its surroundings are wonderful to explore in warmer months as well. The possibilities for hiking and mountaineering are endless in Triglav National Park on the town's southern outskirts, and there aren't many travellers who won't be impressed by a trip over the Vršič Pass (1611m), the gateway to the Soča Valley and the province of Primorska.

Orientation

Kranjska Gora sits at the foot of Mt Vitranc (1631m) and in the shadow of two higher peaks (Razor and Prisojnik/Prisank) that reach up to 2600m. Rateče and Planica, famous for ski-jumping championships, are some 6km to the west while Jasna Lake, Kranjska Gora's doorway to Triglav National Park, is 2km south.

Kranjska Gora is a very small town with some unattractive modern buildings around its periphery and a more romantic older core along Borovška cesta. As you walk along this

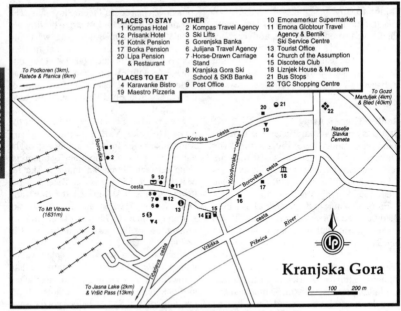

PLACES TO STAY
1 Kompas Hotel
12 Prisank Hotel
16 Kotnik Pension
17 Borka Pension
20 Lipa Pension
   & Restaurant

PLACES TO EAT
4 Karavanke Bistro
19 Maestro Pizzeria

OTHER
2 Kompas Travel Agency
3 Ski Lifts
5 Gorenjska Banka
6 Julijana Travel Agency
7 Horse-Drawn Carriage
   Stand
8 Kranjska Gora Ski
   School & SKB Banka
9 Post Office

10 Emonamerkur Supermarket
11 Emona Globtour Travel
   Agency & Bernik
   Ski Service Centre
13 Tourist Office
14 Church of the Assumption
15 Discoteca Club
18 Liznjek House & Museum
21 Bus Stops
22 TGC Shopping Centre

Kranjska Gora

GORENJSKA

street you might see tanners clipping and scraping sheepskins behind one of the farmhouses. The chair lifts up to the ski slopes on Vitranc are at the western end of Borovška cesta.

The town's bus station (just a couple of stops and a shelter) is 150m west of the big TGC shopping centre at the main entrance to the town from the motorway.

Information
Tourist Office The tourist office (☎ 881 768; fax 881 125), with rather disinterested staff, is at Tičarjeva cesta 2, a few steps east of the Prisank hotel. It has quite a few useful handouts on various activities and sells maps and guides to the surrounding areas (including Triglav National Park). From December to March and in July and August the office is open Monday to Saturday from 8 am to 2 pm and 3 to 7 pm and on Sunday from 9 am to 1 pm. In April, October and November the daily hours are 8 am to 3 pm.

Money SKB Banka has a branch with an ATM next to the ski school at Borovška cesta 99a. It is open weekdays only from 8.30 am till noon and 2 to 5 pm. Gorenjska Banka is in the building behind the ski school and south-west of the entrance to the Prisank hotel. It is open weekdays from 9 to 11.30 am and 2 to 5 pm and on Saturday from 8 to 11 am. You can also change money at the tourist office (3% commission) and post office.

Post & Communications Kranjska Gora's new post office, next to the Emonamerkur supermarket on Borovška cesta, is open weekdays from 8 am to 7 pm and on Saturday till noon. During the high seasons (July and August, and December to March), the hours on Saturday may be extended to 7 pm.

Travel Agencies Most of the big agencies are represented in Kranjska Gora, including Emona Globtour (☎ 881 055) on the corner of Koroška cesta at Borovška cesta 90 and Kompas (☎ 881 661) at Borovška cesta 98-100. In season, Globtour is open Monday to Saturday from 8.30 am to 5 pm and on Sunday from 10 am to 3 pm. Kompas' hours are 7.30 am to 7 pm Monday to Saturday and from 8 am till noon on Sunday.

Liznjek House

One of the very few sights in Kranjska Gora, this late 18th century house at Borovška cesta 63 contains quite a good collection of household objects and furnishings peculiar to this area of Gorenjska. But don't for a minute think that this 'folk baroque' house was typical of the place and time; it belonged to an immensely rich landowner and was probably considered a palace in rural Slovenia 200 years ago. Among the various exhibits are some excellent examples of trousseau chests covered in folk paintings, some 19th century icons painted on glass and a collection of linen tablecloths (the valley was famed for its flax and its weaving).

In the main room are two shuttered 'safes' for valuables; one was meant for the man of the house and one for the woman. The tiny fireplace was intended for light only. The chimney-less 'black kitchen' was used to smoke meat.

Antique carriages and a sledge are kept in the massive barn in the back, which once housed food stores as well as pigs and sheep. The stable reserved for cows below the main building now contains a **memorial room** dedicated to the life and work of Josip Vandot (1884-1944), a writer born in Kranjska Gora who penned the saga of *Kekec*, the do-gooder shepherd boy who, together with his little playmate Mojca and his trusty dog Volkec, battles the evil poacher and kidnapper Bedanec. It's still a favourite among Slovenian kids (and was made into several popular films), but he's a bit saccharine for my tastes. Kekec has become something of a symbol for Kranjska Gora, and there's a wooden statue of the tyke outside the tourist office on Borovška cesta. Oddly, the name of a gay publication in Ljubljana bears the name *Kekec*.

Liznjek House is open year round, except in April and November, Tuesday to Saturday from 10 am to 5 pm (to 4 pm on Saturday and Sunday). Admission costs 250/200 SIT.

Church of the Assumption

While the date on this baroque-looking church, in the nameless little square with the giant linden opposite Borovška cesta 78, says 1758, the net vaulting of the nave inside reveals its true age – the early 16th century. Most of the church is, in fact, late Gothic, and the belfry is even older.

Skiing

The snow-covered slopes of the Sava Dolinka Valley, running for almost 11km from Gozd Martuljek to Rateče and Planica, are effectively one big ski piste. But the main ski centres are in Kranjska Gora and Podkoren, 3km to the west, with ski jumping concentrated at Planica. The season usually lasts from mid-December to late February/early March, and there are snow cannons for making artificial snow on certain slopes.

Skiing in Kranjska Gora is on the eastern side of Vitranc, and some runs join up with those at Podkoren on Vitranc's northern face to an altitude of about 1600m. Kranjska Gora counts two chair lifts and 10 tows; Podkoren, site of the Men's World Cup Slalom and Giant Slalom Competition (Vitranc Cup) in late December, has another two chair lifts and five tows. Generally, skiing is easier at Kranjska Gora than at Podkoren, where the two most difficult slopes – Ruteč and Zelenci – are located. In all, the two centres have 30km of pistes and 40km of cross-country courses.

The ski-jumping centre at **Planica** across the motorway from Rateče has six jumps with lengths of 25, 120 and 180m. The short lift near the Dom Planica hut reaches an altitude of 900m. There are also good possibilities at Planica for tobogganing and for cross-country skiing in the Tamar Valley. The Ski Jumping World Championships are held here every year in March. The 100m mark was reached here by Austrian Josef Bradl in 1936 and the 200m one by the

GORENJSKA

Slovenian teenage champion Primož Peterka in 1994.

Ski passes for Kranjska Gora/Podkoren are DM38 a day for adults and DM27 for children, with a full seven days costing DM216/152. Needless to say, there are a lot of places offering ski tuition and renting equipment, but it's best to stick with the tried and true. Both Kompas and the Bernik Ski Service Centre (☎ 881 470) at Borovška cesta 88a next to Emona Globtour have skis and other equipment for hire; a complete kit should cost about DM20 a day or DM100 a week. Bernik opens daily in season from 8 am to 6 pm. For skiing and snowboarding lessons contact the Kranjska Gora Ski School (☎ 881 385) opposite the post office on Borovška cesta. It does both Alpine and cross-country tuition in groups and on an individual basis. For one-on-one instruction, expect to pay about DM30; it's DM45 for two people.

Hiking

The area around Kranjska Gora is excellent for hikes and walks ranging from the very easy to the difficult. One of the best references available is *Walking in the Julian Alps* (UK£8.99) by Simon Brown and published by Cicerone Press in the UK. It also includes excursions from Bled and Bohinj in Gorenjska and Bovec in Primorska. Another possible source is the dated *Julian Alps* (UK£10.95) by Robin G Collomb published by West Col Publishing (Reading, Berkshire).

Between Podkoren and Planica is a beautiful area called **Zelenci** with a turquoise-coloured lake, the source of the Sava River. You can easily walk here on a path from Kranjska Gora via Podkoren and on to **Rateče** – both attractive Alpine villages with medieval churches, wooden houses and traditional hayracks – in about two hours. If you're still willing to carry on, there's a well marked trail via Planica to *Dom v Tamarju* (☎ 876 055; 1108m) in the **Tamar Valley** 6km to the south. The walk is spectacular, in the shadow of **Mojstrovka** (2366m) to the east and **Jalovec** (2645m) to the south. The

Tamar hut is open every day and has a restaurant and accommodation for 70 people. From here, the **Vršič Pass** is less than three hours away on foot.

Another great walk from Kranjska Gora, and quite an easy one, takes you north and then east through meadows and pasture land to the traditional village of **Srednji Vrh** and **Gozd Martuljek** in a couple of hours. The views of the Velika Pisnica Valley and the Martuljek range of mountains to the south are breathtaking. From Gozd Martuljek, it's only 9km east to Mojstrana, the starting point for the northern approaches to Triglav (see boxed text entitled Climbing Mt Triglav from Mojstrana). The **Triglav Museum Collection** (Triglavska Muzejska Zbirka) in an old inn at Triglavska cesta 50 in Mojstrana deals with the early history of mountaineering and is open mid-May to mid-September from 10 am till noon and 2 to 5 pm daily, except Monday.

Other Activities

Four hotels in Kranjska Gora have indoor swimming pools and saunas, including the Larix (Borovška cesta 99), the Kompas, the Lek (Vršiška cesta 38) and the Relax (Vršiška cesta 23). You can hire one of several tennis courts at the Kompas hotel.

Horse-drawn carriages (☎ 881 082 or ☎ 881 241) seating four people can be hired from the stand behind the ski school on Borovška cesta. Prices are 1500 SIT for a trip to Jasna Lake and back and 3500 SIT for one to Planica. Horses for riding are available at the Porentov Dom (☎ 881 436) just east of Kranjska Gora on the main road at Čičare 2.

Fishing is possible in the Sava Dolinka and Jasna Lake but as always it's not for the budget-conscious. A total of three fish (the daily limit from the Sava) will cost you DM80. See Kompas if you want a fishing licence for the river and the Gostišče Jasna for one for the lake.

Engineers are conducting some exploratory drilling near the Prisank hotel; in the not-too-distant future Kranjska Gora may boast its own thermal spa.

Climbing Mt Triglav from Mojstrana

Mojstrana, 13km west of Kranjska Gora, is another gateway to Triglav, this time via one of the northern approaches. Without going into all the details, which can be gleaned from *How to Climb Triglav* (PZS), the easiest route ascends through the Kot Valley, which is accessible by road 3km south of Mojstrana. The road (and then trail) goes essentially due south past a meadow called Lengrajev Rovt, a spring and a big bowl called Pekel below Spodnja Vrbanova Špica (2299m) before reaching, in about five hours, the *Dom Valentina Staniča* (☎ 064-806 396 or mobile ☎ 0609-614 772) at 2332m. It has 78 beds. *Triglavski Dom na Kredarici* (☎ 064-223 181 or ☎ 061-312 645), the main hut serving the northern routes and at 2515m the highest accommodation in the land, is an hour away and the summit still two hours away. While Triglavski Dom has 126 beds it is often full; the best idea is to spend the night at Staniča Dom and make the ascent in the morning.

Side trips from Staniča Dom via marked and secure trails include: Begunjski Vrh (2461m; 30 minutes); Cmir (2393m; two hours); Spodnja Vrbanova Špica (2299m; 1½ hours); and Rjavina (2532m; two hours).

A more difficult ascent is possible via the Tominšek Trail through the Vrata Valley, passing *Aljažev Dom v Vratih* (☎ 064-891 030), a 180-bed hut at 1015m. The hut can be reached by car from Mojstrana (11km), but the gradient is very steep in parts. Walking should take about three hours, including time for a look at Peričnik Waterfall. You'll probably want to spend the night here as it is among the most beautiful sites in the park, with a perfect view of Triglav's north face. Nearby is a 10m boulder called Mali Triglav (Little Triglav) where you can practise your ascent of The Big One.

From Aljažev Dom it's a 3½ hour walk via the north-west flank of Cmir and below Begunjski Vrh to a spring with excellent drinking water. From the spring you can choose either to walk to Dom Staniča, 30 minutes to the south-west, or to Triglavski Dom, an hour to the south. ■

Places to Stay

Camping The closest camping ground to Kranjska Gora is *Špik* (☎ 880 120) near the Špik hotel in Gozd Martuljek, 4km east of Kranjska Gora. The eight-hectare site is on the left bank of the Sava Dolinka below the peaks of the Martuljek range, and there's an outdoor swimming pool on the grounds. The overnight rate per person is 850 to 1100 SIT, depending on the season.

Private Rooms The tourist office has singles for DM17 to DM30 and doubles for DM30 and DM52, depending on the category and the time of year. There's a 10% supplement for stays of less than three nights. Its apartments for two people run between DM50 and DM66. If the office is closed or you want to check out the premises before you hand over your money, there are a lot of houses with rooms available (look for *sobe* or *Zimmer frei* signs) in the development called Naselje Slavka Černeta south of the TGC centre. The *Vidic* house (☎ 881 375) at No 19 and the small *apartment* at No 23 are especially good deals. There are also lots of private rooms and apartments avail-

able in Rateče. Emona Globtour also has private rooms.

Farmhouses If you want to go rural, you'll have to head out of Kranjska Gora in the direction of Rateče. On the Planica side of the road, the *Kvabišar* house (☎ 876 113) at Rateče 120 has three rooms. *Skubr* (☎ 881 786), with four rooms, is at house No 78 in Podkoren. Both are open all year.

Pensions The *Borka* pension (☎ 881 297) at Borovška cesta 71 has rooms with shower for DM30 to DM35 per person. The attractive *Lipa* pension (☎ 881 101) at Koroška cesta 14 is a little more expensive at DM30 to DM40 per person.

Hotels Kranjska Gora counts about 10 hotels that are within easy walking distance of the ski lifts. Among the cheapest is the pension-like *Kotnik* (☎ 881 564; fax 881 859), one of only three private hotels in Slovenia. It has 15 double rooms costing from DM40 to DM50 per person, depending on the season, and is at Borovška cesta 75, in the centre of town.

The *Prisank* hotel (☎ 881 472; fax 881 359) has a total of 220 beds in two buildings at Borovška cesta 93 and 95. Singles range from DM48 to DM80, with doubles from DM68 to DM126.

Singles at the 156-room *Kompas* (☎ 881 661; fax 881 176), Borovška cesta 98-100, Kranjska Gora's biggest hotel, start at DM66 and DM92 with doubles from DM102 to DM154.

Places to Eat

One of the cheapest places for a quick meal in Kranjska Gora is the *Karavanke Bistro* behind Gorenjska Banka with pizza, pasta and simple grills. More pizza is available at the *Lipa* pension's lovely glassed-in café-restaurant at Koroška cesta 14, open daily from 10 am to 11 pm, and at the *Maestro* opposite at No 16. The latter has dozens of varieties of pizza and a good choice of fish dishes. The restaurant at the *Borka* pension at Borovška cesta 71 has set menus (including roast suckling pig and fish dishes) for 900 SIT. It's open daily to 11 pm.

The restaurant at the *Kotnik*, one of Kranjska Gora's better eateries with bits of painted dowry chests on the walls, serves grilled meats (pepper steak a speciality) for about 1000 SIT that should keep you going for a while.

The huge *Emonamerkur* supermarket across from the Prisank hotel on Borovška cesta is open Monday to Saturday from 7 am to 7 pm. The *Delikatesa* supermarket in the TGC centre at Naselje Slavka Černeta 33 has a better selection of meats, cheeses and fruit. It is open Monday to Saturday from 8 am to 7 pm and on Sunday to 11 pm.

Entertainment

The *Discoteca Club* just east of the Church of the Assumption on Borovška cesta is Kranjska Gora's most popular late-night venue. The *Hit Casino Kranjska Gora* (☎ 881 333) at the Relax hotel south of the town centre, on the road to Jasna Lake, is open from 6 pm Monday to Friday and from 3 pm at the weekends.

Getting There & Away

Bus Buses depart frequently for Rateče-Planica (via Podkoren) and Jesenice and once an hour for Ljubljana via Mojstrana, Jesenice, Lesce, Radovljica and Kranj. Other destinations include Villach in Austria (daily during the summer), Tarvisio in Italy (twice a day, except Sunday, at 9.35 and 11.45 am) and Zagreb in Croatia (one a day at 4.25 am).

On Saturday and Sunday in September and daily from late June to August, a bus from Ljubljana links Kranjska Gora with Bovec via the Vršič Pass. The first bus departs at 7.30 am and the last one leaves Bovec for Kranjska Gora at 5.30 pm.

Car Emona Globtour rents cars.

Getting Around

Bernik, Kompas and Julijana (☎ 881 325), a small travel agency in a kiosk west of the Prisank hotel, all rent bicycles. Bernik's rates are 400 SIT per hour, 1000 SIT for half a day and 1600 SIT for a full day. Julijana's bikes cost a bit more.

TRIGLAV NATIONAL PARK

Though there are two dozen regional parks in Slovenia, this is the country's only gazetted national park and it includes almost all of the Julian Alps lying in Slovenia. The centrepiece of the park is, of course, Mt Triglav, but there are many other peaks here reaching above 2000m as well as ravines, canyons, rivers, streams, forests and pastures. Triglav National Park (Triglavski Narodni Park) is especially rich in fauna and flora, including blossoms like the pink Triglav rose, blue Clusi's gentian, yellow hawk's beard, Julian poppy and purple Zois bell flower.

The idea for a park was first mooted in 1908 and realised in 1924, when 14 hectares in the Triglav Lakes Valley were put under temporary protection. The area was renamed Triglav National Park in 1961 and expanded 20 years later to include most of the eastern Julian Alps. Today the park covers about 84,000 hectares and stretches north from Kranjska Gora to Tolmin in the south and from the Italian border on the west almost to Bled in the east. The bulk of the park lies in Gorenjska province, but once you've crossed the awesome Vršič Pass and begun the descent into the Soča Valley, you've entered Primorska.

Excellent marked trails in the park lead to innumerable peaks and summits beside Triglav, and favourite climbs include those to **Mangart** (2678m) on the Italian border (the 12km road that descends to the Predel pass is the highest road in Slovenia), the sharp ridge of **Razor** (2601m) and the needle-

point of **Jalovec** (2645m) in the north. But the Triglav National Park is not only about climbing mountains. There are easy hikes through beautiful valleys, forests and meadows too. Two excellent maps to consult are the Alpine Association of Slovenia's 1:50,000-scale *Triglavski Narodni Park* (1000 SIT) and Freytag and Berndt's 1:50,000 *Julische Alpen Wanderkarte*.

The park has a number of rules and regulations and most of the 'don'ts' are as clear as Triglav on a clear day: no littering, no plucking flowers, no setting fires etc. But

GORENJSKA

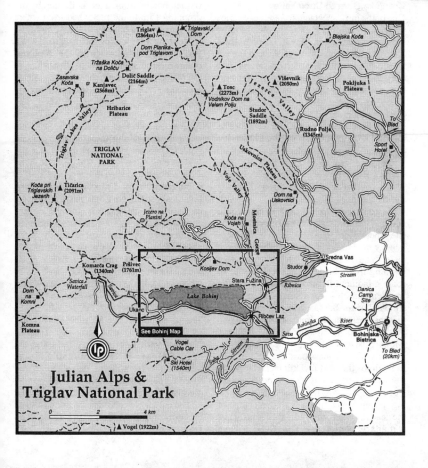

Julian Alps & Triglav National Park

also remember that this is a very fragile landscape, and there is no camping, mountain bikes are banned from trails and the park tradition is to greet everyone you pass. That can get a bit tiresome after a while but a simple *'Dober dan'* ('Hello') and/or a smile will suffice. You may notice that the roads running through the park aren't in such great shape. The park commission refuses to upgrade them for fear that half of Europe would descend on this little paradise.

For more information about Mt Triglav, see the Bled and Bohinj sections.

Kranjska Gora to Soča Valley

One of the most spectacular – and easy – trips in Triglav National Park is simply to follow the paved road, open May to October, from Kranjska Gora via the Vršič Pass to Bovec, about 50km to the south-west and just outside the park. Between June and September, you can do the trip by bus. At other times, you'll need your own transport – be it a car or mountain bike.

The first stop from Kranjska Gora is **Jasna Lake**, about 2km south of town. It's a beautiful, almost too-blue glacial lake with white sand around its rim and the little Pivnica River flowing alongside. A bronze statue of that irascible old goat Zlatorog stands guard.

As you zigzag to just over 1100m, you'll come to the **Russian Chapel** erected on the site where more than 400 Russian war prisoners were buried in an avalanche in March 1916. The POWs were in the process of building the road you are travelling on, so spare a moment in remembrance. The little wooden church is on a small hill and very simple inside. Services in memory of the victims were held jointly by the Russian patriarch and the archbishop of Ljubljana, Alojzij Šuštar, for the first time here in 1994.

The road meanders past a couple of huts as it climbs the next few kilometres to **Vršič Pass** (1611m), about 13km from Kranjska Gora. The area was the scene of fierce fighting during WWI, and a high percentage of the dead lay where they fell (at 1525m there's a **military cemetery**). The Tičarjev Dom

mountain hut is 50m away. To the west is Mojstrovka, to the east Prisojnik/Prisank; to the south the valleys of the Soča and Mlinarica rivers point the way to Primorska.

A hair-raising descent of about 10km ends just short of the **Julius Kugy Monument**. Kugy (1858-1944) was a pioneer climber and author whose books eulogise the beauty of the Julian Alps. He is shown meditating on the Trenta Mountains to the north-west. From here you can take a side trip along the Soča Trail (Soška Pot) of about 2.5km north-west to the **source of the Soča River** (Izvir Soče). Fed by an underground lake, the rivulet bursts from a dark fissure before dropping 15m to the rocky bed from where it begins its long journey to the Adriatic.

Not long after joining the main road again you'll pass the entrance to the **Alpinum Juliana**, a botanical garden established in 1926 and showcasing the flora of all of Slovenia's Alps (Julian, Kamnik, Savinja and Karavanke) as well as the Karst. The elongated mountain village of **Trenta** (662m) is about 4km to the south.

Trenta has a long tradition of mountain guides; shepherds and woodsmen made the first ascents of the Julian Alps possible in the 19th century and their bravery and skill is commemorated in a plaque just below the botanical garden. Na Logu, in the upper part of Trenta, is the gateway for the eastern approach of Triglav – a much less frequented and steeper climb than most of the others. It's about a four-hour walk from here to the Dolič Saddle (2164m) and the *Tržaška Koča* mountain hut (mobile ☎ 0609-614 780), where you join the route from Savica Waterfall near Bohinj to the *Dom Planika* (mobile ☎ 0609-614 773) and Triglav. In lower Trenta at house No 34 the *Dom Trenta* (☎ 065-89 330) contains the Triglav National Park Information Centre and the **Trenta Museum** (500/350/250 SIT for adults/students/children) dedicated to the Trenta guides, the pioneers of Slovenian alpinism and the park's flora and fauna.

The equally long village of **Soča** (480m) is another 8.5km down the river. The **Church of St Joseph** from the early 18th century has paintings by Tone Kralj (1900-75). Completed in 1944 as war still raged in central Europe, one of the frescoes depicts Michael the Archangel struggling with Satan and the foes of humanity, Hitler and Mussolini. The colours used are those of the Slovenian flag. Outside stands a lovely old linden tree and opposite, through the potato fields, the narrowing Soča flows past.

Bovec, the recreational centre of the Upper Soča Valley (Gornje Posočje), is 12km west of Soča. For details, see the following Primorska chapter.

Places to Stay & Eat The *Gostišče Jasna* overlooking Jasna Lake is a great place for a meal or a drink before pushing on for the Vršič Pass and points beyond. A lovely terrace at the back is open in the warmer months.

There are several mountain huts on or near the Vršič road. *Mihov Dom na Vršiču* (☎ 064-881 190), a hut with food and accommodation at 1085m on the Vršič road and just before the Russian Chapel, is open most of the year. The next one – at 1525m – is *Erjačeva Koča* (mobile ☎ 0609-610 031), also open all year. *Tičarjev Dom na Vršiču* (mobile ☎ 0609-634 571), right on the pass, is open from May to October. A bed in a room

for three is 2100 SIT, 1500 SIT in rooms with four to six beds and a bed in the attic is only 1050 SIT. Beyond the Tičarjev Dom at 1688m is the *Poštarski Dom* (☎ 061-313 168 in Ljubljana or mobile ☎ 0609-610 029).

Near the source of the Soča River at 886m, the *Koča pri Izviru Soče* (☎ 064-81 291) is open from May to October.

Trenta and Soča count a number of camping grounds, including *Bolčina* (mobile ☎ 0609-615 966), open all year, at Trenta 60a and charging 770 SIT per person; *Komac* (☎ 065-89 318) at Soča 8 open May to September and charging 675 to 805 SIT; and *Korita* (☎ 065-89 338) at Soča 38 open June to October and charging 600 to 800 SIT. *Kamp Klin* (☎ 065-89 356), about 4.5km to the south-west of Soča at the start of the Lepena Valley, is open May to September and charges 750 to 850 SIT.

Koča Zlatorog (☎ 065-89 382), a mountain hut at Trenta 53 that marks the start of the eastern approach of Mt Triglav, is open all year.

The staff at the Dom Trenta (☎ 065-89 330), Trenta 34, can book *private rooms* and *appartments*. *Penzion Julius* (☎ 065-89 355) at house No 31 in Soča has accommodation and there's a decent restaurant attached.

Primorska

It may come as a surprise to many that Primorska, the long slender province that extends from Austria and Triglav National Park to Istria and the Adriatic Sea, means 'Littoral' in Slovene. With Slovenia's coastline measuring only 47km long, why such an extravagant name?

It all has to do with weather. Almost all of Primorska gets the warm winds from the coast that influence the valleys as far as Kobarid and Bovec and inland. As a result, the climate and the flora here are distinctly Mediterranean right up to the foothills of the Alps. Yet the province has four distinct regions: the Soča Valley (partly covered in the Triglav National Park section of the Gorenjska chapter); central Primorska with its rolling Cerkno and Idrija hills; the unique Karst and the coast (sometimes called Slovenian Istria).

Primorska is a magical province offering unlimited activities and sights; it really is 'Europe in miniature'. In one day you can climb mountains or kayak in the Soča Valley, tour the wine-growing areas of the Vipava Valley or Brda Hills near Nova Gorica, explore the Škocjan Caves or ride Lipizzaners in the Karst or laze on the beaches of Piran or Portorož. Primorska is also an excellent gateway to Italy (eg from Nova Gorica or Ankaran) and Croatian Istria from Sečovlje and Sočerga.

The Soča Valley

The region of the Soča Valley (Posočje) stretches from Triglav National Park to Nova Gorica, including Bovec, Kobarid, Tolmin and Most na Soči. Its most dominant feature is the 96km Soča River, which can widen to 500m and narrow to less than a metre but always stays that deep, almost unreal aquamarine colour. The valley has more than its share of historical sights and important

---

HIGHLIGHTS

- Try kayaking on the aquamarine Soča River
- Sample wines from the Vipava and Brda regions
- Take a tour of the Škocjan Caves
- View the *Biblia pauperum* frescoes at the Church of the Holy Trinity in Hrastovlje
- Survey Piran and the Adriatic from the bell tower of the Church of St George
- Visit the salt pans of Sečovlje south of Portorož
- Savor a seafood meal at the Topli Val restaurant in Kobarid
- Experience high-altitude Alpine skiing at Kanin near Bovec

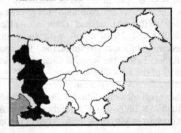

---

artwork but most people come here for such recreational pursuits as rafting, hiking and skiing.

The Soča Valley has been an important trade route between the Friulian Plain and the Alpine valleys since early times. It was the site of several Hallstatt settlements, evidenced by the rich archaeological finds unearthed at Most na Soči, Tolmin and Kobarid. During Roman times the valley was on the important Predel road between Noricum and the province of Histria, but it lost its importance when the Romans left.

The proximity of Venice and the Napoleonic wars of the late 18th and early 19th centuries restored the valley's strategic role. The railway to Bohinj brought modern transport between the Sava Valley and Gorica for

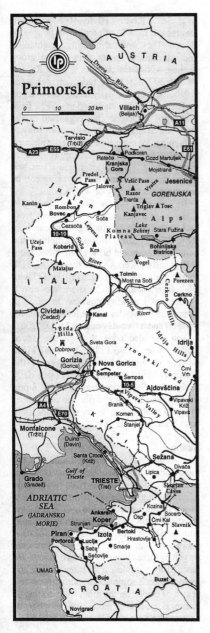

Primorska

0   10   20 km

the first time in 1906 and during WWI millions of troops were brought here to fight on the battle front stretching from the Karst to Mt Rombon. Between the wars, Primorska and the Soča Valley fell under Italian jurisdiction. Many Italians were expelled or left the province voluntarily after WWII.

BOVEC

• *pop 1775* • *area code ☎065* • *postcode 5230*

The 'capital' of the Upper Soča Valley (Gornje Posočje) has a great deal to offer adventure-sports enthusiasts. With the Julian Alps above, the Soča River below and Triglav National Park at the back door, you could spend a week hiking, kayaking, mountain biking and, in winter, skiing at Slovenia's highest ski station without ever doing the same thing twice.

History

The area around Bovec (Plezzo in Italian; Pletz in German) is first mentioned in documents dating back to the 11th century. At that time it was under the direct rule of the Patriarchs of Aquileia but was later transferred to the Counts of Gorica and, in about 1500, to the Habsburgs. The Turks passed through the basin on their way to the Predel Pass in the 15th century, and on two occasions (in 1797 and again in 1809) Napoleon's army attacked Austria from here.

Bovec suffered terribly in the fighting around the Soča Valley during WWI. Much of the town was destroyed, but its reconstruction by the architect Max Fabiani in the 1920s gave Bovec an interesting combination of traditional and modern buildings. Further reconstruction took place after a severe earthquake in 1976.

Except for a period in the 17th and 18th centuries when the Bovec area was a centre of iron mining and forging, the people here have traditionally worked as sheep and goat herders, climbing high into the mountains in search of pasture. The knowledge of these herders was highly prized by early Alpinists, and many of them became guides – a tradition that continues to this day.

PRIMORSKA

Orientation

Bovec, 483m above sea level, lies in a broad basin called the Bovška Kotlina at the meeting point of the Soča and Koritnica valleys. Towering above are several peaks of well over 2000m including Mt Rombon (2208m) and Mt Kanin (2587m). The Soča River flows past Bovec 2km to the south at Čezsoča and widens from about a metre to almost 500m. The Italian border is 16km to the south-west via the pass at Učeja and 17km north at Predel.

The centre of Bovec is Trg Golobarskih Žrtev, about the only named 'street' in Bovec. Actually it's a long square that forms the main east-west drag and runs northward to the neo-Romanesque Church of St Urh and the holiday village of Kaninska Vas. Buses stop on Trg Golobarskih Žrtev in front of the Letni Vrt restaurant at No 1.

Information

Money There's a Komercialna Banka branch next to the Alp hotel at Trg Golobarskih Žrtev 47, open from 8 am to 6 pm weekdays and till noon on Saturday. The Avrigo travel agency next door also changes money but takes a 2% commission.

Post & Communications The post office is at Trg Golobarskih Žrtev 8 at the foot of the hill leading to the church and Kaninska Vas. It is open from 8 am to 6 pm on weekdays and till noon on Saturday.

Travel Agencies Bovec has no official tourist office but two agencies can handle all your needs. The very knowledgeable staff at the Alpkomerc agency (☎ 86 370) at the Alp hotel will arrange virtually any outdoor activity you can think of. The Avrigo agency (☎ 86 123) between the Alp hotel and the bank can do the same, and is particularly good with accommodation and transport. Avrigo is open Monday to Saturday from 8 am to 6 pm (8 pm in July and August) and on Sunday from 9 am till noon.

Boating

Rafting, kayaking and canoeing on the beau-tiful Soča River (10 to 40% gradient; Degrees I to VI) attract most people to Bovec. They are exhilarating, frightening and educational sports. The largest group dealing with these pursuits is Soča Rafting (☎ 196 200) next to the reception area at the Alp hotel. It is open daily from 9 am to 6 pm.

The season for these sports lasts from mid-April to October, but organised excursions are available daily only from May to September. At other times, they take place on Saturday and Sunday. Rafting is done in groups of six to eight (leaving at 10 am and 2 pm) while canoeing and kayaking can be practised individually or with a guide.

Rafting trips on the Soča of about 1½ hours with a distance of 10km cost from DM50 to DM55 (including neoprene long john, wind cheater, life jacket, helmet and paddle). You should bring along a swimsuit, T-shirt and a towel. A canoe for two is DM58 for the day and a kayak is DM30 (DM37 with life jacket, helmet etc). There are also a number of kayaking courses on offer in summer (eg a two-day course for beginners for DM100 and a five-day course for DM200).

You can also book through the Bovec Rafting Team (☎ 86 128) in the small kiosk on Trg Golobarskih Žrtev opposite the Martinov Hram restaurant. It is open daily June to late September from 8 am to 8 pm. In April and May and from late September to mid-October it is open weekends only from 9 am to 7 pm.

Skiing

The **Kanin** ski centre (☎ 86 022) in the mountains north-west of Bovec has skiing up to almost 2300m – the only real high-altitude Alpine skiing available in Slovenia. As a result, the season can be long (God and Jack Frost providing) with good spring skiing in April and even May. The ski fields, 14km of pistes and some 12km of cross-country runs served by three chair lifts and two T-bars, are reached by a cable car in three stages; the lower station is some 600m south-west of the centre of Bovec on the main road. Skiing at Kanin is generally more difficult than at centres like Kranjska Gora in Gorenjska and

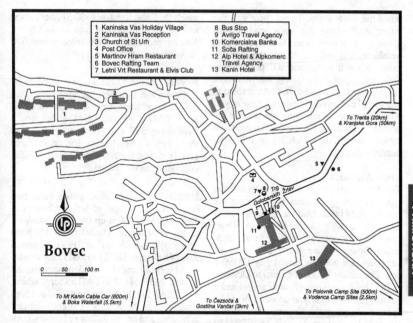

1 Kaninska Vas Holiday Village
2 Kaninska Vas Reception
3 Church of St Urh
4 Post Office
5 Martinov Hram Restaurant
6 Bovec Rafting Team
7 Letni Vrt Restaurant & Elvis Club
8 Bus Stop
9 Avrigo Travel Agency
10 Komercialna Banka
11 Soča Rafting
12 Alp Hotel & Alpkomerc Travel Agency
13 Kanin Hotel

To Trenta (20km) & Kranjska Gora (50km)

Bovec

0   50   100 m

To Mt Kanin Cable Car (600m) & Boka Waterfall (5.5km)

To Čezsoča & Gostilna Vančar (3km)

To Polovnik Camp Site (500m) & Vodenca Camp Sites (2.5km)

PRIMORSKA

Rogla in Štajerska. You can rent the complete kit (skis, poles, boots) from the Alpkomerc agency.

The cable car runs constantly during the skiing season; in July and August it runs hourly from 8 am to 4 pm and every second hour from Thursday to Sunday in June and September. It's a lovely place to go when the weather is clear and from the cable car's upper station you could make the difficult three-hour climb of **Mt Kanin** or reach the **Prestreljenik Window** (2499m) in about 1½ hours. For your troubles, you'll see all the way to Trieste and the Julian Alps.

Hiking
The 1:25,000-scale map called *Bovec z Okolico (Bovec and Surroundings)* lists a number of walks and hikes ranging from a two-hour stroll south to **Čezsoča** and the protected gravel deposits in the Soča to an ascent of **Mt Rombon**, which would take a good four hours one way. *Walking in the*

Julian Alps (Cicerone Press; UK£8.99) by Simon Brown also lists a half-dozen walks in the area, including an easy one to the source of the Soča River and the difficult ascent of Kanin. The Alpkomerc agency also has a lot of guided walks available such as the one to the **Mangrt Saddle** (2072m) along the highest road in Slovenia and to **Krn Lake** above the Lepena Valley. They're expensive at about DM40 per person, but you certainly won't get lost. The agency also has a mountain walking tour of medium difficulty that follows the Soča Front lines (see the Kobarid section) to Rombon, passing trenches, old caverns, bunkers and observation posts. It takes between eight and 10 hours and costs DM80.

The most popular do-it-yourself walk in the area is to **Boka Waterfall** some 5.5km to the south-west of Bovec. The waterfall drops more than 100m from the Kanin Mountains into the valley and is almost 30m wide – it's an impressive sight, especially in late spring when the snow melts. To get there you can either walk along the main road toward Tolmin, which more or less follows the Soča, or take the bus and get off after the Gostilna Žikar, a small restaurant and pub in Pod Čela. The trip up to the falls (850m) and back takes about 1½ hours but the path is steep in places and can be very slippery. Those of you who are not up for climbing can stand at the bridge on the main Bovec-Tolmin road and look up at the falls which are on full – but distant – display.

Other Activities

The Alpkomerc and Avrigo agencies sell two types of fishing licences for hooking the famous Soča trout. One for the area east of Čezsoča, as well as the Lepenjica River, costs DM120 per day. To fish in the Soča below Bovec, where there is a lot more kayaking and boating, you'll pay DM90 a day. The season lasts from April to October.

Tandem paragliding (ie with a pilot and a passenger), in which you descend from the upper cable-car station down 2000m into the Bovec Valley or from Mangrt, costs DM130 with Soča Rafting and there are hourly lessons in paragliding for DM30 available in March and April and again from August to October.

You can also learn to pothole – descending with a guide through tunnels into the bowels of the earth – in the Kanin Mountains. This is real adventure stuff – there are no pretty stalactites or stalagmites or easy trails to keep you going here. But prices are steep: from DM100 for one person, DM160 for two and DM180 for three.

Places to Stay

Camping The closest camping ground to Bovec is the *Polovnik* camp site (☎ 86 069) about 500m south-east of the Kanin hotel. It's small but is in an attractive setting. Polovnik, which is open from April to September, costs between 720 and 850 SIT per person, depending on the month. The little *Liza* camp site (☎ 86 073) is farther afield in Vodenca, some 2.5km south-east of the town centre at the point where the Koritnica River

meets the Soča. It charges 830 SIT per person and is open from April to mid-October. Nearby and right on the river is the *Toni* 'kayak camp' (☎ 86 454).

Private Rooms These are easy to come by in Bovec and the agencies have more than 300 beds on their lists. A single will cost about DM21, a double DM38, but you'll have to pay 30% extra for stays of less than three nights. Apartments for up to three people cost between DM62 and DM68, depending on the season.

Hotels The Alpkomerc group runs two hotels and a 'village' of holiday houses at Kaninska Vas, 500m up the hill north-west of the town centre. The 93-room *Alp* hotel (☎ 86 040; fax 86 081) at Trg Golobarskih Žrtev 48 charges DM75 to DM95 for singles with breakfast and shower, depending on the season, and DM110 to DM150 for doubles. The *Kanin* hotel (☎/fax same), about 150m south-east of the Alp, is in slightly quieter surrounds and has an indoor swimming pool and a sauna. It has 122 rooms. Single rates are DM78 to DM106, depending on the season and whether your room has a balcony. Doubles are DM116 to DM172.

The *Kaninska Vas* complex (☎ 86 022; fax 86 081) has apartments for two people for between DM48 and DM57, depending on the season.

Places to Eat

The *Letni Vrt* (Summer Garden) opposite the Alp Hotel has pizza, grilled dishes and trout at affordable prices. Its garden is lovely in summer and there is also the *Club Elvis* disco here, should you want to kick up your heels after dark. *Martinov Hram* at Trg Golobarskih Žrtev 27 specialises in seafood and grills. It is open from 10 am to 11 pm every day but Monday.

If you want to go where local people do, head for *Vančar* in Čezsoča (house No 48), about 3km south of Bovec. It is open from 11 am to 10 pm but closes Monday and Tuesday.

Getting There & Away

Buses are frequent to Kobarid and Tolmin, with some eight departures a day (a lot less at the weekend). There are also four buses a day to Ljubljana via Tolmin and Most na Soči and three to Nova Gorica. In July and August there are up to five daily buses to Kranjska Gora via the Vršič Pass, one of which carries on to Bled.

Getting Around

Alpkomerc and Soča Rafting rent bicycles and mountain bikes. The latter costs 1200 SIT for a half day, 1800 SIT for a full day and 7200 SIT for five days. They also organise group bike trips of varying lengths and degrees of difficulty: DM80 for three hours for between two and eight cyclists and DM180 for seven hours.

KOBARID

• *pop 1460* • *area code* ☎*065* • *postcode 5222*

Only a few things have changed since the American writer Ernest Hemingway described Kobarid (then Caporetto) in his novel depicting the horror and suffering of WWI, *A Farewell to Arms* (1929). It was 'a little white town with a campanile in a valley,' he wrote, 'a clean little town and there was a fine fountain in the square'. The bell in the tower still rings on the hour, but the fountain has disappeared; you can locate it (and hear the water rushing below) in the courtyard behind Trg Svobode 15, north of the rather striking statue of the poet and priest Simon Gregorčič (1844-1906), who was born in nearby Vrsno.

Kobarid did have a history before WWI and things have happened since. It was a military settlement during Roman times, was hotly contested in the Middle Ages and hit by a devastating earthquake in 1976 which destroyed some historical buildings and farmhouses with folk frescoes (preserved in the Kobarid Museum). But the world will always remember Kobarid as Caporetto and the decisive battle of 1917 in which the combined forces of the Central Powers defeated the Italian army.

Orientation & Information

Kobarid, some 21km south of Bovec, lies in a broad valley on the right bank of the Soča River. Though it is surrounded by mountain peaks of more than 2200m, Kobarid feels

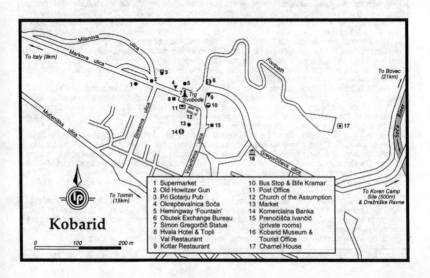

Kobarid

1 Supermarket	10 Bus Stop & Bife Kramar
2 Old Howitzer Gun	11 Post Office
3 Pri Gotarju Pub	12 Church of the Assumption
4 Okrepčevalnica Soča	13 Market
5 Hemingway 'Fountain'	14 Komercialna Banka
6 Obutek Exchange Bureau	15 Prenočišča Ivančič
7 Simon Gregorčič Statue	(private rooms)
8 Hvala Hotel & Topli	16 Kobarid Museum &
Val Restaurant	Tourist Office
9 Kotlar Restaurant	17 Charnel House

0 100 200 m

more Mediterranean than Alpine. The Italian border at Robič is only 9km to the west and Cividale, where a good many people from Kobarid commute to work every day, is another 18km to the south.

The centre of Kobarid is Trg Svobode, dominated by the Gothic Church of the Assumption and that famous bell tower. Buses stop in front of the Bife Kramar on the eastern side of the square at No 9. There is a schedule posted.

The tourist office (☎/fax 85 055) is on the ground floor of the Kobarid Museum at Gregorčičeva ulica 10 and keeps the same hours as the museum. There's a Komercialna Banka branch in the market at Trg Svobode 4 open weekdays from 8 am to 6 pm and on

Saturday till noon, and a *bureau de change* called Obutek at Trg Svobode 12 is open Monday to Saturday from 8 am to 7.30 pm. The post office, to the west of the church at Trg Svobode 2, is open weekdays from 8 am to 6 pm, with a couple of half-hour breaks, and on Saturday till noon.

Kobarid Museum

This museum, which opened to great fanfare in 1990 and has won several European awards, is located in the 18th century Mašer House at Gregorčičeva ulica 10. It is devoted almost entirely to the Soča Front and deals with the tragedy of the 'war to end all wars'.

Among the collection are 500 photographs documenting the horrors of the Soča

---

Soča (Isonzo) Front

The breakthrough in the Soča Front (more commonly known to historians as the Isonzo Front) by the combined Austrian, Hungarian, German and Slovenian forces near Kobarid in October 1917 was one of the costliest battles in terms of human life that the world has ever known. By the time the fighting had stopped 17 days later, hundreds of thousands of soldiers lay dead or wounded, writhing and screaming in the blood-drenched earth, gassed and mutilated beyond recognition, with limbs and faces torn away.

In May 1915, Italy declared war on the Central Powers and their allies and moved its army across the south-western border of Austria to the strategically important Soča Valley. From there, they hoped to move eastward to the heart of Austria-Hungary. By then, however, the Austrians had fortified the lines with trenches and bunkers for some 80km from the Adriatic and the Karst to the mountain peaks overlooking the Upper Soča Valley as far north as Mt Rombon. The First Offensive launched by the Italians was successful and they occupied Kobarid and Mt Krn to the north-east, where they would remain for 29 months.

The Italians, commanded by General Luigi Cadorna, launched another 10 offensives over the ensuing months, but the difficult mountain terrain turned it into a war of attrition between two entrenched armies. Territorial gains were minimal but the fighting was horrific, involving a total assault of light artillery, anti-aircraft guns, trench mortars and gas-mine throwers. With the stalemate, much of the fighting shifted to Gorica (Gorizia) on the edge of the Karst.

On 24 October 1917 the stalemate was broken. By then the Italians had become dispirited by their lack of success and the weaker Austrian forces knew this. So the Austrians formulated an unusual plan of attack based on surprise and moved hundreds of thousands of troops, arms and materiel (including six German divisions) into the area between Trnovo and Kobarid. The 12th Offensive – the first by the Austrians – began with heavy bombardment.

The 'miracle of Kobarid' routed the Italian army and pushed the fighting back to the Friulian Plain as far as the Piave River, where the war continued for another year. The sketches of the breakthrough by one Lieutenant Erwin Rommel, who later became known as the 'Desert Fox' while commanding Germany's North African offensive in WWII, are invaluable for understanding the battle. But nothing is more vivid than the description of the Italian retreat in Ernest Hemingway's *A Farewell to Arms*. The novelist himself was wounded on the Gorica battlefield in the spring of 1917 while driving an Italian ambulance.

The 12th Offensive was the greatest breakthrough in World War I. It was also the most difficult mountain battle and the first successful 'lightning war' (blitzkrieg) in the history of European warfare. The Italians alone lost 500,000 soldiers and another 250,000 were taken prisoner. But if we count the casualties on the Soča Front for the entire 1915-17 period, that number grows to almost a million, including soldiers on the battlefields and men, women and children behind the lines. ■

or Isonzo Front (see boxed text entitled The Soča (Isonzo) Front), military charts, diaries and maps and two large relief displays showing the front lines and offensives through the Krn Mountains and the positions in the Upper Soča Valley the day before the decisive breakthrough. There's also a 22-minute 'multivision presentation' (slides with commentary) describing the preparations for the final battle, the fighting and its results. The observations made by soldiers on both sides are the most enlightening parts.

The museum is divided into about 18 rooms on three floors and the displays are labelled in four languages, including English. The entrance hall on the ground floor has photographs of soldiers, tombstone crosses, mortar shells and the flags of all the countries involved in the conflict.

The rooms on the 1st and 2nd floors have themes: the **Black Room** shows horrible photographs of the dead and dying; the **White Room** describes the particularly harsh conditions of waging war in the mountains in the snow and fog; and the **Rear Lines Room** explains what life was like for soldiers during pauses in the fighting and for the civilian population uprooted by war and famine. The **Breakthrough Room** deals with the events over three days (24-27 October 1917) when the combined Austrian and German forces met up near Kobarid and defeated the Italian army. In one room an Italian soldier sits in his cavern shelter writing a letter to his father while the war rages outside.

The Kobarid Museum is open daily from 9 am to 7 pm. Admission costs 450 SIT for adults and 250 SIT for students and children.

Italian Charnel House

This huge ossuary (kostnica in Slovene), containing the bones of more than 7000 Italian soldiers killed on the Soča Front, stands on the **Hill of St Anthony** east of Trg Svobode. You can reach it in about 10 minutes by following the footpath leading north from Trg Svobode and lined with the Stations of the Cross.

After the war Austrian, German and Italian cemeteries littered the entire Soča Valley. During the Italian occupation of Primorska between the wars, the authorities in Rome decided to collect what Italian remains they could and bury them at the charnel house. The dedication in September 1938 was attended by Benito Mussolini.

The charnel house comprises three stacked octagons, each smaller than the one before it, and is topped with the 17th century **Church of St Anthony**, moved here in 1935. Only one of several frescoes painted by Jernej Vrtav (1647-1725) survived the move.

Third Italian Defence Line

From the ossuary, a path several kilometres long leads east along the remains of the 3rd Defence Line built to **Kozjak Waterfall** by the Italians in 1915. The path crosses the Soča over a copy of the bridge that was originally built by the French during the period of the Illyrian Provinces in the early 19th century. Though the original was destroyed in May 1915, it is still called **Napoleon Bridge**.

After a short distance the path heads north and joins the cleared trenches that lead to gun emplacements, observation posts and a cavern used as shelter – not unlike the one in the Kobarid Museum in which the young soldier writes his letter home. About 500m after you cross a stone bridge over the **Kozjak Stream** you reach the waterfall.

Places to Stay

Wherever you stay in Kobarid that infamous church bell is likely to keep you awake at least part of the night. Not only does it ring on the hour every hour but two minutes later as well!

The small *Koren* camp site (☎ 85 312) is about 500m north of Kobarid on the left bank of the Soča and just before the turn to Drežniške Ravne, a lovely village with traditional farmhouses, at the foot of Mt Krn. Koren is open from mid-March to October and costs 720 SIT per person.

In Kobarid, the tourist office has a short list of families offering *private rooms* including *Prenočišča Ivančič* (☎ 85 307) between the museum and Trg Svobode at Gregor-čičeva ulica 6c (but enter via the driveway from Volaričeva ulica south of the main square). They charge 2000 SIT per person without breakfast. The Hvala hotel (see below) also has two private doubles available for DM30 to DM35, which includes breakfast.

The only hotel in town is the 32-room *Hvala* (☎ 85 311; fax 85 322), a wonderful metamorphosis of the run-down Matajur hotel at Trg Svobode 1. It has a bar, one of the best restaurants in the country, a back garden which is open in summer and it even sells permits for fishing in the Soča. Singles are DM50 to DM63, depending on the season, and doubles are DM80 to DM106.

Places to Eat

The *Okrepčevalnica Soča*, opposite the Hvala hotel at Trg Svobode 12, has drinks and snacks, including pizza. A more salubrious sit-down option is the *Kotlar* restaurant at Trg Svobode 11, open Thursday to Monday to 11 pm (midnight on Friday and Saturday).

One of Slovenia's finest restaurants is in Kobarid – the *Topli Val* at the Hvala hotel open daily from noon to midnight. With a name meaning 'Warm Wave' and owners from Portorož, the speciality here has got to be seafood. It's excellent but not cheap: a shellfish starter for two is 1900 SIT and Soča trout and other fish main courses cost around 2000 SIT. Expect to pay about 8000 SIT for two with a decent bottle of wine (eg Goriška Chardonnay).

There's a large *supermarket* at Markova ulica 1, open daily from 7 am to 7 pm (to 3 pm on Thursday and 8 pm daily in summer).

Entertainment

The *Pri Gotarju* pub in a shady garden at the start of Milanova ulica is a pleasant place for a drink – especially in the courtyard in summer. In the grassy area near the petrol station opposite is a rusting 150mm Howitzer weighing more than 5000kg and built by Krupp-Eassen in 1911. It was fished out of the Soča River after WWI.

Getting There & Away

Buses are frequent to Bovec and Tolmin, 15km to the south-east. Other destinations include Cerkno (up to five a day), Ljubljana via Idrija (six) and Nova Gorica (four).

NOVA GORICA

• *pop 14,800* • *area code ☎065* • *postcode 5000*

When the town of Gorica, capital of the former Slovenian province of Goriška, was awarded to the Italians under the Treaty of Paris in 1947 and became Gorizia, the new socialist government in Yugoslavia set itself to building a model town on the eastern side of the border 'following the principles of Le Corbusier', the Swiss functionalist architect who has a lot to answer for. Appropriately enough they called it 'New Gorica' and erected a chain-link barrier between the two towns.

'Where the Latin and the Slavic worlds shake hands in the name of friendship' and other tourist-brochure malarkey notwithstanding, Nova Gorica itself offers travellers little more than a game of chance and an easy doorway into or out of Slovenia. With the Italian frontier running right through what was once united Gorica and a couple of flashy casino-hotels dominating the place, most people arrive here to try their luck or move on – sometimes both and in that order. But Nova Gorica isn't all bad. It's a surprisingly green place with a couple of lovely parks and gardens and its immediate surrounds – eg the Franciscan monastery at Kostanjevica nad Gorico to the south and the ancient settlement of Solkan in the north, with several baroque manor houses – offer some startling contrasts. Slovenian, Venetian, Friulian and Austrian influences can be felt everywhere in the hinterland.

Nova Gorica straddles two important wine-growing areas: the Brda Hills to the north-west and the wide Vipava Valley to the south-east. It's also an excellent springboard for some of Slovenia's most popular destinations: the Soča Valley, Bled and Bohinj in Gorenjska and the beautiful Karst region leading to the coast.

Orientation

Nova Gorica sits on a broad plain south of the Soča River. Across the Italian region of Goriziano to the north-west are the Brda Hills (Goriška Brda). The Vipava Valley (Vipavska Dolina) lies to the south-east. The Karst region is south and south-east of the town.

Nova Gorica is an unusually long town, running about 5km from the border crossing at Rožna Dolina (Casa Rossa) in the south to Solkan in the north. The bus station is in the centre of town at Kidričeva ulica 22, some 400m south-west of the Perla hotel. The train station is on Kolodvorska ulica, about 1.5km to the west. To get to the train station from Kidričeva ulica, walk south-west on Erjavčeva ulica. When you reach the Italian border and checkpoint follow Kolodvorska ulica north to No 6.

Neither this border checkpoint nor the one farther north at Solkan is open to foreigners (ie non-Slovenes and non-Italians). To cross into Italy you must travel 4km south to Rožna Dolina or another 2km to Vrtojba (Santa Andrea).

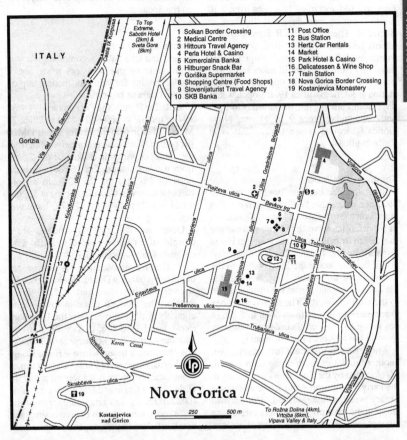

1	Solkan Border Crossing	11	Post Office
2	Medical Centre	12	Bus Station
3	Hittours Travel Agency	13	Hertz Car Rentals
4	Perla Hotel & Casino	14	Market
5	Komercialna Banka	15	Park Hotel & Casino
6	Hitburger Snack Bar	16	Delicatessen & Wine Shop
7	Goriška Supermarket	17	Train Station
8	Shopping Centre (Food Shops)	18	Nova Gorica Border Crossing
9	Slovenijaturist Travel Agency	19	Kostanjevica Monastery
10	SKB Banka		

ITALY

To Top Extreme, Sabotin Hotel (2km) & Sveta Gora (8km)

Gorizia

Cesta IX Korpusa

Via del Monte Santo

Kolodvorska ulica

Prvomajska

ulica

Rejčeva ulica

Ulica Gradnikove Brigade

Bevkov trg

Cankarjeva ulica

Vojkova cesta

Ulica Tolminskih — Puntarjev

Delpinova ulica

Kidričeva ulica

Gregorčičeva ulica

ulica

Erjavčeva

Prešernova ulica

Trubarjeva ulica

Koren Canal

Smetiška Pot

Vojkova cesta

Škrabčeva ulica

Kostanjevica nad Gorico

Nova Gorica

0   250   500 m

To Rožna Dolina (4km), Vrtojba (6km), Vipava Valley & Italy

Information

About the only sources of information in Nova Gorica are travel agencies. Slovenija-turist (☎ 26 012) is a couple of hundred metres north-west of the bus station at Erjavčeva ulica 4 and keeps 'Italian' hours: from 9 am till noon and from 3 to 6 pm on weekdays and on Saturday morning. Hittours International (☎ 28 202), a travel agency owned by the Hit hotel and casino group at Bevkov trg 6, may answer your questions but won't be all that keen to do so. The office is open weekdays from 8 am to 7 pm and till 1 pm on Saturday.

Komercialna Banka, south of the Perla hotel at Kidričeva ulica 11, opens from 7.30 am to 6 pm on weekdays and till noon on Saturday. There's an SKB Banka with a Cirrus-linked ATM at Ulica Tolminskih Puntarjev 4. The bank itself is open weekdays only from 8.30 am till noon and 2 to 5 pm. The post office is opposite the bus station at Kidričeva ulica 19. It's open weekdays from 7 am to 7 pm, on Saturday to 1 pm and on Sunday from 9 to 11 am. Nova Gorica's medical centre (☎ 22 122) is at Rejčeva ulica 4.

Things to See & Do

Neither the neo-baroque **basilica** built in 1927 nor yet another **WWI museum** perched atop **Sveta Gora** (Monte Santo) 8km north of Nova Gorica is worth the trip; you can see the church from the town anyway. But if you do walk up the 681m hill on a clear day, you'll be able to see the Soča Valley to the north and the impossibly blue ribbon that is the Soča River, and across the Friulian Plain to the Gulf of Trieste. The museum is open Wednesday to Friday from noon to 5 pm (4 pm in winter) and on Saturday and Sunday from 11 am to 7 pm (4 pm in winter).

The **Kostanjevica Monastery**, on another hill 800m south of the train station, was founded by the Capuchin Franciscans in the early 17th century and has a wonderful library which can be visited. The narrow, single-nave **church** nearby has interesting stuccos and in the spooky **crypt** lie the mortal remains of the last members of the French house of Bourbon, including Charles X (1757-1836), who was overthrown in the July Revolution of 1830 in Paris. The monastery is open Monday to Saturday from 9 am till noon and from 2 to 5 pm.

If you have a few hours on hand and always did want to try bungee jumping, Top Extreme (☎ 22 006 or mobile ☎ 0609-620 636) at Vojkova ulica 9 in Solkan will have you flying from the Solkan Bridge over the Soča River in a few hours. The mini-course and jumps are organised on Saturday and Sunday between April and October. It also organises rafting, kayaking and canyoning on the Soča.

Places to Stay & Eat

Decent and affordable accommodation is at a premium in this transient town and if you're looking for value for money, hop on the next train or bus out.

In Rožna Dolina, the *Pertout* family (☎ 32 194 or mobile ☎ 0609-624 452) at Ulica 25 Maja 23 has *private rooms* for about DM20 per person. The house is scarcely 200m from the border crossing. In Solkan, about 2.5km from the bus station, the 16-room *Sabotin* hotel (☎ 28 221; fax 26 430), in an old baroque manor at Cesta IX Korpusa 35, has doubles with shower for DM72, including breakfast.

Other than that, the only choices are a couple of expensive hotels, both with casinos. The 84-room *Park* (☎ 28 225; fax 22 381) at Delpinova ulica 5 is the cheaper of the two, charging DM110 for a single with shower and breakfast and DM160 for a double. The flashiest place in town – and arguably in all of Slovenia – is the 105-room *Perla* hotel (☎ 12 630; fax 28 886) at Kidričeva ulica 7. A favourite with Italians, this place could be anywhere – Hong Kong, Las Vegas, Disneyland Paris – and it's something local people are just a wee bit proud of. DM133 for a single and DM200 for a double (DM270 for a suite) gets you the run of the place (pool, sauna, tennis courts, casino) and breakfast. The Perla's expensive restaurant (with an emphasis on Italian dishes – surprise, surprise) is quite good.

The shopping centre north of the bus station is a warren of cafés, pubs and fast-food places, including the ever-popular *Hitburger*. There's also a large supermarket here called *Goriška* open Monday to Saturday from 7 am to 7 pm. The outdoor *market* is just off Delpinova ulica east of the Park hotel. A good place for picnic supplies is *Delikatesa Ideja* on the corner of Delpinova ulica and Prešernova ulica, open Monday to Saturday from 7.30 am to 7 pm. The *Goriška Brda Vinoteka* next door (open 10 am to 5 pm weekdays, 8 am to 1 pm on Saturday) has an excellent selection of local wines.

Entertainment

The *Perla Hit Casino* (☎ 28 890) is the company store – nothing makes more money in this town, and it's all in lire from Italians across the border. So if you want to gamble along with thousands of *italiani*, by all means beat a path to Kidričeva ulica 7 – it's open 24 hours a day. The *Park Hit Casino* (☎ 27 221) is also open 24 hours with the exception of the roulette tables (open 3 pm to 4 am). Both casinos offer all the usual games – roulette, blackjack, poker, baccarat – with a total of almost 800 slot machines.

Getting There & Away

Bus From Nova Gorica you can expect buses to Ajdovščina every half-hour and at least one an hour to Ljubljana, Postojna, Šempeter and Tolmin. Other destinations and their daily frequencies include: Bovec (three), Celje (two), Dobrovo (two), Idrija via Tolmin or Ajdovščina (two), Koper (three), Maribor (two), Piran (two) and Sežana via Komen or Branik (six). In July and August there are three buses a day to Kranjska Gora via Bovec and the spectacular Vršič Pass.

Up to five buses a day cross the Italian border to Gorizia, and there's a daily bus at 6.30 am to Trieste. There's also a daily departure at 7.15 am for Rijeka in Croatia.

Train About half a dozen trains head north-east each day for Jesenice (89km; 1¾ hours) via Most na Soči, Bohinjska Bistrica (61km; 70 minutes) and Bled Jezero (79km; 1½ hours) on what is arguably the country's most beautiful train trip. In the other direction, an equal number of trains go to Sežana (40km; 55 minutes), where you can change for Ljubljana or Trieste in Italy.

Nova Gorica is linked to Ajdovščina, 26km to the south-east, by two trains a day from Monday to Saturday, year round except during school holidays.

Getting Around

Local buses serve Solkan, Rožna Dolina, Šempeter and Vrtojba from the main station. Hertz (☎ 28 711) at Delpinova ulica 12 rents cars and is open from 7 am to 7 pm weekdays and to 1 pm on Saturday. You can order a taxi on ☎ 22 059 or ☎ 22 300.

AROUND NOVA GORICA
• *area code* ☎ 065

If you want to have a look at **Goriška Brda**, the hilly wine region that stretches from Solkan west to the Italian border, catch a bus to **Dobrovo**, 13km to the north-west. The town has a **Renaissance castle** dating from about 1600 that is filled with period furnishings and exhibits on the wine industry. Dobrovo Castle on Grajska cesta also has a very good restaurant and a vinoteka where you can sample the local vintages: white Rebula and Chardonnay or the Pinot and Merlot reds. The very full red Teran (made from the grape varietal Refošk) is more closely associated with the Karst region than here. Goriška Brda is also known for its fabulous cherries in early June.

This area has been under the influence of northern and central Italy since time immemorial and you'll think you've crossed the border as you go through little towns with narrow streets, houses built of karst limestone and the remains of feudal castles. One good example is **Šmartno** (San Martino), a pretty little fortified village with stone walls and a tower from the 16th century.

South-east from Nova Gorica is the wide and fertile **Vipava Valley**, also famous for its wines; indeed, the first wine cooperative in Slovenia was established here in 1894. Some of the reds here are world-class and Vipava Merlot is among the best wines in central Europe. They also do a decent rosé. The valley's mild climate encourages the cultivation of delicate stone fruits like peaches and apricots and in autumn, when the red sumac changes colour, the valley can look as if it is in flames.

The Vipava Valley is where the Romans first launched their drive into the Danube region, and it was overrun by the Goths, Huns and Langobards from the 4th to 6th centuries before the arrival of the early Slavs. Along the way though the valley, about 22km south-east of Nova Gorica, is **Vipavski Križ** (Santa Croce), a walled medieval village with a ruined castle, a Gothic church and a 17th century monastery with some wonderful illuminated medieval manuscripts.

Another 4km to the west is **Ajdovščina** (Aidussina). This was the site of Castra ad Fluvium Frigidum, a Roman fort on the River Frigidus (Vipava) and the first important station on the road from Aquileia to Emona (Ljubljana). The border between Goriška and Kranjska (Carniola) provinces once ran nearby.

The town of **Vipava** (Vipacco), the centre of the valley 6km to the south-east, is full of stone churches below **Mt Nanos**, a karst plateau from where the Vipava River springs. Be sure to make a side trip 2km to **Zemono Palace** (☎ 65 129), a summer mansion built around 1700 by one of the Counts of Gorica. Today the mansion, built in the shape of a cross inside a square with arcaded hallways and a raised central area, houses a posh restaurant and wine cellar and is used for wedding ceremonies and banquets. Have a peek at some of the **baroque murals** near the entrance. They portray a phoenix and a subterranean cave – symbols of fire and water. There are some excellent views down into the fertile valley from Zemono.

Central Primorska

This is an area of Primorska often overlooked by travellers heading for the 'sexier' Alps, Karst or beaches. Central Primorska is a land of steep slopes, deep valleys and innumerable ravines with plenty of good hiking, the lovely Idrijca River and a couple of interesting towns.

Central Primorska is dominated by the Cerkno and Idrija hills, which eventually join the Škofja Loka Hills in Gorenjska to the east. They are foothills of the Julian Alps. A major tectonic fault line runs below the region and Idrija was the epicentre in the catastrophic quake of 1511. It was at the time no more than an upstart mining town of wooden buildings and the damage was less severe than at Škofja Loka.

Nowhere in Slovenia can cultivated fields be found on such steep slopes and human dwellings in such remote locations as in the regions around Idrija and Cerkno. The ravines and valleys were very useful to the Partisans during WWII and the region is dotted with monuments testifying to their presence: the hospitals of Pavl and Franja (near Cerkno) and the Partisan printing house called Slovenija at Vojsko, some 14km north-west of Idrija.

IDRIJA
• *pop 6200* • *area code* ☎*065* • *postcode 5280*
When most Slovenes think of Idrija, three things come to mind: žlikrofi, lace and mercury. The women of Idrija have been taking care of the first two for centuries, stuffing the crescent-shaped 'Slovenian ravioli' with a savoury mixture of bacon, potatoes and chives as fast as they spin their web-like *čipka*. The men, on the other hand, went underground to extract the 'live silver' (*živo srebro*) that would make this town one of the richest in Europe in the Middle Ages.

History
Mercury was first discovered in 1490 at the site where the Church of the Holy Trinity

now stands. The legend is that a man who made *suha roba*, or traditional wooden products, was busy at work on some tubs he was going to sell at the market in Škofja Loka. After he'd finished soaking them in a spring to ensure they wouldn't leak, he tried to lift one up but it was too heavy. At the bottom was a mass of silvery material that he'd never seen before. But some of the people at the market in Loka where he took the stuff had seen mercury before and the 'mercury rush' to Idrija (Ydria in German) began.

The first mine opened at Idrija in 1500, making it the second-oldest mercury mine in the world after the one in Almadén in central Spain. By the 18th century, Idrija was producing 13% of the world's mercury, thought to be the purest and of the best quality. Its biggest markets were Venice, Trieste, Amsterdam and towns in Germany.

All that meant money – for both the imperial court in Vienna and Idrija. Because of the toxic effects of mercury, doctors and lawyers flocked here to work. The Idrija miners faced many health hazards, but the relatively high wages attracted workers from all over the Habsburg Empire. In 1769, Idrija built Slovenia's first theatre and later could boast two of its finest schools. By the turn of the century, Idrija was second in size only to Ljubljana among the towns of Carniola.

The market bottomed out on mercury in the 1970s and production of this once precious element has all but ceased in Idrija. The last pit will close very soon and most miners now work in factories north of town at Spodnja Idrija or Cerkno.

The mine has left the town a difficult and expensive legacy. Idrija sits on something like 700km of shafts that go down 15 levels to 32m below sea level. The first four have now been filled with water and more have to be loaded with hard core and debris to stabilise the place. Otherwise the town might sink.

Some destinations in Slovenia just have the right feel, and Idrija is one of them.

PRIMORSKA

On the Wings of Mercury

Why was mercury so important in the Middle Ages when they hadn't yet invented the thermometer? Well, mercury (or quicksilver as it was then called in English) had a lot of other important uses – as it still does today.

Alchemists, who named it after the fleet-footed messenger of the Roman gods because of its fluidity, were convinced that all metals originated from mercury. They used it extensively in their search to obtain gold from other metals. But the biggest boon came in the 16th century, when amalgam processes for obtaining silver and gold were introduced by the *conquistadores* in Mexico and Peru. Since mercury bonds as an alloy to many metals, it could separate gold or silver from the rock or ore.

Mercury was used as a medicine – it was an early antidote to syphilis – and in another form as an antiseptic. The Venetians needed it to make their famous mirrors and later milliners used it to lay felt for making hats. Mercury is a highly toxic substance and can affect behaviour; occupational mercurialism from vapours and absorption by the skin is a serious disorder. As a result many milliners went crazy and thus was the inspiration for the Mad Hatter in *Alice's Adventures in Wonderland* by Lewis Carroll in 1865. Idrija's miners weren't immune to mercurialism and one of the largest mental hospitals in the country is in the hills to the north of town.

In modern times, mercury has been used in industry to obtain caustic soda and chlorine and to make drugs. It is an important element in certain light bulbs, batteries, laboratory monitoring equipment and power control switches. It has a role in the electrical industry, as a conductor, and in the paper industry and has been used with silver to make amalgam for tooth fillings.

Its uses have not always been for peaceful purposes; it is a crucial ingredient in some detonators and bombs. Indeed, during the Vietnam War the USA was one of the biggest importers of Idrija mercury from what was then socialist (and neutral) Yugoslavia.

Mercury mining in Idrija is coming to an end for several reasons. The use of heavy metals has been abandoned by many industries in favour of more environmentally friendly substances, and protective measures have been in place in some countries since the 1970s. More importantly, a 2.5L flask (about 34kg) of mercury that went for approximately US$800 in the 1970s was worth only $100 a decade later. Such prices no longer even covered production costs. ■

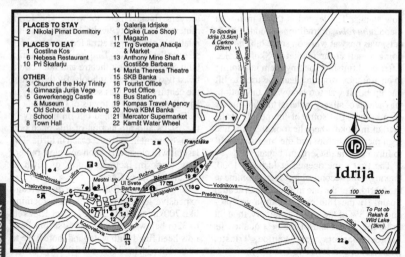

PLACES TO STAY
2 Nikolaj Pirnat Dormitory

PLACES TO EAT
1 Gostilna Kos
6 Nebesa Restaurant
10 Pri Škafarju

OTHER
3 Church of the Holy Trinity
4 Gimnazija Jurija Vege
5 Gewerkenegg Castle
& Museum
7 Old School & Lace-Making
School
8 Town Hall
9 Galerija Idrijske
Čipke (Lace Shop)
11 Magazin
12 Trg Svetega Ahacija
& Market
13 Anthony Mine Shaft &
Gostišče Barbara
14 Maria Theresa Theatre
15 SKB Banka
16 Tourist Office
17 Post Office
18 Bus Station
19 Kompas Travel Agency
20 Nova KBM Banka
21 Mercator Supermarket
22 Kamšt Water Wheel

Idrija

Walking through the shaft where miners toiled for almost five centuries, across Mestni trg to the town's well preserved castle or along the Idrijca River and its canal to pristine Wild Lake on a warm summer's evening, you might just think so too.

Orientation

Idrija sits snugly in a deep basin at the confluence of the Idrijca and Nikova rivers. Surrounding the valley are the Idrija and Cerkno hills which eventually join the Škofja Loka Hills in Gorenjska to the east.

The centre of Idrija is Mestni trg but everything of a practical nature is to the east on Lapajnetova ulica. The bus station is nearby between Vodnikova ulica and Prešernova ulica.

Information

Idrija's tourist office (☎ 71 135) is at Lapajnetova ulica 7, a few steps west of the post office. It is open weekdays from 8 am to 4 pm and, from June to August, on Saturday and Sunday from 9 am to 5 pm as well. The staff at Kompas (☎ 71 700) to the east of the post office on Lapajnetova ulica may also be

able to help. They are open from 7 am to 3 pm on weekdays (to 5 pm on Wednesday) and on Saturday till noon.

The Nova KBM Banka branch in the shopping centre opposite the bus station at Lapajnetova ulica 13 is open weekdays from 7.30 am to 6 pm and on Saturday till noon. There's an SKB Banka with an ATM at Ulica Svete Barbare 3 open weekdays only from 8.30 am till noon and 2 to 5 pm. The post office at Lapajnetova ulica 3 is open weekdays from 8 am to 7 pm and on Saturday till noon.

Municipal Museum

This excellent museum, which won the coveted Micheletti Prize for 'Best Technical Museum in Europe' in 1997, is housed in the enormous Gewerkenegg Castle on top of the hill to the west of Mestni trg at Prelovčeva ulica 9. Because the castle was purpose-built for the mine administration in 1533, local people call it Rudniški Grad from the Slovene word *rudnik* for mine. Visit the museum before you go into the Anthony Mine Shaft; you'll understand a whole lot more.

The collections, which deal with mercury and lace but, sadly, not žlikrofi, are exhibited in three wings centred around a courtyard. The **rococo frescoes** of plants, scrolls and columns framing the windows and arcades date from the 18th century.

Mercury (Hg on the periodic table) is the only metal that reaches a liquid state at room temperature. It comes in a 'free' state (looking pretty much like the stuff in an average thermometer) and can also be bound up with a bright-red mineral called cinnabar, which must be burned at very high temperatures or treated with lime to free the silvery element inside. As the wood-worker discovered, mercury is a very heavy metal, even heavier than iron and in the castle's north wing, amid a jungle of minerals and fossils, is a large cauldron of mercury with an iron ball floating in the middle.

Part of the **ethnographical collection** in this wing shows rooms in a typical miner's house at various times in history (including the 1960s). A miner's job carried status and they earned more than double the average salary in this part of Slovenia; the furnishings are more than adequate. The miners were well organised and socialism was popular in the late 19th and early 20th centuries.

In the Rondel Tower of the east wing there's a mock-up of the 'call man', the unspeakable so-and-so who summoned miners to work every day at 3.30 am in the town centre by hitting a hollow log with a mallet. There's also an ingenious 'walking tour of Idrija' set up here. Paintings and old photographs spaced between the windows allow you to compare old Idrija with the town that now lies below you. At the bottom of the new **Mercury Tower** at the start of the south wing is a 320kg plexiglass cube filled with drops of mercury.

One large room in the south wing is given over entirely to *klekljana čipka*, the **bobbin lace** woven in broad rings with distinctive patterns. Motifs, numbering up to 40, run the gamut from the usual hearts and flowers to horseshoes, crescents and lizards. Check the table covering measuring 3 by 1.80m. It took 5000 hours to make and was intended for Madame Tito until she was banished into

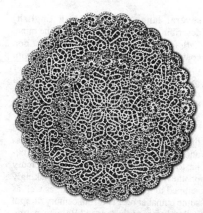

Lace-making is a centuries-old craft in Idrija and the end product is prized the world over.

political limbo after the death of her husband in 1980.

Another room is dedicated to the life and work of the novelist France Bevk (1890-1970), born in the village of Zakojca near Cerkno. One of Bevk's finest works is *Father Martin Čedermac* about the persecution of an Italian-Slovene priest and his struggle against the Fascists just before WWII.

The Municipal Museum is open daily, year round, from 9 am to 6 pm. Admission is 300 SIT (200 SIT for students and children).

Anthony Mine Shaft

Antonijev Rov, a 'living museum' on Kosovelova ulica south of Trg Svetega Ahacija, allows you to get a brief feel for what working conditions were like for the mercury miners of Idrija. The entrance is the Anthony Shaft, built in 1500, which led to the first mine: 1.5km long, 600m wide and 400m deep.

The tour, lasting about 1¼ hours, begins in the 'call room' of an 18th century building where miners were selected each morning and assigned their duties. Just imagine sitting on those hard, cold benches at 4 am with 10 hours underground to look forward to. There's an excellent 20-minute video in

PRIMORSKA

several languages (including English) describing the history of Idrija and the mine.

Before entering the shaft, you must don coats with the miners' insignia, helmets with torches attached and wish each other 'Srečno!' ('Good luck!'), the traditional miners' farewell. You'll be thankful for those helmets every time you knock your head against one of the shaft's support beams.

As you walk into the shaft there's a good display of the mine's levels done with glass and light underfoot. As you follow the circular tour you'll see samples of live mercury on the walls that the miners painstakingly scraped to a depth of about 5cm, as well as some cinnabar ore. The 18th century **chapel** in the shaft is dedicated to St Barbara, patron of miners, and St Ahac, on whose feast day (22 June) rich deposits of cinnabar ore were discovered.

You can visit the mine with a guide on weekdays at 10 am and 4 pm only. On Saturday, tours depart at 10 am, 3 pm and 4 pm, on Sunday at 11 am, 3 pm and 4 pm. Admission is 700/500 SIT for adults/children.

Other Sights

There are several fine neoclassical buildings on Mestni trg, including the **town hall** at No 1. To the west of the square opposite Prelovčeva ulica 1a is the **Lace-making School** (Čipkarska Šola) in the Stara Šola (Old School), built in 1876. Lace-making is still a required subject for girls in elementary school in Idrija. Visitors are welcomed daily from noon to 4 pm. The **Gimnazija Jurija Vege** (1901), to the north-west on Študentovska ulica, educated many Slovenes who later rose to national prominence, including the painter Božidar Jakac (1899-1989).

The large 18th century building on the north side of Trg Svetega Ahacija, the centre of town in the Middle Ages, is the **Magazin**, a granary and warehouse where the miners, who were paid in food as well as in cash, kept their stores. It now houses a gallery and the city library. To the east, at Trg Svetega Ahacija 5, is the **Maria Theresa Theatre**, the oldest in the country. Today it functions as a cinema.

Laid out across the slopes encircling the valley are Idrija's distinctive **miners' houses**. Large wooden A-frames with cladding and dozens of windows, they usually had four storeys with living quarters for three or four families. They must have appeared massive when they were first built in the 17th century.

North of Mestni trg is the **Church of the Holy Trinity** (1500) on the site where mercury was first discovered by our friend the tub-maker more than 500 years ago. To the north-east off Grilčeva ulica in the district of **Frančiške** is the last mine still functioning in Idrija. A warehouse nearby contains a mass of mining equipment from before WWI that still works on compressed air. If you're interested, ask the staff at the Municipal Museum about a tour.

One of the most interesting bits of mining technology that still exists is the **Kamšt**, a 13.6m water wheel made of wood that was used to pump the water out of the flooded mines from 1790 until 1948. It is about 1.5km south-east of Mestni trg off Vodnikova ulica. You could combine a visit here with a walk along the Idrijca River Canal to Wild Lake, about 3km south.

Wild Lake

An excellent trail called Pot ob Rakah follows the Idrijca River Canal from the Kamšt to Wild Lake (Divje Jezero), a tiny, impossibly green lake fed by a karst spring more than 80m under the surface. After a heavy rainfall, water gushes up from the tunnel like a geyser and the lake appears to be boiling. Perhaps that's not the right word; the surface temperature never exceeds 10°C. Three cave divers have drowned at Wild Lake over the past several years – two in 1995 and one in 1997 – trying to find the source.

The lake has been declared a natural monument and little signboards around the shore (which should take you about 15 minutes to circle if you go at a snail's pace) identify the plants and trees and point out the lake's unique features. That body of water flowing from Wild Lake into the Idrijca just happens to be the shortest river in Slovenia. The Jezernica River is a mere 55m long.

If you followed the canal for 15km to the south-west you'd come to the first of the barriers *(klauže)* of stacked wood and stones that dammed the Idrijca and Belca rivers to float timber in the old days. They were once called 'Slovenian pyramids' because of their appearance. Wood was an important commodity for two reasons. First, something had to support those 700km of mine shafts and second, the heat needed to extract mercury from cinnabar required a lot of fuel. The dams continue for some 12km down the Belca River.

The area of the Idrijca near the suspension bridge is good for swimming in summer, when the water averages about 20°C.

Special Events

The big event in Idrija is the annual Lace-making Festival in late August. The highlight is a contest in which up to 100 people compete.

Places to Stay & Eat

In summer the *Nikolaj Pirnat Dijaški Dom* (☎ 71 052) at Ulica IX Korpusa 6 has 56 beds available in multi-bed rooms.

Since the closure of the decrepit Ydria hotel at the eastern end of Lapajnetova ulica, the only standard accommodation now in Idrija is the six-room *Gostišče Barbara* (☎ /fax 71 142) above the mine shaft museum at Kosovelova ulica 3. Singles/doubles with shower are 4500/7200 SIT.

Pri Škafarju ('At the Sign of the Tub') is a very friendly restaurant at Ulica Svete Barbare 9, open weekdays and on Sunday to 10 pm and to 11 pm on Friday and Saturday. Pizza baked in a beautiful wood-burning tile stove is why most people come here, but there are plenty of other things on the menu as well.

Pri Škafarju does decent enough žlikrofi, but the best place to have this most Idrijan of specialities is at *Kos*, a little pub and restaurant at Tomšičeva ulica 4, not far from the Ydria hotel. Don't be put off from entering what looks at first like a private club; the

natives are friendly. It is open Monday to 3 pm, Tuesday to Saturday to 10 pm. *Nebesa* by the bridge over the Nikova River at Prelovčeva ulica 5 is a central place for lunch or a snack (sandwiches, hotdogs and, of course, žlikrofi).

There's a large *Mercator* supermarket at Lapajnetova ulica 45 open weekdays from 7.30 am to 7 pm and to 6 pm on Saturday. A *market* is held in Trg Svetega Ahacija on the 15th and 20th of every month.

Entertainment

Evenings of classical, folk and jazz concerts take place in the courtyard of Gewerkenegg Castle every second Friday or so in July, August and September. Contact the museum (☎ 71 135) for schedules and information.

Things to Buy

Idrija lace is among the finest in the world and a small piece, though not cheap, makes a great gift or souvenir. The best place to buy it is at a shop called Galerija Idrijske Čipke at Mestni trg 16. It is open weekdays from 10 am till noon and 4 to 7 pm and on Saturday morning. The Vanda shop at Trg Svetega Ahacija 7 has a smaller selection. It is open from 9 am till noon and 4 to 7 pm on weekdays and on Saturday morning.

Getting There & Away

Idrija is not the easiest place in the world to reach. The town is not on a train line and the bus service is fairly limited. There are at least hourly departures to Cerkno and Ljubljana, about three buses a day to Bovec, eight to Črni Vrh, eight to Tolmin, three to Ajdovščina and one (at 5.30 am) to Nova Gorica, which then carries on into Italian Gorizia.

CERKNO

• *pop 2170* • *area code* ☎065 • *postcode 5282*

Until recently this town could not claim the historical importance of its celebrated neighbour Idrija, 20km to the south. But with the recent discovery of what is considered to be the oldest known musical instrument on

Stone Age Music

The image of our Neanderthal ancestors sitting around a campfire making beautiful music together is not an easy one to conjure up, but it's a lot easier now, following a major discovery in a mountain cave near Cerkno.

Paleontologists were messing around in the area in 1995 and collecting Stone Age tools when a local pundit who happened to pass by told them he knew where they'd find lots more. He led them to Divje Babe, a cave some 200m above the main road linking Cerkno with the Tolmin-Idrija highway, and they began digging. Among the buried tools was a piece of cave bear femur measuring 10cm long and perforated with four aligned holes – two intact and two incomplete – at either end. It looked exactly like a flute.

Because objects of such antiquity cannot be dated by the usual radiocarbon techniques, the flute was sent to the City University of New York to undergo electron spin resonance, which measures the small amounts of radiation absorbed by objects from the time of their burial. And the verdict? According to the researchers, the flute is anywhere between 45,000 and 82,000 years old, depending on how much moisture – which inhibits the absorption of radiation – the cave floor had been exposed to. One thing is certain, however – Slovenia can now claim the oldest known musical instrument on earth. The flute will eventually be put on display at the Cerkno Museum and – just in case you were wondering – it still works. ∎

earth (see boxed text entitled Stone Age Music) that has changed.

In any case, Cerkno has two other claims to fame. It is the home of the *Laufarija*, the ancient Shrovetide celebration in which the key players wear artfully crafted wooden masks and 'execute' the Old Year. If you don't get a chance to come to Cerkno for Mardi Gras to see the famous show, you'll have to be content with looking at the masks in the town's museum. Cerkno is also known for its strange dialect in a land where there are something like 50 of them. People from outside the Cerkno region (Cerkljanska) always seem to smile when they hear what is the equivalent of an American southern drawl.

Orientation & Information

Cerkno lies in the Cerknica River Valley 4km north-east of the main road linking Idrija with the Soča Valley. Glavni trg, the main square, is where the buses stop.

The tourist office (☎ 745 222) is at Bevkova ulica 24 to the north-west of Glavni trg past the Cerkno Museum. If it is closed, seek assistance from the helpful and knowledgeable staff at the Cerkno hotel. The Nova KBM bank branch (open weekdays from 8 am to 6 pm and Saturday till noon) is at Glavni trg 5. The post office, in Sedejev trg

next to the Cerkno hotel, keeps the same hours as the bank, with a couple of half-hour breaks in the morning and afternoon.

Cerkno Museum

The Cerkno Museum (Cerkljanski Muzej) is about 150m south-west of Glavni trg at Bevkova ulica 12. A large section of this small museum is given over to the work done by the WWII Partisans in secret hospitals and printing presses around the region, but those displays are black, white and grey at best and labelled in Slovene only. Step into the room with the Laufarji masks. It's a lot brighter.

Ethnologists believe that the Laufarija tradition and the masks came from Austria's South Tyrol hundreds of years ago. *Lauferei* means 'running about' in German and that's just what the players do as they nab their victim. The masks with the crazy, distorted faces on display here are originals bought from one of the Laufarji clubs. Only one elderly man in Cerkno still makes them.

Groups of boys and young men (and now a few girls and women) belonging to Laufarji societies (like the Mardi Gras clubs in New Orleans) organise the event every year and about two dozen perform. Those aged 15 and over are allowed to enter, but they must prove themselves worthy apprentices by sewing costumes. These costumes – though not masks – must be made fresh every year because many of them are made out of leaves, pine branches, straw or moss stitched onto a burlap (hessian) backing and can take quite a beating during the festivities.

The action takes place on the Sunday before Ash Wednesday and again on Shrove Tuesday (Pustni Torek). The main character is the Pust, whose mask is horned and who wears a moss costume weighing up to 100kg. He's the symbol of winter and the old year – he must die.

The Pust is charged with a long list of crimes – a bad harvest, inclement weather, lousy roads – and, of course, is found guilty. Some of the other two dozen Laufarji characters represent crafts and trades (the Baker, the Thatcher, the Woodsman), while the rest have certain character traits or afflictions such as the Drunk and his Wife, the Bad Boy, Sneezy and the Sick Man, who always plays

One of the colourful Laufarji masks on display in Cerkno Museum

the accordion. The Old Man, wearing Slovenian-style lederhosen and a wide-brimmed hat, executes the Pust with a wooden mallet and the body is rolled away on a caisson.

The Cerkno Museum shows a dated video of the Laufarija in Slovene, but it is entertaining and illustrates how the masks and costumes are made and how events unfold at Mardi Gras. It is open daily, except Monday, from 9 am to 2 pm and admission is 250 SIT (150 SIT for children).

Franja Partisan Hospital

This hospital, hidden in a canyon near Dolenji Novaki about 5km north-east of Cerkno, treated wounded Partisan soldiers from Yugoslavia and other countries from late 1943 until the end of WWII. Franja Hospital really has nothing to do with political or economic systems; it is a memorial to humanism, courage and self-sacrifice. It is a moving and very worthwhile place to visit, and the most popular WWII museum in Slovenia.

The complex, named after its chief physician, Dr Franja Bojc-Bidovec, was built in December 1943 for the needs of the IX Corps which included seven brigades and a large number of companies – a total of some 10,000 soldiers. By May 1945 it counted some 13 structures, including treatment sheds, operating theatres, X-ray rooms and bunkers for convalescence. More than 500 wounded were treated here with a mortality rate of only about 10%.

The complex, hidden in a ravine by the Pasica Stream with steep walls riddled with caves, had an abundance of fresh water that was also used to power a hydroelectric generator. Because of the hospital's isolated position, noise was not a problem. Local farmers and Partisan groups provided food that was lowered down the steep cliffs by rope; medical supplies were diverted from hospitals in occupied areas or later air-dropped by the Allies. The hospital came under attack by the Germans twice – once in April 1944 and again in March 1945 – but it was never taken.

PRIMORSKA

The Franja Partisan Hospital is open April to September daily from 9 am to 6 pm and to 4 pm in March, October and November. From December to February it is open from 9 am to 4 pm on Saturday, Sunday and holidays only. Admission costs 300/200 SIT.

Ravne Cave
The snow-white aragonite crystals in the Ravne Cave (Ravenska Jama) at Ravne, about 7km south-west of Cerkno, are a very rare phenomenon. They are formed by karst springs containing magnesium as well as calcium and are very beautiful, resembling ice, needles, even hedgehogs. The cave is a total of 682m long and you get to see about half of it in three galleries. But to visit, you must seek permission from the Srečko Logar Caving Club (no telephone) at Ljubljanska cesta 5 in Idrija or from the Municipal Museum (☎ 71 135).

Hiking
The Cerkno Hills (Cerkljansko Hribovje) are simply tailor-made for hiking and the English-language *Cerkno Map of Local Walks*, available from the Cerkno hotel, lists some eight walks, most of them pretty easy. They include walks to the **Franja Partisan Hospital** (No 7; 3½ hours return) and **Ravne Cave** (No 2; four hours). The highest peak in the area is **Mt Porezen** (1632m) to the north-east, which has a mountain hut called *Dom na Poreznu* (1590m; ☎ 75 135 or mobile ☎ 0609-615 245) with accommodation. It is open daily from June to September and at the weekend only during the rest of the year.

Skiing
The **Cerkno Ski Centre** (☎ 17 420), 10km north-east of Cerkno, is situated on Črni Vrh (1290m) and covers 50 hectares of ski slopes. In normal snow conditions four tows and three chair lifts operate but there are cannons for making artificial snow. The closest accommodation is at Cerkno or Dolenji Novaki so you'll have to make it a day trip via one of the special ski buses operating during normal snow conditions.

Special Events
The Laufarija festival in late February/early March takes place outdoors both in Glavni trg and Sedejev trg near the Cerkno hotel.

Places to Stay & Eat
The 75-room *Cerkno* hotel (☎ 17 420; fax 75 207) with some 140 beds is in a modern building in the heart of town at Sedejev trg 8. It's a comfortable enough place with an indoor pool (600 SIT for nonresidents), sauna, gym and three clay tennis courts. Singles with breakfast and shower are DM85, while doubles are DM140. The hotel offers discounts for stays of more than two nights.

The *Gostilna V Logu* (☎ 745 188) in Dolenji Novaki (house No 1) not far from the Franja Partisan Hospital is very popular with local people, particularly for lunch at the weekend. It is open Wednesday to Sunday from 11 am to 11 pm. V Logu also has four rooms where you can stay for about DM25 per person.

Getting There & Away
There are hourly departures by bus to Idrija (eight a day on Saturday and Sunday), up to five a day to Ljubljana and three to Bovec via Most na Soči, Tolmin and Kobarid. Another 10 or so (three at the weekend) go just to Tolmin, where you can change for Nova Gorica and the coast. There's one direct bus to Nova Gorica from Cerkno on weekdays at 6.04 am.

Karst Region

The Karst region is a small limestone plateau stretching from Nova Gorica south-east to the Škocjan Caves, west to the Gulf of Trieste and east to the Vipava Valley. Because it was the first such area to be researched and described in the 19th century, it is called the Classic, Real, True or Original Karst and always spelled with an upper-case 'K'. Other karst areas (from the Slovene word *kras*) around the world are similar but they get a downgraded 'k'.

Millions of years ago this part of Europe was covered by a deep sea that left thick layers of limestone deposits. When the sea dried up, craters and fissures began to appear, growing deeper and creating large stone fragments that were bleached white by the sun. Because most of the soil blew away, vegetation is scarce, giving the landscape a desolate, somewhat wild appearance.

Rivers, ponds and lakes can disappear and then resurface in the porous limestone through sinkholes and funnels. Some go on to produce large underground caverns like the caves at Škocjan. The calcium bicarbonate from the dripping water below creates stalactites (the ones that hang down) and stalagmites (the ones that shoot up). When these underground caverns collapse – and they do periodically – they form a depression *(polje)* which collects soil (mostly red clay, the *terra rossa* of the Karst) and then vegetation. They are cultivated and, because of all the sink holes and underground water, they tend to flood quickly in the heavy rain.

The Karst, with its olives, ruby-red Teran wine, air-dried *pršut* ham, old stone churches and red-tiled roofs, is some people's favourite region of Slovenia. You can explore Rihemberk Castle near Branik or the walled village of Štanjel with its magnificent Ferrari Gardens to the north, but the areas with the most to see and do are to the south.

Though the weather is very pleasant for most of the year, with lots of sun and low humidity, don't be fooled into thinking it's all sweetness and light all the time. The bora *(burja* in Slovene), a fiercely cold northerly wind from the Adriatic Sea, can do a lot of damage in winter, ripping off roofs, uprooting trees and blowing away topsoil. It does give the pršut its distinctive taste, though.

ŠKOCJAN CAVES
• area code ☎067 • postcode 6215
The karst caves at Škocjan are far more captivating and 'real' than the larger one at Postojna, some 33km to the north-east in Notranjska province. If you can imagine climbing the concrete Matterhorn at Disneyland and then scaling the real thing, you'll get the picture. For many travellers, a visit here will be one of the highlights of their trip to Slovenia – a page right out of Jules Verne's *A Voyage to the Centre of the Earth*. Heed the words of a French speleologist who wrote in 1955: 'In the Postojna Cave the

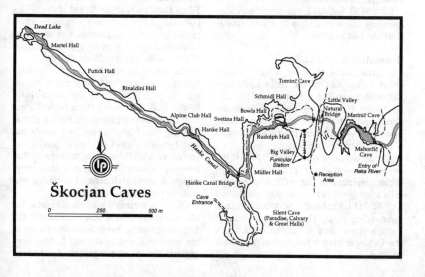

Škocjan Caves

speleologist sees everything he could desire, but the Škocjan Caves have no comparison in the world.'

The Škocjan Caves (Škocjanske Jame), 5km long and 250m deep, were carved out by the Reka River, which originates in the foothills of Mt Snežnik to the south-east. The Reka enters the caves in a gorge below the village of Škocjan (San Canziano in Italian) and eventually flows into the Dead Lake (Mrtvo Jezero), where it disappears. It surfaces again – this time as the Timavo River – at Duino in Italy, some 40km to the north-west, before emptying into the Gulf of Trieste.

The caves – or at least their entrances – were known by prehistoric people who sheltered in them or used them to make sacrifices to the gods of the underworld. Janez Vajkard Valvasor described them and the phenomenon of the disappearing Reka in his encyclopaedic work *The Glory of the Duchy of Carniola* in the late 17th century, but real exploration did not start until the mid-19th century. Organised visits followed soon afterward, but the caves never became the tourist mecca that Postojna did; electric lighting was not even installed until 1959. Today, visitors can explore about 2km of these spectacular caves.

UNESCO included the caves and surrounding nature reserve in its World Natural Heritage List in 1986.

Orientation & Information

The caves are at Matavun, a small village about 1.5km east of the main Ljubljana-Koper highway. The closest town of any size is Divača (pop 1750), about 5km to the north-west. Divača's train station, where buses stop as well, is on Trg 15 Aprila about 600m west of this highway.

The information office (☎ 31 361) at the caves' reception area is open from 9 am until the last tour departs. The small shop opposite sells a few good guides and maps (including a UNESCO 1:5000-scale one) to the caves and surrounding areas. There's a post office in Divača at the start of Kraška cesta and a Banka Koper branch just west of the Risnik pension.

The Caves

If you have some time to spare before your tour departs, follow the path leading north and down some steps from the reception area for 300m to the **lookout** (it is signposted 'Razgledišče/Belvedere' in Slovene and Italian). Extending before you is a superb vista of the Velika Dolina (Big Valley) and gorge where the Reka starts its subterranean journey (and close to where you will emerge from the caves). Across the 180m-deep gorge to the east is the village of **Škocjan** and the 17th century **Church of St Cantianus**. St Cantianus is the protector against evil spirits and floods and is also the caves' namesake. He's a good man to know in this volatile part of Slovenia.

Visitors to the caves assemble around the picnic tables across from the restaurant at the reception area and walk with their guides for about 500m down a gravel path to the main entrance in the Gločak Valley. Through an artificial tunnel built in 1933, you soon reach the head of the **Silent Cave** (Tiha Jama), a dry branch of the underground canyon that stretches for 500m. The first section, called **Paradise**, is filled with beautiful stalactites, stalagmites and flow stones; the second part (called **Calvary**) was once the river bed. The Silent Cave ends at the **Great Hall** (Velika Dvorana), 120m wide and 30m high. It is a jungle of exotic dripstones and deposits; keep an eye open for the stalagmite called the **Giant** and the one named the **Organ**.

The sound of the Reka River rushing through cascades and whirlpools below signals your entry into the astonishing **Müller Hall**, with walls 100m high. To get over the Reka you must cross **Hanke Canal Bridge**, 45m high, narrow, and surely the highlight of the trip. Count your blessings as you do (or don't) look down; the catwalk that allowed visitors to cross over into long, narrow **Svetina Hall** before this bridge was built 60 years ago was 20m higher.

Only experienced speleologists are allowed to explore the caves and halls in the 5km-long siphon that extends downward to the north-west ending at Dead Lake. Every century or so the siphon gets blocked and the caves are flooded. This happened most recently in 1965.

From Svetina Hall you climb up a path hewn into the stone to **Bowls Hall**, remarkable for its rare bowl-like pans which were formed from calcium deposits when water flooding the cave churned and swirled up to the ceiling. They look like troughs or rice terraces. The final section, **Schmidl Hall**, opens on to the Velika Dolina. From here you walk past **Tominč Cave**, where finds from a prehistoric settlement have been unearthed, and over a walkway near the **Natural Bridge** to the funicular, which carries you 90m up the rock face to close to the reception area.

You may be surprised to learn that the Škocjan Caves are home to an incredible amount of flora and fauna: 250 varieties of plants and five different types of bats. The temperature in the caves is constant at about 13°C so you should bring along a light jacket or sweater. Good walking shoes (the way can get pretty wet and slippery in the high humidity) and a torch (flashlight) are also recommended.

The caves can be visited seven times a day from June to September at 10 and 11.30 am and on the hour from 1 to 5 pm. In April, May and October there are tours at 10 am and at 1 and 3.30 pm. From November to March, visits are allowed on Sunday and holidays at 10 am and 3 pm only. The entry fee is 1500 SIT for adults and 1200 SIT for children. The tours, much less structured than at Postojna Cave, are given in five different languages (the guides will separate you) and take about 1½ hours.

Activities

The Farma Diomed (☎ 60 003) in Lokev (house No 230), halfway between Divača and Lipica, has horses for hire. An excellent excursion would be to ride for a couple of kilometres north-west to 803m-long **Vilenica Cave** (Jama Vilenica), the first karst cave to open to the public in the early 19th century and still welcoming guests every Sunday at 3 pm. **Divača Cave** (Divaška Jama), about 3km north-east on the road to Divača, is open only by arrangement. It is only 672m long but has excellent drip-

stones and rock formations. Enquire at the Lipica Stud Farm or the Škocjan Caves reception areas.

Places to Stay & Eat

The closest *camp site* (☎ 82 611) to the caves is at Kozina, 7km south of Divača. It's a tiny place, barely covering a hectare, and is full of caravans and cars. It's open from May to September and costs 800 SIT per person.

Divača is the only place to stay near the caves unless you want to head for Sežana, a dull place 9km to the north-west where there are two small hotels: the *Tabor* (☎ 31 551) near the train station at Kolodvorska ulica 4 or the *Triglav* (☎ 31 361) at Partizanska ulica 1. They are both fairly nondescript but reasonable at about 3600 SIT for a single with shower and breakfast and 5400 SIT for a double.

In Divača, the *Risnik* pension (☎ 60 008; fax 73 384) at Kraška cesta 24, about 400m north of the main highway to the caves and the coast, has 10 dark and dingy rooms for which they ask an outrageous 4250/6500 SIT for singles/doubles. With the highway so close, a busy petrol station opposite and buses and trains heading for the station, it is very noisy here.

The Risnik has a gloomy restaurant that serves fairly decent food. A much more pleasant place to eat in Divača is the *Klunov Hram*, a cellar restaurant 150m to the north-east at Kraška cesta 32. It has some good pasta dishes like njoki and pizza (around 950 SIT) as well as its own home-made Teran wine. The Klunov Hram is open daily from 11 am to 10 pm (though the pesky mini casino adjoining the dining room stays open to 2 am). Nearby at Kraška cesta 26 is the 17th century Škratelj House, the oldest traditional Karst house in Slovenia. It's now a gallery, open Saturday and Sunday only from 2 to 4 pm.

There's a restaurant called *Pri Jami* at the caves' reception area open daily from 9 am to 8 pm.

Getting There & Away

The Škocjan Caves are about 5km by road south-east of the Divača train station.

PRIMORSKA

Getting there by public transport can be tricky, but the driver of any bus heading along the highway to/from the coast will let you off at the access road if you ask in advance (there are huge signs announcing the caves). From there you can walk the remaining 1.5km to the caves' entrance. All in all, it's probably easier to go there on foot via a 3km path that leads south-east from Divača and through the village of Dolnje Ležeče to Matavun.

About half a dozen buses a day (12 in July and August) pass through Divača from Ljubljana and Postojna on their way to the coast and destinations in Croatia. The first leaves Divača at 7 am, the last at 7.05 pm.

Divača is on the rail line linking Ljubljana (104km; 1½ hours) with Sežana (9km; 10 minutes). Divača is also the railhead for eight trains a day to Koper (49km; 50 minutes) via Hrpelje Kozina as well as up to five daily trains to Buzet and Pula in Croatia.

LIPICA
• *pop 125* • *area code ☎067* • *postcode 6210*

The impact of Lipica, some 10km south-west of Divača, on the world of sport has been far greater than its tiny size would suggest. In 1580, in what was then called Lipizza, the Austrian Archduke Charles, son of Ferdinand I, established a stud farm *(kobilarna)* to breed horses for the Spanish Riding School in Vienna.

The riding school had been founded eight years earlier to train horses for the imperial court and was looking for a lighter, more elegant breed for parades and military purposes (which would later lead to the development of dressage). Andalusian horses from Spain were coupled with the local Karst breed that the Romans had once used to pull chariots – and the Lipizzaner was born. But they weren't quite the snow-white beauties we know today. Those didn't come about for another 200 years when white Arabian horses got into the act.

It's easy to see why both Charles and the nags liked the place. Though very much part of the region, this 'oasis in the barren Karst' (as Lipica is called) feels like Eden after all

that limestone. Indeed, the word *lipica* in Slovene means 'little linden', after the trees that grow in such profusion here. The moderate, dry climate allows ideal conditions for breeding horses with speed, strength and stamina.

The stud farm remained the property of the court in Vienna until the end of WWI when the Italians took control of Primorska province. Herds were moved to Hungary and then Austria but the change in climate took its toll. In 1943, with WWII still raging, the Germans moved more than 200 horses to the Sudetenland in Bohemia (now the Czech Republic). When the area was liberated by American forces in 1945, most of the horses and the stud farm's archives were shipped off to Italy. Sadly, only 11 horses returned when operations resumed at Lipica in 1947.

Today, there are 200 Lipizzaners remaining at the original stud farm while 'genuine' Lipizzaners are bred in various locations around the world: Croatia, Hungary, Italy, Slovakia and even in the American state of Illinois. The stud farm at Piber, north-east of Graz in Austria, now breeds the horses for the Spanish Riding School.

Orientation & Information
Lipica lies 2km west of the Italian border and 5km south of Sežana. The centre of everything, of course, is the stud farm in the south-west corner of the village and the two hotels nearby.

The tourist information office (☎ 31 580; fax 72 818) at the entrance to the stud farm can change money, but it takes a 2% commission.

Lipica Stud Farm
Tours of the 311-hectare stud farm begin opposite the information and ticket office; simply wait by the sign bearing the name of the language you want to hear it in (English, German, French, Italian or Slovene). The guide will find you.

A visit covers the stables, one of which dates from 1703, and the riding halls to give you an idea of what it's like to learn dressage and control a very large animal. But frankly,

Dancing Horses of Lipica

Lipizzaners are considered to be the finest riding horses in the world – sought after for *haute école* dressage – and with all the trouble that's put into producing them, it's not surprising. They are very intelligent, sociable horses, quite robust and graceful.

Breeding is paramount, and it is carried out with all the precision of a well organised crime. A half dozen equine families with 16 ancestors can be traced back to the early 18th century and their pedigrees read like those of medieval royalty. When you walk around the stables at Lipica you'll see charts on each horse stall with complicated figures, dates and names like 'Maestoso Allegra' and 'Neapolitano'. It's all to do with the horse's lineage.

Lipizzaners foal between January and May and the colts and fillies suckle for six or seven months. They remain in the herd for about three years. They are then separated for training, which takes another four years.

Lipizzaners are not white when they are born but grey, bay or even chestnut. The celebrated 'imperial white' does not come about until they are between five to 10 years old, when their hair loses its pigment. Think of it as just part of the old nag's ageing process. Their skin remains grey, however, so when they are ridden hard enough to sweat, they become mottled and are not so attractive.

A fully mature Lipizzaner measures about 15 hands (about 153cm) and weighs between 500 and 600kg. They have long backs, short, thick necks, silky manes and expressive eyes. They live for 25 to 30 years and are particularly resistant to disease. They will nuzzle you out of curiosity if you approach them while they graze.

Lipizzaners are bred at Lipica, in Austria and in the USA as riding and show horses; they are known for their beauty, elegance and agility. Lipizzaners bred at Szilvásvárad near Eger in Hungary and at Jakovo near Osijek in Croatia, however, are raised primarily as carriage horses and are bigger and stronger. ∎

PRIMORSKA

the tour is a little boring with endless facts, figures and horse pedigrees.

The highlight of a visit (if you can time it right) is the performance of these elegant horses as they go through their complicated paces with riders *en costume*. It's not as complete a show as the one at the Spanish Riding School in Vienna or in such ornate surroundings, but watching great white horses pirouetting and dancing to Viennese waltzes sort of makes up for it. If you miss the performance, at least try to be around when the horses are moved from the stables to pasture (usually before 9 am) and again in the late afternoon. It's stunning to see them gallop past.

You can visit the Lipica Stud Farm throughout the year and it's open from 8 am to 6 pm. From April to October, tours, which are mandatory, leave at 10 and 11 am and then hourly from 1 to 5 pm weekdays with an additional tour at 9 am at the weekend. In July and August there are tours on the hour seven days a week from 9 to 11 am and 1 to 6 pm. From November to February there are only two tours on weekdays (at 11 am and 3 pm) with two more at 1 and 2 pm at the weekend. In March, weekday tours are at 11 am and 1, 2 and 3 pm and at the weekend at 10 and 11 am and hourly from 1 to 4 pm. Tickets cost DM8 to DM10 for adults, depending on the season, and DM4 or DM5 for children.

Exhibition performances take place from May to September at 3 pm on Tuesday, Friday and Sunday; in April and October they are at 3 pm on Friday and Sunday only. Admission to the performance, which includes the tour of the stud farm, is DM20 for adults and DM10 for children.

Activities
Some 60 horses are available for riding both in the ring and the open countryside at 8.30 and 9.30 am and then at 5 and 6 pm from June to September and at 9.30 and 10.30 am and 3.30 and 4.30 pm from October to March. The cost for riding in a guided group is DM25 per hour. There is also a large choice of courses including group classes for beginners (DM35) and intermediate riders (DM30) and individual classes in dressage (DM100). There are week-long courses too: six two-hour lessons for beginners (DM336), classes for advanced riders (DM300) and dressage classes (DM540; minimum L-level). For the kids and/or the timid there are pony rides (DM12) and half-hour/hour carriage jaunts for DM14/25.

The nearby Lipica Golf Course (☎ 72 930) has nine holes for a par 36, a driving range and a couple of putting greens. The green fees are DM30/46 on weekdays/at the weekend and you can rent a full set of clubs for DM10.

Renting one of the five tennis courts near the Maestoso hotel costs between DM12 and DM16, depending on the time and day. A racquet/set of balls costs DM6/3 per hour.

Places to Stay & Eat
There are two hotels in Lipica, both managed by one company and costing the same: singles with breakfast and shower are DM56 to DM82, depending on the season, and doubles DM82 to DM120. But these prices are discounted heavily for stays of a week or more if you are taking a riding course.

The 65-room *Maestoso* (☎ 31 580; fax 31 409 or 72 818) has most of the amenities, including an indoor swimming pool (closed Tuesday; DM7/6 for adults/children), sauna (DM11) and tennis courts nearby etc. The 80-room *Klub* (☎/fax same) is generally reserved for those staying for longer periods.

It has a pool (closed Sunday in summer) and is slightly closer to the stud farm.

The Maestoso has a *snack bar* with a terrace café open from 8 am to 11 pm. The best (and most expensive) eatery in the complex is the *Lipica* wine cellar restaurant.

Entertainment
The *Casino Lipica* (☎ 72 368) at the Maestoso hotel is open from 3 pm to 2 or 3 am Monday to Saturday (noon to 2 am on Sunday). The hotel also has a disco/nightclub called the *Pegas Klub* open daily from 11 am to 5 pm.

Getting There & Around
Most people visit Lipica as a day trip from Divača or Sežana, both of which are on the rail line to Ljubljana. You can reach them on up to five buses a day during the school year, between two and three buses in summer and on holidays.

The Maestoso hotel has bicycles for rent for DM5 per hour (DM8 for two hours) or DM15 a day.

HRASTOVLJE
• *pop 425* • *area code ☎067* • *postcode 6275*
Hrastovlje lies near the source of the Rižana River, whose valley effectively forms the boundary between the Karst and the coast. From here, northward to the village of Črni Kal and on to Osp, a row of fortresses were built below the limestone plains during the Bronze Age, which the Illyrian tribe of Histrians later adapted to their needs. The valley and the surrounding areas would prove to be safe havens for later inhabitants during the Great Migrations and the Turkish invasions.

The Romanesque church in this tiny village in a valley between the Karst region and the Slovenian coast is the Istrian equivalent of St John the Baptist's Church in Bohinj. OK, so it's not on a lake. But it is small, surrounded by medieval walls with corner towers and covered inside with extraordinary 15th century frescoes.

Church of the Holy Trinity

This church, with a nave and two aisles, was built between the 12th and 14th centuries in the southern Romanesque style though the fortifications were added in 1581 in advance of the Ottomans. As you approach this structure of grey Karst stone at the south-eastern end of the village, just imagine the fear in the hearts of the men, women and children who scrambled to protect what they must have considered to be the most important thing in their lives.

The sombre exterior does not prepare you for what's inside; the complete interior of the church is festooned with **narrative frescoes** painted by Johannes de Castuo (John of Kastav near Rijeka) around 1490. The paintings are a *Biblia pauperum* – a 'Bible of the poor' – to help the illiterate understand the Old Testament stories, the Passion of Christ and the lives of the saints. It is a unique way to see and understand how our ancestors viewed their lives, joys, hopes and sufferings some five centuries ago. Spare the 20 minutes it takes to listen to the taped commentary that will guide you around the little church in English, German, Italian or Slovene. It's dull with a capital 'D', but there are a lot of things you'd miss otherwise.

Facing you as you enter is the main altar, carved in the 17th century, and the central apse with scenes from the Crucifixion on the ceiling and portraits of the Trinity and the Apostles. On the arch, Mary is being crowned Queen of Heaven. To the right of the central aisle are episodes from the **seven days of Creation**, to the left the story of Adam and Eve, as well as the murder of Abel by Cain – all easy stories for an unschooled 15th century peasant to comprehend. On the ceilings of the north (left) and south (right) aisles are scenes from daily life (sowing, hunting, fishing, making wine) as well as the **calendar year** and its seasonal duties. **Christ's Passion** is depicted at the top of the southernmost wall, including his descent into hell, where devils are attacking him with blazing cannons.

Yes, I've saved the best bit for last. Below the Passion is what attracts most people to Hrastovlje and its little church – the famous **Dance of Death fresco** (also called the Danse Macabre) showing 11 skeletons leading the same number of people forward to a freshly dug grave, a pick and shovel at the ready. A 12th skeleton holds a list of the 'invited'. The line-up includes a child, a beggar, a soldier, a banker, a merchant, a monk, a bishop, a nun, a queen, a king and an emperor. Under the nun you can see graffiti left by a visitor in 1640.

Ghoulish and strange though the Dance of Death may appear to be at first, it carries a simple message – we are all equal in the eyes of God no matter how important we (or others) think we are in this mortal life. It was a radical concept, perhaps, for the late 15th century in a remote part of Europe, and it remains a sobering and thought-provoking one today.

Out in the courtyard, have a look around at the two corner towers and ancient walls, which are at least a metre thick. The strange cliffs of loose rock to the north make up the Kraški Rob – the very 'Edge of the Karst' – above the village of Črni Kal, marking the end of the stony limestone plateau and the start of a green valley leading to the sea. Could it be that this little church between two worlds was placed in this geographical limbo on purpose?

Entry to Holy Trinity Church costs 300 SIT for adults and 150 SIT for students and children. It is usually open every day from morning to dusk but should you find it locked, get the key from house No 30 in the village. It's a five-minute walk from the church.

Getting There & Away

Hrastovlje is 31km south-west of Divača off the main highway to the coast; Koper is 18km to the north-west. Any bus heading along this road in either direction will drop you off just west of Črni Kal, but it's still another 6km south to Hrastovlje. One of the three daily buses from Koper to Buzet in Croatia could get you closer, but without a car or bicycle (or a horse or bullock cart) the only sure way of making it to Hrastovlje is by train.

Unfortunately, the trains do not have a very extensive or flexible schedule. A train leaves Divača daily at 7.43 am, arriving at Hrastovlje station at 8.16 am; the church is about 1km to the north-west. The next train of any kind through this backwater is the 7.13 pm from Koper, which gets into Hrastovlje 20 minutes later. The train carries on to Divača, Postojna and Ljubljana.

If you're driving south to the coast on highway No 10, take the first left after Črni Kal, which is the road heading south for Buzet and Pula in Croatia, and follow the signs for Hrastovlje.

The Coast

Slovenia's very short coast (47km) on the Adriatic Sea is both an area of history and recreation. Three important towns full of Venetian Gothic architecture and art (Koper, Piran, Izola) will keep even the most indefatigable of sightseers busy, and there are beaches, boats for rent and rollicking discos in those towns as well as at Portorož and Ankaran.

But the coast is not everybody's cup of tea. It is very overbuilt, jammed from May to September and the water is not especially clean. Many Slovenes give it a miss in favour of the unspoiled beaches of Istria or Dalmatia, leaving it to German, Italian and Austrian tourists. If you want solitude, head for the hinterland to the south or east where 'Slovenian Istria' still goes about its daily life. Or spend an afternoon at the eerily tranquil salt pans of Sečovlje.

The Koper wine-producing area is known for its white Malvazija and Chardonnay and red Refošk. A number of cultural events take place during the Piran Musical Evenings and Primorska Summer Festival in Koper, Izola, Piran and Portorož in July and the first half of August. Bear in mind that many of the hotels, camp sites, tourist offices and restaurants close down during the off-season (from November to March or as late as April).

KOPER
• *pop 24,400* • *area code ☎066* • *postcode 6000*
Koper is a workaday port city that hardly gives tourism a second thought. It is much less crowded and uppity than its ritzy cousin Piran, 17km down the coast, but despite the surrounding industry, container ports and high-rise buildings, Koper has managed to preserve its compact medieval centre. Its recreational area, the seaside resort of Ankaran, is to the north across Koper Bay.

History
Koper has been known by many names through its long and turbulent history. As an island separated from the mainland by a canal, it was called Aegida by ancient Greek sailors, Capris by the Romans (who found it being used to raise goats) and Justinopolis by the Byzantines. The Patriarchs of Aquileia, who took over the town in the 13th century and made it the base for their estates on the Istrian peninsula, renamed it Caput Histriae – 'Capital of Istria' – from which its Italian name Capodistria is derived. They fortified the town and erected some of Koper's most beautiful buildings, including its cathedral and palaces.

Koper's golden age, though, came during the 15th and 16th centuries under the domination of the Venetian Republic. Trade increased and Koper became the administrative and judicial centre for Istria as far as Buzet to the south-east and Novigrad on the coast. It also had a monopoly on salt, which Austria so desperately needed. But when Trieste, some 20km to the north-east, was proclaimed a free port in the early 18th century and the Habsburgs opened a railway line between Vienna and Trieste in 1857, Koper's fate was sealed. Many of the coastal people moved inland to raise grapes, olives and stone fruits.

Between the two world wars, Koper was administered by the Italians, who launched an aggressive program of Italianisation, closing bilingual schools and keeping close tabs on Slovenian intellectuals. After the defeat of Italy and Germany in WWII, the disputed area of the Adriatic coast – the so-called Free Territory of Trieste – was divided into two zones. Under the London Agreement of 1954, Zone B and its capital Koper went to Yugoslavia while Zone A, including Trieste, fell under Italian jurisdiction.

Up to 25,000 Italian-speaking Istrians fled to Trieste, but 3000 stayed on in Koper and other coastal settlements. Today Koper is the centre of the Italian ethnic community of Slovenia and Italian is widely spoken here. Indeed, Koper is one of the few places in Slovenia where English and German is often of little use when dealing with middle-aged and older people.

Koper has developed rapidly since the 1950s. Not only is it Slovenia's sole port (and Austria's main shipping outlet) but also a business and industrial centre. It is the largest town by far on the coast.

Orientation

Koper's semi-circular Old Town was an island until the early 19th century when it was joined to the mainland by a causeway and later by landfill. Today it's difficult to imagine it as a separate entity as you travel from the combined bus and train station just over 1km to the south-east at the end of Kolodvorska cesta.

The centre of the Old Town is Titov trg, a marvellous Gothic-Renaissance square with Venetian influences. The marina and tiny city beach are to the north-west.

Information

Money Banka Koper, which doesn't charge a commission on travellers cheques, has a branch at Kidričeva ulica 21 a few doors west of the regional museum. It is open from 8.30 am till noon and from 3 to 5 pm weekdays and Saturday morning. There's an SKB Banka with a Cirrus-linked ATM at Ferrarska ulica 6 to the south-east of the Old Town. There are also a couple of private exchange offices on Pristaniška ulica. Maki at No 13 next to the Hertz office is open Monday to Saturday from 7.30 am to 7 pm. Feniks, in the east wing of the large shopping complex and market across the street, is open weekdays from 7 am to 7 pm and on Saturday to 1 pm.

Post & Communications The main post office is next to the train and bus station. It is open from 7 am to 8 pm on weekdays, to 7 pm on Saturday and from 8 am till noon on Sunday. Telekom Slovenije is in the next building. Much more convenient is the post office branch at Muzejski trg 3 near the regional museum. It is open weekdays from 7 am to 7 pm and on Saturday till 1 pm.

Travel Agencies There is no tourist office as such in Koper; seek assistance from Slovenijaturist (☎ 271 358), opposite the marina at Ukmarjev trg 7 and open weekdays from 9 am to 1 pm and 4 to 7 pm on weekdays and on Saturday morning, or from Kompas (☎ 272 346) opposite the outdoor market at Pristaniška ulica 17 and open weekdays from 8 am to 7.30 pm and to 1 pm on Saturday. Slovenijaturist also has a counter inside the train station open weekdays from 6 am to 7.30 pm and on Saturday and Sunday from 6 am to 3 pm then again from 6 to 7.15 pm. They change travellers cheques for a 3% commission.

Consulate The Italian Consulate is at Belveder 2 opposite the bath house.

Walking Tour

The easiest way to see almost everything of interest in Koper's Old Town is simply to walk from the marina on Ukmarjev trg east along Kidričeva ulica to Titov trg and then south down Čevljarska ulica, taking various detours along the way.

The first stop is **Carpacciov trg** behind the Taverna restaurant where the **Column of St Justin** commemorates Koper's contribution – a galley – to the Battle of Lepanto in which Turkey was defeated by the European powers in 1571. Nearby is a large Roman covered basin.

On the north side of Kidričeva ulica you'll pass several disused churches and, at No 20, the 16th century **Totto Palace** with a relief of the winged lion of St Mark taken from Koper's medieval fortress. Opposite, at Kidričeva ulica 33, are some wonderful old

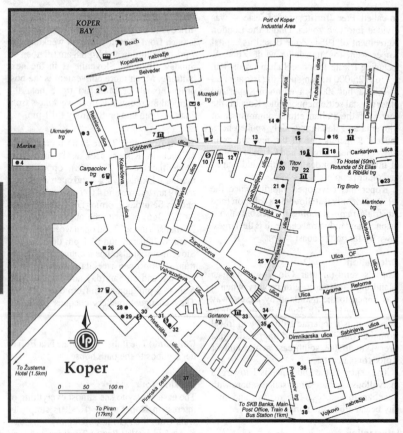

PLACES TO STAY	6	Elite Disco &	20	Town Hall
9 Private Rooms		Carpaccio Pub	21	Široka Jewellery Shop
26 Triglav Hotel	7	Totto Palace	22	Praetorian Palace
	8	Post Office	23	Fontico
PLACES TO EAT	10	Banka Koper	27	Forum Café & Pub
5 Taverna Restaurant	11	Belgramoni-Tacco	28	Vegetable Market
12 Bife Nanos		Palace & Museum	29	Supermarket
24 Atrij Pizzeria	13	Burek Shop	30	Feniks Exchange
25 Bife Diana	14	Theatre		Bureau
34 Istrska Klet Restaurant	15	Loggia & Café	31	Maki Exchange Bureau
		& Gallery	32	Kompas Travel Agency
OTHER	16	Baptistery		& Hertz
1 Bath House		(Carmine Rotunda)	33	Almerigogna Palace
2 Italian Consulate	17	Brutti Palace	35	Keramika Koper Shop
3 Slovenijaturist	18	Cathedral of	36	Da Ponte Fountain
Travel Agency		St Nazarius	37	Department Store
4 Customs Wharf	19	City Tower	38	Muda Gate

BOGDAN KLADNIK

STEVE FALLON

STEVE FALLON

A	B
C	

A: Laufarji mask in Cerkno, Primorska
B: Kayaking on the Soča River, Soča Valley, Primorska
C: Limestone 'bowls' at the Škocjan Caves in the Karst region, Primorska

STEVE FALLON

STEVE FALLON

DUŠAN PODGORNIK

A: Garden courtyard, Hvala Hotel, Kobarid, Primorska
B: Section of the Dance of Death fresco, Church of the Holy Trinity, Hrastovlje, Primorska
C: Working the salt pans at Sečovlje, near Portorož, Primorska

medieval town houses with protruding upper storeys painted red, gold and green.

The **Koper Regional Museum** in 16th century Belgramoni-Tacco Palace at Kidričeva ulica 19, has old maps and photos of the port and coast, 16th to 18th century Italianate sculptures and paintings and copies of medieval frescoes. The museum is supposed to be open April to October, Tuesday to Sunday from 9 am to noon and again from 3 to 6 pm (afternoon hours in July and August are 4 to 7 pm), but it's generally a hit-or-miss situation here. At least have a look at the wonderful bronze door knocker of Venus arising from a seashell.

Titov trg, the centre of old Koper, is a beautiful square full of interesting buildings; mercifully, like much of the Old Town's core, it is closed to traffic. On the north side is the arcaded Venetian Gothic **Loggia** built in 1463. It now contains a coffee house and the **Koper Gallery**, open from 10 am to noon and from 5 to 8 pm Tuesday to Saturday and Sunday morning. To the south, directly opposite at No 3, is the sparkling white **Praetorian Palace**, a mixture of Venetian Gothic

and Renaissance styles dating from the 15th century and now the symbol of Koper. The façade of the palace, once the residence of Koper's mayor who was appointed by the doge in Venice, is chock-a-block with medallions, reliefs and coats of arms of the rich and famous. The Praetorian Palace was once two separate buildings with the Loggia in the centre. When the latter was moved across the square to its current location, the two wings of the palace were joined and the battlements added later.

On the square's western side at No 4, the **town hall** occupies what was an armoury some four centuries ago. Opposite is the **Cathedral of St Nazarius** and its separate belfry, now called the **City Tower**. You can climb this 36m tower daily between 9 am and 1 pm and again between 3 and 7 pm.

The cathedral, partly Romanesque and Gothic but mostly dating from the 18th century in its present state, is the sixth church on this spot. It has a white classical interior with a feeling of space and light that belies the sombre exterior. The **carved stone sarcophagus** behind the main altar is that of the

Koper's landmark Praetorian Palace is a mixture of Venetian Gothic and Renaissance styles and dates from the 15th century.

cathedral's (and town's) patron, a 6th century bishop. Among the furnishings are choir stalls made from olive wood, an ornate 18th century **bishop's throne** on the north side and **paintings by Vittore Carpaccio** (1465-1526), a native of Koper. The cathedral doors are open daily from 7 am till noon and from 3 to 7 pm.

Behind the cathedral to the north is a Romanesque **Baptistery** (also called the Carmine Rotunda) dating from the 12th century.

Trg Brolo, which joins Titov trg on its eastern side, is another square of fine old buildings, including the baroque **Brutti Palace** to the north, and on the eastern side, at No 4, the **Fontico**, a granary where the town's wheat was stored in the 14th century. **Ribiški trg**, a 10-minute walk to the north-east from here, is an old fishing quarter with narrow streets and houses dating back to the 14th century. To get there from Trg Brolo, walk east along Cankarjeva ulica and turn north on to Dijaška ulica. Along the way you'll pass the **Rotunda of St Elias**, a pre-Romanesque structure that could date back as far as the 9th century. Bosadraga ulica, the next street on the right, leads into Ribiški trg.

From Titov trg continue the tour by walking south along **Čevljarska ulica** (Shoemaker's Street). As you walk under the arch of the Praetorian Palace, have a look to the right. The little hole in the wall with the Italian inscriptions was the town's so-called lion's mouth, where anonymous denunciations of officials and others could be made.

Čevljarska ulica, a narrow pedestrian street, leads into Župančičeva ulica (Mayor's Street). Just below it, down the stairs in Gortanov trg at No 13 is the **Almerigogna Palace**, a painted Venetian Gothic palace and arguably the most beautiful building in Koper. It's now a pub.

The Italian family who erected the **fountain** in Prešernov trg in the 17th century was named Da Ponte; thus it is shaped like a bridge (*ponte* in Italian). At the southern end is the **Muda Gate**, erected in 1516 and the last of a dozen such entrances to remain standing. On both sides of the archway you'll see the city seal – the face of a youth in a sunburst.

Activities
Koper's tiny – and dirty – beach is on the north-west edge of the Old Town on Kopališko nabrežje. It has a small bath house, a grassy area for lying in the sun, a restaurant and a snackbar. It's open daily from 8 am to 8 pm in season.

Places to Stay
Camping The closest camp sites are at Ankaran, about 10km to the north by road, and at Izola, 8km to the west. See those sections for details.

Private Rooms Slovenijaturist and Kompas have private singles available for between DM17 and DM29, depending on the category and the season, while doubles are DM26 to DM49. Apartments for two start at DM50 and DM70. You must pay a surcharge of 50% if your stay is less than three days. The vast majority of the rooms are in the new town beyond the train station but not all; the family at Kidričeva ulica 16 has great rooms for rent in an old town house.

Hostel Koper has one of Slovenia's six official hostels – but, as it is a student dormitory, most of it is open in summer only. *Dijaški Dom Koper* (☎ 391 154), a modern five-storey building at Cankarjeva ulica 6 in the Old Town, about 50m east of Trg Brolo, rents beds in triple rooms at DM18 per person, including breakfast, in July and August. The rest of the year only a handful of beds are available. An HI card may get you a small discount.

Hotels The only hotel in the Old Town, the 80-room *Triglav* (☎ 23 771; fax 23 598), Pristaniška ulica 3, is relatively affordable: singles with shower and breakfast are DM40 to DM65, depending on the season, and doubles DM54 to DM98. The 100-room *Žusterna* (☎ 284 385; fax 284 409), the Triglav's sister hotel about 1.5km west on the main coastal road (Istrska cesta), is cheaper, with singles/doubles from as low as DM37/55 to DM52/68. The Žusterna has a swimming pool on the edge of the sea.

Places to Eat

The *Bife Nanos* at Kidričeva ulica 17 next to the regional museum has very basic food and a small courtyard in the back. It's open Monday to Saturday to 10 pm. For fried dough on the go, head for the *burek shop* at No 8 in the same street.

A decent place for a cheap and fast meal is the little *Bife Diana* at Čevljarska ulica 36 with čevapčiči, hamburgers and so on. It's open to 10 pm daily. A pizzeria called *Atrij* at Triglavska ulica 2 is open most days till 10 pm.

One of the most colourful places in Koper for a meal is the *Istrska Klet* in an old palace at Župančičeva ulica 39. Filling set lunches go for 850 SIT, and there's draught wine straight from the barrel. This is the place to try Teran, the hearty red (almost purple) wine from the Karst and coastal wine-growing areas. Istrska Klet is open till 9 pm.

The *Taverna* in a 15th century salt warehouse at Pristaniška ulica 1, almost opposite the marina, is one of Koper's more upmarket restaurants and serves some decent fish dishes.

The large shopping centre and outdoor *market* (open most days from 7 am to 2 pm), also on Pristaniška ulica, contains a *supermarket* and various *food shops*.

Entertainment

Koper's *theatre* (☎ 271 027), north of Titov trg at Verdijeva ulica 3, puts on plays, dance performances and concerts.

Koper often feels more Italian than Slovenian and at dusk, as in most cities and towns across the Adriatic, the *passaggiata* – a lot of strolling and strutting – begins. You can watch some of it from the lovely *Loggia Caffè* at Titov trg 1 (open Monday to Saturday to 10 pm), but the outdoor *Forum* café/pub at the west wing of the market on Pristaniška ulica facing a little park and the marina, is where you'll see most of the action.

The *Elite* is a high-class nightclub and disco at Carpacciov trg 6 (closed Sunday). The *Carpaccio Pub* next door is pleasant for a drink.

Things to Buy

Koper has some very fine shops selling jewellery, textiles and folkcraft at the eastern end of Kidričeva ulica near Titov trg. Most shops close for siesta between about 1 and 4 pm (or even later). The Široka jewellery shop (open 9 am to 1 pm and 4 to 8 pm weekdays and from 8 am till noon on Saturday) at Čevljarska ulica 4 has lovely Art Deco pieces in silver and onyx, coral etc. For ceramics, try Keramika Koper at Župančičeva ulica 41. It is open from 9 am to noon and 5 to 7 pm weekdays and from 9 am till noon on Saturday.

Getting There & Away

Bus Although train departures are limited, the bus service to and from Koper is excellent. There are departures almost every 20 minutes on weekdays to Izola, Strunjan, Piran and Portorož and every 40 minutes at the weekend. The buses start at the train and bus station and stop at the market on Pristaniška ulica before continuing on to Izola.

About nine buses a day leave Koper for Ankaran and Lazaret and between nine and 12 for Ljubljana via Divača and Postojna. Other destinations include: Branik (one or two buses a day), Celje (five), Črna na Koroškem (one), Gračišče (two to four), Ilirska Bistrica (four to six), Maribor (four), Murska Sobota (two), Nova Gorica (one or two), Sežana (three), Velenje (one) and Vrhnika (up to six).

Frequent service (up to 17 buses a day during the week but only one on Saturday) to and from nearby Trieste makes Koper an easy entry/exit point for Italy. Buses run from 6 am to 7.30 pm weekdays (at 7.30 pm only on Saturday). The bus station in Trieste is immediately south-west of the train station in Piazza Libertà.

Koper also provides an excellent springboard for Istria. Destinations on the Croatian

PRIMORSKA

peninsula and their daily departures include: Buzet (three), Novigrad and Poreč (two to three), Pula (one or two), Rijeka (one) and Rovinj (one). There are also three buses a day to Zagreb.

Train Koper is on a minor rail line linking it with Ljubljana (153km; 2¼ hours) via Postojna and Divača. To get to Buzet and Pula in Croatia from here, you must change at Divača or Hrpelje-Kozina for one of up to five trains a day.

Car Kompas Hertz (☎ 22 558) has rental cars available from its office at Pristaniška ulica 15. Parking in much of the Old Town is restricted – or banned – between 6 am and 8 pm. Generally, you can only park on the ring road or in the pay car park near Trg Brolo.

Getting Around
Local buses Nos 1, 2 and 3 go from the main bus and train station to the eastern edge of Cankarjeva ulica in the Old Town with a stop not far from Muda Gate.

To order a taxi in Koper ring ☎ 21 451.

ANKARAN
• *pop 2820* • *area code ☎066* • *postcode 6280*
With Koper concerned primarily with container ships, the role of city playground has fallen to Ankaran (Ancarano in Italian), a seaside holiday village 10km by road to the north. There's not much at Ankaran – the first of the Slovenian coastal resorts – apart from a large tourist complex with a camp site, hotels and a shopping centre. But it's a lush, very green place with a mild subtropical climate, and Italy is right around the corner. Just follow the main road north-west for 3.5km to the checkpoint at Lazaret (Lazzaretto). Trieste is directly across Muggia Bay (Miljski Zaliv) to the north.

Orientation
Ankaran lies on the southern side of the hilly Milje Peninsula which is shared by Slovenia and Italy. The 'town' is essentially a stretch of the road (Jadranska cesta) leading from the coastal highway to Italy and the scattered

houses and vineyards above it. Buses stop in front of the shopping centre on Jadranska cesta. The Adria resort and camp site are opposite.

Information
There's a tourist information kiosk (☎ 526 116; fax 527 158) in the car park of the shopping centre on Jadranska cesta, open from May to mid-September. At other times, seek assistance from the reception desk at the entrance to the Adria tourist complex.

Banka Koper has a branch in the shopping centre open weekdays from 8.30 am till noon and 3 to 5 pm and on Saturday morning. The post office is on the western side of the shopping centre at Regentova ulica 1. It is open on weekdays from 8 am to 7 pm and on Saturday to 1 pm.

Activities
The Adria holiday village, which can accommodate up to 700 people at its hotel, cottages, bungalows and camp site, has a small pebble beach below a cement promenade, two large swimming pools (one faces south-east to the Istrabenz refinery; 1000 SIT) and sporting facilities, including tennis courts, minigolf, table tennis, basketball court and a fitness centre.

Ankaran is the start (or finish) of the Slovenian Alpine Trail that goes all the way to Maribor via the Škocjan Caves, the Cerkno and Idrija hills, the Julian Alps, the Kamnik-Savinja Alps and the Pohorje Massif. The whole trip would take a very fit person a month of walking, eight hours a day. Needless to say, most people find another way to get to Štajerska from here. One of the first stops from Ankaran is **Mt Slavnik** (1028m), which is about 8km north-east of Hrastovlje. There's accommodation at the *Tumova Koča na Slavniku* mountain hut (☎ 25 320 or mobile ☎ 0609-621 791) near the summit.

Places to Stay
Adria Camping (☎ 528 323) extends over an area of 12 hectares on the eastern side of the Adria resort and down to the sea. The price

per person ranges from DM10 to DM14 depending on the season, and guests get to use all the facilities at the resort. Adria Camping is open from May to September.

The *Adria* resort complex (☎ 528 444; fax 528 321) contains a half-dozen different types of accommodation, ranging from cottages with balconies to self-contained seaside bungalows for five people. The cheapest place to stay at the resort just happens to be the most interesting. It's a two-storey hotel dead in the centre called the *Adria Convent*. It was once a Benedictine monastery and later became the summer residence of the aristocratic Madonuzza family from Koper. The price for a single is 3050 to 4280 SIT for a room with breakfast and shared shower, and 4700 to 6580 SIT for a double; the differential depends on the season and the direction in which your room faces. Singles/doubles with private bath range from 3420/5260 SIT to 5250/8080 SIT. The Convent is open year round; most of the other accommodation at the resort is available from May to September only.

The flashy 25-room *Biser* hotel (☎ 526 050; fax 526 057), opposite the large (and quite famous) orthopaedic hospital at Jadranska cesta 86a, charges from DM50 to DM70 per person, depending on the season. Suites start at DM70 and jump to DM90 in July and August. All rooms have air conditioning, direct-dial telephones and satellite television. There's a fitness centre and a night club here as well.

Places to Eat

The *Bistro Adria* at Regentova ulica 2 has light meals and snacks, but the emphasis is on liquid refreshment. The *Jestvina* supermarket behind the post office is open Monday to Saturday from 8 am to 7 pm and to 6 pm on Saturday.

Have you ever eaten a pizza in church? The desanctified monastery chapel next to the Adria Convent hotel is now the *Pizzeria Convent*.

The *Vera Gostilna*, about 1km west of the Adria resort at Jadranska cesta 66, is one of the few independent eateries on the peninsula and popular with local people. It's open daily from 9 am to 11 pm.

Entertainment

There are a couple of popular night spots at the Adria resort including the *Disco Club* near the entrance, with its own huge car park, open from 10 pm and the *Taverna* restaurant with music near the camp site looking out over the Adriatic.

Getting There & Away

Buses make the run from the centre of Ankaran to the Italian border crossing at Lazaret between eight and 11 times a day. Up to nine buses go to Koper. If you're heading for Trieste from Ankaran you'll have to change buses just over the border. All in all, it's probably easier to catch a direct bus from Koper.

IZOLA

• *pop 10,300* • *area code ☎066* • *postcode 6310*

Izola, a somewhat scruffy fishing port 7km south-west of Koper, is the poor relation among the historical towns on the Slovenian coast, but it wasn't always that way. The Romans built a port called Haliaetum at Simon's Bay (Simonov Zaliv) south-west of the Old Town, and they say you can still see parts of the original landing when the tide is very low.

History

The vicissitudes of Izola in the Middle Ages are closely tied to those of Koper and, to a lesser degree, Piran. Struggle among various groups (and a brief period of independence in the 13th century) led to the supremacy of Venice. At first, Izola – at that time an island, which explains its name *(isola* means island in Italian) – flourished, particularly in the trade of olives, fish and its celebrated wine, which was distributed as far away as Germany. But a devastating plague in the 16th century and the ascendancy of Trieste as the premier port in the northern Adriatic destroyed the town's economic base. During the period of the Illyrian Provinces in the early 19th century, the French pulled down the town walls and used them to fill the channel separating the island from the mainland. Many of the medieval churches and buildings were also razed.

After several fish canneries were opened at Izola this century, the town began to industrialise. It remains the country's foremost fishing port, but its glory days seem a million years ago as you walk through the narrow streets whose houses look as if they could topple over in the slightest of winds – or because of the noise of all the rebuilding currently going on. Still, Izola has its charms along with some of the best seafood in Slovenia. It's definitely worth a visit as long as you don't mind a slight fishy smell and some very fat cats underfoot.

Orientation

Almost everything of a practical nature is centred around Trg Republike. Buses stop in front of the Slavnik Koper transport office at Cankarjev drevored 2 on the south-eastern edge of the square.

To reach the Old Town and its main square, Veliki trg, which faces a circular inner harbour, walk north along the waterfront promenade called Sončno nabrežje.

Information

The staff at the tourist office (☎ 62 901; fax 746 101) at Sončno nabrežje 4 are as indifferent and uninterested as you're likely to find on the coast – a very sad change from the way things used to be run here. The office is open daily from 9 am to 1 pm and 4 to 8 pm (to 10 pm in July and August).

Banka Koper has a branch at Drevored 1 Maja 5 open from 8.30 am till noon and from 3 to 5 pm on weekdays and till noon on Saturday. A Banka at Pittonijeva ulica 1, the side street next to the bus office, is open from 8 am to noon and 5 to 7 pm weekdays and on Saturday from 8 to 11 am. The Šifra exchange office at Sončno nabrežje 16 is open weekdays from 7 am to 8 pm and on Saturday to 1.30 pm.

The post office and telephone centre, open from 7.30 am to 7 pm weekdays and to 1 pm

on Saturday, is opposite Slavnik Koper at Cankarjev drevored 1.

Things to See & Do

Izola isn't overly endowed with important historical sights; Napoleon's finest took care of that. But there are one or two things at least worth a brief look, such as the 16th century **Church of Saint Maurus** and its detached bell tower on the hill above the town, the **Municipal Palace** on Veliki trg and the Venetian Gothic **Manzoli House** (1470), owned by a chronicler of Istria in the 16th century, on Manzoli trg near the waterfront (now under renovation).

Izola's most beautiful building, though, is the rococo **Besenghi degli Ughi Palace** on the corner of Gregorčičeva ulica and Bruna ulica below the church. Built between 1775 and 1781, the mansion has windows and balconies adorned with stuccos and wonderful wrought-iron grilles painted light blue. Inside, a stairway decorated with illusionist paintings leads to a salon with a curious wooden balcony running just below the ceiling. The palace is now a music school and headquarters of the local Italian Society.

There are beaches to the north and southeast of the Old Town, but the best one is at Simon's Bay about 1.5km to the south-west. It has a grassy area for sunbathing and a water slide.

The tourist office sells daily fishing licences for 900 SIT a day and can organise a boat for under 1000 SIT per person.

Places to Stay

Camping There are two camp sites within easy reach of Izola. *Jadranka* (☎ 61 202), a small site on the waterfront at Polje cesta 8 some 1200m south-east of the Old Town, is open from May to October. But it's right off the noisy coastal road and fills up quickly in summer. The per-person charge is 450 to 810 SIT, depending on the month.

Belvedere Izola (☎ 605 100), on a bluff 3km west of Izola with wonderful views of the port and the Adriatic, is larger than Jadranka, covering an area of three hectares and accommodating 700 happy campers

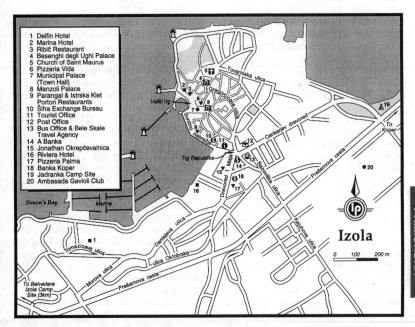

1 Delfin Hotel
2 Marina Hotel
3 Ribič Restaurant
4 Besenghi degli Ughi Palace
5 Church of Saint Maurus
6 Pizzeria Vida
7 Municipal Palace
   (Town Hall)
8 Manzoli Palace
9 Parangal & Istrska Klet
   Porton Restaurants
10 Šifra Exchange Bureau
11 Tourist Office
12 Post Office
13 Bus Office & Bele Skale
   Travel Agency
14 A Banka
15 Jonathan Okrepčevalnica
16 Riviera Hotel
17 Pizzeria Palma
18 Banka Koper
19 Jadranka Camp Site
20 Ambasada Gavioli Club

Izola

0   100   200 m

PRIMORSKA

among the trees. It is open from May to October and costs from 600 to 1100 SIT. The holiday village surrounding the camp has a large swimming pool.

Private Rooms The tourist office can arrange private rooms and apartments throughout the year, but the biggest choice is available in summer. Single rooms are DM17 to DM29, depending on the category and the season, while doubles are DM26 to DM49. Apartments for two start at DM50 and DM70. Breakfast (when available) is usually DM6 extra, and you must pay a surcharge of 50% if your stay is less than three days.

Hotels Izola's cheapest hotel is the four-storey *Riviera* (☎ 62 925; fax 65 495) overlooking the marina at Prekomorskih Brigad ulica 7. The catch is that its 174 beds are only available from mid-June to August; the rest of the year it serves as a dormitory

for students attending Izola's catering and tourism school. Singles and doubles with breakfast and communal shower are 3069 SIT and 5766 SIT. Rooms with their own bathroom are 3627 SIT and 5952 SIT.

The most central hotel in town is the 45-room *Marina* (☎ 65 325; fax 62 012) at Veliki trg 11. Singles start at DM68 in the low season, rising to DM98 in July and August. Doubles are DM88 and DM122.

If you don't mind being a bit out of the centre but still near the water, the *Delfin* (☎ 63 554; fax 63 411), Tomažičeva ulica 10, may be for you. It's a pleasant enough place on a hill about a kilometre south-west of Trg Republike and has its own pool. But it's big, with well over 100 rooms, caters largely to tour groups and is not cheap. Prices start at about 5500 SIT per person.

Places to Eat
Jonathan Okrepčevalnica at Drevored 1 Maja 6 has fast food in less-than-salubrious

surroundings, but it's pretty cheap. *Pizzeria Palma* next to the Banka Koper at Drevored 1 Maja 3 has decent pizza but *Pizzeria Vida*, at Alietova ulica 3, with garden seating out the back, is a better bet.

Why not skip a meal and have a blow-out at one of the fish restaurants? Izola has a large selection of them but not all are reasonably priced or even very good. Stick with the local favourites: *Parangal* just up from the tourist office at Sončno nabrežje 20 or *Ribič* at Veliki trg 3, both of which are open to about 11 pm. But do be careful when you order (especially at Ribič) and ask the exact price of the fish. As seafood is sold by decagramme (abbreviated as *dag* on most menus), you may end up eating (and paying) a lot more than you expected. For a list of fish dishes see Food in the Facts for the Visitor chapter. Be sure to have a glass or two of Malvazija, the pale yellow local white that is light and reasonably dry.

If you want to try Istrian specialities like Istrska rižota (risotto with shellfish and white wine) and pašta fažol (thick bean soup with noodles), head for the *Istrska Klet Porton* at Sončno nabrežje 18, open daily from 11 am till midnight.

Entertainment

The top rave centre on the coast is Izola's *Ambasada Gavioli*, which features some of the top DJs and bands in the country. It's in the industrial area south-west of the port on Industrijska cesta and opens Wednesday (summer only), Friday and Saturday from midnight to 7 am. Such talent doesn't come cheap, though, and you'll pay 1800 SIT to get in, including the first drink. Ring ☎ 61 122 for more information and what's on.

Getting There & Away

Buses leave for Koper and for Strunjan, Piran and Portorož every 20 minutes during the week and every 40 minutes on Saturday and Sunday. Other destinations from Izola (via Koper) include: Celje (three buses a day), Črna na Koroškem (one), Ljubljana (up to 12), Maribor (three), Murska Sobota (two) and Nova Gorica (two).

International routes include eight buses a day (weekdays only) to Trieste in Italy and two to Pula and Zagreb in Croatia.

Like most of the towns on the coast, parking is severely restricted in Izola and you'll have to pay about 100 SIT per hour for the privilege. The full day rate is 1000 SIT.

Getting Around

From June to August a minibus does a continuous loop from the Belvedere Izola holiday village west of the Old Town to Simon's Bay, Izola Marina, Trg Republike and the Jadranka camp site and back.

The Bele Skale travel agency (☎ 65 206) near the bus office at Cankarjev drevored 2 rents bicycles for 800 SIT per day. It is open weekdays from 9 am to 2 pm and from 4 to 7 pm. On Saturday it closes at noon.

AROUND IZOLA
Strunjan

For centuries, the people who lived at Strunjan, a peninsula halfway between Izola and Piran, were engaged in making salt, and you'll see the disused pans spread out before you as you descend along the main road from the Belvedere tourist complex. Today the area, protected as a regional park, attracts large numbers of waterfowl.

Though there has been much development around Strunjan Bay to the south-west, much of the peninsula is remarkably unspoiled. It is bounded by a high cliff – **Cape Ronek** (Rtič Ronek) – at its northernmost point and there are plans to turn the area into a nature reserve. The 16th century **Church of St Mary** nearby is a place of pilgrimage on 15 August.

The *Strunjan Health Resort* (Zdravilišče Strunjan; ☎ 474 100; fax 782 036) has all types of accommodation on offer, but the cheapest are the *Salinera* hotel bungalows for two starting at 4000 SIT during the low season and more than doubling in summer. Along with a beach, the resort has an indoor pool filled with heated sea water as well as tennis courts and other sport facilities. Much use is made of the salty mud found nearby for beauty and therapeutic purposes. The *Strunjan* camp site (☎ 782 076), which is open all year, has space for 350 campers. It charges 750 to 900 SIT per person, 300 SIT per car and 300 SIT for a caravan.

PIRAN
• *pop 4800* • *area code ☎066* • *postcode 6330*
Picturesque Piran (Pirano in Italian), sitting at the tip of a narrow peninsula, is everyone's favourite town on the Slovenian coast. It is a gem of Venetian Gothic architecture and full of narrow streets, but it can be mobbed at the height of summer. Some people might find the best thing to do at that time of year is to get out of the town, though I'm not one of them.

History
Piran has been settled since ancient times, and it is thought that the town's name comes from the Greek word for fire *(pyr)*. In those days, fires were lit at Punta, the very tip of the peninsula, to guide ships to the port at Aegida (now Koper). The Romans established a settlement here called Piranum after their victory over the Illyrians and Celts. They, in turn, were followed by the early Slavs, the Byzantines, the Franks and the Patriarchs of Aquileia.

Venetian rule began in the late 13th century and lasted in one form or another for more than 500 years. Unlike Koper and Izola, whose citizens rose up against the Venetians time and time again, Piran threw its full support behind Venice in its struggles with Aquileia and Genoa. (The fact that Venice was Piran's biggest customer for the salt it produced was certainly an incentive.) The Venetian period was the town's most fruitful, and many of the town's most beautiful buildings and its fortifications were erected then.

Economic stagnation under Austrian and, particularly, Italian rule from the early 19th century until after WWII meant Piran was able to preserve – at a price to the affluence of its citizens – its medieval character. Today it is one of the best preserved historical towns anywhere on the Adriatic and is entirely protected as a cultural monument.

Orientation
Piran's Old Town is situated on the westernmost point of Slovenian Istria. Strunjan Bay is to the north; Piran Bay and Portorož, Slovenia's largest beach resort, lie to the south.

Tartinijev trg, north of Piran Harbour and the small marina, is the centre of the Old Town today but in the Middle Ages the focal point was Trg 1 Maja (also written Prvomajski trg) in what is the oldest part of the Old Town. The bus station is along the waterfront, about 400m to the south of Tartinijev trg at Dantejeva ulica 6. There is no left-luggage office here.

Information
Money Banka Koper at Tartinijev trg 12 changes travellers cheques and cash weekdays from 8.30 am till noon and 3 to 5 pm and on Saturday morning. Outside the bank is an automatic exchange machine that accepts banknotes from 13 countries. It's in operation 24 hours a day.

Post & Communications The new post office at Cankarjevo nabrežje 5 is open weekdays from 7.30 am to 7 pm and till noon on Saturday.

Travel Agency Surprisingly, for a town that receives so many visitors, Piran does not have a tourist office (the one in Portorož handles Piran as well). Head for the Maona travel agency (☎ 746 228) at Cankarjevo nabrežje 7, whose helpful and knowledgeable staff can organise private rooms, an endless string of activities and boat cruises (see the Cruises section). From May to October, it is open Monday to Saturday from 9 am to 7 pm (9 pm in July and August) and on Sunday from 9 am to 1 pm and 5 to 7 pm. In winter, the opening hours are 9 am to 2 pm every day, except Sunday.

Maritime Museum
This museum in a lovely 17th century palace on the waterfront at Cankarjevo nabrežje 3 is named in honour of Sergej Mašera, a Slovenian naval commander whose ship was blown up off the Croatian coast in WWI.

The museum's excellent exhibits, labelled in Slovene and Italian only, focus on the three 'Ss' that have been so important to Piran's development over the centuries: the sea, sailing and salt-making. The salt pans at Sečovlje, south-east of Portorož, get most of the attention downstairs. There are some excellent old photographs showing salt workers going about their duties in coolie-like straw hats as well as a wind-powered salt pump and little wooden weights in the form of circles and diamonds that were used to weigh salt under the Venetian Republic.

The **antique model ships** upstairs are very fine (especially the 17th century galleon and 18th century corvette); other rooms are filled with old figureheads and weapons, including some very lethal-looking blunderbusses. The folk paintings are **votives** that were placed by sailors on the altar of the pilgrimage church at Strunjan for protection against shipwreck.

The palace, with its lovely moulded ceilings, parquet floors and marble staircase, is worth a visit in itself. The museum is open every day, except Monday, from 9 am till noon and from 3 to 6 pm from April to June and in September and October. In July and August the afternoon hours are from 4 to 7 pm. The admission charge is 300/200 SIT for adults/children.

Tartinijev Trg

The statue of the nattily dressed gentleman in the centre of this oval-shaped, marble-paved square, which was the inner harbour until a landfill in 1864, represents local composer and violinist Giuseppe Tartini (1692-1770). To the east and opposite the **Church of St Peter** (1818), Tartini's birthplace at No 7 contains the **Tartini Memorial Room** on the 1st floor open weekdays, except Monday, from 10 am till noon and 5 to 7 pm and at the weekend in the morning only.

The red **Venetian House** (Beneške Hiša), a lovely Venetian Gothic structure from the 15th century with tracery windows and a balcony is at No 4. There is a story attached to the stone relief of the lion with a ribbon in its mouth and the inscription *Lassa pur dir* above it. A wealthy merchant from Venice fell in love with a beautiful local girl. But she soon became the butt of the local gossips. So to shut them up and keep his lover happy, the merchant built her this little red palace complete with a reminder for her loose-lipped neighbours: 'Let them talk.'

The classical 19th century **town hall** and the **court house** with two 17th century doors are to the west. The **Aquarium**, less than 100m along the harbour at Tomažičeva ulica 4, may be small, but there's a tremendous variety of sealife packed into its two dozen tanks. It's open from 9 am to 8 pm and costs 300/200 SIT.

The two 15th century **flag poles** at the entrance to the square bear Latin inscriptions praising Piran as well as the town's coat of arms, and reliefs of St George, the patron, to the left, and St Mark with the lion symbol, on the right.

Church of St George & Around

This Renaissance and baroque church, Piran's most eye-catching structure, stands on a ridge north of Tartinijev trg above the sea.

To the east runs a 200m stretch of the 15th century **town walls**. Climb them for superb views of Piran and the Adriatic. The walls once ran from the sea all the way to the harbour and seven crenellated towers remain pretty much intact.

The church was founded in 1344 and was rebuilt in baroque style in 1637. It's wonderfully decorated with paintings, a magnificent altar and a statue of St George slaying the dragon, with a woman curiously holding the monster by a lead.

The free-standing **bell tower** (1609) was modelled on the campanile of San Marco in Venice and can be climbed daily for excellent views of the town and harbour. Next to it, the octagonal 17th century **Baptistery** contains altars, paintings and a Roman sarcophagus from the 2nd century later used as a baptismal font.

On your way up to the church from Tartinijev trg, have a quick look inside **Our**

PRIMORSKA

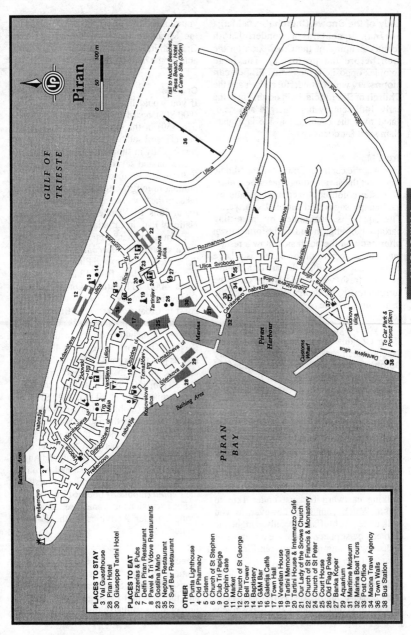

Piran

0   50   100 m

GULF OF
TRIESTE

PIRAN
BAY

Piran
Harbour

Trail to Nudist Beaches,
Fiesa Beach Hotel
& Camp Site (300m)

To Car Park &
Portorož (5km)

PLACES TO STAY
3 Val Guesthouse
28 Piran Hotel
30 Giuseppe Tartini Hotel

PLACES TO EAT
2 Pizzerias & Pubs
7 Delfin Piran Restaurant
8 Pavel & Tri Vdove Restaurants
23 Gostilna Mario
35 Neptun Restaurant
37 Surf Bar Restaurant

OTHER
1 Punta Lighthouse
4 Old Pharmacy
5 Cistern
6 Church of St Stephen
9 Club Tri Papige
10 Dolphin Gate
11 Market
12 Church of St George
13 Bell Tower
14 Baptistery
15 G&M Bar
16 Galerija Caffè
17 Town Hall
18 Venetian House
19 Tartini Memorial
20 Tartini House & Intermezzo Café
21 Our Lady of the Snows Church
22 Church of St Francis & Monastery
24 Church of St Peter
25 Court House
26 Old Flag Poles
27 Banka Koper
29 Aquarium
31 Maritime Museum
32 Marina Boat Tours
33 Post Office
34 Maona Travel Agency
36 Town Walls
38 Bus Station

Lady of the Snows Church (Sveta Marija Snežna). It contains a wonderful 15th century painting of the Crucifixion on the arch before the presbytery. The large complex opposite is the former **Franciscan monastery** with a wonderful cloister and the **Church of St Francis**, built originally in the early 14th century but enlarged and renovated over the centuries. Inside is a giant clam shell for donations.

Trg 1 Maja

This was the centre of Piran until the Middle Ages and the surrounding streets are a maze of pastel-coloured 'overhanging' houses, vaulted passages and arcaded courtyards. The square is surrounded by interesting baroque buildings including the former town **pharmacy** on the north side (now a restaurant). In the centre of the square is a large **cistern** that was built in the late 18th century to store fresh water; rain water from the surrounding roofs flowed into it through the fish borne by the stone cherubs in each corner.

If you're going to Tartinijev trg, walk along Obzidna ulica, one of Piran's oldest streets, which passes under the 15th century **Dolphin Gate** (Dolfinova Vrata). **Židovski trg**, the centre of Jewish life in Piran in the Middle Ages, is a couple of hundred metres to the north-west.

Swimming

Piran has several 'beaches' – rocky areas along Prešernovo nabrežje – where you might dare to get your feet wet. They get a little better after Punta, the 'point' with a lighthouse and an old church, but I'd keep walking eastward for just under 1km to **Fiesa**. Watch your step, however, as you walk under the bluffs, especially at night; the path can be slippery. There are a number of nudist swimming areas between Piran and Fiesa and Fiesa and Strunjan.

The beach at Fiesa is one of the cleanest and prettiest on the Slovenian coast, essentially because boating is very restricted here. It is terribly small though and is positively jammed with bathers in summer. From here you can see Strunjan and on a really clear day the Miramare Castle in Trieste and even Grado in Italy. Kayaks and canoes are available by the hour on the beach.

Cruises

If you would like a tour of Piran Harbour (800 SIT), board the *Marina* (mobile ☎ 041-676 359) at the small pier on Cankarjevo nabrežje just south of the Maritime Museum. It sails daily in summer.

Maona and several other travel agencies in Piran and Portorož can book you on any number of longer cruises – from a loop that takes in the towns along the coast to day-long excursions to Venice, Trieste or Brioni National Park in Croatia.

From about late March to October, the large catamaran *Marconi* glides between Trieste (35 minutes) and Piran on Thursday; the excursion lasts from 12.30 to 8 pm and costs 4000 SIT return. On Wednesday, Friday and Sunday, it goes down the Istrian coast in Croatia as far as the Brioni Islands and the national park there (2¼ hours; 9600 SIT return including lunch), with a stop at Rovinj. The boat leaves at 9.40 am and returns just after 6 pm. On Wednesday, Maona also organises a 'fishing picnic' trip (11 am to 4.30 pm; 4500 SIT) as well as a 'romantic night cruise' (9 to 11.30 pm; 2000 SIT).

The *Delfin* (mobile ☎ 0609-628 491) boat sails from Piran to the marina at Portorož via the Bernadin tourist complex (one hour; 1000 to 1200 SIT) between six and 11 times a day from April to October. In July and August the loop also takes in Fiesa and Strunjan. Another boat offering a similar excursion is the *Pepina* (mobile ☎ 0609-613 628).

For excursions to Venice, see Boating & Cruises under Activities in the Portorož section.

Special Events

Some events of the Piran Musical Evenings/Primorska Summer Festival in July and the first half of August take place on Friday in the vaulted cloister (*križni hodnik*) of the former Franciscan monastery.

Places to Stay

Camping The closest camp site is *Camping Jezero Fiesa* (☎ 73 150) at Fiesa, 4km by road from Piran (but less than 1km if you follow the coastal trail east of the Church of St George). It's in a quiet valley by two small, protected ponds and close to the beach, but it gets very crowded in summer. There's a small supermarket here open daily in summer from 7 am to 7 pm. The camp is open from June to September.

Private Rooms The tourist office in Portorož (☎ 747 015) and the Maona travel agency can arrange private rooms and apartments throughout the year, but the biggest choice is available in summer. Single rooms are DM17 to DM29, depending on the category and the season, while doubles are DM26 to DM50. Apartments for two start at DM44 in the low season and DM55 in July and August. You usually have to pay a surcharge of 50% if your stay is less than three days.

Pension One of the cheapest and very central places to stay in Piran is the hostel-like *Val* guesthouse (☎ 75 499; fax 746 911) at Gregorčičeva ulica 38 on the corner of Vegova ulica. Open from late April to October, it has about two dozen rooms with shared shower for between 2600 and 2900 SIT.

Hotels Piran has only two central hotels. The cheaper of the two, the *Piran* (☎ 746 110; fax 746 101) at Stjenkova ulica 1, has about 77 rooms, many of them facing the sea. Singles and doubles with breakfast and shower start at DM40 and DM60 in the lowest season but jump to a minimum DM65 and DM100 in July and August.

The 45-room *Giuseppe Tartini* hotel (☎ 746 221; fax 746 324) at Tartinijev trg 15 has singles and doubles with views in the high season for DM95 and DM150, but they're only half that in the lowest season.

Though not in Piran itself, one of the nicest places to stay in the area – if not in all of Slovenia – is the *Fiesa* (☎ 746 897; fax 746 896), a 22-room hotel overlooking the sea near the Jezero Fiesa camp site. This pleasant four-storey hotel charges 3750/6000 SIT for singles/doubles in the low season, rising to 7125/11,400 SIT in July and August. From May to September you'll pay 400 SIT extra for a room with a balcony facing the sea, but it's well worth it. The hotel's restaurant is excellent.

Places to Eat

Have a pizza at *Punta* or *Flora* east of the Punta lighthouse along Prešernovo nabrežje and enjoy the uninterrupted views of the sea. There are also several pubs in the area.

The *Surf Bar* restaurant at Grudnova ulica 1, a small street north-east of the bus station, is a good place for a meal or drink. It has a 'photo-album menu' with some 60 dishes and lots of pizzas; the staff are multilingual. It's open daily from 10 am to 11 pm.

Gostilna Mario is a pleasant little restaurant with an outside terrace up the steps from St Peter's Church at Kajuhova ulica 6. It specialises in fish dishes and is open daily, except Wednesday, until 11 pm.

Piran has a heap of seafood restaurants along Prešernovo nabrežje but most (including *Pavel* and less so *Tri Vdove*) are fairly pricey; expect to pay about 5000 SIT for a meal for two, with drinks. Instead, try the local favourites *Delfin Piran* near Trg 1 Maja at Kosovelova ulica 4, or the more expensive *Neptun* at Župančičeva ulica 7 behind the Maona travel agency.

Two decent cafés to check are the *Galerija Caffè* opposite the Venetian House on Tartinjev trg and the clubby *Intermezzo* Italian café in the Tartini House (enter from Kajuhova ulica 12). The latter is open Tuesday to Sunday from 9 am till noon and 6 to 9 pm.

There's an outdoor *market* in the small square behind the town hall.

Entertainment

Piran is not exactly raging but the pamphlet produced by the Erazem student travel agency in Ljubljana a couple of years back wasn't entirely fair when it said that 'nothing really exciting here has happened since the

Venetian Republic'. The *G&M* bar at Ulica IX Korpusa 9 (open to midnight) is a popular meeting place. *Club Tri Papige*, Prešernovo nabrežje 2 near the Piran hotel, is a night-club-cum-disco that attracts, well, working girls. It's open at the weekend to 4 am.

Getting There & Away

Bus Buses head for Portorož and for Strunjan, Izola and Koper about every 20 minutes in season and every 40 minutes at the weekend. Other destinations that can be reached from Piran include: Beli Križ near Fiesa (up to seven a day), Celje (five), Črna na Koroškem (one), Ljubljana via Postojna (six to 10 a day), Maribor (three), Murska Sobota (two), Nova Gorica (two) and Sečovlje via Seča (10).

About six buses go to Trieste in Italy on weekdays, and there's a daily departure for the Croatian capital of Zagreb. One bus a day heads south for Croatian Istria, stopping at the coastal towns of Umag, Poreč and Rovinj.

Car Traffic is severely restricted in Piran and spaces are at an absolute premium. All cars must pay a stiff parking fee if they intend to stay in the town for more than an hour. Leave your car behind or in the municipal lot south of the bus station which charges 60 SIT per hour up to 600 SIT for the full day.

Getting Around

Bus Minibuses run by a company called I&I go from Piran to Portorož and as far as the camp sites at Lucija continuously year round. In summer there is also service to the beach and camp site at Fiesa.

Taxi For a local taxi in Piran, call ☎ 73 555.

PORTOROŽ

• *pop 2980* • *area code ☎066* • *postcode 6320*

Every country with a sea coast has got to have a honky-tonk beach resort – a Blackpool, a Bondi or an Atlantic City – and Portorož is Slovenia's very own. The 'Port of Roses' is essentially a solid strip of high-rise hotels, restaurants, bars, travel agencies,

shops, discos, beaches with turnstiles, parked cars and tourists, and it is not to everyone's liking. A senior Slovenian tourism official calls it 'Portobeton' (Port of Cement) while another says he hasn't been there for over three decades, preferring (like the vast majority of Slovenes) to holiday in Croatian Istria or along the Dalmatian coast.

But Portorož (Portorose in Italian) isn't all bad. The sandy beaches are the largest on the coast and relatively clean, there is a pleasant spa where you can take the waters or cover yourself in curative mud, and the list of other activities goes on and on. If you take it for what it is and let your hair down, Portorož can be a fun place to watch Slovenes, Italians, Austrians, Germans and others at play and in various states of undress. You may just want to join in the fun.

History

Portorož may look as if it was born yesterday, but that's not the case. Though most of the development along the main drag Obala (Beach Road) dates from the late 1960s and 1970s, the settlement was first mentioned in the 13th century and its sheltered bay was fiercely contested over the next 200 years. In 1689, Portorož Bay was the centre of a pan-Istrian sailing competition in which over 100 galleons participated.

But Portorož didn't achieve real fame until the late 19th century when Austro-Hungarian officers came here to be treated with the mud collected from the salt pans at Sečovlje (see Around Portorož). Word spread quickly and the Palace Hotel (1912) was established. This once luxurious pile is just opposite the main beach on Obala and currently under renovation.

Orientation

Portorož skirts a sandy bay about 5km south-east of Piran. The main development looks onto the bay from Obala, but there are satellite resorts and hotel complexes to the north-west at Bernadin and south near the Portorož Marina at Lucija.

The bus station is opposite the main beach on Postajališka pot, while Portorož airport

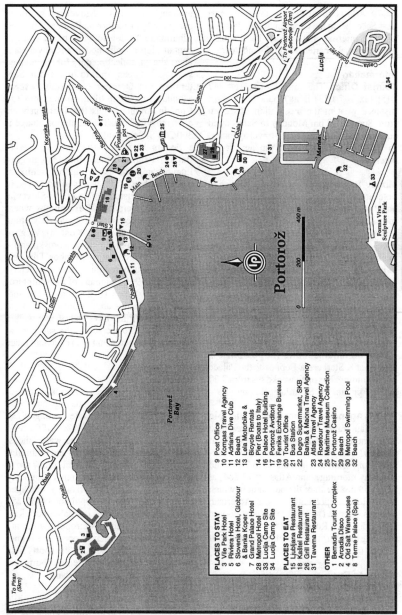

PRIMORSKA

Portorož

0   200   400 m

Portorož Bay

To Piran (5km)

To Portorož Airport & Sečovlje (7km)

Lucija

PLACES TO STAY
3 Vile Park Hotel
5 Riviera Hotel
6 Slovenia Hotel, Globtour & Banka Koper
7 Grand Palace Hotel
28 Metropol Hotel
33 Lucija Camp Site
34 Lucija Camp Site

PLACES TO EAT
15 Ljubljana Restaurant
18 Kaštel Restaurant
26 Grill Restaurant
31 Taverna Restaurant

OTHER
1 Bernadin Tourist Complex
2 Arcadia Disco
4 Old Salt Warehouses
8 Terme Palace (Spa)
9 Post Office
10 Kompas Travel Agency
11 Adriana Dive Club
12 Beach
13 Lela Motorbike & Bicycle Rentals
14 Pier (Boats to Italy)
16 Palace Hotel Building
17 Portorož Avditorij
19 Feniks Exchange Bureau
20 Tourist Office
21 Bus Station
22 Degro Supermarket, SKB Banka & Maona Travel Agency
23 Atlas Travel Agency
24 Roseiour Travel Agency
25 Maritime Museum Collection
27 Portorož Casino
29 Beach
30 Metropol Swimming Pool
32 Beach

(☎ 79 001) is about 7km to the south-east near Sečovlje on the Croatian border. It is one of three international airports in Slovenia, but only small chartered aircraft land there.

Information
Tourist Office The tourist office (☎ 747 015; fax 747 013) is at Obala 16, a short distance west of the bus station. It's open from 8 am to 10 pm Monday to Saturday in summer but, like most of the travel agencies, in winter it's closed by 1 pm and at the weekend.

Money Banka Koper, below the Slovenija hotel at Obala 33, is open from 8.30 till noon and 3 to 5 pm on weekdays and on Saturday morning. It has an automatic exchange machine outside which accepts the bank-notes of 17 countries. There are private exchange offices everywhere. Feniks, a *bureau de change* next to the tourist office, gives a good rate and does not charge commission. Best of all, it's open from 9 am till midnight seven days a week in season. The SKB Banka at Obala 53 has a Cirrus-linked ATM.

Post & Communications The post office is located at K Stari cesta 1 opposite the Palace hotel building. It is open weekdays from 7.30 am to 7 pm and on Saturday till noon.

Travel Agencies Almost all of the big Slovenian travel agencies are represented here, including Kompas (☎ 747 032) at Obala 41 below the post office (open week-days from 9 am to 1 pm and 3 to 7 pm and Saturday morning), and Atlas (☎ 73 264) at Obala 55 just south of the bus station, which is the local representative for American Express. Maona (☎ 746 423) is next door at Obala 53 and Rosetour (☎ 667 5291) is opposite the Maritime Museum Collection at Obala 16a.

Things to See
The **Maritime Museum Collection** in the Villa San Marco, Obala 58, is a branch of the museum in Piran. This time, though, the emphasis is on the Slovenian shipping company Splošna Plovna Piran and its contribution to the development of the coast. It contains lots of ship models and naval paraphernalia – a collection only for the devoted sea dog. It's open April to June and in September and October every day, except Monday, from 9 am till noon and from 3 to 6 pm. In July and August the afternoon hours are from 4 to 7 pm. The admission charge is 300/200 SIT for adults/children.

Forma Viva atop the Seča (Sezza in Italian) Peninsula near the 1st category Lucija camp site is an outdoor sculpture garden with over 100 works of art carved in stone. This is just one of several in Slovenia. They were international exhibitions where sculptors worked with local materials: stone at Portorož, wood at Kostanjevica in Dolenjska, iron at Ravne in Koroška and – God help us – concrete in Maribor. This one, which is vaguely reminiscent of a cemetery, dates from 1961 and many of the sculptures are in sad shape. To be honest, the real reasons for coming are the fantastic views of Portorož and Piran bays and, if you walk a short distance to the south, the salt pans at Sečovlje. The peninsula is an excellent place for a picnic.

Activities
Swimming The beaches at Portorož, including the main one accommodating some 6000 fried and bronzed bodies, are 'managed', so you'll have to pay 290 SIT (200 SIT after 1 pm) to use them. They have water slides, outside showers, beach chairs and umbrellas for rent (400 SIT) and are open from 7 am to 7 pm in season. On a hot summer's day they can be real zoos. The privately managed beach opposite the Metropol hotel (350/250 SIT for adults/children) is smaller but nicer.

The large outdoor Metropol swimming pool next to the beach is open in summer (500/300 SIT admission). In the sports field attached there's minigolf, tennis courts and bowling (10 am to midnight daily).

Diving The Adriana Dive Club (mobile ☎ 0609-639 306), in the little round building near the beach and opposite the Riviera hotel, rents scuba equipment and gives lessons; you can make arrangements with the diving instructor daily between 9 and 10 am daily in season. For about DM55 you get the entire kit – wet suit, mask, flippers, tank and regulator – and a single dive for absolute beginners is DM70. Remember, though, that you're diving for the sport here; there ain't a whole lot in those waters.

Boating & Cruises The Atlas travel agency rents out boats and you can also hire them on the grassy beach area directly west of the Metropol hotel. Rosetour has 'safari canoes' for rent (4000 SIT a day).

On Friday, Saturday and Sunday between late March and October the *Prince of Venice*, a 40m Australian-made catamaran seating 330 passengers, sails from Portorož to Venice (2½ hours; DM90 return). The boat leaves Portorož from the pier below the Ljubljana restaurant, Obala 14, at 8 am and leaves Venice for the return journey at 5.30 pm. For information in Portorož contact Kompas. The Kompas office in Venice (☎ 041-528 6545) is at San Marco 1497. The *Prince of Venice* also sails to Poreč and Rovinj in Croatia for about the same fare on other days, but verify this and the schedule with any Kompas office before making plans.

Another boat making return trips to Venice five times a week (Tuesday to Saturday) between late May and September from Portorož is the *Santa Eleonora* catamaran (☎ 73 583 in Portorož; ☎ 041-520 8966 in Venice). The trip takes only 1½ hours and costs DM95 to DM110 return. On other days the *Santa Eleonora* sails down the coast to various towns in Croatia, including Rovinj, Umag, Poreč, Pula and Lošinj.

If you'd like to see what's *below* the water rather than on or above it, board the *Sub-aquatic* (mobile ☎ 0609-636 371) from the Bernadin tourist complex daily at 10 am or at 2, 4, 6 or 9 pm daily in season. The trip costs between 1800 SIT (2500 SIT for the night cruise).

Spa The Terme Palace spa (☎ 747 041), located on K Stari cesta next to the post office, is famous for thalassotherapy, treatment using sea water and by-products like mud from the salt flats. The spa offers warm sea-water baths (900 SIT per half-hour), brine baths (2200 SIT), Sečovlje mud baths (2800 SIT), massage (3500 SIT for 45 minutes) and a host of other therapies and beauty treatments. It is open Monday to Saturday from 7 am to 7 pm. The palatial indoor swimming pool here is open daily, except Monday, from 7 am to 9 pm.

Panoramic Flights Sightseeing by ultra-light plane is available at the Portorož airport near Sečovlje from April to September from 8 am to 8 pm and between 3 and 5 pm the rest of the year. Flights over Portorož and Piran or the whole coast (15 minutes) cost DM45 (minimum two passengers). There are also 45-minute flights taking in places farther afield like Lipica and the Škocjan Caves (DM108) and the Julian Alps and Triglav (DM210).

Special Events
Portorož Night in July and Istrian Night in early August – evenings of celebration and fireworks – recall the sailing competition held in the bay here in the 17th century. Many special events in summer are held in the large open-air theatre at the Portorož Avditorij (☎ 747 230), an auditorium at Senčna pot 12 a block behind the bus station.

One very unusual event held in Portorož is the Mariners' Baptism of new recruits to the naval school held in early September. It involves a lot of pageantry.

Places to Stay
Camping The *Lucija* camp site (☎ 771 027) has two locations. The 2nd category site is south-east of the marina at the end of Cesta Solinarjev less than 2km from the bus station. The 1st category site, 600m to the west, is on the water. Both camps are open from May to September and get very crowded in summer. The charge per person ranges from DM12 to DM15, depending on the site and the month.

PRIMORSKA

Private Rooms The tourist office, Atlas and Kompas all have private rooms and apartments. You can also book them through Rosetour as well as at Globtour (☎ 73 356) below the Slovenija hotel at Obala 33. Generally single rooms range from DM19 to DM30, depending on the category and the season while doubles are DM32 to DM50. Apartments for two go for a minimum of DM50 and DM70. Some of the rooms are up on the hillside, quite a walk from the beach. Getting a room for less than three nights (for which you must pay a 50% supplement) or a single any time is difficult, and in winter many owners don't want to rent at all due to the low off-season rates in force.

Hotels Portorož counts some 20 hotels, not including the 'olde world' Palace under renovation at Obala 45, the Art Nouveau hotel that put Portorož on the map. Hotels in Portorož can be very expensive during the warmer months. Many close for the winter in October or November and do not reopen until April or even May.

The cheapest hotels in Portorož are the central *Riviera* (☎ 747 051; fax 747 239) and *Slovenija* (☎ /fax same), side by side but sharing the same address at Obala 33, and the *Vile Park* (☎ 475 0000; fax 76 481) in the Bernadin tourist complex. The Riviera and the Slovenija, with 352 and 272 beds respectively, charge from 4760 to 7565 SIT for singles, depending on the season and category, and from 6800 to 11,390 SIT for doubles. The 386-bed Vile Park – that's the plural of 'villa' in Slovene not a comment on the establishment's quality – has singles for 5200 to 8000 SIT and doubles for 7400 to 11,400 SIT. The Riviera is closed from January to March and the Vile Park from mid-October to mid-April. The Slovenija stays open all year.

Places to Eat
Fast-food and pizza/pasta restaurants line Obala. If you want a proper sit-down meal, the terrace at the *Taverna* in the sports field at Obala 22 looks out over the marina and the bay. It's open daily from 11 am till midnight.

The *Grill* restaurant, often with something large being roasted on a spit near the entrance, faces the main beach at Obala 20. Main courses are 800 to 1400 SIT, and there's a set menu for 1100 SIT. The *Kaštel* restaurant sits under an enormous marquee in the warmer months almost opposite the tourist office on Obala. The *Gostilna Ribič* in Seča (house No 143) south of the Forma Viva sculpture park has a wonderful setting and good fish dishes. It is open daily from noon to 11 pm but closes in February.

The *Degro supermarket* is a few steps away from the bus station. It is open weekdays from 7 am to 8 pm, Saturday to 7 pm and Sunday from 8 am to 11 am.

Entertainment
The *Arcadia*, near the old church tower in the centre of the Bernadin tourist complex northwest of the centre, is a popular disco. For more 'mature' entertainment, there's also the *J&B Club Venus* below the Riviera Hotel and the *Tivoli Club* at the Grand Hotel Palace.

The *Portorož Casino* (☎ 746 934) at the Metropol hotel, popular with Italian daytrippers, is open daily from 5 pm.

Getting There & Away
Bus Buses leave Portorož station for Piran, Strunjan and Izola about every 20 minutes on weekdays in season and every 40 minutes on Saturday and Sunday.

Other destinations from Portorož and their daily frequencies include: Celje (five), Črna na Koroškem (one), Ljubljana via Postojna (12), Maribor (three), Murska Sobota (two), Nova Gorica (two) and Sečovlje via Seča (10). International destinations include Poreč (three), Pula (one or two) and Zagreb (two) in Croatia and Trieste (eight a day on weekdays) in Italy.

Car Kompas Hertz (☎ 76 170), Obala 41, and Atlas have cars for hire. There are quite a few smaller agencies along Obala so stroll along and compare prices. You must 'pay and display' to park in Portorož. Four hours costs 100 SIT, a full day 300 SIT.

Salt of the Sea

Although salt-making went on for centuries along the Slovenian coast at places like Sečovlje and Strunjan, the technique changed very little right up to 35 years ago when harvesting on a large scale came to an end.

Traditionally, sea water was channelled via three in-flow canals – the 'salt roads' – into shallow ponds separated by dikes, which were then dammed up with small wooden paddles. Wind-powered pumps removed some of the water and the rest evaporated in the sun and the wind as the salt crystalised from the remaining brine. To stop the salt from turning into a foul-tasting, reddish-brown material, workers lined the pans with a hard, compressed material of microorganisms and gypsum called *petola* so that the salt would not mix with the mud and clay. The procedure dated back to the 13th century.

The salt was collected, drained, washed and, if necessary, ground and iodised. It was then loaded onto to the heavy wooden barge called a *maona* and pulled to salt warehouses at various locations on the coast. Examples of these old *skladišča soli* can still be seen on Obala between Portorož and the Bernadin tourist complex.

Salt is necessary for the human body to enable it to retain water. Once, salt was one of the only things which could preserve meat. Sea salt later became prized because it tastes stronger and more pleasant than mined salt, which can be somewhat metallic, and because it dissolves more quickly. Sea salt was used in the 19th century to treat rheumatism and other muscular disorders at the thermal spa at Portorož and elsewhere.

The lifestyle of the salt workers didn't change much over the years. Salt harvesting was seasonal work, lasting from April to September, when the autumn rains came. During that time most of the workers (both those who controlled the water and those who harvested the salt) lived with their families in the houses you see lining the canals at Sečovlje. They rented the houses and their 'salt funds' – the pans around each house – and divided the profits equally with the landowner.

The set-up of each house was pretty much the same. The large room downstairs served as a storehouse and had two doors so that salt could come in from the fields and then be carried out again on boats in the canal. Upstairs there were two bedrooms and a combination living room and kitchen. All the windows and doors opened on both sides so that workers could observe changes in the weather – as crucial to them as to sailors. Rain and wind could wipe out the entire harvest if the salt was not collected in time.

In September or during rainy periods, the workers returned to their villages to tend their crops and vines. For this reason – and because they lived both on the land and 'at sea' – Slovenian salt workers were said to be 'sitting on two chairs.' ■

Getting Around
Bus I&I minibuses make the loop from the Lucija camp sites to central Portorož and Piran throughout the year.

Taxi For a local taxi in Portorož ring ☎ 73 555 or hail one by the post office.

Car & Motorcycle Atlas and Rosetour rent motor scooters for between 4500 and 5400 SIT a day. You can also rent mopeds/buggies from an outfit called Lela at Obala 127 for 1500/3500 SIT per hour. Lela has a rental kiosk in season near the beach opposite the Grand Palace hotel.

Bicycle Atlas and Rosetour rent bicycles for 1600 to 1800 SIT per day. They cost 1000 SIT for two hours from the Lela rental kiosk.

AROUND PORTOROŽ
Sečovlje
The abandoned salt pans at Sečovlje, stretching some 650 hectares from Seča to the Dragonja River on the Croatian border, have been turned into a regional park and nature reserve. In the centre is the wonderful **Saltworks Museum**, ranked in the top 12 by the European Museums Association.

The area, crisscrossed with dikes, channels, pools and canals, was once a hive of activity and was one of the biggest moneyspinners on the coast in the Middle Ages. Today, it looks like a ghost town with its empty grey-stone houses and pans slowly being taken over by hardy vegetation. Part of a **nature park**, Sečovlje is eerily quiet except for the occasional cry of a gull, an egret or a heron – among the 150 species that flock here.

Sečovlje is right on the border with Croatia and to reach it you must pass through Slovenian immigration and customs first (don't forget your passport). Before you cross the Croatian checkpoint, though, you make a sharp turn to the right (east) and continue along an unsealed road for just under 3km. The two museum buildings stand out along one of the canals; they are the only renovated houses of the many still standing at Sečovlje.

The exhibits relate to all aspects of saltmaking and the lives of salt workers and their families: tools, weights, water jugs, straw hats, baking utensils and the seals used to mark loaves of bread baked communally. They are not in themselves very interesting, but the surroundings are and you do begin to get a feeling of how the *solinarji* (salt workers) lived and worked (see boxed text entitled Salt of the Sea). Out among the pans south of the museum is a **wind-powered pump** (just follow the earthen dikes to reach it) that still twirls in the breeze. The museum staff make use of it and other tools to produce a quantity of salt – about 180 tonnes – every year, in the traditional way.

The museum is open Tuesday to Sunday from 9 am till noon and 3 to 6 pm. Admission is 350 SIT for adults and 250 SIT for children.

Getting There & Away Buses stop at the town of Sečovlje (Sicciole in Italian), about 1.5km north of the border, so it would be best to catch a bus heading into Istria if you can and get off just before the Croatian frontier.

Notranjska

'Inner Carniola' is the least developed of Slovenia's eight traditional provinces. It is largely covered in forest – the setting of many of the country's myths and legends (see boxed text entitled Big Men for Big Times) – but its most distinguishing characteristic is its karst caves below the ground.

Notranjska is the most typical Dinaric region of Slovenia, but its karst is different from that of Primorska. Abundant rain and snow fall here, but the ground is like a great Gruyère cheese; the water vanishes into the ground and resurfaces on the fringes of karst fields called *polje*. Notranjska is also known for its underground rivers (eg Unica, Pivka, Ljubljanica, Rak) and 'intermittent' lakes at Cerknica and Planina.

Notranjska had – and to a certain extent still has – poor communications links, which stunted development. Transport through the deep forests and valleys of this isolated province has been difficult for centuries and when the railway linking Trieste and Ljubljana opened in 1857, it sidestepped much of Notranjska. Notranjska was hit by massive emigration (especially around Cerknica) from the turn of the century up to WWII. Today much of the province is given over to logging, especially on the Bloke Plateau – the birthplace of skiing in Europe, according to some – and in the Lož Valley.

There is a move to make a 60 sq km piece of land around Lake Cerknica, west to Postojna, east to Snežnik and south to the border with Croatia into 'Notranjska Regional Park'. Much of the country's wildlife (and most aggressive animals) live in this region. There are already small regional parks at the Rakov Škocjan Gorge and around Snežnik Castle.

POSTOJNA

• *pop 8200* • *area code ☎067* • *postcode 6230*

The karst cave at Postojna, one of the largest in the world, is among Slovenia's most popular attractions. As a result, it is very

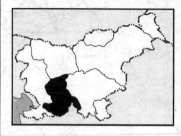

commercialised and crammed most of the year with coaches and tour groups; many travellers prefer the less visited caves north of the town or the ones at Škocjan in Primorska. It's not the end of the world if you miss Postojna; go to Škocjan and you'll see something much more wonderful.

The Postojna Cave (Postojnska Jama) system, a series of caverns, halls and passages some 27km long and 2 million years old, was hollowed out by the Pivka River, which enters a subterranean tunnel near the cave's entrance. The river continues its deep passage underground, carving out several series of caves, and emerges again as the Unica River. The Unica meanders through a sunken field of porous limestone – the Planinsko Polje (Planina Plain) – which becomes Lake Planina in the rainy season. But, as is the nature of what is called a *ponor* river, it is soon lost to the underground. It reappears near Vrhnika as the Ljubljanica

213

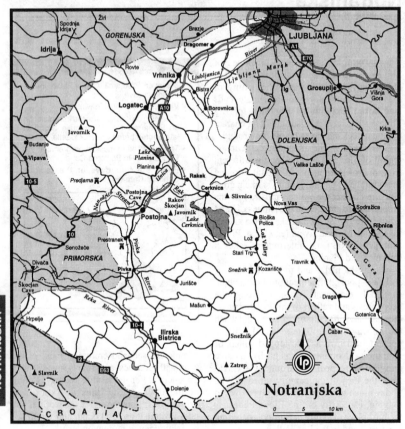

Notranjska

0   5   10 km

River and continues its journey northward to the capital.

History

The town of Postojna (Adelsberg in German) dates back to the 12th century, but there is little of interest here except for a very small collection in the Karst Museum at Titov trg 2.

Postojna Cave has been known – and visited – by residents of the area for centuries; one need only look at the graffiti dating back seven centuries in the Gallery of Old Signatures by the entrance. But people in the Middle Ages knew only the entrances. The inner parts were not explored until April 1818, just days before the arrival of Habsburg Emperor Franz I (ruled 1792-1835). The following year the Cave Commission accepted its first organised tour group, including Archduke Ferdinand, and Postojna's future as a tourist destination was sealed.

Even in those early days, the very poor region of Notranjska saw the potential economic benefits, and in 1823 a guidebook was published to Postojna, which also included the Škocjan and Vilenica caves as well as the mercury mine at Idrija. Since then some 27 million people have visited Postojna.

Orientation

The town of Postojna lies in the Pivka Valley at the foot of Sovič Hill (677m). The Pivka River, once lined with water mills, and the entrance to the cave are about 1.5km north-west of Titov trg, the centre of town.

Postojna's bus station is at Titova cesta 36, about 250m south-west of Titov trg. The train station is on Kolodvorska cesta about 1km to the south-east of the square. If you're walking, the fastest way to get to the town centre from the train station is to go down the steps at the southern end of the station and follow Pod Kolodvorom to Ulica 1 Maja, which leads into Titov trg.

Information

Tourist Offices The tourist office (☎ 25 041; fax 24 870), by the entrance to Postojna Cave at Jamska cesta 30, is open April to September from 9 am to 6 pm daily. In town seek assistance from the helpful staff at Kompas (see Travel Agency).

Money Banka Koper has a branch at Tržaška cesta 2. It is open weekdays from 8.30 am till noon and 3 to 5 pm and on Saturday morning. SKB Banka at Ljubljanska cesta 5a has an ATM. Stil Turizem at Tržaška cesta 4 changes money without taking a commission. It is open weekdays from 8 am to 6 pm and Saturday to 1 pm. You can also change money at Kompas, but the commission there is 3%.

Post & Communications The post office is at Ulica 1 Maja 2a, a short distance south of Titov trg. It is open weekdays from 7.30 am to 7 pm and on Saturday from 8 am till noon.

Travel Agency Kompas (☎ 25 439) at Titov trg 2a is open weekdays from 8 am to 8 pm (7 pm in winter) and on Saturday from 9 am to 1 pm.

Postojna Cave

Visitors get to see about 5.7km of the cave on 1½-hour tours, but the lazy or infirm shouldn't fret – about 4km are covered by a circular electric train that will shuttle you through the so-called Old Passage. The remaining 1700m is on foot. Before you enter the cave, have a look at the Pivka River just opposite as it finds its way underground. That water has created everything you are about to see.

First you board the mini-train, just beyond the entrance, that runs for about 3km to the **Big Mountain** (Velika Gora) cavern. Here you stand under one of the five signs identifying your language, and a guide escorts you through halls, galleries and caverns.

These are dry galleries, decorated with a vast array of white stalactites shaped like needles, enormous icicles and even fragile spaghetti. The stalagmites take familiar shapes – pears, cauliflower and sand castles – but there are also bizarre columns, pillars and translucent curtains that look like rashers of bacon. All in all, it could be a nightmare for anyone who saw monsters in the dark as a child.

Many of the dripstones are colourfully (and artificially) lit in reds, oranges, browns and whites. Only one of the halls is completely devoid of them. It was here that the Partisans blew up a Nazi fuel dump in 1944, and you can still see the blackened walls.

From the Velika Gora cavern you continue across the **Russian Bridge**, built by prisoners of war in 1916, through the 500m-long **Beautiful Caves** (Lepe Jame) filled with wonderful stalactites and stalagmites shaped like ribbons. In case you were wondering, it takes 10 years to produce 1mm of a stalactite. The halls of the Beautiful Caves are the farthest point you'll reach; from here a man-made tunnel stretches to the **Black Cave** (Črna Jama) and **Pivka Cave**, but you'll have to visit them from the entrance at the Pivka Jama camp site to the north.

The tour continues south through the **Winter Hall** (Zimska Dvorana) past the **Brilliant Stalagmite** and the **Pillar Column**, which have become the symbols of the cave (and which look pretty silly when reproduced graphically on the guides' badges and on bumper stickers). You then enter the **Concert Hall** (Koncertna Dvorana), which is the largest in the system and can accommodate 10,000 people for musical performances.

NOTRANJSKA

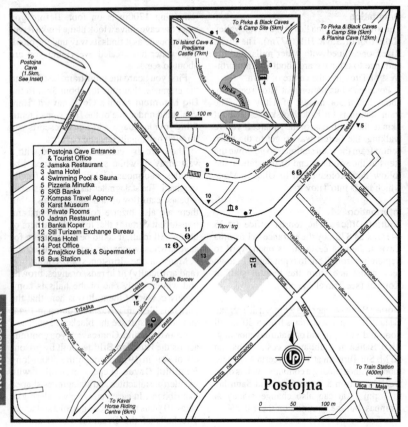

1 Postojna Cave Entrance & Tourist Office
2 Jamska Restaurant
3 Jama Hotel
4 Swimming Pool & Sauna
5 Pizzeria Minutka
6 SKB Banka
7 Kompas Travel Agency
8 Karst Museum
9 Private Rooms
10 Jadran Restaurant
11 Banka Koper
12 Stil Turizem Exchange Bureau
13 Kras Hotel
14 Post Office
15 Zmajčkov Butik & Supermarket
16 Bus Station

Postojna

One of the last things you'll see before boarding the train for the trip back is a tank filled with pink salamanders. These bizarre (and rather rude-looking) little things are *Proteus anguinus*, a unique 'human fish' that was first described by Janez Vajkard Valvasor as the 'dragon's offspring' (see boxed text entitled Proteus Anguinus, the Human Fish). The salamander is just one of 190 species of fauna (beetles, bats, cave hedgehogs etc) found in the cave and studied at the Biospeleological Station here.

The cave has a constant temperature of 8°C and humidity of 95% so a waterproof

jacket is essential. Don't worry if you haven't brought one along; green-felt cloaks can be hired at the entrance for 100 SIT. Shoes are not as big an issue here as they are at the Škocjan Caves and a torch (flashlight) is not necessary; the cave has been lit by electricity since 1884 when many European cities were still using gas.

From May to September, tours leave daily on the hour between 9 am and 6 pm. Admission at this time is 1900/950 SIT for adults/students and children. In March and April and again in October there are tours at 10 am, noon, 2 and 4 pm with an extra daily one at 5 pm in April and tours at the weekend in October at 11 am and 1, 3 and 5 pm. Between November and February, tours leave at 10 am and 2 pm on weekdays with extra ones added at noon and 4 pm at the weekend and public holidays. Admission during the early and late seasons is 1600/800 SIT.

Other Caves

To the north of Postojna lie several smaller but equally interesting caves created by the Pivka River and still part of the Postojna system. They too are open to the public.

Island Cave (Otoška Jama), a half-hour walk north-west from Postojna Cave, is very small (632m in total) and the tour takes only 45 minutes, but its stalagmites and stalactites are very impressive. There's no electric lighting so you'll need a torch and the temperature is also 8°C.

The most popular caves after Postojna – **Pivka** and **Black caves** – are about 5km to the north and the entrance is in the Pivka Jama camp site. You reach the 4km-long system by descending a couple of hundred stairs. A walkway has been cut into the wall of a canyon in Pivka Cave, with its two siphon lakes and a tunnel, and a bridge leads to Black Cave. This is a dry cavern and, as its name implies, its dripstones are not white. A tour of both caves takes 1½ hours.

Planina Cave, 12km to the north-east

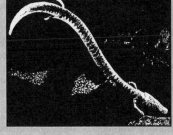

Proteus Anguinus, the Human Fish

Proteus anguinus is one of the most mysterious creatures in the world. It's a kind of salamander but related to no other amphibian and is the largest permanent cave-dwelling vertebrate known to man. The blind little fellow lives hidden in the pitch black for up to a century and can go years without food. *Proteus anguinus* is now the symbol of Postojna and has been added to the town seal (just below the imperial eagle).

The 17th century chronicler Valvasor wrote about the fear and astonishment of local people when an immature 'dragon' was found in a karst spring near Vhrnika, but he judged it to be 'an underground worm and vermin of the kind that is common in some parts'. Several other reports about this four-legged 'human fish' (*človeška ribica* as it's called in Slovene) were made before a doctor in Vienna realised its uniqueness in 1768. In announcing its existence to the scientific world, he called it 'Proteus anguinus', after the protector of Poseidon's sea creatures in Greek mythology and the Latin word for 'snake'.

Proteus anguinus measures about 25 to 30cm long and is a little bundle of contradictions. It has a long tail fin that it uses for swimming but also can propel itself with its four legs (the front pair have three little 'fingers' and the back one two 'toes'). Though blind, with atrophied, almost invisible eyes, *Proteus anguinus* has an excellent sense of smell and is sensitive to weak electric fields in the water. It uses these to move around in the dark, locate prey and communicate. It breathes through frilly, bright-red gills at the base of its head when submerged but also has rudimentary lungs for breathing when it is outside the water. The human-like skin has no pigmentation whatsoever but it looks pink in the light due to blood circulation.

The question that scientists have asked themselves for three centuries is: How do they reproduce? This has never been witnessed in a natural state, and the crafty little things haven't been very cooperative in captivity. But it is almost certain that they hatch their young from eggs and that they don't reach sexual maturity until the age of 16 or 18.

Animal-rights activists will be happy to learn that the beasties in the tank in Postojna Cave call it home for only two or three months and are then returned to the 'wild'. Others aren't so lucky. The export of live *Proteus anguinus* is banned in Slovenia but that hasn't stopped unscrupulous dealers and the little creatures keep appearing for sale in aquariums and pet shops in other European countries. The biggest customers, it is said, are scientists. ■

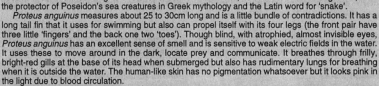

NOTRANJSKA

near the unpredictable Lake Planina, is the largest water cave in Slovenia and a treasure trove of fauna (including *Proteus anguinus*). This is where the Pivka and Rak join forces to form the Unica River. The cave's entrance is at the foot of a 100m rock wall. It's over 6km long and you get to visit about 900m of it in an hour. There are no lights so take a torch. Many parts of the cave are accessible only in low water or by rubber raft.

These caves are all open from June to September and can be visited between two and four times every day (weekends only at the Island Cave). For information about the Island, Pivka and Black caves, call the tourist office (☎ 25 041) at Postojna. For Planina Cave, ring ☎ 57 686. Admission is 1000/500 SIT adults/students and children for each cave.

Horse Riding

The Kaval Horse Riding Centre (☎ 54 506) at Prestranek Castle, about 6.5km south of Postojna, is one of the most professional stables in Slovenia and an excellent place for learning to ride or improving your skills. (The history of horse breeding at the castle goes back to the early 18th century.) The centre is open daily from 9 to 11 am and 4 to 8 pm in summer and 10.30 am to 12.30 pm and 2 to 5 pm in winter.

Special Events

Musical performances are staged in the Concert Hall at Postojna Cave in summer and on various holidays throughout the year, especially the week between Christmas and New Year. This is also the time when the 'Live Christmas Crib' – the Christmas story performed by actors – takes place in the cave.

Places to Stay

Camping The *Pivka Jama* camp ground (☎ 25 382) is located on a 2.5-hectare site in a pine forest near the entrance to Pivka and Black caves. It is open from May to September and costs 1400 SIT per person. The 20 box-like bungalows with four beds each are 10,000 SIT, apartments for four are 12,000 SIT. If you're in a group this is a pleasant, friendly place to stay, and there's a swim-ming pool. You can walk to the camp site through the forest from Postojna along a marked trail in about 45 minutes.

Private Rooms Kompas can organise private rooms in and around Postojna for about 2000 SIT per person. The *rooms* available at Tomšičeva ulica 3 above Titov trg are very central.

Hotels The only hotel in Postojna town is the 54-room *Kras* (☎ 24 071; fax 24 431) facing Titov trg at Tržaška cesta 1. Singles with breakfast and shower start at 5000 SIT, doubles at 8000 SIT.

Some 200m south-east of the entrance to Postojna Cave at Jamska cesta 28, the 136-room *Jama* (☎ 24 172; fax 24 431) costs from 6200 SIT for a single and from 10,000 SIT for a double. There is little reason to stay out here though, unless you want to be the first person in the cave in the morning. The hotel has an indoor swimming pool (400 to 500 SIT), sauna (700 to 1000 SIT) and fitness centre open weekdays from 4 to 9 pm and at the weekend from 10 am to 8 pm.

Places to Eat

The *Jadran* restaurant on Titov trg in Postojna town has a good selection of fish dishes, but they can be pricey.

Pizzeria Minutka, with a terrace outside at Ljubljanska cesta 14, is a local favourite open daily to 11 pm. The fast-food *Zmajčkov Butik* next to the *supermarket* at Tržaška cesta 9 has sandwiches, mini-pizzas etc available daily from 7.30 am to 7 pm.

There are many places to eat in the tourist complex near Postojna Cave, including a *pizzeria* and two *self-service restaurants*. The *Jamska* restaurant in a 1920s-style building next to the entrance to the cave has three-course set menus for 1200 and 1500 SIT.

Getting There & Away

Bus All the buses travelling between Ljub-ljana and the coast stop at Postojna. Count on a bus about every half-hour to the capital and hourly to Pivka, a town south of Postojna (and not the camp site).

Other destinations and their daily frequencies include: Celje (six), Cerknica (one to four), Koper (10), Koper via Ilirska Bistrica (one), Maribor (six), Murska Sobota (two), Izola (one), Nova Gorica (one to four), Piran (eight or nine), Sežana (three to five) and Stari Trg pri Lož (one).

International destinations include Poreč (one bus a day), Rijeka (one) and Zagreb (three) in Croatia and Trieste (two from Monday to Saturday) in Italy.

Train Postojna is on the main line linking Ljubljana (67km; one hour) with Sežana and Trieste via Divača (37km; 40 minutes). As many as 20 trains a day make the run from the capital to Postojna and back. You can also reach here from Koper (86km; 1½ hours) on one of up to eight trains a day.

Getting Around

For a taxi in Postojna, call ☎ 23 941. The Pivka Jama camping ground has bicycles for rent.

PREDJAMA CASTLE
• *area code* ☎*067* • *postcode 6230*
Situated in the gaping mouth of a cavern halfway up a hillside, about 9km north-west of Postojna, this four-storey castle has one of the most dramatic settings anywhere. Although traces of other structures can be dated back to the early 13th century, the castle as you see it today is from the 16th century. Then – as now – it looked unconquerable, perched in the centre of a 123m cliff.

Ah, but along came one Erazem Lueger, a 15th century robber baron who, like Robin Hood, waylaid wagons in the deep forest, stole the loot and handed it over to the poor. During the wars between the Hungarians (under good King Matthias Corvinus) and the Austrians (behind the wicked Frederick III), Lueger supported the former. He holed himself up in the castle and continued his daring deeds with the help of a secret passage that led out from behind the rock wall. Frederick was livid.

NOTRANJSKA

The four-storey Predjama Castle, 9km north-west of Postojna, has a spectacular setting perched in the centre of a 123m-high cliff.

In the autumn of 1483, the Austrian army attacked the castle, but it proved impregnable for months. All the while Erazem mocked the soldiers and showered them with fish, the occasional roast ox and even cherries to prove that he came and went as he pleased.

But Erazem proved to be too big for his breeches and met an ignoble fate. Having gone 'to where even the sultan must go alone' (as Valvasor described it), Erazem was hit by a cannon ball as he sat on the toilet. A turncoat servant, it seems, had betrayed his boss by marking the location of the water closet with a little flag for the Austrian soldiers.

The castle is not in very good shape nowadays and the eight **museum rooms** contain little of interest except for a portrait of Erazem and an oil painting of the 1483-84 siege. But Predjama's striking position and the views of the valley below are incomparable. And it does have all the features a castle should have: a drawbridge over a raging river, holes in the ceiling of the entrance tower for pouring boiling oil on intruders, a very dank dungeon, a 16th century chest full of treasure (unearthed in the cellar in 1991) and an eyrie-like hiding place at the top called **Erazem's Nook**. Just watch out when walking and climbing over the very uneven surfaces.

The **cave** below the castle, carved out by the Lokva and Nanoščica streams, is actually a 7km network of galleries spread over five levels. Much of it is open only to speleologists, but casual visitors can see about 900m. There is no electric lighting, and the trail is only partially constructed so you will need to don rubber boots and carry torches, both of which are available at the entrance. For information, contact Postojna Cave (☎ 25 041) or the castle directly (☎ 59 260).

Predjama is open daily year round. From June to August the hours are 9 am to 7 pm; in May and September the castle closes an hour earlier. In March and April and again in October the daily hours are 10 am to 5 pm. In winter – November to February – it opens Tuesday to Friday from 10 am to 4 pm and at the weekend to 5 pm. Admission is 500/250 for adults/students and children.

Short circular tours of Predjama Cave leave at 11 am and at 1, 3 and 5 pm from May to September and cost 600/300 SIT or 900/450 SIT for both the castle and the cave. Longer tours – to the end of the cave's Eastern Passage (3000 SIT) or the recently reopened Erazem's Gallery (Erazmov Rov; 1600 SIT) are available by prior arrangement only.

If you want or need to stay out here (transport is tricky), the *Gostilna Požar* near the ticket kiosk has rooms. There's also accommodation available at the *Erazem* motel (☎ 59 185) about 3km south-east near the village of Belsko.

Predjama is difficult to reach by public transport. As close as you'll get by local bus from Postojna (and during the school year only) is Bukovje, a village about 2km northeast of Predjama. A taxi from Postojna plus an hour's wait at the castle costs 5000 SIT.

CERKNICA
• pop 3500 • area code ☎061 • postcode 1380

This is the largest town on the lake that isn't always a lake – one of Slovenia's most unusual natural phenomena. Cerknica itself is not important as a destination, but it is close to the 'intermittent' Lake Cerknica, the regional park around Rakov Škocjan Gorge, Mt Snežnik and Snežnik Castle.

The area around the lake has been settled since prehistoric times, and a trade route once ran over the Bloke Plateau to the east, linking Slovenia and Croatia. During the Roman period, Cerknica (Cirkniz in German) was a stopover on the road leading from Emona (Ljubljana) to the coast. Cerknica was given town status in the 11th century.

But Cerknica is a good example of how important communication lines are for the development of a town. The railway linking Trieste and Ljubljana opened in 1857, but it dodged Cerknica in favour of Rakek, 5km to the north-west. The highway from Ljubljana toward the coast follows the same route, and Cerknica remains something of a backwater. With some of Notranjska's most beautiful forests and their fragile ecosystems in the town's back yard, that may not be such a bad thing.

Orientation & Information

Cerknica lies north of Lake Cerknica and about 16km north-east of Postojna. Cesta 4 Maja, the main street, is the centre of town. The bus station is on Čabranska ulica about 100m to the south-west.

Cerknica's tourist office (☎ 793 636; fax 791 201) is at Cesta 4 Maja 51. It is open weekdays from 7.30 am to 3 pm and on Saturday from 8 am till noon. Nova Ljubljanska Banka has a branch in the Mercator shopping centre at Cesta 4 Maja 64. It is open from 8 to 11 am and 2 to 5.30 pm weekdays and on Saturday morning. SKB Banka, open weekdays only from 8.30 am till noon and 2 to 5 pm, is at Partizanska cesta 1. The post office, next door to the tourist office at Cesta 4 Maja 52, is open from 8 am to 7 pm weekdays and on Saturday till noon.

Parish Church of Our Lady

Sitting atop a gentle slope 200m north of Cesta 4 Maja, this church is the only real attraction right in Cerknica. To reach it, walk up the street simply called Tabor, which runs to the east of the shopping centre. This was called 'Road of the Patriarchs' in medieval

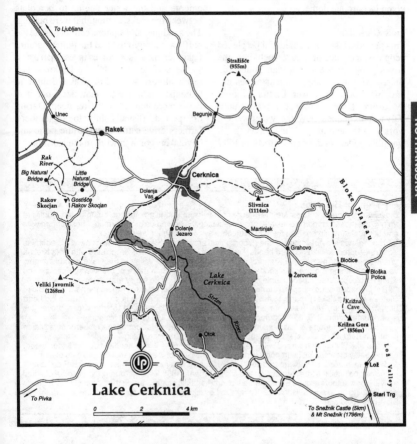

NOTRANJSKA

Lake Cerknica

To Ljubljana
Stražišče (955m)
Unec
Begunje
Rakek
Rak River
Cerknica
Big Natural Bridge
Little Natural Bridge
Dolenja Vas
Rakov Škocjan
Gostišče Rakov Škocjan
Slivnica (1114m)
Bloke Plateau
Dolenje Jezero
Martinjak
Grahovo
Bločice
Žerovnica
Bloška Polica
Veliki Javornik (1268m)
Lake Cerknica
Stržen
Križna Cave
Križna Gora (856m)
Lož Valley
Otok
River
Lož
Stari Trg
To Pivka
0 2 4 km
To Snežnik Castle (5km) & Mt Snežnik (1796m)

times when Cerknica was the centre of Aquileia's estates in the area.

The church sat in the middle of a fortified settlement, and the ramparts and two towers, built to withstand Turkish raids in the late 15th century, remain intact. On the Latin plaque in the wall, the number 4 of the year 1472 is written with a loop – the top half of an 8 – because 4 was considered unlucky in the Middle Ages, as it still is in much of Asia.

Completed in the early 16th century, this is a hall church – with nave and aisles of equal height – and not unlike the one at Kranj in Gorenjska. In the 18th century two side chapels were added, and the bell tower was given its baroque dome.

Lake Cerknica

This periodic lake has baffled and perplexed people since ancient times, including the Greek geographer and historian Strabo (63 BC-24 AD) who called the mysterious on-and-off body of water Lacus Lugeus (Mourning Lake). However, it wasn't until Valvasor explained how the water system worked at the end of the 17th century that it was fully understood. For his efforts, in 1697 this great Renaissance man was made a member of the Royal Society in London, the premier scientific institution in the world at the time.

Cerknica is a polje, a field above a collapsed karst cavern full of sinkholes, potholes, siphons and underground tunnels that can stay dry for much of the year but then floods. From the south, the polje is fed by another one of those disappearing ponor rivers, the Stržen, and to the east and west it collects water underground from the Bloke Plateau and the Javornik Mountains. During rainy periods in the autumn and spring, all this water comes rushing into the polje. Springs emerge and the water begins to percolate between the rocks, as though it were boiling. The sinkholes and siphons cannot handle the outflow underground and the polje becomes Lake Cerknica – sometimes in less than a day.

The surface area of Lake Cerknica can reach almost 40 sq km (Lake Bohinj in Gorenjska is a quarter that size), but it is never more than a few metres deep. During dry periods (usually July to September), farmers drive cattle down to the polje, and haymakers come to work in the sunshine.

Big Men for Big Times

Slovenian folklore and tales are rife with fairies, witches and things that go bump in the night, but among the most common stories are those describing the derring-do of 'supermen' whose strong wills and unusual strength enabled them to overcome evil and conquer their enemies.

The legends are not limited to one geographical area. Peter Klepec, who swept away his enemies with trees uprooted with his bare hands, lived on the Kolpa River and is associated with Bela Krajina province. Another hero called Kumprej ruled the Upper Savinja Valley in Štajerska with his mighty voice and fearsome blade. His shoes were five times larger than those of the average person and when he disappeared a poor couple made footwear for their entire family from them.

But perhaps the most popular stories revolve around the feats of Martin Krpan, the hero of the Bloke Plateau in Notranjska. Krpan's traits and characteristics are familiar. He is an outlaw with a big heart hunted by the imperial guard for smuggling salt. When he is arrested, Martin Krpan proves his super-human strength to the emperor in Vienna by picking up and carrying his horse.

Realising his fortune at having such a powerful giant under his control, the emperor sets Martin Krpan on Berdavs, the local scourge and personification of the marauding Turk. Martin Krpan defeats Berdavs and chops off his head with his magic axe – complete with a handle made of linden wood. For his pains the imperial court confers on him the privilege of the free transport and sale of salt.

The tales of Martin Krpan are traditional but reached a wider audience when the writer Fran Levstik collected and published them under the title *Martin Krpan* in 1858. This was during the period of national revival when authors around Europe were writing Romantic stories, raising the status of local legends and, in doing so, the local language. Thanks to Levstik, Slovenia had for the first time a hero that all Slovenes could admire. ■

Lake Cerknica is a beautiful place – whether dry and under cultivation, full of water (and anglers and windsurfers and swimmers) or frozen solid. In fact, it is in winter that the lake becomes most glorious. The waves of the lake freeze into eerie ice formations, and mallard ducks and wild geese drift to and fro. A lot of people skate here then.

The lake really begins at the village of **Dolenje Jezero** about 2.5km south of Cerknica. If you continue south along a trail following the Stržen River, you'll come to a little island called **Otok** with farmland and a little village.

Rakov Škocjan

This gorge 6km west of Cerknica has been under protection as a regional park since 1949. The Rak River, en route to join the Pivka at Planina Cave, sculpted out 2.5km of hollows, caves, springs and its big and little natural bridges – the **Veliki Naravni Most** and the **Mali Naravni Most**. To the south lie the Javornik Mountains, including its tallest peak, **Veliki Javornik** (1268m). If you're coming from Rakek, you can reach the Gostišče Rakov Škocjan restaurant on foot from the train station in about one hour.

Activities

When it's full, Lake Cerknica becomes a vast playground for boaters, anglers and swimmers. Ask the tourist office in Cerknica about fishing licences (1900 SIT a day) and boat rentals.

The tourist office can also help arrange tours of the lake by horse-driven carriage. The Kontrabantar farmhouse (☎ 792 253) in Dolenja Vas (house No 72), a village 2km south-west of Cerknica, has half a dozen horses for rent for 1200 SIT per hour from Thursday to Sunday as well as offering lessons (1200 SIT per hour) and guided coach tours into the countryside for four to five people (3000 SIT per hour). It's difficult to imagine a more enjoyable way of exploring Lake Cerknica and the surrounding hills.

The area around Cerknica is excellent for hikes, and the **Cerknica Mountain Trail** will

lead you to the most interesting peaks in a very full two-day walk. The trail heads south-west from Cerknica to thickly forested Veliki Javornik; from here you can take a side trip of about two hours to Rakov Škocjan. The trail then skirts the southern shore of Lake Cerknica and carries on north to Križna Gora (856m) and its nearby cave and north-west to Slivnica (1114m). Slivnica, home of the witch Uršula and other sorcerers, has accommodation in a mountain hut. The next day you walk north to Stražišče (955m) and back to Cerknica.

You can do just parts of the walk, such as the stages to Rakov Škocjan, Veliki Javornik or Slivnica. Cerknica's tourist office sells the useful *Karst of Notranjska* 1:50,000-scale map for 1000 SIT.

Special Events

Cerknica is famous for its Carnival (Pustni Karneval), which takes place for four days before Ash Wednesday in February or early March. This is the time when the enormous masks of Uršula, who makes her home on Mt Slivnica, and a half-dozen other legendary characters are dusted off and paraded up and down Cesta 4 Maja while being provoked by upstarts with pitchforks. It wasn't such a laughing matter during the Reformation, though. Valvasor reports that this part of Notranjska was the centre of witch-hunting and executions even in his day.

Places to Stay

The choice of accommodation is very limited in Cerknica. The *Turšič* guesthouse (☎ 791 354) between the tourist office and the Church of Our Lady at Partizanska ulica 14 has two basic rooms with shared shower for 1500 SIT per person and a large *apartment* with five beds in Dolenje Jezero for 7600 SIT a night. The *Zabukovec* house (☎ 793 226) at Partizanska cesta 5 also has accommodation in two rooms.

The *Dom na Slivnici* mountain hut (mobile ☎ 0609-619 489) on Mt Slivnica has 37 beds and is open year round except in July. Singles/doubles with breakfast cost 1950/3900 SIT.

Places to Eat

Cerknica has a couple of decent restaurants, including *Valvasorjev Hram*, with its own wine cellar, opposite the tourist office at Partizanska cesta 1 (open daily), and the *Gostilna Peščenek*, some 250m east of the centre on the main road. There's a very basic self-service restaurant in the *Mercator* shopping centre open weekdays from 7 am to 7 pm, on Saturday to 1 pm and on Sunday to 11 am. The supermarket here is open weekdays from 8 am till noon and 3 to 7 pm and on Saturday morning.

Jezerski Hram in Dolenje Jezero is a good place for a meal while having a look at the lake. There's a scale model inside. The *Gostišče Rakov Škocjan* is a short walk from the Little Natural Bridge (Mali Naravni Most) and the Zelške Caves at Rakov Škocjan.

Getting There & Away

Bus As is the case in this part of Notranjska, bus service to and from Cerknica is not great. Buses run hourly to Ljubljana and up to five times a day to Lož, Rakek and Stari Trg, but other destinations are few and far between. They include Bloška Polica (two buses a day), Hrib-Loški Potok (one on weekdays), Nova Vas (up to three), Postojna (three) and Snežnik Castle (one or two).

Train Luckily, there's a train station at Rakek, about 5km to the north-west of Cerknica, and it's on the line connecting Ljubljana with Sežana. About 15 trains a day stop at Rakek to or from the capital. Heading south, all of these stop at Postojna and Pivka, but only about half carry on to Divača and Sežana.

Getting Around

The Notranjska Ecology Centre (☎ 791 064) above the tourist office at Cesta 4 Maja 51 rents bicycles for 1200/2000/3500/5000 SIT for half a day/full day/three days/five days.

SNEŽNIK CASTLE

This 16th century Renaissance castle below the village of Kozarišče, some 21km south-east of Cerknica, is one of the loveliest and best-preserved castles in Slovenia. Because of its secluded position in the Lož Valley (Loška Dolina), it has been able to escape the fate of most other castles in the country, and it looks almost exactly the way it did more than four centuries ago.

Things to See & Do

Snežnik Castle (Schneeberg in German), which houses a **museum**, stands in a large and protected park. The entrance is through a double barbican with a drawbridge and a moat. The exhibits in the main building are essentially the entire household inventory of the Schönburg-Waldenburg family, who used the castle as a summer residence and hunting lodge until WWII. The castle is full of tasteful period furniture; one room is done up in Egyptian handicrafts presented to Herman Schönburg-Waldenburg by a friend early in the century. The castle also contains an **art gallery**.

Adjacent to the castle, a 19th century building that once served as a dairy now contains a small **Dormouse Museum** (see Special Events). There's not much you won't know about this incredible-edible fellow's life and habits after a visit here.

Snežnik Castle is open mid-April to mid-November, Wednesday to Friday, from 10 am to 1 pm and 3 to 6 pm. On Saturday and Sunday it is open the same hours with no break. Admission is 500/350 SIT for adults/students and children.

16th century Snežnik Castle is one of the best preserved in Slovenia.

STEVE FALLON

JOCO ŽNIDARŠIČ

STEVE FALLON

A: 16th century Renaissance Snežnik Castle, near Kozarišče, Notranjska
B: Cycling is a wonderful way to tour around Notranjska
C: The beautiful and mysterious 'disappearing' Lake Cerknica

A	
B	C
D	

A: Riding along the Krka River, near Otočec Castle, Dolenjska

B: Žužemberk Castle ruins, Krka River Valley, Dolenjska

C: Buildings at Baza 20, Kočevski Rog, Dolenjska

D: Mobile beehive, Kočevski Rog, Dolenjska

Snežnik Castle would make an excellent bicycle trip from Cerknica. If you make the necessary preparations in advance, you could stop at **Križna Cave**, about a kilometre or so after you turn off the main Cerknica road. The cave, which was carved out by water from the Bloke Plateau, is 8.5km long and counts some 22 underground lakes filled with green and blue water as well as a unique 'forest' of ice stalagmites near the entrance. It is one of the most magnificent water caves in the world and can be explored by rubber raft. But in order to do so you must contact the man in charge, Alojz Troha, in Bloška Polica (house No 7) or ring ☎ 061-798 149. It's a long tour if you elect to do the entire cave. You should be dressed warmly and carry a torch as Križna Cave does not have electric lighting.

Lož, the next village, is a picturesque place in a valley with the ruins of a mighty 13th century castle and a fortified church.

A stage of the E6 European Hiking Trail leads from near Snežnik Castle to **Mt Snežnik** (1796m), whose peak remains snowcapped until well into the spring. Snežnik, about 15km south-west of Kozarišče, is the highest non-Alpine mountain in Slovenia and on a clear day you can see forever (well, as far as Trieste and Venice, the Julian Alps, the Karavanke on the Austrian border and the Pohorje Massif).

There is accommodation at the *Zavetišče na Velikem Snežniku* (mobile ☎ 0609-615 356), open on Saturday, Sunday and holidays from June to October and daily in August.

Special Events

Summer concerts are held as part of the Snežnik Evenings festival from July to September. Contact the museum (☎ 707 814 or ☎ 708 400) or the tourist office (☎ 793 636) in Cerknica for details. The big occasion in these parts is Dormouse Night (Polharska Noč) held in late September during the brief period when it's open season to trap the edible dormouse or loir *(polh)*, a tree-dwelling nocturnal rodent not unlike a squirrel that grows to about 30cm and sleeps through several months of the year. The dormouse is a favourite food in Notranjska (in fact, it was once a staple), and the hunting and eating of it is tied up with a lot of tradition. According to one Slovenian belief, the dormouse is shepherded by Lucifer himself and thus deserves its fate in the stew or goulash pot.

Getting There & Away

Snežnik's isolation makes it tough to reach by public transport. Without a car, bicycle or horse, you'll have to take a bus (up to five a day) to Stari Trg pri Lož and walk 4km. The one or two direct buses to Snežnik depart at very inconvenient times.

NOTRANJSKA

Dolenjska

'Lower Carniola' is a charming area of gently rolling hills, vineyards, forests and the Krka River flowing south-eastward into Croatia. Those white hilltop churches with their red tile roofs you'll see everywhere once protected the people from marauding Turks and other invaders; the ones on the flat lands are newer – built in the baroque style and painted the mustard colour ('Maria Theresa yellow') so common in central Europe. The castles along the Krka are some of the best preserved in Slovenia as are the many monasteries and abbeys. You can't miss the distinctive 'double hayracks' *(toplarji)* of Dolenjska; they're here in spades.

Many people say that the 'purest' Slovene is spoken in Dolenjska – around the village of Rašica, south of the town of Krka, to be precise. But this may have more to do with the fact that Primož Trubar (1508-86), the 'father of the Slovenian literary language', was born here.

Dolenjska is the cycling centre of Slovenia. The E6 and E7 European Hiking trails pass through Dolenjska, and there are lots of chances to do some kayaking or canoeing on the Krka. The province is also famous for its thermal spas.

History

Dolenjska was settled early on and is well known for its Hallstatt ruins and tombs, especially near Stična, Šmarjeta and Novo Mesto. The Romans eventually made the area part of the province of Upper Pannonia (Pannonia Superior) and built roads connecting Emona (Ljubljana) with smaller settlements at Praetorium Latobicorum (Trebnje), Acervo (Stična) and Neviodonum (Drnovo).

In the Middle Ages, the people of Dolenjska clustered around the many castles along the river (eg at Žužemberk and Otočec) and at parish centres like Šentvid. Monasteries sprung up at Stična, Kostan-

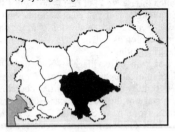

jevica na Krki and near Šentjernej. Much of the region was part of the Slovenska Krajina, the 'Slovenian March' that became part of Carniola (Kranjska) in the 13th century.

Dolenjska declined after the Middle Ages and progress only came in the late 19th century when a railway line linked Novo Mesto with Ljubljana. This was extended (via Bela Krajina) to Karlovac in Croatia in 1914.

RIBNICA
• *pop 3300* • *area code ☎061* • *postcode 1310*

Though Ribnica is the oldest and most important settlement of western Dolenjska and just over the hills from the border with Notranjska, people in this region have traditionally affiliated with neither province. As far as they are concerned, this is Kočevsko, a forested, sparsely inhabited area with a unique history.

Ribnica is 16km north-west of the town of

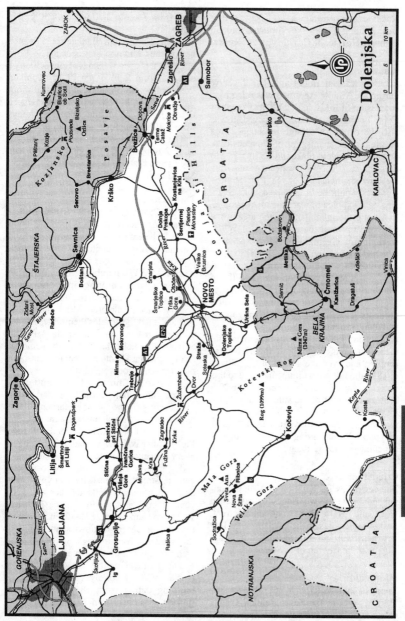

Kočevje, another gateway to Kočevski Rog (see Around Dolenjske Toplice), and on highway No 6 to the Croatian port of Rijeka.

History

Ribnica was an important feudal centre during the Middle Ages and was ruled by a succession of lords, including the Counts of Celje, before the Habsburgs arrived. It was also the centre of a large missionary area during the Christianisation of Slovenia. Like neighbouring Notranjska and Bela Krajina to the south-east, Kočevsko suffered greatly from the Turkish invasions of the 15th century. Bonfires would be lit atop peaks like Sveta Ana near Ribnica to warn the townspeople.

Among the inhabitants of the area at the time and up until the early days of WWII were many German-speaking *Kočevarji* who had been brought to Kočevsko by feudal lords a century before. Because the karst soil was too poor to make an adequate living from farming year round, the Kočevarji supplemented their income with wooden products *(suha roba*, literally 'dry goods') that they produced at home: pails, sifters, baskets and kitchen utensils. The men sold these products throughout the Habsburg Empire, and even the advent of the railway in 1893 did not put an immediate end to this itinerant way of life. Until well into the 20th century the sight of the suha roba pedlar – his products piled high on his back and a staff in hand – was as Slovenian as a *kozolec* (hayrack). Woodcarving remains an important cottage industry today.

Orientation

The town lies in the Ribnica Valley sandwiched between two ridges called Velika Gora and Mala Gora. The main street, Šeškova ulica, lies on the left bank of the tiny Bistrica River and runs parallel to it. Buses stop near the Church of St Stephen.

Information

There's a tourist office (☎ 861 063 or ☎ 861 909) of sorts in the Zavarovalnica Triglav office at Šeškova ulica 9c. It is open week-days from 7 am to 2.30 pm (to 4.30 pm on Thursday).

Nova Ljubljanska Banka has a branch next to the Church of St Stephen at Šeškova ulica 9b. It is open weekdays from 8.30 to 11 am and from 2 to 5 pm (3 to 6 pm on Wednesday). SKB Banka, at the Ideal shopping centre on Kolodvorska ulica 9a, has a Cirrus-linked ATM and opens weekdays from 8.30 am till noon and 2 to 5 pm.

The main post office is at Kolodvorska ulica 2 opposite the shopping centre. It is open from 8 am to 7 pm weekdays and on Saturday till noon.

Things to See

Ribnica Castle, on the right bank of the Bistrica at Gallusovo nabrežje 1, was originally built in the 10th century but was transformed and expanded over the centuries. Only a small section – a Renaissance wall and two towers – survived WWII bombing. Today the castle houses a small **ethnograpic collection** showcasing the traditional wood crafts and pottery made in the area. More interesting, perhaps, than the articles themselves are the tools that made them. The castle, set in an attractive semicircular park with memorial statues and markers to Slovenian greats, is a popular venue for weddings.

The **Parish Church of St Stephen** on Šeškova ulica, built in the latter part of the 19th century on the site of an earlier church, would not be of much interest were it not for the two striking towers added by Jože Plečnik after WWII. As usual, Plečnik mixed every conceivable style – to great success.

The plaque on the house opposite the church, **Steklič House** (Stekličkova Hiša) at Šeškova ulica 26, tells us that the 19th century poet and patriot France Prešeren spent two years here (1810-12) in what was then the region's best known school, attracting students from throughout Slovenia as well as from Trieste and Croatia.

The cultural centre at Miklova Hiša (☎ 861 938), a lovely cream-and-white building dating from 1858, has a small **gallery**. It is open from 10 am to noon and from 3 to 6 pm.

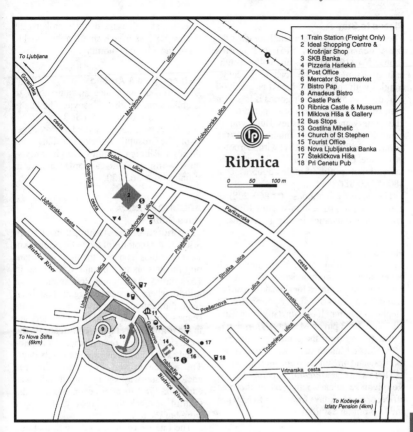

1 Train Station (Freight Only)
2 Ideal Shopping Centre & Krošnjar Shop
3 SKB Banka
4 Pizzeria Harlekin
5 Post Office
6 Mercator Supermarket
7 Bistro Pap
8 Amadeus Bistro
9 Castle Park
10 Ribnica Castle & Museum
11 Miklova Hiša & Gallery
12 Bus Stops
13 Gostilna Mihelič
14 Church of St Stephen
15 Tourist Office
16 Nova Ljubljanska Banka
17 Šteklíčkova Hiša
18 Pri Cenetu Pub

Ribnica

0   50   100 m

Activities

Ribnica is the base for several excellent walks. A well marked 'educational' trail leads north of the town for about 4.5km up Mala Gora ridge to Sveta Ana, a rock wall or cliff *(stena)* some 963m high with fantastic views of Ribnica and the Ribnica Valley. Along the way you'll pass the entrance to France Cave, the hilltop Church of St Anne and two huts selling food and drink.

From the Jasnica recreational centre (on the way to Kočevje), where horses are available for hire, a more difficult path leads north about 6km to the junction with the Ribnica Alpine Trail. This eventually joins up with the E7 European Hiking Trail about 5km west of Velike Lašče.

A trail into the Velika Gora ridge west of Ribnica that leads to a comfortable mountain hut is more easily accessible from Nova Štifta (see the Around Ribnica section).

Special Events

Ribnica's main event is the Dry Goods & Pottery Fair (Ribniški Semenj Suhe Robe in Lončarstva) held on the first Sunday in September, though the entire weekend is given over to music, drinking and, of course, buying and selling.

Places to Stay

The only accommodation near Ribnica is the *Izlaty* pension (☎ 864 515) in Prigorica (house No 115), which is about 4km southeast of Ribnica on the road to Kočevje. Singles with shower and breakfast are 3000 SIT, doubles 5000 SIT. Prigorica is less than 1km from Dolenja Vas, a town noted for its clay pottery and clay whistles. But if you've come this far, continue on another 4km to the *Jasnica* pension (☎ 854 101) with 27 rooms in Gornje Ložine (house No 26) near the recreational centre. Singles/doubles cost 4800/7200 SIT.

The *Boltetni* farmhouse (☎ 860 208) at house No 8 in Dane, 4km west of Ribnica, offers accommodation in July and August.

Places to Eat

Ribnica's catering options are not much better than its accommodation. One of the very few central places for a meal is *Gostilna Mihelič* on Šeškova ulica opposite St Stephen's Church. It is open daily from 9 am till 10 pm (to 3 pm on Monday). *Harlekin* is a pizzeria, north of the centre at Gorenjska cesta 4, open Monday to Saturday from 10 am to 11 pm and on Sunday from noon to 10 pm.

There's a big *Mercator* supermarket on Kolodvorska ulica, south-west of the post office, open weekdays from 7 am to 6.30 pm and to 5 pm on Saturday.

Entertainment

The less than salubrious *Pri Cenetu* at Šeškova ulica 24 has 300 years of history under its belt but little else. Head instead for the modern *Bistro Pap* at No 34 of the same street or the convivial *Amadeus*, a 'garden bistro' on the other side of the street at No 21.

Things to Buy

You'll see a fair number of household articles made of wood for sale in Ribnica and the odd piece of pottery from nearby Dolenja Vas. The Krošnjar shop at the Ideal shopping centre at Kolodvorska ulica 9a has a large

selection as well as handwoven baskets. It's open weekdays from 8 am till noon and 4 to 7 pm and Saturday morning.

Getting There & Around

Buses run at least once an hour north to Ljubljana and south to Kočevje. The bus to Sodražica is good for Nova Štifta.

Ribnica is no longer served by passenger train. The Grosuplje-Kočevje line that passes through Ribnica handles freight only – mostly timber. You can order a taxi in Ribnica on ☎ 863 120.

AROUND RIBNICA
Nova Štifta

The **Church of the Assumption** at Nova Štifta, in the foothills of the Velika Gora 6km west of Ribica, is one of the most important pilgrimage sites in Slovenia. Completed in 1671 during the Counter-Reformation on a hilltop where mysterious lights had been seen, the baroque church is unusual for its shape – both the nave and the presbytery are in the form of an octagon. The arcade on the west side fronting the entrance accommodated extra pilgrims on important holy days. The church proved so popular that the enclosed stairway on the north side was added in 1780 to allow even more of the faithful to reach the clerestory, the upper storey of the nave.

The interior of the church, with its three golden altars and pulpit carved by Jurij Skarnos, is blindingly ornate. Look for the painting of an aristocratic couple on stained glass on the north side of the presbytery. In the courtyard opposite the Franciscan monastery (where the church key is kept) stands a linden tree, planted in the mid-17th century, complete with tree house.

Dom na Travni Gori (☎ 866 333 in Ravni Dol), a guesthouse 890m up with restaurant and accommodation, can be reached by a marked trail heading south-west from Nova Štifta in about 1½ hours. In winter one of Slovenia's smallest ski centres, **Travna Gora**, operates nearby with a 200m-long piste and one T-bar tow.

Under the Linden Trees

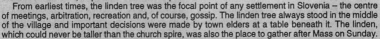

If cities can have municipal animals – where would Rome be today without the she-wolf that suckled Romulus and Remus? – and American states proclaim 'official drinks' (like tomato juice in New Jersey), why can't a country have a national tree? It's the linden (or common lime) in Slovenia and its heart-shaped leaf is often used as a symbol.

The stately linden *(lipa* in Slovene) can be found in abundance in central Europe and was the most common tree in England thousands of years ago. Normally it grows slowly for about 60 years and then suddenly spurts upward and outwards, living to a ripe old age. It is said that a linden grows for 300 years, stands still for another 300 and takes 300 years to die.

Linden wood was used by the Romans to make shields and, as it is easy to work with, artisans in the Middle Ages carved religious figures from it, earning linden the title *sacrum lignum*, or 'sacred wood'. Tea made from the linden flower, which contains aromatic oils, has been used as an antidote for fever and the flu at least since the 16th century.

But the linden's ubiquity, longevity and many uses are not the only reasons it is so honoured by the Slovenes. For them, its past is even more important.

From earliest times, the linden tree was the focal point of any settlement in Slovenia – the centre of meetings, arbitration, recreation and, of course, gossip. The linden tree always stood in the middle of the village and important decisions were made by town elders at a table beneath it. The linden, which could never be taller than the church spire, was also the place to gather after Mass on Sunday.

So sacred has the linden tree become to Slovenes that its destruction is considered a serious offence. In discussing the barbarous acts committed by the Italians during the occupation of Primorska between the wars, one magazine article passionately points out that 'Kobarid had to swallow much bitterness ... The Fascists cut down the linden tree etc.' Arbicide, it would appear, is a grave crime in these parts.

In today's Slovenia the linden represents not just hospitality but democracy too – something that has not been lost on seekers of high office. Few politicians facing an election fail to waltz around Slovenia's oldest linden, the Najevska Lipa under Mt Peca in Koroška. ■

STIČNA

• *pop 1150* • *area code* ☎*061* • *postcode 1295*

The abbey at Stična (Sittich in German) is the oldest monastery in Slovenia and one of the country's most important religious and cultural monuments. At only 35km from Ljubljana and within easy walking distance of the train station at Ivančna Gorica (pop 2060), Stična can be visited on a day trip from the capital or en route to Novo Mesto, the valley of the lower Krkva or Bela Krajina.

The monastery was established in 1136 by the Cistercians, a branch of the Benedictines that had been founded less than four decades before in France. The monks worked as farmers, following a vow of silence and communicating only through sign language. It became the most important religious, economic, educational and cultural centre in Dolenjska.

The lives of the monks were disrupted continuously in the second half of the 15th century during the Turkish invasions. Ultimately the abbey was surrounded by 8m-high walls and fortified with towers. But more damaging to the Cistercians was the edict issued by Emperor Joseph II in 1784 dissolving all religious orders – many of them very powerful and corrupt – in the Habsburg Empire. Stična was abandoned, and the order did not return until 1898.

Stična monastery has undergone steady reconstruction since WWII – much of it paid for by the government – and today almost the entire complex is again in use. There are five priests (including the abbot) and seven monks in residence.

DOLENJSKA

Orientation & Information

The village of Stična is about 2.5km north of Ivančna Gorica, where the train station is located. The clergy and staff at the monastery will be able to help you if you need information.

Stična Abbey

The entrance to the walled abbey, an incredible combination of Romanesque, Gothic, Renaissance and baroque architecture, is on the east side across a small stream. This leads on to a large open courtyard bordered on the west by the Abbey Church and to the north by the Old Prelature, a Renaissance building dating from about 1600.

The **Old Prelature**, once the administrative centre of the abbey, contains exhibition rooms on two floors. The collection is a hotchpotch of antique clocks, paintings, furniture and farm implements mixed with chalices, monstrances and icons. (One particularly gruesome statue shows Saint Perpetua holding her two amputated breasts on a platter.) There are a few 16th century missals and medical texts in Latin and German, but all the medieval documents are facsimiles of the originals carted off to libraries in Vienna and Ljubljana when the order was banned in the 18th century, including the 15th century *Stična Manuscript*, one of the earliest writings in Slovene. It is now kept at the National University Library in the capital. One room is devoted to the accomplishments of the missionary Frederick Baraga (1797-1868), who was born in Trebnje to the south-east. Baraga taught among the Chippewa (or Ojibwa) Indians of Michigan and composed the first grammar of their language in 1843.

The video that the abbey shows visitors at the start of their tour is well produced and available in five languages, including English.

If you want to drop out of the tour early, you can exit under the **Upper Tower**, which is a few steps to the north-east of the Old Prelature. Just make sure you look up as you pass through. The ceiling is covered in stuccos from 1620 showing scenes of Christ's Passion and the Last Judgment.

Otherwise, across the courtyard to the west of the Abbey Church, a door leads to Stična's celebrated **vaulted cloister**, which mixes Romanesque and early Gothic styles. The cloister, which was once made of wood with stone corner pillars, served as an ambulatory for monks in prayer and connected the church with the monastery's other wings. The arches and vaults are decorated with frescoes of the prophets and Old Testament stories as well as allegorical subjects like the Virtues, the Four Winds etc. Look for the carved stone faces on the west side that were meant to show human emotions and vices – upon which the clergy were expected to reflect.

On the south side of the cloister is a typically baroque monastic **refectory** with an 18th century pink ceiling and decorative swirls and loops made of white stucco. One floor above is the much impoverished library. **Neff's Abbey**, built in the mid-16th century by Abbot Volbenk Neff, runs to the west. The arches in the vestibule on the ground floor are painted with a dense network of leaves, blossoms, berries and birds. You can gain access to the church through a doorway in the north-east corner of the cloister.

The **Abbey Church**, consecrated in 1156, was built as a buttressed, three-nave Romanesque cathedral. But except for the small windows at the top, you'd be hard-pressed to see much of that style today through all the baroque reconstruction that took place in the early 17th century and again in the mid-18th century, just a few decades before the order was forced to quit the premises. Apart from the ornate main altar and 11 side ones, the church contains several interesting elements. Look for the Renaissance red-marble tombstone of Abbot Jakob Reinprecht (who initiated the first baroque reconstruction) in the north transept and the blue organ cupboard with eight angels (1747) in the choir loft. But the greatest treasures here are the **Stations of the Cross** painted by Fortunat Bergant in 1766. The artist signed the last one – 'Jesus is Laid into the Sepulchre' – spelling his surname with a 'W'.

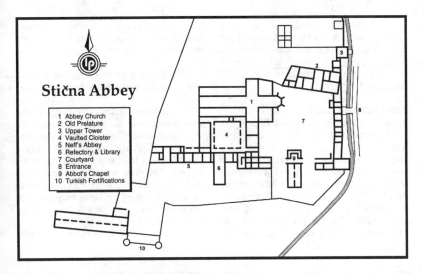

One final building worth a look is the outer wing **Abbot's Chapel** closing off the southern portion of the courtyard. Built in the late 18th century as a kind of replacement to the grandiose halls seen in palaces and some larger monasteries, it contains a double staircase and a hall chapel of incredible lightness and vivacity.

The abbey can be visited from 8 am to noon and from 2 to 6 pm Tuesday to Saturday and on Sunday afternoon. Guided tours (available in Slovene, English and German) leave at 8.30 and 10 am, and 2 and 4 pm Tuesday to Saturday and on Sunday and holy days at 2 and 4 pm. The entry charge is 400/200 SIT for adults/students and children. The abbey can be very crowded with visiting school children from April to June and September to November.

Places to Stay & Eat
It is possible to spend the night at the monastery *guesthouse* (☎ 777 100) for less than 2000 SIT per person, but you should make prior arrangements with the abbot.

Much more comfortable is *Grofija* (☎ 778 141), a 19th century farmhouse with accommodation, scarcely 1km south-east of Stična in the village of Vir pri Stični (house No 30). Its four rooms cost about DM30 per person for bed and breakfast. Grofija (meaning 'county') is a working farm and horses are available for hire. Of historical note, a major Hallstatt settlement dating from 800 BC once stood near the site of the tennis court at Grofija. Grofija can also be reached directly from Ivančna Gorica (2.5km) on the Šentvid bus.

In Ivančna Gorica, about 150m west of the train station at Ljubljanska cesta 38, *Gostilna Krjavelj* serves local Dolenjska favourites to a much appreciative local crowd.

Things to Buy
The Cistercians sell many home-made products under their own label – bread, honey, wine, herbal teas and liqueurs – in a small shop in the Old Prelature. It's open Monday to Saturday from 8 am to 12.30 pm and 1 to 4 pm (3 pm on Saturday).

Getting There & Away
Stična is served by up to 16 buses a day from Ljubljana, but the number is halved on Saturday, and there are only three on Sunday.

DOLENJSKA

Ivančna Gorica is on the rail line linking Ljubljana with Novo Mesto, Črnomelj and Metlika in Bela Krajina and Karlovac in Croatia. Up to 14 trains a day leave the capital, and the 37km trip to Ivančna Gorica takes about one hour.

BOGENŠPERK CASTLE

About 20km north of Stična is Bogenšperk Castle, in many respects the secular equivalent of Stična Abbey. Here the Slovenian polymath Janez Vajkard Valvasor (see boxed text entitled Valvasor, Slovenia's Renaissance Man) spent the most productive two decades of his life, writing and eventually publishing *The Glory of the Duchy of Carniola* (1689), his encyclopaedic work on Slovenian history, geography and culture.

Note that Bogenšperk is only accessible from Ivančna Gorica by car or bicycle; even the public transport options from Ljubljana, 40km to the west, are not good. Frequent trains and buses go to Litija, but it's still another 7km south to Bogenšperk – much of it uphill.

Bogenšperk Castle was built in the Renaissance style in the early 16th century by the aristocratic Wagen family, who named the place Wagensberg. Valvasor bought Bogenšperk in 1672 and installed his printing press, engraving workshop and extensive library here. But due to the enormous debts incurred in getting his *opus magnus* published, he was forced to sell the castle in 1692. He died a year later in Krško.

The castle passed from family to family

Valvasor, Slovenia's Renaissance Man

Most of our knowledge of Slovenian history, geography, culture and folklore before the 17th century comes from the writings of one man, Janez Vajkard Valvasor, and more specifically his *The Glory of the Duchy of Carniola*. Not only did this truly great Renaissance man map large areas of Carniola and its towns for the first time, he also explained the mystery of disappearing karst lakes and rivers, 'discovered' the unusual amphibian *Proteus anguinus*, introduced the world to Erazem Lueger, the 15th century Robin Hood of Slovenia, and catalogued early Slovenian folk tales and dress.

Valvasor, whose name comes from the *valvassores*, the burghers who lived in the towns of the Holy Roman Empire in the early Middle Ages, was born in Ljubljana in 1641 of a noble family from Bergamo. After a Jesuit education there and in Germany, he joined Miklós Zrínyi, the Hungarian count and poet, in the wars against the Turks. Valvasor travelled widely for a man of his time, visiting Germany, Italy, North Africa, France and Switzerland. He collected data on natural phenomena and local customs as well as books, drawings, mineral specimens and coins.

In 1672 Valvasor installed himself, his books and his precious collections at Bogenšperk Castle, where he conducted scientific experiments (including alchemy) and wrote. In 1689 he completed his most important work. Published in German at Nuremburg under the title *Die Ehre des Herzogthums Crain* it ran into four volumes, containing 3500 pages with 535 maps and copper engravings. *The Glory of the Duchy of Carniola* remains one of the most comprehensive works published in Europe before the Enlightenment, a wealth of information on the Slovenian patrimony that is still explored and studied to this day.

As is so often the case with great men and women in history, Valvasor did not live to enjoy the success of his labour. Publishing such a large work at his own expense ruined him financially and he was forced to leave Bogenšperk in 1692. Valvasor died a year later at Krško, a town 65km to the east on the Sava River. ■

and the last owners, the Windisch-Grätz family, left it in 1943. During WWII, Bogenšperk was spared the total destruction that befell other castles in the area like Lichtenberg, Pogonik and Slatna since German soldiers were billeted here.

The castle, with its rectangular courtyard and three towers (the fourth burned down in Valvasor's time), was renovated in 1972 and today houses a museum devoted to the great man, his work and Slovenian culture. Valvasor's **library** is now used as a wedding hall (complete with a cradle, as is traditional in Slovenia), but his **study**, with its beautiful parquetry and painted ceiling, is pretty much the way he left it when he did his last alchemy experiments here.

Other rooms contain examples of Valvasor's cartography and etching, four original volumes of his work donated by a Slovene from Trieste in 1993, a printing press similar to the one Valvasor used (the real one is in Munich) and the inevitable collection of hunting trophies, including a 132kg brown bear shot in Kočevski Rog in 1978.

The most interesting exhibits, though, are the ones that deal with folk dress (life-size mannequins sport costumes modelled exactly on Valvasor's illustrations, right down to the boots that have neither a right nor a left), superstition and folk medicine through the ages in Slovenia. There are endless recipes to break spells, red crosses to ward off witches, votives and good-luck charms and vials of herbs and elixirs. The **Knights' Hall** situated on the ground floor is often used for banquets and conferences, and the **castle chapel** near the entrance has now been renovated.

Autumn Serenade concerts take place at the castle every Sunday in September at 5 pm. The entrance to *Gostišče Valvasor*, a small restaurant with a vaulted ceiling, is by the fountain in the courtyard.

Bogenšperk is open daily in summer from 9 am to 7 pm and in winter from 9 am till sunset Tuesday to Sunday. The entrance fee is 450/300 SIT for adults/students and children.

KRKA RIVER VALLEY

The Krka River springs from a karst cave south-west of Stična, near the village of Trebnja Gorica, and runs to the south-east and east until it joins the mightier Sava River near Brežice. At 94km, it is Dolenjska's longest and most important waterway and one of the cleanest rivers in Slovenia.

If you are continuing on to other towns in Dolenjska and/or Bela Krajina and have your own transport, the ideal way to go is to follow the road along the Krka, which cuts a deep and picturesque valley along its upper course. The road is also excellent for cycling. From Ljubljana most buses and the train heading for Dolenjska follow the old medieval road, today's route No 1 (E70). Opt instead for the bus going to Žužemberk.

Muljava

• *pop 706* • *area code ☎061* • *postcode 1295*

This picturesque town of double hayracks and beehives (a few with their original painted panels) is about 5km south of Ivančna Gorica and just north of a tributary of the Krka. Muljava's claim to fame is twofold: it is the birthplace of the writer Josip Jurčič (1844-81), whose *The 10th Brother* is considered the first full-length novel in Slovene, and is home to a small Gothic church with 15th century frescoes.

The Kranjič beehive has removable boxes, creating a series of individual hives.

DOLENJSKA

Things to See & Do The **Church of the Assumption** lies east of the main road at the start of the village, and the key is available from the woman who lives next door (she's the bell ringer too). Not all of the paintings in the presbytery and on the vaulted arches are very clear – they show Cain and Abel making their sacrifices, symbols of the Apostles (including the winged lion of St Mark) and St Margaret – but the fresco depicting the death of the Virgin Mary on the south wall is still vibrant. The frescoes are signed by Johannes de Laibaco (John of Ljubljana) and dated 1456. The gilded main altar portraying the Assumption dates from the late 17th century.

Josip Jurčič's birthplace, a small cottage typical of the region, is west of the main road and open Tuesday to Friday from 8 am to noon and from 1 to 5 pm and afternoons only on Saturday and Sunday. Entry is 300/200 SIT. In front of the house is a beehive with painted front panels *(panjske končnice)* from the 19th century; behind it is an open-air theatre in a dell where some of Jurčič's works are staged in summer.

One of the most popular places in Slovenia for fishing is the 9km stretch of the Krka from its mouth to Zagradec, about halfway to Žužemberk. The season lasts from March to November and brown and rainbow trout and grayling abound. But it's not a sport for the poor: a daily fishing licence costs 10,500 SIT and a three-day one is 26,250 SIT. Permits are available from the Magovac pension (☎ 786 049) in Krka village (house No 13) and the Gostišče Pod Lipo (☎ 068-87 007) in Žužemberk.

Places to Eat If you're hungry, *Gostilna Pri Obrščaku* serves up hearty Slovenian fare like klobasa in zelje (sausage with sauerkraut). It is on the main road in the village centre (house No 22) and is open daily, except Wednesday, to 10 pm.

Krka Cave

Krka Cave, 2km from the main road and just west of the village of Trebnja Gorica, ain't in the same league as Postojna or Škocjan caves (see the Notranjska and Primorska chapters), but you do get to see some stalactites shaped like ribbons and fragile-looking 'spaghetti', a 100-year-old specimen of the *Proteus anguinus* amphibian in a tank (see boxed text in the Notranjska chapter entitled Proteus Anguinus, the Human Fish) and a siphon lake that is the source of the Krka River.

From the kiosk marked 'Pri Izviru', a guide will escort you through fields to the entrance of the cave and as far as the lake (190m – a bit more than half the total length). The depth of the lake is 17m, but in winter – depending on the rain and the snowfall – the lake can rise almost as high as the ceiling. Krka Cave is open March to October daily from 9 am to 7 pm. During the rest of the year the hours are 11 am to 3 pm. Admission is 200/100 SIT for adults/students and children. Bring a jacket with you as the temperature is a constant 9.6°C and the humidity is high.

Žužemberk

• *pop 3930* • *area code ☎068* • *postcode 8360*

Once the site of a mighty fortress from the early Middle Ages perched on a cliff over the Krka, Žužemberk is about 17km from Muljava. The castle was completely rebuilt and the old walls fortified with round towers in the 16th century but was all but flattened during more than 20 air raids in WWII. Only one round tower has been reconstructed, but the sheer enormity and might of the place can still be seen from the opposite bank of the Krka. Note the iron well in the central square. It came from Dvor, a town to the south-east known for its ironwork.

Activities Kayaking and canoeing are excellent on the fast-flowing Krka, and Žužemberk is a good spot from which to set out. The Žužemberk Kayak and Canoe Club (☎ 87 055) in Prapreče (house No 1a), 1km north-west of Žužemberk, can help with rentals and routes. Or contact the larger Rafting Club Gimpex (☎ 83 171) near Straža (Pod Srobotnikom 12) or Carpe Diem (☎ 061-786 011) in Krka (house No 27).

Special Events The Summer Castle Performances (Poletne Grajske Prireditve) are a series of concerts held in the Castle Cellar (Grajska Klet) between June and September.

Places to Eat *Gostilna Župančič* at Grajski trg 5 is a pizzeria with an outside terrace overlooking the Krka and is open till 10 pm (11 pm on Friday and Saturday) every day, except Tuesday. The *Gostišče Pod Lipo* sits under a rather sick-looking linden in front of the castle at Grajski trg 4 and is open daily till 10 pm.

Getting There & Away The bus stop is near the post office at Grajski trg 28. Up to 10 buses a day go to Ljubljana, with some six to Dolenjske Toplice (13km) and Novo Mesto (23km), two or three to Črnomelj, two to Vinica, two to Metlika and one to Celje.

DOLENJSKE TOPLICE
• *pop 800* • *area code ☎068* • *postcode 8350*

Within easy striking distance of Novo Mesto (13km to the north-east), this thermal resort is the oldest and one of the few real spa towns in Slovenia. Located in the karst valley of the Krka River below the wooded slopes of Kočevski Rog, Dolenjske Toplice is an excellent place in which to hike, cycle, fish or simply relax.

History
Although the curative powers of the thermal springs were known as early as the 14th century, the first spa was not built until 1658 when Ivan Vajkard, a member of the aristocratic Auersperg family, opened the Prince's Bath. The Kopališki Dom (Bathers' House), complete with three pools, was built in the late 18th century when the first chemical analysis of the thermal waters was done. Within a century, Dolenjske Toplice had 30 rooms, basic medical facilities and its very own guidebook, but tourism did not really take off until 1899 with the opening of the Zdraviliški Dom (Health Resort House). Strascha Töplitz, as it was then called (after the nearby town of Straža), was a great favourite of Austrians from around the turn of the century up to WWI.

The complex was used as a military treatment centre in the 1920s and 1930s and part of it was a Partisan hospital during WWII.

Orientation & Information
Dolenjske Toplice lies about 1.5km south of the Krka River on an undulating stream called the Sušica. Virtually everything – including the two hotels of the thermal resort – are on or just off the main street, Zdraviliški trg. Buses stop just south of or opposite the post office. Dolenjske Toplice is not on a rail line.

The helpful staff at the Kopališki Dom hotel (☎ 65 230) will answer all your questions about the spa and surrounding area. Dolenjska Banka has a branch at Zdraviliški trg 8 and is open from 8 am to noon and 2 to 4.30 pm weekdays. The post office is north across the car park at No 3. It is open from 8 am to 5 pm weekdays and on Saturday till noon.

Thermal Spas
Taking the waters is the *sine qua non* of Dolenjske Toplice, and you don't have to be a hotel guest to do so; outsiders pay 1000 SIT for the privilege. It's actually taken very seriously. The warm mineral water (36-38°C) gushing from 1000m below the two covered pools at Kopališki Dom is ideal for locomotive ailments such as rheumatism, but a recreational soak is still a lot of fun and can avert backache. The health resort also offers any number of other types of therapy, from underwater massage (1800 SIT) to magnetic therapy (1100 SIT).

The outdoor thermal pool *(športni bazen)* is 300m north of the two hotels and can be reached through a lovely little park. The unusual carved wooden statues of curling snakes and elongated (and shackled) human figures suggest the traditional occupations of this area: logging and woodcarving. The pool, which is open from 9 am till 7 pm in summer, has 27°C water. Admission is 800 SIT on weekdays and 900 SIT at the weekend.

DOLENJSKA

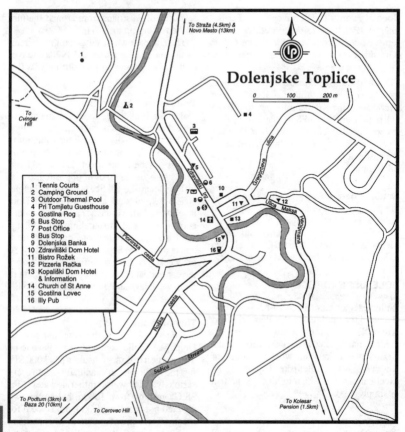

Dolenjske Toplice

1 Tennis Courts
2 Camping Ground
3 Outdoor Thermal Pool
4 Pri Tomjletu Guesthouse
5 Gostilna Rog
6 Bus Stop
7 Post Office
8 Bus Stop
9 Dolenjska Banka
10 Zdraviliški Dom Hotel
11 Bistro Rožek
12 Pizzeria Račka
13 Kopališki Dom Hotel
    & Information
14 Church of St Anne
15 Gostilna Lovec
16 Illy Pub

Hiking

A number of short (under 5km) and easy walks can be made from Dolenjske Toplice, or you might consider hiking in the virgin forests of Kočevski Rog, with Baza 20, the Partisan nerve centre during WWII, or even Veliki Rog (1099m) as your destination (see the Around Dolenjske Toplice section).

Walks marked on the Dolenjske Toplice town map include a 3km one south through the forest to Cerovec Hill (276m), with the Church of the Holy Trinity atop, affording pleasant views of the town, and a hike of 4km west to Cvinger (263m), where Hallstatt

tombs and iron foundries have been unearthed. Nature lovers may be interested in the 'educational forest walk' just west of Podturn (2km), which also takes in a small cave and the ruins of Rožek Castle.

Other Activities

The tennis courts on the hill north-west of the camping ground can be hired for 700 SIT (500 SIT for hotel guests) per hour between 7 am and 8 pm. See the staff at the Kopališki Dom about renting racquets.

Daily permits (3800 SIT) valid for fishing in the Sušica and the middle course of the

Krka, famous for its salmon and trout, are available from the hotels.

The ski centre of Rog-Črmošnjice (☎ 25 250), 16km south of Dolenjske Toplice, is under renovation but may be open again by the time you read this. In the past the centre has operated five T-bar tows on the slopes of Mt Gače at altitudes of between 730 and 930m between December to the end of March (depending on the snowfall).

Places to Stay

The three-hectare *Dolenjske Toplice* camp site (☎ 66 012) is just off the northern end of Zdravilíški trg, more or less opposite the outdoor swimming pool. It is open from May to September and can accommodate up to 120 guests. Daily charges are 500 to 600 SIT per person, 320 SIT per car and per tent and 390 SIT per caravan.

Pri Tomjletu (☎ 65 023) is a cosy guest-house behind the open-air pool at Zdravilíški trg 24. None of the eight rooms has its own bathroom but all have sinks, and cooking facilities are available. The per-person charge including breakfast is about DM25.

The eight-room *Kolesar* pension (☎ 65 003) is an even better deal – 2200 SIT per person with bathroom and breakfast – and there's a very popular gostilna on the ground floor. But it's in Dolenje Sušice (house No 22), about 2km south-east of Dolenjske Toplice, with no chance of catching a late-night bus.

The two spa hotels (☎ 65 230; fax 65 662) run by the Krka Health Resorts company – the four-star *Kopališki Dom* with 176 beds at Zdravilíški trg 11 and the three-star *Zdravilíški Dom* with 104 beds north across the plaza at No 19 – share the same facilities, including two indoor thermal pools, two saunas, a fitness centre etc. Of the two, the Kopališki Dom has much better rooms and public areas. Singles with breakfast start at 8000 SIT, doubles at 12,200 SIT. The Zdravilíški Dom has a large restaurant with a wonderful painted ceiling, but its rooms are in need of upgrading. Singles with breakfast here are from 7000 SIT, with doubles 10,200

SIT. Both hotels offer discounted weekend and week-long packages.

Places to Eat

The health resort's main restaurant is the ornately decorated dining room of the *Zdravilíški Dom* where most guests on half or full pension take their meals. Otherwise the choice in the immediate area is limited to two gostilne: the *Lovec* (open to 11 pm or midnight), just south of the Gothic Church of St Anne (with a fine baroque altar) and the small bridge over the Sušica, and the *Gostilna Rog* on the edge of the park near the outdoor pool at Zdravilíški trg 22. Frankly, the 'Hunter' and the 'Horn' are much of a muchness though the Rog, open daily to 10 or 11 pm, has decent salads. *Račka*, in a renovated village house at Ulica Maksa Henigmana 13, to the east of the centre, serves decent pizza and pasta daily until 11 pm.

If you've got two or more wheels or don't mind walking 3km, head south-west for *Gostilna Štravs* (☎ 65 390) in Podturn (house No 28). It's one of the best small restaurants in the area and specialises in freshwater fish and game. It also has accommodation.

Entertainment

The *Rog* has Slovenian folk music Tuesday to Friday from 8 pm. Otherwise it's generally early to bed and early to rise in this healthy place. The *Rožek* is a glassed-in bistro in the plaza between the two hotels, though Dolenjske Toplice's young bloods tend to congregate at the *Illy Pub* south-west of the Kopališki Dom at the start of Pionirska cesta.

Getting There & Around

There are hourly buses to Novo Mesto between 7 am and 10 pm and six or seven a day to Žužemberk. Up to half a dozen go to Črnomelj (two via Novo Mesto, one via Semič), one to Maribor, two or three to Metlika (via Novo Mesto), one or two to Vinica and five or six to Ljubljana (via Straža and Žužemberk).

The health resort has bicycles for rent for 400 SIT per hour.

AROUND DOLENJSKE TOPLICE
Kočevski Rog

One of the most pristine areas in Slovenia, Kočevski Rog has been a protected nature area for more than 100 years, and six virgin forests, covering an area of more than 200 sq hectares, are preserved here.

The region was – and still is – so remote and filled with limestone caves that during the early days of WWII the Partisans, under the command of Marshal Tito, headquartered here building bunkers, workshops, hospitals and schools, and even setting up printing presses. The nerve centre was the so-called **Baza 20** (Base 20), about 10km south-west of Dolenjske Toplice, which was reconstructed and turned into a national monument after the war.

During the former regime, Baza 20 was a favourite 'pilgrimage' spot for many Slovenes and other Yugoslavs, and busloads of 'the faithful' paid their respects every day. Nowadays Baza 20 is a shadow of its former self – its two dozen buildings are ramshackle, the access trail unkempt and the indicator maps all but illegible. Still, as an indication of how Slovenes view the recent past both under communism and now, it's worth a visit.

A plaque erected near the site in 1995 diplomatically pays homage to everyone involved in the 'national liberation war', presumably including the thousands of Domobranci (Home Guards) murdered here by the Partisans in 1945.

There is no scheduled bus service to Baza 20, but it is easily reached by sealed road on foot or bicycle from Podturn, 7km away. From the car park and *Gostišče Baza 20* (open 10 am to 10 pm daily), it's a 15-minute walk up a mountain path to the site. The road south to Črmošnjice is unsealed and pretty rough; if you're heading for Črnomelj or Metlika, it's easier to return to Podturn first.

The range's tallest peak, **Veliki Rog** (1099m) is about 5km to the south-west. The area is a popular hunting ground (brown bear, wild cat, boar etc) for rich Italian tourists and was a favourite of Tito and his cronies.

NOVO MESTO

• *pop 22,400* • *area code ☎068* • *postcode 8000*

Situated on a sharp bend of the Krka River, the inappropriately named 'New Town' is the political, economic and cultural capital of Dolenjska and one of its prettiest towns. For Slovenes, Novo Mesto is synonymous with the painter Božidar Jakac (1899-1989), who captured the spirit of the place on canvas, and the writer Miran Jarc (1900-42) who did the same in prose with his autobiographical novel *Novo Mesto*. For the traveller, Novo Mesto is an important gateway to the historical towns and castles along the lower Krka, the karst forests of the Gorjanci Hills to the south-east, Bela Krajina and Croatia. Indeed, Zagreb is a mere 74km east of Novo Mesto via route No 1 (E70).

Today's Novo Mesto shows two faces to the world: the Old Town, which is perched high up on a rocky promontory above the left bank of the Krka, and a new town to the north and south, which thrives on the business of Krka, a large pharmaceutical and chemical company, as well as Revoz, which produces Renault cars and is the country's largest exporter.

History

Novo Mesto was settled during the late Bronze Age around 1000 BC, and helmets and decorated burial urns unearthed in surrounding areas suggest that Marof Hill above the Old Town was the seat of Hallstatt princes during the early Iron Age. The Illyrians and Celts came later, and the Romans maintained a settlement in this region until the 4th century AD, when it was then overrun by Germanic tribes during the Great Migrations.

During the early Middle Ages, Novo Mesto flourished as a market because of its location and later became the centre of the estates owned by the Cistercian abbey at Stična. In 1365, Habsburg Archduke Rudolf IV raised it to the status of a town, naming it Rudolphswert. By the 16th century, some 15,000 loads of freight passed through Novo Mesto each year. But plague, fires and raids by the Turks on their way to Vienna took a toll on the city and, within a hundred years, Novo Mesto's main square had become grazing land for cattle. Despite Novo Mesto's decline, Janez Vajkard Valvasor wrote in his opus *The Glory of the Duchy of Carniola* that it was still 'the most remarkable town of the duchy after Ljubljana'.

Prosperity returned in the 18th and 19th centuries: a college was established in 1746, Slovenia's first National Hall (Narodni Dom) opened here in 1875 and a railway line linked the city with Ljubljana in the 1890s. After the capitulation of the Habsburgs in 1918, Novo Mesto began to industrialise. Bombardments during WWII, particularly in 1941 and 1943, severely damaged the city, however.

Orientation

Almost everything of interest in Novo Mesto is in the toe-shaped Old Town above the Krka River and dominated by the belfry of the Chapter Church. Glavni trg is a large, cobbled square – bigger than any in Ljubljana, local people like to point out – lined with arcaded shops and public buildings. A bridge at its southern end leads to the suburbs of Kandija, Šmihel and Grm.

The bus station is south-west of the Old Town across the Krka on Topliška ulica; to reach Glavni trg, follow Kandijska cesta for 800m and cross the bridge. Novo Mesto has two train stations: the main one about 2km north-west of the Old Town and tiny Novo Mesto-Center, at the start of Ljubljanska cesta at the western edge of the Old Town. From here it's a five-minute walk eastward to Novi trg, which has been converted into a pedestrian mall and business centre. Another 350m along Rozmanova ulica will take you to Glavni trg.

Information

Tourist Office The tourist office (☎ /fax 322 512) is in the town hall at Glavni trg 6. Try to get the Slovenian Tourist Board's free pamphlet *Europe's Sleeping Beauty: Heritage Trails through Dolenjska & Bela Krajina*, which lists more than two dozen of the top sights in the region.

Money The most centrally located banks are SKB Banka at Glavni trg 10 and another SKB Banka branch with an ATM at Novi trg 3. They are open weekdays only from 8.30 am to noon and from 2 to 5 pm. A Banka's Novo Mesto branch is at Rozmanova ulica 38 just north of Novi trg.

Post & Communications The main post office is at Novi trg 7 and open weekdays from 7 am to 8 pm, Saturday to 1 pm and Sunday from 9 to 11 am. Next door at No 7a is Telekom Slovenije.

Travel Agencies Agencies in Novo Mesto include Kompas (☎ 321 338) at Novi trg 6 and Emona Globtour (☎ 323 376) at Rozmanova ulica 19, both of which are open from 7 or 8 am until 4 pm weekdays and till noon on Saturday.

Bookshop Mladinska Knjiga at Glavni trg 9, open from 7 am till 7 pm weekdays and till noon on Saturday, sells regional maps and guides.

Chapter Church of St Nicholas

Perched above the Old Town on Kapiteljska ulica, this Gothic church is Novo Mesto's most visible historical monument. And, with a 15th century presbytery and crypt, painted ceiling, a belfry that had once been a medieval defence tower and an altar painting of the eponymous saint supposedly done by the Venetian master Jacopo Tintoretto (1518-94), it is also the city's most important. But what strikes many visitors most is the nave; it actually doglegs by some 17°C before reaching the main altar.

The cream-coloured building to the northwest of the church is the **Provost's House**, built in 1623. If the church is locked, you'll find the key here. A section of the town's **medieval walls** can be seen just west of the church. It dates from the 14th century.

Dolenjska Museum

Below the Chapter Church about 100m to the east at Muzejska ulica 7, the Dolenjska Museum complex is divided into five parts.

DOLENJSKA

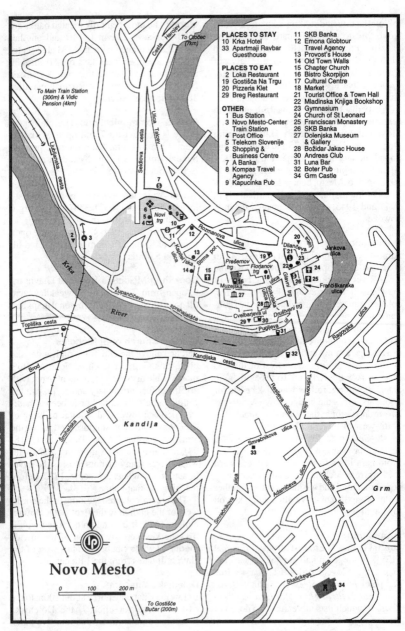

PLACES TO STAY
10 Krka Hotel
33 Apartmaji Ravbar
   Guesthouse

PLACES TO EAT
2 Loka Restaurant
19 Gostišča Na Trgu
20 Pizzeria Klet
29 Breg Restaurant

OTHER
1 Bus Station
3 Novo Mesto-Center
   Train Station
4 Post Office
5 Telekom Slovenije
6 Shopping &
   Business Centre
7 A Banka
8 Kompas Travel
   Agency
9 Kapucinka Pub

11 SKB Banka
12 Emona Globtour
   Travel Agency
13 Provost's House
14 Old Town Walls
15 Chapter Church
16 Bistro Škorpijon
17 Cultural Centre
18 Market
21 Tourist Office & Town Hall
22 Mladinska Knjiga Bookshop
23 Gymnasium
24 Church of St Leonard
25 Franciscan Monastery
26 SKB Banka
27 Dolenjska Museum
   & Gallery
28 Božidar Jakac House
30 Andreas Club
31 Luna Bar
32 Boter Pub
34 Grm Castle

Novo Mesto

0   100   200 m

DOLENJSKA

The oldest building, which once belonged to the knights of the Teutonic Order, houses a valuable collection of archaeological finds unearthed in the southern suburb of Kandija in the late 1960s. The museum is divided into four periods: the Neolithic and Bronze ages; the Hallstatt (early Iron Age) period; the Celtic era; and Roman Dolenjska.

You can't miss the Hallstatt helmet dating from 800 BC with two enormous axe blows at the top, the fine bronze situlae (or pails) from the 4th century BC embossed with battle and hunting scenes, and the Celtic ceramics and jewellery (particularly the bangles of turquoise and dark-blue glass) from Beletov Vrt.

The **Dolenjska Gallery** hosts the Biennial of Slovenian Graphic Art, held during even-numbered years (the 4th Biennale was in 1996, the 5th in 1998 etc), but occasionally accepts non-Slovenian guests. The gallery's permanent collection includes regional works from the 16th to 20th centuries.

Other collections in the complex include one devoted to the Liberation Front and the Partisans during WWII and a small but excellent **ethnographic collection** with farm implements, commemorative jugs presented at weddings, decorated heart-shaped honey cakes and icons painted on glass. Take a look at the almost lifesize wooden statue of a French soldier from the Illyrian Provinces era. It was used as a beehive.

The museum also administers the **Božidar Jakac House** about 100m east at Sokolska ulica 1. The peripatetic and prolific Jakac visited dozens of countries in the 1920s and 1930s, painting and sketching such diverse subjects as Parisian dance halls, Scandinavian port towns, African villages and American city skylines. But his best works are of Novo Mesto: markets, people, churches and rumble-tumble wooden houses clinging precariously to the banks above the Krka. One unusual work is the almost surreal *Odkrivanje (Revelation)* of a man hiding his face before a parted curtain.

In summer, the Dolenjska Museum is open Tuesday to Friday from 8 am to 5 pm, on Saturday from 10 am to 5 pm and on Sunday from 9 am till noon. During the winter, weekday hours are 8 am to 4 pm, on Saturday 9 am to 1 pm and on Sunday 9 am till noon. The Božidar Jakac House is open Tuesday to Saturday from 9 am to 1 pm (from 10 am on Saturday). Entrance to the Dolenjska Museum is 300/150 SIT for adults/students and children or 500/300 SIT for both the museum and the Božidar Jakac House.

Other Sights

Novo Mesto's other interesting buildings are mostly on or just off Glavni trg. At No 6, the neo-Renaissance **town hall**, out of step with the square's other arcaded buildings, ostentatiously calls attention to itself at all hours with its bells and odd façade but especially at noon, when an ear-piercing siren is sounded. The coat of arms on the front is that of Archduke Rudolf IV, the town's founder.

South of the town hall on Frančiškanska ulica is the **Church of St Leonard**, which was originally built by Franciscan monks fleeing the Turks in Bosnia in 1472 but with an unusual neo-Gothic/Moorish gable added in the 19th century, and the **Franciscan monastery**. The monastery library's collection of rare manuscripts, including many important 12th century incunabula, are now in Ljubljana. The **Gymnasium** founded by Maria Theresa in 1746 is to the north at Jenkova ulica 1. Today it houses a music school, a public library and the provincial archives.

The only historical structure of note on the right bank of the Krka is **Grm Castle**, a manor house at Skalickega ulica 1, with an ornately stuccoed central hall. A Habsburg stone eagle and a socialist seal with sheaves of wheat, grapes and a hammer and sickle on the outside reveal its later incarnations – a public building from the late 19th century and then an agricultural school. It contains some government offices but is still in a general state of disrepair.

Activities

Boating The Luna bar (☎ 321 612) rents canoes during the summer months, but don't expect to get very far along the Krka from this point; you can only paddle about 2km upstream and 200m downstream. More serious canoeing and kayaking are available 9km south-west on the Krka at the Rafting Club Gimpex (☎ 83 171) near Straža at Pod Srobotnikom 12.

Flying The Novo Mesto Aeroclub (☎ 321 107) at Prečna, 5km west of Novo Mesto, offers sightseeing flights over Novo Mesto and the Krka Valley in Cessna 172s and Piper 28-Warriors daily between 9 am and 7 pm. A 15-minute flight costs 4200 SIT for three passengers. Flying lessons are also available. The airfield is just over a kilometre from the centre of Prečna, which is served by bus from Novo Mesto.

Horse Riding The Novo Mesto Sport Equestrian Centre (☎ 28 166) in the village of Češča Vas, about 3km south of Prečna, has Holsteiners and Arabians for riders of all levels. You can ride on any day, but you should book first. There's also horse riding at the Struga Riding Centre (☎ 75 627) near Otočec Castle, 7km to the north-east (see the Otočec section).

Places to Stay

The accommodation options in Novo Mesto are not great and can be quite expensive. The closest *camping grounds* are at Otočec and Dolenjske Toplice, 7km and 12km away respectively. Emona Globtour has a few *private rooms* on its books, but they are quite a distance from town.

Apartmaji Ravbar (☎ 342 700), a family-run guesthouse at Smrečnikova ulica 15-17 across the Krka in Kandija, has five modern, spotlessly clean apartments with kitchen and two rooms for about DM30 per person. It's a very quiet area, full of trees and people walking their dogs. Farther afield (about 4km north-west of the Old Town), the *Vidic* pension (☎ 321 822) at Ljubljanska cesta 51 charges DM50/80 for singles/doubles.

The only other place to stay in Novo Mesto itself is the *Krka* (☎ 323 711; fax 313 000) at Novi trg 1, a renovated 50-room business hotel run by the Krka group. Singles with shower and breakfast are 11,000 SIT, doubles 14,800 SIT. The Krka has a decent restaurant and a pub open till 10 pm.

Places to Eat

The *Pizzeria Klet*, tucked away in a cellar at Dilančeva ulica 7, is open from 9 am to 10 pm on weekdays and till midnight at the weekend.

Gostišča na Trgu, the 'Inns on the Square' at Glavni trg 30, have no accommodation but count three eateries and a *kavarna*. On the ground floor there's a café with sidewalk terrace, a pizzeria and an ice-cream parlour. Upstairs the 'classic' restaurant has set-lunch menus from 650 SIT. The self-service restaurant on the same floor, with pleasant seating on a narrow balcony overlooking a courtyard, is much cheaper.

For better (and more expensive) food, head deeper into the Old Town for the *Breg* restaurant at Cvelbarjeva ulica 7, birthplace of Božidar Jakac and once an important spot for artists and writers. Try kurja obara z ajdovimi žganci (chicken stew with buckwheat groats) or pečenica in zelje (bratwurst with sauerkraut) along with a glass or two of Cviček, the uniquely Slovenian light red wine from Dolenjska. There's garden seating available in the warmer months. Expect to pay about 1250 SIT for two courses and a drink.

Loka, at Župančičevo sprehajališče 2, is on the Krka with restful views across the river. The speciality here is fish, particularly trout, and the restaurant is open daily from 9 am till midnight. French workers at the Renault factory frequent the *Gostišče Bučar*, south-west of the Old Town at Šmihelska ulica 14 opposite the Church of St Michael in Šmihel. It's not cheap, but if the *Francozi* give the thumbs up, it just has to be good. Bučar is open weekdays to 11 pm and till midnight on Friday and Saturday.

There is an outside *market* on Monday, Wednesday and Friday selling fruit and vegetables on Florjanov trg in the centre of the Old Town.

Entertainment

The *cultural centre* (☎ 321 214) at Prešernov trg 3-5 has a cinema (screenings at 4, 6.15 and 8.30 pm) and sponsors occasional theatrical and musical performances. Ask the staff about summer concerts held in the atrium of the Provost's House.

Like the province of Bela Krajina to the south, Dolenjska has a tradition of folk music, and flyers and posters around town are always announcing folk ensemble performances at music halls and cultural centres in neighbouring towns and villages.

Glavni trg has a number of small pubs and cafés (eg *Klub Vida* at No 14) with outside terraces that would be pleasant in the warm months if the traffic through the square wasn't so heavy. Leave them behind and head for *Luna* at Pugljeva ulica 2 or *Boter* behind Kandijska cesta 4, two outdoor café-pubs on opposite sides of the river. The Luna, with its lovely back garden and open daily to 11 pm, is more pleasant, but the Boter has better views of the Old Town from across the Krka. They could be straight out of a Jakac painting.

The *Andreas Club* next to the Breg restaurant on Cvelbarjeva ulica and the *Kapucinka* pub at the eastern end of Novi trg opposite Rozmanova ulica 32 are decent late-night places for a drink. Another recommended venue is the *Bistro Škorpijon* opposite the Dolenjska Museum on Muzejska ulica. It's open daily till 11 pm.

Getting There & Away

Bus Bus service to and from Novo Mesto is good. There are very frequent departures to Dolenjske Toplice, Otočec, Šentjernej and Šmarješke Toplice and at least 10 a day to Brežice, Kostanjevica na Krki and Ljubljana (via Trebnje or Žužemberk). Other destinations served from Novo Mesto include: Bled (one bus a day), Celje (one), Črnomelj (six), Koper (two or three), Kranjska Gora (two), Krško (six), Maribor (one), Metlika (six), Prečna (three), Trebnje (eight) and Vinica (five). You can also reach Zagreb on three buses a day.

Train Up to 14 trains a day serve Novo Mesto from Ljubljana (75km; 1¾ hours) via Ivančna Gorica and Trebnje. Many of these continue on to Črnomelj (32km; 45 minutes) and Metlika (47km; one hour), where you can make up to three connections a day for Karlovac in Croatia. To reach anywhere else of importance in Slovenia by train from Novo Mesto, you'll have to go to Ljubljana.

OTOČEC

• *pop 1885* • *area code ☎068* • *postcode 8222*

The castle at Otočec (Wördl in German), occupying a tiny island in the middle of the Krka River, 7km north-east of Novo Mesto, is one of Slovenia's loveliest and most complete fortresses. Unfortunately, someone else thought so too and turned it into an upmarket and very expensive hotel. But the area around Otočec, the gateway to the lower Krka and the Posavje region, has become something of a recreational centre, and there is a wide choice of accommodation and activities.

History

The first castle at Otočec almost certainly stood on the right bank of the river. But during the Mongol onslaught in the mid-13th century (or even a century later during the wars with the Hungarians), a canal was dug on the south side, thereby creating an artificial island. The present structure probably lost its military significance almost as soon as it was built in the early 16th century since the frontier had moved southward by then. In 1560 the castle was purchased by Ivan Lenkovič, the commander of the Vojna Krajina (Military March) who went on to defeat the Turks at Kostanjevica na Krki three years later.

Orientation

The castle – now the posh Grad Otočec hotel – is 1km east of Otočec village on a secondary road running parallel to route No 1 (E70) and the river. You reach the castle via a rickety wooden bridge that probably should not handle cars. Cheaper accommodation is available up the hill a few steps north of the bridge and across the main road. The camping ground is south-west of the island on the right bank.

Information

Staff at the reception of the castle hotel (☎ 75 170 or ☎ 321 911) can provide information about the recreational facilities at Otočec and help with equipment rentals. You can change money here, at the reception of the Šport hotel, at the camp site or at the post office in Otočec village.

Otočec Castle

Though you probably won't be staying at the castle hotel, there's no harm in having a look around this historical site and perhaps having a drink or cup of coffee at the terrace café in the courtyard if the weather is warm. The castle, which contains elements of late Gothic and Renaissance architecture, consists of two wings connected by a wall. There are four squat, rounded towers with very thick walls and narrow loopholes at each end.

Activities

Otočec (and the Krka Valley in general) is a cycling centre. The tennis centre by the Šport hotel has bicycles and mountain bikes for rent for 500 SIT per hour. The tennis centre has three indoor courts (1800 to 3000 SIT per hour) and six outdoor ones (500 to 800 SIT) as well as a sauna and steam room (900 SIT) and fitness centre (600 SIT per hour).

The camping ground rents canoes, rowing boats and rafts for use on the Krka. (The best areas for rowing are downstream from Struga.) The per-hour fee is 600 SIT.

While not as rich as the upper Krka, the river around Otočec is a popular fishing spot and more than likely will yield a couple of pike, perch or carp. Fishing permits from the hotel cost 2800 SIT per day.

The Struga Riding Centre (☎ 75 627) on the right river bank about 1.5km north-east of the Otočec camp site has a number of horses available for dressage, cross-country riding and coach excursions. One hour of riding is DM22, lessons are DM26 per hour and a half-hour ride in an old coach is DM35.

The centre, which is housed in another medieval castle complete with chapel, is open from 8 to 11 am and 5 to 9 pm every day, except Tuesday. To get there from the castle, cross the second bridge, walk east for 600m on the paved road and then another 900m north on the unsealed one.

Places to Stay

All the accommodation listed here shares the same contact numbers: ☎ 321 911; fax 323 413.

The *Otočec* camp site is on a two-hectare strip of land running along the right bank of the Krka and can accommodate 200 people. To reach it from the castle, cross the second bridge, turn left (east) and walk for 300m. It has its own tennis and pool and there's a 'beach' along the river. Daily charges are 500 SIT per person, 250 SIT per car, 300 SIT per tent and 350 SIT per caravan. It is open from May to September.

An unattractive area north of the castle includes the *Šport* hotel, a concrete-and-glass box at Grajska cesta 2 with a cocktail bar, disco and 78 rooms. Singles with shower and breakfast are 9500 SIT, doubles are 12,400 SIT. The *bungalows* nearby in the complex cost 5000/9000 SIT.

The *Grad Otočec* is one of the most attractive and luxurious hotels in Slovenia. Its two dozen rooms are enormous and have polished parquet floors, Oriental carpets, marble-topped tables and large baths. But don't expect all that to come cheap – singles with bath and breakfast are 15,400 SIT, doubles 21,000 SIT.

If you want something a bit more rural and affordable, the *Šeruga* farmhouse (☎ 85 656) in the village of Sela pri Ratežu (house No 15) about 2km south of Otočec village has doubles and triples (some with kitchen) for about DM35 per person for bed and breakfast.

Places to Eat

The *Otočec* restaurant north of the castle has a large terrace that is very popular in summer. If you can't handle the crowds, try the small eatery at the camp site or the one at the Struga Riding Centre.

The *Castle* restaurant and the smaller *Knights' Hall* at the Grad Otočec hotel will be out of most people's price range, but the ancient stone walls, chandeliers and game and fish specialities make them worth a splurge.

Entertainment
The *Diskoteka Otočec* at the Šport hotel is open till late on Thursday, Friday and Saturday. The *Hit Casino Otočec* (☎ 75 700), with black jack, poker, American roulette and slot machines, is open from 5 pm to 2 am daily.

Getting There & Away
The bus linking Novo Mesto and Šmarješke Toplice stops at the bridge leading to the castle about once an hour on weekdays but less frequently at the weekend.

AROUND OTOČEC
There are a couple of excellent excursions accessible from Otočec on foot, mountain bike or even horseback. The first is to the vineyards of **Trška Gora** (428m), which can be reached by road and trail from Mačkovec, about 5km south-west of Otočec on the main road to Novo Mesto. The walk (or ride) is quite straightforward from there. Follow the road north for 1km to Sevno and then continue along the winding track for another 2km to Trška Gora and the **Church of St Mary**. From here there are wonderful views of the Gorjanci Hills, Kočevski Rog and the Krka Valley. Below the church is Krkin Hram, a 100-year-old wine cellar open to groups only.

Farther afield is **Gospodična** (828m) in the Gorjanci Hills and the *Dom Vinka Paderšiča na Gorjancih* (☎ 24 920 or ☎ 23 391), a mountain lodge with a restaurant and accommodation, open daily from May to September and at weekends only the rest of the year. Gospodična and the lodge are about 13km south-east of Otočec in the shadow of **Trdinov Vrh** (1178m), the highest peak in the Gorjanci. This densely forested area is known for its mushrooms and a 'magic spring' in which first-time visitors are supposed to wash. The route from Otočec goes for 5km south-east to **Velike Brusnice**, famous for its cherries and cherry festival in spring, then to Gabrje (4.5km) and on to Gospodična (3.5km).

ŠMARJEŠKE TOPLICE
• *pop 1860* • *area code* ☎*068* • *postcode 8220*
If all that Cviček wine is taking its toll on you, consider taking a break at Šmarješke Toplice, a spa in a small, lush valley about 5km north of Otočec. While it doesn't have anything close to the history or atmosphere of Dolenjske Toplice, 25km to the southwest, it has lovely grounds and more than enough facilities to keep you busy and help recharge those batteries.

The three natural pools that once stood on the site of the spa were used by local people as far back as the 18th century and were collectively known as the Lake Spa. Development did not come until 1950, when the first hotel was built, but even that remained a rather exclusive facility reserved for the *nomenklatura* (communist honchos) with ailing hearts. Only in the last decade has Šmarješke Toplice really made it on the map as a serious therapy centre for those with cardiovascular problems as well as promoting relaxation and a healthier lifestyle.

Orientation & Information
The spa complex and its hotels are north of the tiny village of Šmarješke Toplice; the road to it passes a thermal stream and a pond with giant waterlilies. Buses stop in front and opposite the Gostilna Prinovec, a restaurant and grocery store. The post office, where you can change money, is nearby and open from 8 am to 5 pm weekdays and till noon on Saturday.

Activities
The spa counts four pools fed by 32°C spring water rich in carbon dioxide and minerals. Two are indoor ones at the hotel complex and used for therapy. Nearby is a sauna, solarium and modern gym.

The larger outdoor pool is below the sports centre. Visitors not staying at the spa pay 800 SIT (900 SIT at weekends). Because the basin of the older (and smaller) pool nearby is made of wood, the water temperature is 2°C warmer.

The sports centre has four clay tennis courts available for hire (500 to 700 SIT per hour) and racquets can be rented. One of the courts is covered and illuminated at night. There are also facilities for table tennis, minigolf and lawn bowls.

The wine-growing areas surrounding Šmarješke Toplice make for excellent walking and there are trails and foot paths south-west to Trška Gora (see Around Otočec) and north-east to Vinji Vrh.

Places to Stay

All the accommodation at Šmarješke Toplice has the same numbers: ☎ 73 230; fax 73 107.

The J-shaped main complex is divided into three hotels. The *Toplice*, dating from 1950, is normally reserved for long-term guests with more serious medical problems. The *Krka*, the middle section built in 1983, costs from 8300 SIT per person with full board. The *Šmarjeta*, the newest (1991) and most attractive of the three hotels, costs 10,700/17,600 SIT for singles/doubles with full board or 9500/14,900 SIT for bed and breakfast. Some of the rooms at the Krka and the Šmarjeta have small balconies with views of nearby hills and forests.

A cheaper alternative to staying at the spa is the 18-room *Domen* pension (☎ 73 051) in Družinska Vas (house No 1), about 1.5km south-east of Šmarješke Toplice. Singles/doubles are 4000/7000 SIT. The Domen has a tennis court, a football pitch and a decent restaurant.

Places to Eat

Most guests take all their meals at the huge hotel restaurant, but if you are visiting or not staying on a full-board program, try the *Topliška Klet* cellar restaurant in the complex.

In Šmarješke Toplice village, *Gostilna Prinovec* is a pleasant, inexpensive place for a meal with an outside grill in summer and open to 11 pm or midnight. The grocery store next door is open Monday to Saturday from 7.30 am to 7 pm and on Sunday from 8 am til noon. The restaurant at the *Domen* pension is open every day, except Tuesday, from 10 am till 10 pm.

Getting There & Away

Bus service is very frequent to Novo Mesto and Otočec, Šmarjeta and Brežice. There's also at least one bus a day to Ljubljana, Mokronog and Sevnica.

Getting Around

The sports centre and the Domen pension rent bicycles for about 300 SIT per hour.

KOSTANJEVICA NA KRKI
• *pop 765* • *area code ☎0608* • *postcode 8311*

Situated on an islet just 500m long and 200m wide in a loop of the Krka River, Kostanjevica is Slovenia's smallest town. And with a charter that dates back to 1252, it is also one of its oldest.

Kostanjevica was an important commercial centre in the Middle Ages and even had its own mint in the 13th century called Moneta Landestrostensis (Kostanjevica is still called Landstrass in German). Its coins were in circulation as far as what is now western Romania. In 1563, after repeatedly attacking the town, the Turks were defeated by Ivan Lenkovič, supreme commander of the Military March.

Kostanjevica's glory days have long since passed, however, and today the town is so sleepy it is almost comatose. Though it is dubbed 'the Venice of Dolenjska' by the tourist industry and under full protection as a cultural monument, most of its buildings are in very bad condition. The only one in the area that seems to be getting any attention is the former Cistercian monastery 1.5km south of town.

Still, Kostanjevica is an important art centre and its location is magical. If you don't manage to flag down a helicopter to view the town from on high, at least take a look at the photographs of the town in *Slovenia from the Air* (Založba Mladinska Knjiga) by Matjaž Kmecl et al.

Orientation & Information

Though most of Kostanjevica's historical sights are on the island, some others and things of a more practical nature are on the mainland to the north-west or south-east, reached by two small bridges. Buses stop opposite the Pod Gorjanci guesthouse and restaurant.

Nova Ljubljanska Banka has a branch at Oražnova ulica 3. It's open weekdays from 8 am to 2.30 pm and on Saturday from 7.30 to 11 am. The post office is at Kambičev trg 5 and is open weekdays from 8 am to 5 pm and till noon on Saturday.

Walking Tour

No one is going to get lost or tired on a walking tour of Kostanjevica – some 500m up one street and 500m down another and you've seen the lot.

On Kambičev trg, across the small bridge from the bus stop and splitting the street in two, stands the **Church of St Nicholas**, a tiny late Gothic structure dating from the late 16th century. The brightly coloured frescoes in the presbytery of scenes from the Old and New Testaments were painted by Jože Gorjup (1907-32). You can see more of this expressionist's work, including the wonderful *Bathers* series, at the **Jože Gorjup Gallery** back over the bridge at Gorjanska cesta 2.

If you walk north-west along Oražnova ulica for about 100m, you'll reach a 15th century manor house at No 5 that now contains the **Lamut Art Salon** (presently under renovation). The painter and graphic artist Vladimir Lamut (1915-62) completed a large portion of his work here in Kostanjevica.

Continue along Oražnova ulica, passing a lovely *fin-de-siècle* house at No 24, to the **Parish Church of St James**, a 13th century Romanesque building at the island's north-western tip with a mostly baroque interior. Above the carved stone portal on the western side, you can just make out geometric shapes and decorative plants and trees. On the north side is a 15th century depiction of Jesus rising from the tomb.

Talcev ulica, the island's other street, leads south-east back to St Nicholas Church and is lined with crumbling but quite attractive 'folk baroque' houses. About halfway down on the left is the 200-year-old **St Nicholas Pharmacy**. The **birthplace of Jože Gorjup** is farther along at No 8.

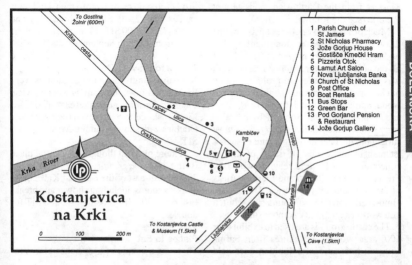

1 Parish Church of St James
2 St Nicholas Pharmacy
3 Jože Gorjup House
4 Gostišče Kmečki Hram
5 Pizzeria Otok
6 Lamut Art Salon
7 Nova Ljubljanska Banka
8 Church of St Nicholas
9 Post Office
10 Boat Rentals
11 Bus Stops
12 Green Bar
13 Pod Gorjanci Pension & Restaurant
14 Jože Gorjup Gallery

To Gostilna Žolnir (600m)

Krška cesta

Talcev ulica

Oražnova ulica

Kambičev trg

Krka River

Kostanjevica na Krki

0   100   200 m

To Kostanjevica Castle & Museum (1.5km)

Ljubljanska cesta

Gorjanska

To Kostanjevica Cave (1.5km)

DOLENJSKA

Kostanjevica Castle

The former Cistercian monastery – what most people here call Kostanjevica Castle – was begun in the mid-13th century and, through donation deeds from the rulers of Hungary and Bosnia, remained a very wealthy institution in the Middle Ages. It was abandoned by the order in the late 18th century and was severely damaged during WWII and again in an earthquake in 1984. Today it houses a large and important art gallery. The castle is about 1.5km south-west of the Pod Gorjanci restaurant on Grajska cesta 45.

The main entrance through two painted towers leads to an enormous courtyard enclosed by a **cloister** with some 260 arcades on three floors. To the west stands' the disused **Church of the Virgin Mary** containing elements from the 13th to 18th centuries – and a lot of free-flying sparrows. A set of steps near what was once the altar leads to the **museum**.

The **Božidar Jakac Gallery** contains 16th century frescoes taken from the church below, works by such Slovenian artists as the impressionist Jakac and the brothers France (1895-1960) and Tone Kralj (1900-75). There is also a permanent collection of Old Masters from the Carthusian monastery at Pleterje (see the following section).

Much of Jakac's work here consists of line drawings done while documenting the underground Partisan movement in 1943. Of all the artists, the expressionist France Kralj was the most versatile and prolific, turning out hundreds of works in oil, ink, bronze and wood; don't miss his sculptures *The Reapers* and *Mother and Child*. Some of Tone Kralj's early work (like *Veined Sunset)* is almost surreal but his later move to a kind of socialist realism obliterates all traces of it. The collection from Pleterje features works by French, German, Italian and Flemish artists of the 16th and 18th centuries. The oils are almost all portraits of saints and church noteworthies and pretty sombre stuff.

The castle grounds are used to exhibit over 100 large wooden sculptures from Forma Viva, an international exhibition once held in several places in Slovenia from 1961 to 1988 whereby sculptors worked with materials associated with the area. Here it was oak, in Portorož stone, iron at Ravne in Koroška and (shudder) concrete in Maribor. The castle is open every day, except Monday, from 9 am till 6 pm from April to October. During the rest of the year it closes at 4 pm. The entry fee is 400/200 SIT for adults/students and children.

Kostanjevica Cave

This small cave, on an unsealed road about 1.5km south-east of town, has half-hour tours (400/300 SIT) at the weekend from 10 am to 6.30 pm between mid-April and October (daily from June to August). The guide will lead you some 300m in (only 1550m of the cave have been fully explored), past a small lake, several galleries full of stalactites and stalagmites and, no doubt, a couple of specimens of *Paladilhiopsis kostanjevicae*, a snail unique to the cave that seems to thrive in the 12°C temperature. There's a shaded picnic area in front of the cave on tiny Studena Stream.

Boating

The little ice-cream kiosk next to the bridge just before you cross over to the island rents canoes (450/2500 SIT per hour/day) and kayaks (350/2000 SIT) for excursions on the Krka from April to September.

Places to Stay

Not surprisingly, accommodation is very limited in a town as small as Kostanjevica. The *Pod Gorjanci* guesthouse (☎ 87 046) at Ljubljanska cesta 5 has seven rooms in total. Doubles with shower and breakfast are 5600 SIT.

A more pleasant though less central place is the *Gostilna Žolnir* (☎ 87 133) about 700m north-east of the island at Krška cesta 4. Its six rooms, including shower and breakfast, cost 3900 SIT for singles, 5200 SIT for doubles.

Places to Eat

There are a couple of bare-bones places for

a quick meal or drink on the island, including *Pizzeria Otok* and the old-style *Gostišče Kmečki Hram*, both on Oražnova ulica. The *Green Bar* in an attractive old baroque building next to the Pod Gorjanci pension is a pleasant place for a drink.

The restaurant at *Pod Gorjanci* is very popular and the back garden is often crowded in summer. But for my money I'd head for the *Žolnir*, Krška cesta 4, whose owners are very serious about the food they serve. It's open daily till 10 pm. A speciality of Kostanjevica is duck served with little mlinci pancakes and, of course, accompanied by Cviček wine.

Getting There & Away
There are departures from Kostanjevica to Novo Mesto, Brežice and Šentjernej. Other destinations and their daily frequencies include Ljubljana (six), Krško (two) and Orešnje (one).

PLETERJE MONASTERY
You'll see more of the treasures of Pleterje, a huge monastery just over 3km south of Šentjernej, at Kostanjevica Castle than you will *in situ*. Pleterje (Pletariach in German) belongs to the Carthusians, the strictest of all Roman Catholic monastic orders. The Gothic **Holy Trinity Church** (also called the Old Monastery Church) is the only part of the complex open to the general public at present. But the monastery's location in a narrow valley between slopes awash in vines and the Gorjanci Hills is so attractive and peaceful, it's worth a visit. The Pleterje Trail is a 1½-hour walk in the hills around the monastery complex.

The monastery was founded in 1407 by Herman II, one of the Counts of Celje, and its construction was supervised by an English abbot called Prior Hartman. The complex was fortified with ramparts, towers and a moat during the Turkish invasions and all but abandoned during the Protestant Reformation, which swept Dolenjska in the 16th century. The Carthusian order, like all monastic communities in the Habsburg Empire, was abolished in 1784. When the

monks returned to Pleterje over a century later, they rebuilt the complex according to the plans of the order's charterhouse at Nancy in France.

You may catch a glimpse of the dozen or so white-hooded monks quietly going about their chores – they take a strict vow of silence and are vegetarians – or hear them singing their office from the old monastery church at various times of the day. But the ubiquitous signs reading *Klavzura – Vstop Prepovedan* ('Seclusion – No Entry') remind you that everything apart from the church – the ornate chapels, the inner courtyard, the cloisters and the library rich in medieval manuscripts – is off limits.

Above the ribbed main portal of the austere church, built in 1420 and one of the most important Gothic monuments in Slovenia, is a fresco depicting Mary and the Trinity. Inside, the rib-vaulted ceiling with its heraldic bosses and the carved stone niches by the altar are worth a look, but what is most interesting is the medieval rood screen, the low wall across the aisle that separated members of the order from the rest of the faithful.

At the monastery office in the main sand-coloured building, you can see a 30-minute video (200 SIT, five people minimum) in one of six languages, including English, that describes the Carthusian way of life and the history of Pleterje. The monks also sell some of their own products here, including packs of beeswax candles (450 SIT), honey (750 SIT), Cviček and Chardonnay wines (400 SIT and 950 SIT a litre) and four types of brandy: *sadjevec* (apple; 1000 SIT), *slivovka* (plum; 1250 SIT), *brinovec* (juniper; 1900 SIT) and – everyone's favourite – *hruška* (pear; 3400 SIT). If you're wondering how they got that whole pear inside the bottle, it's simple – the bottle is placed over the immature fruit while still on the tree. When the pear ripens inside, the bottle is removed and filled with brandy. The shop is open Monday to Saturday from 7.30 am to 5 pm and from 8 am on Sunday.

Šentjernej is 6km west of Kostanjevica and can be reached on the Novo Mesto bus

DOLENJSKA

(return to Kostanjevica on one of two direct daily buses or on any of the dozen or so headed for Brežice). There are also up to six buses a day to Ljubljana and one each to Krško and Zagreb. Buses stop in front of the *Gostilna Majzelj* at Trg Gorjanskega Bataljona 5, which is open daily, except Tuesday, till 10 pm (Sunday to 1 pm). Accommodation can be arranged in town or in a vineyard cottage. You'll have to make your way on foot to Pleterje from the bus stop, though, as there is no local service; it's just over 3km. The post office, where you can change money, is on the square opposite the gostilna. It is open weekdays from 8 am to 6 pm and till noon on Saturday.

POSAVJE REGION

Most of what is called Posavje, the area 'on the Sava River' as far as the border with Croatia, is in Štajerska, the large province north of Dolenjska. But historically and geographically, Posavje is closely tied to Dolenjska and easily accessible from many of its towns.

History

Like Dolenjska, Posavje was settled early and is rich in archaeological finds from the Hallstatt, Celtic and Roman periods. The Sava, of course, was paramount and, while Jason and the Argonauts probably did not navigate the 'Savus' upstream as legend tells us, the Romans certainly did, building a major port called Neviodunum near today's Drnovo. Slavic graves unearthed in the area date from the 7th century.

Posavje took centre stage during the Turkish invasions starting in the 15th century – which explains the large number of heavily fortified castles in the region – and again 100 years later during the Slovenian-Croatian peasant uprisings and the Protestant Reformation. River traffic increased in the 19th century after a 20km stretch of the Sava was regulated, and the arrival of the railway in 1862 linking Ljubljana and Zagreb helped the region develop industrially.

Posavje had more than its share of suffering during WWII. In a bid to colonise the area, the occupying German forces engaged in a brutal program of 'ethnic cleansing' and expelled more than 15,000 Slovenes. Many of them were interned at a camp in Rajhenburg Castle at Brestanica before being deported to Serbia, Croatia or Germany.

Brežice

• *pop 6900* • *area code ☎0608* • *postcode 8250*
Brežice is not the largest town in Posavje – that distinction goes to Krško, 12km upriver – but from a traveller's point of view, it is the most interesting. The town lies between the Orlica Hills to the north and the Gorjanci to the south, and opens onto a vast plain to the east. The climate is milder and drier than elsewhere in Dolenjska.

History Situated in a basin just north of where the Krka flows into the Sava, Brežice (Rhain in German) was an important trading centre in the Middle Ages and was granted a town charter in 1354. Brežice's dominant feature has always been its castle, mentioned in documents as early as 1249, with a strategic position some 400m from the Sava. In the 16th century the original castle was replaced with a Renaissance fortress to strengthen the town's defences against the Turks and marauding peasants who, during one uprising, beheaded nobles at the castle and impaled their heads on poles.

The castle was built with the help of Italian masters and is not dissimilar to the ones at Otočec, Sevnica and Mokrice in design. Over a century later, the castle's new owners, the Counts of Attems, renovated the building in the baroque style and added several sumptuous rooms, including the largest function room in Slovenia. Today the castle houses the Posavje Museum.

Orientation & Information Brežice's main street is Cesta Prvih Borcev. Heading south it becomes Prešernova cesta and crosses the Sava. Going north it changes names to Trg Izgnancev and Cesta Bratov Milavcev. The main artery going eastward is Bizeljska ulica.

The bus station is behind the big shopping

centre on Cesta Svobode, 200m north of Bizeljska ulica. The train station is farther afield on Trg OF, about 2.5km north of the town centre.

There is no tourist office in Brežice, but the staff at the Posavje Museum will help you with any questions you have. There's a Nova Ljubljanska Banka branch at Cesta Prvih Borcev 31, open on weekdays from 7 am to 6 pm and till noon on Saturday. SKB Banka, which has an ATM, is farther north at No 39. The post office is at Trg Izgnancev 1a and is open from 7 am to 7 pm weekdays and till noon on Saturday.

Posavje Museum Housed in the Renaissance castle at Cesta Prvih Borcev 1, this is one of provincial Slovenia's best museums, and its archaeological and ethnographic collections are particularly rich.

From the courtyard you ascend a staircase illustrated on the walls and ceiling with Greek gods, the four Evangelists and the Attems family coat of arms. The first rooms contain bits and pieces from earliest times to the arrival of the Slavs; don't miss the skeletons from the 9th century BC unearthed near Dobova, the 5th century BC bronze bridle, the Celtic and Roman jewellery and a dented helmet that suggests the legionnaire wearing it got kicked in the head by a mule. In the ethnographic rooms, along with the carved wooden bowls, decorated chests and plaited loaves of bread, is a strange beehive in the shape of a soldier from the early 1800s. On the top he's French and on the bottom Croatian.

Other rooms cover life in the Posavje region in the 16th century (focusing on the peasant uprisings in the area and the Protestant Reformation) and the time of the two world wars, with emphasis on the deportation of Slovenes by the Germans during WWII. There's also a collection of baroque

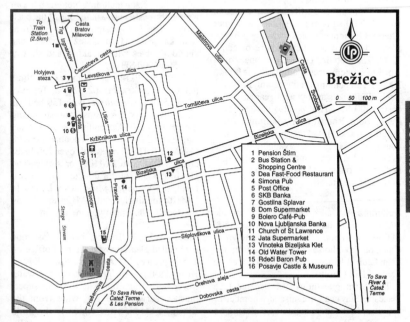

Brežice

0   50   100 m

1 Pension Štim
2 Bus Station & Shopping Centre
3 Dea Fast-Food Restaurant
4 Simona Pub
5 Post Office
6 SKB Banka
7 Gostilna Splavar
8 Dom Supermarket
9 Bolero Café-Pub
10 Nova Ljubljanska Banka
11 Church of St Lawrence
12 Jata Supermarket
13 Vinoteka Bizeljska Klet
14 Old Water Tower
15 Rdeči Baron Pub
16 Posavje Castle & Museum

DOLENJSKA

oil paintings. Check out the ornate tile stoves in many of the rooms.

But the museum's real crowd-pleaser is the **Knights' Hall** (Viteška Dvorana), an Italian baroque masterpiece where everything but the floor is painted with landscapes, gods and heroes from Greek and Roman mythology, allegories, the Muses etc. You may vaguely recognise the place; some scenes from the TV miniseries *The Winds of War* were filmed here.

The Posavje Museum is open Monday to Saturday from 8 am to 1 pm and on Sunday from 9 am till noon. The admission charge is 300/150 SIT.

Čatež Terme Rheumatics have been bathing in the thermal spring at Čatež (pop 1005), 3km south-east of Brežice, since the late 18th century. Today, while the huge spa complex still attracts those suffering from such aches and pains, it is every bit as much a recreational area. The spa counts nine thermal-water (27-36°C) outdoor pools with huge slides, fountains and artificial waves over an area of 8000 sq metres. Indoors the Winter Thermal Riviera complex measures 1200 sq metres with a water temperature of about 32°C. The outdoor complex is open from April to September and admission is 900 to 1000 SIT depending on the day of the week. The indoor pools are open all year and entry costs 1300 SIT. The spa also has saunas, a steam room, Roman bath, solarium, gym, a jogging track along the river and tennis courts. A guide is made available to guests every day between 9 and 11 am; tell him or her where you want to go and what you want to see and you're off.

Activities At Čatež, along with taking the waters, you can rent a boat or a bicycle (500 SIT for two hours). In the nearby town of Čatež ob Savi, horses can be hired from the Zean Club at Rimska cesta 22 and ridden up Šentvid Hill (386m).

The Štirn guesthouse in Brežice (see Places to Stay) can organise any number of activities in the area, including canoeing on the Krka, fishing in the Sava or Krka, horse riding and tennis.

Special Events The Festival of Early Music, which for many years had been held in Radovlje in Gorenjska, is a series of concerts of ancient music held in Brežice during the first half of August and one of the country's most prestigious cultural events. The concerts take place in the Knights' Hall.

Places to Stay The huge *Čatež Terme* camp site (☎ 35 000) is not cheap at DM16 to DM18 per person, depending on the season, but campers get use of the outdoor swimming pools. It is open from April to October. There are also *bungalows* nearby costing DM59/84 and DM66/94 for singles/doubles, depending on the season, and *apartments* for up to five people for DM120 to DM140.

In Brežice, the *Štirn* pension (☎ 65 613) at Trg Izgnancev 7 is an attractive little guesthouse with 22 beds that's been around for more than 70 years. Expect to pay about DM25 per person including breakfast. It's on a rather busy street so ask for one of the back rooms. The *Les* guesthouse (☎ 61 100) at Rimska cesta 31 in Čatež ob Savi has singles/doubles with breakfast and shower for 3500/6000 SIT.

The Čatež Terme spa complex has three hotels (☎ 35 000; fax 62 721) at Topliška cesta 35. The *Zdravilišče*, with 130 beds, is generally reserved for those who are taking the spa seriously. Depending on the season, singles are DM76 to DM87, doubles DM108 to DM124. The *Terme*, with over 250 beds, charges DM96 to DM109 for singles and DM140 to DM168 for doubles. The newest hotel, the 48-bed *Toplice*, costs DM89 to DM102 for singles and DM134 to DM154 for doubles, depending on the season.

Places to Eat In Brežice, there's a fast-food café called *Dea* opposite the post office on Trg Izgnancev. *Vinoteka Bizeljska Klet* at Bizeljska ulica 10, just past the old water tower (1914) and opposite the *Jata* supermarket, serves food and wine from the Bizeljsko-Sremič wine region to the north and west of Brežice. Another possibility is the *Gostilna Splavar* at Cesta Prvih Borcev 40.

The gostilna at the *Štirn* pension specialises in fish and seafood. The Laški Rizling, a slightly fruity, medium-dry wine from Bizeljsko, is not a bad accompaniment. The gostilna is open daily for lunch and dinner (except Sunday) to 9 pm.

The *Dom* supermarket at Cesta Prvih Borcev 35 is open weekdays from 7 am to 7 pm and on Saturday till 1 pm.

Entertainment The *Knights' Hall* in the Posavje Museum has near-perfect acoustics and concerts are held there throughout the year. The *Rdeči Baron* pub at Cesta Prvih Borcev 2 and the *Bolero* café-pub at No 33 of the same street are popular places for a drink, open daily to 11 pm or midnight. The *Simona* pub at Holyjeva steza 1 attracts a very young crowd. It's open till late.

Getting There & Away Buses run hourly from Brežice to Bizeljsko, Cerklje, Dobova, Kostanjevica, Krško, Novo Mesto and Čatež Terme and up to eight times a day to Ljubljana. Other destinations and their daily frequencies include: Celje (one bus a day on weekdays), Krško via Drnovo (three), Orešje (three) and Senovo (three). Some of these buses, like the ones to Čatež, can be boarded at the train station in Brežice. There's a bus to Munich on Tuesday, Thursday and Sunday.

As many as 15 trains a day serve Brežice from Ljubljana (107km; 1¾ hours) via Zidani Most, Sevnica and Krško. Many of these trains then cross the Croatian border near Dobova and carry on to Zagreb.

Getting Around Buses run between the bus station and the train station every half-hour throughout the day.

Mokrice Castle

Mokrice, about 10km south-east of Brežice, is the loveliest castle in the Posavje region and has been completely renovated and turned into a 30-room luxury hotel. With one of Slovenia's few golf courses, a large stable

with horses for rent, a 20-hectare 'English park' full of rare plants, and a large orchard of pear trees, it makes a delightful excursion from Brežice.

The castle as it stands today dates from the 16th century, but there are bits and pieces going back to Roman times (inscription stones, part of a tower etc) built into the structure. Like many other castles in the region, it was built as a defence against the Turks and later turned into a baronial manor. The 19th century German writer Count Friedrich von Gagern was born here, and some of his novels are set in the castle and surrounds.

There are a couple of interesting stories about the castle, one of which tells of a 17th century countess named Barbara who fell in love with a sailor called Marko. When he went to sea and failed to return, poor Barbara committed suicide. Her ghost still stalks the castle's secret passageways and staircases at night, and she is particularly active on the feast day of St Barbara (4 December). The castle's coat of arms may strike you as odd; it portrays a raven with an arrow piercing its throat. Apparently a Turkish janissary shot the bird as it squawked to warn the inhabitants of an invasion in the 15th century.

Mokrice, the finest castle in the Posavje region, dates from the 16th century.

DOLENJSKA

The small Gothic **Chapel of St Ann** in the castle grounds not far from the drawbridge has some interesting baroque stucco work inside. The park is filled with baroque statues.

If you want to stay at the *Grad Mokrice* hotel (☎ 57 000; fax 57 007), be prepared to shell out a minimum of DM144 for a single with breakfast and DM160 for a double. One of the 240 sq metre suites goes for DM320 to DM340, depending on the season. The rooms have beamed ceilings and period furniture, and some suites have fireplaces. The castle restaurant is pretty formal with fancy game and fish dishes and classical music; the cellar has 60 different Slovenian wines available by the glass or bottle. Try some *viljamovka*, Mokrice's famous pear brandy.

The green fee for a round of golf at Mokrice's 18-hole course is DM45 on weekdays and DM50 at weekends (less for hotel guests). A half set of clubs costs DM15 to rent. There's also a pro giving lessons (DM35 an hour). Horse riding is available and a carriage ride to Čatež Terme (7km) and back costs DM30 per person.

You can reach Mokrice on the bus to Obrežje, but the ideal way to go would be by bicycle from Čatež, following the secondary road running parallel to route No 1 (E70).

Bizeljsko-Sremič Wine District

Cycling all the way to **Bizeljsko** (Wisell in German; population 1940) through the heart of the Bizeljsko-Sremič wine country might be pushing it for some (it's 18km from Brežice), but there's a bus leaving every hour or so, allowing you to get off whenever you see a gostilna or wine cellar *(vinska klet*; marked by a red, yellow and brown sign) that takes your fancy. In Bizeljsko, try some of the local medium-dry whites and reds at the *Vinska Klet Pinterič* at house No 115 or at *Gostilna Šekoranja* at No 72, or visit the *Istenič* cellars in the nearby village of **Stara Vas** (house No 7). They are open Monday, Wednesday and Thursday from noon to 7 pm and from Friday to Sunday till 9 pm. A tour and a wine tasting costs 800 SIT.

From Bizeljsko you can either return to Brežice or continue north for 7km past Bizeljska Vas and the ruins of the 15th century **Bizeljsko Castle** to Bistrica ob Sotli. From here, buses go north-west to Kozje via the village of **Podsreda**, site of the oldest castle in Slovenia (see the Štajerska chapter).

A: Entrance to Kostanjevica Castle, a former Cistercian monastery, Dolenjska
B: The ornate Italian baroque Festive Hall, in Brežice Castle, Posavje Region, Dolenjska

STEVE FALLON

STEVE FALLON

STEVE FALLON

| A |
| B |
| C |

A: Churches of the Tri Fare (Three Parishes), Rosalnice, Bela Krajina
B: 19th century painted beehive panels, Maribor Regional Museum, Štajerska
C: Centuries-old grapevine, Lent district, Maribor, Štajerska

Bela Krajina

The 'White March' of south-eastern Slovenia takes its name from the endless stands of birch trees that cover this little province. It is a treasure trove of Slovenian folklore, and you'll see more traditional dance and hear more music here than anywhere else in the country, particularly around Črnomelj and Adlešiči. Many of the stringed instruments – the *tamburica*, the *berdo* (contrabass), the guitar-like *brač* and the *bisernica* (lute) – are unique to the region or originated here.

Like Dolenjska, Bela Krajina is famous for its Hallstatt and Roman sites; a 3rd century shrine to the god Mithra (or Mithras) near the village of Rožanec is one of the best preserved in Europe. In the Middle Ages, Bela Krajina was the most remote part of Slovenia, and in some ways it still feels like that. Many of the peasant uprisings of the 15th and 16th centuries started here or across the border in Croatia.

METLIKA
• *pop 3300* • *area code ☎068* • *postcode 8330*
One of Bela Krajina's two most important towns, Metlika (Möttling in German) lies in a valley at the foot of the Žumberak Hills and is surrounded by Croatia on three sides. The Kolpa River is 2km to the south.

History
The area around Metlika was inhabited during prehistoric times, and there was a major Hallstatt settlement here during the early Iron Age. The Romans came too, establishing an outpost here, and Metlika was on a road leading to the important river port of Sisak in Croatia. In medieval times *reggio que Metlica dicitur* (the region called Metlika) included most of today's Bela Krajina, and the Metlika March was an important frontier region. Only a few kilometres from the pilgrimage site of Tri

HIGHLIGHTS
• Visit the Three Parishes pilgrimage churches in Rosalnice
• Experience the Jurjevanje festival in Črnomelj in mid-June
• Go kayaking on the rapid-water run on the Kolpa River from Stari Trg to Vinica
• Discover Bela Krajina folk music, especially around Adlešiči

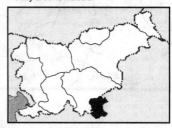

Fare at Rosalnice, Metlika grew into a market town and was given a charter in 1365.

Metlika was in the front lines during the wars with the Hungarians in the 14th century. The Turks attacked some 17 times beginning in 1408 and actually occupied the town in 1578 – something its rival Črnomelj points out never happened to it. For many years, Metlika was the last outpost of Christianity in this part of Europe. Prosperity came briefly during the Protestant Reformation, but the Žumberak Hills sheltered outlaws and brigands from Croatia, who would continue to harass the town for centuries.

The Italians occupied Metlika during WWII, and by the end of the war some 120 buildings had been burned to the ground. Though the kernel of the Old Town counts some buildings dating back several centuries, most of Metlika was rebuilt after 1945.

Orientation
Metlika's Old Town, consisting of three squares, stands on a ridge between a small

stream called the Obrh and the main street, Cesta Bratstva in Enotnosti (Avenue of Fraternity and Unity). You can reach it from the main street by walking up Ulica na Trg to Trg Svobode and then Mestni trg.

The modern bus station is 650m south of the Old Town on Cesta XV Brigade. To get to the train station, walk south along Cesta XV Brigade for 600m and then turn east on Kolodvorska ulica.

Information

The staff at the information window in the town hall (☎ 58 135) at Mestni trg 24 may be able to help you out or you can try the reception at the Bela Krajina hotel.

Dolenjska Banka has a branch at Trg Svobode 7, open from 8 am to 6 pm and till noon on Saturday, and another one with reduced hours (weekdays only from 8 am till noon and 2 to 4.30 pm) in the shopping complex in Naselje Borisa Kidriča opposite the bus station. The post office, open from 7 am to 7 pm weekdays and till noon on Saturday, is in the same shopping centre. The medical centre (☎ 58 259) is at Cesta Bratstva in Enotnosti 71.

Things to See

Metlika Castle, with its L-shaped arcaded courtyard at Trg Svobode 4, houses the **Bela Krajina Museum**. The collection, exhibited in 18 rooms, includes archaeological finds taken from the area such as Hallstatt buckles, bracelets and amulets from Pusti Gradac south of Črnomelj and a copy of the Mithraic relief from the Roman period found at Rožanec near Črnomelj. Artefacts collected from more recent periods are displayed in a mock-up of an old pharmacy and photo studio.

Much emphasis is placed on agriculture in Bela Krajina – everything you've ever wanted to know about beekeeping, fruit cultivation, viniculture, fishing and animal husbandry is here – as well as folk art peculiar to the region, including decorated Easter eggs, glass paintings and religious icons in bottles. The artist and sculptor Alojzij Gangl, who was born in Metlika, is given pride of place.

A small building west of the castle entrance (Trg Svobode 5) contains the **Fire Brigades Museum**. Metlika was the first town in Slovenia to have a fire brigade and has thus earned the right to such a shrine. It's a lot more interesting than it sounds, displaying old fire trucks with enormous wheels, ladders and buckets but no Dalmatians (on four legs anyway). Firefighters, by the way, are considered the 'party animals' of Slovenia, hosting dances, fêtes and other booze-ups outside the *gasilski dom* throughout the summer. Some Slovenes say that's all they ever seem to do. The **defence tower** opposite the Fire Brigades Museum dates from the 16th century.

The Bela Krajina Museum is open from 8 am to 4 pm on weekdays, till 2 pm on Saturday and from 9 am till noon on Sunday. The Fire Brigades Museum is open Monday to Saturday from 9 am to 1 pm and on Sunday till noon. The entrance fee to both is 300/200 SIT for adults/children.

Mestni trg is a colourful, leafy square of 18th and 19th century buildings, including the neo-Gothic **town hall** (1869) at No 24. At the southern end of the square is the so-called **Komenda** (Commandery), which once belonged to the knights of the Teutonic

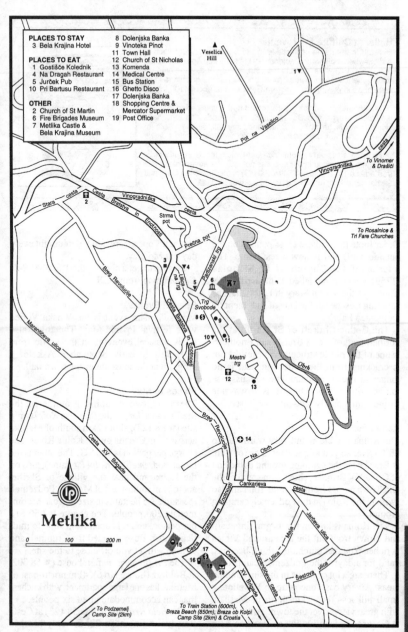

PLACES TO STAY
3 Bela Krajina Hotel

PLACES TO EAT
1 Gostišče Kolednik
4 Na Dragah Restaurant
5 Jurček Pub
10 Pri Bartusu Restaurant

OTHER
2 Church of St Martin
6 Fire Brigades Museum
7 Metlika Castle &
Bela Krajina Museum

8 Dolenjska Banka
9 Vinoteka Pinot
11 Town Hall
12 Church of St Nicholas
13 Komenda
14 Medical Centre
15 Bus Station
16 Ghetto Disco
17 Dolenjska Banka
18 Shopping Centre &
Mercator Supermarket
19 Post Office

Metlika

0   100   200 m

Hallstatt Culture in Slovenia

Hallstatt is the name of a village in the Salzkammergut region of Austria where objects characteristic of the early Iron Age (from about 800 to 500 BC) were found in the 19th century. Today, the name is used generically for the late Bronze and early Iron Age cultures that developed in central and western Europe from about 1100 to 450 BC.

Many parts of Slovenia were settled during this period, particularly Bela Krajina and Dolenjska. Burial grounds and forts have yielded swords, helmets, jewellery and especially situlae – pails (or buckets) that are often richly decorated with battle and hunting scenes.

Hallstatt art is very geometric, and typical motifs include birds and figures arranged in pairs. It was not until the advent of the late Iron Age La Tène culture (450 to 390 BC) of the European Celts that S-shapes, spirals and round patterns developed. ■

Order (note the Maltese cross painted on the outside wall) and is now a rest home. The interior of the **Church of St Nicholas** (1759), which is modelled on the Križanke's Church of the Virgin Mary in Ljubljana, has sobering frescoes of the Day of Judgment by Domenico Fabrio.

The Gothic **Church of St Martin** at the northern end of Cesta Bratstva in Enotnosti is one of the oldest structures in Metlika but is cracking from the bottom up and is no longer in use. It contains late Renaissance tombs with reliefs. Outside is a wayside shrine with a barely recognisable fresco.

Activities

The Kolpa is a clean and very warm (up to 28°C) river so you might want to go for a dip at Breza near the camping ground at the end of Cesta XV Brigade, about 2km south of the Old Town across from Croatia. You can also swim in the Kolpa at the Podzemelj camping ground.

The Kolpa is known for its grayling, carp and brown trout but the area around Vinica is richer. You can purchase fishing licences, valid for a day, at the Podzemelj camp site.

There are a lot of walks in the surrounding areas. A very easy one is up to **Veselica**, a small hill less than 1km north of Metlika, with great views over the town. You can stop at *Gostišče Kolednik* at Pot na Veselico 5 for lunch. It's open from noon to midnight every day but Monday.

Be sure to get a copy of the 1:50,000 *Bela Krajina* map from GZS.

Special Events

Metlika's main event is the Vinska Vigred wine festival in mid-May. The town also holds musical evenings in the castle from early July to early September. Ask for a program at the museum or the town hall.

Places to Stay

There are two camping grounds in the Metlika area. One is the *Breza ob Kolpi* camp site (☎ 58 123), about 2km south of Metlika across from Croatia on the Kolpa River. The charge per person is 450 SIT. The other is the larger *Podzemelj ob Kolpi* (☎ same), also on the Kolpa and near the village of Škrilje, about 7km south-west of Metlika. Podzemelj measures 1.5 hectares in size and can accommodate 200 people. The charge is 650 SIT per person, and it is open from June to mid-September. Buses headed for Črnomelj and Griblje will let you off close to the site.

The *Pri Bregarjevih* farmhouse (☎ 58 302) at Boldraž (house No 6), 4km north-east of Metlika, has one large apartment, with kitchen, that can accommodate up to six people.

The *Bela Krajina* (☎ /fax 58 123) at Cesta Bratstva in Enotnosti 28, the only hotel in town, has 24 fairly shabby rooms and charges 2500/4600 SIT for singles/doubles with shared shower and 3400/5800 SIT for rooms with showers. Prices include breakfast.

Places to Eat

Pri Bartusu at Mestni trg 6 is a pleasant place for a meal and centrally located. It is open daily, except Thursday, until 10 pm. The town's largest restaurant is the *Na Dragah* at Cesta Bratstva in Enotnosti 45, opposite the Bela Krajina hotel. It's open to 10.30 pm weekdays and till midnight at the weekend. The *Jurček* pub on Partizanski trg 21 has cheap pizzas from 400 SIT.

There's a wonderful place called *Gostilna Veselič* (☎ 57 156) in Podzemelj (house No 17), not far from the camp site. It's a favourite of local people and has accommodation.

If you want to try some Bela Krajina wine but don't have time to get out into the country, head for the *Vinoteka Pinot* at Trg Svobode 28, where you can sample Pinot Blanc, Chardonnay, Rieslings and sweet Gold Muscatel. It's open daily to 11 pm.

There's a large *Mercator* supermarket in the shopping complex in Naselje Borisa Kidriča, open Monday to Thursday from 6.30 am to 8 pm, to 9 pm on Friday, to 7 pm on Saturday and from 8 am to 11 pm on Sunday.

Entertainment

There's a disco called the *Ghetto* at the shopping centre in Naselje Borisa Kidriča, open Thursday to Sunday from 8 pm to 4 am.

Getting There & Away

Destinations served by bus from Metlika include Božakovo (two or three buses a day), Črnomelj (eight), Drašiči (two on weekdays), Griblje (one), Jugorje (seven), Karlovac in Croatia (three on weekdays), Ljubljana (four), Novo Mesto (eight), Radoviča-Ostriž (four on weekdays) and Vinica (five).

Metlika is served by up to a dozen trains daily from Ljubljana (122km; 2¾ hours) via Novo Mesto and Črnomelj. Four trains a day head for Karlovac in Croatia.

AROUND METLIKA

Rosalnice

The **Three Parishes** (Tri Fare) in this village 2.5km east of Metlika is a row of three graceful little churches that have been important pilgrimage sites for seven centuries. Though they were originally built in the late 12th century by the Templars, today's churches date from the 14th and 15th centuries. The one to the north – the largest of the three – is the **Church of the Sorrowful Virgin** and has a Gothic presbytery. The church in the middle – **Ecce Homo** – has a large tower rising above its porch. The one on the south with the buttresses and another Gothic presbytery is the **Church of Our Lady of Lourdes**. Many of the gravestones in the churchyard are decorated with carved vines and grape leaves.

To the west of the churchyard entrance at house No 80 is *Gostilna Pri Treh Farah*, a pleasant place for lunch or a snack. There is actually a train station in Rosalnice south of the Three Parishes and the bus to Božakovo stops here, but it is just as easy to walk from Metlika. From the Old Town, head north-east along Navratilova pot and follow Ulica Janka Brodariča eastward for 600m, where you'll turn south. After 200m turn east and continue on straight to the churches.

Metlika Wine District

The hills to the north and north-east of Metlika are one of the most important wine-producing areas in Bela Krajina and produce such distinctive wines as Metliška Črnina, a very dark red – almost black – wine and a late-maturing sweet 'ice wine'. They are also superb areas for easy walking.

On the way to **Vinomer** and **Drašiči**, two important wine towns about four and 6km respectively from Metlika, you'll walk through *steljniki*, stands of birch trees growing among ferns in clay soil. For Slovenes, these 'forests' are the very symbol of Bela Krajina.

Drašiči is famous for its folk architecture – old peasant houses built over wine cellars. You can sample some local wines at several places, including the *Mavretič* farmhouse

(☎ 58 644) at Drašiči 2b. Call in advance as everyone might be out in the vineyards.

ČRNOMELJ
• *pop 5400* • *area code ☎068* • *postcode 8340*

The capital of Bela Krajina and its largest town, Črnomelj is situated on a promontory in a loop where the Lahinja and Dobličica rivers meet. The town is not overly endowed with important sights, but it is Bela Krajina's folk 'heart' and its Jurjevanje festival attracts hundreds of dancers and singers from around the region.

Legend has it that Črnomelj (a corruption of the words for 'black mill') got its name when a beggar, dissatisfied with the quality of the flour he'd been given, put a curse on the local miller. Perhaps the town's symbol – a smiling baker holding a pretzel – knew better than the miller the real threat of a 'beggar's curse'.

History
Like Metlika, Črnomelj (Tschernembl in German) was settled very early on, and the Roman presence is evident from the Mithraic shrine at Rožanec, about 4km north-west of the town. Črnomelj was an important market town and a bishopric as early as the 13th century, and was given a charter in 1407.

During the Turkish invasions in the 15th and 16th centuries, the town was attacked incessantly, but due to its strong fortifications and excellent hilltop lookouts at Stražnji Vrh and Doblička Gora to the west, it was never taken. In fact, trade thrived under such protection, and Črnomelj enjoyed something of a golden age in the 16th century. With the establishment of the Military March and the fort at Karlovac in Croatia in 1579, however, Črnomelj lost its military significance and prosperity. The town did not begin to develop again until 1914 with the opening of the railway between Novo Mesto and Karlovac.

Črnomelj played an important role during WWII. After Italy's surrender in 1943, the town functioned for a time as Slovenia's capital and was the centre of the Slovenian National Liberation Council and of Partisan activity.

Orientation & Information
Buses to and from Črnomelj stop on Trg Svobode in the heart of the Old Town. The train station is about 200m north of the Lahinja hotel at Kolodvorska cesta 1.

By now the *občina* (community) government may have opened a tourist office in Črnomelj Castle on Trg Svobode as planned; ring ☎ 52 040 or ☎ 51 363 (fax 51 117) for information. Otherwise seek assistance from the new town museum in Črnomelj castle or from the staff at the Lahinja hotel. Keep your eyes open for the freebie pamphlet *Europe's Sleeping Beauty: Heritage Trails through Dolenjska & Bela Krajina* produced by the Slovenian Tourist Board.

Dolenjska Banka has a branch at Trg Svobode 2 open from 8 am to 6 pm weekdays and till noon on Saturday, and another one at Kolodvorska cesta 32b, next to the post office, open weekdays only from 8 am till noon and 2 to 4.30 pm. There's an SKB Banka in the new shopping centre just off Belokranjska cesta at Zadružna cesta 16.

The post office, at Kolodvorska cesta 30, is open from 7 am to 7 pm weekdays and till noon on Saturday. Črnomelj's medical centre (☎ 51 131) is at Delavska pot 4.

Things to See & Do
Črnomelj Castle (Črnomaljski Grad), parts of which date from the late 12th century, houses government offices, a restaurant and the new **Town Museum Collection** of items and documents related to the history of Črnomelj and Bela Krajina. It is open weekdays only from 9 am to 2 pm.

The foundations of **Stonič Castle** (Stoničev Grad), to the south at Ulica Staneta Rozmana 4, go back to the 12th century as well; this is where the town's original castle stood. The **Komenda** (Commandery) of the Teutonic knights, to the south-east across Trg Svobode, is a more recent structure, originally built in 1655 with alterations made in the 19th century.

The history of the **Parish Church of St Peter**, almost opposite Stonič Castle on Ulica Staneta Rozmana, also goes back more than seven centuries, but what you'll see today

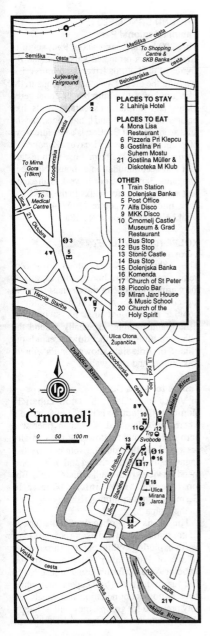

PLACES TO STAY
2 Lahinja Hotel

PLACES TO EAT
4 Mona Lisa
  Restaurant
6 Pizzeria Pri Klepcu
8 Gostilna Pri
  Suhem Mostu
21 Gostilna Müller &
  Diskoteka M Klub

OTHER
1 Train Station
3 Dolenjska Banka
5 Post Office
7 Alfa Disco
9 MKK Disco
10 Črnomelj Castle/
  Museum & Grad
  Restaurant
11 Bus Stop
12 Bus Stop
13 Stonič Castle
14 Bus Stop
15 Dolenjska Banka
16 Komenda
17 Church of St Peter
18 Piccolo Bar
19 Miran Jarc House
  & Music School
20 Church of the
  Holy Spirit

Črnomelj

is a standard-issue baroque structure with a single spire. You can still see Roman tombstones built into the walls, and the fresco on the western exterior of St Christopher, the patron saint of travellers, was meant to remind passers-by that they, too, walked with God.

The Gothic **Church of the Holy Spirit** (1487) at the southern end of Ulica Mirana Jarca is undergoing extensive renovations. The novelist and poet Miran Jarc (1900-42) was born in the house at No 3 of the same street. It is now a music school.

One of the most popular hikes in this part of Bela Krajina starts at the northern end of Ulica 21 Oktobra and carries on over hill and dale for 18km north-west to **Mirna Gora** (1047m). Accommodation is available year round at the *Planinski Dom na Mirni Gori* (☎ 56 330 or ☎ 68 573).

A popular wine road *(vinska cesta)* runs from Tanča Gora, 5km south-west of Črnomelj, northward through Doblička Gora, Stražnji Vrh and Ručetna Vas to Semič. Try some of the local Bela Krajina wines, especially the Chardonnay.

Semič (pop 753), 9km north of Črnomelj, is an attractive little town with the ruins of a castle, the 13th century **Church of St Stephen** and, to the south-east, the **source of the Krupa River**.

Special Events

Jurjevanje, a three-day festival in mid-June of music, dance and bonfires held at the fairground near the train station, is one of the most important celebrations of folklore in Slovenia. This is the time of the Zeleni Jurij (Green George), when boys dressed in greenery go from house to house singing. Another big event is the Florjanovo, the firefighters' festival on 4 May. For information about both events ring ☎ 361 000.

There are concerts in Črnomelj Castle in July and August.

Places to Stay

The *Podzemelj* camp site on the Kolpa River is about 10km north-east of Črnomelj; see the Metlika section for details.

The only hotel in Črnomelj is the nondescript

BELA KRAJINA

30-room *Lahinja* (☎ /fax 51 141) near the train station at Kolodvorska cesta 60. It charges 2200/4000 SIT for singles/doubles with shared shower and 4200/6000 SIT for rooms with private bath. Prices include breakfast. The hotel's terrace café is a pleasant enough meeting place in warm weather.

Places to Eat

The *Grad* restaurant in the castle at Trg Svobode 3 is an old-style eatery that hasn't changed a lot since the 1960s, and still serves pretty solid fare. For pizza, try the *Pri Klepcu* on Ulica Otona Župančiča next to the Alfa disco, or *Mona Lisa* on Kolodvorska cesta opposite the post office. Another option for snacks is the *Gostilna Pri Suhem Mostu* at Kolodvorska cesta 5 open daily to 11 pm.

The best place for a meal in Črnomelj is the *Gostilna Müller* south-east of the Old Town at Ločka cesta 6 and overlooking the Lahinja River. It closes on Monday.

Entertainment

Črnomelj has several popular late-night venues, including the *Alfa* disco at Ulica Otona Župančiča 6, open weekdays till midnight and on Friday and Saturday till 4 am; *Diskoteka M Klub* at the Gostilna Müller (Ločka cesta 6); and *MKK* on Trg Svobode, which attracts a younger crowd on Friday and Saturday from 10 pm to 4 am. The *Piccolo* at the start of Ulica Mirana Jarca is the most popular place in town for a quiet drink.

Getting There & Away

Departures by bus to Metlika and Vinica via Dragatuš are frequent, with up to a dozen a day. Other destinations with less frequent service include Adlešiči (three), Dolenjske Toplice (one), Griblje (one), Jesenice (one at the weekend), Ljubljana via Semič or Novo Mesto (two or three), Maribor via Žužemberk and Ljubljana (one), Novo Mesto (five), Semič (eight) and Žuniči (three).

Črnomelj is served by up to a dozen trains a day from Ljubljana (107km; 2½ hours) via Novo Mesto and Semič. Four trains daily depart Črnomelj for Karlovac in Croatia.

AROUND ČRNOMELJ
Lahinja Regional Park

This 200-hectare park, about 9km south of Črnomelj, is a protected karst area and the source of the Lahinja River, with trails crisscrossing the area. Two small swamps in the park are home to a number of endangered plants and animals, especially birds like orioles, nightingales and kingfishers, and the area around **Pusti Gradac** is a treasure trove of prehistoric finds and caves. *Župančičev Hram* (☎ 57 347), a farmhouse with restaurant and accommodation at house No 22 in Dragatuš, 3km to the north-west, is an excellent starting point for walks in the park. The park information centre (☎ 57 428) is in Veliki Nerajec at house No 18a.

KOLPA RIVER VALLEY
• *area code* ☎ 068

The 118km-long Kolpa, which forms Slovenia's south-eastern border with Croatia, is the warmest and one of the cleanest rivers in the country. As a result, it has become a popular recreational area for swimming, fishing and boating, especially around the village of **Vinica**. Farther downstream is the village of **Adlešiči**, known for its vibrant folk culture and easy walks.

Things to See & Do

In Vinica (pop 2288), the **Oton Župančič Memorial Collection** is in the house at No 9 where the celebrated Slovenian poet was born in 1878, and the tower of the partially preserved **castle** from the 16th century has an interesting Gothic chapel and offers commanding views of the valley and Croatia. But most people visit Vinica (Weinitz in German) to go swimming, fishing or boating on the Kolpa.

The ruins of **Pobrežje Castle** about 1.5km north-east of Adlešiči (pop 938) are worth exploring. While passing through the village of Purga after Adlešiči, visit the **Čebelar Adlešič** farmhouse at house No 5. The family here are beekeepers and, while there is no accommodation and meals are only prepared for groups, they will be happy to show you around. They will explain all things apiarian and give you a sample of their honey or *domača medica*, home-made mead that has a kick like a donkey.

Activities

The Kolpa camping ground (☎ 64 018) in Vinica is the best source of information for all sporting activities in the area, and there is a decent grass beach adjacent to it. Žagar, a company with an office at the camp site, rents canoes and water scooters. The ambitious, though, will look into making the rapid-water kayak run from Stari Trg, 20km upriver, to Vinica. Fishing is good, especially around Dol to the north-west, and the Kolpa is particularly rich in grayling, carp and brown trout. The camp site can sell you a daily fishing licence.

From Adlešiči, two easy hikes to nearby hills afford great views of the Kolpa, vineyards and surrounding towns. To get to **Mala Plešivica** (341m), walk south along a marked trail for about half an hour. A short distance to the west is a sinkhole with a water source called **Vodenica** which, according to local lore, was walled in by the ancient Illyrians. Steps lead down to the source, where you'll find a large stone vault.

Velika Plešivica (363m) is about an hour's walk north-west of the Adlešiči. At the foot of the hill is a chapel dedicated to Mary; during attacks by the Turks, the faithful hid in the cave below it. On top of Velika Plešivica is another church dating back to the 12th century. This one is dedicated to St Mary Magdalen.

You can rent horses from the RIM farmhouse (☎ 57 718) in Jankoviči (house No 12) for about DM20 per hour. There is a swimming area on the Kolpa just south of Pobrežje Castle.

Places to Stay

There are several camping grounds in the area. The *Kolpa* camp site (☎ 64 018) on the river at Vinica 19a covers an area of about 1.5 hectares and can accommodate up to 300 people. The charge is 720 SIT per person, and the camp site is open from April to mid-October. The *Jankovič* camp site (☎ 57

814) on the Kolpa at the southern end of Adlešiči (No 24a) is open from June to September, as is the *Dragoši* site (☎ 57 787) to the north at Dragoši 4, between Jankoviči and Griblje.

Among the accommodation in Adlešiči is the *Grabrijanovi* farmhouse (☎ 57 715) at house No 5. It has four rooms and is open all year.

Places to Eat

The *Kolpa* camp site has a full restaurant as well as a pub/snack bar open till 11 pm weekdays and till midnight at the weekend.

In the centre of Adlešiči, *Gostilna Milič* at house No 15 is one of the oldest eateries in Bela Krajina. Its drawing card is a large baker's oven that produces anything from pizzas to roast suckling pig.

Gostilna Kapušin (☎ 57 154) in Krasinec (house No 55), about 2km north of Griblje, has excellent fish dishes and is highly recommended by locals. It closes on Monday. It has accommodation in six rooms.

Things to Buy

The Čebelar Adlešič farmhouse sells honey, mead, beeswax and pollen. An interesting souvenir is a vial of propolis, the sticky substance collected from certain trees by bees to cement their hives. It is supposed to be an elixir.

The RIM farmhouse contains a gallery of locally produced leather goods as well as some hand-woven linen, painted Easter eggs and other folk craft. It also has a range of local wines (including the sweet 'ice' variety) and brandies in beautifully crafted hand-blown bottles.

Getting There & Away

Bus connections with Črnomelj, Metlika and Novo Mesto from Vinica are very good. There are also three buses a day that pass through those towns en route to Ljubljana.

There are three buses a day making the run from Črnomelj to Adlešiči, 12km to the south-east, and Žuniči, another 8km to the south-east.

Štajerska

It is difficult to characterise Štajerska (Styria in English, Steiermark in German). Though it is Slovenia's largest province, it does not have as much variety as Gorenjska and Primorska. A lot of Štajerska is field, but there are plenty of mountains too, such as the Pohorje Massif. Štajerska has more big farms than any other part of Slovenia (hops for making beer are an important crop as are wheat, potatoes and grapes for the province's excellent wines), but it also contains some of the country's largest and most historical cities and towns: Maribor, Celje and that little gem, Ptuj.

Štajerska has been at the crossroads of Slovenia for centuries and virtually everyone has 'slept here' – at least for a time: Celts, Romans, early Slavs, Habsburgs and Nazi German occupiers. In the 14th century the Counts of Celje were among the richest and most powerful feudal dynasties in central Europe and challenged the Austrian monarchy's rule for 100 years. Štajerska suffered terribly under the black leather boot of Nazism in WWII and many of its inhabitants were murdered, deported or forced to work in labour camps.

Some Slovenian guidebooks divide up Štajerska simply as the 'Maribor area' and the 'Celje area'. Here we've split it into many more sections: the Kozjansko region in the south-east; the spa town of Rogaška Slatina above Kozjansko; historic Ptuj; Maribor, Slovenia's second largest city; the Pohorje Massif; the central city of Celje; and the Upper Savinja Valley bordering Gorenjska.

The geographical centre of Slovenia is at Spodnja Slivna, north of Litija in Štajerska.

KOZJANSKO REGION
Kozjansko is a remote region along the eastern side of the Posavje Mountains and the 80km-long Sotla River, which forms the border with Croatia. It is an area of forests, rolling hills, vineyards and scattered farms.

Kozjansko's isolation made it suitable for

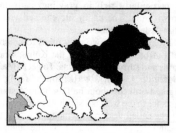

HIGHLIGHTS

- Try cycling or riding in Logarska Dolina
- Discover Ptuj, one of the oldest towns in Slovenia
- Visit Podsreda Castle in the Kozjansko region
- View the 15th century carved Misericordia statue at the church in Ptujska Gora
- Enjoy farm holidays in the central Pohorje region
- Tour the Jeruzalem-Ljutomer wine road, with frequent stops, from Ormož to Ljutomer

---

settlement during the Great Migrations. In the Middle Ages it became the frontier region between Austrian Styria and Hungarian Croatia, which accounts for the large number of castles (for example, at Podsreda, Podčetrtek, Bistrica ob Sotli) and it became Slovenia's 'stormy corner' during the peasant uprisings of the 16th century.

Today, Kozjansko remains an underdeveloped region but with much to offer travellers: spas, castles, hiking and excellent wine.

Podčetrtek
• *pop 474* • *area code ☎063* • *postcode 3254*
The town of Podčetrtek is situated less than 1km west of the Sotla River on a little bump of land extending into Croatia. Its castle, originally built in the 12th century, was an important fortification during the wars with the Hungarians 300 years later. Podčetrtek's name comes from the Slovene word for

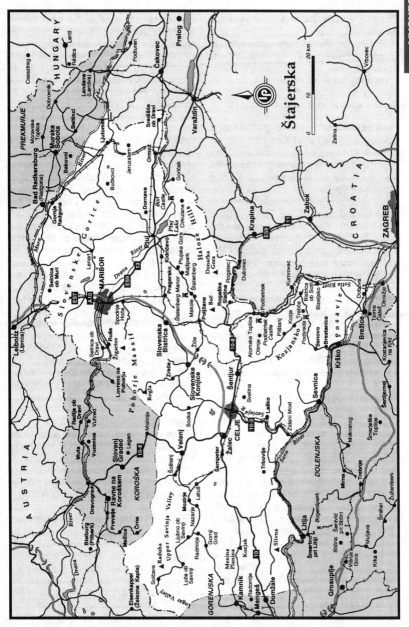

Thursday – the day the market took place and the court sat.

The castle, the Minorite monastery at Olimje and wonderful hikes into the surrounding hills are Podčetrtek's major drawcards, but most people visit the town these days to relax at the Atomske Toplice thermal spa a short distance from the centre.

Orientation The centre of Podčetrtek is actually the junction of four roads: to the west is Olimje; to the north-east, the Atomske Toplice spa complex; to the north-west, the castle; and to the south, the town of Bistrica ob Sotli.

All buses stop at the crossroads as well as at the spa and the camp site. There are three train 'stations'. For the town centre and the castle, get off at 'Podčetrtek'. 'Atomske Toplice' is good for the hotel, Atomska Vas and the Terme pool complex. 'Podčetrtek Toplice' is the correct stop for the camp site.

Information The staff at the Atomske Toplice hotel (☎ 829 000; fax 829 024) can answer questions, make bookings and change money. The post office, open from 8 am to 6 pm and till noon on Saturday, is at Trška cesta 23, about 150m north of the main junction on the left. It too has exchange facilities.

Podčetrtek Castle The giant castle on the hilltop to the north-west of town is not the original one. That was built by the Krško bishops in the 13th century but razed in the 15th century during the wars with the Hungarians. The present castle went up some time in the mid-16th century but it too was badly damaged – this time by an earthquake in 1974. The castle can be easily reached on foot by a trail from town marked 'Grad'. Along the way you'll pass the **Church of St Lawrence** with baroque frescoes inside.

Atomske Toplice Though a serious thermal spa in its own right (the 28° to 36°C water is full of magnesium and calcium and recommended for those recovering from surgery or trying to cure rheumatism), this 'health and holiday resort' about 1200m north-east of

Podčetrtek puts most of the emphasis on recreation these days with a total of eight pools, sauna, steam room, solarium and sports facilities. The indoor and outdoor pools connected by an underwater passage at the Terme complex alone cover an area of 2000 sq metres, and there's a section reserved for naturists. The only drawback to the complex is that it overlooks a rather busy road.

Olimje The **Minorite monastery** 3km west of Podčetrtek was built as a Renaissance-style castle in about 1550. When Pauline monks took over what was then called Wolimia in German about a century later, they added the baroque **Church of the Assumption**, which retains its original ceiling paintings in the presbytery and the unbelievably ornate **Chapel of St Francis Xavier**. On the ground floor of one of the four corner towers is the monastery's greatest treasure; a 17th century **pharmacy** – the third oldest in Europe – painted with religious and medical scenes. One of the best ones shows the cunning serpent tempting a rather plump Eve with Adam in attendance. The church and the pharmacy are open at 10 am, 3 pm and 4 pm daily, except Wednesday. Admission is 200/100 SIT for adults/children.

The **Ježovnik Deer Farm** (Jelenov Greben; ☎ 829 046) at house No 90 is about 500m along the main road above the monastery.

Horse Riding Some 2.5km on the road to Olimje and another 500m south is the Amon Riding Centre (☎ 829 042) at Olimje 23 with horses for both beginners and the advanced. An hour in the paddock costs 1500 SIT, riding in the open countryside costs 2500 SIT per hour and half-hour lessons are 3000 SIT.

Hiking & Cycling Some of the most rewarding hikes and bike trips in Slovenia can be made in this area and the 1:18,000-scale *Podčetrtek-Atomske Toplice Tourist Map* lists dozens of excursions for walkers, cyclists and mountain bikers. The easiest walks on marked trails take an hour or two (though the circuitous one north-east to the hilltop Church of St Emma lasts about four

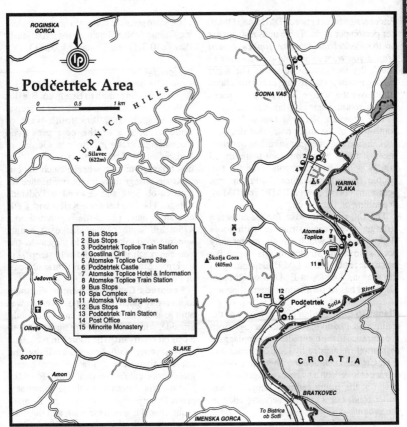

Podčetrtek Area

0   0.5   1 km

ROGINSKA GORCA

RUDNICA HILLS

Silavec (622m)

SODNA VAS

HARINA ZLAKA

Atomske Toplice

Škofja Gora (405m)

Ježovnik

Olimje

SOPOTE

Amon

SLAKE

Podčetrtek

Sotla River

CROATIA

BRATKOVEC

To Bistrica ob Sotli

IMENSKA GORCA

1 Bus Stops
2 Bus Stops
3 Podčetrtek Toplice Train Station
4 Gostilna Ciril
5 Atomske Toplice Camp Site
6 Podčetrtek Castle
7 Atomske Toplice Hotel & Information
8 Atomske Toplice Train Station
9 Bus Stops
10 Spa Complex
11 Atomska Vas Bungalows
12 Bus Stops
13 Podčetrtek Train Station
14 Post Office
15 Minorite Monastery

hours) and there are bicycle routes all the way to Kozje, Podsreda and Rogaška Slatina. The more demanding mountain bike routes head north to the forest-covered Rudnica Hills in the 600m range, but there are some easier ones down through the Olimje forest and through the vineyards of Virštanj, Selo and Imeno.

Places to Stay The *Atomske Toplice* camp site (☎ 829 000; fax 829 024 for all accommodation at the spa) is just under 1km north of the main spa complex on the edge of the Sotla River; if you've checked in and you've

got a guest card, you can take the shortcut to the spa through Croatia! The camp site covers an area of two hectares and can accommodate 500 guests. It's far enough off the main road and the train line running close by doesn't get much use. For the DM14 or DM16 (seasonal) charge, campers get to use the site's three outdoor thermal pools as well as the pools at the spa complex. The camp site is open from May to August.

The staff at the reception desk of the Atomske Toplice hotel have a list of families offering *private rooms* in Podčetrtek and Sodna Vas, 2km north of the spa complex.

Prices range from between DM15 and DM20 per person per night. The names also appear on the *Podčetrtek-Atomske Toplice Tourist Map* if you want to do your own hunting or check the facilities in advance. The other private rooms on the list are in Harina Zlaka, a hop over the narrow Sotla and a few paces inside Croatia. There is no border check here.

The *Atomska Vas* is a tourist 'village' south-west of the main hotel that does not look unlike an American suburban development; if that's what you want there are 25 houses with 136 apartments. One for two people (including kitchen, bathroom and bedroom) costs between DM70 and DM94, depending on the season.

The 150-room *Atomske Toplice* hotel is a strange, five-storey structure with roofs sloping off every which way and has recently been renovated. Singles in this expensive place start at DM90 or DM95, depending on the season, doubles at DM138 or DM146. The hotel has its own indoor thermal pool.

Places to Eat *Gostilna Ciril* at No 10 of the main road (Zdraviliška cesta) across from the entrance to the camp site is a popular grill restaurant frequented by local Slovenes and their Croatian neighbours. The vine-covered terrace is lovely on a warm evening. *Gostilna Amon* at the riding centre (Olimje 23) has better food, but it can get very crowded in the evening.

Getting There & Around Up to eight buses a day cruise by Podčetrtek and Atomske Toplice on their way to Bistrica ob Sotli and Celje. You can also reach Kozje (one bus a day), Maribor (three), Rogaška Slatina (three) and Virštanj (one).

Podčetrtek and Atomske Toplice are on the rail line linking Celje (via Stranje) with Kumrovec in Croatia. Up to six trains leave the main Podčetrtek station every day for Celje (47km; 45 minutes) with one departing for Kumrovec in Croatia via Imeno.

You can call a taxi on ☎ 829 382 or ☎ 813 924. There's also a van service available at Atomske Toplice hotel reception or directly from the driver (☎ 823 122 or mobile ☎ 0609-610 086) to points of interest in the area, including Olimje (250 SIT per person), Kozjanski Park (650 SIT) and Virštanj (400 SIT).

Podsreda

• *pop 672* • *area code ☎063* • *postcode 3257*

If you're heading south to Bizeljsko, Brežice in Posavje or to Dolenjska, be sure to stop at Podsreda about 20km south-west of Podčetrtek, site of the best preserved Romanesque castle in Slovenia. Getting to Podsreda from Podčetrtek is tricky if you don't have your own wheels: catch the bus to Kozje, change there for the one headed for Bistrica ob Sotli and descend at Podsreda village. The bus between Krško and Celje also stops here. The castle is perched on a 475m hill south of the village. A rough, winding road (5km) leads to the castle, but you can reach it via a relatively steep 2km trail from Stari Trg, less than 1km south-east of Podsreda village.

Podsreda Castle (Herberg in German) looks pretty much the way it did when it was built in about 1200. A barbican on the southern side, with walls some 3m thick, leads to a central courtyard. The rooms in the castle wings, some with beamed ceilings and ancient chandeliers, now contain a dull glassworks exhibit (crystal from Rogaška Slatina, vials from the Olimje pharmacy, green Pohorje glass), but the tiny Romanesque chapel is worth the wait, and there's a wonderful collection of prints of Štajerska's castles and monasteries taken from *Topographii Ducatus Stiria* (1681) by Georg Mattäus Vischer (1628-96). The view from the castle windows of the surrounding countryside and the pilgrimage church on Svete Gore above Bistrica ob Sotli are superb. A Musical Summer festival takes place in July and August.

The castle is open May to September every day, except Monday, from 10 am to 6 pm and to 4 pm in April and October. It is closed in winter. The entry fee is 500/350 SIT. If you've built up an appetite climbing up and down those hills, there's a small gostilna called *Pri Martinu* in Podsreda village that has a vine-covered terrace.

Kozjanski Park, some 2.5km north-east of Podsreda at Trebče, honours the Partisan effort during WWII and the pivotal role played by Josip Tito. Tito was born in the Croatian village of Kumrovec just over the border from Bistrica ob Sotli in 1892 to a Slovenian mother and a Croatian father.

ROGAŠKA SLATINA
• *pop 8586* • *area code ☎063* • *postcode 3250*
Rogaška Slatina is Slovenia's oldest and largest spa town, a veritable 'cure factory' with almost a dozen hotels, therapies ranging from 'pearl baths' to dreadful-sounding 'lymph drainage' and some 30,000 visitors a year. It's an attractive place set among scattered forests in the foothills of the Macelj range, whose two highest peaks, Boč and Donačka Gora, are visible from the centre. The border crossing into Croatia at Rogatec is 7km to the east.

Legend tells us that the magnesium-rich spring was discovered by the Muses' winged horse Pegasus when Apollo advised the steed to eschew the 'make believe and glitter' of the magic Hippocrene fountain on Mt Helicon and drink instead at Roitschocrene. And the rest is history.

Well, not really. While it's true that the spring was known in Roman times, Rogaška Slatina didn't make it onto the map until 1574 when the governor of Styria, one Wolf Ungnad, took the waters on the advice of his physician. A century later a publication entitled *Roitschocrene* examined the curative properties of the Slatina springs and claimed they had helped the ailing viceroy of Croatia. The news spread to Vienna, visitors started to arrive in droves and inns were opened. By the early 19th century Rogaška Slatina (Rohitsch-Sauerbrunn in German) was an established spa town.

Today this 'Vichy of Slovenia' is as popular as a recreational and beauty resort as it is for health treatments, with a host of sporting facilities available. But Rogaška Slatina is going through a lot of changes at present – in the process of being privatised and sold, in fact – so standards may not be as high as they once were. Hiking and cycling in the area is particularly good.

Orientation
The heart of Rogaška Slatina is the spa complex, an attractive – and architecturally important – group of neoclassical, Secessionist and Plečnik-style buildings surrounding a garden. This is called Zdraviliški trg or 'Health Resort Square'. The unattractive hotels and Terapija building to the north and north-east are late 1960s and 1970s vintage and not in keeping with the rest of the lovely square.

Rogaška Slatina's bus station is south of Zdraviliški trg on Celjska cesta, not far from the post office. The train station is about 300m farther south on Kidričeva ulica.

Information
The helpful tourist office (☎ 811 5731; fax 811 5733) at Zdraviliški trg 1 is open weekdays year round from 9 am to 5 pm and till noon on Saturday.

Banka Celje is at Kidričeva ulica 5 and is open from 8 am to 1 pm and 1.30 to 5 pm. On Saturday it closes at 11.30 am. Otherwise, try the Srečko exchange office (☎ 813 340) in the little pavilion just opposite (open weekdays from 7.30 am to 6 pm, on Saturday till noon). The post office next door to Banka Celje at Kidričeva ulica 3 has exchange facilities and is open weekdays from 8 am to 7 pm and till noon on Saturday.

Rogaška Spa
First and foremost, the mineral water (called Donat Mg here) is for drinking. The stuff is bottled and sold throughout Slovenia for both curative and refreshment purposes, but you might find the real thing here a bit too salty and metallic. The water, which also contains calcium, sulphates, lithium and bromide, is said to eliminate stress, aid digestion and stimulate weight loss. The magnesium alone, I was told, regulates 200 bodily functions (most of which I didn't know were working for me).

You can engage in a 'drinking cure' of your own at the **Pivnica**, the round, glassed-in building just beyond the gazebo-like **Tempel**, which was built in the early 19th century above the central Slatina spring. A pass, valid for three days, costs DM10, but be sure you follow the advice in the pamphlet entitled *Catch Your Drop of Health* – you wouldn't want to overdo it. The Pivnica is open daily from 7 am to 1 pm and from 3 to 7 pm.

The centre of real action at the spa is the 12-storey **Terapija** building where those pearl baths are being taken and those lymphs (shudder) are being drained. Between the Donat hotel and the Zdravilišče building with the Grand hotel there's a beauty centre as well as an indoor thermal pool (700 SIT), sauna, steam room and gym. An outside

swimming pool complex is under construction next to the modern Sonce shopping centre at Celjska cesta 7.

The former administration building at Zdravilíški trg 4, the oldest structure at the spa, houses the little **Museum of Graphic Arts** (Muzej Grafične Umetnosti), a collection of etchings and drawings from the 16th to the 19th centuries that was donated by a satisfied Swiss patient named Kurt Müller. It's open on Tuesday, Thursday and Saturday only from 10 am till noon and from 2 to 6 pm. Entrance is 200 SIT.

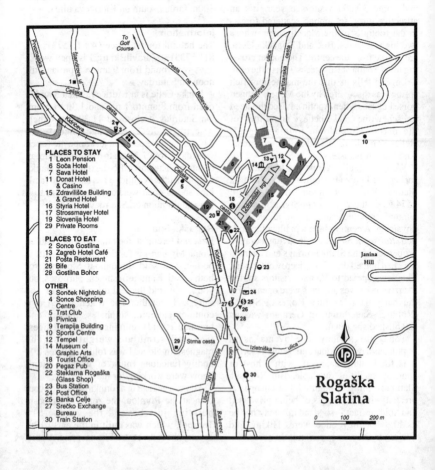

PLACES TO STAY
1 Leon Pension
6 Soča Hotel
7 Sava Hotel
11 Donat Hotel
   & Casino
15 Zdravilišče Building
   & Grand Hotel
16 Styria Hotel
17 Strossmayer Hotel
19 Slovenija Hotel
29 Private Rooms

PLACES TO EAT
2 Sonce Gostilna
13 Zagreb Hotel Café
21 Pošta Restaurant
26 Bife
28 Gostilna Bohor

OTHER
3 Sonček Nightclub
4 Sonce Shopping
   Centre
5 Trst Club
8 Pivnica
9 Terapija Building
10 Sports Centre
12 Tempel
14 Museum of
   Graphic Arts
18 Tourist Office
20 Pegaz Pub
22 Steklarna Rogaška
   (Glass Shop)
23 Bus Station
24 Post Office
25 Banka Celje
27 Srečko Exchange
   Bureau
30 Train Station

To Golf Course

Janina Hill

Rogaška Slatina

0   100   200 m

Other Activities

The sports centre (☎ 811 6386), a couple of hundred metres east of the Donat hotel and up the hill, has six outdoor and four indoor tennis courts available for hire. Prices range from DM13 to DM25 depending on whether you're outside or inside and the time of day. A racquet and balls costs DM3, and there's a squash court for hire at DM7. Bicycles cost DM6/10/13 per hour/half day/day. There's also minigolf, table tennis, archery and lawn bowling. There's a new nine-hole pitch and putt course (☎ 811 6479) open daily in summer on Cesta na Bellevue.

South of the sport centre on Janina Hill is a tiny ski slope with 3km of trails and two tows. A day pass costs about 1200 SIT; skis, poles and boots are another 800 SIT.

There are 10 marked trails which fan out from Rogaška Slatina into the surrounding hills and meadows, and the hikes can be as short as 2km or as long as 20km. No 8, for example, leads 14km to the **Church of St Florian**, on a hill north-east of the spa, and to Ložno, from where you can continue on another 4km to **Donačka Gora** (883m). If you want to do it an easier way, take a bus or train to Rogatec, then walk to Donačka Gora in about two hours. Accommodation there is at the *Rudljev Dom* (☎ 827 128 or mobile ☎ 0609-331 001) at 590m. It's open on weekends and holidays from May to the end of January.

In **Rogatec** (pop 1621), one of the oldest towns in Slovenia, there's an interesting **open-air ethnographic museum** with traditional Pannonian farmhouses on display.

The walk to **Boč** (979m) north-west of Rogaška Slatina takes about four hours, though you can drive as far as *Dom na Boču* (☎ 824 617), a mountain hut a couple of kilometres south of the peak.

Special Events

The Rogaška Musical Summer is a series of concerts held in the Crystal Hall (Kristlana Dvorana) of the Zdravilišče, where Franz Liszt tickled the ivories in 1846, and in the Pivnica. Other concerts are held *en plein air* at the Tempel pavilion. Concerts take place every two to three days at 8.30 pm from late June to late September. The tourist office or the festival information office (☎ 811 6424) on the 2nd floor of the Zdravilišče building (Zdraviliški trg 11) will provide you with a list.

Places to Stay

The tourist office can arrange *private rooms* in the town and surrounding area for between DM14 and DM25 for a single and DM22 and DM38 for a double, depending on the season (busiest time is July and August) and the room category. There's a list of private accommodation in the window if the office is closed. It includes the *Herček* family (☎ 816 603) at Strma cesta 7, a couple of hundred metres west of the train station.

With the exception of the high-priced *Sava* (☎ 811 4000; fax 811 4732) and *Donat* (☎ 811 3000; fax 811 3732), two enormous and modern hotels with over 400 rooms at the end of Zdraviliški trg, prices at most of the spa hotels are standard: from DM43 to DM59 for a single with shower and breakfast and DM67 to DM99 for a double. Full board is recommended though not mandatory.

The hotels in the Zdravilišče (☎ 811 2000; fax 811 2711) – the *Styria*, *Grand* and *Strossmayer* – have seen better days though many of their rooms look out on to the lovely park. Choose instead the 90-room *Slovenija* (☎ 811 5000; fax 811 6427) at Celjska cesta 1, which is central to everything.

If you're in a group, you might try *Leon* (☎ 815 099; fax 471 652), a pension at Šlandrova ulica 1a with apartments for five people costing DM130 to DM170, depending on the season.

Places to Eat

There's an inexpensive *bife* at Kidričeva ulica 15, open from 7 am to 7 pm weekdays and till 2 pm on Saturday. Don't expect *cordon bleu* though.

Gostilna Bohor at Kidričeva ulica 23 has fish dishes and pizzas in the 600 to 800 SIT range. The 'Farmer's Pizza' (Kmečka Pizza), with virtually everything from the barnyard on it, is good. The Bohor is open daily from 9 am to 10 or 11 pm. The *Pizzeria Vrh* in the

Sonce shopping mall at Celjska cesta 7 and open 9 am to 10 pm daily is another choice.

The *Pošta* restaurant at Zdraviliški trg 23 has a pleasant terrace for dining under the chestnut trees, but the awful synthesizer music might drive you away. If so, head for the *Sonce*, a pleasant little gostilna with fish dishes at Celjska cesta 9, open till 11 pm.

One of the most pleasant places for a drink and a snack in the spa complex is the Kavarna Zagreb in what used to be the Zagreb hotel next to the Museum of Graphic Arts at Zdraviliški trg 5. It's open daily till midnight.

Entertainment

The *HIT Casino Rogaška Slatina* (☎ 814 960) at the Donat hotel is open nightly from 8 pm till 3 am. The *Kavarna Zagreb* has ballroom dancing Thursday to Sunday to 11.30 pm while on Wednesday night the venue switches to the more elegant *Crystal Hall* in the Zdravilišče.

Most visitors to Rogaška Slatina spend their evenings in the spa's bars and cafés; the *Pegaz* pub attached to the Pošta restaurant and facing Celjska cesta is especially popular as is the *Kavarna Veking* in the Sonce shopping centre on Celjska cesta. There's also a couple of night clubs: the *Trst Club* at Celjska cesta 3 and a strip joint called the *Sonček* beneath the Sonce restaurant. The latter is open daily from 10 pm to 4 am. It also has a mini casino open from 8 pm.

Things to Buy

Rogaška Slatina is almost as celebrated for its crystal as it is for its mineral water. A showroom (Steklarna Rogaška) on the southern end of the Pošta restaurant building has a large selection of stemware, vases and bowls. It is open weekdays from 8 am to 7 pm and on Saturday till noon (also 3 to 7 pm from May to September).

Getting There & Away

Buses to Celje and Rogatec leave Rogaška Slatina at least once an hour. Otherwise, the bus service is no more than adequate. The following destinations can also be reached from Rogaška Slatina: Bistrica ob Sotli (one bus a day), Dobovec and the Croatian border (up to six a day), Gornja Radgona (one), Ljubljana (three), Ljutomer (two), Maribor (five), Ormož (two), Podčetrtek (three), Ptuj (four) and Radenci (one).

Rogaška Slatina is on the train line linking Celje via Dobovec with Zabok in Croatia, where you can change for Zagreb. Up to six trains a day go to Celje (36km; 45 minutes) with the same number heading eastward for Rogatec and Dobovec.

PTUJ

• *pop 11,300* • *area code ☎062* • *postcode 2250*

Ptuj, one of the oldest towns in Slovenia, equals Ljubljana in terms of historical importance. Ptuj's compact medieval core, with its castle, museums, monasteries and churches, can easily be seen in a day. But there are so many interesting side trips and activities in the area that you may want to base yourself here for a while.

History

Ptuj, which, when pronounced in English, sounds vaguely like someone spitting from a great distance, began life as a Roman military outpost on the right (or southern) bank of the Drava River and later grew into a civilian settlement on the opposite side called Poetovio. Unlike so many other Slovenian towns, Ptuj doesn't have to put a spade into the ground to prove its ancient origins; Tacitus mentioned it by name in his *Historiae* as having been in existence as early as 69 AD.

Poetovio, then the largest Roman township in what is now Slovenia, lay on a major road linking Pannonia and Noricum provinces. It was famous for its large stone bridge spanning the Drava near today's Dominican monastery. An aqueduct brought water down from the distant Pohorje Massif. In the 2nd and 3rd centuries, Ptuj was the centre of the Mithraic cult, a new religion with origins in Persia that was popular among Roman soldiers and slaves (see boxed text entitled Mithra & the Great Sacrifice). Several com-

Mithra & the Great Sacrifice

Mithraism, the worship of the god Mithra, originated in Persia. As Roman rule extended into Asia, the religion became extremely popular with traders, imperial slaves and mercenaries of the Roman army and spread rapidly throughout the empire in the 1st and 2nd centuries AD. The Roman emperors eventually accepted the new faith and Mithraism was the principal rival of Christianity until Constantine came to the throne in the 4th century.

Mithraism was a mysterious religion and its devotees were sworn to secrecy. What little is known of Mithra, the god of justice and social contract, has been deduced from reliefs and icons found in temples, like the ones near Črnomelj and at Ptuj in Štajerska. Most of these portray Mithra clad in a Persian-style cap and tunic sacrificing a white bull in front of Sol, the sun god. From the bull's blood and semen sprout grain, grapes and living creatures. Sol's wife Soma, the moon, begins her cycle and time is born.

Mithraism and Christianity competed strongly because of a striking similarity in many of their rituals. Both religions involved the birth of a deity on 25 December, shepherds, death and resurrection and a form of baptism. Devotees of Mithraism knelt when they worshipped and a common meal – a 'communion' of bread and water – was a regular feature of the liturgy. ■

plete temples have been unearthed in the area.

But all this came to a brutal end when the Goths attacked the town in the 5th century. They were followed by the Huns, Langobards, Franks and then the early Slavs.

The hilltop castle at Ptuj (Pettau in German) was attacked by the Magyars in the 10th century but was not taken. Ptuj received its town rights in 977 and over the next several centuries it grew rich through trade on the Drava. By the 13th century it was competing with the 'upstart' Marburg (Maribor), some 26km upriver, in both crafts and commerce. Two monastic orders – the Dominicans and the Franciscan Minorites – settled here and built important monasteries. The Hungarians attacked and occupied Ptuj for most of the 15th century though each of the half-dozen raids by the Turks were thwarted.

When the railroad reached eastern Slovenia from Vienna on its way to the coast in the mid-19th century, the age-old rivalry between Maribor and Ptuj turned one-sided – the former was on the line and the latter missed out altogether. Though Ptuj was rescued from oblivion in 1863 when the train to Budapest passed through it, the town remained essentially a provincial centre with a German majority and very little industry until WWI.

Orientation

Ptuj lies on the left bank of the swift-flowing Drava, which widens into the artificial Ptuj Lake (Ptujsko Jezero) to the south-east. To the south are the Haloze Hills, among the best wine-growing regions in Slovenia. The castle, with its irregular shape and ancient walls, dominates the town from a 300m hill to the north-west. Though there is no real centre to Ptuj, much of historical interest lies on or near Slovenski trg while Minoritski trg could be considered the gateway to the town. Terme Ptuj, a spa and recreational area across the river, is a tempting place to visit on one of Ptuj's very hot summer days.

The bus station is about 450m north-east of Minoritski trg on Osojnikova cesta. The train station is another 200m farther along the same street.

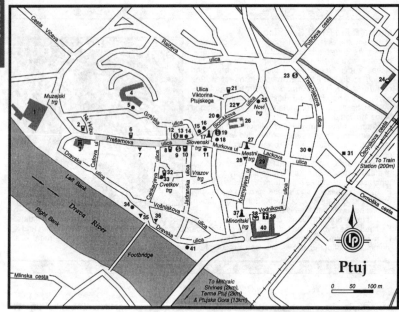

Ptuj

0   50   100 m

Information

Tourist Offices The tourist office (☎ 771 569; fax 773 534) is located at the bottom of the City Tower at Slovenski trg 14. It is open daily from 8 am to 6 pm, from 8 am till noon and 1 to 6 pm on Saturday, and from 10 am to 3 pm on Sunday. It can organise guided tours for 500 SIT per person (minimum five people). Anyone planning to spend more than a day or two in Ptuj should pick up a copy of *Ptuj: A Guide to the Town* (2000 SIT) from the tourist office. It contains a wealth of information on Ptuj and neighbouring areas. The Ptuj Alpine Society (☎ 777 151) at Prešernova ulica 27 has information about hiking in the area, but it is only open on Tuesday and Friday from 4 to 6 pm.

Money Nova Ljubljanska Banka has a branch next to the Mitra hotel at Prešernova ulica 6. It is open on weekdays from 8.30 am till noon and from 2.30 to 5 pm (on Saturday 8 to 11 am). A Banka, in the lovely Late

Gothic House at Prešernova ulica 1, is open weekdays from 8 am till noon and 2.30 to 5 pm and till 11 am on Saturday. SKB Banka, which has a Cirrus-linked ATM at Trstenjakova ulica 2, keeps the same hours as A Banka but closes on Saturday.

Post & Communications The main post office is at Minoritski trg 1a. It is open from 7 am to 7m (to 1 pm on Saturday) and has exchange facilities.

Ptuj Castle

Parts of the castle complex date back to the first half of the 12th century (notably the tower on the western edge of the hill), but what you see here is an agglomeration of styles from the 14th to the 18th centuries put into place by one aristocratic owner after another. The castle houses the collection of the **Ptuj Regional Museum** on its three arcaded floors, but a trip is worth it for the views alone.

As you enter the castle, you can't help but

PLACES TO STAY		4	Ptuj Castle & Museum	21	Pav Nightclub
13	Mitra Hotel	5	Peruzzi Portal	23	SKB Banka
31	Super Li Hotel	6	Bistro Julija	24	Bus Station
		8	Sima & Orfej Cafés	25	Market
PLACES TO EAT		9	Late Gothic House &	26	Church of St George
7	Slonček Pizzeria		A Banka	27	St Florian Column
22	Pivnica Zlatorog	10	Bistro Piramida	29	Town Hall
28	Evropa Café	11	Teater III	30	Vinska Klet
35	Ribič Restaurant	12	Nova Ljubljanska		(Wine Cellar)
36	Bambusov Gozd		Banka	32	Metulj Disco
	Chinese Restaurant	14	Romanesque House	33	Kino Ptuj (Cinema)
		15	Ljutomer House	34	Anka Travel Agency
OTHER		16	Former Town Hall	37	Plague Pillar
1	Dominican	17	Orpheus Monument	38	Post Office
	Monastery &	18	Ptuj Theatre	39	Church of Sts Peter
	Museum	19	City Tower &		& Paul
2	Amadeus Pub		Tourist Office	40	Minorite Monastery
3	Little Castle	20	Provost's House	41	Drava Tower & Gallery

notice the red-marble **tombstone of Frederick V**, the last lord of Ptuj who died in 1438. It was brought here from the Dominican monastery. The ground floor castle contains a fascinating exhibition of musical instruments from the 17th to 19th centuries – flutes, horns, drums, lutes, violas, harps, clavichords etc. As you approach each case, a tape plays the music the instruments make.

The 1st floor is given over to period rooms, each with its own style, as well as an impressive **Knights' Hall**. The rooms are treasure troves of tapestries, painted wall canvases (many from Dornava Castle, 8km to the north-east of Ptuj), portraits, weapons and furniture left by the castle's last occupants, the Herbertsteins. You'll probably notice a coat of arms containing three buckles and the motto 'Grip Fast' in English. It belonged to the Leslies, a Scottish-Austrian family who owned the castle from 1656 to 1802. The buckles are said to have been added to the family escutcheon when one of their number saved a countess who had fallen into a well by pulling her up with belts buckled together.

Among some of the more interesting bits and pieces are the Chinoiserie decorations and wallpaper (whose figures have curious Caucasian features), the beautiful porcelain stoves fuelled through pipes from the outside corridors and the large collection of clocks, including an astronomical one from the 18th century, in the Music Room.

The 2nd floor is a gallery of Gothic statues and oil paintings from the 16th to the 19th centuries. Have a look at the scene of Ptuj in winter by Franc Jožef Fellner (1721-70). There is also one from the early 19th century of the Church of St George, marred by graffiti in German. Two fine statues – one of St Catherine (with a wheel) and the other of St Barbara (with a tower) – carved from sandstone in about 1410 in the 'soft' Gothic style, are among the museum's most priceless possessions. Check the faces of the guards torturing Christ in the crucifixion scene nearby; they really seem to be enjoying themselves.

The museum also has the largest collection of **Turkerie portraits** in Europe. They are paintings of Turkish aristocrats, generals and courtiers commissioned by Count Johann Herbertstein in 1665 and painted in a western style. Partly because of these paintings, Turkish dress became all the rage for a time in the 18th century.

The museum is open from 9 am to 4 pm in winter and to 6 pm in summer. Entry is 450/200 SIT (130/70 SIT extra with guide), and the ticket includes admission to the former Dominican monastery.

Walking Tour

Ptuj's Gothic centre, with its Renaissance and baroque additions, is a joy to explore on foot. It's unlikely that you'll get lost in this small place but if you do, explanatory signs in four languages (including English) will tell you where you are. The arched spans that look like little bridges above some of the narrow streets are to support the older buildings.

Start a walking tour of Ptuj in **Minoritski trg**, which has a 17th century **plague pillar** of Mary and the Infant Jesus that was restored in 1994. This is the site of the **Minorite monastery** that was built in the 13th century. Because the Minorites dedicated themselves to teaching, the order was not dissolved under the Habsburg edict of the late 18th century and it has continued to function in Ptuj for more than seven centuries.

The **Church of Sts Peter and Paul**, on the northern side of the monastery's inner courtyard, was one of the most beautiful examples of early Gothic architecture in Slovenia until it was reduced to rubble by Allied bombing in January 1945. Only the presbytery, with a medieval altar and striking modern stained-glass windows, has been restored.

The arcaded monastery, which dates from the second half of the 17th century, has two things worth seeing. The **summer refectory** on the 1st floor, which somehow managed to escape wartime destruction and served as the chapel until recently, contains beautiful 17th century stucco work and a dozen ceiling paintings of Sts Peter (north side) and Paul (south side). One panel depicts the martyrdom of poor St Stephen, who was stoned to death by a group of pagans including Saul, who was later baptised as Paul. The monastery also contains a rich, 5000-volume **library** of important manuscripts including part of a 10th century codex used to cover a prayer book around 1590 and an original copy of the New Testament (1561) translated by Primož Trubar. It is one of the most valuable documents of the Slovenian patrimony. The monastery doesn't have regular opening hours, but you can ring the bell to the right of the church entrance and ask one of the brothers in residence if you can visit.

If you walk northward on Krempljeva ulica, you'll soon reach Mestni trg, the rectangular square once called Florianplatz in honour of the **St Florian Column** (1745) in the centre. To the east at No 1 is the neo-Gothic **town hall** (1907), designed by an architect from Graz and the most beautiful 'new' building in Ptuj.

Murkova ulica, with some interesting old houses, leads westward to **Slovenski trg**, the heart of old Ptuj. This funnel-shaped square, which is higher than Mestni trg, contains the lion's share of Ptuj's most beautiful buildings.

The most obvious structure here is the **City Tower** (Mestni Stolp), built in the 16th century as a belfry and later turned into a watch tower. Roman tombstones and sacrificial altars from Poetovio were incorporated into the tower's exterior in 1830; you can still make out reliefs of Medusa's head, dolphins and a man on horseback.

In front of the City Tower stands the 5m **Orpheus Monument**, a Roman tombstone from the 2nd century with scenes from the Orpheus myth. It was used as a pillory in the Middle Ages; the guilty were shackled to iron rings attached to the holes at the base.

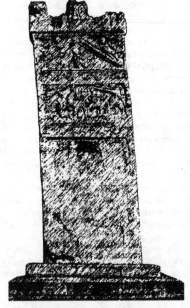

The 2nd century Orpheus Monument was used as a pillory in the Middle Ages.

The attractive building on the right (No 13) is the **Ptuj Theatre**, originally built in 1786. Until 1918 it staged plays only in German. The theatre was well known for its avant-garde productions in the late 1930s.

Behind the City Tower is the **Parish Church of St George**, which reveals a melange of styles from the Romanesque to neo-Gothic. The church contains some lovely 15th century choir chairs decorated with animals, a carved relief of the Epiphany dating from 1515 and frescoes in the middle of the south aisle, a 15th century stone Pietà and, in the baptismal chapel at the start of the south aisle, the so-called **Konrad Laib altar**, a three-winged altar painting from 1460 (presently being restored). In the north aisle, under glass, is a carved 15th century statue of St George slaying the dragon.

On the northern side of Slovenski trg are several interesting buildings including the 16th century **Provost's House** with a rococo facade at No 10, the baroque **former town hall** at No 6 and, next door at No 5, **Ljutomer House**, whose Mediterranean-style loge was built in 1565 by Italian workers who had come to Ptuj to fortify it against the Turks.

The shortest way to the castle from here is to follow narrow Grajska ulica, which leads to a covered wooden stairway and the Renaissance **Peruzzi Portal**. But take time to explore pedestrian **Prešernova ulica**, the town's market in the Middle Ages.

The **Late Gothic House**, dating from about 1400, at No 1 has an unusual projection held up by a black man's head. Opposite at No 4 is the sombre **Romanesque House**, the oldest building in Ptuj. The yellow pile at Prešernova ulica 35 is the **Little Castle** (Mali Grad), home to the Salzburg bishops and a number of aristocratic families over the centuries and recently restored (but marred by a new tile roof). The building to the west housed a **prison** from the 19th century. During WWII many Partisans, including the local hero Jože Lacko, were tortured and died here. From the western end of Prešernova ulica you can follow the gravel path eastward to the castle.

Just past the small park at Muzejski trg 1 is the former **Dominican monastery**, which now contains the Ptuj Regional Museum's **archaeological collection**. The monastery was built in 1226 but abandoned in the late 18th century when Habsburg Emperor Joseph II dissolved all religious orders. The beautiful eastern wing has a cross-ribbed Romanesque window and Gothic cloisters with 15th century frescoes of Dominican monks in their black and white garb. There's also a refectory with 18th century stucco work, a chapter hall and a large Roman coin collection. But the main reason for coming is to see the Roman tombstones, altars and wonderful mosaics unearthed in Ptuj and at the **Mithraic shrines** at Zgornji Breg and Spodnja Hajdina, a couple of kilometres west of town. A guide will explain the significance of all the stones and help bring them to life. Apart from Mithra himself and the Sol deity that looks not unlike the American Statue of Liberty, there are the *nutrices*, the wet nurses who nourished the offspring of Roman aristocrats, and ancient Jewish tombstones. The Dominican monastery collection is open from mid-April to November from 10 am to 4 pm on weekdays and to 5 pm on Saturday and Sunday. Entry is 200/100 SIT (130/70 SIT extra with a guide).

You can return to Minoritski trg by following Dravska ulica to the round **Drava Tower** (Dravski Stolp), a Renaissance water tower built by Italian workers for defence against the Turks in 1551. It now houses a gallery featuring the works of the graphic artist France Mihelič. It is open Tuesday to Friday from 4 to 7 pm only.

Activities

Terme Ptuj (☎ 771 721), a thermal spa about 2km west of town on the right (or south) bank of the Drava at Pot v Toplice 9, is primarily a recreational centre with two outdoor swimming pools, three indoor thermal ones (water temperature is 32° to 34°C) and eight tennis courts. A full-day entrance to the pools is 850/550 SIT for adults/children, 750/500 SIT in the afternoon and 500/400 SIT in the evening. You can also rent bicycles here.

Kurent: Carnival Time in Ptuj

Ptuj – and many towns on the surrounding plain and in the hills – mark Shrovetide by Kurentovanje, a rite of spring and fertility that may date back to the time of the early Slavs. Such celebrations are not unique to Slovenia; they still take place at Mohács in Hungary and in Serbia and Bulgaria. But the Kurentovanje is among the most extravagant of these celebrations.

The main character of the rite is Kurent, god of unrestrained pleasure and hedonism – a 'Slovenian Dionysus'. The Kurents (there are many groups of them) are dressed in sheepskins with cowbells dangling from their belts. On their heads they wear huge furry caps decorated with feathers, sticks or horns and coloured streamers. The leather face masks have eyeholes outlined in red, trunk-like noses and enormous red tongues that hang down to the chest.

The Kurents move from house to house in procession scaring off evil spirits with their bells and wooden clubs topped with hedgehog spines. A devil, *(hudič)*, covered in a net to catch souls, leads each group. Young girls present the Kurents with handkerchiefs (which they then fasten to their belts), and people smash little clay pots at their feet for luck and good health. ■

Licences for river fishing are available from the Anka travel agency (☎ 776 020) at Dravska ulica 10 near the Ribič restaurant.

Special Events

Kurentovanje, a rite of spring celebrated for 10 days leading up to Shrove Tuesday, is the most popular and best known folklore event in Slovenia. Ask the tourist office for details about this year's festivities.

There is a September series of concerts in Ptuj called Glasbeni September. Venues include the Minorite monastery refectory, the Church of St George, the Knights' Hall in Ptuj Castle and Ptuj Theatre.

Three traditional fairs taking place in Novi trg in Ptuj are those dedicated to St George (Jurij) in late April, St Oswald (Ožbalt) in early August, and St Catherine (Katarina) in late November.

Places to Stay

The crowded camp site at the *Terme Ptuj* spa (☎ 771 721) charges between 1250 and 1500 SIT per person and is open from May to September. Prices include use of the pools and other recreational facilities. Terme Ptuj also has *bungalows* available (5225 to 6270 SIT for singles, 7600 to 9120 SIT for

doubles) as well as modern *apartments* in larger villas accommodating two people from 6400 SIT.

The tourist office can arrange *private rooms*, but they're not cheap (about 3000 SIT per person) and most are on the other side of the Drava near Terme Ptuj. *Pri Tonetu* (☎ 771 586), at Zadružni trg 13 on the way to the spa, charges about the same price.

The 22-room *Super Li* (☎ 779 821; fax 779 823) at Trstenjakova ulica 13 is the cheaper of Ptuj's two hotels: bright and airy singles with shower and breakfast are 5200 SIT and doubles are 7300 SIT. The Super Li is not a bad place, but the disco and large pub below may make sleep just a tad difficult.

The 21-room *Mitra* hotel (☎ 771 281; fax 771 111) at Prešernova ulica 6 is one of provincial Slovenia's more interesting hotels – complete with Mithraic artefacts. Though the guestrooms are fairly ordinary, they are certainly large. You can't beat the location but the prices are high: 7000 SIT for a single with shower and breakfast, 9000 SIT for a double and 12,000 SIT for a suite.

Places to Eat

The *Evropa* is a small restaurant-cum-café in an 18th century town house at Mestni trg 2.

It's open daily from 7 am to 9 pm and on Sunday from 9 am to 8 pm.

Slonček, behind an interesting marble fountain at Prešernova ulica 19, serves pizza and some meatless dishes every day from 9 am to 10 pm. *Pivnica Zlatorog* at Slomškova ulica 20 also has pizza and is open weekdays from 9 am to 10 pm and on Sunday from noon.

Grajska Kavarna in the castle courtyard serves drinks and snacks weekdays from 9 am to 9 pm and at weekends till 11 pm.

One of the best restaurants in Ptuj, with excellent food, service and location, is the *Ribič* facing the river at Dravska ulica 9. The speciality here is fish – especially boiled or fried trout (1225 SIT) – and their mushroom and seafood soups (350 SIT) are exceptional. If the oil on the salad tastes odd (nutty, a little smoky) that's because it's pumpkin-seed oil (bučno olje), a speciality of the Drava Plain region and available in most shops. Ribič, which has a group playing Slovenian folk music some nights, is open from 11 am to 11 pm (till 10 pm on Sunday).

Ptuj now boasts a Chinese restaurant, the *Bambusov Gozd* (Bamboo Grove) almost opposite the Ribič at Dravska ulica 7. Starters are 250 to 450 SIT, main meat dishes like crispy duck cost 1290 SIT, vegetable ones about 790 SIT.

Vinska Klet (☎ 772 821) at Trstenjakova ulica 10 is the place to go if you want to buy or taste (1300 SIT for up to 10 types) wine – it's one of the largest cellars in Slovenia. If you can't make it to the wine-growing regions to the south or east, try some Haloze Chardonnay, Šipon or Laški Rizling here. The cellar also has stocks of Zlata Trta, the 'Golden Vine' sweet wine dating from 1917. It is the oldest vintage in Slovenia. The 'Wine Cellar' is open weekdays from 7 am to 7 pm and on Saturday till noon.

There's a *market* selling fruit, vegetables and more on Novi trg. It's open daily from very early in the morning to about 3 pm.

Entertainment
Teater III at Slovenski trg 1 opposite the City Tower stages avant-garde productions (eg *Psiha* by Emil Filipčič) most weekdays in season at 8 pm. The *Kino Ptuj* (☎ 773 326) in Cvetkov trg has a couple of screenings a day, usually at 6 and 8 pm.

Prešernova ulica has several decent pubs and cafés, including *Sima Kava Bar* at No 3, *Orfej* at No 5, *Bistro Julija* at No 20 and, opposite the Little Castle, *Amadeus* at No 36. The large pub at the *Super Li* hotel is open daily from 9 am till midnight. Another popular watering hole is *Bistro Piramida* at the northern end of Jadranska ulica, open from 9 pm till late.

There's a disco called *Metulj* at Cvetkov trg, which can be reached by walking south along Cankarjeva ulica from Prešernova ulica. It's open on Friday and Saturday from 10 pm to 3 am. The *Pav* at Ulica Viktorina Ptujskega 4 is a nightclub for a more sleazy crowd, with a 'nude show' on Friday at 10 pm.

Getting There & Away
Bus Buses are frequent from Ptuj to Cirkulane, Kidričevo, Maribor, Majšperk, Ormož and Poljčane, but count on only about a half dozen on Saturday and far fewer on Sunday.

Other destinations and their daily frequencies include Apače (11), Celje (one via Maribor, three via Pragersko, two via Rogaška Slatina), Ljubljana (one via Maribor, two via Pragersko or two via Rogaška Slatina), Ljutomer (six), Murska Sobota (one), Pragersko (two), Rogaška Slatina via Rogatec (three), Slovenska Bistrica (five) and Vurberk (two).

Two buses a week (on Monday and Friday) head for Graz in Austria. For destinations in Croatia, count on six buses a day to Varaždin and three to Zagreb (via Varaždin or Krapina).

Train You can reach Ptuj up to a dozen times a day by train from Ljubljana (155km; three hours) via Zidani Most and Pragersko. Up to nine trains go to Maribor (37km; one hour). Four trains a day head for Murska Sobota via Ormož.

Getting Around
Book a taxi on ☎ 786 171.

AROUND PTUJ

Ptujska Gora

• *pop 1136* • *area code* ☎*062* • *postcode 2323*

The pilgrimage **Church of the Virgin Mary** in this village some 13km south-west of Ptuj, contains one of the most treasured objects in Slovenia – a 15th century carved **Misericordia** of the Virgin Mary and the Child Jesus sheltering both rich and poor under an enormous cloak held up by seven angels. The carving, which is above the main altar, is as important an historic document as it is a work of art. Among the lifelike faces of the faithful are the Counts of Celje (Frederick II and the three Hermans). It rivals the altar carving (1489) by Wit Stwosz in Kraków's Church of Mary for its grace and beauty.

The church itself, built in the late 14th century, is the finest example of a three-nave Gothic church in Slovenia. Among some of the other treasures inside is a small wooden **statue of St James** on one of the pillars on the south aisle, **15th century frescoes** of Christ's Passion, under the porch and to the right as you enter, medieval paintings of saints, including St Nicholas and St Dorothy. The abstract stained glass windows date from this century. Look behind the modern tabernacle in the chapel to the right of the main altar for frescoes of St Peter and St Michael the Archangel.

The church, open daily in summer from 7 am to 7 pm and to 3 pm in winter, perches atop Black Hill (Črna Gora), an easy 10-minute walk from where the bus headed for Majšperk will let you off. The Galerija Paleta, to the north of the church at house No 38, has some interesting artwork and souvenirs for sale, and there's a small eatery called *Gostišče Dragica* at No 37.

Štatenberg

• *pop 173* • *area code* ☎*062* • *postcode 2322*

About 9km south-west of Ptujska Gora in the Dravinja Valley is Štatenberg, site of an 18th century baroque manor house. The manor has impressive stucco work, frescoes and rooms full of antique (if moth-eaten) furniture and tapestries, but the main reason for coming is to spend the night in a castle – on a budget.

Štatenberg was built in the first half of the 18th century not far from the site of another castle that had been occupied and razed by Slovenian and Croatian peasants under Matija Gubec in 1573. It was designed by an Italian architect for the Attems family.

The manor consists of a landscaped central courtyard enclosed by two side wings and the central building. On the ground floor of the latter is an arcaded hall with baroque stucco work; seven residential rooms and the lovely **Great Hall** are on the 1st floor. The Great Hall has a frescoed ceiling with mythological scenes as well as statues of Greek and Roman gods in the corners. The other rooms contain carved armoires, rugs, 19th century portraits and a bed in which Empress Maria Theresa once slept. Štatenberg is open Friday, Saturday and Sunday from 11 am till dark. The entrance fee is 200/150 SIT for adults/children.

The *guestrooms* (☎ 818 916 or ☎ 830 308) are in the west wing and cost DM20 per person or DM100 for an apartment accommodating nine people. There's also a small restaurant in the main building. The surrounding park has four small fishing ponds, and there are a couple of other restaurants in the area. The one on the main road across from the entrance to the castle is called *Gostilna Marof*. The other, *Gostilna Lesjak Karel*, is at house No 36 in Makole, a village on the Dravinja River about 1.5km to the south-west.

Štatenberg can be reached on the Poljčane bus from Ptuj.

Wine Routes

Ptuj is within easy striking distance of two important wine-growing areas: the **Haloze** district and the **Jeruzalem-Ljutomer** district. They are accessible on foot, by car and, best of all, by bike.

The Haloze Hills extend for about 30km from Makole south-west of Ptuj to Goričak on the border with Croatia. The footpath taking in this land of gentle hills, vines, corn and sunflowers is called the Haloze Trail (Haloška Pot) and is accessible from near Štatenberg Manor. But it's much easier to pick up the trail near **Borl Castle**, 11km south-east of Ptuj.

Borl was originally built in the 13th century and fell to the Hungarians until the late 15th century. It changed ownership again and again and was used as a detention centre both by the Nazis and then the communists after the war. It was even a hotel and restaurant for a while. Today there's not much here but an old baroque altar in a disused church and a few Kurent masks scattered about though concerts are sometimes held in the courtyard in summer. There's a small restaurant near the entrance where you can try the local Haložan wine, and the surrounding parkland (with an unofficial camping ground) is lovely.

A road called the **Wind Rattle Route** (after the unusual wind-powered noise-makers called *klopotci* which are used to scare the crows away from the vines) follows a 50km course from Ptujska Gora to Zavrč via Dolena, Gorca and the fine town of Cirkulane. Ask the tourist office in Ptuj for a map.

The Jeruzalem-Ljutomer wine road begins at Ormož and continues for 18km north to Ljutomer (pop 3700), the main seat in the area, via the hilltop village of Jeruzalem. There are quite a few cellars and small restaurants along the way, especially around Ivanjkovci, where you can sample any of the region's local whites. They include the *Jože Kupljen* cellar (☎ 714 001) in Veličane (house No 63).

MARIBOR

• *pop 134,000* • *area code ☎062* • *postcode 2000*
Though it is the nation's second largest city, Maribor counts less than half the population of Ljubljana and, frankly, feels more like a large provincial town than north-east Slovenia's economic, communications and cultural centre. It has the country's only university outside the capital and boasts an important museum, a number of galleries, a theatre built in 1786 and an attractive Old Town along the Drava River. Maribor is also the gateway to the Maribor Pohorje, a hilly recreational area to the south-west, and the Slovenske Gorice wine-growing region to the north and the east.

History
Maribor has been inhabited continuously since the Neolithic period, but it did not rise to prominence until the Middle Ages when a fortress called Marchburg was built on Piramida, a hill north of the present-day city, to protect the Drava Valley from the Magyar invasions. The settlement that later developed along the river was given town status in 1254. It grew wealthy through the timber and wine trade, financed to a large degree by the town's Jewish community, and the waterfront landing (Pristan) in the Lent district became one of the busiest ports in the country.

The town was fortified with walls in the 14th century to protect it first against the Hungarians and then the Turks; four defence towers still stand along the Drava. Though its fortunes declined somewhat in later centuries – the Jews were expelled from the town in the late 1400s and it competed in commerce with Ptuj – most of the town's important buildings were erected then.

The tide turned in 1846 when the railroad from Vienna reached here – the first town in Slovenia to have train connections with the imperial capital – and by 1861 three main routes linking Vienna, Budapest and Trieste intersected at Pragersko to the south. The town, by then known as Maribor, became the centre of Slovene-speaking Styria, a kind of counter-balance to German Graz in Austria, and began to industrialise. The bishopric was moved from Šent Andraž (now St Andrä near Wolfsberg in Austria) to Maribor in 1859, and two important Slovenian newspapers began publication.

Maribor remained Slovenian within the Kingdom of Serbs, Croats and Slovenes after WWI, due to the efforts of General Rudolf Maister, and it continued to develop in the 1920s and 1930s. But the air raids during WWII devastated the city and by 1945 two thirds of it lay in ruin. New areas were opened up on the right bank of the Drava, and in the 1950s Maribor was one of Slovenia's most 'proletarian' cities. Much of that is still evident from the factories and housing estates south of the Old Town.

Orientation

Maribor sits on both sides of the Drava River but the Lent waterfront area and other parts of the Old Town are on the left bank. There are several main squares, with funnel-shaped Grajski trg the historical centre. The Maribor Pohorje lies to the south-west.

Maribor's enormous postmodern bus station – a 1980s urban 'prestige project' if there ever was one and now somewhat decayed – is east of Grajski trg on Mlinska ulica. The train station is about 400m north on Partizanska cesta. Maribor airport (☎ 691 541) at Skoke, about 8km south-east of the Old Town, is one of only three international ones in the country, but there are no scheduled flights.

Information

Tourist Office The Maribor Tourist Information Centre (MATIC; Glvani trg 13; ☎ 211 262; fax 25 271), one of the few real tourist offices in Slovenia, doesn't offer much in the way of information – it doesn't even post its hours (usually 9 am to 6 pm weekdays, till noon on Saturday). It does, however, publish a monthly calendar of events (*Koledar Prireditev/Veranstaltungskalender*) in Slovene and German only.

Money A Banka has a branch at Glavni trg 17 in the passageway connecting Gosposka ulica with Vetrinjska ulica. It is open from 8 am till noon and 2 to 5 pm on weekdays and to 11 am on Saturday. There's an SKB Banka with a Cirrus-linked ATM at Gosposka ulica 10 next to the Kvik supermarket. To the right of McDonald's on Grajski trg and down a small passageway, the Enka exchange counter is open from 8 am to 6 pm on weekdays and till noon on Saturday. If you arrive in town without local currency on a Sunday, go to the Slovenijaturist office at the train station.

Post & Communications The main post office is near the train station at Partizanska cesta 54 and is open 24 hours a day seven days a week. A more convenient branch is at Slomškov trg 10. It's open from 7 am to 8 pm on weekdays and till 1 pm on Saturday.

Travel Agencies Slovenijaturist (☎ 28 990) has an office next to the Orel hotel at Grajski trg 3a open from 9 am to 5 pm weekdays and on Saturday morning till noon. Its train station branch (☎ 211 222), however, is open every day from 6 am till 8.30 pm. Kompas (☎ 26 751), on the east side of Maribor Castle at Trg Svobode 1, and Globtour (☎ 25 582) at the Slavija hotel (entrance on Sodna ulica) keep the same hours: 8 am to 5 pm on weekdays and till noon on Saturday.

Bookshop Mladinska Knjiga at Gosposka ulica 28 sells regional and city maps and a few guides in English. It also has the 1:50,000-scale map *Pohorje* from GZS, which includes the Maribor Pohorje. MK is open weekdays from 9 am to 6 pm and on Saturday from 8 am till noon.

Walking Tour

Start a walking tour of Maribor in **Grajski trg**, the centre of the Old Town and closed to traffic. In the middle of the square stands the 17th century **St Florian Column**, dedicated to the patron of fire-fighting. **Maribor Castle**, a successor to the Piramida fortress of medieval times, is on the north-east corner at Grajska ulica 2.

Along with the exhibits of the **Maribor Regional Museum** (Pokrajinski Muzej Maribor), the 15th century castle contains a **Festival Hall** with a remarkably disproportionate ceiling painting, a **baroque chapel** and a magnificent **rococo staircase** near the exit. The staircase, with its pink walls, stucco work and figures arrayed on the bannisters, is worth a visit in itself.

The museum's collection, one of the richest in Slovenia, is arranged on two levels. On the ground floor there are archaeological, ethnographic and clothing exhibits with 19th century beehive panels painted with Biblical scenes from the Mislinja and Drava valleys, models of Štajerska-style hayracks, Kurent costumes and wax votives from the area around Ptuj, and heaps about the wine industry.

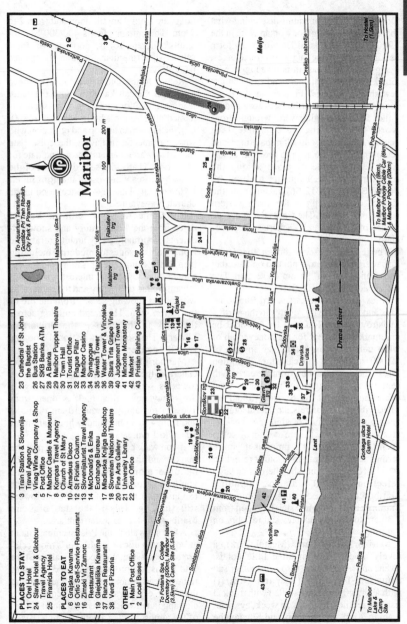

Maribor

0   100   200 m

PLACES TO STAY
11 Orel Hotel
24 Slavija Hotel & Globtour
   Travel Agency
25 Piramida Hotel

PLACES TO EAT
6 Grajski Kavarna
15 Orlic Self-Service Restaurant
16 Zimski Vrt Zamorc
   Restaurant
19 Glejdališka Kavarna
37 Ranca Restaurant
38 Verdi Pizzeria

OTHER
1 Main Post Office
2 Local Buses
3 Train Station & Slovenija
   Travel Agency
4 Vinag Wine Company & Shop
5 Post Office
7 Maribor Castle & Museum
8 Kompas Travel Agency
9 Church of St Mary
10 Amadeus Disco
12 St Florian Column
13 Slovenijaturist Travel Agency
14 McDonald's & Enka
   Exchange Bureau
17 Mladinska Knjiga Bookshop
18 Slovenian National Theatre
20 Fine Arts Gallery
21 University Library
22 Post Office
23 Cathedral of St John
   the Baptist
26 Bus Station
27 SKB Banka ATM
28 A Banka
29 Maribor Puppet Theatre
30 Town Hall
31 Tourist Office
32 Plague Pillar
33 Maribor Casino
34 Synagogue
35 Jewish Tower
36 Water Tower & Vinoteka
39 Stara Trta Grape Vine
40 Judgement Tower
41 Minorite Monastery
42 Market
43 Pristan Bathing Complex

To Aquarium Terrarium,
Gostišče Pri Treh Ribnikih,
City Park & Piramida

To Fontana Spa, College
Dormitory (500m), Maribor Island
(3.5km) & Camp Site (5.5km)

To Maribor
Lake &
Camp
Site

To Maribor Airport (8km),
Maribor Pohorje Cable Car (8km)
& Maribor Pohorje (20km)

To Hostel
(1.5km)

Don't miss the mannequins displaying what the well dressed Maribor woman wore in the 19th century or Marshal Tito's dress uniform as commander of the Yugoslav armed forces.

Upstairs you'll pass through a loggia with Greek and Roman statuary and 14th century Jewish gravestones. Farther on there are rooms devoted to Maribor's history and its guilds and crafts (glassware, wrought ironwork, clockmaking), a complete 18th century pharmacy and altar paintings and sculptures from the 15th to the 18th centuries. Taking pride of place among the sculptures are the exquisite **statues by Jožef Straub** (1712-56) taken from the Church of St Joseph in the south-western suburb of Studenci. The works depicting the Angel of Grapes and Zacharias are especially fine.

The regional museum is open Tuesday to Friday from 10 am to 5 pm and on Saturday and Sunday from 10 am to 2 pm. The entrance fee is 300/100 SIT.

A few steps to the east is **Trg Svobode**. This and the two leafy squares to the north – Maistrov trg and Rakušev trg – would be unremarkable except for the honeycomb of **wine cellars** below that cover an area of 20,000 sq metres and can store 7 million litres. The cellars, dating from the early 19th century, are managed by the Vinag wine export company at Trg Svobode 3 and are filled with old oak barrels, steel fermentation tanks and an 'archive' of vintage wine – all at a constant 15°C. There's a small cellar open to the public till 7 pm, but if you're serious about wine, ask for a tour at reception (☎ 212 161). The wine shop here has a large selection of local vintages, including Mariborčan, Laški Rizling, Chardonnay, Traminer and Gold Muscatel. It is open from 7.30 am to 7 pm weekdays and to 2 pm on Saturday.

Maribor's **City Park** (Mestni Park), a lovely arboretum with three little ponds, swans and a bandstand, also has a rather sad **Aquarium-Terrarium** (Akvarij-Terarij) with about 40 small tanks filled with tropical fish and reptiles. It's open on weekdays from 8 am to 7 pm. On Saturday and Sunday the hours are from 9 am till noon and from 2 to 7 pm. The entrance fee is 400/300 SIT for adults/children. To the north-east is **Piramida**, where the titans of Marchburg once held sway.

Return to the Old Town via Trubarjeva ulica and Gledališka ulica, with the latter leading into **Slomškov trg**. The square is named after Anton Martin Slomšek (1800-62), the Slovenian bishop and politician who was instrumental in having the episcopate moved to Maribor and is now a candidate for sainthood. That's him seated in front of the cathedral just south-west of the **light pillar**, a 16th century lantern that once stood in the church graveyard.

The **Cathedral of St John the Baptist** dates from the 13th century and shows elements of virtually every architectural style from Romanesque to modern (including inept 19th century attempts to 're-Gothicise' certain bits). Of special interest is the flamboyant Gothic presbytery and the choir stalls with reliefs showing scenes from the life of the patron saint. The grand building across the park to the west is the **University Library**. The **Slovenian National Theatre** is on the northern side.

Maribor's **Fine Arts Gallery** (Umetnostna Galerija), the most complete of the many in town, is south-west of Slomškov trg at Strossmayerjeva ulica 6. It is open from Tuesday to Saturday from 10 am till noon and from 4 to 8 pm. Sunday hours are from 10 am to 1 pm.

If you walk across Koroška cesta past the market and the dilapidated remains of the **Minorite monastery** to the waterfront, you'll come to the round **Judgement Tower** (Sodni Stolp), the first of four defence towers still standing. This is the start of Lent, Maribor's historical waterfront area.

A few steps along the Pristan embankment at Vojašniška ulica 8 is Maribor's most celebrated possession, a grapevine called **Stara Trta** that is still producing some 35 litres of red wine each year after being planted more than four centuries ago. It is tended by a city-appointed viticulturist and small bottles of the almost black Žametna Črnina (Black

Velvet) are distributed to visiting dignitaries as 'keys' to Maribor. Some people say it has a sourish taste.

Glavni trg, Maribor's market place in the Middle Ages, is north-east of here. In the centre of the square is perhaps the most extravagant **plague pillar** found anywhere in central Europe. Designed by Jožef Straub and erected in 1743, it includes the Virgin Mary surrounded by a half-dozen saints. At No 14 of the square is the **town hall**, built in 1565 by Venetian craftsmen living in Štajerska. The **Maribor Puppet Theatre** is at No 2 of the lovely arcaded courtyard behind called Rotovški trg.

Running north from Glavni trg is **Gosposka ulica**, once the residential area of well-to-do burghers and now a fashionable shopping street for pedestrians. To the east is **Židovska ulica**, the centre of the Jewish district in the Middle Ages. The 15th century **synagogue** at No 4 has been under renovation for several years now while the square **Jewish Tower** (Židovski Stolp) nearby is now the headquarters of the local photographers' club.

Opposite at Usnjarska ulica 10 is the five-sided **Water Tower** (Vodni Stolp), a 16th century defence tower containing Slovenia's oldest vinoteka. You can taste up to 300 different Slovenian wines here from Tuesday to Saturday between 9 am and 10 pm.

Activities

A great deal of the outdoor activities available in the Maribor area are centred in the Maribor Pohorje. See the following Around Maribor section for details.

Maribor has several outdoor swimming pools, but the most pleasant ones are on Maribor Island (Mariborski Otok), a sand bank at the end of a dammed-off portion of the Drava River called Maribor Lake (Mariborsko Jezero) about 4km west of the Old Town. Swimming in the river is allowed here and a sunbathing area has been reserved for nude bathing. It's open from June to September only, from 9 am to 7 pm. Local bus No 15 from the train station will drop

you off at the start of the footpath leading to the bridge and the island.

The latest arrival is the Fontana Terme Maribor (☎ 223 254), a huge spa complex west of the centre at Koroška cesta 172. It has thermal pools and whirlpools with a water temperature of 39° to 44°C, sauna, solarium, fitness centre and massage. The Fontana complex is open year round from 9 am to 9 pm and entry is 1800 SIT for four hours, 2500 SIT for eight hours. A much less flash bathing complex is the Pristan pool complex (☎ 26 740) on the river west of Lent (entrance from Ob Bregu or Koroška cesta 33). It has a pool, sauna, gym and massage. The pool is open from 7 am to 6 pm on weekdays and from 8 am to 7.30 pm at the weekend. The sauna is open from 8 am to 8 pm from Wednesday to Saturday.

The Maribor Flying Centre (☎ 691 506) at the airport in Skoke, about 8km south-east of the Old Town, has several sightseeing flights available including one that takes in Maribor, Ptuj and Slovenska Bistrica for about DM35 per person or DM100 for a group of five.

Special Events

Maribor hosts a lot of events throughout the year, including the International Trade Fair and Slovenian Choir Competition in April, the Puppet Theatre Festival throughout most of the summer and the annual Theatre Festival in the second half of October. But the biggest event on the city's calendar is the Lent Festival, a two-week celebration of folklore, culture and music in late June/early July when stages are set up throughout the Old Town. Among the most colourful ceremonies is the 'baptism' of the rafts on the Drava and the International Jazz Festival is held here at the same time. Grapes are harvested in early October from Stara Trta, the 'Old Vine' in Lent.

Places to Stay

Camping The *Jezero* camp site (☎ 621 640), in Bresternica, about 6km west of town on Maribor Lake, is a pleasant enough place with a large amount of space (five hectares) for the 150 people the organizers say they can accommodate. The camp site is open from March to October. Local bus No 15 will drop you off outside reception.

Private Rooms The MATIC and Slovenijaturist can organise private rooms for about DM20.

Hostel The *Dijaški Dom 26 Junij* (☎ 511 800) at Železnikova ulica 12 on the right bank of the Drava in the south-eastern suburb of Pobrežje accepts travellers in July and August. From the train station take bus No 3 (which may have a Hostelling International symbol on the front of it) and get off at the cemetery stop. The price is 1800 SIT per person.

Hotels Maribor's three big hotels cater almost exclusively to business travellers from Austria and Germany and charge accordingly; for cheaper hotel accommodation you'll have to head for the hills of the Maribor Pohorje (see Around Maribor) or try the new 75-bed *Garni Hotel Tabor* (☎ 104 224; fax 104 225) at Ulica Heroja Zidanška 18 in Studenci to the south-west across the Drava. Singles/doubles with shower are 6300/9800 SIT.

The most central of the three city hotels, the rather gloomy 231-bed *Orel* (☎ 26 171; fax 28 497) at Grajski trg 3a, charges from 9500 SIT for a single with shower and breakfast and 13,000 SIT for a double. The 170-bed *Slavija Best Western* (☎ 227 560; fax 222 857), a modern 10-storey block facing a busy street at Ulica Vita Kraigherija 3, has singles for 9000 to 11,500 SIT and doubles for 12,000 to 14,500 SIT. The *Piramida* (☎ 25 971; fax 25 984), due east at Ulica Heroja Šlandra 10, is a former 164-bed tourist hotel tarted up with a bit of paint and marble. Singles with shower and breakfast start at 10,000 SIT, doubles at 17,000 SIT.

Places to Eat
One of the cheapest places in Maribor is the *Orlic* self-service restaurant on Volkmerjev prehod, the narrow passage on the south side of the Orel hotel. It is open weekdays only from 9 am to 2 pm. There's a *McDonald's* at Grajski trg 1.

For pizza, head for *Verdi* just off Pristan at Dravska ulica 8; look for the sign with the three rats! Verdi is open from 10 am to midnight daily. Nearby at Vojašniškova ulica 4 and facing the Drava, *Ranca* serves simple Balkan grills like pleskavica and čevapčiči for between 500 and 700 SIT and is open daily from 8 am to 11 pm.

The otherwise expensive *Ribja* restaurant at the Slavija hotel has good set lunches (including some vegetarian ones) for between 700 and 1000 SIT. The upmarket *Zimski Vrt Zamorc*, a 'Winter Garden' restaurant with lots of marble, hanging vines and an atrium, is around the corner from the Orel hotel at Gosposka ulica 30. It's open daily, except Sunday, from 11 am to 11 pm.

A great place for a meal if you want to get out of the city but don't feel like travelling is *Gostišče Pri Treh Ribnikih* (☎ 211 371) near the three fish ponds above City Park at Ribniška ulica 3. Oddly, their specialities are cheese štruklji (dumplings) and game dishes – not fish. The restaurant is open daily from 10 am to 10 pm.

Two lovely cafés in Maribor are the *Grajska Kavarna* in the castle at Trg Svobode 2 (open Monday to Saturday from 8 am to 10 pm) and the *Glejdališka Kavarna* next to the Slovenian National Theatre on Miklošičeva ulica (open weekdays from 8 am to 2 am, on Saturday from 10 am to 2 pm and 7 pm to 2 am, and on Sunday from 7 pm to 2 am). The Glejdališka Kavarna attracts a gay crowd.

There's a *market* selling produce at Vodnikov trg.

Entertainment
The *Slovenian National Theatre* (Slovensko Narodno Gledališče; SNG) in Maribor has one of the best reputations in the country and its productions, including *Faust* directed by Tomaž Pandur, have received critical acclaim throughout Europe. The city's ballet and opera companies also perform here. The ticket office (☎ 224 421 or ☎ 221 206), on

STEVE FALLON

STEVE FALLON

STEVE FALLON

JOCO ŽNIDARŠIČ

A: Looking across Savinja River to
   Celje Castle, Štajerska
B: Wayside shrine, Logar Valley,
   Štajerska

C: Wooden suspension bridge,
   Upper Savinja Valley, Štajerska
D: Cycling in the Logar Valley,
   Štajerska

JOCO ŽNIDARŠIČ

TOMO JESENIČNIK

RENATA PICEJ

STEVE FALLON

A	B
C	D

A: Wine cellar, Trg Svobode, Maribor, Koroška

B: Drying corn with a religious theme, Koroška

C: Church of the Ascension, designed by Jože Plečnik, Bogojina, Prekmurje

D: 13th century church in Spodnja Muta, Koroška

the theatre's north side at Slovenska ulica 27, is open weekdays from 10 am to 7 pm (to 5 pm on Monday), to 1 pm on Saturday and two hours before the performance. Maribor's second famous theatre is the *Maribor Puppet Theatre* (Lutkovno Gledališče Maribor) (☎ 26 748), with productions year round, at Ratovški trg 2.

Concerts are held in several locations, including the castle's Festival Hall and the cathedral. Ask the tourist office for a list. The *Jazz Club Satchmo* meets in the Fine Arts Gallery building at Strossmayerjeva ulica 6, nightly from 9 to 1 am.

The pubs and restaurants along the Drava in Lent are pretty lively on summer evenings. The beer in these parts is Gambrinus, brewed in Maribor for more than two centuries. If you're looking to bop, you can try *Amadeus*, a disco down a little alleyway at Slovenska ulica 20 (open Tuesday to Sunday from 7 pm to 4 am) or *Paradiso* at Čurfarjeva cesta 21 on the other side of the Drava not far from the hostel (open Monday to Saturday from 9 pm to 4 am). One of the hottest places in town is *Martin Krpan* at Ulica Heroja Šaranoviča 27 in Melje, east of the train station, a district not unlike the Metlikova squat in Ljubljana. Martin Krpan rages on Friday and Saturday from 9 pm to 4 am.

Maribor Casino, at Glavni trg 1, is open daily from 6 pm to 2 pm and offers slot machines, American and French roulette and blackjack.

Getting There & Away
Bus You can reach virtually any large centre in Slovenia (and destinations in Austria, Hungary, Croatia and even Germany) from Maribor. The bus station is huge, with some 30 stands, shops, bars, cafés and a large left-luggage office open from 7 am to 9 pm.

Bus service is frequent to Celje, Dravograd, Gornja Radgona, Lenart, Lendava, Ljubljana, Ljutomer, Lovrenc, Murska Sobota, Ptuj, Radenci, Selnica and Slovenska Bistrica.

Other destinations and their daily frequencies include the Areh hotel in the Maribor Pohorje (two), Gornji Grad (one), Koper (three), Majšperk (two), Moravske Toplice (two), Nova Gorica (two), Novo Mesto (one), Ormož (six), Podčetrtek (three), Postojna (five), Rogaška Slatina (five), Slovenj Gradec (seven) and Velenje (three).

Two buses a day go to Varaždin and Zagreb in Croatia and there's a daily bus to Graz in Austria at 7.30 am. Five buses a week leave for Frankfurt and three for Stuttgart in Germany. For Lenti in Hungary there's a bus at 8 am on Thursday and Saturday and one for Budapest at 20 minutes after midnight on Wednesday, Friday and Saturday.

Train Maribor is on the train line linking Zidani Most and Celje with the Austrian cities of Graz and Vienna. From Ljubljana (156km; 2¾ hours), you can reach Maribor on any of 20 trains a day. About a half-dozen trains a day, originating in Maribor, go east from Pragersko to Ormož (59km; 1¼ hours), from where you can make your way into Croatia. Connections can be made at Pragersko for trains to Murska Sobota and Hungary.

About four trains head west each day for Dravograd (64km; 1½ hours) and other stops in Koroška. Two of those trains cross the Austrian border at Holmec and carry on to Klagenfurt (Celovec).

Car & Motorbike Kompas Hertz (☎ 225 252) has an office at the Slavija hotel open from 7 am to 7 pm on weekdays and to 1 pm on Saturday.

Getting Around
Bus Maribor and its surrounds are well served by local buses. They depart from the stands about 200m north of the train station's main entrance.

Taxi For a local taxi, ring ☎ 27 755.

AROUND MARIBOR
Maribor Pohorje
• *area code* ☎062 • *postcode 2208*
Maribor's green lung and its central playground, the eastern edge of the Pohorje Massif (Mariborsko Pohorje in Slovene) can

be easily reached by car, bus or cable car from town. The area has any number of activities on offer – from skiing and hiking to horse riding and mountain biking – and is a welcome respite from the city, especially in summer.

Skiing The ski grounds of the Maribor Pohorje stretch from the Habakuk hotel near the lower cable-car station to Žigartov Vrh (1347m) west of the Areh hotel. With some 60km of slopes, 25km of cross-country runs and 16 ski lifts, this is Slovenia's largest ski area and long waits for tows, which can be a problem in Slovenia, are virtually nonexistent here.

The season generally lasts from December to March, but there are snow cannons along the 870m run where the Women's World Cup Slalom and Giant Slalom Competition (Golden Fox trophy) take place in January.

Ski equipment can be rented at the Bellevue hotel (1050m) or from the small cabin between the Areh hotel and the pretty little 17th century pilgrimage church nearby. A daily ski pass costs around 3100 SIT (2200 SIT for children) and a weekly one is 14,500 SIT (10,200 SIT). There's also a ski school.

Hiking There are heaps of easy walks in every direction from the Areh hotel, but following a stretch of the marked Slovenian Alpine Trail (which originates in Maribor) west and then south-west for 5km will take you to the two **Šumik waterfalls** and **Pragozd** – one of the few virgin forests left in Europe. Another 6km to the south-west is **Black Lake** (Črno Jezero), the source of the swift-running Lobnica River, and Osankarica, where the Pohorje battalion of Partisans was wiped out by the Germans in January 1943. This is a remarkably beautiful hike and the joy of it is that with all the streams around you don't have to carry as much water as you normally would while hiking in summer.

Other Activities You can rent horses from the Bellevue hotel for about 500 SIT if you are content to sit in the paddock. It costs 1500 SIT per hour to take them outside. Both the Areh and the Bellevue hotels also have mountain bikes, an ideal way to explore the back roads and trails of the Maribor Pohorje. The rental charge is 400 SIT per hour or 2000 SIT for the day. The Poštarski Dom mountain lodge has tennis courts.

Places to Stay & Eat There are plenty of places to stay in the Maribor Pohorje, including more than a dozen *mountain lodges* and *holiday homes*, many of them run by the Branik Ski Club (☎ 221 810 or ☎ 222 152). Its main office in Maribor at Mladinska ulica 29 will provide you with a list and basic map. Places close to main roads include *Ruška Koča pri Arehu* (☎ 603 264) and *Poštarski Dom* (☎ 222 152). Most have cooking facilities and are open all year.

The 84-bed *Areh* hotel (☎ 603 260; fax 226 866) is a very pleasant ski lodge with rustic, wood-panelled rooms, a pleasant restaurant and helpful staff. Singles with shower and breakfast cost 2900 SIT, doubles 5400 SIT. The hotel has cupboards with locks in the basement for storing skis and bicycles.

The 75-bed *Bellevue* (☎ 603 215; fax 603 210), near the upper cable-car station, is not as nice as the Areh but it has pleasant outside terraces for eating and drinking in warm weather. Its rates are about the same as those at the Areh.

Getting There & Away You can drive or, if ambitious, cycle the 20km from the Old Town in Maribor south past the Renaissance-style Betnava Castle, turning west at Spodnje Hoče before reaching a fork in the road at a small waterfall. Go left and you'll reach the Areh hotel after about 5km. A right turn and less than 4km brings you to the Bellevue hotel.

A much easier – and more exhilarating – way to get to the Bellevue and the heart of the Maribor Pohorje is to take the cable car (*vzpenjača*; ☎ 631 850 for information) from the station on Pohorska ulica in Zgornje Radvanje 6km south-west of the Old Town.

The Hayrack: A National Icon

Nothing is as Slovenian as the *kozolec*, the hayrack seen almost everywhere in the country except in Prekmurje and parts of Primorska. Because the ground in Alpine and hilly areas can be damp, wheat and hay are hung from racks, allowing the wind to do the job faster and more thoroughly.

Until the late 19th century, the kozolec was looked upon as just another tool to make a farmer's work easier and the land more productive. Then the artist Ivan Grohar made it the centrepiece of many of his impressionist paintings, and the kozolec became as much a part of the cultural landscape as the physical one. Today it is virtually a national icon and a sure way to reduce *zamejci* (ethnic Slovenes living outside the national borders) to nostalgic tears is to send them a postcard or Christmas card of a kozolec on a distant slope covered in snow.

There are many different types of Slovenian hayracks: single ones standing alone or with sloped 'lean-to' roofs, parallel and stretched ones and double hayracks *(toplarji)*, often with roofs and storage areas on top. Simple hayracks are not unknown in other parts of Alpine central Europe, but toplarji, decorated or plain, are unique to Slovenia.

Hayracks were made of hardwood (usually oak) from the early 17th century. Today, however, the hayrack's future is in concrete, and the new stretched ones can go on forever. ∎

The ride above the chestnut trees lasts only 15 minutes but offers excellent views of the city and surrounding countryside. There are even clamps on the outside of each carriage for skis and mountain bikes. Regular buses make the run between the Bellevue and Areh hotels.

From the train station in Maribor take local bus No 6, which leaves about every 20 minutes, and get off at the terminus. The cable car runs every half-hour from 7 am to 7 pm with one last trip again at 10 pm.

CENTRAL POHORJE REGION
• *area code* ☎*063* • *postcode 3214*

Travellers can easily sample Pohorje's recreational offerings along its eastern and western fringes from Maribor and Slovenj Gradec in Koroška. But the pear-shaped massif's most beautiful and highest area is in the centre.

While it's true that the Pohorje peaks can't hold a candle to those of the Julian and the Kamnik-Savinja Alps – most here barely clear the 1500m mark – this is the only part of the country where you can appreciate the sheer vastness of the mountains without feeling hemmed in or vertiginous. What's

more, hiking and trekking in the winter here is as good as it is in the summer. Though the Pohorje was once covered in forests, lumberjacks and charcoal makers exploited the woods for the sawmills, forges and glassworks of Štajerska and Koroška in the 19th century. Many of the hillsides have been cleared and are now given over to brush, pasture and meadows. Others were replanted with oak trees.

Zreče (pop 3575), about 40km south-west of Maribor, is the springboard for the central Pohorje region. Though certainly not Slovenia's most attractive town (the Unior tool-manufacturing company dominates the place), it has the modest Terme Zreče spa and is within easy striking distance of the ski and sport centre around Rogla (1517m), 16km to the north. The central Pohorje region is also very well developed for rural tourism, with dozens of local farmhouses offering accommodation.

Information
Staff at the Dobrava hotel, Cesta na Roglo 15, at Terme Zreče, which is owned by the Unior Turizem travel group (☎ 768 1117; fax

762 446), can help with information. There's a Banka Celje branch next to Zreče's small bus station in the shopping centre to the north-east, about 150m from the spa's main entrance. It is open from 8 am to 1 pm and 1.30 to 5 pm weekdays and on Saturday to 11.30 am. The bus station also has an exchange office. The post office, opposite the bank to the west, is open weekdays from 8 am to 6 pm and till noon on Saturday.

Terme Zreče

The thermal spa at Zreče is a serious treatment centre for post-operative therapy and locomotor disorders (especially those involving sports injuries), but it is also a place where you can have fun. Along with an indoor thermal pool (water temperature is 32°C) and a couple of jacuzzis, there's a large covered recreational pool and two outdoor ones. A fee of 1200 SIT gets you use of the pool, saunas and steam room; it's 900 SIT for the pool alone. The spa complex also has a very well equipped gym (700 SIT entry). You won't soon forget a massage with aromatic oils or the medicinal mud treatment.

Rogla

Rogla is a true sports centre and many teams – including Slovenian and Croatian Olympic teams – come here to train. With all those spruce trees producing so much oxygen there's enough to go around for everyone. No matter where you look it seems that someone is bouncing, lifting or pushing something, and the hiking and skiing are excellent.

Hiking The *Rogla Foothpaths* hiking map produced by Unior Turizem and available everywhere in Zreče and Rogla outlines seven trails (most of them open to mountain bikes) from Rogla. They all follow well marked circular paths and are as short as 2km (30 minutes) and as long as 32km (eight hours). The latter is hike No 5 and covers much of the hike described in the earlier Around Maribor section – Šumik waterfalls, Black Lake, Osankarica – but from the other side. Another good one is the 12km hike No 3 (three hours) that leads north-west to the

Lovrenc Lakes (Lovrenska Jezera), a turf swamp with 19 lakes that are considered a natural phenomenon. This area is also known for its unique vegetation.

Skiing Rogla's 15km of slopes and 30km of cross-country trails are served by two chair lifts and 11 tows. The season is a relatively long one – from late November till April – and there are cannons for artificial snow. A daily ski pass in full season costs 3100/2200 SIT for adults/children and a seven-day one is 14,500/10,200 SIT. There's also a ski school (☎ 420 4468; 3000 SIT for one-hour individual lessons), and you can rent equipment at the Planja hotel. In recent years Rogla has become the centre in Slovenia for snow-boarding; lessons for individuals cost 3000 SIT per hour.

Horse Riding The Rogla Equine Centre (☎ 775 210 or ☎ 754 322) is about 3km north-east of Rogla at Koča na Pesku, a mountain hut with a small restaurant, and opens daily from 10 am to 5 pm. An hour's ride in the hills costs 1500 SIT, a lesson 2000 SIT. A 45-minute horse-drawn sleigh ride in winter is 2000 to 4000 SIT, depending on the destination, and they also have sleighs pulled by huskies.

Other Activities The sports centre at Rogla has an indoor pool open from 9 am to 8 pm, a covered stadium for all kinds of team sports (including basketball and volleyball), jogging tracks, lawn bowls, squash and badminton courts and indoor and outdoor tennis courts. The tennis courts cost 1000 to 2600 SIT an hour to rent, depending on the type and the time of day. A racquet is 150 SIT. Mountain bikes can be rented for 500 SIT an hour or 1500 SIT for four hours.

Places to Stay & Eat

The cheapest place to stay at the Rogla holiday centre (☎ 42 040; fax 766 010) is the *Jelka* hostel, open from June to mid-October and December to March. For DM21, you get a bed in one of four dormitory rooms and breakfast.

The *Brinje*, a poky annexe of the Planja hotel, charges 6400 SIT for a double in summer and 7800 SIT through most of the winter, while the hotel *bungalows* for two people are 6700 to 8800 SIT. The most expensive accommodation at Rogla is at the *Planja* hotel, which has a three-star wing with 176 beds and a four-star one with 75 beds. Frankly, the cheaper wing's rooms are brighter and more attractive but even they aren't a bargain: expect to pay a minimum of 4800 SIT for one and 7200 SIT for two in the very low season, with prices shooting up to 8200 SIT and 14,000 SIT in the high season.

A much better deal is available at the many *farmhouses* in the region, particularly along Cesta Kmečnega near Resnik, about 7km south-west of Rogla. The *Pačnik* farmhouse (☎ 762 202), for example, at No 21 is open in summer and in winter and has five rooms while *Kočnik-Kovše* (☎ 760 728) at No 33 has four rooms and is open all year. There are more farmhouses with accommodation in nearby Skomarje and Padeški Vrh and, closer to Zreče, Stranice and Križevec. The usual farmhouse prices apply: from about DM30 per person in a 2nd category room with shared bath and breakfast in the low season to DM45 per person for a 1st category room with private bath and meals in the high season.

There's no particular reason for staying at Terme Zreče (☎ 76 820; fax 762 446); all the fun is up in Rogla anyway. But if you're a serious disciple of things thermal, the spa's 54-room *Dobrava* hotel, an unexceptional block near the entrance, has singles with shower and breakfast for 7000 to 10,700 SIT, depending on the season, and doubles for 11,200 to 17,600 SIT. Make sure you get one of the rooms with a balcony, though. More pleasant are the 10 *villas* with four apartments each in a small wooded area behind the main spa building. Each apartment has a kitchen, eating area, sitting room and one or two bedrooms. Prices are 9400 to 16,800 SIT for an apartment for two.

If you get tired of the restaurant at Terme Zreče and its *Zreška Klet* wine cellar, try the *Gostilna Jančič* opposite the shopping centre at Cesta na Roglo 4b or the *Kavarna Težak* with lighter fare next door at No 4c. Both are open daily to 10 or 11 pm. There's a big *Emona Mercator* supermarket in the shopping centre at Cesta na Roglo 11.

The pizza and pasta dishes at the *Macarena*, en route to Rogla from Zreče at Boharina cesta 2, can be recommended. In Rogla there's a cheap *self-service restaurant* in the Planja hotel and a *pizzeria* just north of the hotel near the ski lift. The *Stara Koča* is a rustic little bistro in one of Rogla's original wooden buildings.

Getting There & Away

There are regular connections from Zreče to Celje, Planina, Slovenske Konjice and Velenje. Two buses a day from Celje and at least three from Slovenske Konjice stop at Zreče and then carry on to Rogla. Local buses make the runs from Zreče bus station to Rogla and to Resnik. In winter there are special ski buses from both Zreče (eg five up and five down per day) as well as Celje and Slovenske Konjice. Terme Zreče runs four morning buses up to Rogla for its guests, the same number returning in the afternoon.

CELJE

• *pop 41,000* • *area code* ☎*063* • *postcode 3000*

Celje (Cilli in German) is not the largest city in Štajerska – Maribor, 60km to the northeast, has more than three times as many people – nor is it the province's most attractive centre. But it has played a pivotal role in Slovenian history on at least two occasions.

History

Celje was settled by the Illyrians and the Celtic tribes who were subdued by the Romans in about 15 BC. As Celeia, it was the administrative centre of the Roman province of Noricum between the 1st and 5th centuries, and roads linked it with other Roman settlements at Virunum (near Klagenfurt in Austria), Poetovio (Ptuj) and Emona (Ljubljana). Celeia was an affluent town as is evident from the large baths, mosaics and temples unearthed in the area. In fact, it flourished to such a degree that it gained the nickname *Troia secunda*, the 'second Troy'. Celeia's glory days came to an end when it was sacked by the Huns in 452 and overrun by subsequent tribes during the Great Migrations.

Celje's second Camelot came in the mid-14th century when members of the Žonek family took control of the area. The Counts – later the Dukes – of Celje, one of the richest and most powerful feudal dynasties in central Europe, were the last on Slovenian soil to challenge absolute rule by the Habsburgs, and they united much of Slovenia for a time. Under their rule, which lasted for just a century, Celje acquired the status of a town, and they built the castles, town fortifications and most of the churches still standing today. The counts left Celje and the nation an invaluable legacy and a part of their emblem – three gold stars forming an inverted triangle – has been incorporated into the Slovenian state flag and seal.

Celje was never able to repeat those glory days and plagues, floods, invasions and revolts struck the town over the ensuing centuries. Celje was in fact more German than Slovene until the end of WWI when the town government passed into local hands for the first time.

Orientation

Celje's compact Old Town – encompassing just about everything of interest to travellers – is bordered by Levstikova ulica and Gregorčičeva ulica to the north and north-west, the area around the Lower Castle to the west, the train tracks to the east and the Savinja River to the south.

The town has two main squares: Glavni trg at the end of Stanetova ulica (a pedestrian street where most of the action is) and Krekov trg opposite the train station. The main bus station is 400m north of the train station opposite the Church of St Maximilian on Aškičeva ulica. Local and suburban buses stop south of the train station on Ulica XIV Divizije.

Information

Tourist Office The tourist office (☎/fax 481 062) is at Prešernova ulica 17 in the same building as the Museum of Recent History. It has a lot of brochures and will sell you a map and the useful *Celje Guide* (1300 SIT) published by EPSI. The office is open Tuesday to Friday from 10 am to 6 pm (5 pm in winter) and on Saturday from 9 am till noon.

Money Banka Celje has a branch office at Vodnikova ulica 2 open from 8.30 am to 1 pm and 1.30 to 5 pm weekdays, to 11.30 am on Saturday. A Banka, at Krekov trg 7 opposite the train station, is open from 8 am till noon and 2 to 5 pm weekdays and to 11 am on Saturday. The SKB Banka branch in the Blagovna Hiša at Gubčeva ulica 1 has a Cirrus-linked ATM.

Post & Communications The main post office is at Krekov trg 9 and is open from 7 am to 8 pm Monday to Saturday and from 8 to 11 am on Sunday.

Travel Agencies Kompas (☎ 443 300), in a lovely Renaissance house at Glavni trg 1, can arrange accommodation and rents cars. It is open weekdays from 8 am to 5 pm and till noon on Saturday. Slovenijaturist (☎ 484 902), at the train station in Krekov trg, is open weekdays from 9 am to 4 pm and till noon on Saturday. Globtour (☎ 442 511) has an office at Razlagova ulica 1 next to the Evropa hotel. It keeps the same hours as Kompas.

Bookshop Mladinska Knjiga at Stanetova ulica 3 sells regional maps and guides including the *Celje Guide*. Another good place for maps is Naša Knjiga across the same street at No 10. Both are open weekdays from 7.30 am to 7 pm and on Saturday from 8 am till noon.

Walking Tour

You can begin an easy walking tour of Celje, which takes in virtually everything of importance and interest in the town, from the main bus station.

Opposite, on the western side of Aškičeva ulica, is the **Church of St Maximilian**, named after the bishop who was beheaded in Celje in the 3rd century. The church was built in the Gothic style in the 15th century (as was the small **chapel** to the south-west) but has undergone many changes and additions since then.

Continue southward along Stanetova ulica, past the **Banka Celje** building designed by Jože Plečnik in 1929 and the spot where the town gates stood in the Middle Ages. The shop on the corner of the next intersection with Prešernova ulica was once the **Merkur coffee house**, the most important gathering spot for Celje intellectuals in the 19th century. Prešernova ulica leads eastward to Krekov trg, where you'll find the **Hotel Evropa**, Celje's oldest, and **Celje Hall** (Celjski Dom), the social centre for the city's German citizens at the turn of the century.

South along Razlagova ulica you'll pass a medieval **defence tower** on the right and, about 150m farther on, the **Water Tower**, part of the city wall and ramparts and built between 1451 and 1473. Many of the blocks used are of Roman origin.

From the Savinja embankment, at the point where the old Capuchin Bridge once stood, there's an excellent view of **Celje Castle** perched on an escarpment to the south-east. Directly opposite is **City Park** (Mestni Park), the **Capuchin Church of St Cecilia** in Breg and, high up on a hill, the **Church of St Nicholas**.

A walk up to the castle, Slovenia's largest, via a footpath from Cesta na Grad takes about half an hour from here. The castle was originally built in the early 13th century and went through several transformations, especially under the Counts of Celje in the 14th and 15th centuries. When the castle lost its strategic importance it was left to deteriorate and subsequent owners used the stone blocks to build other structures, including parts of the Lower Castle and the Old County Palace. A surprisingly large portion remains intact, however, and has been restored, including the 35m **Frederick Tower**.

On your way back to the Old Town you can walk up to Nicholas Hill for a wonderful view of the castle, the Old Town and the Savinja River. Or you can explore the Breg area. A stairway with 90 steps at Breg 2 leads to the **Church of St Cecilia**. The Germans used the nearby monastery (now apartments) as a prison during WWII. Between the church and the City Park off Maistrova ulica is the reconstructed Roman **Temple of Hercules** dating from the 2nd century. A birch-lined park along the Savinja's northern embankment has a **lapidary** of Roman remains unearthed in the Celje area. Just behind it, at Muzejski trg 1, is the 16th century **Old County Palace**, a Renaissance building with a two-level arcade around a courtyard. The palace now contains the **Celje Regional Museum** (Pokrajinski Muzej Celje).

Needless to say, the museum puts much emphasis on Celeia and the Counts of Celje, right down to exhibiting 18 of the nobles' skulls in glass cases. (They were taken from the Minorite church in 1956; the one belonging to Ulric is particularly gruesome.) The museum has 13 rooms, many of them done up in styles from different periods (baroque, neoclassical, Biedemeier, Secessionist), painted with various scenes and filled with fine furniture. Don't miss the 18th century cabinet with hunting scenes inlaid with ivory, the 20-drawer 'bank' desk and the neoclassical clock/music box that still works. But the museum's main attraction is the **Celje Ceiling**, an enormous *trompe l'oeil* painting in the main hall of columns, towers, frolicking angels, noblemen and ladies looking down at you looking up at them. Completed in about 1600 by a Polish artist, the mural was meant to lift the ceiling up to the sky and it does just that. Other panels represent the four seasons and show scenes from Roman and Greek mythology. The museum is open from 10 am to 6 pm Tuesday to Friday and from 9 am till noon on Saturday. The entry fee is 600/400 SIT.

Trg Celskih Knezov leads north from the western end of Muzejski trg. At the start of the square you'll find the **Lower Castle**, built in the 14th century as a residence for the Celje counts, and at No 9 the **National Hall** (Narodni Dom), the cultural and social centre for Celje's Slovenes at the turn of the century.

ŠTAJERSKA

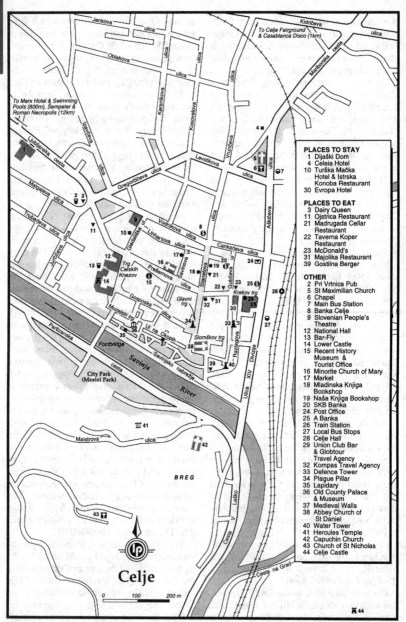

Jenkova ulica

ulica

Kidričeva
ulica

To Celje Fairground
& Casablanca Disco (1km)

Oblakova ulica

Mariborska cesta

To Merx Hotel & Swimming
Pools (800m), Šempeter &
Roman Necropolis (12km)

Kersnikova

Kosovelova ulica

Vrunčeva

Ljubljanska cesta

Levstikova ulica

Ipavčeva

4

5

6

7

Malgajeva ulica

Gregorčičeva ulica

2 3

Trubarjeva ulica

Jurčičeva ulica

11

Vodnikova ulica

9

Linhartova ulica

Gledališka ul.

10

8

Aškičeva

Cankarjeva ulica

20

19

Stanetova

Globočeva

24

12

Trg
Celskih
Knezov

16

Prešernova

17

18

21

22

13

15

23

25

26

14

Gospoška

Glavni
trg

32

31

Krekov trg

30

29

28

27

Muzejski trg

Glavni
trg

36

35

Partizanska

Footbridge

cesta

Savinja

Ul. na Okopih

37

34

33

Slomškov trg

38

Razlagova

Ulica XIV Divizije

City Park
(Mestni Park)

Savinjsko nabrežje

39

40

River

Maistrova ulica

41

42

Cesta V Lasko

BREG

43

Cesta na Grad

Celje

0   100   200 m

44

PLACES TO STAY
1 Dijaški Dom
4 Celeia Hotel
10 Turška Mačka
    Hotel & Istrska
    Konoba Restaurant
30 Evropa Hotel

PLACES TO EAT
3 Dairy Queen
11 Ojstrica Restaurant
21 Madrugada Cellar
    Restaurant
22 Taverna Koper
    Restaurant
23 McDonald's
31 Majolika Restaurant
39 Gostilna Berger

OTHER
2 Pri Vrtnica Pub
5 St Maximilian Church
6 Chapel
7 Main Bus Station
8 Banka Celje
9 Slovenian People's
    Theatre
12 National Hall
13 Bar-Fly
14 Lower Castle
15 Recent History
    Museum &
    Tourist Office
16 Minorite Church of Mary
17 Market
18 Mladinska Knjiga
    Bookshop
19 Naša Knjiga Bookshop
20 SKB Banka
24 Post Office
25 A Banka
26 Train Station
27 Local Bus Stops
28 Celje Hall
29 Union Club Bar
    & Globtour
    Travel Agency
32 Kompas Travel Agency
33 Defence Tower
34 Plague Pillar
35 Lapidary
36 Old County Palace
    & Museum
37 Medieval Walls
38 Abbey Church of
    St Daniel
40 Water Tower
41 Hercules Temple
42 Capuchin Church
43 Church of St Nicholas
44 Celje Castle

Both buildings now contain art galleries open from 10 am till 1 pm and from 4 to 6 pm Tuesday to Friday and on Saturday morning.

Walking eastward along Prešernova ulica, you'll pass the **Museum of Recent History** in the former town hall building (1830) at No 17. The museum gives glory to our friends, the Counts of Celje, and is a jumble of items like postcards, weighing scales, weapons from WWII and – egad! – a dental surgeon's collection. It also contains **Herman's Den** (Hermanov Brlog), the first children's museum in Slovenia. The Museum of Recent History keeps the same hours as the Celje Regional Museum.

Opposite the museum is the **Minorite Church of Mary**, where the bones of the Celje counts once rested. Until recently a relief depicting the Madonna and Child and the counts Herman I and Herman II hung above the doorway leading from the nave into the sacristy, but that too has disappeared. Nothing is forever, it seems, in the Church of Mary.

Prešernova ulica leads to **Glavni trg**, the heart of the Old Town. It is filled with lovely 17th and 18th century town houses and, in summer, outdoor cafés. In the centre of the square, where a pillory once stood, is the requisite **plague pillar** (1776) dedicated to Mary.

In Slomškov trg, a few steps to the southeast, you'll find the **Abbey Church of St Daniel** dating from the early 14th century. The church has some magnificent frescoes and tombstones, but its most important item is the 15th century carved wooden **Pietà** in the Chapel of the Sorrowful Mother. The walls are decorated here with carved stone and the vaults with frescoes are from the early 15th century.

Parts of Celje's **medieval walls and ramparts** can be seen along Ulica na Okopih, west of the Abbey Church of St Daniel.

Activities

There are a couple of open-air swimming pools behind the Merx hotel on Ljubljanska cesta and an indoor one at the Celje Fairground at Dečkova cesta 1, north-east of the Old Town. If you're not satisfied with these,

you might consider a day trip 10km south to the spa (☎ 731 312) at **Laško**, a town equally celebrated for the beer which has been brewed here since 1825 and for a renovated castle called **Tabor**. Some Slovenes say the gourmet restaurant there (Na Taboru; ☎ 731 600) is the country's finest.

The Šeško Riding Centre (☎ 778 282) at Socka (house No 33), 15km north of Celje, has horses available for hire for experienced riders and offers lessons to beginners. The centre is in stunning countryside on the edge of the Pohorje Massif. It is open in summer from 8 to 11 am and 4 to 8 pm and in winter from 9 am to noon and from 2 to 6 pm.

The *Celje Guide* lists a number of walks and hikes into the surrounding countryside lasting between one and four hours. The longest one (28km) leads south-east to **Mt Tovst** (834m) and the picturesque village of Svetina via the Celjska Koča mountain hut. This can also be done by car or bicycle.

Places to Stay

The *Dijaški Dom* (☎ 484 420) at Ljubljanska cesta 21, 300m west of Dairy Queen, accepts travellers in July and August.

The cheapest hotel in Celje is the 60-bed *Celeia* (☎ 443 151; fax 485 160), an ugly, nine-storey brick block just a little north of the bus station at Mariborska cesta 3. Singles and doubles with shared shower and breakfast are 4000 and 8000 SIT; if you want your own shower, add 1000 SIT to both rates.

The evocatively named *Turška Mačka* (Turkish Cat; ☎ 442 908; fax 483 410), a 26-room hotel hard by the Slovenian People's Theatre at Gledališka ulica 7, is the nicest place to stay in Celje with small but comfortable rooms, a good seafood restaurant and friendly staff. Singles with shower, TV and breakfast are 5500 SIT, doubles are 9000 SIT.

The *Evropa* (☎ 443 400; fax 443 434) hotel, with 60 rooms, has seen better days and, despite its good location near the train station at Krekov trg 4 and its pleasant, helpful staff, it remains a gloomy and very dated place. Singles with breakfast, shower and TV are 6700 SIT, doubles are 9800 SIT.

The far-flung *Merx* hotel (☎ 452 218; fax 452 018) at Ljubljanska cesta 39, has only 36 beds and may not be very convenient to the Old Town, but it is as close as you'll get to the Savinja River. There are also public swimming pools behind the hotel. Singles/doubles with shower and breakfast are 6000/10,000 SIT.

Places to Eat

Two pizza places at the eastern end of Prešernova ulica can be recommended. The nothing-special *Majolika* at No 3 is open daily from 9 am to 9 pm, with pizzas in the 470 to 570 SIT range. *Taverna Koper* at No 2, and about two centuries younger in style and atmosphere, has both pizza and pasta dishes. It is open weekdays from 9 am to 7 pm and on Saturday from 11 am to 2 pm. Set lunches go for 650 and 750 SIT. The *Gostilna Berger* at the southern end of Razlagova ulica has set menus of hearty Slovenian food from 690 SIT.

The *Ojstrica* at Ljubljanska cesta 5 is one of the oldest eateries in Celje, but its claim to fame – it was the meeting place of an important Slovenian cultural society in the late 19th century – does nothing for the food. If you want something a bit more up-to-date, cross Jurčičeva ulica to the *Dairy Queen*. It's open till 11 pm (10 pm on Sunday). You'll find a *McDonald's* on Krekov trg.

One of the most interesting places for a meal in Celje is the *Istrska Konoba* restaurant at the Turška Mačka hotel, which specialises in Istrian fish dishes and wine and was designed by the Karst artist Lojze Spacal (check the lovely stained glass). It's open till 11 pm. Another upmarket place is the *Madrugada* cellar restaurant at Stanetova ulica 4. This would be a good place to try some of the better whites from the Ljutomer wine-growing region to the east of Celje. It's open Monday to Saturday from 11 am till midnight.

There's an outdoor *market* selling fresh fruit, vegetables and other foodstuffs daily on the corner of Savinova ulica and Linhartova ulica behind the Minorite church.

Entertainment

The *Slovenian People's Theatre* (Slovenski Ljudsko Gledališče; SLG) at Gledališki trg 5 stages six plays a season, not always in Slovene. The box office (☎ 442 910 or ☎ 441 861) is open weekdays from 9 to 11 pm and from 5 to 7 pm.

A couple of popular discos are *Jungle* in the north-west suburb of Lava (No 7), open most days till 3 am, and *Casablanca* at the Celje Fairground at Dečkova cesta 1, open Friday and Saturday from 10 pm to 5 am. The *Pri Vrtnica* pub and café next door to the Dairy Queen is a popular hangout as is the central *Union Club* bar in the Celjski Dom on Krekov trg. The *Bar-Fly* pub behind the Lower Castle on Trg Celskih Knezov is open from 9 pm till very late.

Getting There & Away

Bus For places like Šempeter (stand No 4), Škofja Vas (stand No 1) and Šentjur (stand No 3), go to the bus stops south of the train station on Ulica XIV Divizije.

Intercity buses, which leave from the main station, run at least once an hour to Dobrna, Hrastnik, Laško, Ljubljana, Maribor, Rimske Toplice, Rogaška Slatina, Slovenske Konjice and Velenje. Other destinations accessible by bus from Celje and their daily frequencies include Bled (one), Bistrica na Sotli (seven), Črnomelj (one), Črna (two), Dravograd (three), Gornji Grad (two), Koper (four), Kranj (two), Krško (five), Lendava on the Hungarian border (four), Logarska Dolina (two to five), Murska Sobota (six), Mozirje (eight), Nova Gorica (two), Novo Mesto (one), Ormož (three), Piran (four), Podčetrtek (eight), Ptuj (five), Sevnica (two), Vinski Vrh (four) and Zreče (three). International destinations include Varaždin in Croatia (at 8.20 am on Saturday and Sunday) and Lenti in Hungary (Thursday and Saturday at 6.55 am).

Train Celje is one of the few rail hubs in all of Slovenia and, for once, you have a real choice between taking the train or the bus. Celje is on the line linking Zidani Most (connections to and from Ljubljana and

Zagreb) with Maribor and the Austrian cities of Graz and Vienna. From Ljubljana (89km; 1¼ hours) you can reach Celje up to 24 times a day. Just as many buses leave Celje for Maribor (67km; 70 minutes).

A spur line links Celje with Velenje (38km; 50 minutes) via Šempeter up to 10 times a day in each direction. A third line connects Celje with Zabok in Croatia via Rogaška Slatina (36km; 50 minutes), Rogatec and Dobovec. Up to six trains arrive and depart each day.

Car & Motorbike Both Kompas and Globtour rent cars.

Getting Around
Parking can be difficult in Celje's Old Town and you will have to pay handsomely for the privilege – up to 1000 SIT per day. For a local taxi ring ☎ 442 200.

AROUND CELJE
Šempeter
• *pop 3935* • *area code* ☎*063* • *postcode 3311*
Some 12km west of Celje and accessible by bus and train, Šempeter is the site of a **Roman necropolis** reconstructed between 1952 and 1966. The burial ground contains four complete tombs and scores of columns, steles and fragments carved with portraits, mythological creatures and scenes from daily life.

The marble stones, quarried in the Pohorje near Slovenska Bistrica between the 1st and 3rd centuries, were washed away and buried when the Savinja River flooded in 268 AD. They have been divided into about two dozen groups linked by footpaths.

Tomb No 1, the oldest of them all, was commissioned by Gallus Vindonius, a Celtic nobleman who lived on a nearby estate in the 1st century. The largest is the **Priscianus tomb** (No II), raised in honour of a Roman official and his son. (Notice the kidnapping scene on the side relief.) The most beautiful is the **Ennius tomb** (No III) with reliefs of animals and, on the front panel, the princess Europa riding a bull. If you compare these three with the more recent tomb erected in

about 250 in honour of Secundanius, it is obvious that Roman power and wealth in these parts was already very much on the decline in the middle of the 3rd century.

The necropolis is open daily from 8 am to 6 pm and costs 600/400 SIT to visit. There's a small *bistro* near the entrance but, if you want something more substantial, the *Gostišče Štorman* (☎ 701 585), one of the first private restaurants to open in Slovenia under the former regime, is at Šempeter 5a, about 2km east of the site on the road to Celje. It is open from 7 am till midnight, except on the first Sunday of every month.

UPPER SAVINJA VALLEY
• *area code* ☎ *063*
The Upper Savinja Valley (Zgornja Savinjska Dolina) refers to the drainage areas and tributaries of the Savinja River from its source in the eastern Savinja Alps to a gorge at Letuš, some 12km north-west of Šempeter. Bounded by forests, ancient churches, traditional farmhouses and Alpine peaks of more than 2000m, the valley is a land of incomparable beauty. There are activities here to suit every taste – from hiking, mountain biking and rock climbing to fishing, kayaking and swimming in the Savinja.

The Savinja begins its rapid flow above Rinka, at 90m Slovenia's highest waterfall, then enters Logarska Dolina (Logar Valley) and continues past isolated hamlets and farmland. The region beyond the gorge at Ljubno is quite different, with a number of towns – really overgrown villages – of historical importance, including Radmirje, Gornji Grad, Nazarje and Mozirje.

Tools found in a cave at Mt Olševa, north-west of Solčava village, suggest that the Upper Savinja Valley was inhabited during the Stone Age. Remains of three Roman settlements have also been unearthed around Mozirje. The valley has been exploited for its timber since the Middle Ages, and until WWII the Savinja was used to power some 200 sawmills. Raftsmen transported the timber from Ljubno to Mozirje and Celje and some of the logs travelled as far as Romania. The trade brought wealth and special rights to the valley, evident from the many fine buildings still standing here.

The following itinerary follows the 45km valley road from Mozirje to Rinka Waterfall, with a side trip to Radmirje and Gornji Grad. It can be done by bus or car but it is tailor-made for a bicycle trip.

Orientation & Information

The small English-language brochure entitled *Zgornja Savinjska Dolina – The Short Guidebook* is helpful if you intend spending a fair bit of time in the area. It lists numerous trails, the best places for rock climbing, isolated farmhouses with accommodation etc. Serious hikers should pick up a copy of the 1:50,000 map *Zgornja Savinjska Dolina* from GZS.

In Mozirje, the Kozorog pension (☎ 831 022) at Na Trgu 32 can provide information. Nova Ljubljanska Banka has a branch in the centre of town at Na Trgu 9; it's open weekdays from 7.30 am to 6 pm and till noon on Saturday. The post office is 200m to the south around the bend in the road at Savinjska cesta 3, and the bus station is on the main road opposite the Savinjski Gaj botanical garden.

In Nazarje there's a Nova Ljubljanska Banka in the building next to Vrbovec Castle on Savinjska cesta, open from 8 to 11 am and 1.30 to 3.30 pm on weekdays and from 7.30 to 11 am on Saturday.

In Gornji Grad the little kiosk near the courtyard, west of the massive baroque church, houses a tourist information centre in summer. Buses stop in the main square – Attemsov trg – in front of the church. The Nova Ljubljanska Banka on the square is open weekdays from 8 am till noon and from 3 to 4 pm. The post office is nearby at house No 79. It is open weekdays from 8 am to 6 pm with a couple of half-hour breaks, and on Saturday till noon.

The Logarska Dolina tourist office (☎ 846 111; fax 846 024) is at the Plesnik hotel at Logarska Dolina 9. You can also seek information from the staff at the entrance to the regional park.

Things to See & Do

Mozirje The administrative centre of the Upper Savinja Valley on the river's left bank, Mozirje (pop 1900) is a town with a long history. Yet it has little to show for its past

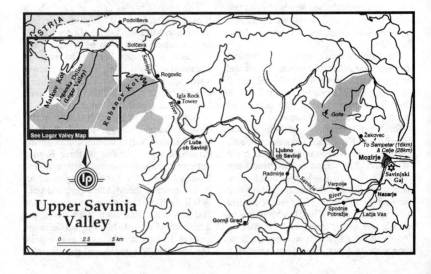

Upper Savinja Valley

except the much rebuilt Gothic **Church of St George** at the western end of Na Trgu just after you cross the small Trnava Stream. You might walk over to **Savinjski Gaj** (Savinja Grove), a botanic park with an **open-air ethnographic museum** south of town across the river (open April to October). In winter, continue 4km north-west to Žekovec where a cable car runs to the ski centre at **Golte** (☎ 831 111). There are slopes of up to 1500m and 12.5km of ski trails. Otherwise, there's little to hold you in this one-horse town.

Nazarje The town of 'Nazareth' (pop 1835) is 2km due south of Mozirje on the Savinja. **Vrbovec Castle**, a 15th century pile at the confluence of the Savinja and Dreta rivers, has a couple of large towers; today the castle houses a music school and offices of the Glin logging company, the industry that built Nazarje.

Towering above the town on a hill called Gradišče is the **Franciscan monastery** and its **Church of the Virgin Mary**, which were all but flattened by Allied bombs during WWII but have since been rebuilt. The twin-spired church has a choir loft with fine grill work; the original chapel, built by Bishop Tomaž Hren of Ljubljana in the early 17th century, now serves as the presbytery. The monastery has a lovely garden surrounded by

This water-wheel is part of the display at the open-air ethnographic museum near Mozirje.

an arcaded courtyard. You can drive up to the monastery or climb to it up 200-odd steps.

The Burger Horse Riding Centre (☎ 831 265) at Lačja Vas (house No 22), in a beautiful valley 3km south-west of Nazarje, has horses for rent. Carriage rides are also available if there are enough people interested.

Radmirje The road to Radmirje (pop 440), a village 9km to the west, is very picturesque with Štajerska-style hayracks, little white churches and stone farmhouses larger than the average in Slovenia. About 500m before the turn-off to Radmirje and Kamnik, the Prodnik Sports Centre (☎ 841 317) on the main road at Juvanje 1 organises kayak (2900 SIT), canoe and raft trips on the Savinja and also rents equipment.

Radmirje is famous for two churches. The **Church of St Michael** in the centre of town dates from the late 14th century. The **Church of St Francis Xavier**, on Straža Hill to the south-west, has been rebuilt several times over the centuries; the present structure is only about 200 years old. It was established as a pilgrimage church by the bishop of Gornji Grad during a period of great fires and the plague. European monarchs paid homage at the site and the church's rich **treasury** contains Mass vestments donated by the kings of Poland and France and a gold chalice from Habsburg Empress Maria Theresa. There's an old wayside shrine *(znamenje)* with folk paintings in the little dale below the church.

Gornji Grad This windy town (pop 1845) in the Zadrečka Valley 6km south-west of Radmirje was the site of a large castle until the last days of WWII when it was flattened. Today, all that is left is the entrance to the fortification and two defence towers.

Gornji Grad (Oberburg in German) was associated for centuries with the Ljubljana diocese. The **former Benedictine monastery**, for example, was converted into a manor house for Ljubljana's bishops in the 15th century. Today, one of its towers (at Attemsov trg 2) contains a small **folk collection** with everyday objects relating to life on the Menina Planina, an area of mountain pastures and slopes south of town. It is open weekdays from 11 am to 4 pm.

In the same complex, the large baroque **Church of Sts Hermagoras and Fortunatus** was built in the mid-18th century and modelled after the cathedral in Ljubljana. Its enormous, 56m-high dome notwithstanding, the interior of the church is surprisingly light and airy. The side altar pictures by the 18th century Austrian artist Martin Johann Kremser-Schmidt (1718-1801) are especially fine. Outside, near the entrance, are bits and pieces from an earlier church, including a 16th century altar portraying the crucifixion of St Andrew. The fountain in the courtyard still appears to be a meeting place for local people. The church is open daily from 9 am to 7 pm.

Ljubno After this town the Upper Savinja Valley begins to feel – and smell – truly Alpine, with the mountains so close you can almost touch them, the houses built entirely of wood and the heady scent of pine in the air. The road continues along the winding Savinja, past wooden bridges, more hayracks and, in a gorge 4km beyond **Luče** and visible from the main road, a curious rock tower called **Igla** (Needle). Just before **Rogovilc**, the usual starting point for canoe and kayak trips on the Savinja, there's a turn south to **Robanov Kot**, a pristine valley and protected park with trails and farmhouse accommodation.

To the north-east of Robanov Kot and below Mt Raduha (2062m) there's an ice cave called **Snežna Jama** (actually 'Snow Cave'; ☎ 723 211 for information) open to the public at the weekend in summer. It is accessible by car via a forest road.

Solčava At 642m the highest town in the valley, Solčava has some lovely road markers with folk icons and painted barns. To the north is the Alpine village of **Podolševa**, where you can spend the night. The road from Solčava to Podolševa, which continues west and down into Logarska Dolina, is one of the most panoramic in Slovenia.

Logarska Dolina Most of the glacial 'Forester Valley' – about 7.5km long and no more than 500m wide – has been a regional park since 1987.

This 'pearl of the Alpine region' is a wonderful place to explore for a few days with more than 30 natural attractions such as caves, springs, peaks and waterfalls.

The park is open every day from April to September (at the weekend only in October). Cars and motorcyclists entering the park must pay 700 SIT; cyclists and hikers get in free. A single road goes past a small chapel and through the woods to **Rinka Waterfall**, the main event here, but there are plenty of trails to explore and up to 20 additional waterfalls in the area.

The bottom of Rinka Waterfall is only about 10 minutes on foot from the car park and you can climb to the top in about 20 minutes. It's not very difficult, but it can get slippery; you'll probably encounter several people using ski poles for balance. From the top of the falls to the west you can see three peaks reaching higher than 2200m: Kranjska Rinka, Koroška Rinka and Štajerska Rinka. Until 1918 they formed the triple border of Carniola (Kranjska), Carinthia (Koroška) and Styria (Štajerska).

Opposite Dom Planincev is a trail leading to **Sušica Waterfall** and **Klemenča Cave**.

Another magnificent and much less explored valley, the 6km-long **Matkov Kot**, runs parallel to Logarska Dolina and the border with Austria. You can reach here by road by turning west as you leave Logarska Dolina. Some think this valley was once a lake. There are several farmhouses in the valley with accommodation.

The tourist office at the Plesnik hotel can organise any number of activities – from horse riding (1300 SIT per hour) and coach rides for up to five people (2500 SIT) to paragliding (4000 SIT), guided mountaineering (10,000 SIT for four people) and rock climbing up to grade IV (16,000 SIT). It also rents mountain bikes for 400 SIT per hour (1800 SIT for six hours). Nonresidents can use the swimming pool and sauna at the Plesnik hotel for 1400 SIT a day.

Places to Stay & Eat

In Mozirje, the *Kozorog* guest house (☎ 831 022) at Na Trgu 32 has a dozen double rooms priced at DM20 per person. The restaurant (open to 11 pm, 10 pm on Sunday) is a simple but inexpensive affair; for something better try the *Gaj* restaurant at the botanic garden. The *Levec* farmhouse (☎ 831 861), not far from Savinjski Gaj in Loke (house No 19), has five rooms and is open all year.

Some 3km west of Nazarje you'll find a couple of camp sites on opposite sides of the river. *Menina* (☎ 831 787), which charges

950 SIT per person, is in Varpolje on the left bank while *Savinja* (☎ 831 463; 650 to 800 SIT) is in Spodnje Pobrežje on the right. In Nazarje, the *Gostišče Grad Vrbovec* restaurant is in the complex next to the castle at Savinjska cesta 8. You'll also find the simple *Okrepčevalnica Izoles* and a pizzeria called *Panda* here.

In Gornji Grad, the 25-bed *Trobej* guesthouse (☎ 843 006) at Attemsov trg 12 has double rooms with showers for DM60. The decent *Pizzeria 902* is at Attemsov trg 25, but if you need something more substantial, try

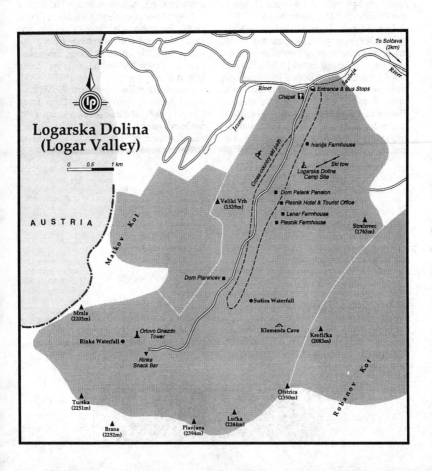

Gostilna Pri Jošku at house No 77, one of the oldest traditional eateries in Slovenia. Its specialities are boiled beef with horseradish and žlikrofi (Slovenian 'ravioli' made with cheese, bacon and chives). Pri Jošku is open daily, except Wednesday, till 10 pm.

In Logarska Dolina, the *Logarska Dolina* camp site (☎ 846 086) lies about 1.5km from the park entrance at Logarska Dolina 8. The *Ivanija* farmhouse (☎ 846 070) nearby also offers accommodation for DM28 per person. A couple of kilometres farther south are two more farmhouses charging the same rate – *Lenar* (☎ 846 103) at Logarska Dolina 11 and *Plesnik* (☎ 846 220) at No 13.

The 24-bed *Dom Palenk* guesthouse (☎ 846 088) nearby is a bit upmarket (DM40 per person) but nothing comes close to the new 64-bed *Plesnik* hotel (☎ 846 024; fax 846 110) at Logarska Dolina 10, one of only three private hotels in the country. Hopefully, it indicates the direction that the Slovenian hotel industry will be taking in future. It has a pool, sauna, a fine restaurant and lovely public area, but don't expect all that to come cheaply: the single rates are DM90 to DM100, the double ones DM150 to DM160.

There's no shortage of places to eat here either. Along with the upmarket restaurants at the *Plesnik* hotel and the *Dom Palenk* is the *Dom Planincev*, 2.5km from Rinka, which has a relaxed, rustic feel to it. There's a simple snack bar called *Rinka* near the car park close to the waterfall and another in a tall wooden tower called *Orlovo Gnezdo* (Eyrie) overlooking the falls.

Getting There & Away

From Mozirje, there is an hourly bus service to Celje. There are five buses a day to Gornji Grad, one to Kamnik, three to Solčava and six to Velenje. Up to three buses a day originating in Celje continue along the valley road to Logarska Dolina and the Rinka Waterfall car park.

From Gornji Grad, buses go to Celje (three a day), Kamnik (up to five), Ljubljana (five), Ljubno (four), Maribor (one), Mozirje (10), Šmiklavž (eight) and Velenje (two). There's an early morning bus on Sunday to Logarska Dolina from May to September only.

Koroška

Koroška (Carinthia in English, Kärnten in German) is Slovenia's smallest province – a mere shadow of what it once was. Until the end of WWI, Carinthia included a very large area as well as the cities of Klagenfurt (Celovec) and Villach (Beljak), both now in Austria.

Koroška, a region of dark forests, mountains and highland meadows, is essentially just three valleys bounded by the Pohorje Massif on the east, the last of the Karavanke peaks (Mt Peca, where good King Matjaž is said to be resting) on the west and the hills of Kobansko to the north. The Drava Valley runs east to west and includes the towns of Dravograd, Muta and Vuzenica. The Mežica and Mislinja valleys fan out from the Drava; the former is an industrial area with towns like Ravne and Prevalje while the latter's main centre is Slovenj Gradec.

Koroška is an excellent area for outdoor activities, including skiing, flying, horse riding and especially hiking. The E6 European Hiking Trail running from the Baltic to the Adriatic enters Slovenia at Radlje, and the Slovenian Alpine Trail from Maribor to Ankaran passes through the heart of Koroška. Parts of these trails can be easily covered from many towns in the area.

History

Koroška has a special place in the hearts and minds of most Slovenes. The Duchy of Carantania (Karantanija), the first Slovenian – and Slavic, for that matter – state dating back to the 7th century, was centred here, and the word 'Carinthia' is derived from that name. The region was heavily fortified with castles during the Middle Ages and, from the 12th century onward, was an important cultural and artistic centre. Development came to western Koroška in the early 19th century with the opening of iron mines at Prevalje and Ravne na Koroškem; in 1863 a railway linked Maribor with Klagenfurt via the mountain pass at Holmec.

In the plebiscite ordered by the victorious

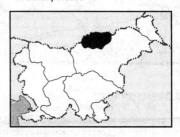

HIGHLIGHTS

- View the paintings of Jože Tisnikar at the Gallery of Fine Arts in Slovenj Gradec
- Experience a sightseeing flight of the Mislinja Valley from the Koroški Aeroclub south of Slovenj Gradec
- Visit the Rotunda of St John the Baptist at Muta, one of the oldest churches in the country
- See the 15th century frescoes of the Final Judgment in the Church of the Holy Spirit in Slovenj Gradec

Allies after WWI, Slovenes living on the northern side of the Karavanke, the 120km-long rock wall that separates much of north-west and north-central Slovenia from Austria, voted to put their economic future in the hands of Vienna, while the mining region of the Mežica Valley went to Slovenia. Understandably, the results of that vote have never sat very well with the Slovenes on the southern side of the mountains. In fact, under the communist regime, school children were taught a very different version of what actually took place in 1920.

The fact remains that the Slovenian nation lost 90,000 of its nationals to Austria (along with 400,000 to Italy and 5000 to Hungary – some 37% of its total population of 1.3 million people at the time) and it still rankles. In one popular guide to Slovenian art and architecture published in Ljubljana, Slovenian Koroška is referred to as the 'Carinthian corner'.

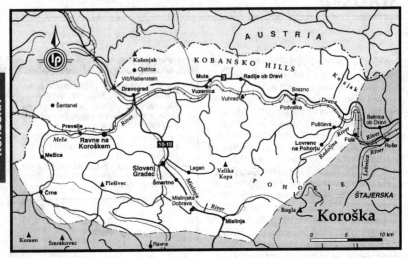

SLOVENJ GRADEC

• *pop 6800* • *area code ☎0602* • *postcode 2380*

Slovenj Gradec is not the capital of Koroška – that distinction goes to the industrial centre of Ravne na Koroškem to the north-west – but it is certainly the province's cultural and recreational centre. A number of museums, galleries and historical churches line its main square, and the sporting opportunities in the Pohorje Massif to the east are endless. It is a wonderful place for a brief stopover en route to Štajerska or Austria.

History

The history of Slovenj Gradec is closely tied to Stari Trg, a suburb south-west of the Old Town where there was a Roman settlement called Colatio from the 1st to the 3rd centuries. At that time an important Roman road from Celeia (Celje) to Virunum (near Klagenfurt in Austria) passed through Colatio. A castle called Grez to the west of the Old Town is first mentioned in the late 11th century though a fort had probably stood on the site as early as the late Iron Age.

Slovenj Gradec came into its own when the settlement shifted to an area between the Mislinja and Suhodolnica rivers in the 12th century. It was an important trade centre in the Middle Ages and minted its own coins. Later it became an important cultural and artistic centre with many artisans and craft guilds. But the town did have its share of troubles: the Turks attacked several times from the 15th century; the Mislinja Valley was ravaged by locusts in 1477; and Slovenj Gradec was captured by the Hungarians under King Matthias Corvinus 11 years later.

Among the prominent Habsburg nobles based in Slovenj Gradec over the centuries were members of the Windisch-Grätz family, a variant of the German name for the town (Windisch Graz). *Windisch* (or *wendisch*) was the general German word for 'Slavic' until the 19th century. 'Gradec' is Slovene for 'Graz'.

Orientation

Slovenj Gradec's main street is Glavni trg, a colourful 'square' of old town houses and shops. Castle Hill (Grajski Grič) and Stari Trg are to the west and south-west; the northern side of the Old Town is scarred by saw mills and paper factories.

The bus station is about 400m north-east of the tourist office at Pohorska cesta 15. Slovenj Gradec is not on a train line.

Information

The tourist office (☎/fax 41 940) on the ground floor of the former town hall at Glavni trg 24 can provide information and arrange accommodation. It sells guides to the region, including the useful (but expensive at 1500 SIT) *Guide to Mislinjska Valley* in English. The office is open weekdays from 9 am to 4 pm and till noon on Saturday. Kompas (☎ 41 152), Glavni trg 38, will answer general questions and book private rooms. It is open from 8 am to 1 pm and 4 to 6 pm weekdays and till noon on Saturday.

Nova Ljubljanska Banka at Glavni trg 30 is open from 7.30 am to 5.30 pm weekdays and till noon on Saturday. The A Banka branch in the former Rotenturn mansion at Šolska ulica 5 is open from 8 to 11 am and 2 to 7 pm weekdays and till 11 am on Saturday. SKB Banka has a branch at Francetova cesta 7 open weekends from 8.30 am till noon and 2 to 5 pm.

The post office is at the northern end of Glavni trg on Francetova cesta. It is open Monday to Friday from 8 am to 6 pm and till noon on Saturday.

KOROŠKA

Slovenj Gradec

0   100   200 m

PLACES TO STAY
17   Kompas Hotel

PLACES TO EAT
1   Pizzerija Turist

OTHER
2   Bus Station
3   SKB Banka
4   Cultural Centre
5   Post Office
6   Pod Velbom Café-Pub
7   Pik Bar
8   Mladinska Knjiga Bookshop
9   Rotenturn Mansion
10   A Banka
11   Tourist Office & Museums
12   Venetian Horse Statue
13   Nova Ljubljanska Banka
14   Salon Maj Shop
15   Kompas Travel Agency
16   Hugo Wolf House
18   Soklič Museum
19   Church of St Elizabeth
20   Church of the Holy Spirit
21   Medical Centre

Mladinska Knjiga, the bookshop at Glavni trg 6, has regional maps if you've arrived in Koroška unprepared and want to do some hiking. It is open from 7.30 am to 6.30 pm weekdays and till noon on Saturday.

Slovenj Gradec's medical centre (☎ 41 031) is south-east of Glavni trg at Partizanska pot 16.

Museums

The former town hall at Glavni trg 24, where the tourist office is located, contains two important museums. The **Koroška Regional Museum** (open 9 am to 6 pm Tuesday through Friday and till noon on Saturday; 200 SIT) has exhibits on the 2nd floor devoted to the history of Slovenj Gradec and the Koroška region – from local sport heroes' awards and farm implements to models of wartime hospital rooms and schools – and a very good archaeological collection on the ground floor.

Most of the latter deals with the Roman settlement of Colatio and includes jewellery and other effects taken from a Slavic burial ground at Puščava near Castle Hill. This part of the town hall served as a German prison during WWII.

The **Gallery of Fine Arts** on the 1st floor is open on the same days as the regional museum but closes between noon and 3 pm on weekdays and admission is 300 SIT. It has rotating exhibits but counts among its permanent collection African folk art, bronze sculptures by Franc Berneker (1874-1932) and naive paintings by Jože Tisnikar (1928-). Tisnikar is among the most interesting and original artists in Slovenia, and his obsession with corpses, distorted figures and oversized insects (perhaps inspired by that locust attack in the late 15th century) is at once disturbing and funny. Don't miss *Rojstva in Smrt (Birth and Death)* and *Stopala (Feet)*. The paintings are all very black and blue.

The interesting **sculpture** in the courtyard is of the French poet Guillaume Apollinaire done by Ossip Zadkine in 1946. Outside the town hall is the odd, life-size **Venetian Horse** by contemporary sculptor Oskar Kogoj. It has become something of a symbol for the town.

The items on display at the **Soklič Museum** in the church rectory at Trg Svobode 5 were amassed by Jakob Soklič (1893-1972), a priest who began squirrelling away bits and bobs in the 1930s. Among the mediocre watercolours and oils of peasant idylls and the umpteen portraits of Hugo Wolf (a Slovenian composer who was born at Glavni trg 40 in 1860) are green goblets and beakers from nearby Glažuta (an important glass-manufacturing town in the 19th century), local embroidery and linen, religious artefacts and some 18th century furniture. The statue of a saint holding a chalice with a snake coming out of it represents St John the Evangelist. (In quite a reversed role for a biblical reptile, a serpent once warned the apostle that he was about to quaff poisoned wine.) The museum is open on request; ask at the regional museum or the tourist office.

Churches

The sombre **Church of St Elizabeth** (1251), the town's oldest structure, is at the end of Trg Svobode. But aside from the Romanesque nave and a couple of windows, almost everything here is baroque, including the massive gold altar and the altar paintings done by local artist Franc Mihael Strauss (1647-1740) and his son Janez Andrej Strauss (1721-82). Far more interesting is the 15th century **Church of the Holy Spirit** next door with an interior covered with Gothic frescoes by Andrej of Otting. The 27 panels on the north wall represent the Passion of Christ; the scenes on the archway are of the Final Judgment. As always, the most disturbing scenes are those of the devil leading the damned down, down, down ...

Stari Trg, where the Romans once frolicked, is nothing but an empty field now, but on Castle Hill (530m) there is the lovingly restored 13th century **Parish Church of St Pancras**, the oldest hall church in the country, with a bell tower that is part of the 17th century fortifications. The house to the left of the church holds the key. Castle Hill is about a 25-minute walk to the north-west from Stari Trg; just follow the **Calvary** and its baroque **Stations of the Cross** up the hill. If you continue along the path past the church you'll reach Puščava, site of an early Slavic burial ground.

Activities

There are plenty of opportunities for recreation near the airfield in Mislinjska Dobrava some 6km south-east of Slovenj Gradec; take the Velenje road (No 10-10) for 5km and then turn east for another 800m. The bus to Mislinja or Velenje will drop you off along the main road.

First you'll come to the Slovenj Gradec Riding Club (☎ 53 547), which has horses for rent both within the hippodrome and cross-country, and tennis courts. Next is the Koroški Aeroclub (☎ 53 630), which offers 10-minute sightseeing flights of the Mislinja Valley for 2500 SIT for one person (4800 SIT for up to three); 15-minute ones of Ravne, Velenje and Dravograd for 3700 SIT (6900 SIT for three); and 20-minute flights over Mozirje and Radlje for 4800 SIT for one person (9000 SIT for three).

The Cross Country Club (☎ 53 058 or ☎ 53 110), 2km south-east of Slovenj Gradec on Legenska cesta, also has horses for riding (1000 SIT per hour).

Three ski slopes are within striking distance of Slovenj Gradec, but the closest is Kope (☎ 42 391 for information), 1380m above the Mislinja Valley on the western edge of the Pohorje Massif. The ski grounds have 9km of runs and seven lifts on Mala Kopa and Velika Kopa peaks. To reach Kope, follow the Velenje road for 3km south and then turn east. The ski area is another 13km at the end of the road. Special ski buses make the run in winter, depending on the snowfall.

The *Guide to the Mislinjska Valley* outlines a number of hikes and bicycle trips in the area, including some along sections of the E6 European Hiking and Slovenian Alpine trails. Pohorje is unique in Slovenia in that there is no real 'off season' for hiking; the meadows and paths are generally as good in the winter as they are in summer.

The Slovenian Alpine Trail passes through Stari Trg and the centre of Slovenj Gradec

before continuing up to Mala Kopa (1524m), where it meets the E6. There is a mountain hut at 1102m to the north-west – *Koča pod Kremžarjevim Vrhom* (☎ 44 883 or ☎ 41 038) – which is open daily June to October and weekends only the rest of the year. The E6 heads north through Vuhred and Radlje ob Dravi to Austria while the Slovenian Alpine Trail carries on eastward to Rogla and Maribor. There is more accommodation on Velika Kopa (1543m) at the *Grmovškov Dom* (☎ 53 410), which is open all year. If you are going to do a fair amount of hiking in the western Pohorje, pick up a copy of the 1:50,000-scale *Pohorje* GZS map before setting out.

Special Events

The Slovenj Gradec Summer Festival of music and other activities takes place from June to September. There is a bonfire and celebrations on Midsummer Night (Kresna Noč) on 23 June.

Places to Stay

The *Medeni Raj* camp site (☎ 53 483) is just beyond the airfield in Mislinjska Dobrava. 'Sweet Paradise' is a small, friendly place set among pine trees and costs about DM10 per person. The camp site also has bungalows (singles/doubles DM40/60 including breakfast), and the small restaurant there is open till 10 pm.

The tourist office can arrange accommodation in *private rooms* both in and out of town for about DM25 per person, but the list is very short.

The only hotel option in town is the 68-room *Kompas* (☎ 42 295; fax 43 179) at Glavni trg 43. Singles with shower and breakfast are 5000 SIT, doubles 9000 SIT. The rooms are no great shakes and the dark corridors seem to go on forever, but some of the public areas, including a pleasant courtyard out back, have been redone.

Places to Eat

The *Pizzerija Turist* at Francetova cesta 14 serves something round and doughy with tomato sauce on top that some people might call pizza. Still, it's cheap enough and the people are friendly. It's open till 9.30 pm. *Gostilna Murko*, about 400m north at Francetova cesta 24, is a rather chi-chi establishment popular with Austrian tourists on the go. It's open daily till 10 pm.

If you've got wheels, the *Tina* restaurant at the Bošnik farmhouse, about 4km northwest of Slovenj Gradec in Gmajna (house No 30), is an excellent choice. Among the specialities of the house is obara z ajdovimi žganci, a rich stew with buckwheat groats. In Stari Trg at house No 251 *Gostilna Markus* has fish specialities and wine from its own vineyard.

Entertainment
Classical music concerts are sometimes held at the Church of St Elizabeth on Trg Svobode and the Slovenj Gradec Cultural Centre (☎ 41 193) at Francetova ulica 5. If you're interested in chatting up Austrian business people, head for the *nightclub* at the Kompas hotel between 10 pm and 3 am. Otherwise, the best places for meeting people include the *Pod Velbom* café-pub at the start of Poštna ulica, open daily to 11 pm or midnight, and the *Pik Bar* next to Mladinska Knjiga at Glavni trg 6.

Things to Buy
A shop called Salon Maj at Glavni trg 32 has a good range of honeys – a speciality of this region – and other products produced in part by our little stinging friends, including heart-shaped honey cakes and beeswax candles.

Getting There & Away
Buses are frequent to Črna, Dravograd, Mislinja, Radlje ob Dravi, Ravne na Koroškem and Velenje. Other destinations served by bus from Slovenj Gradec include Celje (three a day), Gornji Grad (one), Legen (eight), Ljubljana (four to five), Maribor (eight), Piran (one on weekdays) and Vuhred (four).

DRAVOGRAD
• *pop 3500* • *area code* ☎*0602* • *postcode 2370*
Situated on the left bank of the Drava,

Slovenia's second longest river (144km), 'Drava Castle' is much smaller than its sister city 12km to the south but just as old, with a recorded history that dates back to the 12th century. It was then that the castle, the ruins of which can be seen on the hill to the north of town, was built. Situated on a bend in the Drava at the point where the smaller Meža and Mislinja rivers flow into it, the castle and the town were of great strategic importance for centuries.

Today, Dravograd is a sleepy place with few sights of its own. But it is a good springboard for exploring the Kobansko Hills to the north and the Drava Valley to the east. The Austrian border (crossing at Vič/Rabenstein) is just 3.5km north-west of Dravograd.

Orientation & Information
While Dravograd's historical centre and its main street, Trg 4 Julija, is on the left bank of the Drava, the bus and train stations are about 1km to the south-east on the right bank.

Nova Ljubljanska Banka, open from 7.30 am to 5.30 pm weekdays and till noon on Saturday, is at Trg 4 Julija 42 two doors east of the Church of St Vitus. The post office is at the eastern end of Trg Julija just before you cross the bridge over the Drava. It is open from 8 am to 6 pm and till noon on Saturday.

Things to See & Do
The **Church of St Vitus** at the western end – ie the top – of Trg 4 Julija is one of the most important Romanesque buildings extant in Slovenia. Built in the second half of the 12th century and only recently renovated, it is a solid structure of light brown stone with a high tower between the nave and the small circular presbytery. While the occupants in the house next door are more than happy to hand you the key, there's not much to see inside except for a beamed ceiling and a fresco of St Cyril and St Methodius. The church is used almost exclusively for wedding ceremonies; Mass is said only on the patron's feast day in June. The Gothic-style **Church of St John** on a bend in the

Drava, a short distance to the west of St Vitus, has a fine baroque interior.

The basement of the **town hall** at Trg 4 Julija 7 was used as a Gestapo prison and torture chamber during WWII. The hydroelectric dam on the Drava nearest Dravograd was built by German soldiers during the war, and many of them were lodged in town. The remains of a bombed-out bridge run parallel to the new one over the Drava.

It's an easy hike north from Dravograd to the **castle ruins** (not much more than a wall); just turn up Pod Gradom, a lane just before the Apolon Bar at Trg 4 Julija 22. The more energetic may want to carry on farther into the **Kobansko Hills**, where you just might encounter some traditional charcoal burners. A circular section of the Kozjak Mountain Trail leads north past Goriški Vrh to Mt Košenjak (1522m) and returns to Dravograd via Ojstrica. There is accommodation on weekends at the *Planinski Dom Košenjak* (☎ 83 504).

Places to Stay

The 16-room *Kudrnovsky* pension (☎ 84 370), which recently metamorphosed from a depressing old communist-style hotel, is at Meža cesta 3 by the train and bus stations. The cost for singles/doubles here is 2800/4800 SIT, and there's a pleasant restaurant with an outside café in summer open daily to 10 pm.

A bit out of town – about 1.5km northwest of Trg 4 Julija at Koroška cesta 48 – is the new *Traberg* hotel (☎ 84 440) with 63 beds. Singles/doubles are 7000/9000 SIT and its *Al Capone* nightclub (open 10 pm to 4 am) with 'erotic shows' was clearly set up to entice *Avstrijci* from over the border.

If you have your own transport and would like to get away from it all, consider spending a night or two in one of the dozen or so farmhouses in the picturesque village of Šentanel in the Mežica Valley, 6km northwest of Prevalje. Prevalje is 12km southwest of Dravograd and easily accessible by bus and train. The *Ploder* farmhouse (☎ 31 104) at Šentanel 3 has 15 rooms and is open in July and August, while the more isolated

Marin farmhouse (☎ 31 409), at Šentanel 8 and open all year, has 11. Both charge between DM30 and DM45 per person, depending on the season and room category.

Places to Eat

Trg 4 Julija has a handful of bistros, cafés and small restaurants, including the *Taverna Pagat* at No 34 and the *Bistro Wolf* at No 36. More pleasant, though, is the *Na Klancu* restaurant at Trg 4 Julija 27 with a back terrace facing the Drava.

Getting There & Away

If you're headed for Črna, Maribor via Radlje, Prevalje, Slovenj Gradec or Velenje, count on a bus about every half-hour or so. Three buses a day go to Celje, one to Gornji Grad, five to Ljubljana and two to Piran. There's also a daily bus to Klagenfurt (Celovec) in Austria.

Dravograd is on the rail line linking Maribor and Bleiburg (Pliberk) and Klagenfurt (Celovec) in Austria. Up to five trains a day depart for Maribor (64km; 1½ hours) via Vuzenica and Vuhred. The same number leave for Ravne na Koroškem and Prevalje (12km; 20 minutes), two of which cross the border into Austria.

AROUND DRAVOGRAD

An excellent bike trip follows the spectacular Drava Valley through the Pohorje and Kobansko Hills, 60km east to Maribor. The river, whose highest flow is reached at the start of the summer, is at its most scenic at Brezno and just above Fala, where it narrows into a gorge. Just before Maribor the Drava widens into a lake with the help of a major dam.

You don't have to go that far to see some great scenery, though. **Vuzenica** and **Muta**, two very attractive villages, are just 14km from Dravograd. The two towns can also be reached on the Maribor bus.

The **Church of St Nicholas** at Vuzenica (pop 2916), on the Drava's right bank, was built in the 12th century and expanded later. Its outstanding features include a star-vaulted ceiling typical of Koroška, 15th century frescoes in the porch and an original fortified wall surrounding the churchyard. The ruins of a 16th century **castle** can be seen on Pisterjev Vrh north-east of town.

Muta (pop 3727), a two-tier village across the Drava from Vuzenica, has churches on both levels, but you want the one in the lower town (Spodnja Muta) near the main road. The **Rotunda of St John the Baptist**, one of the oldest churches in Slovenia, is an austere round structure built in the early 1200s. Its shape, wooden roof and steeple are typical of the province, and the tiny church appears quite content with itself sitting in a field with the hills far behind it. There are fragmented reliefs on the east side of the apse and near the west entrance; if you can manage to wrest the key from the farmhouse next door at Liverska ulica 12, you'll get to see the 14th century frescoes in the choir. The larger **Church of St Margaret** up in Zgornja Muta is 'new', dating from the 17th century.

Prekmurje

Prekmurje, Slovenia's 'forgotten' corner, is mostly a broad plain that extends for kilometres 'beyond the Mura River'. Its isolation is rooted in history; until 1924 not a single bridge spanned the sluggish Mura River and crossings were made by ferry. As a result, Prekmurje has preserved some traditional music, folklore and even architecture in its distinctive Pannonian-style farmhouses.

Until the end of WWI, almost all of Prekmurje belonged to the Austro-Hungarian crown and a sizeable Magyar minority still lives here, especially around the spa town of Lendava, Slovenia's easternmost city and its oil capital, and in Murska Sobota, which Hungarians call Muraszombat. In many ways Prekmurje looks and feels more like Hungary than Slovenia, emphasised by the abundance of white storks, large thatched farmhouses with attached barns and other

HIGHLIGHTS

- Visit Plečnik's masterful Church of the Ascension in the flower-bedecked village of Bogojina
- See the last of Prekmurje's celebrated floating mills on the Mura River near Veržej
- Admire the wonderful 14th century frescoes at the Church of St Martin in Martjanci
- Watch for the arrival of the white storks in spring

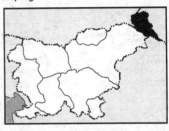

PREKMURJE

farm buildings under a single roof (see boxed text entitled The Farmhouses of Prekmurje), a substantial Gypsy population – especially around the village of Pušča west of Murska Sobota – and the occasional Hungarian-style *čarda* (inn).

For most Slovenes, Prekmurje means a local version of *golaž* (goulash) cooked with paprika, a rich pasty called *gibanica* and a people who are generally more volatile and quick-tempered than most others in the nation. For travellers the province is a springboard into Austria or Hungary and a place to relax and enjoy one of the many thermal spas in the region. Winters can be very cold on the plain, though, and summers extremely hot.

White storks make good use of Prekmurje's large thatched farmhouses and barns.

MURSKA SOBOTA

• *pop 13,900* • *area code ☎069* • *postcode 9000*
The capital and administrative centre of Prekmurje, Murska Sobota is a scruffy industrial town with little to recommend it, except for

313

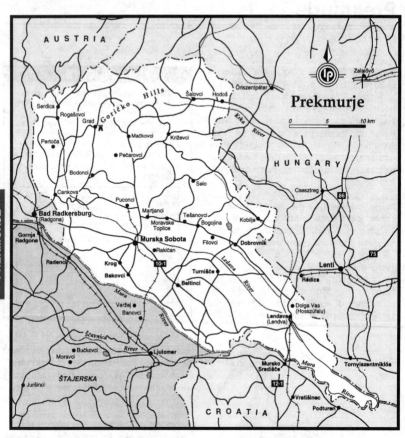

an odd architectural mix of neoclassical, Secessionist and 'socialist baroque' buildings. But the surrounding countryside, potters' villages and thermal spas make it a good starting point for travellers to the region.

History

Murska Sobota was little more than a market town – its name means 'Mura Saturday', indicating when the market took place – until two pivotal events this century.

The first was the opening of the railway (1907), which linked Murska Sobota with Hungary proper via Šalovci to the south. The second event was ultimately even more significant for the city. With the formation of the Kingdom of Serbs, Croats and Slovenes in 1918 and the transfer of territory, Murska Sobota found itself more or less in the centre of Prekmurje and development really began. The area was occupied by Hungary during WWII.

Orientation

The centre of Murska Sobota, Trg Zmage (Victory Square), lies south-east of large, shady City Park (Mestni Park). The bus station is some 400m due south of the square on Slomškova ulica next to the Diana hotel. The train station is about 600m south-east of Trg Zmage. Just follow Slovenska ulica, the main street lined with fruit stands and kiosks, southward and turn east on Ulica Arhitekta Novaka.

Information

Murska Sobota still does not have a tourist office. Seek assistance from the helpful staff at the tourist office in Moravske Toplice, 7km to the north-east. Failing that, the folks at Slovenijaturist (☎ 21 296) at Slovenska ulica 1 or at Kompas (☎ 21 312) in the Diana hotel should be able to help you with questions and arrangements. Slovenijaturist is open from 8.30 am to 2.30 pm weekdays only while Kompas opens from 8 am to 4 pm Monday to Friday and till noon on Saturday.

Pomurska Banka has a big branch at Trg Zmage 7 and is open from 7.30 am to 5 pm weekdays and Saturday to 11.30 am. The SKB Banka at Kocljeva ulica 14 has an ATM and is open weekdays from 8.30 am till noon and 2 to 5 pm.

The main post office, which is next door to Pomurska Banka on Trg Zmage and faces City Park, is open weekdays from 7 am to 7 pm, on Saturday to 1 pm and on Sunday from 9 to 11 am.

Dobra Knjiga, a bookshop at Slovenska ulica 11, has a decent selection of regional maps if you plan to do any hiking in the area. It is open from 7 am to 7 pm on weekdays and till noon on Saturday.

Sobota Castle

This late 15th century manor house is in the centre of City Park at the end of Trubarjev drevored and houses the recently renovated **Murska Sobota Regional Museum** on the 2nd floor; enter from the north side. The largest collection of the museum is an ethnographic one devoted to the culture and traditional lifestyles of the Prekmurje region. Anyone who has visited such collections in southern Transdanubia just across the border will find the farm implements, painted jugs, costumes and woodcarvings in the vaulted rooms almost identical to their Hungarian counterparts. The museum is open Tuesday to Friday from 10 am to 5 pm and on Saturday and Sunday to 1 pm.

The castle itself, with Renaissance and baroque elements, is interesting. Have a walk around the outside to spot the two Atlases supporting the balcony on the east side, the older chapel on the west and the lovely baroque gable with a clock on the north side.

Other Sights

You may be surprised to see heavy artillery guns and statues of Yugoslav and Soviet soldiers at the eastern entrance of **City Park**. This is the **Liberation Monument**, which somehow managed to stay in place despite the 'house cleaning' that the rest of Slovenia did after independence.

Opposite the park entrance is the neo-Gothic **Evangelical Church**, the main Lutheran seat in Slovenia. Prekmurje has long been a Protestant stronghold, and the majority of Slovenian Protestants live in this province. The church dates only from 1910, but its ceilings painted with geometric shapes and muted shades of blue and green are a welcome relief from the overwrought baroque gold and marble décor found in most Catholic churches.

The **Parish Church of St Nicholas** near the train station is a turn-of-the-century structure built around a Gothic presbytery with 14th century frescoes.

The **Murska Sobota Gallery** at Kocljeva ulica 7 has revolving exhibits and is arguably the best gallery in Prekmurje. It's open weekdays from 8 am to 6 pm (to 4 pm on Monday), from 10 am till noon on Saturday and from 9 am till noon on Sunday.

Activities

The Rakičan Castle Riding Centre (☎ 32 413) is located in the grounds of a historical castle 2km south-east of Murska Sobota at Lendavska ulica 28. It's all pretty serious stuff, with experienced riders trotting along the Mura or into the Goričko Hills to the north for about DM20 per hour, but absolute beginners can give it a go in the paddock for DM15. The centre is open daily, except Monday, from 9 am till noon and 2 pm to 8 pm. There's a very nice *café* in a wing of the castle open till 10 pm.

Special Events

The castle courtyard is the site of occasional concerts and at least one folklore festival in summer; ask at the Moravske Toplice tourist office or at one of the travel agencies as to what's going on.

Places to Stay

The closest *camp site* to Murska Sobota is at Moravske Toplice (see that section). The *Terme Banovci* (☎ 87 067) camping ground at a small spa near Veržej, about 13km south of Murska Sobota, is one of the few naturist camp sites in Slovenia. It's open April to October (Indian summer providing) and costs 1190 to 1390 SIT per person. Nearby on the Mura River is the last of the region's celebrated floating mills. The *Dijaški Dom Murska Sobota* (☎ 21 043 or ☎ 22 168), a student dormitory south-west of the centre at

Murska Sobota

0   200   400 m

To Martjanci (4km),
Moravske Toplice
(7km) &
'Potter's Road'
(9km)

Lendava River

City Park
(Mestni Park)

Trubarjev
drevored

Trg
Zmage

To Pušča
(3.5km)

To Rakičan Castle
Riding Centre (2km)

To Bakovci (5km)

PLACES TO STAY
18 Diana Hotel &
    Kompas Travel Agency

PLACES TO EAT
1   Taša Restaurant
2   Prekmurski Hram
    Restaurant
3   Rajh No 1 Mini-Restaurant
9   Former Zvezda Hotel
    & Restaurant
15 Bife

OTHER
4   Slovenijaturist Travel
    Agency
5   Dobra Knjiga
    Bookshop
6   Sobota Castle &
    Regional Museum
7   Liberation Monument
8   Evangelical Church
10 Pomurska Banka

11 Post Office
12 SKB Banka
13 Murska Sobota
    Gallery
14 Market
16 Rdeči Baron Pub
17 Bus Station
19 Church of
    St Nicholas
20 Train Station

PREKMURJE

Tomšičeva ulica 15, accepts travellers in summer only.

With the closure of the central Zvezda hotel on Trg Zmage, Murska Sobota's hotel accommodation options have been cut in half – and its budget ones reduced by 100%. The only central place is the expensive *Diana* hotel (☎ 32 530; fax 32 097), a garishly painted concrete block with 97 rooms at Slovenska ulica 52. Its singles with shower and breakfast are DM69, doubles are DM114. At those rates, you should indeed get 'unlimited use' of the indoor swimming pool as advertised.

The *Čarda* motel (☎ 48 118), about 2.5km north of town in the village of Nemčavci, charges about DM30 per person.

Places to Eat

There's an inexpensive *bife* in the market south of Trg Zmage open weekdays from 6.30 am to 4 pm and on Saturday till noon. The restaurant in the *Zvezda* hotel building at Trg Zmage 8 is no great shakes, but in warmer months the outside terrace under the chestnut trees becomes the focal point of Murska Sobota. It is open to 10 pm (till midnight on Friday and Saturday). *Grajski Hram* at the Sobota Castle is open weekdays only from 9 am to 8 pm.

You'll find better restaurants along Lendavska ulica, a few minutes walk to the north-east from Trg Zmage. *Prekmurski Hram* at No 35a has regional specialities; this is a good place to try some of the local Laški Rizling wine from one of Prekmurje's wine-growing areas. *Taša* at No 39e has simple dishes while the *Rajh No 1* 'mini-restaurant' on the corner of Lendavska ulica and Cvetkova ulica is an upmarket špagetarija and picerija. All are open till about 10 pm.

If you're under your own steam, head for the *Gostilna Rajh* at Soboška ulica 32 in Bakovci, a village 5km south-west of Murska Sobota. The Rajh specialises in local food and boasts a huge cellar of regional wines; President Kučan eats at this country inn whenever he's in the neighbourhood. Dishes to consider include the bograč golaž (Hungarian-style goulash 'soup'); roast suckling pig served with 'twice-cooked' noodles; and, of course, the gibanica.

Entertainment

A couple of pleasant pubs can be found along Slovenska ulica including *Rdeči Baron* (no prizes for guessing that *rdeč* means 'red' in Slovene) at No 42, open Monday to Thursday to 11 pm and on Friday and Saturday till midnight. The *disco* at the Diana hotel rages till 4 am on Friday and Saturday.

Getting There & Away

Bus Buses leave Murska Sobota at least 10 times a day for Dobrovnik, Gornja Radgona (via Radenci) on the Austrian border, Lendava near the Hungarian border, Ljutomer, Mačkovci, Maribor, Moravske Toplice, Petrovci, Rakičan and Turnišče (via Dobrovnik or Beltinci). Other destinations include Beltinci (up to five departures daily), Celje via Ljutomer (seven), Grad (six), Hodoš on the Hungarian border (eight), Ljubljana via Maribor or Ljutomer (eight), Ormož (five), Piran (two) and Ptuj (two).

A bus headed for Lenti in Hungary leaves Murska Sobota Thursday to Saturday at 9.10 am.

Train Murska Sobota is on a spur that connects it with a main line (to Ljubljana, Maribor, Vienna and Budapest) at Ormož (39km; 45 minutes). There are up to nine departures a day, and the train stops at Beltinci, Ljutomer and sometimes Veržej.

AROUND MURSKA SOBOTA
Martjanci

The **Parish Church of St Martin** in this village 4km north of Murska Sobota, on the road to Moravske Toplice, contains wonderful 14th century frescoes painted on the presbytery's vaulted ceiling and walls by Johannes Aquila of Radgona. They depict angels bearing inscriptions, the Apostles, scenes from the life of St Martin and even a self-portrait of Master Johannes himself. Not to be outdone by the artist, the church's benefactor had his likeness appear in several scenes on the north arch and west wall.

PREKMURJE

MORAVSKE TOPLICE
• *pop 700* • *area code* ☎069 • *postcode 9226*

The thermal spa of Moravske Toplice, 7km north-east of Murska Sobota, boasts the hottest water in Slovenia: 72°C at source and cooled to 38°C for use in its many pools and basins. Though it's one of the newest spas in the country – the spring was discovered in 1960 during exploratory oil drilling – many young Slovenes consider the clientele too geriatric for their liking, preferring the small *au naturel* spa at Banovci. But Moravske Toplice is every bit a health resort geared for recreation, with enough sport facilities to cater to every taste.

Information
The tourist office (☎ 48 940; fax 48 765) is at No 3 on Kranjčeva ulica, the main thoroughfare running east-west through town, and a short distance north-west of the spa complex. It is open Monday to Saturday from 8 am to 8 pm (6 pm in winter) and on Sunday to 2 pm.

There's a Pomurska Banka branch near the entrance to the spa open weekdays from 8 am to 2.30 pm (5 pm on Wednesday) and on Saturday to 11.15 am. The post office, near the tourist office on Kranjčeva ulica, is open from 7 am to 6 pm and till noon on Saturday.

Thermal Spa
The resort counts nine indoor and outdoor pools filled with thermal water and two large outdoor ones with ordinary heated water. The thermal water is recommended for relief of rheumatism and certain minor skin problems, and there are enough therapies and beauty treatments available to keep you occupied for a week. Many visitors, though, simply come to sit in the warm water, cycle in the countryside or walk in the nearby vineyards. If you're staying at the resort, you get use of the pools for free; otherwise you'll have to pay between 700 and 1500 SIT for the privilege. The spa resort also has several tennis courts, a fitness room/gym and saunas.

Places to Stay & Eat
The tourist office can organise *private rooms* for between DM20 and DM29 per person, depending on the season and the category. If you're going freelance, there are rooms available at Kranjčeva ulica 16 and at No 30 of the same street. *Apartments* booked through the tourist office cost DM33 per person.

All the accommodation at the Moravske Toplice resort complex shares the same contact numbers (☎ 48 210; fax 48 607).

The five-hectare *camp site* can accommodate 200 guests and is open all year except December. Use of the swimming pool nearby is included in the daily charge (DM17 per person).

The resort's two hotels – big modern structures of little interest – are expensive. Singles with shower and breakfast at the 274-bed *Ajda* are DM106 to DM115 and doubles are DM168 to DM186, depending on the season. The 252-bed *Termal*, while cheaper, is still going to cost you a minimum of DM86 to DM93 for a single and DM138 to DM152 for a double.

The only other option at the resort is to stay in one of the attractive *bungalows* done up to look like traditional Prekmurje peasant cottages, with thatched or tiled roofs and cool whitewashed walls. They cost DM65 to DM77 for one person and DM96 to DM120 for two, depending on the time of year.

The *Flisarovi* farmhouse (☎ 48 411), about 3km north of the resort at Dolga ulica 213, has nine rooms costing DM25 to DM30 per person. Closer to the resort, at house No 5b in Moravske Toplice village, is the *Gostilna Kuhar* (☎ 48 215), a restaurant with accommodation.

There's a basic *pizzeria* next to the Pomurska Banka at the entrance to the spa open daily from 1 to 8 pm. A good place in which to sample Prekmurje's food specialities is *Popotnik*, a couple of kilometres north of the spa at Dolga ulica 116. It is open daily, except Tuesday, from 9 am till midnight.

Getting There & Around
Buses leave hourly from Kranjčeva ulica for Murska Sobota, and there are about a dozen a day to Dobrovnik. Other destinations

include Kobilje (six buses a day), Lendava via Turnišče (six), Ljubljana (one via Maribor) and Maribor. The tourist office rents bicycles for 250 SIT an hour.

AROUND MORAVSKE TOPLICE

An excellent bike trip (also accessible on the Dobrovnik and Kobilje buses) is what could be called **potters' road** which runs southeast from the spa. The road passes through the villages of Tešanovci, Bogojina and Filovci; to the north are the low Goričko Hills covered in vineyards. This is not Prekmurje's most important wine-growing region – that distinction goes to the areas around Lendava to the south-east and Gornja Radgona to the west – but it is just as lovely.

Tešanovci (pop 1080), less than 2km from Moravske Toplice, is noted for its pottery *(lončarstvo)*, and you can visit workshops at house Nos 51 and 53 on the main road. Otherwise, Tešanovci is not an especially interesting place; carry on another 2.5km to **Bogojina** (pop 1530), which should get an award for being the most attractive and tidiest village in Prekmurje.

The main attraction here is the **Parish Church of the Ascension**, redesigned by Jože Plečnik between 1926 and 1927. The church is at the northern end of the village on a low hill; from the main road proceed

Jože Plečnik's impact on Slovenian architecture has been extraordinary.

past peasant houses bedecked with flowers and storks nesting on chimneys and telephone poles to No 147. To the original Romanesque and baroque structure, Plečnik added two asymmetrical aisles and a round

PREKMURJE

The Farmhouses of Prekmurje

Along with *gibanica* cake and storks, Prekmurje is known for its traditional L-shaped farmhouses, among the most uniform regional dwellings in Slovenia. Anyone who has crossed the border into Hungary will recognize them; they are not dissimilar to the *kerített házak* ('fenced-in houses') found in Transdanubia.

The thatched roof of a Prekmurje farmhouse extended into the central courtyard, and this sheltered 'portico' *(podsten)* allowed access from the outside to all the rooms when it rained. It was also used as a work area and a place to gossip with the family or neighbours on a warm summer afternoon.

The main living area consisted of a central entrance hall, which also served as the kitchen. The large open hearth was used to cook and also to heat the tile stoves in the rooms on either side: the 'first room' *(prva izba)*, with table and chairs, decorated trousseau chests and religious icons, and the 'back room' *(zadnja izba)*, used for sleeping. Connected to the house (though accessible only from the portico) were the work and storage shed, the barn and the stable.

Another distinctive feature of Prekmurje houses (though not uncommon in south-western Hungary) were the floral designs stencilled on the outside walls about a metre from the ground. They gave a little colour to the stark, whitewashed walls and varied from one house to another. ∎

tower reminiscent of a crow's nest on a ship. The interior is an odd mixture of black marble, brass and wood; the oak-beamed ceiling is fitted with ceramic plates and jugs collected from the area.

Filovci (pop 522), another 2km beyond Bogojina, is famed throughout Slovenia for its *črna keramika* (black pottery), which can also be found in parts of southern and eastern Hungary. One of the best workshops to visit is at house No 29, where the Bojnec family work the wheels and fire their pots and pitchers in an old brick oven. The workshop is about 200m south-west of the main road past the small church and over the bridge.

If you get hungry, there are a couple of decent gostilne in **Dobrovnik**, 3.5km beyond Filovci. *Pri Lujzi* is at house No 273a. *Lipot*, almost opposite at No 277a, has outside seating. Both are open till 10 or 11 pm.

RADENCI
• *pop 5750* • *area code ☎069* • *postcode 9252*
Strictly speaking, Radenci is not part of Prekmurje province because it is not 'beyond the Mura'. In fact, it lies about a kilometre from the river's right bank and is thus really 'on the Mura' (Pomurje). But let's not get technical ... Radenci has always been closely tied historically and geographically with Prekmurje, and it is easily accessible from Murska Sobota, 13km to the east.

Radenci is best known for its health resort, parts of which still feel like a full-of-itself 19th century spa town. Indeed, as one Slovenian wag put it: 'Radenci remains the preserve of highbrow intellectuals and rumble-tumble chamber music.' But when most Slovenes hear the name they think of Radenska Tri Srca – the Radenci Three Hearts mineral water bottled here that is consumed in every restaurant and café in the land.

Orientation & Information
Radenci lies west and north of the Radgona-Kapel wine-growing area. To the north is a triangle of Austrian territory inhabited mostly by ethnic Slovenes. The border crossing is at Gornja Radgona/Bad Rakersburg, 6km north-west of Radenci.

For general information, go to reception in the Radin hotel (☎ 65 331) or to the Marika travel agency (☎ 65 889) at the bus station, which is south-east of the spa complex. The latter also does exchange and is open from 8 am to 5 pm weekdays and till noon on Saturday.

Pomurska Banka has a branch at Panonska cesta 5-7 open weekdays from 7.30 am to 5 pm and on Saturday to 11.30 am. The post office, open from 7 am to 7 pm weekdays and till noon on Saturday, is on the same street opposite the Vikend restaurant.

Thermal Spa
The health resort has three claims to fame: water rich in carbon dioxide for drinking; thermal water high in minerals for bathing that comes out at 41°C at source; and sulphuric Negova mud for smearing all over yourself. All three play a role in the therapeutic and beauty treatments so popular here.

Springs of mineral water were discovered in the early 19th century, and the bottling of Radenska water began in 1869. By the turn of the century, the water had become so popular that it was sent to the imperial court in Vienna and to the pope in Rome. The spa itself opened in 1882.

Today, three modern (and ugly) blocks overlook the older Victorian-style buildings and a large wooded park with paths, a chapel, pavilions and tame red squirrels. The complex counts several pools, including an indoor recreational one, an outdoor thermal one with a temperature of about 34°C and an outdoor Olympic-size one. Guests can use the pools at will; outsiders pay 500 to 1000 SIT depending on the pool.

There's a small **museum** in the park devoted to the history and development of the spa and its famous mineral water (open daily from 10 am till noon and again, on Tuesday, from 3 to 4 pm).

Activities
The tennis courts just south of the hotel complex can be rented for 900 SIT per hour (1200 SIT at night). Racquets (300 SIT) and balls are available from the small kiosk there

from 8 am to noon and 2 to 8 pm. Lessons cost 1500 SIT per hour. For badminton, table tennis and minigolf, go to the large outdoor pool. Mountain bikes are available for rent.

Excellent cycling excursions can be made into the surrounding wine country; head south-west along the 'wine road' *(vinska cesta)* for about 4km to Janžev Vrh and an old vineyard cottage called Janžev Hram or even farther south to Kapelski Vrh and Ivanjski Vrh. Almost all the wines produced here are whites; try the popular local one called Janževec or the Zlata Radgonska Penina sparkling wine.

Special Events

The spa puts on its famous chamber music concerts in summer.

Places to Stay

There are lots of *private rooms* available on Panonska cesta to the west and south of the spa's main entrance, including some at house No 23. The price should be about DM25 per person. The *Vikend* restaurant (☎ 65 996) at Panonska cesta 2 has rooms available for 1600 SIT per person.

The three spa hotels (☎ 65 331; fax 66 594), with a total of more than 500 beds, are much of a muchness and certainly no bargain. Singles at the cheapest of the three – the *Terapija* – range from DM65 to DM80, depending on the season, with doubles

DM110 to DM140. Prices at the three-star *Miral* and four-star *Radin* are generally about 20% and 50% higher respectively.

Places to Eat

Radenci is supposed to have some of the best food in Slovenia, but great cuisine proved elusive for me; perhaps you'll be luckier. The *Park* restaurant in the middle of the resort's large wooded park is a pleasant place for a meal in summer, but the mosquitoes may consume you first. It closes on Monday. The *Vikend* restaurant is a big, raucous place at Panonska cesta 2 and open every day.

For something a little more colourful, head north-west for about 3km on the road to Austria to *Gostilna Klobasa* in Šratovci at house No 8 or to *Gostilna Adanič* in Mele at house No 27a. They're both open till about 10 pm.

Getting There & Away

Bus services are frequent to Maribor, Murska Sobota and Gornja Radgona. Other destinations include Celje (six a day), Koper (two), Lendava (up to 10), Ljubljana (up to eight), Ljutomer (six), Nova Gorica (one), Ormož (two), Piran (one or two) and Rogaška Slatina (one).

Passenger trains do not operate on the Ljutomer-Gornja Radgona line that passes through Radenci; it is used for freight only.

Alternative Place Names

ABBREVIATIONS

(C) Croatian
(Cz) Czech
(E) English
(G) German

(H) Hungarian
(I) Italian
(S) Slovene

Adriatic Sea (E) – Jadran, Jadransko Morje (S)
Aquileia (I) – Oglej (S)

Bad Radkersburg (G) – Radgona (S)
Bela Krajina (S) – White March (E)
Bleiburg (G) – Pliberk (S)
Budapest (H) – Budimpešta (S)

Cividale (I) – Čedad (S)

Dolenjska (S) – Lower Carniola (E)

Eisenkappel (G) – Železna Kapla (S)

Gorenjska (S) – Upper Carniola (E)
Gorizia (I) – Gorica (S)
Graz (G) – Gradec (S)
Gulf of Trieste (E) – Tržaški Zaliv (S),
   Golfo di Trieste (I)

Hrvatska (C) – Croatia (E), Hrvaška (S)

Istria (E) – Istra (S)
Italia (I) – Italy (E), Italija (S)
Izola (S) – Isola (I)

Karnburg (G) – Krnski Grad (S)
Klagenfurt (G) – Celovec (S)
Kobarid (S) – Caporetto (I)
Koper (S) – Capodistria (I)
Koroška (S) – Carinthia (E), Kärnten (G)
Kras (S) – Karst (E)
Kranjska (S) – Carniola (E), Krain (G)

Leibnitz (G) – Lipnica (S)

Lendava (S) – Lendva (H)
Ljubljana (S) – Laibach (G)

Magyarország (H) – Hungary (E), Madžarska (S)
Mediterranean Sea (E) – Sredozemlje,
   Sredozemsko Morje (S)
Monfalcone (I) – Tržič (S)
Montenegro (E) – Črna Gora (S)
Murska Sobota (S) – Muraszombat (H)

Notranjska (S) – Inner Carniola (E)

Österreich (G) – Austria (E), Avstrija (S)

Piran (S) – Pirano (I)
Portorož (S) – Portorose (I)
Prague (E) – Praga (S), Praha (Cz)
Prekmurje (S) – 'Beyond the Mura' (E)
Primorska (S) – Littoral

Rijeka (C) – Reka (S), Fiume (I)
Rome (E) – Rim (S), Roma (I)

Serbia (E) – Srbija (S)
Soča (S) – Isonzo (I)
Štajerska (S) – Styria (E), Steiermark (G)

Tarvisio (I) – Trbiž (S)
Trieste (I) – Trst (S)

Udine (I) – Videm (S)

Venice (E) – Benetke (S), Venezia (I)
Vienna (E) – Dunaj (S), Wien (G)
Villach (G) – Beljak (S)

322

Language Guide

Slovene *(slovenščina)* is a South Slavic language closely related to Croatian and Serbian and written in the Roman alphabet. Linguists have counted no fewer than 50 dialects and sub-dialects in little Slovenia though the 'purest' form of the language is said to be spoken in north-west Dolenjska.

Slovene is a grammatically complex language with six cases for nouns and adjectives, three genders and four verb tenses. In addition to singular and plural, Slovene also has a separate 'dual' form to indicate 'two' of something: *miza*, 'one table', *mize*, 'three or more tables', but *mizi*, 'two tables'.

There are many irregularities in verb conjugations and noun declensions but adjectives precede the noun as in English and there are no articles: 'a table' or 'the table' is just 'table', *miza*.

The Slovenian alphabet has 25 letters – the 'q', 'w', 'x' and 'y' of the English alphabet are not used but it contains the letters 'č', 'š' and 'ž' in both upper and lower case. (The little mark on top is called a *strešica*, or 'little roof', in Slovene.)

Pronunciation

Like English, Slovene is not a 'one letter-one value' language. The pronunciation of some vowels and consonants (eg 'v' or 'l') can change from word to word even though the same letter is used in the spelling. Stress – where the emphasis falls on a word – is also irregular and, as in English, has to be learned for individual words. The following should be seen only as an approximate guide to Slovene pronunciation.

Consonants Most Slovene consonants are pronounced more or less as they are in English. The following are the main exceptions:

c	as the 'ts' in 'hats'
č	as the 'ch' in 'church'
j	as the 'y' in 'yes'
l	as 'w' if at the end of a syllable or before a vowel; elsewhere as the 'l' in 'lie'
lj	as the 'li' in 'million'
nj	as the 'ni' in 'onion'
r	a slightly trilled Spanish or Scottish 'r'
š	as the 'sh' in 'she'
šč	as the 'sh' and 'ch' in 'fresh chips'
v	as 'w' if at the end of a syllable or before a vowel; elsewhere as the 'v' in 'via'
ž	as the 's' in 'pleasure'

Don't be fazed by vowel-less words like *trg*, 'square', or *vrt*, 'garden' (which are pronounced something like 'terg' and 'vert'), or by consonant clusters such as *ključ*, 'key' (which is pronounced 'klyooch').

Vowels The five basic vowels in Slovene are 'a', 'e', 'i', 'o', 'u', but each can have several different pronunciations, depending on whether it's stressed, unstressed, long or short. The letter 'e', for example, can sound like the 'a' in 'gate', the 'e' in 'there' or the 'e' in 'bet'. Slovenian dictionaries often mark these differences with accents (é, ê, è), but they never appear elsewhere in the written language. Don't worry though, as you shouldn't have too much trouble being understood even if your pronunciation is slightly off.

The following is a very rough guide to the pronunciation of Slovenian vowels.

a	as in 'far' or as the 'u' in 'cut'
e	as in 'bet'
i	as in 'hit' or as the 'ee' in 'feet'
o	as in 'hot' or as in 'go'
u	as the 'oo' in 'soon' but shorter

For more words and phrases in Slovene, see the Food and Drinks sections in the Facts for the Visitor chapter or the Glossary that follows this Language Guide. For a more in-depth look at the language get hold of Lonely Planet's *Mediterranean Europe phrasebook*.

Useful Words & Phrases

Hello.	*Dober dan.* (polite)
Hi.	*Živio/Zdravo.* (informal)
Goodbye.	*Na svidenje.*
Good morning.	*Dobro jutro.*
Good day/ afternoon.	*Dober dan.*
Good evening.	*Dober večer.*
Good night.	*Lahko noč.*
Please.	*Prosim.*
Thank you (very much).	*Hvala (lepa).*
You're welcome.	*Prosim/Ni za kaj.*
Yes.	*Ja.*
No.	*Ne.*
Maybe.	*Mogoče.*
I'm sorry. (forgive me)	*Oprostite.*
How are you?	*Kako ste?* (polite) *Kako si?* (informal)
Fine, thanks.	*Dobro, hvala.*

Essentials

Please write it down.	*Prosim, zapišite si.*
Please show me (on the map).	*Prosim pokažite mi (na mapi)*
I understand.	*Razumem.*
I don't understand.	*Ne razumem.*
I don't speak …	*Ne govorim …*
Do you speak English?	*Ali govorite angleško?*
Does anyone speak English?	*Ali kdo govori angleško?*
Where are you from?	*Od kod ste?*
I'm from …	*Sem iz …*
How old are you?	*Koliko ste stari?*
I'm … years old.	*Imam … let.*
I have a visa/permit.	*Imam vizum/ dovoljenje.*

surname	*priimek*
given name	*ime*
date/place of birth	*datum/kraj rojstva*
nationality	*državljanstvo*
male/female	*moški/ženska*
passport	*potni list*

Small Talk

What is your name?	*Kako vam je ime?* (polite) *Kako ti je ime?* (informal)
My name is …	*Ime mi je …*
I'm a tourist/student.	*Sem turist/študent.*
Are you married?	*Ali ste poročeni?*
Do you like …?	*Ali imate radi …?*
I like it very much.	*Imam zelo rad.*
I don't like …	*Ne maram …*
Just a minute.	*Samo trenutek.*
May I?	*Ali lahko?*
It's all right.	*Je v redu.*
No problem.	*Brez problema.*
How do you say … in Slovene?	*Kako se reče … po slovensko?*
What does this mean?	*Kaj to pomeni?*

Getting Around

I want to go to …	*Rad bi šel v …*
I want to book a seat for …	*Rad bi rezerviral sedež za …*
What time does the … depart/arrive?	*Ob kateri uri je odhod/prihod …*
Where does the … leave from?	*Od kje pelje …*
bus/tram	*avtobusa*
train	*vlaka*
boat/ferry/ hydrofoil	*ladje/trajekta/ gliserja*
plane	*letala*
How long does the trip take?	*Koliko dolgo traja potovanje?*
The train is delayed/early.	*Vlak ima zamudo/je zgodnji.*
The train is on time.	*Vlak prihaja pravočasno.*
The train is cancelled.	*Vožnja je stornirana.*
Do I need to change?	*Ali moram presesti?*
You must change trains/platform.	*Presesti morate vlak/peron.*

left-luggage office/locker	*garderoba*
one-way ticket	*enosmerna vozovnica*
platform	*peron*

return ticket	*povratna vozovnica*
(bus/train) station	*(avtobusna/železniška) postaja*
ticket	*vozovnica*
ticket office	*blagajna*
timetable	*vozni red*
I'd like to hire a …	*Rad bi najel …*
bicycle/motorcycle	*kolo/motorno kolo*
car	*avto*
guide	*vodiča*
horse	*konja*

Directions

How do I get to …?	*Kako pridem do …?*
Where is …?	*Kje je …?*
Is it near/far?	*Ali je blizu/daleč?*
What street/road is this?	*Katera ulica/cesta je to?*
What town/what village is this?	*Katero mesto/ katera vas je to?*
(Go) straight ahead.	*(Pojdite) naravnost naprej.*
(Turn) left/right at the …	*(Zavijte) na levo/ desno …*
traffic light	*pri semaforju*
next/second/ third corner	*pri naslednjem/ drugem/tretjem ovinku*
up/down	*zgoraj/spodaj*
behind/opposite	*za/nasproti*
east/west	*vzhod/zahod*
north/south	*sever/jug*

here/there/ everywhere	*tu/tam/povsod*

Around Town

Where is the/a …?	*Kje je …?*
bank	*banka*
city centre	*središče mesta/ center*
embassy	*ambasada*
entrance/exit	*vhod/izhod*
exchange office	*menjalnica*
hospital	*bolnišnica*
market	*tržnica*
police	*policija*
post office	*pošta*
public toilet	*javno stranišče*
restaurant	*restavracija*
tourist information office	*turistični informacijski center (TIC)*
I want to make a telephone call.	*Rad bi telefoniral.*
I'd like to change some money/ travellers cheques	*Rad bi zamenjal nekaj denarja/ potovalne čeke*
abbey	*opatija*
beach	*plaža*
bridge	*most*
castle	*grad*
cathedral	*stolnica*
church	*cerkev*
hospital	*bolnišnica*
island	*otok*

Useful Signs

CAMPING GROUND	*KAMP/KAMPING*	POLICE STATION	*POLICIJSKA POSAJA*
ENTRANCE	*VHOD*	PROHIBITED	*PREPOVEDANO*
EXIT	*IZHOD*	PULL	*VLECI*
ADMISSION	*VSTOPNINA*	PUSH	*RINI*
FULL/OCCUPIED	*POLNO/ZASEDENO*	ROOMS AVAILABLE	*SOBE PROSTE*
GUESTHOUSE	*GOSTIŠČE/PENZION*	TOILETS	*STRANIŠČE/WC*
INFORMATION	*INFORMACIJA*	LADIES/GENTS	*ŽENSKE/MOŠKI*
OPEN/CLOSED	*ODPRTO/ZAPRTO*	TRAIN STATION	*ŽELEZNISKA POSTAJA*
POLICE	*POLICIJA*	YOUTH HOSTEL	*POČITNIŠKI DOM*

lake	*jezero*
main square	*glavni trg*
manor	*dvorec*
market	*tržnica*
old city	*staro mesto*
palace	*palača*
ruins	*ruševine*
sea	*morje*
square	*trg*
tower	*stolp*

Accommodation

I'm looking for …	*Iščem …*
a youth hostel	*počitniški dom*
a camping ground	*kamping*
a hotel	*hotel*
a guesthouse	*gostišče/penzion*
the manager/owner	*direktorja/lastnika*

What's the address?	*Na katerem na slovu je?*
Do you have a … available?	*Ali imate … prosto?*
bed	*posteljo*
cheap room	*poceni sobo*
single/double room	*enoposteljno/dvopost eljno sobo*

for one night/ two nights	*za eno noč/ za dve noči*
How much is it per night/per person?	*Koliko stane na noč/na osebo?*
Is breakfast included?	*Ali je zajtrk vključen?*
Is service included?	*Ali je postrežba vključena?*
Can I see the room?	*Lahko vidim sobo?*
Where is the toilet?	*Kje je stranišče?*
It's very dirty/ noisy/expensive.	*Je zelo umazana/ hrupna/draga.*
I'm/We're leaving now.	*Danes odhajam/ odhajamo.*

Do you have (a) …?	*Ali imate …?*
clean sheet	*čisto rjuho*
hot water	*toplo vodo*
key	*ključ*
shower	*tuš*
towel	*brisača*

Food

I'm hungry/thirsty.	*Lačen/žejen sem.*
breakfast	*zajtrk*
lunch	*kosilo*
dinner	*večerja*
set menu	*meni*
grocery store/ delicatessen	*samopostrežba/ delikatesa*
market	*tržnica*
restaurant	*restavracija*
waiter/waitress	*natakar/natakarica*

I'd like the set lunch, please.	*Lahko dobim meni, prosim?*
Is service included in the bill?	*Ali je napitnina vključena?*
I'm a vegetarian.	*Vegetarijanec sem.*
I'd like some …	*Rad bi nekaj …*
Another, please.	*Še enkrat, prosim.*
The bill, please.	*Račun, prosim.*
I don't eat …	*Ne jem …*

beef	*govedina*
beer	*pivo*
bread	*kruh*
butter	*maslo*
cheese	*sir*
chicken	*piščanec*
coffee	*kava*
eggs	*jajca*
fish	*riba*
food	*hrana*
fruit	*sadje*
fruit juice	*sadni sok*
meat	*meso*
milk	*mleko*
mineral water	*mineralna voda, Radenska (brand-name)*

pepper	*poper*
pork	*svinjina*
salt	*sol*
soup	*juha*
sugar	*sladkor*
tea	*čaj*
vegetables	*zelenjava*
wine	*vino*

hot/cold	*topel/hladen*
with/without	*z/brez*

Shopping

How much is it?	*Koliko stane?*
I'd like to buy it.	*Rad bi kupil.*
It's too expensive for me.	*Predrago je za mene.*
Can I look at it?	*Ali lahko pogledam?*
I'm just looking.	*Samo gledam.*
I'm looking for …	*Iščem …*
Do you take travellers cheques?	*Ali vzamete potovalne čeke?*
Do you have another colour/size?	*Ali imate drugo barvo/velikost?*

chemist	*lekarno*
clothing	*oblačila*
souvenirs	*spominke*
big/bigger	*velik/večji*
small/smaller	*majhen/manjši*
more/less	*več/manj*
cheap/cheaper	*poceni/cenejši*

Time & Dates

When?	*Kdaj?*
today	*danes*
tonight	*danes zvečer*
tomorrow	*jutri*
the day after tomorrow	*pojutrišnjem*
yesterday	*včeraj*
all day/every day	*ves dan/vsak dan*

Monday	*ponedeljek*
Tuesday	*torek*
Wednesday	*sreda*
Thursday	*četrtek*
Friday	*petek*
Saturday	*sobota*
Sunday	*nedelja*

January	*januar*
February	*februar*
March	*marec*
April	*april*
May	*maj*
June	*junij*
July	*julij*
August	*avgust*
September	*september*
October	*oktober*
November	*november*
December	*december*

What time is it?	*Koliko je ura?*
It's … o'clock	*Ura je …*
in the morning	*zjutraj*
in the evening	*zvečer*
1.15	*četrt na dve* (lit: one quarter of two)
1.30	*pol dveh* (lit: half of two)
1.45	*tri cetrt na dve* (lit: three quarters of two)

Numbers

0	*nič*
1	*ena*
2	*dve*
3	*tri*
4	*štiri*
5	*pet*
6	*šest*
7	*sedem*
8	*osem*
9	*devet*
10	*deset*
11	*enajst*
12	*dvanajst*
13	*trinajst*
14	*štirinajst*
15	*petnajst*
16	*šestnajst*
17	*sedemnajst*
18	*osemnajst*
19	*devetnajst*
20	*dvajset*
21	*enaindvajset*
22	*dvaindvajset*
30	*trideset*
40	*štirideset*
50	*petdeset*
60	*šestdeset*
70	*sedemdeset*
80	*osemdeset*
90	*devetdeset*
100	*sto*
101	*sto ena*
110	*sto deset*
1000	*tisoč*
one million	*milijon*

Health

I'm diabetic/
  epileptic/
  asthmatic.

*Sem diabetik/
  epileptik/
  astmatik.*

I'm allergic to
  penicillin/
  antibiotics.

*Alergičen sem na
  penicilin/
  antibiotike.*

antiseptic
aspirin
condoms
contraceptive

*antiseptičen/razkužilo
aspirin
kondomi
kontracepcijsko
  sredstvo*

diarrhoea
medicine
nausea
sunblock cream

tampons

*driska
zdravilo
slabost
zaščitna krema
  proti soncu
tamponi*

Emergencies

Help!
Go away!
Call a doctor/the
  police.

*Na pomoč!
Pojdite stran!
Pokličite zdravnika/
  policijo.*

Glossary

If you can't find the word you're looking for here, try the Language Guide, the Food and Drinks sections in the Facts for the Visitor chapter or the Addresses & Place Names section in the Getting Around chapter.

AMZS – Avto-Moto Zveza Slovenije (Automobile Association of Slovenia)
avtocesta – motorway, highway

bife – snack and/or drinks bar
bivak – bivouac (basic shelter in the mountains)
breg – river bank
burja – bora (cold north-east wind from the Adriatic Sea)

c – abbreviation for *cesta*
čakalnica – waiting room
cenik – price
cerkev – church
cesta – road
CPTS – Center za Promocijo Turizma Slovenije (Slovenian Tourist Board)

delovni čas – opening/business hours
dijaški dom – student dormitory, hostel
dolina – valley
dom – house; mountain cottage or lodge
Domobranci – anti-Partisan Home Guards during WWII
drevored – avenue

fijaker – horse-drawn carriage

gaj – grove, park
garderoba – left-luggage office, coat check
gora – mountain
gostilna – inn-style restaurant
gostišče – inn-style restaurant usually with accommodation
gozd – forest, grove
grad – castle
greben – ridge, crest
GRS – Gorska Reševalna Služba (Mountain Rescue Service)

GZS – Geodetski Zavod Slovenije (Geodesic Institute of Slovenia)

Hallstatt – early Iron Age Celtic culture (800-500 BC)
hrib – hill

izhod – exit
izvir – source (of a river, stream etc)

jezero – lake
jug – south

kamnolom – quarry
Karst – limestone region of underground rivers and caves in Primorska
kavarna – coffee shop, café
knjigarna – bookshop
knjižnica – library
koča – mountain cottage or hut
kot – glacial valley, corner
kotlina – basin
kozolec – hayrack distinct to Slovenia
kras – karst
krčma – drinks bar (sometimes with food)

La Tène – late Iron Age culture (450 to 390 BC)
LPP – Ljubljanski Potniški Promet (Ljubljana city bus network)

moški – men (toilet)
most – bridge

na – on
nabrežje – embankment
naselje – colony, development
nasip – dike, embankment

občina – administrative division; county or commune
obvoz – detour (road sign)
odhod – departure
odprto – open
okrepčevalnica – snack bar
Osvobodilne Fronte – anti-Fascist Liberation Front in WWII

329

otok – island

panjska končnica – beehive panel painted with Slovenian folk motifs
PD – prometni davek (sales tax on goods and services; VAT)
pivnica – pub, beer hall
planina – Alpine pasture
planota – plateau
pod – under, below
polje – collapsed limestone area under cultivation
pot – trail
potok – stream
prehod – passage
prekop – canal
prenočišče – accommodation
pri – at, near, by
prihod – arrival
PZS – Planinska Zveza Slovenije (Alpine Association of Slovenia)

reka – river
restavracija – restaurant
rini – push (door)
rob – escarpment, edge

samopostrežna restavracija – self-service restaurant
samostan – monastery
Secessionism – art and architectural style similar to Art Nouveau
sedežnica – chair lift
sedlo – pass, saddle
sever – north
SIT – tolar (international currency code)
slaščičarna – shop selling ice cream, sweets
sobe – rooms available (sign)
soteska – ravine, gorge
sprehajališče – walkway, promenade
stena – wall, cliff
steza – path

SŽ – Slovenske Železnice (Slovenian Railways)

terme – Italian for 'spa' (commonly used in Slovenia)
TIC – Tourist Information Centre
TNG – Triglavski Narodni Park (Triglav National Park)
toplar – double-linked hayrack unique to Slovenia
toplice – spa
trg – square

ul – abbreviation for *ulica*
ulica – street

vas – village
vhod – entrance
vila – villa
vinoteka – wine bar
vinska cesta – wine road
vinska klet – wine cellar
vleci – pull (door)
vozni red – timetable
vozovnica – ticket
vrh – summit, peak
vrt – garden, park
vrtača – sinkhole
vzhod – east
vzpenjača – cable car, gondola

zahod – west
zaprto – closed
zavetišče – mountain 'refuge' with refreshments and sometimes accommodation
zdravilišče – health resort, spa
žegnanje – a patron's festival at a church or chapel
ženske – women (toilet)
žičnica – cable car
znamenje – religious road sign, wayside shrine
zdravstveni dom – medical centre, clinic

Index

ABBREVIATIONS

MAPS

TEXT

Maps are in **bold** type

LONELY PLANET PHRASEBOOKS

Building bridges,
Breaking barriers,
Beyond babble-on

Listen for the gems

Speak your own words

Ask your own
questions

Master of
your
own
image

- handy pocket-sized books
- easy to understand Pronunciation chapter
- clear and comprehensive Grammar chapter
- romanisation alongside script to allow ease of pronunciation
- script throughout so users can point to phrases
- extensive vocabulary sections, words and phrases for every situation
- full of cultural information and tips for the traveller

'...vital for a real DIY spirit and attitude in language learning' – Backpacker

'the phrasebooks have good cultural backgrounders and offer solid advice for challenging situations in remote locations' – San Francisco Examiner

'...they are unbeatable for their coverage of the world's more obscure languages' – The Geographical Magazine

---

Arabic (Egyptian)
Arabic (Moroccan)
Australia
  *Australian English, Aboriginal and
  Torres Strait languages*
Baltic States
  Estonian, Latvian, Lithuanian
Bengali
Brazilian
Burmese
Cantonese
Central Asia
Central Europe
  *Czech, French, German, Hungarian,
  Italian and Slovak*
Eastern Europe
  *Bulgarian, Czech, Hungarian, Polish,
  Romanian and Slovak*
Ethiopian (Amharic)
Fijian
French
German
Greek

Hindi/Urdu
Indonesian
Italian
Japanese
Korean
Lao
Latin American Spanish
Malay
Mandarin
Mediterranean Europe
  *Albanian, Croatian, Greek,
  Italian, Macedonian, Maltese,
  Serbian and Slovene*
Mongolian
Nepali
Papua New Guinea
Pilipino (Tagalog)
Quechua
Russian
Scandinavian Europe
  *Danish, Finnish, Icelandic, Norwegian
  and Swedish*

South-East Asia
  *Burmese, Indonesian, Khmer, Lao,
  Malay, Tagalog (Pilipino), Thai and
  Vietnamese*
Spanish (Castilian)
  Basque, Catalan and Galician
Sri Lanka
Swahili
Thai
Thai Hill Tribes
Tibetan
Turkish
Ukrainian
USA
  *US English, Vernacular,
  Native American languages and
  Hawaiian*
Vietnamese
Western Europe
  *Basque, Catalan, Dutch, French,
  German, Irish, Italian, Portuguese,
  Scottish Gaelic, Spanish (Castilian)
  and Welsh*

LONELY PLANET JOURNEYS

JOURNEYS is a unique collection of travel writing – published by the company that understands travel better than anyone else. It is a series for anyone who has ever experienced – or dreamed of – the magical moment when they encountered a strange culture or saw a place for the first time. They are tales to read while you're planning a trip, while you're on the road or while you're in an armchair, in front of a fire.

JOURNEYS books catch the spirit of a place, illuminate a culture, recount a crazy adventure, or introduce a fascinating way of life. They always entertain, and always enrich the experience of travel.

THE GATES OF DAMASCUS
Lieve Joris
Translated by Sam Garrett

This best-selling book is a beautifully drawn portrait of day-to-day life in modern Syria. Through her intimate contact with local people, Lieve Joris draws us into the fascinating world that lies behind the gates of Damascus. Hala's husband is a political prisoner, jailed for his opposition to the Assad regime; through the author's friendship with Hala we see how Syrian politics impacts on the lives of ordinary people.

Lieve Joris, who was born in Belgium, is one of Europe's leading travel writers. In addition to an award-winning book on Hungary, she has published widely acclaimed accounts of her journeys to the Middle East and Africa. *The Gates of Damascus* is her fifth book.

'Expands the boundaries of travel writing' – Times Literary Supplement

KINGDOM OF THE FILM STARS
Journey into Jordan
Annie Caulfield

Kingdom of the Film Stars is a travel book and a love story. With honesty and humour, Annie Caulfield writes of travelling in Jordan and falling in love with a Bedouin. Her book offers fascinating insights into the country – from the traditional tent life of nomadic tribes to the first woman MP's battle with fundamentalist colleagues. *Kingdom of the Film Stars* unpicks some of the tight-woven Western myths about the Arab world, presenting cultural and political issues within the intimate framework of a compelling love story.

Annie Caulfield, who was born in Ireland and currently lives in London, is an award-winning playwright and journalist. She has travelled widely in the Middle East.

'Annie Caulfield is a remarkable traveller. Her story is fresh, courageous, moving, witty and sexy!' – Dawn French

LONELY PLANET TRAVEL ATLASES

Lonely Planet has long been famous for the number and quality of its guidebook maps. Now we've gone one step further and produced a handy companion series: Lonely Planet travel atlases – maps of a country produced in book form.

Unlike other maps, which look good but lead travellers astray, our travel atlases have been researched on the road by Lonely Planet's experienced team of writers. All details are carefully checked to ensure the atlas corresponds with the equivalent Lonely Planet guidebook.

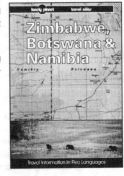

The handy atlas format means no holes, wrinkles, torn sections or constant folding and unfolding. These atlases can survive long periods on the road, unlike cumbersome fold-out maps. The comprehensive index ensures easy reference.

- full-colour throughout
- maps researched and checked by Lonely Planet authors
- place names correspond with Lonely Planet guidebooks
  – no confusing spelling differences
- legend and travelling information in English, French, German, Japanese and Spanish
- size: 230 x 160 mm

Available now:
Chile & Easter Island • Egypt • India & Bangladesh • Israel & the Palestinian Territories •Jordan, Syria & Lebanon • Kenya • Laos • Portugal • South Africa, Lesotho & Swaziland • Thailand • Turkey • Vietnam • Zimbabwe, Botswana & Namibia

---

LONELY PLANET TV SERIES & VIDEOS

Lonely Planet travel guides have been brought to life on television screens around the world. Like our guides, the programmes are based on the joy of independent travel, and look honestly at some of the most exciting, picturesque and frustrating places in the world. Each show is presented by one of three travellers from Australia, England or the USA and combines an innovative mixture of video, Super-8 film, atmospheric soundscapes and original music.

Videos of each episode – containing additional footage not shown on television – are available from good book and video shops, but the availability of individual videos varies with regional screening schedules.

Video destinations include: Alaska • American Rockies • Australia – The South-East • Baja California & the Copper Canyon • Brazil • Central Asia • Chile & Easter Island • Corsica, Sicily & Sardinia – The Mediterranean Islands • East Africa (Tanzania & Zanzibar) • Ecuador & the Galapagos Islands • Greenland & Iceland • Indonesia • Israel & the Sinai Desert • Jamaica • Japan • La Ruta Maya • Morocco • New York • North India • Pacific Islands (Fiji, Solomon Islands & Vanuatu) • South India • South West China • Turkey • Vietnam • West Africa • Zimbabwe, Botswana & Namibia

The Lonely Planet TV series is produced by:
Pilot Productions
The Old Studio
18 Middle Row
London W10 5AT UK

For video availability and ordering information contact your nearest Lonely Planet office.

Music from the TV series is available on CD & cassette.

PLANET TALK

Lonely Planet's FREE quarterly newsletter

We love hearing from you and think you'd like to hear from us.

When...is the right time to see reindeer in Finland?
Where...can you hear the best palm-wine music in Ghana?
How...do you get from Asunción to Areguá by steam train?
What...is the best way to see India?

For the answer to these and many other questions read PLANET TALK.

Every issue is packed with up-to-date travel news and advice including:

* a letter from Lonely Planet co-founders Tony and Maureen Wheeler
* go behind the scenes on the road with a Lonely Planet author
* feature article on an important and topical travel issue
* a selection of recent letters from travellers
* details on forthcoming Lonely Planet promotions
* complete list of Lonely Planet products

To join our mailing list contact any Lonely Planet office.

Also available: Lonely Planet T-shirts. 100% heavyweight cotton.

LONELY PLANET ONLINE

Get the latest travel information before you leave or while you're on the road

Whether you've just begun planning your next trip, or you're chasing down specific info on currency regulations or visa requirements, check out Lonely Planet Online for up-to-the minute travel information.

As well as travel profiles of your favourite destinations (including maps and photos), you'll find current reports from our researchers and other travellers, updates on health and visas, travel advisories, and discussion of the ecological and political issues you need to be aware of as you travel.

There's also an online travellers' forum where you can share your experience of life on the road, meet travel companions and ask other travellers for their recommendations and advice. We also have plenty of links to other online sites useful to independent travellers.

And of course we have a complete and up-to-date list of all Lonely Planet travel products including guides, phrasebooks, atlases, Journeys and videos and a simple online ordering facility if you can't find the book you want elsewhere.

www.lonelyplanet.com
or
AOL keyword: lp

LONELY PLANET PRODUCTS

Lonely Planet is known worldwide for publishing practical, reliable and no-nonsense travel information in our guides and on our web site. The Lonely Planet list covers just about every accessible part of the world. Currently there are nine series: *travel guides, shoestring guides, walking guides, city guides, phrasebooks, audio packs, travel atlases, Journeys* – a unique collection of travel writing and *Pisces Books* - diving and snorkeling guides.

EUROPE

Amsterdam • Austria • Baltic States phrasebook • Berlin • Britain • Canary Islands• Central Europe on a shoestring • Central Europe phrasebook • Czech & Slovak Republics • Denmark • Dublin • Eastern Europe on a shoestring • Eastern Europe phrasebook • Estonia, Latvia & Lithuania • Finland • France • French phrasebook • Germany • German phrasebook • Greece • Greek phrasebook • Hungary • Iceland, Greenland & the Faroe Islands • Ireland • Italian phrasebook • Italy • Lisbon • London • Mediterranean Europe on a shoestring • Mediterranean Europe phrasebook • Paris • Poland • Portugal • Portugal travel atlas • Prague • Romania & Moldova • Russia, Ukraine & Belarus • Russian phrasebook • Scandinavian & Baltic Europe on a shoestring • Scandinavian Europe phrasebook • Slovenia • Spain • Spanish phrasebook • St Petersburg • Switzerland •Trekking in Spain • Ukrainian phrasebook • Vienna • Walking in Britain • Walking in Italy • Walking in Switzerland • Western Europe on a shoestring • Western Europe phrasebook

Travel Literature: The Olive Grove: Travels in Greece

NORTH AMERICA

Alaska • Backpacking in Alaska • Baja California • California & Nevada • Canada • Chicago • Deep South• Florida • Hawaii • Honolulu • Los Angeles • Mexico • Mexico City • Miami • New England • New Orleans • New York City • New York, New Jersey & Pennsylvania • Pacific Northwest USA • Rocky Mountain States • San Francisco • Southwest USA • USA phrasebook • Washington, DC & the Capital Region

Travel Literature: Drive thru America

CENTRAL AMERICA & THE CARIBBEAN

•Bahamas and Turks & Caicos •Bermuda •Central America on a shoestring • Costa Rica • Cuba •Eastern Caribbean •Guatemala, Belize & Yucatán: La Ruta Maya • Jamaica

SOUTH AMERICA

Argentina, Uruguay & Paraguay • Bolivia • Brazil • Brazilian phrasebook • Buenos Aires • Chile & Easter Island • Chile & Easter Island travel atlas • Colombia Ecuador & the Galápagos Islands • Latin American Spanish phrasebook • Peru • Quechua phrasebook • Rio de Janeiro • South America on a shoestring • Trekking in the Patagonian Andes • Venezuela

Travel Literature: Full Circle: A South American Journey

ISLANDS OF THE INDIAN OCEAN

Madagascar & Comoros • Maldives• Mauritius, Réunion & Seychelles

AFRICA

Africa - the South • Africa on a shoestring • Arabic (Moroccan) phrasebook • Cairo • Cape Town • Central Africa • East Africa • Egypt • Egypt travel atlas• Ethiopian (Amharic) phrasebook • Kenya • Kenya travel atlas • Malawi, Mozambique & Zambia • Morocco • North Africa • South Africa, Lesotho & Swaziland • South Africa, Lesotho & Swaziland travel atlas • Swahili phrasebook • Tunisia • Trekking in East Africa • West Africa • Zimbabwe, Botswana & Namibia • Zimbabwe, Botswana & Namibia travel atlas

Travel Literature: The Rainbird: A Central African Journey • Songs to an African Sunset: A Zimbabwean Story

MAIL ORDER

Lonely Planet products are distributed worldwide. They are also available by mail order from Lonely Planet, so if you have difficulty finding a title please write to us. North American and South American residents should write to 150 Linden St, Oakland CA 94607, USA; European and African residents should write to 10a Spring Place, London NW5 3BH; and residents of other countries to PO Box 617, Hawthorn, Victoria 3122, Australia.

NORTH-EAST ASIA

Beijing • Cantonese phrasebook • China • Hong Kong • Hong Kong, Macau & Guangzhou • Japan • Japanese phrasebook • Japanese audio pack • Korea • Korean phrasebook • Mandarin phrasebook • Mongolia • Mongolian phrasebook • North-East Asia on a shoestring • Seoul • Taiwan • Tibet • Tibet phrasebook • Tokyo

Travel Literature: Lost Japan

MIDDLE EAST & CENTRAL ASIA

Arab Gulf States • Arabic (Egyptian) phrasebook • Central Asia • Central Asia phrasebook • Iran • Israel & the Palestinian Territories • Israel & the Palestinian Territories travel atlas • Istanbul • Jerusalem • Jordan & Syria • Jordan, Syria & Lebanon travel atlas • Lebanon • Middle East • Turkey • Turkish phrasebook • Turkey travel atlas • Yemen

Travel Literature: The Gates of Damascus • Kingdom of the Film Stars: Journey into Jordan

ALSO AVAILABLE:

Brief Encounters • Travel with Children • Traveller's Tales

INDIAN SUBCONTINENT

Bangladesh • Bengali phrasebook • Delhi • Goa • Hindi/Urdu phrasebook • India • India & Bangladesh travel atlas • Indian Himalaya • Karakoram Highway • Nepal • Nepali phrasebook • Pakistan • Rajasthan • Sri Lanka • Sri Lanka phrasebook • Trekking in the Indian Himalaya • Trekking in the Karakoram & Hindukush • Trekking in the Nepal Himalaya

Travel Literature: In Rajasthan • Shopping for Buddhas

SOUTH-EAST ASIA

Bali & Lombok • Bangkok • Burmese phrasebook • Cambodia • Ho Chi Minh City • Indonesia • Indonesian phrasebook • Indonesian audio pack • Jakarta • Java • Laos • Lao phrasebook • Laos travel atlas • Malay phrasebook • Malaysia, Singapore & Brunei • Myanmar (Burma) • Philippines • Pilipino phrasebook • Singapore • South-East Asia on a shoestring • South-East Asia phrasebook • Thailand • Thailand's Islands & Beaches • Thailand travel atlas • Thai phrasebook • Thai audio pack • Thai Hill Tribes phrasebook • Vietnam • Vietnamese phrasebook • Vietnam travel atlas

AUSTRALIA & THE PACIFIC

Australia • Australian phrasebook • Bushwalking in Australia • Bushwalking in Papua New Guinea • Fiji • Fijian phrasebook • Islands of Australia's Great Barrier Reef • Melbourne • Micronesia • New Caledonia • New South Wales • New Zealand • Northern Territory • Outback Australia • Papua New Guinea • Papua New Guinea phrasebook • Queensland • Rarotonga & the Cook Islands • Samoa • Solomon Islands • South Australia • Sydney • Tahiti & French Polynesia • Tasmania • Tonga • Tramping in New Zealand • Vanuatu • Victoria • Western Australia

Travel Literature: Islands in the Clouds • Sean & David's Long Drive

ANTARCTICA

Antarctica

THE LONELY PLANET STORY

Lonely Planet published its first book in 1973 in response to the numerous 'How did you do it?' questions Maureen and Tony Wheeler were asked after driving, bussing, hitching, sailing and railing their way from England to Australia.

Written at a kitchen table and hand collated, trimmed and stapled, *Across Asia on the Cheap* became an instant local bestseller, inspiring thoughts of another book.

Eighteen months in South-East Asia resulted in their second guide, *South-East Asia on a shoestring*, which they put together in a backstreet Chinese hotel in Singapore in 1975. The 'yellow bible', as it quickly became known to backpackers around the world, soon became *the* guide to the region. It has sold well over half a million copies and is now in its 9th edition, still retaining its familiar yellow cover.

Today there are over 350 titles, including travel guides, walking guides, language kits & phrasebooks, travel atlases and travel literature. The company is the largest independent travel publisher in the world. Although Lonely Planet initially specialised in guides to Asia, today there are few corners of the globe that have not been covered.

The emphasis continues to be on travel for independent travellers. Tony and Maureen still travel for several months of each year and play an active part in the writing, updating and quality control of Lonely Planet's guides.

They have been joined by over 80 authors and 200 staff at our offices in Melbourne (Australia), Oakland (USA), London (UK) and Paris (France). Travellers themselves also make a valuable contribution to the guides through the feedback we receive in thousands of letters each year and on our web site.

The people at Lonely Planet strongly believe that travellers can make a positive contribution to the countries they visit, both through their appreciation of the countries' culture, wildlife and natural features, and through the money they spend. In addition, the company makes a direct contribution to the countries and regions it covers. Since 1986 a percentage of the income from each book has been donated to ventures such as famine relief in Africa; aid projects in India; agricultural projects in Central America; Greenpeace's efforts to halt French nuclear testing in the Pacific; and Amnesty International.

'I hope we send people out with the right attitude about travel. You realise when you travel that there are so many different perspectives about the world, so we hope these books will make people more interested in what they see. Guidebooks can't really guide people. All you can do is point them in the right direction.'

– Tony Wheeler

LONELY PLANET PUBLICATIONS

Australia
PO Box 617, Hawthorn 3122, Victoria
tel: (03) 9819 1877 fax: (03) 9819 6459
e-mail: talk2us@lonelyplanet.com.au

USA
150 Linden St
Oakland, CA 94607
tel: (510) 893 8555 TOLL FREE: 800 275-8555
fax: (510) 893 8572
e-mail: info@lonelyplanet.com

UK
10a Spring Place,
London NW5 3BH
tel: (0171) 428 4800 fax: (0171) 428 4828
e-mail: go@lonelyplanet.co.uk

France:
71 bis rue du Cardinal Lemoine, 75005 Paris
tel: 01 44 32 06 20 fax: 01 46 34 72 55
e-mail: bip@lonelyplanet.fr

World Wide Web: http://www.lonelyplanet.com
or *AOL keyword: lp*